T0366343

Investing in
Asset-Backed Securities

Frank J. Fabozzi, Ph.D., CFA
Editor

Published by Frank J. Fabozzi Associates

© 2000 By Frank J. Fabozzi Associates
New Hope, Pennsylvania

ISBN: 1-883249-80-5

Table of Contents

Contributing Authors

James S. Anderson	First Union Securities, Inc.
Ryan Asato	
Nichol Bakalar	Deutsche Banc Alex. Brown
Joel W. Brown	Stein, Roe & Farnham, Inc.
Arthur Chu	Lehman Brothers
Kristina L. Clark	First Union Securities, Inc.
Patrick Corcoran	J.P. Morgan Securities Inc.
Ralph DiSerio	
Frank J. Fabozzi	Yale University
Todd Fasanella	Credit Suisse First Boston
Christopher Flanagan	
Sunil Gangwani	Deloitte & Touche LLP
Laurent Gauthier	Prudential Securities Inc.
Lang Gibson	First Union Securities, Inc.
Laurie Goodman	PaineWebber
Rich Gordon	First Union Securities, Inc.
Jeffrey Ho	PaineWebber
Oliver Hsiang	Morgan Stanley Dean Witter
R. Russell Hurst	First Union Securities, Inc.
John N. McElravey	Banc One Capital Markets, Inc.
Neil McPherson	Credit Suisse First Boston
James Mountain	Deloitte & Touche LLP
Joseph Philips	Morgan Stanley Dean Witter
Joshua Phillips	Nomura Securities International
James Nimberg	Deutsche Banc Alex. Brown
Shrikant Ramamurthy	Prudential Securities Inc.
W. Alexander Roever	Banc One Capital Markets, Inc.
Anthony B. Sanders	The Ohio State University
Charles Schorin	Morgan Stanley Dean Witter
Glenn M. Schultz	Banc One Capital Markets
Scott H. Shannon	First Union Securities, Inc.
Andrew A. Silver	Moody's Investors Service
Weisi Tan	
Allen S. Thomas	Deloitte & Touche LLP
William M. Wadden IV	Stein, Roe & Farnham, Inc.
Karen Weaver	Deutsche Banc Alex. Brown
Steven Weinreich	Morgan Stanley Dean Witter
Stephanie Whitten	Deutsche Banc Alex. Brown
Lisa N. Wilhelm	Banc One Capital Markets, Inc.
Eugene Xu	Deutsche Banc Alex. Brown
Thomas Zimmerman	PaineWebber

Chapter 1

Overview of ABS Portfolio Management

Karen Weaver, CFA
Managing Director
Global Head of Securitization Research
Deutsche Banc Alex. Brown

Stephanie Whitten
Associate
Deutsche Banc Alex. Brown

Eugene Xu, Ph.D.
Director
Deutsche Banc Alex. Brown

INTRODUCTION

Asset-backed securities (ABS) are securities backed by a pool of assets, typically loans or accounts receivable originated by banks, specialty finance companies, or other credit providers. ABS have grown from a niche market product in the 1980s to a mainstay of today's fixed income portfolios. ABS have the broadest investor base of any spread product. Investors employ ABS to suit a spectrum of needs — from a cash or Treasury surrogate in their most liquid forms, to a yield enhancer in their more esoteric ones. Here, after an overview of some of the common ABS investor types, we'll discuss constraints, guidelines and risks in ABS investing, as well as relative value assessment and methods used to monitor and measure ABS performance.

INVESTOR TYPES AND STRATEGIES

Investment advisors and money managers often benchmark the performance of their portfolios against an index, such as the Lehman Aggregate or Salomon Broad Index. "Indexers" are those who seek to match the index's performance. Definitionally, a portfolio constructed to exactly mimic the index will perform in line with the index (i.e., no better and no worse). Other portfolio managers seek to *beat* an index's performance. Portfolio managers typically try to outperform an index

1

by one of several ways. They can underweight portions of the index they think are rich, or overweight portions they think are cheap. They may even buy something that is not in the index because they expect it to perform better than the index. In addition, a portfolio manager may choose a longer or shorter duration than the index, based on a belief about the direction of interest rates. Lastly, a portfolio manager might chose a higher or lower credit profile than the index against which he or she is measured, based on a belief about credit spreads and/or the economy.

In any event, the starting point is a portfolio that mimics the index. Portfolio managers either try to match the index with the starting portfolio, or make adjustments to it in hopes that, by placing slightly different bets, they will outperform the index benchmark. For example, ABS currently represent a very small fraction of most fixed-income indices (e.g., 2% or less). Many argue that ABS are underrepresented in the indices, in part due to the quirks of the index guidelines relating to minimum deal and/or tranche sizes. As a result, most managers who use ABS are substantially overweighted (e.g., with 8 or 10% or more of their portfolios in ABS versus the 2% in the index). Historically, such an overweighting has proven beneficial.

Because performance is measured on a total return basis, these investors may trade actively and are concerned not just about credit, but also about price performance. They often invest in liquid ABS with short-duration and AAA ratings, although money managers are active across the spectrum.

Federal agencies, like FNMA and FHLMC, use ABS in two ways. First, they use their expertise in the mortgage market to assess mortgage-related ABS, e.g., home equities and manufactured housing. They are one of the largest investors in this sector, often buying entire deals and/or having deals structured to suit their portfolio needs. The yields on these mortgage-related ABS products are typically higher than the agencies' traditional mortgage investments. Because the agencies' own credit quality is so strong, they are especially important buyers in market crises, because they can still fund themselves at attractive levels and use the proceeds to buy what they perceive to be "cheap" ABS.

FNMA and FHLMC also run what are referred to as "liquidity portfolios." As the name might suggest, these portfolios are used as a place to hold cash and cash substitutes for general purposes. In their liquidity portfolios, FNMA and FHLMC are unlikely to hold mortgage-related assets, and generally buy large, highly-rated on-the-run ABS deals, especially credit cards and autos.

Insurance companies and *pension funds* invest to meet a stream of future liabilities (death benefits, annuity benefits, pension benefits, etc.) Generally these investors try to "match" the assets they buy to their liabilities. If they "cash flow match," they simply buy assets with cash flows scheduled to be paid when the liability is due. For example, assume an insurance company actuarially estimates that it will pay out $1 million per quarter in death benefits. The cash flow matched portfolio would include assets with quarterly sinking fund payments of $1 million. This approach to selecting investments is difficult and cost prohibitive, not to mention that liability cash flows can sometimes be dynamic and generally involve some estimation error. For this reason, most insurance companies and pension funds do not use cash flow matching. They either "horizon match" or "immunize." "Immunization," refers to matching the duration of their investments (assets) with the duration of their products (liabilities). "Horizon matching" is a hybrid approach, whereby the first few years of liabilities are cash flow matched, with the remaining years of liabilities immunized.

Both insurance companies and pension funds tend to be "buy-and-hold" investors. That is, once they find an investment that suits their liabilities, they are less likely to actively trade. Their main objective is to find the best relative value that funds their liabilities and, in the case of insurance companies, allows them to sell competitive products.

As the ABS market has matured, the product has evolved to, in floater form, a cash surrogate and, in fixed rate form, often a Treasury surrogate. Many *corporate treasuries* and *monetary authorities* use ABS in this way. The extraordinary credit quality and liquidity of the most commoditized ABS (credit card floaters especially) provides a higher yielding substitute for other liquid assets. Corporate treasuries and monetary authorities usually buy ABS product in maturities of five years and in.

The goal of a *leveraged fund* is to maximize the difference between the yield on its portfolio and its funding cost. A significant portion of a leveraged fund's portfolio is usually invested in ABS because of their spread relative to other investment options. Leveraged funds invest mostly in investment-grade securities, and historically the credit risk of their portfolios has been, on average, AA. The portfolios are fully hedged to protect against interest rate and currency related risks. The high quality and liquidity of the underlying assets, diversification, and the funds' equity capital enable the funds to issue AAA paper to fund themselves. Leveraged funds raise financing through the issuance of rated commercial paper (CP), medium-term notes (MTNs), and bonds.

Securities lenders lend out clients' investment portfolios, typically portfolios of Treasuries and agencies. The cash they receive is then invested in accordance with guidelines agreed upon with the clients, and the returns are shared with the clients. These guidelines typically stipulate very high credit quality and maturities of 2 to 3 years (though in some cases as long as 5 years). In the early stages of the ABS market, these guidelines were stipulated in legal final maturity terms. This initially precluded the use of many ABS products. In recent years, most investors have come to accept the expected final maturity as the true final maturity. Today, ABS floaters are very popular with securities lenders. Because the clients of securities lenders generally preclude securities lenders from taking credit risk, the only alternatives to ABS floaters are highly rated bank floating-rate notes (FRNs). As long as floating ABS continue to offer a pick-up to these alternatives, securities lenders will continue to be a major force, particularly in floater ABS inside of 3 years.

Hedge funds are mutual funds that involve speculative investing. They generally are yield-driven, which makes them willing to go out the curve, down in credit, and buy esoteric asset types. In addition, hedge funds use leverage and so their ability to finance ABS at attractive levels is paramount. Hedge funds are most active in ABS floaters with maturities of 5 years or longer.

Asset-backed commercial paper (ABCP) conduit facilities buy ABS for various reasons. Some conduits are considered arbitrage programs and participate in spread investing. These conduits purchase assets, including ABS and other debt securities, that meet a number of criteria to be considered eligible under various capital monitoring, hedging, and other calculations. The assets are bought with the proceeds raised by the issuance of ABCP and/or MTNs. The pool of assets securitizes the conduits' issuance, and hedge contracts are used to limit the change in the value of the pool. Conduits can also purchase hard-to-place tranches (i.e., subordinate classes) of asset-backed deals, funding them temporarily until another investor can be found.

Companies who issue *guaranteed investment contracts* (GICs) often use ABS for "cash flow matching." A GIC is a secured obligation of a limited liability company that pays holders a specified rate of return over the life of the contract. The GICs can be secured by an investment portfolio, sometimes containing ABS, that is hedged to match the investment contract's liability.

Some ABS investors seek to maximize their total return on investments. This "total return" strategy is concerned not just with income, but price performance as well. These investors are opportunistic and may speculate on price movements by purchasing bonds with the intent of flipping them for a profit. This strategy obviously is used when it is anticipated that an issue will be in great demand. Many investors who do not trade per se will still mark-to-market their portfolios in order to measure performance.

CONSTRAINTS AND GUIDELINES

Portfolio managers all have different constraints impacting their use of ABS. These constraints are often dictated externally, by industry or government regulation, by prospectus or by client directive. When selecting securities for investment, portfolio managers must consider questions with regard to diversification, duration, credit risk, liquidity, and cash flow variability, among others.

Some investors (insurance companies, for example) must take into consideration the duration of their liabilities, and when investing select ABS whose own durations roughly match their liabilities. Other types of portfolio managers, like investment advisors, try to match an index and choose ABS with durations comparable to their benchmark, thereby attempting to use their portfolios to achieve results similar to, or better than, the index.

Portfolio managers who are able to take a certain degree of credit risk can make credit plays by collateral, originator or tranche. By investing in ABS secured by sub-prime collateral or in subordinate pieces, portfolio managers can often achieve a significant spread pick-up versus competing products. Moreover, ABS issued by out-of-favor or financially weak seller/servicers offer spread pick-ups.

Exhibit 1: Types of Constraints and Guidelines in ABS Portfolios

Characteristic	Comment
Exposure Limits	By issuer, by wrapper and by sector
Duration	Versus an index or versus a liability
Credit Quality	Weighted average or absolute minimum
Form of Offering	Public, Private, 144A, Reg. S
Size of Each Investment	Minimum size to efficiently manage portfolio and for trading liquidity
Sovereign Risk Limitations	Some structures ameliorate exposure
Currency	Both at the collateral level and the bond level (if swapped)
Bullet vs. Amortizers	Z-spread analysis; systems issues
Risk Weighting	Varies in jurisdictions
Asset Type	Based on perceived risk/reward
Tax Issues	Withholding tax can apply for some investors in junior tranches
Senior vs. Subordinated	Subordinated bonds not always ERISA-eligible and are less liquid
Hybrid (corporate guaranty bonds, credit-linked notes)	Some portfolio managers prefer "pure" ABS
Legal jurisdiction	"Bankruptcy remoteness" and other bedrock legal ABS concepts are not universal
Financing	Repo-able or not, and at what level?

Source: DB Global Markets Research

The need for liquidity factors into a portfolio manager's investment decisions. Does a manager need to have the ability to raise cash quickly, or does he operate under a "buy-and-hold" strategy? Corporate treasurers, for example, often invest in credit card floaters as a cash substitute. On the other hand, insurance companies are more willing to buy less liquid paper because their long-lived liabilities do not require them to actively trade.

Portfolio managers vary in their ability and/or willingness to accept cash flow variability. Broadly speaking, there are two types of cash flow variability. Cash flow variability that is correlated with interest rates (for example, the risk that cash will be returned early if rates fall and a mortgage borrower refinances) is more difficult to manage than random cash flow variability. Interest rate-related variability is more damaging because the portfolio manager gets money back early to reinvest at a time when rates are low. Investors typically require additional spread to take on cash flow variability, particularly if the variability is correlated to interest rate movements.

Of course, portfolio managers are sensitive to their customers. Some customers may be very averse to headline or credit risk, therefore a portfolio manager's investments may be limited to AAA-rated, plain-vanilla ABS. The size of a portfolio manager's staff also plays a role in dictating ABS selected for investment. A portfolio management team with a large staff devoted to analyzing, monitoring, and trading ABS can more easily invest in complex, off-the-run securities than can a smaller team.

Exhibit 1 provides a summary of the types of constraints and guidelines in ABS portfolios.

IDENTIFYING ABS RISKS

The risks in ABS investing, as with investing in any spread product, include *fundamental risks* as well as *technical risks*. "Technicals" are largely supply and demand factors and do not directly impact the securitized collateral, whereas the "fundamentals" largely relate to collateral performance. Fundamentals can be broken up into credit quality and cash flow considerations.

Fundamentals

The most obvious credit quality fundamentals are *collateral risk* and *structural protection*. Although the rating agencies perform extensive analysis when assigning a rating, portfolio managers should perform their own analyses as well. To assess collateral risk, a portfolio manager should look at past performance of previous deals. For deals secured by installment loans (auto loans and leases, home equity and manufactured housing loans, and student loans), *static pool analysis* gives the best indication of past loss experience. Static pool analysis isolates a particular pool of collateral and plots the cumulative net loss experience (gross losses or defaults net of recoveries) over time. This is preferable to an "income statement" approach, whereby losses are expressed simply as a percent of the outstanding portfolio, because rapid portfolio growth can mask losses. The past performance should then be compared to future expectations to see if the expectations are reasonable. However, comparisons must take into account differences in underwriting, servicing, and the economy.

The structural protection in a transaction, or its "credit enhancement," protects ABS investors from losses on the underlying collateral and thus allows the securities to achieve credit ratings as high as AAA. Credit enhancement is determined by the rating agencies such that the collateral pool can experience many multiples of the expected level of losses before the senior bonds experience any loss of principal. The higher the rating, the greater the multiple of expected losses the bond can withstand. Credit enhancement can take many forms, including subordinated notes or certificates, cash reserve funds, overcollateralization, excess servicing, and surety bonds. The riskier the underlying collateral, the greater the credit enhancement required to earn a given rating.

Although the cornerstone premise of ABS has been bankruptcy-remoteness (i.e., achieving structures whose creditworthiness is separate and insulated from the seller/servicer's credit risk), the seller/servicer can have both a technical and a fundamental impact. On the fundamental side, deteriorating quality and stability of the seller/servicer can translate into *operational risk* and negatively impact collateral performance. When assessing servicer risk, portfolio managers should consider the servicer's operations and financial health. A wrapped transaction, for example, is insulated from servicer impact on fundamentals, since the wrap provider backs up the collateral performance, but the bond might still trade poorly if the seller/servicer falters (technical risk). The seller/servicer has the greatest impact on fundamentals for servicing-intensive assets, for unusual assets (where back-up servicers are hard to find), and in subordinated investments (because the servicer's skills can have a bigger impact for investors who are disproportionately exposed to collateral losses).

ABS structures do contemplate the transfer of servicing in the event the original servicer is unable to fulfill its duties. A specified stream of funds is allocated in a transaction's waterfall that is sized by the rating agencies to be sufficient to attract another party to service. Oftentimes arrangements are made to employ the Trustee as a back-up servicer. If the Trustee is not acting as back-up servicer, the Trustee will usually control a bidding process to sell the servicing rights of a troubled portfolio to a new servicer. Portfolio managers should also perform due diligence with respect to a servicer's operations (size, employee training, technology, specialization) and financial statements.

Surety bonds (or wraps) are bond insurance policies purchased from third parties, which guarantee the timely payment of interest and the ultimate full recovery of principal. Wraps are common in home equity, manufactured housing, and sub-prime auto ABS. Wrapped ABS are subject to surety provider risk, a unique type of credit risk. In some ways the business risk of wrappers is similar to a bank's in that they invest in a portfolio of credits. However, unlike a bank, or any corporate credit for that matter, their credit rating is their livelihood. A financial guarantor that loses its AAA rating is, arguably, out of business. For this reason, the interests of management are uniquely aligned with the interests of AAA bond investors. Although the possibility of a downgrade does exist, a wrapper's credit risk is tied to a diversified portfolio of not just ABS, but other credits as well, and that risk is further buffered by their substantial capital.

Prior to 1998, downgrades in the ABS world were very rare (analysis of corporate downgrades shows that, in the past decade, anywhere from 5% to 15% of the corporate universe was downgraded annually), and downgrades due to collateral performance were virtually unheard of. In fact, an analysis of downgrades (as measured by the Moody's rated universe) shows that there were only seven collateral-related ABS downgrades for the entire period 1986-1997. Collateral-related downgrades increased to 45 in 1998, and downgrades for external reasons (servicer or guarantor downgrades) numbered 115.[1] Taken together, ABS downgrades as a percentage of the ABS universe amounted to 3%[2] in 1998 versus 0.45% on average in the prior 5 years. The marked increase in collateral-related downgrades in 1998 was primarily due to the performance of sub-prime auto ABS and CBOs with emerging market content. There is significant precedent for major ABS issuers to protect their programs prior to a rating agency action. Issuers have protected imperiled ABS transactions prior to a downgrade by adding/removing collateral, adding credit enhancement, buying out loans and transferring servicing. Exhibit 2 outlines ABS downgrade activity by year.

---

[1] Each tranche downgraded equals one downgrade. An issuer may have multiple series and each series may have multiple tranches which may be downgraded multiple times. Historically, the number of tranches per downgrade averages 1.8.

[2] This is calculated by dividing the total number of downgrades by the difference of ratings outstanding as of January 1 and ½ of ratings withdrawn. By subtracting ½ of ratings withdrawn, Moody's assumes the ratings were withdrawn at a steady pace throughout the year.

Exhibit 2: Moody's ABS Downgrade Activity by Year (Based on Number of Ratings)

Year	Ratings O/S as of Jan. 1	Downgrade Reason		Total Downgrades		Comments
		Collateral	External	Number	Percentage**	
1986	4	0	0	0	0.00%	
1987	25	0	0	0	0.00%	
1988	63	0	15	15	25.21%	13 GMAC deals due to GM downgrade (corporate guarantee structure) and 2 Household deals due to downgrade of third party enhancer
1989	126	0	0	0	0.00%	
1990	194	0	13	13	7.05%	All related to downgrade of third party enhancer
1991	359	0	12	12	3.51%	All related to downgrade of third party enhancer
1992	535	2	30	32	6.21%	2 classes of a CBO downgraded for collateral. All others related to downgrade of third party enhancer
1993	734	0	12	12	1.74%	All related to downgrade of third party enhancer
1994	1,021	0	3	3	0.31%	All related to downgrade of third party enhancer
1995	1,564	1	0	1	0.07%	Long Beach subordinated home equity bond downgraded due to California housing market
1996	2,378	0	0	0	0.00%	
1997	3,549	4	0	4	0.12%	3 separate subprime auto deals (one deal had 2 tranches downgraded)
1998	5,351	45	115	160	3.06%	101 of the external-downgrade incidents related to two waves of Green Tree corporate downgrades. 17 of the collateral-related downgrades related to CBOs, primarily those with emerging markets exposure. The remaining 29 collateral-related downgrades were related mainly to subprime autos and charged-off credit cards
1999*	N/A	59	0	59	N/A	28 of the downgrades were due to poor performance of UCFC MH transactions, 13 were CBO-related and the remainder were related to subprime auto, home equity, charged-off credit card, and other MH deals

* Through June 30, 1999

** Calculated by dividing the total number of downgrades by the difference of ratings outstanding as of January 1 and ½ of ratings withdrawn. By subtracting ½ of ratings withdrawn, Moody's assumes the ratings were withdrawn at a steady pace throughout the year

Source: Compiled from Moody's Investors Service, "Rating Changes in the U.S. Asset-Backed Securities Market: An Update," August 7, 1998 and "Rating Changes in the U.S. Asset-Backed Securities Market: August 1999 Update," August 6, 1999

Cash flow risks include *early amortization/payout risk, prepay and extension risk, cap risk,* and *basis risk.* Although rare (only two credit card payouts, totalling 0.2% of outstandings, have occurred in the market's 15-year history), early amortization/payout risk is particularly applicable to revolvers, such as credit card ABS. Early amortization occurs when the revolving period ends ahead of schedule and the transaction begins to pay out early. Generally, early amortization/payout can happen when there is negative excess spread in the transaction, when the seller's interest falls below the minimum amount required, when the seller/servicer goes bankrupt or declares insolvency or when there is a breach of contract. The early amortization/payout feature is actually a protection for investors, acting as a *de facto* credit "put." If a portfolio is deteriorating, principal collections should not be reinvested in new receivables, but should be returned to the investor to reduce the risk of loss. Issuers can (and have) taken steps to prevent early amortization.

Mortgage-related ABS (home equity and manufactured housing) entail some degree of prepayment risk. When interest rates fall, home equity borrowers can refinance into a new, lower rate loan and prepay their old loan — and the investor is left to find an alternate investment in a lower yield environment. The extent of this risk (i.e., borrowers' sensitivity to changes in interest rates) varies considerably among different types of collateral and at different points in time. The yield paid to investors in mortgage-related ABS compensates for this risk (and its corollary, extension risk, when rates back up).

Although cap risk is not common in ABS, it does exist in some transactions, usually in the home equity and manufactured housing sectors. Types of caps found in ABS include *available funds caps*[3] and *nominal caps.* When investing in capped ABS, portfolio managers must understand the caps and price them in. Portfolio managers should also be aware of basis risk, occurring in transactions where the underlying collateral pays off one benchmark but the securities issued pay off another benchmark. Credit enhancement and/or the use of swaps usually mitigate basis risk.

Technicals

While not directly affecting a deal's underlying collateral, technical risks should not be discounted. Technicals include supply and demand, headline risk and liquidity. Supply and demand affect prices in all markets. As it relates to ABS, investors try to understand supply and demand dynamics for ABS and competing products in order to predict price movements. On the supply side, there are seasonal patterns to consider (quarter-ends have traditionally been a popular time for issuers who wish to maximize quarterly gain-on-sale earnings). More broadly, ABS supply forecasts are a function of the growth of the underlying collateral

---

[3] Available funds caps, often found in student loan ABS, are caps tied to the blended average coupon of the loans, less servicing fees. To the extent that the cap is less than the bond coupon in any given period, an interest shortfall results, and is recouped in future periods, usually from excess spread.

(i.e., rising new car sales translates into more auto ABS, refinancing booms equate to more home equity ABS, etc.) and the financing choices of the seller/servicers. The decisions of seller/servicers to fund themselves by issuing ABS will depend on cost, control, structural ease, and their funding alternatives.

ABS demand is a function of competing supply as well as the breadth of the investor base. Investors who wish to assess demand for a particular ABS need to understand who buys the bonds and why, as well as understand flow of funds. If a particular investor type encounters troubles (e.g., many hedge funds faltered in the 1998 liquidity crisis), an investor might expect spreads to widen in the products the investor type favored (in that instance, subordinated bonds). On the other hand, regulatory changes (risk weightings, for example) can broaden the demand.

Increasingly, performance in ABS has been affected by the perceived quality and stability of the issuer. Part of this has been due to "headline risk," (i.e., news events regarding the issuer and not necessarily directly impacting the collateral). Transaction liquidity is another technical risk. Tranche size, frequency of issuance, the form of offering (public, private, or 144A) and the size of the underwriting group are all factors unrelated to collateral that affect a transaction's liquidity. The most liquid transactions are those issued in the public market by frequent issuers with large underwriting groups and sizable tranches. Credit cards have historically been viewed by investors as the most liquid asset class in the ABS market.

Exhibit 3 summarizes fundamental and technical risks by major asset type.

MONITORING ABS PORTFOLIOS AND MEASURING PERFORMANCE

ABS are more fungible than corporates and as such, may be easier to monitor. Portfolio managers should review the remittance reports produced on a regular basis by the servicers of the ABS deals in which they invest. The rating agencies also offer regularly updated summaries of deal collateral performance. Other information sources exist (e.g., Bloomberg, Passport, Lewtan) and many issuers are starting to put electronic copies of their remittance reports on the Web. Tracking actuals and trends in excess spread, losses, and delinquencies (and, for revolving ABS, payment rates and portfolio yields as well) provides important information about the performance of the ABS in a manager's portfolio. Analyzing these percentages on a 3-month rolling average basis, rather than a straight monthly basis, will help smooth any month-to-month volatility and distinguish between noise and a meaningful trend. Exhibit 4 lists website addresses for various sources of ABS information.

Exhibit 3: Different Asset Classes Have Varying Degrees of Risk

Risk	Credit Card	Auto	MH	HE	Student Loan	CBO	CLO (Delinked)
Fundamental-Credit Quality							
Collateral Risk	High	Variable	High	Moderate	Minimal*	High	Usually Low
Structural Protection	Excellent; Triggered**	Very Good	Very Good	Very Good	Very Good	Excellent Triggered**	Excellent; Triggered**
Servicer Risk (i.e., intensity of servicing)	Moderate	Prime-Low Sub-prime-High	High	Moderate	Moderate	Moderate	Low
Wrapper Risk	NA	Sub-prime-Yes	Some	Some	NA	NA	NA
Downgrade Risk	Lowest, due to early am	Low	Moderate	Low	Low	Low	Low
Fundamental-Cash Flow							
Early Amortization/Payout Risk	Yes	NA	NA	NA	NA	Generally Low	Generally Low
Prepay Risk	NA	NA	Generally Low	Low to Moderate	Very Low	NA	NA
Extension Risk	Very Low	Very Low	Moderate	Low to Moderate	Very Low	NA	NA
Cap Risk	NA	Generally NA	Generally NA	Variable	Variable	NA	NA
Basis Risk	Some	NA	Generally NA	Minimal	Some	Minimal	Minimal
Technical							
Liquidity	Excellent	Excellent	Fair	Good	Excellent	Fair	Fair
Headline Risk	Moderate	Variable	High	High	Low	Low	Low

* Assumes government guaranteed loans

** In order to reduce the risk of loss to investors, credit card ABS can amortize early (i.e., the revolving period ends ahead of schedule and the deal begins to pay out) if a portfolio is deteriorating. For cash flow CBO/CLOs, failure of a transaction's portfolio tests can lead to early payout.

Source: DB Global Markets Research

Exhibit 4: General Data Sources on the Web

Selected Issuers

Credit Card

		Auto	
www.americanexpress.com	www.discovercard.com	www.americredit.com	www.mitsubishicars.com
www.bankofamerica.com	www.firstusa.com	www.bmwusafs.com	www.nissan-usa.com
www.bankone.com	www.fleet.com	www.chryslerfinancial.com	www.onyxacceptance.com
www.capitalone.com	www.mbna.com	www.fordcredit.com	www.toyota.com
www.chase.com	www.providian.com	www.gm.com	www.unionacceptance.com
www.citibank.com	www.wachovia.com	www.honda.com	www.wfsfinancial.com

Equipment

		Home Equity	
www.cat.com	www.dvi-inc.com	www.advanta.com	www.irwinfinancial.com
www.cit.com	www.hellerfinancial.com	www.conseco.com	www.provident-bank.com
www.cnh.com	www.ikon.com	www.countrywide.com	www.rfc.com
www.copelco.com	www.sierracities.com	www.equicredit.com	www.saxonmortgage.com
www.deere.com	www.unicapitalcorp.com	www.gmacmortgage.com	www.superiorbank.com

Manufactured Housing

www.bombardiernv.com
www.clayton.net
www.conseco.com
www.greenpoint.com
www.oakwoodhomes.com

Student Loan

www.keybank.com
www.salliemae.com
www.slfc.com
www.usagroup.com

Rating Agency

		Other	
Duff & Phelps	www.dcrco.com	American Bankruptcy Institute	www.abiworld.org
Fitch	www.fitchibca.com	ABSNet (Lewtan)	www.absnet.net
Moody's	www.moodysresearch.com	EDGAR	www.sec.gov/edaux/formlynx.htm
Standard & Poor's	www.standardandpoors.com	Federal Reserve	www.bog.frb.fed.us
		Securitizaton.net	www.securitization.net

Trustee

Bankers Trust	www.gis.deutsche-bank.com
Bank of New York	www.mbsreporting.com
Bank One	www.bankone.com/commercial/invest/corporate
Chase Manhattan	www.chase.com/sfa
First Union	www.firstunion.com/corptrust
Norwest Bank	www.ctslink.com
U.S. Bank	www.usbank.com/corp_trust/inv_info_reporting.html

Source: DB Global Markets Research

Assembling a *loss curve* from historical data can provide one of the most important tools for monitoring a portfolio of installment loans. A loss curve shows the timing as well as the magnitude of losses and allows the portfolio manager to create a baseline stress scenario for examining the sufficiency of loss protection in a given bond. One should start by graphing the loss curves for as many issues as possible (again using rating agency data or remittance reports). Varying degrees of sophistication can be employed to fit a base curve, from simple hand-drawn curves to spreadsheet-based curve fitting techniques, like nonlinear regression analysis. Exhibit 5 shows the loss experience of a set of collateral pools of different vintages, and a representative curve chosen to analyze an actual issue. For the example in Exhibit 5, to build a representative curve, we weighted the experience of more recent deals more heavily, because we felt that that experience reflected shifts in collateral quality that best matched the bond we were analyzing.

One of the most important parts of curve-fitting is in developing the shape of the curve. Once a reasonable shape exists, modifying the amplitude of the curve (i.e., 1.25×, 1.5×, etc.) is easily done. Portfolio managers should pay special attention to any deal that is not "tracking" along the expected curve.

As mentioned earlier, headline risk is a concern of many ABS investors. Some find it helpful to track issuers' equity performance as a possible early warning indicator of difficulties. Leaving tickers up on the Bloomberg screen is a quick and easy way check up on stock performance. Also important to note is the issuer's credit rating (if such rating exists). Higher rated companies usually have greater funding flexibility than lower rated companies. Diversification of funding is often reflected in an ABS issuer's pricing and trading levels.

In addition to monitoring the performance of a portfolio manager's specific ABS investments, a manager should monitor industry trends within each sector. By reading available research reports and attending conferences, portfolio managers can keep up to date on sector growth and change as well as overall ABS market performance. While these trends may or may not affect a portfolio manager's outstanding portfolio, on a going-forward basis, they may cause portfolio managers to rethink their strategies with regard to ABS.

Portfolio managers who invest in ABS transactions enhanced by surety bonds should pay special attention to credit quality trends of wrap providers. The major rating agencies provide periodic updates on their financial strength.

Exhibit 5: Projected Loss Curve for a Representative Collateral Pool

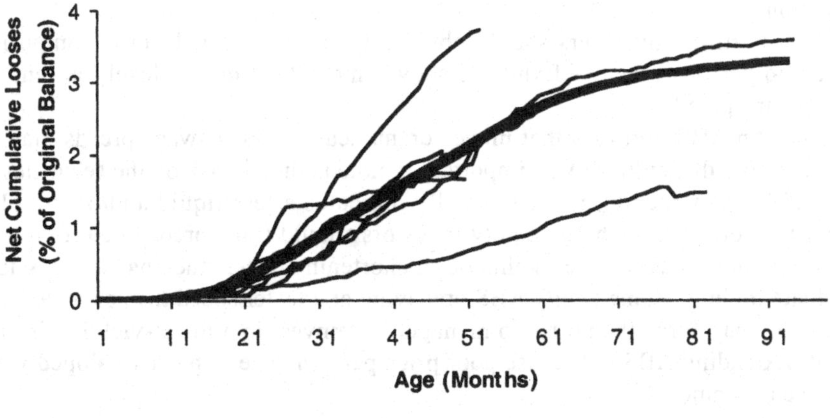

Source: DB Global Markets Research

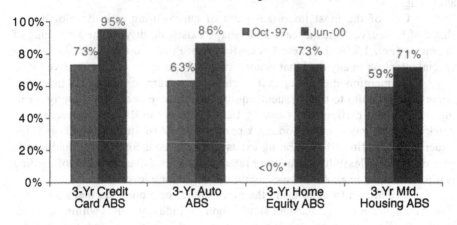

**Exhibit 6: Correlation Between ABS Spreads and Swap Spreads
is Strong and Rising
(October 1997 and June 2000)**

* Negatively correlated.

Source: DB Global Markets Research

Measuring ABS Performance

Part of monitoring a portfolio includes measuring its performance. Several dealers compile and distribute spread information on a weekly basis. Many portfolio managers mark-to-market their portfolios on a regular basis. Various pricing services exist that will mark to market portfolios for a fee. Dealers can provide this information to investors as well. With the mark-to-market information, a portfolio manager can compare his ABS portfolio to other debt products, such as corporates or Treasuries, and he can also compare his ABS portfolio to the ABS universe. In this way, the portfolio manager can evaluate his security selection and his sector selection.

Portfolio managers should obviously be on the watch for decomposing portfolio performance. As Exhibit 6 shows, most ABS move closely in tandem with swap spreads.

An ABS portfolio that moves dramatically versus swap spreads may be experiencing difficulties. Also important to note is the bid/ask on the securities in a portfolio. A widening bid/ask usually indicates a less liquid and/or troubled security. Additionally, home equity investors should track prepayment trends in their portfolio to assess the likelihood of shortening or lengthening, and possibly evaluate trading. Home equity ABS prepaying at a faster speed than expected, for example, may force the portfolio manager to reinvest in a lower-yielding instrument. Extending ABS will cause poor price performance in positive-sloped yield curve environments.

CONCLUSIONS

Asset-backed securities are now a common part of all types of investors' fixed income portfolios. ABS offer many different types of opportunities, from the most liquid, highest quality, least volatile bonds (AAA credit card floaters, for example) to esoteric, complex high-yield instruments (subordinates bonds, future flow deals, etc.). ABS continue to offer investors — rating for rating — incremental spread, inherent diversification, and stable ratings.

Chapter 2

Rating Asset-Backed Securities

Andrew A. Silver, Ph.D.
Managing Director
Moody's Investors Service

INTRODUCTION

Credit ratings are becoming an increasingly important factor for asset-backed security markets around the world. As investors are faced with extremely complex securities from an ever-widening array of familiar and unfamiliar issuers in domestic and cross-border markets, they need a simple, unbiased, accurate, and globally consistent framework for analyzing credit risk. This chapter describes how the Moody's ratings process provides that framework to investors.

ASSET-BACKED SECURITIES

Structured finance is a term that refers to a wide variety of debt and related securities whose promise to repay investors is backed by (1) the value of some form of financial asset or (2) the credit support from a third party to the transaction. Very often, both types of backing are used to achieve a desired credit rating.

Structured financings are offshoots of traditional secured debt instruments, whose credit standing is supported by a lien on specific assets, by a defeasance provision, or by other forms of enhancement. With conventional secured issues, however, it is generally the issuer's earning power that remains the primary source of repayment. With structured financings, by contrast, the burden of repayment on a specific security is shifted away from the issuer to a pool of assets or to a third party.

Securities supported wholly or mainly by pools of assets are generally referred to as either mortgage-backed securities (mortgages were the first types of assets to be widely securitized) or asset-backed securities, whose collateral backing may include virtually any other asset with a relatively predictable payment stream, ranging from credit card receivables or insurance policies to speculative-grade bonds or even stock. Outside the United States, both types of structured financing are often referred to simply as "asset-backed securities," which is the convention that we will employ here.

Types of Structures

There are two types of structures — cash flow structures and market value structures. We discuss each below.

Cash Flow Structures — "Pass-Through" or "Pay-Through"

The support provided in structured financings can take on many forms. In transactions supported by assets, some or all of the cash flows from those assets can be dedicated to the payment of principal and interest. That type of transaction is known as a cash flow structure, which, in turn, may be structured in either of two ways: as a "pass-through" or as a "pay-through." (See Exhibit 1 for a schematic diagram outlining the major elements of a stylized cash flow transaction.)

Pass-through securities are equity instruments, in which the assets are typically sold to a trust. Investors buy shares of the trust and are entitled to interest at a specified pass-through rate of interest and to their share of principal payments.

Pay-throughs are debt obligations. The institution that wants to raise funds pledges or sells assets to a special-purpose, often bankruptcy-remote, "issuer," which issues notes or bonds.

In either type of cash flow structure, the cash flows to investors are secured primarily by the cash flows of the pledged assets. Issuers choose between the two types based on their accounting, tax, and regulatory needs.

Market Value Structures

In market value structures, the liquidation value of the assets is used to support the security. If investors are not paid by the issuer as promised, or if some other "trigger event" occurs (for example, if the market value of the collateral falls below a specified level), the collateral is sold in the secondary markets and investors receive repayment from the proceeds.

Exhibit 1: Cash Flow Transaction
I. Loan Origination and Servicing

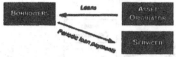

An *asset originator*, such as a bank, a savings bank, or a finance company, makes loans to *borrowers*. Borrowers repay the loans over time in periodic interest and principal payments. The repayments are typically administered by a *loan servicer*, which may be the same organization.

II. Adding the Transaction Structure

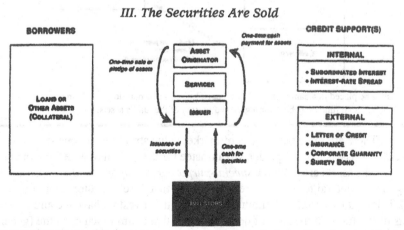

To sell/finance loans, the originator sets up a separate legal entity, the *issuer*. The issuer may be a special-purpose, bankruptcy-remote entity that issues debt, a trust that represents investors' interest in the assets, or another entity. The cash flow from the loans (i.e., the *collateral*) will be used to make interest and principal payments to investors. Credit enhancements may also be included to help reduce the risk of credit loss. These may be *internal*, provided by excess cash flow from the collateral, or *external*, such as a letter of credit from a bank or a financial guarantee from an insurance company.

III. The Securities Are Sold

Investors purchase the securities by making a one-time payment to the issuer. The originator sells/pledges the assets to the issuer, who transfers the proceeds to the originator as a one-time payment for the assets.

Exhibit 1 (Continued)
IV. The Transaction's Cash Flows Over Time

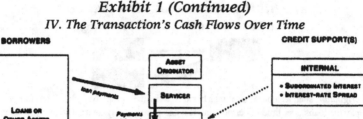

Generally, payments on the underlying collateral are the main source of cash to pay principal and interest. Borrowers continue to make periodic payments to the servicer and those payments are passed through to investors. If cash flow from the collateral is insufficient, then the credit supports may be drawn upon.

Exhibit 2: Market Value Transaction

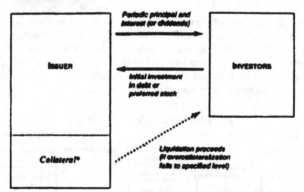

*Assets may be placed in a bankruptcy-remote, special-purpose corporation or held in trust accounts, or, in the case of a mutual fund, may be an unsegregated portion of the fund's assets.

There are three basic types of market value structures. In one structure, debt is backed by assets that are pledged to a trustee for the benefit of investors. In another structure, the assets are sold to a *special-purpose, bankruptcy-remote issuer* and then pledged as collateral for debt or preferred stock. In a third structure, debt or preferred stock is issued by an income (mutual) fund and the investors have a claim on all the assets of the fund. In the case of debt investors, that claim is senior to the (generally substantial) common equity interest in the fund, and in the case of preferred stock investors, the claim is senior to both the common equity and debt positions. (See Exhibit 2 for a schematic diagram outlining a stylized market value transaction.)

Internal Credit Supports

With either a cash flow or market value structure a variety of "internal" credit supports may be used to help to increase the probability that investors will receive the level of returns promised. One common method is overcollateralization, in which additional assets are provided, such that their additional cash flow or market value are available to offset any losses stemming from defaults and delinquencies. For example, in a structure in which the cash flow from 100 mortgages is necessary to meet payments to security holders, the collateral pool might contain 110 mortgages, which would be sufficient to pay off security holders even if some of the mortgages defaulted.

One form of overcollateralization is a senior-subordinated structure, which divides the security into two or more classes, or tranches, with varying credit risk stemming from differences in their sequence of loss allocation. The risk of credit loss is thus shifted toward the lower-credit-quality (but presumably higher-yielding) tranches, while investors in the higher-credit-quality portions of the security are more cushioned against loss. As discussed in detail below, there is a complex array of internal credit supports (such as interest rate spreads) that can reduce the investor's risk of credit loss, typically by either adding collateral or by shifting risks among classes of security holders.

External ("Third-Party") Credit Supports

In addition to support from pledged assets, many structured financings include external credit support from a third party to the transaction, such as a bank or financial guarantor. The support generally takes the form of a corporate guarantee, a letter of credit (from a bank), an insurance policy, or a surety bond. If the third party provides unlimited ("full") credit support, the transaction is called a fully-supported structure. In "direct-pay" fully-supported structures, the third party is the primary source of payment. Alternatively, in "stand-by" fully-supported structures, the asset pool or underlying issuer is the first source of payment and the third party is the second source.

The same third-party credit supports may also be used to enhance the credit quality of conventional bonds, commercial paper programs, or other securities of companies as well as municipalities. The analysis of their value in enhancing credit quality is similar whether the supports are used to back an asset-backed financing or a conventional debt obligation of an issuer. Moody's approach to the analysis of third-party credit supports for either purpose is thus discussed under one heading below.

THE ROLE OF RATINGS

Ratings serve a limited, but important, purpose in the structured finance market, as they do in the other markets that they cover. The ratings are opinions on the credit quality of the securities offered to investors, that is, the level of risk associated with the timely payment of principal and interest on a security over the life of the instrument. They are intended to serve as indicators of the relative risk premiums necessary to compensate investors for bearing the risk of credit loss.

As applied to particular structured finance issues or issuers, ratings are intended as indicators of the relative credit risk that investors may expect for securities rated at a given level. As in the rest of the corporate sector, ratings are forward-looking measures of a security's relative cushion (or level of protection) against credit loss under a variety of plausible scenarios, including both "best" and "worst" case situations that may occur over the life of the rated security. For long-term securities, "credit loss" refers both to the probability of default and to the relative magnitude of loss in the event of default; for short-term securities, only the risk of default is being measured.

As in the rest of the corporate sector, structured finance ratings are used by investors to evaluate whether or not a security meets their credit guidelines, to weigh the level of risk premium needed to offset credit losses, and for other credit-related decisions. In all cases, ratings are not intended to forecast protections against the other major investor concern, market risk (i.e., the risk the value of a security can change because of changes in interest rates, prepayment rates or the value of other call provisions, or foreign exchange rates). It should be noted, however, that ratings on particular structured securities may indirectly reflect market risk, but only to the extent that market risk of the assets backing the security will affect the risk of credit loss on the security itself.

To facilitate risk comparisons across all types of instruments, the same rating symbols are used to rate structured financings and all other types of debt obligations. For international consistency, Moody's sovereign rating ceilings are used to "cap" ratings on structured financings denominated in foreign currencies (i.e., currencies other than that of the issuer's country of domicile). Moreover, Moody's insurance, industrial, and bank letter of credit ratings are used consistently in rating decisions as indicators of the relative strength of all third-party credit supports provided by the same institution.

To further the consistency among ratings in all market sectors, Moody's often compares the "expected" credit loss on a particular structured issue with the credit losses that are consistent with Moody's rating categories. A structured security's expected loss is an average of the losses that the investor would experience under many alternative future scenarios, where each scenario is weighted by its probability of occurring. As noted earlier, for short-term securities, Moody's analyzes the expected default probability instead of the expected loss.

This rating approach has the virtues of being simple, yet comprehensive, and can be applied in a consistent manner across countries, security types, assets, and support mechanisms. Moreover, the system is consistent with that of the traditional corporate bond rating sector, which has a long-standing policy of considering the values added by the presence of collateral protection and/or senior payment position in assigning the debt rating of a corporate issue.

Although it is quantitative to some extent, credit analysis also relies heavily on judgment, requiring that ratings be provided by an independent, experienced organization. To that end, Moody's is a company that is independent of any government or financial institution, such as a commercial or investment bank. Its analysts have no direct involvement in the sale or trading of securities, instead focusing exclusively on credit analysis. Before turning to the many factors that are considered in Moody's credit analyses of the different types of structured securities, the next section presents a general description of the rating process.

THE RATING PROCESS FOR STRUCTURED FINANCINGS

In general, the process of researching credit fundamentals, reaching rating conclusions, and keeping market participants informed is the same for structured financings as for other segments of the credit markets. The entire rating process is scheduled to provide investors with timely rating information. However, unlike traditional unsecured obligations of a corporation, issuers of structured financings are typically in a position to "structure" appropriate investor credit protections to achieve a desired credit rating. Consequently, there may be many iterations of certain aspects of the rating process as issuers restructure the securities into their most profitable form. In addition, it is often possible for issuers to alter the structure over time to maintain a desired credit level as conditions change.

Developing a "Rating Approach" to Specific Types of Financings

Accordingly, the starting point in the rating process is to develop a generalized "rating approach" to particular types of financings. With asset-backed financings, that typically involves developing an understanding of the credit risk characteristics of particular asset types. The credit implications of typical legal and structural facets of the major types of financings are also studied. The information is often published in articles and special reports as part of Moody's Structured Finance service.

Initial Meetings with the Issuer

The rating approach is also useful as a framework for preliminary discussions between Moody's analysts and issuers who are in the process of structuring new securities. Typically, the meetings begin with a brief statement by the issuer's management, which may include an overview of the industry, the corporate strategy, and the purpose and structure of the security, followed by questions from Moody's analysts. A brief presentation of specific aspects of the security may follow: type of structure; collateral; credit supports; legal issues; and implications for the issuer's own credit risk, where appropriate.

Several members of Moody's senior management with direct involvement in the rating process are often present at the meeting. In addition, industry analysts from the "fundamental" areas of Moody's (i.e., the areas that rate the companies in the same industry) are often consulted. Subsequent discussion about the security and Moody's reaction to alternative structures that may be proposed are frequently conducted by telephone. In assigning ratings, Moody's often also works with the issuer's attorneys, investment bankers, and other participants in the transaction in a series of meetings beginning at the very early stages of the transaction. If the issue involves the sale of loans that are not government-guaranteed, Moody's analysts will normally visit the loan originators and servicers to examine underwriting and collection operations.

Rating Assignments

When the security's structure is nearly finalized, a "rating committee" meets to rate the security. The size and composition of the committee varies according to the special characteristics of the issue being rated. Commonly, the rating committee includes the lead analyst or analysts for the type of security being issued along with other Moody's analysts, and, possibly, managing directors with expertise applicable to the issue.

When a decision is reached, the issuer is informed. If changes to the structure are subsequently made, the rating committee generally meets again and informs the issuer about any effect on the rating. At the time of the closing, the issuer receives a letter stating Moody's rating and, where there is special market interest, the rating and a brief rationale are distributed to the relevant financial news media. A concise summary report on the issue and its main credit characteristics may also be published around the time of closing.

Credit Monitoring

Moody's analysts continuously monitor the credit quality of the assets backing each rated issue, looking specifically for rates of default or delinquency that are significantly above the range expected when the issue was originally rated. Data related to this collateral monitoring process are made available to investors in a variety of electronic and print formats. Analysts also maintain continuing surveillance for changes in the legal and regulatory environment, the quality of the servicer, etc. Changes in the credit quality of the issuer or of third-party providers of credit supports may also be a cause for a re-evaluation of the rating.

EVALUATING CREDIT RISK

Although the asset-backed securities market covers a wide range of asset types and structures, each with its own set of special risks, those risks can generally be characterized as belonging to one of four general categories: asset risk, structural (cash flow) risk, legal risk, and third-party risk. *Asset risk* refers to the uncertainty concerning the extent to which the obligors of the underlying assets backing the security will pay as promised. The other three categories of risk refer to the degree to which the transaction is structured so that investors will receive payments as promised.

In this section we will outline the general credit quality issues that Moody's analyzes in each of those categories, as well as some of the major ways in which the analyses must be tailored to take into account the features of specific asset types and structures. The overriding goal, as mentioned earlier, is to provide a consistent analysis of credit risk across all structured financings and all Moody's ratings.

Asset Risks

General Framework
Analysis of the credit quality of any structured security that is backed by assets typically begins with an assessment of the risk in the underlying asset pool. Below we will discuss some of the methods Moody's uses in evaluating those asset pools, along with other asset considerations that may relate to the overall credit quality of the transaction.

Assets Can Supplement the Value of Third-Party Support An evaluation of the assets backing a transaction may be the logical starting point even if the transaction is fully supported by a third party. The assets generally enhance the value of a third party's support.

For a fully supported asset-backed security to default, the third party would have to default on its obligation and the funds from the assets would have to be insufficient to pay off investors as promised. Moreover, in the event of default, the severity of loss is likely to be lower, much as in the case of a traditional secured debt issue, since investors will receive funds from the assets in addition to any payments by the third party. Thus, depending on the quality of the assets and the correlation of that quality with the fortunes of the third party, the credit quality of a transaction that is backed by assets and fully supported by a third party can be higher than the credit quality of the third party itself.

Analogously, the credit quality could also be higher if, in addition to the full support of a third party, the transaction were backed by the promise of the firm raising the funds, instead of by assets. However, although the credit quality of assets and/or the issuer are important aspects of fully-supported transactions, the principal focus is the credit quality of the support provider and the legal structure of the support mechanism.[1]

Cash Flow versus Market Value Analysis The emphasis of collateral analysis is different depending on whether the transaction is based on a cash flow structure or a market value structure. With the former, the objective is twofold:

---

[1] See the discussion of the credit support provider in the Third-Party Considerations section and the discussion of the third-party support mechanisms in the Legal and Regulatory Issues section later in this chapter.

1. To assess the cash flows that investors will ultimately receive from the asset pool, which will depend on the portion of the pool that is ultimately charged off, and
2. To assess the timing of those cash flows, which is influenced by delinquency patterns, among other factors. The importance of timing in the analysis depends on whether the instrument is short term or long term, and on whether the structure allows for the accrual of interest that is owed but not paid because of a shortfall of cash in a particular period.

In the case of market value structures, the focus is on the expected liquidation value of the assets should it be needed to pay off investor claims if the issuer fails to do so. Market perceptions of the expected credit loss on the assets is one factor that will affect that expected liquidation value; in addition, many other factors must be considered, such as expected market liquidity, trends in interest rates, and (for cross-currency issues) foreign exchange rates.

Incentive to Default and the Credit Quality of Obligors Moody's analysis of the credit quality of an asset pool starts with an understanding of the key factors that affect the incentive and ability of obligors to pay off their loans as promised, and the magnitude of the loss if they do not. The incentive to continue payments as promised depends on the net "benefit" to the obligor of, default. If the net benefit is positive, then the obligor will choose to default, whether or not the borrower has the ability to pay.

The net benefit consists of the present value of the monthly cash flows that the obligor would avoid by defaulting, minus the costs of defaulting. Those costs consist of both the value of the asset, if any, that would be repossessed in the event of default, and other costs, such as the impact on the obligor's credit record, the inconvenience of responding to dunning attempts by the creditor, deficiency judgments (i.e., court-ordered payments by a borrower), bankruptcy costs, and the general social attitudes toward, and ramifications of, default.

Moody's weighs the many factors that affect an obligor's incentive to pay. The value of the remaining cash flows on the obligation depends on the original term to maturity and the rate at which the loan amortizes. The value of the asset depends first, of course, on whether there is an asset (i.e., whether the loan is secured), and then on how the asset appreciates or depreciates over time. Our evaluation of the other costs of default depends on an understanding of the general social, institutional, and legal framework that influences defaults, which can vary markedly across countries. However, even if the net benefit of defaulting is negative, the borrower still may default if he or she does not have the ability to pay and if the net value of the asset (i.e., the gross market value minus the cost of disposing of it) is less than the remaining balance on the loan. Therefore, in addition to analyzing the net benefit of default to obligors, it is also important to evaluate the credit quality of the pool of obligors.

Because of the necessarily forward-looking nature of credit ratings, Moody's analysis of those asset considerations does not simply rely on past data and experience. Another element is essential: judgment regarding how the future experience of the current pool can differ from the historical data. Portfolio data are adjusted to account for recent trends, potential changes in overall regional or national economic performance, recent changes in the issuer's underwriting and collection procedures and policies, and any specific selection criteria used in the current pool that might cause its performance to differ from that of past portfolios.

Likely Loss Scenario and the Potential Variability of Loss Moody's overall assessment of each asset pool incorporates both (1) a determination of the most likely asset performance path and (2) a projection of the variability of that estimate, reflected in the many alternative scenarios that we examine in determining the expected (or, weighted average) loss on the security due to credit losses. For example, for cash flow structures, expected losses on the pool and the variability of those losses are weighed. For market value transactions, we would estimate the expected change in market value (including the impact of credit losses) and its variability.

Accounting for the potential variability of asset losses is important in the structured finance rating process because more variable pool losses, with constant expected pool losses, generally implies higher expected losses for investors. For example, suppose the expected loss was 3% of the original pool and the transaction had credit support that covered losses up to the first 5% of the original pool. Now, consider two stylized scenarios. First, assume that we knew the potential pool losses were not very variable. For example, suppose that at the most they could be 4% and, at the least, 2%, and that each of these outcomes had a 50% probability. Then, because of the 5% credit support, investors could never realize a loss; even at the maximum pool loss, the credit support would fully protect investors. Consequently, the credit quality of that security would be very high.

On the other hand, consider a more variable case, in which there was a 50% chance that losses could be 6% and a 50% chance that they would be 0%. Again, the expected pool loss is 3%. In that situation, however, if the maximum pool losses were realized, investors could suffer a loss of 1% (5% credit support minus 6% pool loss). Since, by assumption, we know this will occur with a 50% probability, the expected, or weighted average, loss to investors would be 0.5%. Therefore, as a result of the higher variability, the credit quality of that security would be lower.

The variability of potential pool loss outcomes can be reduced through diversification. Diversification lowers the chance that many of the assets in the pool will perform unfavorably at the same time. Pool diversification can be increased by increasing the number of assets in the pool, or by reducing concentrations in certain attributes, such as geographic location. The less correlated the performance of the assets, the greater the impact of diversification in lowering variability.

In the last section of this chapter, we will describe how Moody's analysts combine their estimates of the expected losses and variability with the credit support, if any, to determine both the expected yield loss attributable to credit losses and the rating. Now, however, we turn to describing some of the structural risks that Moody's evaluates in rating structured securities.

Structural Risks

The ultimate credit quality of a security depends not only on the riskiness of the asset or the borrowing firm, but also on the manner in which the transaction is structured to channel the benefits of the assets, payments from the borrower, or payments from other forms of support to investors.

Credit Support

As noted earlier, many types of credit enhancements can be used to increase the credit quality of a structured financing. Enhancement may be "external" to the security, in the form of an insurance policy, letter of credit, corporate guarantee, or surety bond. Those external enhancements can be used either in structures that are backed by assets or in those that have no asset backing but are fully supported by a third party. In addition, for asset-backed securities, the enhancement may be internal, as in the form of a "senior/subordinated" structure or interest rate spread in cash flow transactions, or overcollateralization in market value structures.

Moody's analysis of the credit support includes an evaluation of the initial size of the enhancement, how the size changes over time, and the conditions under which the enhancement is available to protect investors. In addition, for external forms of credit support, Moody's examines both the rating of the provider and the correlation of the credit strengths of the assets or the issuer/borrower with the entity providing the enhancement.[2]

Commingling

In many structures, funds owed to investors may be "commingled," or mixed together, with the funds of another party involved in the transaction. If that other party becomes insolvent or bankrupt, a bankruptcy court may find it difficult to determine the source and ownership of the commingled funds, so that investors may become unsecured creditors of the insolvent or bankrupt firm. For example, in many cash flow transactions, a servicer receives payments from obligors and is required to pass along a portion to investors. There is a lag, however, between the time funds are collected and paid. During this period, the funds may be commingled with the other funds of the servicer. If the servicer becomes bankrupt or insolvent, investors are at risk for the amount that has been paid to the servicer but not yet passed on to the investor. For servicers rated Prime-1, this risk is negligible. To reduce the risk with lower-rated servicers, the structure can provide for a separate account to receive funds on a daily basis for the benefit of investors, thus protecting against commingling. Alternatively, a letter of credit can be obtained from a third party to back up the servicer's payment obligation.

---

[2] See the section on Third-Party Considerations.

Similarly, in a fully-supported letter-of-credit structure, there may be the risk that payments made under the letter of credit will be commingled with payments by the borrower. That would increase the risk that would normally be associated with the funds from the generally high-credit-quality letter-of-credit provider.

Eligible Investments and Reinvestment Rates

During the period between the time the cash flow is received from the underlying assets or credit support providers of the security and the time it is paid to investors, the funds may be reinvested in financial assets. Moody's analysis examines the credit quality of the investments permitted within the structure, and the amount of reinvestment income that can be expected to be earned and available to investors.

Additional Structural Considerations for Asset-Backed Securities

Loss Allocation The quality of the support provided by assets depends not just on the credit quality of the asset pool itself, but also on the manner in which that support has been structured to be available to different investors. In some transactions, certain classes may have a position that is "senior" to other more "subordinate" classes with respect to losses. In a standard "senior/subordinated" structure, the senior and subordinated classes are backed by a common pool of assets. However, the subordinated class at any point in time absorbs the current losses on the entire pool (i.e., absorbs all chargeoffs) until it is exhausted; only if losses exceed the remaining subordinated principal balance would the senior class experience a loss. In effect, then, the subordinated class is backed by the "worst" portion of the pool (on an *ex post* basis), and the senior class by the "best."

The credit support provided by subordinated classes depends on the transaction's particular loss allocation method, of which there are many. For example, the senior class has less risk if it has a senior claim on both principal and interest payments, rather than on principal payments only.

Cash Flow Allocation A related point that Moody's evaluates in analyzing the credit quality of a multi-tranche structured financing is the payment priorities, or cash flow allocation, for principal and interest cash flows. In some securities, all principal and interest cash flows are initially paid to the "first" class; cash flow in excess of promised interest is used to pay down the balance of that class, while the unpaid interest to other classes accrues. That payment structure can reduce the risk to the first class, since the tranche's accelerated payment reduces exposure to future losses. Of course, any reduction in risk to the first class would be reflected in an increase in risk to another class.

Other cash flow allocation methods are also possible. For example, the first class may receive its pro rata share of principal, but the entire pool's interest payments. Or, it may be allocated only its pro rata share of interest and scheduled principal payments, but all of the prepayments from the pool. Alternatively, it may receive its pro rata interest share, but all of the pool's principal payments (i.e., scheduled payments and prepayments). In each case, the accelerated payments to the first class (vis-à-vis a completely pro rata cash flow allocation method) reduces the risk to the first class to some extent.

The reduction in risk to the first class, however, depends on the loss allocation method. The sharpest reduction occurs in structures in which losses are not allocated until there is a shortfall of cash flow at the end of the transaction, which may occur after the first class has been retired. Risk is reduced to a lesser extent if losses are allocated as they occur and if the allocation depends on original tranche balances instead of current balances.

A reserve fund structure is a somewhat different way of combining cash flow and loss allocation methods. In a reserve fund transaction, the senior tranche receives its pro rata share of interest and principal. However, the remaining principal inflows from the assets (or, principal and interest) are allocated to a reserve fund until it reaches a specified level, at which time excess payments can be paid to the subordinate class. Losses are paid from the reserve fund first and then from the cash flows owed to the subordinated tranche. Since some cash flows are "trapped" in the reserve fund to support the senior tranche, instead of being paid immediately to the subordinated class, the senior class in this senior/subordinated structure would be of higher credit quality than one in a structure that was equivalent except for the fact that the cash flows were allocated strictly on a pro rata basis.

Interest Rate Spread Interest rate spread refers to the difference between the interest earned on the assets and the sum of the (1) interest paid on the security and (2) servicing expenses. In some structures, this difference is available to serve as a cushion against losses, and consequently could lower the additional credit support that would be consistent with a particular rating level.[3]

Generally, interest spread is "worth more" (i.e., provides more effective support) if it is "trapped" in a "spread account" (instead of being distributed to the seller of the assets) and if unpaid pool losses are accrued instead of being taken immediately as a loss by the investor. Trapping the spread makes all past (unused) spread available to cover losses in a particular period; accruing the unpaid losses makes all future spread available to pay for those losses. For example, if losses are concentrated in one period, and if spread is not trapped and losses do not accrue, then the spread from that single period may not be sufficient to cover the (concentrated) losses. On the other hand, if the spread is trapped and losses accrue, the currently accumulated spread will, in general, cover more of the losses, and any future spread will be used to pay down at least some of the portion that was not previously covered.

Interest spread typically is not equal for all contracts in the pool. Therefore, in analyzing the credit-support value of interest rate spread to investors, Moody's adjusts the initial spread percentage for the possibility that "high spread" contracts might prepay before "low spread" contracts.

---

[3] Similarly, in some structures the servicing fees are also available to pay for losses, providing additional enhancement.

Changes in the Size of Credit Enhancement Over Time Credit enhancement levels generally decline as they are called upon to pay for losses. In addition, the dollar amount of credit support will also decline in some structures because it is tied in some way to the amount of outstanding assets. For example, the dollar amounts of some letters of credit and surety bonds over time are a fixed percentage of the total outstanding pool contract balances, so that as the asset pool pays down, the dollar amount of support declines. Similarly, the credit support would decline in senior/ subordinated structures in which the tranches received principal payments on a pro rata basis; in that case, the dollar amount of support provided to the senior class by the subordinated class would decline as the principal was repaid. And, in transactions in which the security receives at least some of its support from interest rate spread, the dollar amount of that support also would fall as the collateral is paid off.

For a given structure, obligor base, and credit enhancement level, allowing the credit support to decline over time weakens the structure of the transaction from the investor's perspective, all else being equal. Investor losses could be higher with declining credit support structures, especially if (1) prepayments are heavy early in the life of the transaction, causing the assets to pay down and the dollar amount of protection to decline, and then (2) heavy losses occur late in the life of the remaining contracts. This can be of particular concern because, with some types of assets, borrowers who prepay tend to be the higher-credit-quality obligors (such as loans for recreational vehicles and manufactured housing).

Modifying the Decline in Credit Enhancement Declines in credit support can be structurally modified in many ways. Declines that occur as the support is used to pay for losses can be "reinstated" by subsequent accumulations of interest rate spread. Declines in subordination levels can be mitigated by alternative cash flow allocation mechanisms, such as distributing all pool principal payments to the senior class until it has been fully paid off, as described earlier. And, instead of setting the enhancement level at a fixed percentage of the outstanding balances, the percentage can be scheduled to change over time, or can be specified in terms of a schedule of fixed dollar amounts.

Even in structures in which the credit enhancement generally is allowed to decline, other protections can be built into the transaction to limit the decline under special circumstances. For example, a "floor," or minimum dollar amount of credit support, can be specified; that is, the credit support generally would be allowed to decline as the contracts pay down, but would stop declining once it reached the floor, except to pay for subsequent losses. In addition, loss and/or delinquency "triggers" can be established; the credit support would only be allowed to decline if loss rates or delinquencies were below some specified levels, except to pay for losses. Another possibility is to allow less of a decline in credit support for prepaid principal than for scheduled principal repayments, thus offsetting to some extent the potential deterioration in pool credit quality that could arise from "adverse" prepayments (i.e., prepayments by obligors of higher average credit quality).

Wind-Down Events for "Revolving" Structures In some structures in which
the assets are usually repaid relatively quickly, such as those backed by credit
card or trade receivables, asset principal payments are normally reinvested in new
receivables during an initial "revolving" period, instead of being paid to investors. After the revolving period, principal is paid to investors during the "amortization" period.

However, to protect investors against the possibility of a protracted
period of deteriorating credit quality, revolving periods can be ended before their
scheduled termination dates if certain "trigger" or "wind-down" events occur.
Those wind-down events are generally designed to be "early warning" signals of
declining credit quality, and the early termination of the revolving period is
intended to reduce investors' exposure to losses that might develop as the asset
quality continues to deteriorate. Typically, the events that can trigger a wind-
down include declines in yield (i.e., finance charge payments and fees), payment
rate, or new purchase rate, increases in losses or delinquencies, or the bankruptcy
of the receivable originator. All else being equal, structures are of higher credit
quality the "tighter" are the wind-down mechanisms (i.e., the less of a deterioration in credit quality necessary to trigger the wind-down).

Repurchase Provisions Another feature that can be incorporated into the
structure to protect investors against losses is a repurchase, or "take-out," or
"clean-up," provision. Typically, such a provision provides that a highly rated
third party repurchase the remaining contracts in the pool at the end of some specified period or when the pool balance has fallen below some specified level, as
long as the credit support is not exhausted. The transaction is therefore effectively
ended for investors at that point, limiting their exposure to subsequent losses on
the underlying pool. That is particularly important late in the life of the pool,
when there may be only relatively few contracts remaining, leading to potentially
highly variable subsequent pool performance. In general, for a particular structure, underlying pool, and credit enhancement level, the shorter the "take-out" or
"call" period, the stronger the protection to investors.

Liquidity Facilities Liquidity facilities are important in structures in which the
cash inflows may not match exactly the required payments to investors. The
liquidity facility provides a temporary source of funds for cash flow that is ultimately expected from another source, in contrast to a credit support provider,
which reimburses investors for shortfalls resulting from actual losses. The timing
mismatches may result from delinquencies on the assets or from other unpredictable delays in asset payment, or, in the case of commercial paper programs, from
an inability to sell new paper. Moody's analyzes the size of a structure's potential
need for liquidity, the conditions under which the structure provides the liquidity,
and the credit quality of the provider.

Legal and Regulatory Considerations

The main legal and regulatory considerations in structured financings are concerned with the potential insolvency of the issuer or other participants in the transaction. The issues that arise are generally those concerning whether the ownership of assets may be recharacterized by the courts or regulatory authorities and the extent to which legal or regulatory action can delay payment to investors.

Laws and regulations vary considerably from country to country, and sometimes across jurisdictions within a country. In many cases, the laws and regulations are developing with the evolving markets. For example, legislation in France created a legal structure (*fonds commune de creances*, or debt mutual funds) specifically for the issuance of asset-backed securities. In other countries, such as the United States, issuers typically have attempted to structure securities to fit into the body of law that existed before the development of the structured finance market, sometimes resulting in uncertainties regarding the way in which courts or regulators would apply the law to the relatively new market. The following is a description of some of the major legal and regulatory issues that arise in evaluating structured securities.

The Nature of Investors' Claims on the Assets

The extent to which investors will be able to realize the benefits of pledged assets depends on the way in which the rights in the assets were transferred. For example, in the United Kingdom, the rights can be transferred through either an equitable assignment or a legal assignment. The major difference is that in a legal assignment, the transfer is recorded and, in some regions, the issuer must notify borrowers of the transfer. The lack of notification in equitable assignments adds a number of risks to the transaction, including the possibility that the borrower may (legally) pay the originator instead of the issuer to whom the asset has been assigned. That would expose investors to the risk that the originator may become insolvent or fail to remit the funds to the issuer and could cause investors to suffer delays in payment or losses.

In the United States, a first-perfected security interest is somewhat analogous to the legal assignment in the United Kingdom. Essentially, the term "first" means that the investor has first priority on the assets. The "perfection" means that the claim has been properly registered to protect the interest. An unperfected security interest is somewhat analogous to the concept in the United Kingdom of equitable assignment. In addition, for transactions that are structured to include a reserve fund, investors can obtain a first-perfected security interest in the fund. In assessing the nature of investors' claims on the assets and reserve funds, Moody's often reviews legal opinions regarding the transfers of those claims.

Bankruptcy-Remote Issuers

Even when investors have a well-established claim in the assets, they are not assured of timely payment if the issuer of the security becomes the subject of an insolvency or bankruptcy proceeding. In that case, investors could be subject to a delay in exercising their rights with respect to the assets while a court sorts out the various claims. As a result, Moody's assesses the likelihood that the issuer will become insolvent or bankrupt. Factors that limit that likelihood include the following:

1. provisions that restrict the purpose of the issuer to that of issuing the securities,
2. provisions that restrict the ability of the issuer to incur additional debt or liabilities,
3. the ability of the issuer to pay for expenses out of capital and its revenue,
4. limitations on the issuer's ability to commence voluntary insolvency proceedings, and
5. limitations on the ability of other creditors to apply to the court system for relief.

"True Sale" of the Assets

In the United States, an investor's access to the benefits of the assets also may be impeded in the event of a bankruptcy filing by or against the seller of the assets. In that case, the court or regulator may rule that the assets were never sold, but merely pledged as collateral for a financing, and thus would possibly become subject to a court delay, or "stay." In addition, the court could allow the seller to substitute other collateral for the assets originally in the transaction. (In other countries, such as the United Kingdom, it is easier to legally establish the "sale" of an asset and hence the risk of delay or substitution is somewhat reduced.)

To determine whether the assets have been transferred in the form of a "true sale," or merely pledged, it is important to assess the extent to which the seller has retained an ownership interest in the assets. For example, Moody's examines the extent of recourse to the seller for defaulted assets, the subordinated interest and servicing fees retained by the seller, and the degree of control the seller has over the assets. In addition, a true sale opinion from a law firm may provide additional comfort that the transaction will be characterized as a transfer of assets rather than as a secured financing.

Substantive Consolidation

If the issuer is a subsidiary of a seller that becomes insolvent, a court may rule that their assets and liabilities must be consolidated in the insolvency proceeding, thereby again subjecting investors to the possibility of an insolvency-related delay. The following factors may mitigate that possibility:

1. the issuer retains a separate office at which it conducts its business,
2. the issuer has directors and executive officers who are not employees of the parent company,
3. the issuer's board of directors holds meetings to authorize all the issuer's corporate actions,
4. the issuer maintains separate corporate records and accounts,
5. the issuer's funds are not commingled with those of the parent,

6. the parent company acknowledges the separate existence of the issuer,
7. all corporate formalities are observed by the parent and the issuer,
8. the issuer is adequately capitalized in light of its business purpose and the transaction itself has a legitimate business purpose,
9. all business dealings between the parent and issuer are conducted on an "arm's-length" basis.

In addition, a legal opinion regarding substantive consolidation would add insight into the risk.

Principles of Fairness and Equity

While legal principles of fraud, fairness, and equity vary from country to country, many legal systems have some provisions for reversing transactions that are subsequently deemed to be unjust in some way. Those situations would typically arise in the event of an insolvency or a bankruptcy of the seller of assets. For example, if assets are deemed to have been sold for less than fair market value by an institution that becomes bankrupt or insolvent, a court may void the transaction, leaving investors with no collateral. In the United States, for example, such a sale could be challenged under applicable "fraudulent conveyance" laws. To protect against this risk, Moody's may use an opinion from a law firm that each transfer of assets is not fraudulent as evidence that the transfers will not be successfully challenged. In addition, Moody's will often examine statements by involved parties that a market price was paid for the assets.

In some countries, certain payments in a transaction also may be reversed if some creditors are deemed by a court to have been paid in a preferential way over other creditors while the payor was insolvent or bankrupt, or during some period immediately prior to insolvency or bankruptcy.[4] In that case, the recipient may be required to return the payment. Thus if an issuer of structured securities became insolvent, investors would be exposed to the risk of a forced return of funds already paid by the issuer.

For example, under United States bankruptcy laws, payments by an entity made while insolvent or within the applicable preference period immediately prior to a bankruptcy filing may be deemed preferential. There are a number of ways to mitigate that risk. First, as noted above, limiting the purpose and scope of activities of the issuer reduces the probability of issuer bankruptcy and therefore reduces the preference risk. Second, if the source of payment to investors is the cash flow from collateral, and if investors have a first-perfected security interest in the proceeds of the collateral, then preference risk is minimal. Third, such entities as banks and thrifts are not subject to the bankruptcy code and therefore are not subject to the same preference risk. However, they are subject to regula-

---

[4] That preference period varies across jurisdictions. In the U. S., it is generally 90 or 123 days, depending on state bankruptcy laws and may be as long as one year in the case of payments to "insiders," as defined in the Bankruptcy Code.

tory authority to avoid (i.e., reverse) payments based on similar principles. Fourth, the structure could incorporate a third-party letter of credit expiring a sufficient number of days after the end of the transaction that could be drawn on to reimburse investors for any payments deemed preferential. Such a letter of credit is often referred to as a "clawback" letter of credit.

Fifth, bankruptcy laws provide that a payment will not be considered preferential if the payment is considered a contemporaneous exchange for new value or:

1. the debt was incurred by the issuer and the investor in the ordinary course of business of the issuer and investor,
2. the payment was made in the ordinary course of business of the issuer and investor, and
3. the payment was made according to ordinary business terms.

To conclude that these conditions were met, the following facts would have to be addressed:

1. the use of the proceeds of the debt,
2. the terms of the repayment to investors,
3. the sources of funds to repay investors,
4. the previous financing sources of the issuer, and
5. the type of investor purchasing the securities.

Application of the so-called "ordinary course" exception to the preference statutes is very sensitive to the particular set of circumstances, and therefore a legal opinion addressing all relevant facts may give Moody's greater comfort that this exception may be relied upon.

Sixth, the trustee could "age" the issuer's funds; that is, the trustee could hold the monies in a segregated account for a sufficient number of days before using the funds to pay investors. As a practical matter, this means that the issuer would have to make the first payment a sufficient number of days prior to the start of the transaction and continue to make advance payments throughout the term of the transaction to ensure that sufficient "aged" funds are always available to pay investors when due.

The preferential payment risk could arise in other contexts as well. For example, if a third-party provider of credit support were to become bankrupt, payments made under the support agreement during the applicable preference period prior to the bankruptcy could be deemed preferential and required to be returned, increasing the severity of the loss caused by the support-provider's bankruptcy.

Third-Party Support

In structures that provide for support by a third party, Moody's evaluates the type of support mechanism and its legal structure to determine the extent to which it allows the support to pass through to investors in an efficient and timely manner. As noted earlier, that is the major ingredient in the analysis of structures that are fully supported by third parties.

The main types of support mechanisms are letters of credit, corporate guarantees, parent company maintenance agreements, surety bonds, and irrevocable credit agreements. Of those, only letters of credit and surety bonds are generally independent of potential defenses by the support provider to avoid payments. Therefore, in evaluating the quality of the support mechanism, Moody's analyzes the extent to which those mechanisms have been specifically designed to limit the defenses to payment.

For example, with some corporate guarantees, the fiduciary is required to first look to the obligor for payment as a condition to collecting on the guarantee, possibly resulting in a delay in payment to investors. Similarly, unless the defense is specifically waived, providers of insurance policies and surety bonds may seek to avoid payment in the event of fraud or failure of consideration. In addition, irrevocable revolving credit agreements typically terminate immediately upon the insolvency of the issuer. That would significantly weaken the support unless the transaction is structured to make the issuer insolvency-remote. Therefore, those agreements tend to be used in structures in which the liquidity but not the insolvency of the issuer is a concern.

Moody's evaluates a number of other risks when the credit support is between affiliated parties, such as in a parent company guarantee or maintenance agreement. Parent guarantees may be deemed unenforceable for a number of reasons, including the absence of an "arm's length" relationship between the parent and the subsidiary. There is also the possibility that the holders, as only indirect beneficiaries of the support, may not be entitled to bring enforcement action. Moreover, there is the risk that payments under the guarantee might be recharacterized by the court or regulatory authority as funds of the issuer and frozen or delayed in the event of the issuer's bankruptcy.

Enforceability and timeliness of payment are also key factors in the analysis of parent company maintenance agreements. Those agreements may be considered executory contracts (i.e., contracts under which the obligations have yet to be performed) by the courts and therefore may not be enforceable in the event of a bankruptcy of the parent or the subsidiary. With respect to timely payment, funds paid from the parent to the subsidiary under the agreement may get trapped in the bankruptcy proceedings of the subsidiary. Another factor that Moody's considers is the cost to the parent of not supporting the subsidiary, which depends on the strategic and financial importance of the subsidiary to the success of the parent and the costs of abrogating an obligation, in terms of damage to the parent's reputation, market access, and business position.

The most fundamental risk for a letter of credit is whether it is drawn as an irrevocable and unconditional obligation of the bank. Moody's analyzes the extent to which the bank may be able to cancel or otherwise avoid its payment obligations.

Consumer Protection Laws

Consumer protection laws can also have an impact on the riskiness of structured securities. In the United Kingdom, for instance, violation of consumer protection laws that apply to consumer debt may make the debt unenforceable. For example, provisions of the Consumer Credit Act of 1974 that apply to loans of less than £15,001 provide for licensing of, and other controls on, participants in the credit-granting process. If those provisions are violated, the loans may be unenforceable.

Regulatory Considerations

For regulated institutions, such as banks and thrifts in the United States, Moody's analyzes the transaction under the regulations of the agency that would become the receiver for a failed institution (e.g., the Federal Deposit Insurance Corporation). Of particular interest, of course, is whether the structures would maintain their integrity upon receivership. Moody's bases its interpretation of likely regulatory response on many factors, among which are verbal discussions with, and/or written assurances from, the appropriate agency and how a court would view the situation.

Evaluating the Credit Quality of Third Parties

The Servicer

In structured finance transactions the issuer often has no employees or facilities and hence must retain a third party, the servicer, to administer the day-to-day operations of the transaction. Those operations include routine asset portfolio administration duties, such as determining interest rates on assets, managing the flow of payments from borrower to issuer, and collecting late payments. Other responsibilities may include advancing funds to provide liquidity to cover loans in arrears, overseeing activities of sub-servicers, and temporarily reinvesting idle cash in short-term investments.

The impact of poor performance, or temporary nonperformance, of the servicing function obviously depends on the servicer's role in the transaction. If the servicer advances funds, for example, alternative sources of liquidity need to be evaluated. Furthermore, in transactions that are backed by the liabilities of lower-credit-quality obligors, which require active collection efforts, a decline in the quality, or a temporary suspension, of the collection effort may lead to a rise in delinquencies and losses. In addition, if a servicer becomes insolvent, funds flowing through the servicer could be tied up in insolvency proceedings; moreover, a liquidator or receiver could use provisions of the bankruptcy or insolvency laws to require the issuer to return sums that were previously paid by the servicer to the issuer.

To assess the likelihood that the servicing functions will be performed satisfactorily throughout the term of the transaction so that investors are paid on a timely basis, Moody's considers the credit quality of the servicer, whether the structure provides for a backup servicer in the event of the primary servicer's insolvency, and the ease with which a substitute servicer could be found, if necessary. The ease with which a backup servicer can be found depends on several key factors, as follows:

1. the complexity of the servicer's role in the transaction,
2. the depth of the secondary market for servicing,
3. the existence of consumer protection laws that might restrict the ready transfer of servicing rights,
4. the performance of the pool and hence the cost of servicing it, and
5. the amount of servicing fees provided for in the transaction.

The Credit Support Provider

In structures that have external forms of credit or liquidity support, the credit quality of the structure is at least partially dependent on the credit quality of the support provider. That dependence is most pronounced for structures that are fully supported by a third party. However, that does not necessarily make third party-supported structures "riskier" than structures that are fully supported internally, such as senior/subordinated transactions. In internally supported structures, the analogous risk is that of a decline in the credit quality of the assets supporting the senior class. Externally supported structures simply substitute the credit quality of the third party for at least some of the support provided internally.

When third-party support is only partial — that is, when the structure is supported partly by assets and partly by the third party — the structure's rating depends on both the size of the enhancement and the rating of the provider. To some extent, more credit support can compensate for a lower rating on a credit support provider. That is because Moody's approach is to weight all kinds of future scenarios in determining a rating. There are some future scenarios in which a lower-quality provider would not fulfill its obligations, leading to some investor losses. However, there are also other possible scenarios in which a higher-quality provider, furnishing less support, would not cover all pool losses, which would also lead to investor losses. Therefore, the average reduction in investor losses could be the same under the two support structures, making them equivalent from a credit analysis perspective.

Furthermore, for structures that depend on the credit quality of an asset pool or the issuer/borrower, as well as the credit quality of the credit enhancement provider, a downgrade of the provider will not necessarily lead to an equivalent downgrade of the structured financing. Whether the structure is downgraded, and the extent of any downgrade, depends on the (1) extent of the downgrade of the provider of the credit support, (2) amount of support provided, (3) performance of the pool or borrower, and (4) paydown of various classes (for asset-backed securities).

In rating a structured transaction, Moody's also looks at the correlation of the credit strengths of the asset pool and of the entity providing enhancement. The less the correlation, the stronger is the degree of protection provided by a given level of credit support. For example, the performance of a foreign bank supplying credit support may not be highly correlated with the credit risk of a pool of U. S. mortgages. If the foreign bank is downgraded, the performance of the assets may not have declined as much, partially offsetting the lower quality of the guarantee. On the other hand, if the two are highly correlated, the support provider may not be in a position to fulfill its obligation exactly in those circumstances in which it will be needed, leading to greater exposure to possible losses.

Other Third Parties

There are a number of other important third parties that provide various commitments and services to a structured transaction, all of which can affect the timely and ultimate payment of principal and interest to security holders. Some of those third parties and a sample of their commitments are the following:

> *Guaranteed Investment Contract Provider* — Insures reinvestment rate on investable funds.
> *Paying Agent* — Pays principal and interest to security holders; may collect and hold funds prior to distribution.
> *Trustee* — Processes payments to security holders, enforces indenture, often provides backup to other third parties, such as Master Servicer.
> *Investment Banker* — Provides fair value representations.
> *Accountants* — Provide auditing checks.
> *Issuer's Counsel* — Provides legal opinions on security interests, ownership interests, and bankruptcy issues.
> *Depository* — Makes payment to security holders, controls issuance of commercial paper.

To assess the impact of a third-party commitment on the risk of a structured transaction, Moody's follows a two-step process. First, Moody's assesses the likelihood that the third party will not fulfill its commitment or may perform it incorrectly. Second, the consequences of an incomplete performance of the commitment are weighed and quantified to the extent possible. To assess the risk of nonperformance by the third party in carrying out its required responsibilities and commitments, Moody's looks at its credit quality, operational experience, and level of expertise.

PUTTING ALL THE PIECES TOGETHER — THE RATING JUDGMENT

As outlined in this chapter, the credit performance of a structured security depends on myriad factors, including the performance of the assets or primary obligor; the extent to which third parties fulfill their obligations; the legal risks; and the structure's flow of funds, which determines the conditions under which third parties would be called upon and allocates the cash flows from the assets and third parties to investors.

In determining a rating, Moody's analyzes a wide range of possible economic and legal scenarios that would determine the amount of cash that would flow into the structure, and assigns a probability to each scenario, depending on the variability of, and correlation among, the various inputs. Then, given the flow of funds structure of the transaction, we analyze the cash flows that investors would ultimately receive under each scenario, and determine whether the payment promises to investors would be kept. As noted earlier, that determination is somewhat different for short- and long-term ratings; for short-term ratings, we simply look at the probability that the promises will not be fulfilled, while for long-term ratings, we also account for the magnitude of any shortfall that might occur.

It is often asserted that ratings represent the ability of a security to "withstand" a "worst case" scenario; for example, a security rated Aaa will withstand a depression and a security rated Aa will withstand a severe recession. Alternatively, a "worst case" may be determined as a multiple of expected losses on an asset pool. However, because Moody's long-term ratings take into account not only the probability of loss but also the severity, that "worst case"-type analysis is, at best, only a rough approximation of our general approach. Two structured financings that perform similarly in a "worst-case" scenario may perform very differently under even slightly altered circumstances. Therefore, "worst-case" performance provides only limited information regarding the overall credit quality of the instrument.

Thus our rating judgment relies on an analysis of multiple future scenarios. While those scenarios sometimes may be based on quantitative models such as regression analysis or Monte Carlo simulations, they nevertheless also depend to a great extent on the judgment of analysts. The asset pool that is currently being analyzed rarely, if ever, has exactly the same characteristics as the assets from which the historical data have been generated. In addition, the current economic and legal environment can also be quite different than that of the past. Consequently, the rating of structured securities requires a blend of quantitative analysis and experienced judgment.

Non-Real Estate Backed ABS

Chapter 3

Securities Backed by Credit Card Receivables

John N. McElravey
Director, ABS Research
Banc One Capital Markets, Inc.

INTRODUCTION

Credit card asset backed securities (ABS) have been issued in the public debt market since 1987. Over the years, they have become the largest and most liquid sector in the ABS market. Average annual new issuance of credit card ABS since 1990 has been $31.5 billion, with a peak amount of $48 billion in 1996. Because of its liquidity and relatively high credit quality issuers, credit card ABS has become something of a safe haven in times of trouble for ABS investors. Indeed, investors making their first foray into ABS generally dip their toes into credit cards before diving in to the many other asset types available.

The size of the credit card ABS sector corresponds with the growth in the credit card market overall as consumers have come to rely on credit cards as a convenient method of payment for an expanding universe of goods and services, and as a means of accessing credit. In this chapter, we summarize the key structural features of credit card securitizations and provide an overview of the credit card ABS market.

SECURITIZATION OF CREDIT CARD RECEIVABLES

The earliest credit card securitizations in the late 1980s were executed as a means of diversifying the funding sources for banks active in the credit card market. In the early 1990s, the banking industry faced the imposition of stricter capital standards by regulators. Securitization provided a vehicle to help meet these new standards by reducing balance sheet assets and thereby improving regulatory capital ratios. Securitization also allowed for the entry and growth of specialized credit card banks into the market. These banks, such as MBNA, First USA, and Capital One, were able to access the credit markets directly and achieve funding costs that were more comparable with established bankcard issuers. Much of the increased competition in the credit card market can be traced to these banks, which could not have grown as rapidly as they did without the benefits afforded by securitization.

BASIC MASTER TRUST STRUCTURE

The structure used for credit card securitization until 1991 was a stand-alone trust formed with a dedicated pool of credit card accounts and the receivables generated by those accounts. Each securitization required a new trust and a new pool of collateral. Since 1991, the master trust has become the predominant structure used in the credit card market (see Exhibit 1). As the name implies, the credit card issuer establishes a single trust. This trust can accept numerous additions of accounts and receivables, and can issue additional securities. All of the securities issued by the master trust are supported by the cash flows from all of the receivables contributed to it. The collateral pool is not segregated to support any individual securities.

For the credit card issuer, this structure lowers costs and provides greater flexibility because a new trust need not be established using a unique set of accounts each time additional securities are issued. From the investors' point of view, assessing the credit quality of a new issue requires less effort because there is only one pool of collateral to review. As the collateral pool grows, it becomes more diversified. While the characteristics of the collateral pool can change over time due to changes in interest rates, underwriting criteria, industry competition, and so on, any change in a master trust would be more gradual than would the differences in stand alone pools.

Exhibit 1: Basic Master Trust Structure

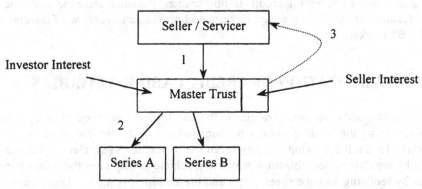

Step 1: Receivables from designated accounts are transferred to the master trust.
Step 2: Pro rata share of charge-offs and cash flows are allocated to investors.
Step 3: Pro rata share of charge-offs and cash flows are allocated to the seller.

Investor Interest/Seller Interest

Credit card master trusts allocate cash flow between the ABS investors and the credit card issuer. The "investor interest" is simply the principal amount owed to investors in the ABS. The "seller interest" is a residual ownership interest that the credit card issuer is required to maintain. This seller interest aligns the incentives of the seller with that of the investors because it has a *pari passu* claim on the cash flows. The minimum required seller interest for most master trusts tends to be 7% of outstanding receivables, though the rating agencies allow the minimum required for some trusts to be lower. The seller interest in a master trust is likely to be higher in practice, in some cases much higher, than the minimum. For example, the First Chicago Master Trust II has a seller interest of close to 50%. The actual level of seller interest will be driven by the issuer's strategy with regard to its use of securitization for its funding needs.

The seller interest absorbs seasonal fluctuations in the amount of outstanding receivables, and is allocated dilutions from returned merchandise and ineligible receivables. The seller interest does *not* provide credit enhancement for the ABS. Credit enhancement for the ABS, discussed more fully below, is provided by subordinated securities, which are part of the investor interest, or by other means provided for in the structure of the series.

As an issuer's credit card business grows, accounts that meet the eligibility criteria can be added to a master trust. An account addition normally requires rating agency approval unless it is a relatively small percentage of the current balance (usually 10% to 15%). Sellers are obligated to add accounts if the seller interest falls below its required minimum level. If the seller is unable to add accounts to the trust, then an early amortization event is triggered and investors begin receiving principal payments immediately. The risk of an early amortization gives the seller a powerful incentive to keep the seller interest above the minimum level.

The Credit Card ABS Life Cycle

Under normal circumstances, the life cycle of credit card ABS is divided into two periods: the *revolving period* and the *amortization period*. We discuss each period below.

Revolving Period

During the revolving period, investors receive interest payments only. Principal collections on the receivables are used to purchase new receivables or to purchase a portion of the seller interest if there are not enough new receivables generated by the designated accounts. The revolving period is used by an issuer to finance short-term credit card loans over a longer time period. The revolving period is used to maintain a stable average life and to create more certainty for the expected maturity date.

Exhibit 2: Class A Controlled Amortization

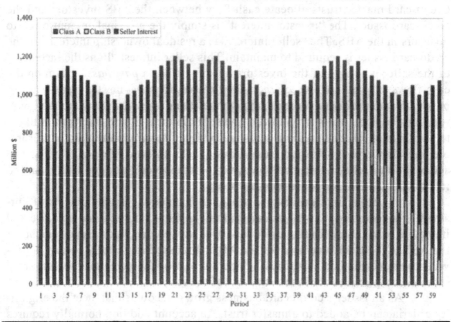

Amortization Period

After the end of the revolving period, the amortization period begins and principal collections are used to repay ABS investors. The amortization period may be longer or shorter depending on the monthly payment rate of the accounts in the master trust. The payment rate is the percentage of the outstanding receivables balance paid each month. Trusts with lower monthly payment rates will require longer amortization periods. For example, credit card ABS with a five year expected maturity might revolve for 48 months, and then enter amortization for the final 12 months of its life. This part of the credit card ABS life cycle is usually accomplished through one of two mechanisms: *controlled amortization* or *controlled accumulation*.

In a controlled amortization, principal is paid to the ABS investors in equal payments (see Exhibit 2). The example assumes one series issued out of the master trust with two classes, a Class A senior certificate and a Class B subordinated certificate. During the 4-year revolving period, investors receive only interest payments. Principal collections are used to purchase new receivables. The total amount of receivables varies over time, and these fluctuations are absorbed by the seller interest. At the beginning of year five, the revolving period ends and a controlled amortization begins. Investors receive principal payments in 12 equal installments. Principal collections not needed to repay ABS investors are used to purchase new receivables. Interest payments continue based on the declining principal balance of the ABS. The Class B amount remains fixed during Class A amortization, and the seller interest grows proportionately until the ABS investors are repaid.

Exhibit 3: Class A Controlled Accumulation

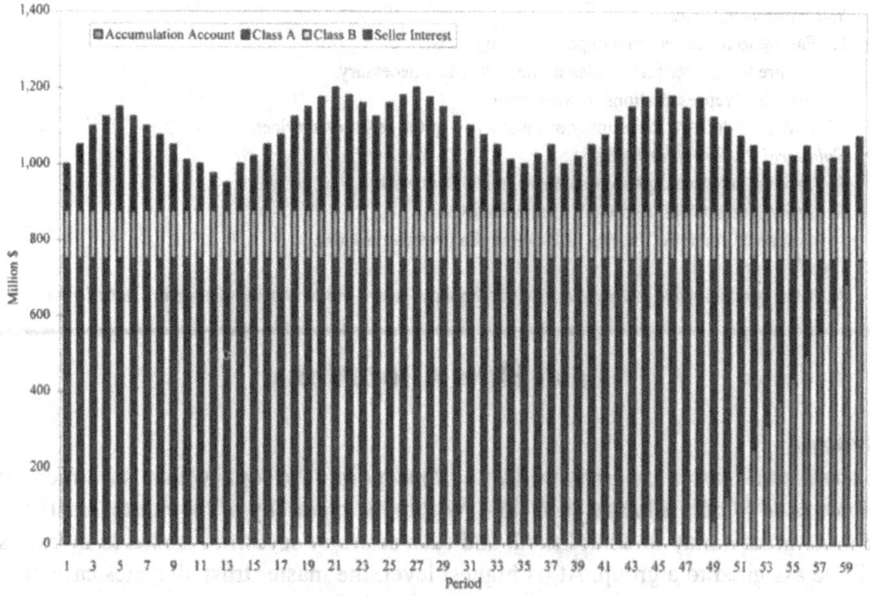

In a controlled accumulation, principal collections needed to repay ABS investors are deposited into a trust account each month and held until maturity after the end of the revolving period (see Exhibit 3). This example again assumes a simple senior/subordinated structure and a 4-year revolving period. After the end of the revolving period, principal collections are trapped in an account in 12 equal installments to be used to repay the Class A investors. Excess principal collections are used to purchase new receivables. Interest payments to investors during the accumulation period are made based on the original outstanding invested amount. A single "bullet" payment of principal is made at maturity to the ABS investors. This structural device developed as a way to emulate the cash flow characteristics of a corporate bond.

Early Amortization

Under certain circumstances, such as poor credit performance or a financially troubled servicer, an early amortization of the ABS could occur. Trigger events are put in place to reduce the length of time that investors would be exposed to a troubled transaction. Exhibit 4 lists common early amortization trigger events found in credit card master trusts. If an early amortization trigger is hit, then a transaction that is in its revolving period stops revolving and immediately begins to pass principal collections through to the ABS investors. One structural enhancement available to protect investors allows for principal to be passed through on an uncontrolled, or rapid amortization, basis. This mechanism diverts principal due to the seller toward payment of the ABS in order to get investors out more quickly.

Exhibit 4: Early Amortization Triggers

Seller/Servicer Issues
1. Failure to make required deposits or payments.
2. Failure to transfer receivables to the trust when necessary.
3. Breach of representations or warranties.
4. Events of default, bankruptcy or insolvency of the seller or servicer.

Collateral Performance Issues
5. Three-month average excess spread falls below zero.
6. Seller interest falls below the minimum level.
7. Collateral portfolio balance falls below the invested amount.

Legal Issues
8. Trust is reclassified as an "investment company" under the Investment Company Act of 1940.

Cash Flow Allocations

Groups

A credit card master trust may utilize the concept of a "group," which is a structural device used to help allocate cash flow. Within the hierarchy of the master trust, one or more groups may be established, and each series of securities issued to investors will be assigned to a group. At its highest level, the master trust allocates cash on a pro rata basis between the investor interest and seller interest. The investor interest is subdivided further on a pro rata basis at the group level. While many trusts have only one group that encompasses all of the series issued, other trusts may have two or more. In trusts with more than one group, series with similar characteristics could be grouped together. For example, a master trust with two groups could place all of the fixed-rate coupon series in one group and all of the floating-rate coupon series in a second group. The sharing of excess principal or finance charge collections, if called for in the master trust structure, will be determined at the group level.

Finance Charge Allocations

The components of the finance charge collected by a master trust include the monthly interest on the account balance, annual or late fees, recoveries on charged-off receivables, interchange,[1] and discounted receivables.[2] When expressed as a percentage of the trust's receivables balance, finance charges are called the *portfolio yield*.

Finance charge collections are allocated by most master trusts pro rata based on the outstanding invested amount of each series. This "floating" allocation adjusts as a series amortizes or accumulates principal collections in a princi-

---

[1] Interchange is a fee paid to the bank that issues the credit card. It compensates the bank for taking on credit risk and allowing a grace period. Interchange is created when a bank discounts the amount paid to a merchant for a credit card transaction. Interchange is shared by the merchant's bank, the bank issuing the credit card, and Visa or MasterCard for clearing the transaction.

[2] Some master trusts allow receivables to be added at a discount. The discount typically ranges between 1% and 5%. When the face amount of the receivable is collected, the discounted portion is included as a finance charge collection. This practice can temporarily increase the portfolio yield on the collateral pool.

pal funding account. Excess finance charge collections may or may not be shared by series in the same group depending on the structure of the master trust. Some master trusts, such as Discover Card Master Trust, utilize a "fixed" allocation of finance charges. In this structure, the proportion to be allocated to a particular series is fixed at the end of the revolving period and is based on the original principal balance of the series. This structure allows for a greater relative proportion of finance charge collections to go to amortizing series. Such a structure can also be used by an issuer in the event of an early amortization to reallocate a portion of the seller's finance charges to investors to cover any potential shortfall.

Master trusts that allocate finance charges pro rata based on the size of the series invested amount are known as "nonsocialized" master trusts. Finance charges are available to each series to cover its allocated charge-offs, servicing fees, and to pay the coupon to the ABS investors each month. Some nonsocialized master trusts do not share excess finance charges. In other nonsocialized trusts, once all of the expenses are covered, the series included in the same group may share excess finance charges. If excess finance charges are shared by the series in a group, then they are distributed to the other series based on need. Any excess finance charges left over are considered excess spread.

The advantage of a nonsocialized master trust is that the risk of early amortization can be isolated at the series level. The disadvantage is that high coupon series are at a relatively greater risk of early amortization if there is a shortfall in finance charge collections. The sharing of excess finance charges helps mitigate, but does not eliminate, this risk. Most master trusts today, such as the Chase Credit Card Master Trust and the Sears Credit Card Master Trust II, are structured as nonsocialized trusts that allow for sharing excess finance charges.

An alternative structure, used by a small number of credit card ABS issuers, is a "socialized" master trust. In such a structure, finance charges are allocated to series within a group based on need. Need is determined by the costs of each series — the coupon, servicing fees, and allocated charge-offs. (Charge-offs are allocated to a series pro rata based on its size within the group.) The expenses for the group are the weighted average of the expenses for each series. Series with higher coupon costs will receive a larger allocation of finance charge collections. The advantage of socialization is that finance charge collections are combined to help support higher cost series, and thus help avoid an early amortization. However, their fates are linked. All series in a group will make payments as expected, or they will all enter early amortization together. Citibank Credit Card Master Trust I and Household Affinity Master Trust I are two prominent examples of socialized master trusts.

Principal Collections

Principal collections are allocated on a pro rata basis to each series in the same group based on the size of its invested amount. The allocation of principal to a series is determined by its point in the ABS life cycle. Series that are in their revolving period receive no principal collections. Their principal collections can be reallocated, and may be shared with other series that are amortizing. Sharing principal collections is a structural enhancement that helps to ensure the timely payment of principal to ABS investors. Principal that is not needed to repay investors is reinvested in new receivables.

For a series in its amortization or accumulation period, principal collections allocated to it will be used to repay investors. The allocation of principal is determined by the size of the invested amount of the series at the end of its revolving period. Even though the certificates are amortizing, the allocation percentage to the series will be fixed based on its original invested amount. If the credit card ABS accumulate principal or amortize over 12 months, then 1/12 of the principal amount of that series will be paid to it. Principal collections in excess of what is necessary for amortization, depending on the structure of the trust, may be shared with other series in the same group as needed to meet their amortization schedules. Otherwise, excess principal is used to purchase additional receivables.

Credit Enhancement

In order to establish an investment grade rating on credit card ABS, credit enhancement is necessary to absorb losses. The amount of credit enhancement needed will vary from one master trust to another based on the desired rating level and the credit performance of an issuer's credit card portfolio. Early credit card transactions carried letters-of-credit from commercial banks as credit enhancement. However, downgrades of a number of credit enhancers exposed ABS investors to downgrades on their investments. While some issuers still rely on surety bonds, internal forms of credit enhancement have become the norm.

Excess Spread

Excess spread is perhaps the most important measure of the health of a credit card master trust, and as such is a key early amortization trigger. Excess spread is simply the cash flow left over each month after the investor coupon, servicing fees, and charge-offs have been allocated to each series. The calculation of excess spread is straightforward, as shown in Exhibit 5, with the values expressed as an annualized percentage of the outstanding receivables balance. If the 3-month moving average of excess spread for a particular series in a non-socialized master trust falls below zero, then an early amortization event with regard to that series has occurred. In socialized master trusts, the excess spread for all series in the same group will be equal because they share finance charge collections based on the weighted-average cost of the group. An early amortization trigger based on a decline in excess spread will, therefore, affect all series in the group.

Cash Collateral Account

A *cash collateral account* (CCA) is a cash reserve account funded at closing and held by the trust. The cash to fund the CCA is usually lent by a third party and invested in high-grade, short-term securities. The CCA is used to protect against short falls in cash flow due to rising charge-offs, and any draws on it are reimbursed from future excess spread.

Exhibit 5: Excess Spread Calculation

Gross Portfolio Yield	19%
Less:	
Charge-Offs	6%
Net Portfolio Yield	13%
Less:	
Investor Coupon	6%
Servicing Fee	2%
Excess Spread	5%

Collateral Invested Amount

An alternative to a cash reserve is a *collateral invested amount* (CIA), which is a privately placed subordinated tranche of a series. The CIA is placed with a third-party investor, and the investor may or may not require a rating on the CIA. The CIA is an improvement for the issuer over the CCA because this tranche is backed by collateral rather than cash. Like the CCA, the CIA is available to protect against short falls in cash flow due to declining excess spread. The CIA tranche has the benefit of a spread account, which is not available as credit enhancement to other investors. Draws on the CIA also are reimbursed through excess spread.

Subordination

As credit card ABS have evolved, structures have become more complex. Letters-of-credit have given way to CCAs or CIAs, which in turn have been replaced by some issuers with rated subordinated securities. The subordinated classes also are placed with public ABS investors and tend to be rated in the single-A or triple-B categories. A typical structure might include AAA-rated Class A senior certificates, a single-A rated Class B subordinated tranche, and then a CIA or CCA. More recently, Class C tranches issued to outside investors have been rated at triple-B levels in place of the CIA (see Exhibit 6). The Class C tranche is credit enhanced by a spread account that can trap additional cash out of excess spread if certain credit performance triggers are tripped. Using subordinated tranches allows the issuer to monetize a larger portion of its collateral portfolio, and allows it to reach a wider investor audience. Some issuers have developed structures that included ERISA-eligible subordinated classes to improve their overall cost of funding. A number of issuers, including Citibank, First USA, MBNA and Chase, have included certificated C pieces in their credit card ABS transactions.

Rating Agency Considerations

Rating agency criteria have evolved over time as new structures, such as rated C-pieces, have been introduced. The structural integrity of credit card ABS is tested by stressing the historical performance of critical variables related to the cash flows. The rating agencies generally require three to five years of historical data, and will examine vintage data in order to estimate loss curves and the ultimate level of charge-offs. Once base line performance is determined, then different cash flow stresses are used depending on the desired rating. The key quantitative variables for analyzing credit card securitizations include portfolio yield, charge-offs, monthly payment rate, monthly purchase rate, and the investor coupon.[3] Each is discussed below.

- Portfolio yield, as noted above, is a measure of the income generated by the credit card receivables. While portfolio yield is driven largely by the APR on accounts and fees, usage by account holders also plays an important role. All else being equal, a portfolio with proportionately more revolving accounts relative to convenience users will translate into a higher portfolio yield.
- Charge-offs are the credit losses experienced by the portfolio, and are taken by most issuers at about 180 days past due. Peak losses for credit card accounts have been observed at about 24 months of seasoning.
- The monthly payment rate is an important variable in the analysis because high payment rates can be a source of strength and implied credit enhancement. A large proportion of convenience users, while depressing portfolio yield, can sharply increase payment rates. A higher payment rate means that investors will be paid out more quickly during an early amortization.
- Related to the payment rate is the purchase rate, which is the generation of new receivables by the designated accounts. Higher purchase rates mean more receivables are being generated to support outstanding ABS. Bankruptcy of the seller, such as a department store chain, is the main risk with regard to the purchase rate because cardholders may stop using the card.

Exhibit 6: Credit Card Series Structure

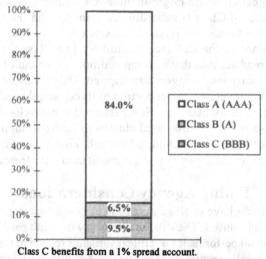

Class C benefits from a 1% spread account.

---

[3] The methodology and variables used are based on Standard & Poor's rating criteria. The other rating agencies perform a similar analysis when rating credit card ABS.

Exhibit 7: Standard & Poor's Benchmark Credit Card Stress Scenarios

	AAA-Rating	A-Rating
Charge-Offs	3-5× steady-state levels	2-3× steady-state levels
Portfolio Yield (1)	11%-12% annual rate	12% annual rate
Payment Rate	45%-55% of steady state level	50%-60% of steady state level
Purchase Rate	0%-5% annual rate	0%-5% annual rate
Investor Coupon (2)	15%	14%

(1) Based on proposed legislative caps.
(2) Coupon for uncapped floaters.

- Floating-rate ABS generally require more credit enhancement than fixed-rate transactions because the agencies assume in their stress scenarios that market interest rates increase dramatically. Higher funding costs reduce the available excess spread.

The stress tests run by the rating agencies force portfolio yields, payment rates, and purchase rates down sharply at the same time that charge-offs rise. This combination compresses excess spread and causes an early amortization of the transaction. Exhibit 7 shows generic stress scenarios for credit card ABS transactions used by Standard & Poor's. The agencies may deviate from these benchmark levels depending on the qualitative factors of the seller's business. Some of the key qualitative elements that go into the rating analysis are new account underwriting, servicing and collections, marketing, card type (private label versus general purpose), geographic diversification, strategic objectives of the firm, account seasoning, and the competitive position of the issuer. These qualitative factors, among others, determine how the generic stress factors will be modified and applied to an individual issuer's credit card portfolio.

THE CREDIT CARD ABS MARKET

Credit card ABS is the largest and most liquid part of the ABS market. Over the 5-year period ending October 22, 1999, total new issuance of credit card ABS has been between $35 billion and $50 billion (see Exhibit 8), and there are over $200 billion of credit card ABS outstanding. The large number of issuers and dollar amount outstanding makes this sector a particularly active secondary market. Consequently, spreads for credit card ABS are a benchmark for other ABS sectors. During the past decade, the credit card industry has experienced rapid growth and increasing competition. That dynamic culminated in sharp increases in outstanding receivables in 1995 and 1996, and was reflected in the amount of new credit card ABS issued during that period. However, rapid growth and intense competition also led to problems with asset quality (see Exhibit 9). Charge-offs rose steadily and excess spreads dropped from the middle of 1995 through the middle of 1997 as consumer bankruptcy rates reached record levels.

Exhibit 8: Public Market Credit Card ABS Issuance

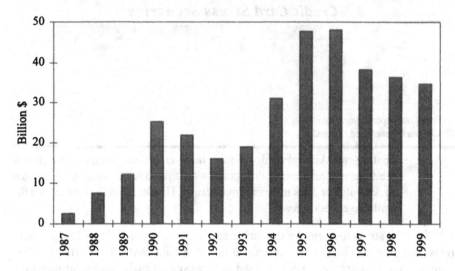

Data through October 22, 1999.

Exhibit 9: Banc One Capital Markets Credit Card Performance Indices

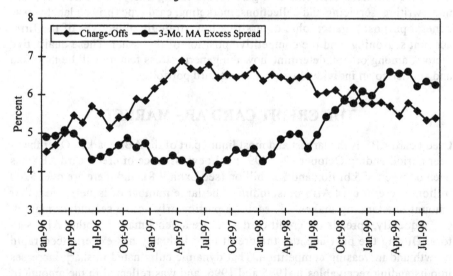

Industry Consolidation

To better meet their credit underwriting and customer service needs, stronger credit card companies invested heavily in technology, and increased their scale of operations to spread the costs of that investment over more accounts. Many smaller or weaker firms have been unable or unwilling to meet the challenge of the new competitive environment, and have decided to exit the business. As a result, consolidation has been one of the key themes in the credit card business for the past few years. To illustrate, at the start of 1987 there were slightly more than $80 billion of credit card receivables outstanding in the U.S., and the top ten credit card companies had a combined market share of about 40%. At the start of 1999, there were about $445 billion of outstanding credit card receivables, and the top ten credit card companies had a combined market share of 75% (see Exhibit 10).

As the credit card industry has consolidated, so has the market for credit card ABS. The three largest credit card issuers accounted for about 58% of credit card ABS outstanding as of year-end 1998, and the top five were responsible for approximately 76%. While consolidation has reduced the number of issuers in the market, the overall credit quality of those that remain has improved. Eight of the top ten sponsors have corporate debt ratings of A2/A or better. From the standpoint of liquidity and issuer quality, this sector is the strongest in the ABS market.

Credit Card Market Segments

The major issuers of credit card ABS fall into four major categories: commercial banks, consumer finance, independents, and retailers. Following are some examples of the issuers in each of these categories.

- *Commercial Banks:* Bank One, Citibank, Chase, BankAmerica
- *Consumer Finance:* MBNA, Household, Capital One, Providian
- *Independents:* Discover, American Express
- *Retailers:* Sears, Dayton Hudson, World Financial Network, Federated

General Purpose Cards

The credit card ABS market is divided into two major segments: *general purpose* and *private label*. The larger of the two segments includes transactions sponsored by issuers of general-purpose credit cards. General-purpose credit cards include both Visa and MasterCard cards issued by commercial banks and consumer finance companies, as well as the independent networks of merchants built by Discover Card and American Express. This group of issuers represents the vast majority of the credit card ABS market. Issuers of general-purpose cards tend to price new ABS at tighter spreads relative to private label issuers. Tiering in that market favors the largest, most frequent issuers with stable credit performance. Citibank and MBNA are generally considered to be the benchmark issuers in this market segment.

Exhibit 10: Top Ten General Purpose Credit Card Issuers

Rank	Sponsor Name	Corporate Ratings (M/S)	Outstanding Receivables ($ bn)	Market Share (%)	Trust Size ($ bn)	Percentage Securitized (%)	Outstanding Securities ($ bn)	As Percent of Market (%)	Series Issued in 1998	Series Issued in 1999
1	Bank One/First USA	Aa3/AA-	69.86	15.7	55.74	74.9	41.77	20.8	11	3
2	Citigroup	Aa3/AA-	69.60	15.6	51.46	70.8	36.44	18.2	9	3
3	MBNA	Baa2/BBB	48.90	11.0	45.02	84.2	37.92	18.9	9	2
4	Discover	Aa3/A+	32.80	7.4	28.11	66.4	18.65	9.3	6	3
5	Chase Manhattan	Aa3/A+	32.20	7.2	21.79	81.6	17.78	8.9	7	0
6	BankAmerica	Aa1/AA-	20.96	4.7	3.57	71.7	2.56	1.3	2	1
7	Amex	Aa3/A+	16.70	3.8	10.63	67.8	7.21	3.6	2	1
8	Fleet/Advanta	A1/A+	15.10	3.4	9.78	34.5	3.37	1.7	1	1
9	Capital One	Baa3/BBB-	14.30	3.2	11.01	85.1	9.36	4.7	4	0
10	Household Bank	A2/A	14.30	3.2	9.81	55.7	5.46	2.7	1	0
	Top Ten Total		334.72	75.2	246.90	69.3	180.53	90.0	52	14
	ABS Market Total		445.00				200.50		62	16

[1] Through December 1998

Teaser Rate Cards

In an attempt to gain market share in the face of fierce competition, credit card issuers devised a number of innovations to establish brand loyalty with new customers. Low-price cards, with no annual fee and up-front "teaser" rates, have been used to lure customers away from competitors. These accounts often allow the new customer to transfer existing balances from other, higher rate cards. The teaser rate usually is in effect for 6 to 12 months, and then steps up to a higher rate based on the borrower's credit risk. Balance transfers have been used to great effect, though many borrowers have become adept at rolling balances from one card to another at the end of the teaser rate period. One of the problems with this approach is the potential for adverse selection in the account base. Borrowers with poor credit are more likely to respond to a teaser rate, and may be less likely to roll balances to a new card in the future because they have less credit options.

Affinity and Co-Branded Programs

One of the uses of the technological investment made by card issuers has been in the customer retention effort. A package of interest rates, credit limits, and other services can be offered to entice customers to stay once the teaser period ends. These packages may come in thousands of possible combinations. The method of mass customization is made possible by the sophisticated computer systems that search for new customers in huge databases, and track the credit performance and profitability of existing customers. Two issuers that practice a mass customization strategy are Capital One and Providian.

Two popular products created by issuers to differentiate themselves in the minds of cardholders and retain them as customers are *affinity* and *co-branded programs*. Affinity cards are issued by a bank in association with a special interest group. This group may be a college alumni association, professional group, or sports team, which receives a fee from the bank. The bank uses its affinity program to attract a certain demographic group to use its card. Co-branded cards are programs that associate a bank's credit card with a particular commercial firm. Customers can earn certain rewards from the commercial firm for making purchases with the card. Earning mileage toward free tickets on airlines is probably one of the most popular bank co-brand programs.

Private Label Credit Cards

The other, much smaller segment of the credit card market includes private label credit cards, which are sponsored by retailers for use in their own stores. This segment has been dominated by issuance from Sears, which represents about one-third of the private label market. Retail credit card accounts are most often viewed by the sponsor as a means to increase sales, and credit underwriting may not be as stringent as it is for general-purpose credit cards. As a result, charge-offs tend to be higher on private label credit card master trusts than on a typical bank card master trust. On the other hand, APRs and portfolio yields do tend to be higher to compensate for the greater risk in the private label portfolio (see Exhibit

11). Because private label transactions tend to be less frequent and somewhat smaller, they tend to price at a concession to the transactions sponsored by general-purpose card issuers. Nevertheless, good value can be found among private label issuers by investors willing to investigate them.

CONCLUSION

The credit card ABS market is the largest, most liquid asset-backed sector with the greatest investor acceptance. For this reason, it can be viewed as a safe haven for ABS investors in stressful market times. A strong economy, healthy consumer balance sheets, and greater acceptance of credit cards for non-traditional uses have led to a sharp increase in outstanding receivables over the past few years. Meanwhile, the market weathered a deteriorating credit situation from 1995 through 1997, and appears fairly strong as of this writing with falling charge-off rates and rising monthly payment rates. Nevertheless, a growing need for technology and intense competition have led to consolidation in the industry, though there seems to be no less competition as a result. Increasing issuance in the European market should produce a more global credit card ABS market in coming years, and additional innovations are sure to follow. While the unbridled growth of the mid 1990s seems unlikely to be repeated, the credit card ABS market should continue to be the benchmark sector for the foreseeable future.

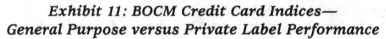

Exhibit 11: BOCM Credit Card Indices—
General Purpose versus Private Label Performance

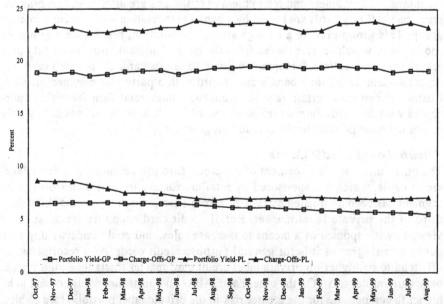

Chapter 4

Securities Backed by Auto Loans and Leases

Neil McPherson
Head of ABS Research
Credit Suisse First Boston

INTRODUCTION

Auto ABS are a substantial part of today's ABS market. As such, they represent a core holding for the majority of United States domestic ABS investors. Indeed, along with credit card ABS, auto ABS are often referred to as "plain-vanilla" or "bread and butter" holdings in an ABS market with ever more complex structures. The bulk of auto ABS offer excellent liquidity, high credit quality and relatively simple cash flows, are free of refinancing risk and generally have predictable prepayments.

THE AUTO ABS MARKET

Of the almost $197 billion in ABS issued in the public market in 1998, auto ABS issuance comprised approximately 18%, with over $35 billion in supply. Auto issuance continued to be strong for the first half of 1999, with almost $22 billion issued. Issuance of auto ABS has grown dramatically since the market's inception in 1985. From 1990 to 1998, the ABS market as a whole has grown at over a 23% compounded annual growth rate (CAGR) while autos have grown at a 15% CAGR. The slower growth rate of auto ABS reflects the rapid development of new asset classes and the growth of the ABS market overall. With the exception of a dip in 1994, auto issuance has shown a steady upward trend. That year, the decline in auto ABS issuance was primarily due to a particularly bearish fixed income market.

Asset-Backed Commercial Paper

Apart from the anomalous lower growth in 1994, the auto ABS market has grown less rapidly than the ABS market overall. Reasons for this include: (1) the increase in lease financing (discussed later) and (2) captive finance companies' increased use of asset-backed commercial paper (ABCP) conduits and single-seller ABCP programs. While measuring the precise amount of auto funding currently obtained by issuers via ABCP is difficult, we know anecdotally that it has grown substantially. Growth in total ABCP issuance has been explosive, from $382 billion outstanding at the end of 1998 to $424 billion by July 1999.

Based on Moody's and CSFB data, at the end of the third quarter of 1997, the top 20 multi-seller, partially-supported ABCP programs[1] (ranked by outstandings) had some $12 billion of their $77 billion (16% of their assets) invested in auto loans and/or ABS. By the end of the first quarter of 1998, the top 20 ABCP programs had almost $21 billion of their $112 billion (19% of their assets) invested in auto finance receivables. Auto finance receivables are a good fit for ABCP conduits because they are high quality, short duration assets. Furthermore, because auto loans have little prepayment variability, they are also easily swapped to LIBOR, which can help alleviate the basis risk between CP funding rates and fixed-rate auto paper. ABCP conduits can buy "raw" loans or pools of securitized assets. ABCP conduits can also be effectively used as warehouse financing for an auto lender, allowing the timing of term securitizations for best execution and also as a balance sheet management tool.

GMAC's ABCP conduit, New Center Asset Trust (NCAT), is a good example. NCAT's outstandings grew from $4.8 billion to $7.8 billion from the third quarter of 1997 to the first quarter of 1998, as presumably GMAC viewed this period as less than optimal for term securitization. World Omni has also has an ABCP vehicle in place to more effectively manage their lease securitizations. Their ABCP conduit has grown to over $1 billion in outstandings as of March 31, 1999.

Auto ABS Investors

Using CSFB historical data on the sales of auto ABS, it appears that the largest segment of the auto ABS investor base is investment advisors. Investment advisors, who are often benchmarked against an index with an intermediate duration such as the Lehman Aggregate or Salomon Broad index, often use auto ABS for their short-duration, liquidity and AAA ratings. Banks, corporations and insurance companies are also major components of the auto ABS investor base. If and when risk-based capital regulations are revised for ABS (current proposals lower the risk weighting from 100% to 20%) and a repo financing market develops, we would expect the investor base to broaden.

AUTO ABS STRUCTURES

In auto loan securitizations, as with other ABS, receivables are sold to a bankruptcy-remote, special-purpose corporation (SPC). The receivables are then trans-

---

[1] Multiseller refers to the ABCP conduit's ability to buy assets from a variety of sources, or seller/servicers. This contrasts with single-seller programs (like NCAT). Partially supported ABCP is CP whose repayment is primarily dependent upon the cash flows from a pool of assets, and is usually combined with credit enhancement and a liquidity facility from third parties. This contrasts with fully supported ABCP, whose repayment is guaranteed via a surety bond, letter of credit or irrevocable liquidity facility.

ferred into a trust, which can take one of a few forms: grantor trust, owner trust and, more recently, Financial Asset Securitization Investment Trust (FASIT).

In practice, all auto securitizations are issued as either grantor trusts or owner trusts. To date, no FASIT auto ABS deals have been issued, as the sale of assets to the trust under FASIT generates an immediately taxable event for the issuer, and any gains on the collateral transfer must be recognized (and taxes paid) immediately. FASIT regulations were designed to provide maximum flexibility for an issuer with regard to asset substitution and also to allow lower classes of securities to be issued as debt (and therefore ERISA-eligible). The economics of a FASIT auto ABS deal are not currently attractive versus the grantor/owner trust structures.

Grantor Trust Cash Flows

From an investor's standpoint, the main distinctions between grantor and owner trusts are in the cash flows. Grantor trusts are passthrough structures where the securities sold are in the form of certificates and represent undivided interests in the pool of receivables securitized. Subordinated tranches in a grantor trust structure are not ERISA-eligible. Passthrough structures have a wide principal payment window, and, typically, cash flows paid to the investor are simply a pro rata share of the cash flows thrown off by the collateral. A typical grantor trust's senior bond backed by auto collateral (shown in Exhibit 1) might have a 1.75-year average life with a 56-month principal window. The structure's subordinated Class B, sized at 5%, has the same window and average life, since the structure is pro rata pay. In a pro rata pay structure, principal collections are allocated proportionally according to the original tranche sizes, with 95% of principal collected each period paying down the senior bond, with the remainder paying down the subordinate bond.

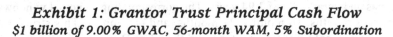

Exhibit 1: Grantor Trust Principal Cash Flow
$1 billion of 9.00% GWAC, 56-month WAM, 5% Subordination

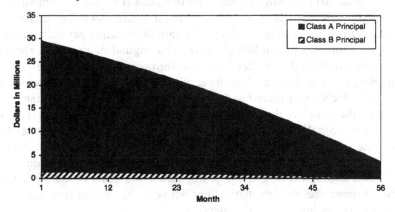

Source: Credit Suisse First Boston.

Exhibit 2: Owner Trust Principal Cash Flow
$1 billion of 9.00% GWAC, 56-month WAM, 5% Subordination

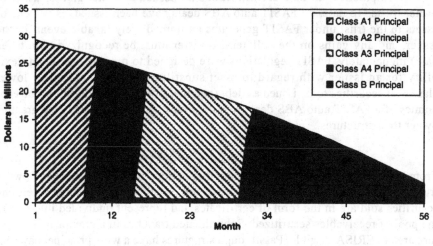

Source: Credit Suisse First Boston.

Owner Trust Cash Flows

By contrast, owner trusts are "time-tranched." By time-tranching the cash flows, the issuer can create several different bonds against one collateral pool, with average lives and principal windows tailor-made to suit investor preferences. For example, a representative owner trust issue (shown in Exhibit 2) might be comprised of four senior class bonds, with average lives of 0.38 years, 1.03 years, 1.92 years, and 3.19 years. The structure's Class B subordinate tranche, also sized at 5%, has an average life of 2.94 years. The corresponding principal windows are 9 months, 8 months, 16 months, 21 months, and 48 months. This structure is a sequential principal payment structure, and the Class B is paid in a "modified pro rata" fashion, only after the Class A1 bond is fully paid down. Essentially, the B class gets some extra principal in its first month of principal payment so that the percentage of subordination is brought back to its original sizing of 5%. The owner trust usually offers slightly better execution for the issuer than a purely pro rata pay structure because the bonds' narrower windows can be sold at tighter spreads.

The decision to issue bonds through either an owner or a grantor trust depends on the structure that results in the lowest all-in-cost ("best execution") for the issuer. Smaller issuers may have less flexibility to use owner trusts because the individual tranches would be too small. Other considerations that impact the choice of owner versus grantor trust might include future liquidity, the issuer's outstanding deals, and competing new issue deals in the marketplace. Exhibit 3 summarizes the key distinctions between the various issuance vehicles and the impacts on investors and issuers.

Exhibit 3: ABS Issuance Vehicles

	Grantor Trust	Owner Trust	Revolving Trust	FASIT
Interest in Trust	Securities represent undivided interest in receivables	Securities represent debt	Securities represent debt	Securities represent debt
Structures	Very limited Ability to tranche cash flows limited to senior/sub structure and "stripped" classes	Multi-class, multiple maturities except for mortgages	Multi-class, multiple maturities except for mortgages	Multi-class, multiple maturities FASIT may issue new securities over time - warehousing concept
Investment of	Very limited	Flexible	Flexible	Flexible
Payments Collected	Principal and interest payments must pass through to investors by next distribution date	Receivable's cash flows may be restructured	Receivable's cash flows may be restructured	Receivable's cash flows may be restructured
Qualifying Assets	Any debt instrument Autos, RVs, boats, trucks	Any securitizable asset Autos, student loans, home equity, equipment loans	May be extended to most assets Most common with wholesale auto, credit cards	Any debt instrument; cash and cash equivalents; foreclosure property; hedging instruments; regular interests in another FASIT or REMIC
Acquisition of Assets	Very limited Prefunding purchase allowed up to 90 days Trustee cannot purchase new assets or substitute assets after prefunding period has expired	Limited Prefunding period varies Trustee cannot purchase new assets or substitute assets after prefunding period has expired	Limited Pre-funding timetable not applicable since collateral may be acquired during revolving period Allows for the addition/ substitution of collateral when debt instruments prepay	Flexible-permitted assets can be added or substituted any time Pre-funding timetable not applicable since collateral may be acquired anytime Allows for the addition/ substitution of collateral when debt instruments prepay
Elimination of Excess Over-collateralization	Very limited Generally, owner may not reacquire assets without liquidating	Flexible Owner can reacquire assets easily	Flexible Owner can reacquire assets easily	Flexible Owner can reacquire assets easily

Exhibit 3 (Continued)

	Grantor Trust	Owner Trust	Revolving Trust	FASIT
Implications for Investors				
Taxability	Own underlying assets—therefore, all income less expenses subject to certain limitations on deductions	Noteholders taxed as holders of debt instruments	Certificateholders taxed as holders of equity instruments	Taxed as holders of debt instruments
	Interest taxed as ordinary income less deductions for expenses (subject to certain limits)			Additionally, holders of high yield interest can not use net operating losses to offset any income derived from FASIT debt
	Principal treated as a return of capital			
Implications to Issuer				
Taxation	Not taxed at the entity level	No entity level tax if formed as a tax partnership; usually part of originator's consolidated tax group	Tax debt of the originator of the trust or its consolidated tax group; often has partnership "back-up"—see Owner Trust	Not taxed at the entity level
Accounting	Generally, sale treatment	Generally, sale treatment	Generally, sale treatment	Generally, sale treatment
Recognition of gains or losses on asset addition	Gain or loss recognized upon sponsor's sale of interest	No tax gain or loss upon issuance of debt; gain or loss upon sale of retained subordinated (equity) interest	No tax gain or loss upon issuance of debt; gain or loss upon sale of retained subordinated (equity) interest	FASIT treated as a sale therefore gain (but not loss) must be recognized
		Accounting gain or loss based on sale treatment	Accounting gain or loss based on sale treatment	

Sources: Stroock, Stroock & Lavan; Dewey Ballantine.

In a positively-sloped yield curve environment, owner trusts can result in better execution for an issuer in the same way REMIC arbitrage profitably produces CMOs from mortgage passthroughs. In an owner trust ABS, shorter average life tranches are typically priced off LIBOR or EDSF. The all-in cost to the issuer from selling a multi-tranche (owner trust) ABS can be lower than from a grantor trust's single tranche passthrough security.

From the investor's perspective, tranches in an owner trust transaction generally trade tighter than grantor trust tranches with a similar average life. Investors typically pay up for the tailored average lives, shorter principal repayment windows, less average life variability and principal lockout of tranched deals. In particular, the principal lockout gives the investor structural call protection and better rolldown performance.

Investors sometimes prefer grantor trusts over owner trusts because, in addition to more spread for the wider window, grantor trusts can offer good liquidity. Because they are single tranches, tranche sizes often exceed $500 million. Especially in relatively flat yield curve environments, rolldown returns are less important and the "spot spread give-up" (discussed later) may be minimal.

Credit Enhancement

Credit enhancement protects ABS investors from losses on the underlying collateral and thus allows the securities to achieve high investment grade ratings. Typically, in an auto ABS transaction, the senior securities are enhanced to AAA levels and subordinate securities are enhanced to A or BBB ratings. To achieve AAA ratings, credit enhancement must be sufficient so that the collateral pool can experience many multiples of the base case, or the expected level of losses, before the senior bonds experience any loss of principal.

For prime auto collateral (discussed later in this chapter), a AAA bond can typically withstand from five to seven times base case loss experience. For an A rating, the multiple of base case losses assumed in sizing credit enhancement may be from two to three times base case losses. Credit enhancement levels also vary according to the issuer and the collateral and many factors are taken into account to establish the base case losses for a given collateral pool.

Determining base case losses is a critical element of the ratings process, as these must be adequately understood before stress cases can be designed for bonds with a given rating. Discussed below are some of the more relevant factors for determining base case losses.

Mix of Borrower/Loan Types —
Prime versus Non-Prime and Sub-Prime

The borrower or loan mix (prime versus non-prime and sub-prime) has obvious implications regarding expected losses. Clearly, the higher the percentage of prime loans in the collateral pool being securitized, the lower the expected loss level, as prime borrowers are less likely to default by definition.

New-Versus-Used Vehicle Mix
The new-versus-used vehicle mix is important in forecasting losses. New vehicles generally are easier to liquidate in the event of default and repossession. Since autos are depreciating assets, this is critical. The percentage of used vehicles may also imply something about the borrower loan mix, as sub-prime borrowers rarely qualify for a new car loan. Some auto ABS issuers have their own used car underwriting guidelines. The bottom line: used vehicle loans generally experience higher default rates than loans on new vehicles (and so, all else equal, require more credit enhancement).

Advance Rates
Advance rates are generally defined as the amount loaned as a percentage of the wholesale value for used cars and as a percentage of the manufacturer's suggested retail price (MSRP) for new cars. (Advanced rates are therefore similar to the LTV concept for mortgage loans.) It is customary that advance rates often exceed 100%, especially if taxes and "add-ons" (car audio systems, alarms, extended warranties and even insurance) are financed by the car buyer. Clearly, a higher average advance rate may have implications for loss severity.[2]

Weighted Average Maturity
Weighted average maturity (WAM) (or more accurately weighted average original loan term) and WAM distribution affect expected losses in that, generally, longer loan terms imply higher loss severity in the event of a defaulted loan.

Longer loan terms amortize the loan balance more slowly. The longer the amortization schedule, all else equal, the less equity an owner will have at any point in time. A borrower may even have negative equity if the car depreciates more rapidly than the loan amortizes. The borrower then has a greater propensity to default and the lender will experience a higher loss severity.

Longer loan terms are also used to reduce the monthly payment for borrowers with lower incomes, who are already more likely to default. While most auto loans are made for terms of less than 60 months, many finance companies offer extended terms. The distribution of WAM is also important to analyze, as two pools with the same WAM but different WAM distribution may have a different loss experience.

Weighted Average Coupon
Weighted average coupon (WAC) is sometimes viewed as an indicator of borrower credit quality, since riskier borrowers are generally charged higher loan rates, all else equal. The WAC distribution is important to review for the same reason as WAM distribution. At times, manufacturers and their captive finance companies offer very low loan rates to promote sales. These loans are termed "subvented" loans (subsidized) and are usually offered to only the most credit-

---

[2] Loss severity is defined as the net loss on a vehicle divided by the defaulted amount of the loan.

worthy borrowers. If these loans are "barbelled" with a pool of relatively high coupon loans to more risky borrowers, the resulting expected losses may be higher than the average coupon would indicate.

Geographical Diversity

Geographical diversity is important in a pool because of the potential for regional economic downturns. Most captives and large bank portfolios, like Chase Manhattan, have excellent geographical diversity. Certain states (Louisiana and Arkansas, for example) have laws that make it more difficult to repossess and liquidate vehicles, which could lead to increased severity in the event of defaults.

According to the latest figures available (1995), the top five states by number of vehicles registered are California (11%), Texas (7%), Florida (5%), New York (5%) and Ohio (4.9%). These data come from the U.S. Department of Transportation and Federal Highway Administration and are published in the *American Automobile Manufacturer's Association Facts and Figures Handbook for 1997*. One might expect that a pool of auto receivables will have comparably diverse geographic concentrations.

Seasoning

Most auto deals are backed by newly originated loans (and oftentimes are prefunded, meaning a portion of collateral has yet to be originated). The use of seasoned collateral would have implications for loss expectations. Because loss curves for auto loans are very steep (losses generally occur early in the life of an auto loan), a well-seasoned pool of loans is likely to experience fewer losses.

Issuer's Historical Experience

An issuer's historical loss experience is a critical component when attempting to project base case losses. Static pool analysis is preferred. Static pool analysis isolates a particular pool of collateral and plots the net cumulative loss experience (gross losses or defaults, net of recoveries) over time. Losses in a static pool are a function of seasoning: they tend to rise over time and then level off. If one looks only at the lender's total portfolio and not a static pool, portfolio growth can hide true loss performance, because there is a long lag between origination of loans and the peak default period. To the extent a portfolio is growing rapidly, actual loss experience as a percentage of loans outstanding can appear artificially low. One therefore should use either static pool loss data or adjust growth by looking at lagged losses (the lag depending upon the type of collateral).

Consistency of loss performance is important. Issuers with volatile loss performance will be assessed differently by rating agencies than issuers with consistent loan performance. Volatile loss performance may be an indicator of a change in underwriting standards or servicing discipline. AmeriCredit is a nonprime issuer with a very consistent loss history, as shown by the static pool loss curves in Exhibit 4.

Exhibit 4: Cumulative Loss Summary for AmeriCredit

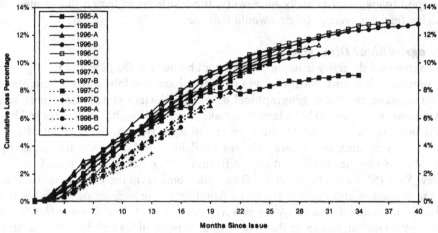

Source: Moody's Investors Service. (As of July 1999.)

Exhibit 5: Generic Lagged Loss Curves

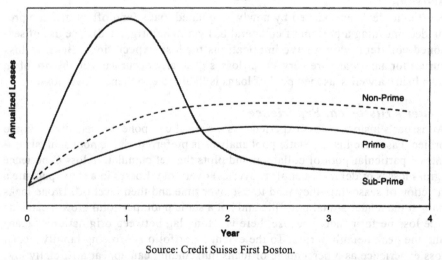

Source: Credit Suisse First Boston.

Looking at a lagged loss curve (Exhibit 5), as opposed to a static pool loss curve, annualized losses typically peak for a sub-prime issuer in the first year. Prime issuers, on the other hand, typically experience peak annualized losses in months 18 to 30.

Forms of Credit Enhancement

Now that we have reviewed some of the drivers of base case losses (the risk), we discuss credit enhancement (the mitigant). Credit enhancement can be internal (provided within the structure of the deal) or external (via third parties). Forms of internal credit enhancement used in auto ABS include: excess servicing, cash reserve funds, overcollateralization, and subordination. External credit enhancement usually entails purchasing insurance in the form of a surety bond from a "wrap provider" like FSA, AMBAC, MBIA, FGIC, etc. A cash collateral account (CCA) can also be used, which is identical to a reserve fund, except that the funds advanced are from a lending institution and do not come from the issuer.

Excess servicing is usually the first line of defense against collateral losses in auto securitizations. It is simply the difference between the gross weighted average coupon on the loan collateral (GWAC) less the sum of the servicing fee and the average coupon paid on the bonds issued. If, for example, the gross WAC of the loan collateral is 10%, the servicing fee is 1% (100bp) and the weighted average bond coupon is 6%, excess servicing is then 3% (300bp). This is illustrated in Exhibit 6. On an outstanding balance of $100 million, assuming no losses or prepayments, excess servicing of 300bp would amount to $250,000 in a month.

A quick, "back-of-the-envelope" way to calculate the amount of cumulative losses that can be covered by excess servicing is to multiply the excess servicing percentage by the average life of the transaction's underlying collateral. As an example, consider a transaction with 3% excess servicing and underlying collateral with a 3-year average life. The excess servicing can cover approximately 9% cumulative losses on the transaction. Rating agencies will not give full credit to excess servicing when determining credit enhancement levels, but instead give a percentage of credit based on rating. For example, a AAA rated bond may receive about 30% credit for excess servicing, while a AA or A rated bond would receive more credit.

Excess servicing amounts remaining after the effect of losses flow back to the seller/servicer (usually referred to as "the issuer"). The excess servicing receivable (ESR) is also called the residual and is the basis of the gain-on-sale calculation. To value the ESR, we use a net present value calculation, assuming a prepayment rate, a loss rate, and a discount rate. Many home equity and manufactured housing issuers have experienced writedowns on their residual portfolios due to overly optimistic prepayment and loss assumptions. Since auto lenders' prepayments are fairly steady and not affected by interest rate changes and because an auto loan's duration is generally very short (average life and duration well under 2 years), the loss rate is the key driver of auto residual valuations.

Exhibit 6: Excess Servicing Calculation — Example

Gross WAC on Pool of Auto Loans	10%
Servicing	1%
Wtd. Average Bond Coupon	6%
Excess Spread	3%*

* If applicable, a surety fee of 0.40% would also be subtracted from the gross WAC, for excess spread of 2.6% in this example.

Source: Credit Suisse First Boston.

Cash reserve funds are cash accounts set up by the issuer for the benefit of the trust to absorb losses and provide liquidity for bond principal and interest payments, in the event that cash flows generated by the pool in a given period are insufficient. Often, the cash reserve account will be only partially funded up front, with the balance funded over time (typically in 6 to 12 months) out of excess spread cash flows. To fully fund the cash reserve, excess spread cash flows are trapped in the cash reserve account by the trustee for the benefit of bondholders. Once the required amount of reserve is met, future excess spread cash flows flow back to the issuer. The cash reserve may also represent part of the issuer's equity interest in an owner trust.

Overcollateralization (OC) exists where the total par amount of the loans exceeds the par amount of bonds issued. Issuers typically use overcollateralization to boost the yield on a portfolio with subvented WAC. In some cases, excess spread is diverted from the issuer to bondholders and applied to pay down principal. This is called "turboing" the bonds to create OC. Excess spread is usually applied to build up the reserve fund first and then to turbo the bonds, creating OC. Turboing continues until overall credit enhancement reaches a specified level (determined by ratings agencies in advance). The resulting overcollateralization is then available to absorb principal losses on the collateral.

Subordination is a technique whereby both senior and subordinated bond classes are issued. Senior classes achieve higher ratings because the junior classes absorb losses first. For senior classes, the effect is identical to overcollateralization, but the issuer sells more bonds and achieves greater proceeds by using subordination instead of overcollateralization as credit enhancement. Of course, the subordinated classes trade at higher spreads.

Subordination is often used in combination with excess spread and a reserve fund (or cash collateral account). This combined enhancement will usually eliminate the need for any external forms of credit enhancement. In most auto ABS transactions, the senior bonds are credit enhanced to a AAA level, and most subordinate securities offered for sale are credit enhanced to a A or BBB level. Issuers may choose to retain all or a portion of the subordinate securities, and the subordinated amount can be "credit tranched." Credit tranching creates multiple levels of subordination, so that bonds of different ratings can be sold, each with ratings that reflect the degree of potential loss exposure.

A simple example of subordination in auto ABS is Honda's 1997-B transaction (Exhibit 7). At issue, the deal was a $904 million grantor trust transaction, with $850 million AAA seniors and subordination of $54 million (6% retained by the issuer). Additional credit enhancement was provided by excess servicing and a cash reserve fund.

Surety bonds (or "wraps") are bond insurance policies, purchased from a third party. Wraps are very common in sub-prime auto ABS. Using a wrapper generally precludes the need to sell a subordinated bond-more difficult for sub-prime issuers. According to *Asset Sales Report*, during the second quarter of

1999, the guarantors wrapped 43 ABS transactions totaling over $15 billion of original par at issuance. The volume of wrapped auto ABS transactions during this time period reached $2.4 billion.

Note that a wrapped transaction is first structured with sufficient credit enhancement so that the risk to the guarantor is at least investment grade (via any of the available forms of credit enhancement mentioned above). Thus, a "wrapper" wraps a bond that is BBB or higher and brings that bond to a AAA level.

With a *cash collateral account* (CCA), funds lent by a financial institution are placed in an account held in the name of the trustee for the benefit of investors. Funds are drawn as required, in the event that finance charges from the collateral are less than the sum of the bond interest plus servicing fee and charge-offs allocated to the bonds. The CCA is usually repaid over time, with excess servicing used to reduce the loan amount.

THE CAR BUYER

Motor vehicles are the most widely-owned asset in the modern household. According to the most recent Survey of Consumer Finance (1995), there were 154.5 million vehicles owned by households. Approximately 84% of all households in 1995 owned a vehicle. The percent of households owning a vehicle tends to rise with a household's income and financial assets. Ownership crests with the 45 to 54 age group. The average age of vehicles owned by households is around 8.0 years. As can be expected, households with relatively low incomes, financial assets, and net worth have older cars.

While still high, the percent of households owning a vehicle fell from 86% in 1992 to approximately 84% in 1995. Tangentially, the percent of households leasing a vehicle rose from approximately 3% in 1992 to almost 5% in 1995. Households with incomes of $50,000 or more reported the greatest increase.

Regional Financial Associates estimates the number of consumer households in the United States to grow by about 10 million over the next ten years. Moreover, RFA expects the number of cars per household to rise from 1.81 in 1995 to 1.91 in 2005. This compares with only 1.25 in 1960.

Exhibit 7: Honda Auto Receivables 1997-B Grantor Trust Credit Enhancement for Senior Bondholders (AAA)

Type	Percentage
Subordination (B-piece)	6.00%
Reserve Fund	0.75%
Excess Servicing	0.71%
Total	7.46%

Source: Credit Suisse First Boston.

Exhibit 8: U.S. Top Selling Automobiles

	U.S. Top Selling Cars	U.S. Top Selling Pick-ups
1.	Toyota Camry	Ford F-Series
2.	Honda Accord	Chevrolet C/K
3.	Ford Taurus	Dodge Ram
4.	Honda Civic	Ford Ranger
5.	Ford Escort	Chevrolet S-10
6.	Chevrolet Cavalier	GMC Sierra
7.	Toyota Corolla	Toyota Tacoma
8.	Saturn	Dodge Dakota
9.	Chevrolet Malibu	Nissan Frontier
10.	Pontiac Grand Am	Chevrolet Silverado

Source: Ward's Automotive Yearbook 1999.

	U.S. Top Selling SUVs	U.S. Top Selling Vans
1.	Ford Explorer	Dodge Caravan
2.	Jeep Grand Cherokee	Ford Econoline
3.	Ford Expedition	Ford Windstar
4.	Chevrolet S-Blazer	Plymouth Voyager

Source: Ward's Automotive Yearbook 1999.

Exhibit 9: Top Selling Cars by Market Segment

	Small	Medium	Large	Luxury
1.	Ford Escort	Toyota Camry	Buick LeSabre	Cadillac Deville
2.	Chevrolet Cavalier	Honda Accord	Mercury Grand Marquis	Lincoln Town Car
3.	Toyota Corolla	Ford Taurus	Ford Crown Victoria	Volvo S70/V70

Source: Ward's Automotive Yearbook 1999.

Retail sales of cars and trucks the have remained relatively steady over the past several years, topping the 15 million mark each year since 1994. Exhibits 8 and 9 show the top selling vehicles in 1998. Exhibit 10 profiles buyers of each vehicle class.

One of the major trends in auto consumption is the growing preference for light trucks, which include pick-up trucks, sports utility vehicles (SUVs) and mini-vans. Automakers have also increased their focus on baby boomers. Baby boomers make up 30% of the population and are benefiting from rising home and financial equity values. They are entering their peak earning years and have been liberated from the responsibility of children, college tuition and mortgage payments.

Going On-Line

The rapid consumer acceptance of the Internet has produced a plethora of Internet sites offering automobile financing, and prospective buyers are increasingly doing research on the Internet before shopping for a car. The number of people using the Internet to help them shop has increased to 40%, up from 25% a year earlier, according to a 1999 J.D. Power and Associates survey. While most of the on-line shoppers are in the market for used cars, the proportion of new-vehicle purchasers using the Internet rose from 1.1% a year ago to 2.6%.

DaimlerChrysler Financial Services was the first captive to operate a direct loan site. The site, Giggo.com, is operated by DaimlerChrysler's debis Financial Services subsidiary and offers direct financing on all vehicle makes.

While car buying is not as easy as ordering books on-line, potential car buyers can use the Internet to research a new or used vehicle. The car-buyer that goes on-line is generally more knowledgeable and therefore more aggressive in negotiations. For example, a car-buyer that has surfed the Web will enter a dealership knowing how much a car cost the dealer, how much markup is reasonable and which options are well-priced. Websites also offer information on dealer incentives, rebates and holdbacks, among other things.

Prices

Exhibit 11 shows the year over year percent change in the Bureau of Labor Statistics' new and used vehicle CPI. While new car prices (in real terms) have remained relatively constant over the years, used car prices have experienced much fluctuation. The last major uptick in prices occurred from 1992 through 1995, as used cars gained in popularity. Rising sticker prices on new cars (in absolute terms) in the early 1990s led more buyers to purchase used cars, and as a result, used car prices rose rapidly. Since 1995, used car prices have plateaued. Vehicles coming off-lease, combined with the use of new car incentives has put downward pressure on used vehicle prices.

Exhibit 10: Profile of the Car Buyer

	Primary Driver	Household Income	Median Age
Pick-up Trucks			
Domestic Full-size	56% Male; 44% Female	$37,500	38
Domestic Small-size	53% Male; 47% Female	$32,800	33
Japanese	45% Male; 55% Female	$36,100	30
Small-Budget Cars			
European	57% Male; 43% Female	$18,810	26
Japanese	50% Male; 50% Female	$17,500	24
Domestic	47% Male; 53% Female	$16,800	24
Minivan			
Domestic Primary	42% Male; 58% Female	$26,600	29
Domestic Secondary	38% Male; 62% Female	$24,100	28
Japanese	44% Male; 56% Female	$33,700	31
Luxury			
European	61% Male; 39% Female	$68,000	49
Japanese	54% Male; 46% Female	$66,000	45
Domestic	74% Male; 26% Female	$59,000	51
SUVs	60% Male; 40% Female	$75,000	44

Sources: Regional Financial Associates; AutoPacific Group, Inc.

Exhibit 11: Percent Change in Consumer Price Indices for New and Used Cars

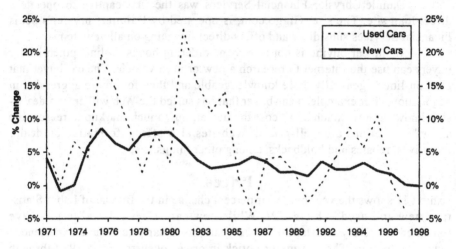

Note: The CPI used car series was discontinued in 1997.
Source: Consumer Price Index.

LEASING

After selecting a vehicle from a dealer, a customer can choose to pay cash or enter into a lease or purchase agreement. Whether financed or leased, the customer must submit a credit application and receive credit approval. If the consumer decides to lease, the vehicle is purchased by a finance company or bank. A certificate of title is issued and filed with the finance company or bank as owner. The customer then enters into a "retail lease agreement" with the finance company or bank as the lessor. The customer agrees to pay the lessor a monthly lease payment for use of the vehicle during the term of the lease. In some states, tax codes make retail balloon contracts more attractive than retail leases. DaimlerChrysler's Gold Key Plus program is a major originator of balloon loan contracts.

At signing, the lessee is typically responsible for the first month's payment, any required down payment, security deposit, acquisition fees, taxes, title and license fees.[3] In addition to the monthly lease payments, the lessee is responsible for maintenance, repairs, "excess wear and tear" and insurance during the life of the lease. Additionally, the lessee is responsible for any excess mileage over the agreed upon limit. At lease end, the customer may purchase the vehicle at the purchase option price plus tax or return the vehicle and pay a disposition fee.

---

[3] Fees and taxes may be rolled into the lease payment.

Components of the Monthly Lease Payment

Each lease payment represents several components: (1) vehicle depreciation (or the decline in the vehicle's value over the lease term), (2) a monthly finance cost, and (3) any unpaid taxes and fees. The vehicle's adjusted capitalized cost, the estimated residual value, the lease term and the finance cost determine the monthly payment amount.

The *adjusted capitalized cost* is equivalent to the negotiated purchase price of the vehicle plus any "rolled fees" and "option charges" minus any "capitalized cost reductions." "Rolled fees" include any fees that the customer wishes to roll into the lease payments; these may include fees for acquisition, preparation, destination, and documentation, among others. "Option charges" may include, but are not limited to, taxes, extended service warranties and non-auto insurance premiums. "Capitalized cost reductions" include down payments, trade-in allowances and dealer incentives such as rebates and discounts. Residual value is the lessor's estimate of a vehicle's worth at the end of the lease term, calculated at the beginning of the lease term. Thus,

> Adjusted capitalized cost
> = Vehicle purchase price + Rolled fees + Option charges
> − Capitalized cost reductions

The bulk of the monthly lease payment covers vehicle depreciation. Monthly depreciation is calculated as the adjusted capitalized cost less the estimated residual value, divided by the term of the lease. The second largest component is the finance cost — the monthly interest paid by the consumer on adjusted capitalized cost of the vehicle plus the estimated residual value. The final components are taxes and fees. Fees vary depending on what the customer has paid for up-front or "rolled" into the payment. The amount of taxes will depend on each state's tax rate.

Lease versus Loan

The differences in leases and loans begins with the initial cash outlay. When purchasing a car, lenders will often require down payments of between 10% to 20% of the negotiated purchase price. The appeal to most consumers is that lease deals do not usually require a down payment per se. Another aspect that appeals to most consumers is the lower monthly payments of leasing.

In September 1996, the Federal Reserve Board approved amendments to Regulation M of the Consumer Leasing Act, which is an amendment to the Truth in Lending Act. The amended regulation went into effect in January 1998 and applies to consumer leases with total contractual obligation equal to or less than $25,000. Regulation M spells out what-and how-disclosures must be made at time of lease, including early termination clauses, warranties and insurance information. This created better information disclosure to the consumer.

Off-Lease Vehicles

At lease end, the lessee is given the option of purchasing the vehicle. If the lessee opts out of the purchase, either the dealer or the lessor takes possession. In this case, the dealer is given choice of either purchasing the vehicle from the lessor (at the same price the lessee would have paid) or returning it to the lessor. ADT Automotive estimates that in 1999, 100% of the vehicles returned to the lessor and 25% of the vehicles returned to the dealer will be remarketed via auctions. According to ADT Automotive estimates, about 22% of off-lease vehicles will be purchased by the lessee, about 21% will be sold by the dealer off lot or to a wholesale broker, and about 57% will be remarketed through the auction process (either by the dealer or the lessor).

Residual Value Risk

As mentioned earlier, residual value is the estimated value of a vehicle at lease end, as forecasted at the beginning of the lease term. Generally, residual values are forecasted using the *Automotive Lease Guide*, or *ALG*, an industry-wide guide that estimates what a used vehicle will bring at auction. The lessor must realize the residual value of the vehicle through the sale or re-lease of the vehicle at the end of the lease term. The potential of a realization less than the residual value assumption is referred to as "residual risk." The residual value will be affected by the car model, the demand for the vehicle in the used car market, the competitiveness of the lessor, the projected miles used, and the dealer incentives offered at the time of the lease signing.

It has been reported that some lenders inflated estimated vehicle residual values, in order to entice potential lessees with lower monthly payments. The result at the end of the lease can be an "upside-down" vehicle — the vehicle's residual value is higher than the ALG value, its retail value or its wholesale auction value. According to Lee & Mason of Maryland Inc., a company that sells residual value insurance, lenders are now losing an average of $1,400 per vehicle and the figure is rising. GM took a $500 million charge in the fourth quarter of 1997 related to residual losses. Rising used-car prices had cushioned the effect of high residuals. But in 1998, used car prices fell below 1997 and the projection is that used-car prices will continue to be flat or slightly down.

Residual Value Risk and Securitization

In a securitized transaction, residual risk is often borne within the structure as long as the principal balance of each contract includes the booked residual value of each leased vehicle. In some cases, this risk is simply factored into credit enhancement and borne by investors. In other cases, residual value risk is addressed separately. There are four methods that have been used to structure residual value support in auto lease securitization transactions: (1) third party residual value insurance, (2) residual value guarantees, (3) reserve accounts, and (4) surety bonds issued by monoline insurers. Most transactions use a combination of these support structures to protect investors against residual value risk.

Exhibit 12: Structure of a Titling Trust

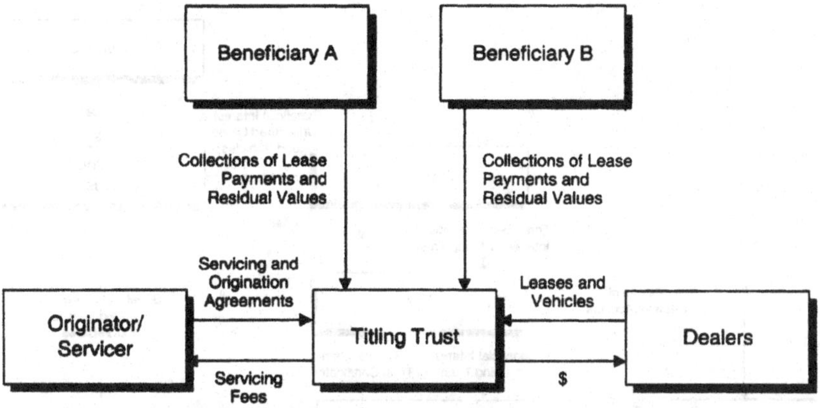

Source: Credit Suisse First Boston.

The Challenge of Securitization —
The Innovation of the Titling Trust

In order to insulate the investor from bankruptcy of the originator, the transfer of assets from the originator to the securitization trust is typically structured as a "true sale" transaction. Additionally, the securitization trust, which is created as a special purpose vehicle specifically for the purchase and issuance of ABS, must "perfect," or legally validate, its interest in the assets. To qualify as a true sale, the originator must treat the transfer as an off-balance sheet sale with limited recourse to the originator. An outside legal counsel must provide an opinion letter confirming this true sale status. For non-auto receivables, this transfer can be completed with a single assignment document. For a motor vehicle, however, transferring of each vehicle's title can be onerous, time-consuming and expensive.

In the case of auto loans, title is issued in the name of the customer as owner, with the finance company listed as lienholder. By transferring the finance company's interest in the vehicle, auto loan securitizations can reach "true sale" status. In the case of an auto lease, title is issued in the name of the finance company. Consequently, in order to perfect title and to meet "true sale" requirements, there must be a transfer of title from the originator.

The titling trust structure was invented to address this burden of retitling. Unlike auto loan ABS structures, the titling trust purchases and holds title to the securitized leased vehicles. The finance company, or the originator of the lease contracts, owns a beneficial interest in leases and vehicles. At the time of securitization, it is the beneficial interest that is transferred to the securitization trust. By creating the titling trust entity, ownership in the vehicles remains with the same party at all times. World Omni 1994-A Automobile Lease Securitization Trust was the first automobile lease securitization to employ the titling trust. Exhibits 12 and 13 illustrate the structure of a typical titling trust and its involvement in a lease securitization.

Exhibit 13: Simplified Securitization Involving a Titling Trust

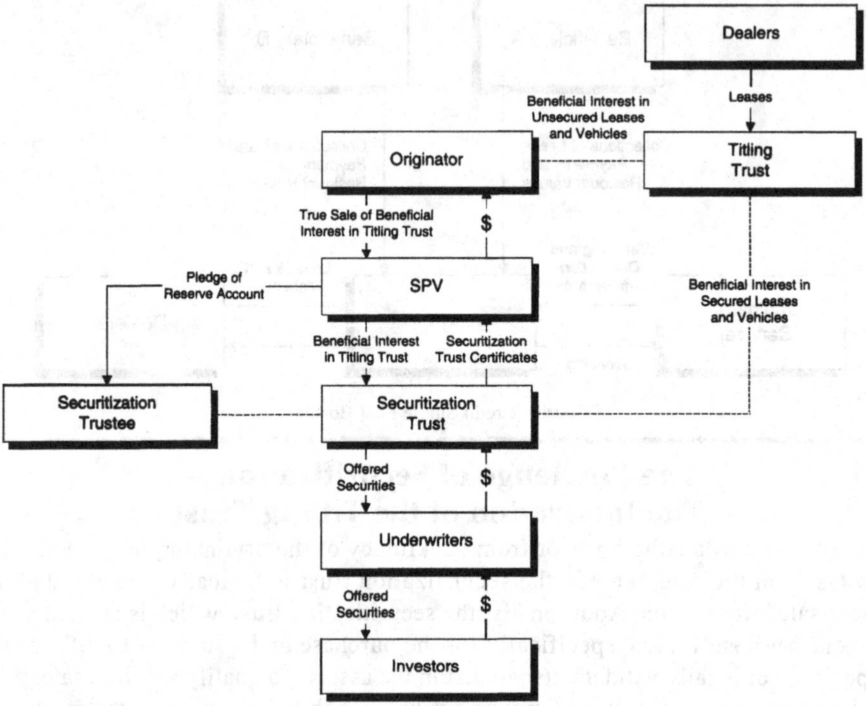

Source: Credit Suisse First Boston.

THE DEALER

As of this writing, there are some 22,400 new franchised auto dealers in the United States and over 58,700 independent used car dealers according to ADT Automotive and NADA. There has been a trend toward consolidation in the past several years; according to ADT Automotive, since 1990, the number of independent used car dealers has dropped by about 16,000 and there are 2,225 fewer new franchised dealers. There has also been a rise in the number of large "megadealer" groups seeking to achieve economies of scale, like H. Wayne Huizenga's AutoNation, Inc. AutoNation, which operates over 400 new car dealerships, has been acquiring new car dealerships since 1996. Auto retailing is an extremely competitive, capital intensive, low margin business. Megadealers like AutoNation are seeking to use size to their advantage to lower costs for advertising, seek better deals from suppliers and lower funding costs by accessing the capital markets for financing inventory.

Dealers are segmented by the number of vehicles sold in a year. In the past 20 years, the number of smaller dealers (those selling fewer than 400 vehicles) has declined dramatically while the number of larger dealers has increased. Roughly 15 million motor vehicles were retailed in each of 1996, 1997 and 1998 according to *Automotive News*. That number is expected to increase in 1999 to between 16.7 million and 16.8 million (according to Ward's *Automotive Reports*). Since 1979, there are 21% fewer new car dealerships, and the number of dealerships selling more than 750 vehicles per year over the same 20-year period has jumped from over 14% of the total number of new car dealerships to 26%.

Despite the current trend toward consolidation, the auto retail business is still a very fragmented industry. According to ADT Automotive, in 1997 the top 100 dealership groups accounted for only 8.8% of the total sales volume.

Dealer Profitability

The NADA Industry Analysis Division reports that the bulk of an auto dealer's revenues (59%) is derived from sales of new cars. Used car sales account for half the (dollar) sales of new cars. However, since the average used car price is roughly half that of the average new car, this would imply almost an equal number of new and used cars sold. The parts and service department provides the balance of revenues.

The profit derived from the sale of new cars is far lower than that for used cars. According to the NADA, used car gross margins in 1998 were 11%, while new car gross margins were only 6.5%. The net margins for used cars were 1.5%, while for new cars net margins were only 0.6%. The differences between net and gross margins are expenses such as advertising, sales commissions, personnel, facilities/rent, floorplan financing, and "back-end" items. Back-end items can also add significant profitability for both new and used car sales. Things like car alarms, audio systems, service contracts, insurance, and financing all would be included. In fact, without them, many new car sales would result in a loss, according to auto dealers' reporting of net profits.

According to the NADA, financing a new vehicle through the dealer usually results in an "acquisition fee" paid by the lender to the dealer of around 2% of the selling price; and for used vehicles this fee is around 4% of the selling price. However, as we mention in the discussion of sub-prime lending, some sub-prime loans are sometimes purchased at a discount, depending on the loan rate and the credit quality of the borrower. On average, however, financing adds significant profitability to vehicle sales. Insurance and service contracts sold through a dealer can also add significantly to the bottom line. For new vehicles, insurance can add 1.5% and extended warranties can add 1.8% in gross profits. For used vehicles, the numbers are better: 2.4% for insurance and 4% for service contracts.

The parts and service department, while the smallest portion of revenues, is the most profitable part of the dealer operation. According to the NADA, gross profits for the average dealership's parts and service department are running at 44%, and net profits are a healthy 5.7%. Parts and service is the largest contributor to the overall net profitability of the average dealer.

Estimates by NADA and ADT Automotive indicate that there has been a downward trend on gross margins for both new and used cars. Note, however, that net profits as reported by dealers may be misleading since they include all allocated costs, including compensation. Since most auto dealers are privately owned, there may be incentives by owners to keep stated profitability low, perhaps for tax purposes.

AUTO ABS ORIGINATORS AND SERVICERS

Auto ABS issuers generally fall into one of three different categories. Captives, including "the Big Three" as well as finance companies such as Honda and Toyota, provide financing primarily for prime borrowers purchasing new cars manufactured by the captive's parent. Banks, such as Chase Manhattan and First Security, also typically lend to prime credit quality borrowers. Issuers like AmeriCredit and Arcadia are considered monolines. As the name suggests, a monoline's sole business is to provide auto financing, often to non-prime used car buyers.

According to the Federal Reserve Board, new car financing (both loan and lease) runs from $250 to $300 billion annually. Only a fraction of the auto loans originated each year become securitized. Total public auto ABS issuance was $35.1 billion in 1998, for example.

The domestic financing subsidiaries of "the Big Three" have accounted for the bulk of auto ABS securitization to date. Ford Motor Credit, General Motors Acceptance and DaimlerChrysler regularly come to market with public deals that become market benchmarks. The next largest issuer is a bank, Chase Manhattan. As Exhibits 14 and 15 show, after that, market share is scattered among smaller banks, non-prime and sub-prime issuers and the smaller captive finance companies.

Exhibit 14: 1985-1998 Percent by Principal Amount
(Total Auto ABS Issuance: $259.3 Billion)

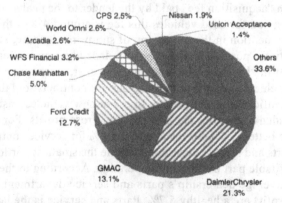

Note: Public transactions only. Includes wholesale, lease, retail and truck loans.
Source: Thomson Financial Securities Data.

Exhibit 15: 1999 1Q-2Q Percent by Principal Amount
(Total Auto ABS Issuance: $21.8 Billion)

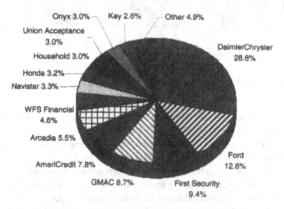

Note: Public transactions only. Includes wholesale, lease, retail and truck loans.
Source: Thomson Financial Securities Data.

Nomenclature: Prime versus Non-Prime and Sub-Prime

Auto loan ABS clearly represent a major component of the ABS market. Generally, auto ABS are viewed as "plain-vanilla" in an ABS market with ever more complex structures and esoteric assets. However, the auto ABS market has evolved over the last few years to include a variety of collateral, namely prime, non-prime, and sub-prime. Auto loan collateral is categorized in this way based upon the *perceived* degree of credit risk in the collateral pool. According to Moody's, prime pools, which represent the bulk of securitizations to date, generally experience cumulative net (static pool) losses[4] lower than 3% over the life of the transaction. Non-prime pools are expected to lose between 3% and 7% cumulative, and sub-prime pools are generally expected to experience losses greater than 7%.

Exhibit 16 summarizes the categorization of auto loan portfolios by expected cumulative losses, the funding discount, the bankruptcy tolerance, the length of the obligors' credit history, the contract APR, and the FICO score. Exhibit 17 shows net loss percentages for selected issuers in the prime, non-prime and sub-prime categories.

Prime loans are typically originated by banks and captive finance companies and are extended to high quality borrowers in good credit standing. Non-prime and sub-prime loans are loans made to borrowers who do not qualify for a loan from a prime lender. Typical reasons for a borrower not qualifying for a prime loan are lack of credit history, poor installment credit history, prior bankruptcy, high ratios of total debt versus income or auto loan payment versus income, or lack of stability with regard to employment or place of residence.

---

[4] Cumulative net losses are net of recoveries on repossessed vehicles. They are analyzed on a static pool basis, which looks at the performance of the same pool of contracts (loans) over a period of time.

Exhibit 16: Classification of Auto Loans

Credit Category	Implied Credit Grade	Static Pool Losses (%)	Discounts (%)a	Bankruptcy Tolerance	Length of Clean Credit[b]	APR (%)[c]	FICO Score[d]
Prime	A+ to B	< 3%	None	None	> 5 yrs	8-12%	680+
Non-prime	B– to C+	3-7	None	> 2 yrs Discharged	2-5 yrs	13-16	620-679
Sub-prime	C to C–	7-15	< 10%	1-2 yrs Discharged	1-2 yrs	17-20	550-619
	D+ to D–	15-25	10-30	< 1 yr Discharged	< 1 yr	> 20	< 550
"EZ"	E to Z	25-50	30-50	Not Considered	None	Usury Limit	Not Considered

a. Discounting occurs primarily in the sub-prime sector, when a finance company purchases a contract from a dealer at less than face value, effectively raising the APR.
b. Clean credit is a relative term and its meaning changes depending on the credit category. In general, however, it refers to the borrower's history of making timely payments.
c. APR, or annual percentage rate, is the annual rate of interest charged on a loan.
d. A FICO score is a credit bureau risk score produced from models developed by Fair, Isaac and Co., Inc. FICO scores are used by lenders to assess the credit risk of prospective borrowers or existing customers in order to help make credit decisions. These scores are derived solely from the information available on credit bureau reports and have a range up to 800.

Sources: Moody's Investors Service; Fitch IBCA.

Exhibit 17: Net Losses as a Percent of Outstanding Principal Balance for Selected Issuers

Issuer	Fiscal Year End[a]						
	1998	1997	1996	1995	1994	1993	1992
AmeriCredit	5.30%	5.50%	5.60%	4.50%	3.80%	0.70%	N/A
Arcadia	4.62%	3.48%	0.99%	0.67%	0.66%	0.52%	0.22%
ASF (formerly AFG)	N/A	8.55%	6.72%	5.39%	3.24%	3.15%	N/A
Chase Manhattan	0.51%[b]	0.44%	0.24%	0.12%	0.12%	0.26%	0.39%
Chevy Chase	1.06%[b]	0.91%	0.62%	0.51%	0.22%	0.44%	0.78%
DaimlerChrysler	1.39%	1.80%	1.68%	1.16%	0.73%	0.75%	0.97%
First Security	1.11%	0.98%	0.94%	0.77%	0.54%	0.38%	0.57%
Ford	1.24%	1.64%	1.53%	0.98%	0.73%	0.82%	1.08%
GMAC	0.83%	1.31%	1.45%	0.89%	0.57%	0.64%	0.89%
Honda	0.91%	0.78%	0.58%	0.43%	0.37%	0.40%	0.51%
Key	2.32%	2.41%	1.36%	0.88%	0.49%	0.44%	N/A
Mitsubishi	2.31%[e]	3.38%	4.87%	1.56%	1.12%	1.43%	0.85%
NationsBank	N/A	N/A	1.22%[d]	0.78%	0.45%	0.38%	0.86%
Nissan	2.71%	3.88%	1.97%	1.55%	1.85%	2.75%	2.19%
Onyx	1.72%	2.03%	1.63%	0.37%	0.00%	N/A	N/A
TMCC	0.66%	0.70%	0.49%	0.44%	0.36%	0.49%	0.69%
Union Acceptance	2.80%	2.40%	1.58%	1.36%	0.69%	0.64%	0.73%
WFS Financial	3.42%	3.02%	2.30%	1.61%	1.09%	1.53%	1.73%

a. Fiscal year end as of December 31 except AmeriCredit (June 30), ASF (June 30), Honda (March 31), Nissan (March 31), TMCC (September 30) and Union Acceptance (June 30).
b. Annualized for the three months ended March 31, 1998.
c. Annualized for the nine months ended September 30, 1998.
d. Annualized for the five months ended May 31, 1996.
e. Annualized for the eleven months ended November 30, 1998.

Source: Credit Suisse First Boston.

Non-prime and sub-prime loans clearly carry higher default risks and are priced accordingly. At current market rates, for example, prime loans are priced in the range of 8% to 12%, non-prime gross coupons are generally in the range of 13% to 16%, and sub-prime loans start at 17% and go up to the highest rate allowable in the state of origination, the usury limit (can be as high as 30%). All finance companies are subject to the usury rate in the state of a contract's origination.

A finance company can effectively increase the yield on loans purchased from a dealer by buying them at a discount to face value. The discount is accreted over time, resulting in a higher yield. Theoretically though, the net effect could allow de facto interest charges above a state's usury limit. Discounting is perfectly allowable, if done properly. Legal problems have arisen, however, in the states of Alabama and Mississippi, whereby the yield increase has been deemed an undisclosed finance charge. In some instances a representative from a finance company was present in a dealer's office at the time of contract origination, agreeing to buy them at a discount as they were being originated. In these cases, the loans originated were looked upon by the courts as direct originations of the finance company rather than indirect originations, and the yield difference as a hidden finance charge. The now-bankrupt Mercury Financial is an example of a finance company sued and fined substantial punitive damages for undisclosed finance charges as a result of buying contracts at a discount.

The Ups and Downs of Non/Sub-Prime ABS

As reported by Moody's, non-prime and sub-prime auto ABS issuance has grown substantially since the early 1990s, as has down-market consumer lending generally (approximately 20% of the auto finance market is sub-prime auto financing). In the early 1990s, sticker prices were rising and the cost of the average new car rose to approximately 50% of the U.S. median family income, up from 36% in 1980. This in turn led used vehicle sales to surpass new vehicle sales at franchised dealers for the first time since World War II, and hence increased financing demand for used vehicles. In 1995, Mercury Finance, then the largest sub-prime lender, was earning 9.4% on assets, approximately six times the ROA of a regional bank, and returning 41.1% on equity, compared to Household International's 16.0%. These operating results and the demand for used vehicle financing attracted additional participants to an increasingly competitive market.

The development and general acceptance of securitization techniques allowed, for a time, new, lesser-capitalized players to enter the market and successfully compete with some of the well-capitalized consumer finance companies that previously dominated this segment of auto lending. The application of computer technology to develop proprietary credit scoring and loan pricing models has also played an important role. This has allowed issuers to better manage risk, service loan portfolios, analyze loan performance, and enhance collection efforts.

In 1998, however, non-prime and sub-prime auto ABS issuance was down about $2.2 billion from the previous year. In addition to the capital markets crisis faced in the fall of 1998, changes at the issuer level led to 1998's decline in volume. The sub-prime market has been stigmatized by bankruptcies and isolated instances of alleged fraud. Bankruptcies have included Jayhawk Acceptance (1997), Mercury Financial (1998), and Eagle Finance (1999), among others. Instances of alleged fraud have included Mercury Financial, First Merchants, and National Auto Credit. The market continues to experience consolidation as acquisitions occur and other participants voluntarily exit this market. The Money Store (1998) and One Hour Acceptance (1998) are included among the participants who have recently exited the sub-prime auto market. These changes have led to a market with fewer participants. The remaining participants are better capitalized and have a significant market presence. We believe this will increase securitization transaction sizes and result in fewer transactions.

Gain on sale (GOS) accounting resulted in increased earnings and profit windfalls leading to easier initial public offerings in the equity market, further capitalizing these smaller lenders. GOS, in effect, acted as a "feedback loop" to reinforce the growth in the market and draw other competitors into the market. Some consumer finance companies, eyeing higher stock market valuations, either spun off their auto finance lending businesses into separate subsidiaries (United Federal Savings Bank/UAC and Western Financial Bank/WFS, for example) or added sub-prime lending to their menu of financial services (like Capital One/ Summit, KeyCorp/ASF, Household Finance/ACC). The tremendous pace of growth has slowed in recent years, as overly aggressive underwriting led to higher than expected losses and problems with liquidity.

The vast majority of non-prime/sub-prime loans are made for used vehicles. As discussed earlier, used vehicles account for more than half of the dollar volume of cars sold in the U.S. and used cars are more profitable for auto dealers as well. The popularity of leasing ensures there will be a growing supply of used cars, and, in fact, the high number of returned (off-lease) vehicles has placed pressure on used car prices. This may lead to higher loss severities down the road. A significant portion of non-prime and sub-prime borrowers are prior bankrupts, a group that unfortunately continues to grow. While there is tremendous competition among non-prime/sub-prime lenders for loans and market share, there is no shortage of lending opportunities.

According to Moody's, auto finance-backed issuance (as rated by Moody's) in 1998 was 61.9% prime loans, 28.6% sub-prime loans, and 9.5% vehicle leases. Thus, prime autos represented the largest subset, but sub-prime/ non-prime issuance has been very strong.

Servicing

Although servicing practices vary from issuer to issuer, general aspects of this process apply across the industry. A typical servicing department is responsible for customer service (usually via a 1-800 call center), insurance verification, billing and collections, payment processing, delinquency follow-up, repossession and liquidation. Different seller/servicers may use different strategies. For example, some servicers may be very aggressive and repossess delinquent cars as soon as possible. Others may prefer to work out a loan and repossess only as a last resort. Both strategies are viable and the choice of strategy may depend on both borrower and collateral quality, as well as the lender's ability to dispose of repossessed collateral. While most lenders dispose of repossessions through wholesale auctions, some use their own retail lots.

Servicing operations can be specialized or can be so-called "cradle-to-grave." In the "cradle-to-grave" approach, the same servicing employee is responsible for the loan over its life, regardless of the loan's status. Alternatively, servicing employees may specialize by loan status (e.g., current or less than 30 days' delinquent loans are handled by one group of employees, while 90-day-plus delinquent loans are serviced by others). The "cradle-to-grave" approach allows for continuity in handling any given account and, sometimes, better control and accountability. By contrast, a specialized approach allows one to build a certain skill set. The skills and personalities most effective for servicing a current borrower who needs a new payment book, for example, are arguably different than those needed to skip-trace a severely delinquent borrower.

Auto loan and lease servicing can be centralized or decentralized. Advantages to having the servicing department in a single location include greater control over the process as well as a lower cost of operations. On the other hand, a decentralized servicing department allows for local accountability, with branch offices servicing all contracts that fall within their region.

Servicing is very much technology driven. Efficient and low cost servicing requires good systems. For example, predictive auto-dialers automatically place phone calls to delinquent borrowers for servicing personnel to field. When the dialer reaches a human, the account history pops up on the screen for the servicing employee to refer to in their conversation. The dialers can be programmed to dial in accordance with algorithms that establish priority by region (time of day), by status of the account (severity of delinquency) or by date since last contact. Predictive auto-dialers can intelligently schedule calls with the highest probability of success by tracking prior borrower responsiveness (e.g., "this borrower is usually found at home weeknights after 7 P.M.").

Servicing operations can be evaluated on several measures in addition to technology, for example, number of accounts per servicing employee. Of course, some collateral is more servicing intensive, and some business strategies are more servicing intensive. Moreover, investments in technology often reduce reliance on human resources. In any case, servicing capacity (in terms of both human resources and capital resources) must be sufficient for the current size of the portfolio as well as for the rate of growth and aging of the portfolio. Servicing income, usually 1.00% for prime and up to 2.50% for non-prime, is at the top of the waterfall in most ABS structures. This stream is protected, so that in the event of problems with the seller/servicer, a new servicer would have the economic incentive to take over the portfolio (although this is extremely rare, one example of this was in 1998, when CSC Logic took over servicing of One Hour Acceptance's portfolio).

Exhibit 18: Sample Repossession Timeline

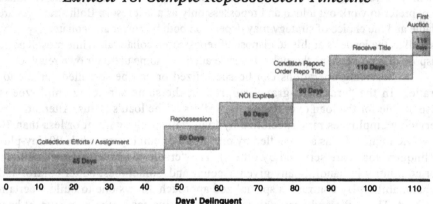

Sources: Fitch IBCA; Credit Suisse First Boston.

Repo Practices

The repossession process is a critical part of loss mitigation in auto ABS. Since autos are a depreciating asset, the faster a vehicle is repossessed and sold, the lower the loss severity. Regulations for repossession vary from state to state, with some states requiring more opportunity for the borrowers to cure their situation and stay in their cars. Lenders will usually exhaust all possibilities to avoid repossession, such as offering payment extensions. While the vast majority of repossessions occur as a result of a loan being delinquent, cars can also be repossessed due to a lapse in insurance coverage by the borrower, even if the loan is current. For lenders, such a lapse in insurance coverage is worse than a lapse in payments because if the car is involved in an accident and totaled, the lender may be exposed to a complete loss.

The Repo Timeline

The repossession timeline usually begins after the second payment is past due, generally when the loan is at or around 45 days' delinquent. When the borrower no longer displays "willingness or ability to pay," the lender orders a repossession (assignment). At this stage, the national credit bureau can run a credit check. The borrower's address can be verified, recent bankruptcy filings can be uncovered and the status of all of the borrower's installment debt can be checked. Servicing personnel use this information to formulate strategy. If the borrower is current on all other obligations except the car loan, perhaps there is a simple reason behind the delinquency.

A sample repo timeline, showing collections efforts through vehicle disposition at auction, for a prime issuer is shown in Exhibit 18. For sub-prime issuers, the timeline can be a bit longer. Sub-prime issuers may allow the delinquency period to be longer, perhaps as long as 90 days, as more exhaustive efforts at avoiding repossession are made. The timeline can also vary by state, depending on regulations governing repossession and the length of time it takes to procure a repo title.

Repo Man

A licensed and bonded repossession company can usually locate and repossess a car within 48 hours. The process can take a bit longer if the borrower is a skip, which means that the borrower has disappeared with the car. (Our discussions with one prime lender indicated that sometimes cars are shipped out of the country, etc.) Depending on the state, costs for repossession vary anywhere from $200 to $500. Some repossession agents are specialists at skip-tracing. Even though some repos are more difficult than others, the fee charged is usually a flat fee. This is probably because there is strong competition among repossession service providers, and there are far more "average repossessions" than more difficult ones.

Dangers in Reposession

Repossession can be a dangerous business. In many states, the laws governing repossession services stipulate only that repossessors "do not breach the peace." Repossessors are allowed to take back a car at any hour of the day or night, without notice, and are allowed access to a vehicle owner's property to do so. There have been incidents of repo men being killed by car owners who mistook them for burglars, and of repo men inadvertently kidnapping sleeping children in the course of their work. Many repo men carry guns for self defense. But in an article in the *American Banker* (in August 1997), it seems many in the business love their work, and with the boom in sub-prime lending, there has been no shortage of it. Repossession may also be recession proof: in bad times business goes up due to higher delinquencies and in good times banks and finance companies extend credit on easier terms.

One Last Chance

After the car is taken by the repo man, a notice of intent (NOI) is delivered to the borrower, a legal document that details the lender's intent to sell the vehicle to satisfy the lien on it. The borrower may be given a period of redemption, which gives him/her a last chance to get his/her car back. The period of redemption usually lasts between 10 and 25 days, and in most states, the entire loan balance must be satisfied in full before the car can be reclaimed. In New York, a "borrower friendly" state, the borrower gets 25 days after the repossession to make all delinquent payments and repossession fees, at which point he/she can get his/her car back.

Once the period of redemption expires, a notice of intent to sell is delivered to the borrower by the lender, which essentially ends his/her chances of getting back the vehicle. At this stage, the car's condition is reported by the repo man, a new title is ordered and the lender moves forward to the auction process. While most repossessed cars show average wear and tear, additional repairs are sometimes required to get the best sale price at an auction.

Wholesale Auctions

Wholesale auctions are arguably the best way to dispose of repossessed vehicles quickly. While selling the vehicle through retail channels (used car lots) can result in higher proceeds, the costs may outweigh the benefits, as the retail disposal process adds delays. Longer times for vehicle disposal mean higher costs for depreciation as well as servicer advances. Servicers are frequently obligated to advance principal and interest payments on delinquent loans not yet charged off, and although they are reimbursed first out of sale proceeds, they do need to fund those advances at some cost. Moreover, many lenders may be obligated by their trustee agreements to use a competitive disposal process, such as an auction, to ensure that they are receiving a fair market liquidation value.

According to ADT Automotive, a leading auto auction house and used car market information provider, wholesale auctions sell about 10 million vehicles a year to new and used car dealers. These vehicles represent approximately one-third of the 30-million-plus used vehicles sold by franchised and independent dealers. Approximately 10% of the 10 million autos sold to new and used car dealers were repossessed vehicles. Of those, 600,000 came from captive finance companies, with the balance coming from banks and specialty auto finance companies.

Used Car Prices

The high numbers of off-lease vehicles coming into the used car market, higher factory incentives for new vehicles and cheaper Asian imports (a result of the strength in the dollar and the current Asian economic situation) have placed pressure on the used car market. To some extent, higher vehicle quality and a reduced stigma surrounding used cars have mitigated these effects.

Blue Book

Used cars trade in a very liquid, commodity-like market. Used cars are easily valued and there are several industry sources of pricing information. The most popular may be the *Kelley Blue Book*, but there is also a popular publication by the National Automobile Dealer's Association, the *N.A.D.A. Official Used Car Guide*® (it's yellow).

Another used vehicle pricing service that offers Internet pricing quotes is *The Black Book*, a Hearst publication. Their data are gathered weekly by attending wholesale auctions, and subjective adjustments to average prices are applied, such as whether the auctions were well attended or if a particular vehicle was in great supply, etc. Aside from a vehicle's make, model, year and mileage, they have various categories of vehicle condition: Xtra Clean, Clean, Average and Rough.

Nevertheless, a used car's "blue book" has come to mean its market value, and in practice, the guides are probably interchangeable, as their prices rarely deviate by significant amounts. The *Kelley Blue Book* provides on-line pricing information on its website (www.kbb.com) and on Bloomberg (KELY), and NADA has a website for its guides (www.nadaguides.com) that provides the same. Although targeted at used car market participants (dealers, lenders, etc.), both NADA and Kelley offer consumer versions of their guides. The information is tailored for specific regions of the country. The *N.A.D.A. Official Used Car Guide*® is published every month for nine different regions of the United States. The *Black Book* is updated weekly.

The process of obtaining used car price appraisals is basically the same for all three guides. We describe the process used with The *N.A.D.A. Official Used Car Guide*®. The inputs are: the region of the U.S. where the car is located, the model year, make and specific model. The output is a base number for three levels of valuation: trade-in, loan and retail. The retail number is the highest and represents the offered side. The loan number is the lowest and is NADA's estimate of the credit that can be obtained based on the trade-in or wholesale number. The trade-in or wholesale number is the bid side. The bid-ask spread for most used cars is between 15% and 20%. All valuations assume the vehicle is in good ("clean") condition. The presence or absence of certain options, particularly high or low mileage, can impact the vehicle's value, and tables are available to estimate these adjustments.

PREPAYMENTS

Prepayments on auto loan ABS are remarkably stable and generally independent of the level of interest rates. There is virtually no refinancing activity in auto loans for two primary reasons. First, the cars used as collateral for the loans depreciate rapidly and the lenders usually have few incentives to provide the borrower a competitive rate for refinancing an existing auto loan. (Loan interest rates for used cars are higher than for new cars.) Also, the borrower has little incentive to refinance as the loan term is so short and the balance so low that changes in interest rates have little impact on monthly payments.

The major causes of auto loan prepayments are:

- *Debt consolidation.* Many financial institutions now offer to consolidate borrowers' credit card and auto loans into home equity loans. Many borrowers often find this attractive. Although a home equity loan does not necessarily carry a lower interest rate than an auto loan does, its term is always much longer than that of the latter, meaning payments are smaller. This creates a payment incentive to refinance. Also, home equity loan interest may be tax deductible.
- *Repossession.* When a borrower becomes seriously delinquent, the lender may repossess the car and the loan will eventually be prepaid out of proceeds from sale of the repossessed car (at a loss, usually).
- *Voluntary prepayment.* A borrower may decide to pay off the loan balance ahead of schedule (in whole or in part).
- *Sale and trade-ins.* Loans are paid off when the car is sold or traded in.
- *Accidents and other casualties.* An insurance policy is required to be in force which will pay off the loan in the event of fire, theft, etc.

Understandably, the causes listed above are functions of time. As a result, the loan age is the most reliable proxy to forecast prepayment rates.

ABS Model

The most commonly used measurement of auto loan prepayments is the absolute (ABS) prepayment rate developed by Credit Suisse First Boston in the mid 1980s. ABS measures the number of loans paid off in a given month, expressed as the percentage of the original number of loans. This measurement suits the auto loan prepayment better than mortgage measurements, such as the single monthly mortality rate (SMM) or conditional prepayment rate (CPR), since it naturally characterizes the prepayment behavior as the underlying loans age.

A prepayment rate has two functions: (1) it measures historical prepayment experience and (2) it characterizes the assumption for future prepayments. For example, a speed since issue is a measurement that summarizes historical prepayments, and a pricing speed is an assumption of future speed. Naturally, we prefer a measurement that can characterize a large part of speed behavior with a single number. ABS is the best way to do this for auto loans.

Exhibit 19 shows graphically the prepayment experience of a representative auto loan deal, measured by ABS, SMM, and CPR. Exhibit 20 shows the measures of variability for the various prepayment measurements. Clearly, ABS has the lowest variability — both characterized by a low max/min ratio and a low proportional deviation.[5] This indicates that using ABS as the prepayment speed measurement for auto loans captures the monthly prepayment activity far closer than CPR and SMM.

Exhibit 19: Various Prepayment Measurements for GMAC 1992-F

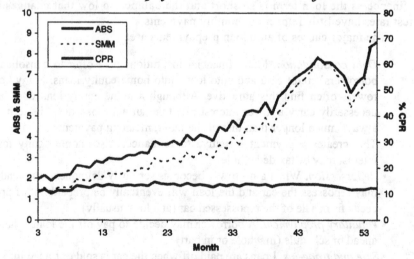

Sources: Bloomberg Capital Markets; Credit Suisse First Boston.

---

[5] Proportional deviation is defined as deviation divided by mean value of the variable.

Exhibit 20: Comparison of Various Prepayment Measurements for GMAC 1992-F

	CPR	SMM	ABS
Average	36.8%	4.0%	1.7%
Life	45.7%	5.0%	1.7%
Max	68.7%	9.2%	1.8%
Min	15.0%	1.3%	1.3%
Max/Min*	4.58%	6.86%	1.45%
Std Dev	15.4	2.1	0.1
Prop Dev	0.42	0.54	0.07

* Ratio expressed as the maximum of a variable divided by the minimum of the variable; the higher the max/min ratio, the greater the dispersion.

Source: Credit Suisse First Boston.

Exhibit 21: Typical Mix of Repossession in Prepayments from Prime and Sub-prime Issuers

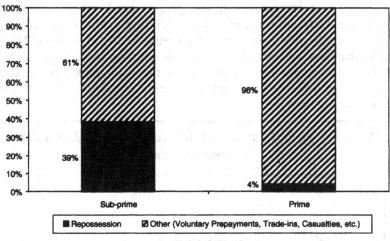

Source: Credit Suisse First Boston.

Repossession

Repossession of vehicles against which the loans in an auto ABS are written will be reflected as prepayments, once the vehicles are sold and proceeds flow through to investors. While repossession constitutes only a small fraction of prepayment in the case of prime auto loans, repossession can represent a considerable portion in sub-prime auto loans' speeds. (See Exhibit 21.)

Loan Age

Loan age is decidedly the single most important proxy for prepayments of auto loans. Our study shows that a high percentage of prepayments can be predicted by loan age.

Of course, this is not to say that loan age per se can drive prepayments. Rather, it means that other factors, such as borrowers' consolidating of loans, selling or trading in cars, encountering accidents and other casualties, or becoming delinquent, etc., are largely correlated with the loan age. In other words, the loan age effect of prepayments is merely a reflection of other borrower behavior that drives prepayments. Exhibit 22 is a typical curve that shows how prepayments change as loans age.

Seasonality

Seasonality for auto prepayments is far less prominent than its counterparts in the mortgage and manufactured housing sectors. Generally, the seasonal highs of prepayments occur around the spring and before the holiday season. Seasonality occurs mostly due to the pattern of consumer spending and car sales. The size of peak-trough difference varies among issuers, with relative changes from trough to peak ranging from 2% to 11%.

Interest Rate Level

The level of interest rates has very little impact on auto loan prepayments. Refinancing is generally not a feature of depreciating assets, especially assets financed over a relatively short term and for relatively small amounts. The little refinancing that does occur usually involves an auto loan being consolidated into another type of consumer loan. In such cases, the major considerations are the longer terms and, hence, lower monthly payments; concern for general interest rate level is only tertiary.

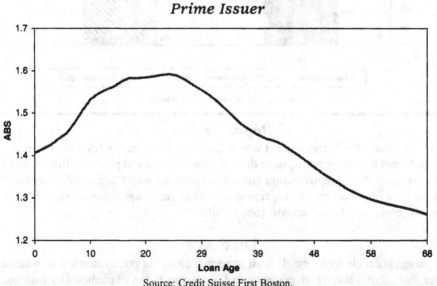

*Exhibit 22: Typical Prepayment Response to Loan Age —
Prime Issuer*

Source: Credit Suisse First Boston.

Exhibit 23: Causality of Prepayments

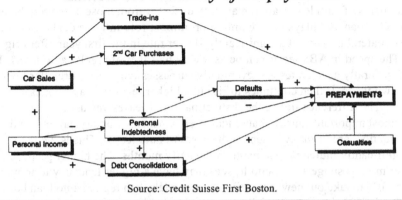

Source: Credit Suisse First Boston.

Interest rates may have an influence on voluntary pay-offs and curtailments of auto loans. These activities represent only a small portion of prepayments, however, and the whole effect is insignificant.

Car Sales

Car sales are positively correlated to prepayments. This is because trade-ins generate prepayments associated with the vehicles that are traded in. We found a clear correlation between retail car sales (both for new and used cars) and auto loan prepayments. Roughly, for an increase of a million units monthly of new car retail sales (to consumers), the seasonally adjusted prepayments will increase about 0.31 ABS; for used cars, it is 0.98 ABS for each million units. The fact that prepayments seem correlated more with used car sales than new car sales may simply reflect the fact that an increase in trade-ins will more likely result in an increase of used car sales.

Personal Income

Overall, personal income is positively correlated with prepayments. On one hand, personal income is directly related to car sales (and hence trade-ins) and the reduction of personal debts (voluntary prepayments). Strong trends in personal income would also strengthen borrowers' ability to consolidate debts. To a smaller extent, however, increases in personal income would result in less repossession and reduce involuntary prepayments.

The statistical relationship between personal income and prepayments, however, is quite complex, and the direct correlation appears to be weak. Each percentage increase of monthly personal income only results in a 0.04 ABS increase of prepayments. This is likely because personal income has many ways to influence prepayments, With some of these links casting a positive impact and others negative, and each with different lags, the overall impact could be deceptively weak.

Exhibit 23 shows the causality of prepayments and qualitative correlation among the causes.

Lease Deals

Prepayments of auto leases are remarkably different from those of the regular auto loans. The loan age plays an even more prominent role in lease deals. Generally, lease collateral prepays at a significantly slower rate in the first year after origination. The speed in ABS terms can be as low as half that of regular auto loans. The speed generally accelerates and eventually surpasses the speed of regular loans in about two years. It then continues to rise to a higher level than auto loans.

The difference lies in the distinct nature of leases versus loans. First, two of the most important causes of auto loan prepayments, voluntary pay-offs and debt consolidation, are virtually absent in the cases of auto leases. This is the reason for the significantly muted prepayments in the early months. The higher prepayments in later months suggest that auto lessees may have a higher tendency to terminate leases early to take out new leases for newer models than regular auto loan borrowers to trade in their cars, especially when the dealers encourage such turn over.

RELATIVE VALUE IN AUTO ABS

In the infancy of the ABS market, ABS products traded at relatively wide spreads. At the time, higher spreads were necessary to attract investors, both to compensate them for the time spent to understand a new product and for the uncertain liquidity of a new sector. For several years, as the ABS market grew into its own, spreads steadily marched downward. The ABS sector has evolved to become a mainstay of fixed income portfolios, and auto ABS, in particular, are among the most liquid and highest quality spread products available.

Today, spreads on auto ABS, as with most spread products, move closely in tandem with swap spreads (see Exhibit 24). Spreads generally have trended higher in recent years, as credit markets have been buffeted by three waves of credit scares. First, in fall 1997, a currency collapse in Asia caused spreads to widen out. The next fall, 1998, default on Russian government debt sent spreads soaring. Once again, in fall 1999, we saw a significant spread widening, this time attributed to concerns over possible economic and financial market impact from the Y2K bug.

Over the entire period shown in Exhibit 24, the pick-up from, for example, 2-year swap spreads to 2-year average life (tranched) auto ABS, has ranged from a high of 43bp in October 1998 to a low of −7bp in August 1997, with an average pick-up of about 10bp. The largest pick-up was during the 1998 crisis, when it reached 43bp (in October 1998).

Prime auto ABS tend to fare better in spread widenings than do non-prime and sub-prime. This is a common thread throughout spread product, whereby in a crisis the most liquid and most straightforward bonds are hurt less and recover soonest. Exhibit 25 shows how the pick-up in prime versus sub-prime widened during the liquidity crunches in the fourth quarter of 1998 and the third quarter of 1999.

Exhibit 24: Various Auto ABS versus 2-Year Swap Spreads

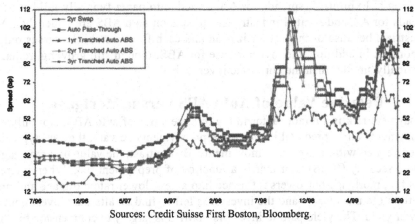

Sources: Credit Suisse First Boston, Bloomberg.

Exhibit 25: Average Spread Pick-Up from Prime to Sub-Prime Auto by Quarter 1998–1999

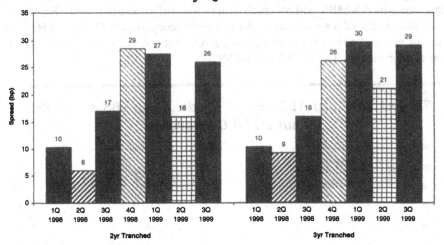

Source: Credit Suisse First Boston.

Relative Value of Auto ABS versus Credit Card ABS and Corporates

Spreads for auto ABS from July 1996 to September 1999 have tracked the same general pattern of ups and downs as spreads for credit card ABS and industrials, again with swap spreads being a primary driver for all of these products. Three-year average life (tranched) auto ABS has traded, on average, 5.7bp wide to 3-year average life credit card ABS, with a high of 20bp wider in December 1997 and a low of 2bp through credit cards (just two months earlier, in October 1997). Looking at Exhibit 26, spreads for AAA rated auto paper typically fall between spreads for AA and A rated industrials. Spreads on auto ABS are wider than AA industrials because of their amortization and cash flow variability versus bullet corporates. In addition, the investor base for ABS, though still growing, remains marginally smaller than the corporate investor base.

Relative Value of Auto ABS versus Mortgages

Prepayment risk is a minor factor in the relative value of auto ABS. Not only are prepayments fairly predictable, but when prepayments do vary, they are typically not correlated with interest rate movements. By contrast, the value of a mortgage-backed security (MBS) is primarily a function of prepayment risk. When interest rates fall, mortgage borrowers refinance into a new, lower rate mortgage and prepay their old mortgage—and the investor is left to find an alternate investment at a lower yield. The yield paid to investors in MBS is largely to compensate for this risk (and its corollary, extension risk, when rates back up).

Some MBS are structured to reduce prepayment risk, and those MBS trade tighter than other MBS as a result. A planned amortization class (PAC) is one example. An MBS without such protection, fully exposed to MBS prepayment risk, is called a sequential. MBS can be "agency" bonds (FNMA, FHLMC, etc.) or can be "non-agency" (still rated AAA, but not via a government-sponsored enterprise such as FNMA or FHLMC).

Exhibit 26: Auto ABS versus Credit Card ABS and 3-Year Industrial Corporates

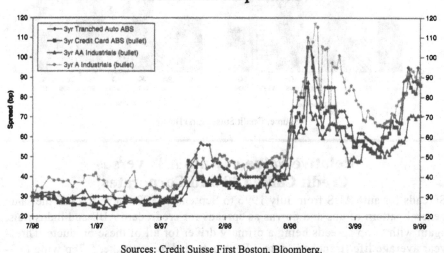

Sources: Credit Suisse First Boston, Bloomberg.

Exhibit 27: Tranched Auto ABS versus PAC and Sequential Mortgages

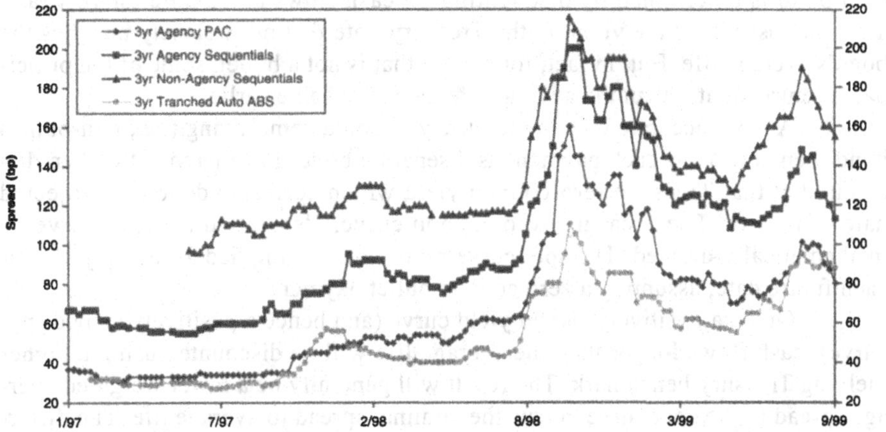

Legend:
- 3yr Agency PAC
- 3yr Agency Sequentials
- 3yr Non-Agency Sequentials
- 3yr Tranched Auto ABS

Source: Credit Suisse First Boston.

In Exhibit 27 we compare auto ABS to some of the MBS alternatives, all with 3-year average lives. All of the unstructured MBS offer significantly wider nominal spreads in order to compensate investors for prepayment risk. The closest alternative in spread is the PAC, which has the least prepayment risk of the MBS shown, but still far more risk that the auto ABS. As the exhibit shows, at times the PAC spread "gaps out" significantly wide to auto ABS (peaking at 65bp in October 1998). This reflects interest rate and/or prepayment uncertainty.

Relative Value within Auto ABS

Within the auto ABS market itself, factors outside of general market conditions affect spreads. "Tiering" has become a significant factor in ABS. Tiering refers to differences in pricing among ABS that have the same rating, average life and cash flow characteristics, but are brought to the market by different issuers. Initially, the ABS market had very little tiering. Because of the bankruptcy-remote status of ABS, the issuer was considered to play a minor role in ABS relative value.

However, performance has in fact varied by issuer and, as a result, not all ABS trades fungibly by issuer name. Issuer characteristics that impact value include: the corporate credit rating of an issuer (and hence their funding flexibility), historical collateral credit performance and the frequency/size of ABS issuance (and hence liquidity).

Spot Spreads and Auto ABS

As mentioned above, some investors prefer bullet repayments of principal (such as in credit card ABS and corporates) to amortizing bonds, which repay principal over a period of time, or "window." Spot spreads (also known as Z-spreads or zero-volatility option adjusted spreads) are used to quantify the value of a principal window relative to a bullet. In calculating a traditional credit spread, the yield on a bond is determined by discounting all cash flows at a single interest rate. That interest rate is the yield on the Treasury note that most closely matches the bond's average life. But, in fact, for a bond that is not a bullet, some of the principal is returned later than the average life date, and some earlier.

A more accurate way to measure yield on an amortizing (i.e., non-bullet) bond then is to view each payment as a separate bond. Each payment is then discounted at that Treasury zero-coupon yield which corresponds to the projected date of receipt. The Treasury zero coupon curve, also called the spot curve, is mathematically derived. The spot curve represents the implied Treasury yield for each future date, assuming a zero coupon bullet payment.

Given a positively sloped yield curve (and hence a positively sloped spot curve), cash flows longer than the average life will be discounted using a higher yielding Treasury benchmark. The result will generally be a lower weighted average spread to the spot curve versus the nominal spread to average life. The difference between this weighted average spread to the spot curve and the nominal spread is the "spot spread give-up." Calculating a spot spread allows an "apples-to-apples" comparison for (amortizing) auto ABS versus bullet alternatives.

Chapter 5

Securities Backed by Recreational Vehicle Loans

Nichol Bakalar
Vice President
ABS Research
Deutsche Banc Alex. Brown

James Nimberg
Associate
ABS Research
Deutsche Banc Alex. Brown

INTRODUCTION

The securitization of recreational vehicle loans began in 1988 with Fleetwood Credit Corp GT 1988-A, making RVs one of the oldest ABS asset classes. Despite its long history, RV securitization has been slow to develop and remains a niche market. This is due to sporadic issuance patterns, a limited number of issuers, and investor unfamiliarity. In addition, limited prepayment information has made assessment of the longer average life classes more difficult for many investors. Recently, investors have shown a preference for mainstream, traditional asset classes to preserve liquidity in their portfolios. This has resulted in increased spread tiering between on-the-run and off-the-run asset classes.

The RV sector offers ABS investors several attractive features. RV owners are among the highest credit quality obligors in the ABS market, which is reflected in the strong credit performance of many RV securitizations. The active securitizers of this product are all well capitalized, diversified and "deep pocket" servicers that are removed from many of the problems experienced by independent finance companies over the past few years. Prepayments are stable and predictable. Based on current ownership trends and projected demographic changes in the United States, RV loan originations should increase and securitizations are likely to mirror this growth.

The authors would like to thank Deutsche Financial Services — in particular the origination, underwriting, servicing and data management staff of DFS' Consumer Finance Group, for providing both extensive source data and numerous operational insights. We would also like to thank everyone in Deutsche Banc Alex. Brown's U.S. ABS Group who helped with this chapter.

This chapter provides an introduction to the RV industry and the securitization of RV loans. In addition, we present results of an extensive loan level study to help investors understand the prepayment and default characteristics of RV loans originated by Deutsche Financial Services (DFS), one of the top three RV lenders.[1]

WHAT IS A RECREATIONAL VEHICLE?

RVs are a well-defined group of towable or motorized vehicles according to the Recreation Vehicle Industry Association (RVIA).[2] RVs provide both transportation and temporary or, semi-permanent living arrangements for travel, recreation and camping. RVs are also known as motor homes or travel trailers. RVs do not include manufactured housing, off-road vehicles, all-terrain vehicles, and snowmobiles. In Exhibit 1 we provide basic descriptions of the various types of RVs offered in the market. Note that the prices in the exhibit represent average base prices for each RV type. The RV industry is quite robust and buyers will often add a wide range of options to their RV, which result in a higher cost. While the average loan size in recent transactions has been in the $35,000 to $45,000 range, the loans in the pools have ranged as high as $350,000 to $500,000 or more in some cases.

Industry Trends

RVs have become increasingly upscale, following quality improvement trends in capital goods categories such as homes and cars. Today, a typical RV will contain luxuries such as cable TV and web access, fine upholstery, a customized kitchen with top-of-the-line appliances, and a "slide-out" wall feature that widens the living space by 2-4 feet when the unit is stationary. Ultra-luxury units are also being constructed as bus conversions with ticket prices starting at $250,000. Even traditionally less expensive products such as travel-trailers have become more elaborate, with many of the same accessories seen in type A motor homes (see the definition in Exhibit 1).

The Who and Why of RV Ownership

The RV industry and lifestyle have played a major role in the recreational lives of Americans for a long time, and are poised for further growth. The demographics of this population have been documented extensively through a periodic (every four years) survey completed by The University of Michigan (UofM) for the RVIA. The information from this study details the strong credit profile and positive characteristics of RV owners and reasons ownership is likely to grow.

For example, in the latest UofM consumer survey from 1997, nearly one in ten vehicle-owning households across America or approximately 8.6 million

---

[1] Readers should be aware that DFS and Deutsche Banc Alex. Brown are both indirect affiliates of Deutsche Bank AG.

[2] The RVIA is an organization dedicated to promoting the interests of the RV industry including manufacturers and suppliers.

families owned an RV. The average age of an RV owner was 48 years. The average income of the owners was $47,000, which is 27% more than the median income for all US households ($37,000). And in 1997, approximately 85% of RV owners were married and owned their own home.

Exhibit 2 shows the demographic breakdown of RV owners by vehicle type. While incomes across age groups are fairly similar, we can draw a few conclusions from this data. The motorhome owner is most likely to be a retired individual with no children while travel trailer and fold-down trailer owners are younger with children still living at home. Generally, the older, retired borrower is considered a better credit risk due to a more stable income versus the younger household with children that may experience more income volatility. In addition, the ability of the motorhome owner to purchase a substantially more expensive vehicle implies stronger credit characteristics. Motorhomes also generally retain their value better than travel trailers.

Exhibit 1: RV Types and Terms with Average Retail Prices as of 1998

Towable Vehicles	Motorized Vehicles
An RV designed to be towed by a motorized vehicle (auto, van, or pickup truck) and of such size and weight as not to require a special highway movement permit. It is designed to provide temporary living quarters for recreational, camping or travel use and does not require permanent on-site hookup.	A recreational, camping and travel vehicle built on or as an integral part of a self-propelled motor vehicle chassis. It may provide kitchen, sleeping, and bathroom facilities and be equipped with the ability to store and carry fresh water and sewage.
Conventional Travel Trailer ($13,878): Ranges typically from 12 feet to 35 feet in length, and is towed by means of a bumper or frame hitch attached to the towing vehicle.	*Motorhome* (Type A, $94,693): The living unit has been entirely constructed on a bare, specially-designed motor vehicle chassis.
Fifth-Wheel Travel Trailer ($25,149): This unit can be equipped the same as the conventional travel trailer but is constructed with a raised forward section that allows a bi-level floor plan. This style is designed to be towed by a vehicle equipped with a device known as a fifth wheel hitch.	*Van Camper* (Type B, $48,023): A panel type truck to which the RV manufacturer adds any of the two following conveniences: sleeping, kitchen and toilet facilities. Also 120-volt hook-up, fresh water storage, city water hook-up and a top extension to provide more head room.
Truck Camper ($12,461): A recreational camping unit designed to be loaded onto or affixed to the bed or chassis of a truck, constructed to provide temporary living quarters for recreational camping or travel use.	*Motorhome* (Type C, $49,863): This unit is built on an automotive manufactured van frame with an attached cab section. The RV manufacturer completes the body section containing the living area and attaches it to the cab section.
Folding Camping Trailer ($5,643): A recreational camping unit designed for temporary living quarters which is mounted on wheels and connected with collapsible sidewalls that fold for towing by a motorized vehicle.	*Conversion Vehicles* ($31,765): Vans, pickup trucks and sport-utility vehicles manufactured by an automaker then modified for transportation and recreation use by a company specializing in conversion vehicles. These changes may include windows, carpeting, paneling, seats, sofas and accessories.

Source: RVIA "Recreation Vehicle Lenders' Experiences Survey & Analysis," 1998.

Exhibit 2: Demographic Breakdown by Vehicle Type

	Median age	Mean income	Children home (%)	% of RVs owned
All Owners	49	$47,000	40	100
Motorhome (Type A, B, and C)	60	$46,000	15	16
Van Conversion	51	$47,000	38	28
Travel Trailer (Conventional and Fifth Wheel)	45	$48,000	43	31
Fold Down	45	$49,000	66	18
Truck Camper	47	$44,000	41	7

Source: "The RV Consumer — A Demographic Profile," A University of Michigan Study for the RVIA, 1997.

"RVing", as it is often termed by members of the RV world, is not just a vacation alternative for people who dislike motels or hate to fly. Increasingly ownership and use of an RV is a fundamental part of the family lifestyle. For example, a typical RV vacation for a retired owner is an extended stay during the winter at an RV park in a warm location, where socializing with other RV owners is the key activity. Looking for others with whom they can share a love for the RV lifestyle, "RVers" are increasingly joining affinity clubs such as The Good Sam Club, which is a million member for-profit confederation of RV owners comparable to AAA. "Good Sammers" command discounts on gas and insurance for their RVs, receive a magazine devoted to the RV lifestyle, get customized roadside assistance, and have their own annual gathering, known as the International Samboree.

Future growth in the RV industry is expected in the coming years as a result of the aging U.S. population. RV ownership is highest in the 55–64 year age group with approximately one in every six vehicle-owning households owning one, followed by the 45-54 year age cohort with an ownership rate of approximately one in eight. The 55-64 year age group is poised to grow significantly as the baby boom generation approaches retirement. Using U.S. Census bureau forecasts and assuming that U.S. consumers purchase RVs in the future at the same rate as prior generations of owners, The UofM estimates that RV ownership in the United States could increase from 8.6 million at the end of 1997 to 10.4 million in 2010.

In addition, replacement of the aging 1970's fleet of RVs will spur sales of new RVs. As of 1997, 24% of the RVs in use were 20+ years old, indicating that these owners are likely candidates to buy either a new RV or another younger used RV.

Another positive trend is the growing push of RV manufacturers into high-end markets. RV sellers compete with other leisure time activities for retirees and near-retirees, such as air-travel and second homes. The availability of high-end units, coupled with the growth in elaborate RV campgrounds (with computer rooms, cable TV hook-ups, and other amenities) is expected to bring the RV lifestyle to more affluent households that have historically viewed RVing as a downscale activity.

Exhibit 3: Comparison of Originator Details

	Fleetwood (subsidiary of Bank of America)*	Deutsche Financial Services**	CIT ***
Managed Portfolio ($ millions)	$2,000	$1,739	$1,816
Number of Contracts (thousands)	62.0	45.5	68.7
Most Recent Securitization Details	1997-B	1999-3	1999-A
Average Contract Size	$24,599	$38,214	$41,639
Range of Contract Size	$2,000 to $305,974	$1,838 to $969,967	$1,952 to $346,889
Average Coupon	9.69%	8.95%	9.30%
Range of Coupons	7.75% to 15.95%	6.99% to 21%	7.50% to 21.24%
Major Geographic Concentrations	CA 19%; OR 10%; TX 9%; FL 7%; AZ 5%	CA 19.78%; FL 8.65%; TX 11.08%	CA 15.05%; FL 7.90%; TX 15.22%
New/Used	76%/24%	57%/43%	65%/35%

* Numbers are approximate based on press release of March 4, 1999
** As of June 30, 1999
*** As of December 31, 1998. Inclusive of only those contracts originated and serviced by CIT. Excludes bulk purchases and subserviced portfolios. Including these other loans, the total portfolio would be $2.5 billion and include approximately 96 thousand contracts

Source: Issue prospectuses and company press release

SECURITIZING RV LOANS

Issuers of RV Loan ABS

The major providers of retail RV loan financings are banks and finance companies. According to the RVIA, as of the end of 1997 (the latest available information), there was approximately $10.9 billion in outstanding RV loans (not including wholesale loans), which represented an increase of approximately 7.9% over the previous year. Of this number, finance companies accounted for 42% and banks accounted for about 51%, with the remaining 7% financed by savings & loans institutions or credit unions.

Based on the RVIA's findings, both finance companies and banks originate roughly 90% of their product through an indirect dealer network. In addition to providing retail financing, finance companies and banks provide wholesale financing for RV dealers with about $1.8 billion in outstanding floor plan loans at the end of 1997. There is also a small but growing direct loan market to existing RV owners, primarily to refinance existing RV loans.

Between December 1988 and July 1999, 35 RV loan securitizations have been completed, totaling $8.9 billion. Over the same period, three companies have dominated the origination and securitization of RV ABS: Fleetwood, CIT, and Deutsche Financial Services (which purchased RV and marine loan originator Ganis Credit Corporation from BankBoston in 1997). The key details of these issuers' managed portfolios and recent securitizations are shown in Exhibit 3, as well as a description of some general differences between the operations of these issuers.

Fleetwood Credit Corp. (FCC) was originally a captive finance company of Fleetwood Enterprises, the leading manufacturer of recreational vehicles, and focused on financing the sales of its parent company's product. In May of 1996, Fleetwood Enterprises sold FCC to Associates First Capital Corp and in 1999 Associates sold FCC to its current owner, Bank of America. Historically Fleetwood has been the most active securitizer in the market, having completed as of this writing 15 transactions totaling $2.2 billion since first entering the market in 1988.

Fleetwood was the pioneer of RV loan securitization but was not active in 1998 and 1999. We believe reentrance by this issuer to the ABS market is possible given its ownership by Bank of America, a regular participant in the ABS market in other asset classes. Fleetwood securitizations are characterized by a significant percentage of motor homes (67% for the 1997-B securitization). These securitizations have exhibited low losses, indicating that Fleetwood's past focus has been on a higher credit quality borrower. Now that Fleetwood is no longer a captive company, any future securitizations would likely include a broader range of RV makes and models. It remains to be seen whether or not the credit quality of the new book of business will change.

CIT is a diversified finance company that focuses on secured commercial (equipment leasing, factoring, etc.) and consumer (RVs, boats, and MH) lending. CIT has been originating RV loans for over 30 years and began securitizing these receivables in 1994. Since then, CIT has completed as of this writing seven RV transactions, totaling about $2 billion. CIT was the first RV loan securitizer to utilize the owner trust structure with sequential-pay tranches. CIT transactions from 1995 forward have exhibited more volatile credit performance than the 1994 issue due to a move to more aggressive lending. For example, cumulative losses on CIT 1994-A stood at 1.06% at the end of September 1999, compared to 2.25% and 2.37% for the 1995-A and 1995-B securitizations, respectively. CIT further adjusted their marketing focus in 1997 to target higher quality and larger balance borrowers, which is reflected in the composition of recent transactions. It is not clear yet how this change will affect the performance of CIT's more recent transactions.

Deutsche Financial Services (DFS) entered the RV lending business in 1997 with its purchase of Ganis Credit Corporation from BankBoston. Ganis has originated RV loans since 1980 and has traditionally focused on high quality obligors. Based on performance statistics and collateral information, we believe DFS has continued similar lending and underwriting practices. Deutsche Financial Services has completed two RV loan securitizations totaling $1.4 billion and is the servicer for the BankBoston Recreation Vehicle Asset Backed Trust 1997-1 which is collateralized by Ganis originated loans.

We expect consistent issuance in the RV sector predominately from CIT and DFS and possibly Fleetwood. These issuers have an established market presence in the RV lending industry. As baby boomers reach retirement age — the most likely age cohort to own an RV — these institutions are poised to win a disproportionate share of new RV loans. In addition, they have established the infrastructure to support securitization, including documentation, servicing, and reporting, and hence can easily use securitization for both balance sheet management and funding diversification. Lastly, while still a niche asset class, the investor base for RV securitizations will become more established as investors see a more regular flow of new transactions and develop a better understanding of the investment characteristics of RV loan ABS.

Loan Characteristics

Across issuers, RV loans are fairly homogenous. RV contracts are generally level payment, fully amortizing, fixed-rate contracts, with 15-year maturities. Recently, there has been an increase in 20-year product, due to increasing prices as buyers purchase more elaborate units. A down payment of between 10% to 20% is usually required depending on the lender, the method of origination, the collateral, and the obligor's history. As Exhibit 4 shows, most pools securitized to date have an average loan size of approximately $25,000 to $35,000, although maximum loan size can approach $1 million.

The size of the loan will be determined by issuer specific underwriting parameters. In Exhibit 5 we show an example of how the typical loan size is calculated. The customer pays the retail ticket price plus taxes, registration fees, and often a warranty. The borrower will then typically pay a 20% down payment of this total amount. However, the LTV on this contract is not 80%. The LTV is figured based on a more conservative valuation which in the case of a new vehicle will be the manufacturer's invoice, and in the case of a used vehicle the wholesale book value. Generally, this LTV will not exceed 115% to 120%.

RV loan borrowers enjoy the same tax benefits as a mortgage obligor. As long as the RV unit offers sleeping, eating, and bathroom facilities, interest may be fully tax deductible. Tax treatment notwithstanding, RV collateral is considered personal property and therefore repossession rather than foreclosure is used when a borrower defaults. This mitigates significantly the length of time necessary to realize liquidation proceeds.

Structural Considerations

Securitization of RV loans has been done through the use of both grantor trust and owner trust structures. In the past, the grantor trust structure had dominated and Fleetwood has thus far only used the grantor trust. A grantor trust structure is a passthrough security that requires pro-rata principal payment on all classes, thereby preventing any maturity tranching. This structure dominated early RV as well as auto securitizations until the early 1990s due to the simplicity of the structure, the ease in gaining debt for tax opinions, and the small size of the early pools.

Exhibit 4: Outstanding Recreational Vehicle Securitizations (Statistics as of Origination)

Issue	Pricing date	Issue size ($mm)	WAC (%)	New/Used (%)	Avg loan size	Wtd avg orig maturity	Wtd avg rem maturity	Seasoning at pricing
Chase Manhattan RV Owner Trust 1997-A	9/22/97	$897	9.31	68.8/31.17	$31,555	168	130	38
CIT RV Grantor Trust 1994-A	1/20/94	$150	9.05	69.9/30.0	NA	154	150	4
CIT RV Owner Trust 1995-A	6/14/95	$200	11.02	41.6/58.4	$23,292	154	152	2
CIT RV Owner Trust 1995-B	8/24/95	$200	10.12	NA	$23,851	155	147	8
CIT RV Owner Trust 1996-A	2/15/96	$250	10.00	67.7/32.3	$25,728	156	148	8
CIT RV Owner Trust 1996-B	8/14/96	$240	10.31	70.4/29.6	$24,247	154	152	2
CIT RV Owner Trust 1997-A	11/20/97	$564	10.10	64.1/35.9	$28,709	163	158	5
CIT RV Owner Trust 1998-A	6/3/98	$400	9.69	64.5/35.5	$35,357	173	170	4
CIT RV Owner Trust 1999-A	5/12/99	$576	9.30	64.77/35.2	$40,876	179	174	5
BankBoston Rec Vehicle Trust 1997-1*	8/13/97	$849	9.37	51.2/47.5	$61,506	194	178	16
Distribution Financial Svcs RV Trust 1999-1	3/12/99	$1,000	8.86	50.5/49.4	$46,803	174	165	9
Distribution Financial Svcs RV Trust 1999-3	7/23/99	$375	8.95	56.9/43.0	$38,214	173	170	3
Fleetwood Credit Corp GT 1992-A	2/19/92	$112	11.05	90.0/10.0	NA	154	147	7
Fleetwood Credit Corp GT 1993-A	1/12/93	$120	9.80	94.0/6.0	NA	156	150	6
Fleetwood Credit Corp GT 1993-B	8/12/93	$94	8.92	95.6/4.4	NA	159	155	4
Fleetwood Credit Corp GT 1994-A	1/12/94	$100	8.98	97.27/2.73	NA	163	146	17
Fleetwood Credit Corp GT 1994-B	6/14/94	$150	8.56	95.0/5.0	NA	160	158	3
Fleetwood Credit Corp GT 1995-A	1/9/95	$150	9.02	91.0/9.0	$30,399	161	158	3
Fleetwood Credit Corp GT 1995-B	7/24/95	$150	10.16	90.0/10.0	$26,286	155	153	3
Fleetwood Credit Corp GT 1996-A	4/11/96	$153	9.50	85.0/15.0	$20,752	156	150	6
Fleetwood Credit Corp GT 1996-B	9/11/96	$205	9.59	81./19.0	$23,977	154	152	2
Fleetwood Credit Corp GT 1997-A	3/6/97	$183	9.53	79.08/20.92	$32,051	160	157	3
Fleetwood Credit Corp GT 1997-B	9/9/97	$350	9.69	76.0/24.0	$24,599	155	149	6

Source: DB Global Markets Research

* Loans were originated by Ganis Credit Corp, which was previously owned by BankBoston and is now owned by Deutsche Financial Services. DFS took over servicing of these loans in the first quarter of 1998.

Exhibit 5: New RV Loan Example

Component	Dollar Amount
Manufacturers' Invoice	$30,000
RV Sales Price	$40,000
Taxes at 5%	$2,000
Registration Fees	$500
Warranty	$500
Total	$43,000
Down Payment (20% × $43,000)	($8,600)
Loan Amount	$34,400
Loan Amt / Mfrs Invoice = LTV	$34,400/$30,000 = 115% LTV

Source: DB Global Markets Research

A combination of growing deal size, investor maturity preferences, and a steep yield curve led to the use of the owner trust structure. In an owner trust transaction principal repayments are allocated sequentially to multiple classes resulting in securities with different average lives and narrower principal payment windows than the grantor trust passthrough structure. Apart from tight payment windows, maturity tranching benefits investors when the yield curve is upward sloping since the principal lock-out on the bonds allows the securities to "roll-down" the curve more quickly, or shorten in average life more quickly than a straight passthrough security. For the most part, the owner trust structure has become the market standard for RV securitizations. While Fleetwood has relied on the grantor trust structure through its last securitization in 1997, we would expect this issuer to utilize an owner trust structure as well, should they return to the ABS market.

A fairly standard security structure has become established in the RV sector. In short, this structure includes four to five senior tranches (triple-A), a mezzanine tranche (single-A), and a subordinate tranche (triple-B). Usually, additional credit enhancement is provided through a reserve fund and possibly over collateralization (OC). Some early RV loan securitizations relied on letters of credit. However, rating downgrades of the insurance providers resulted in downgrades on the related issues and prompted the abandonment of this method of enhancement.

The example in Exhibit 6 is typical of recent transactions with senior and subordinate tranches that extend out as far as five years. A standard 10% clean-up call is likely to be exercised due to the inefficiency of maintaining a reserve account when the collateral pool declines in size. The tight payment windows are similar to an auto loan issue.

Credit Enhancement Mechanics

The reserve fund is typically partially funded at closing and is structured to grow over time to a target level using excess spread. After the reserve fund is fully funded, excess spread is allocated to pay down or "turbo" investor principal and create OC up to a target level.

Exhibit 6: CIT RV Owner Trust 1999-A
(Assuming 1.4% ABS and Exercise of 10% Clean Up Call)

Class	Size ($mm)	Orig Avg Life	Principal Window	Months
A-1	189.94	0.75	6/99 – 12/00	19
A-2	104.36	2.00	12/00 – 11/01	12
A-3	109.68	3.00	11/01 – 12/02	14
A-4	86.48	4.00	12/02 – 11/03	12
A-5	45.22	4.71	11/03 – 3/04	5
B	28.50	4.82	3/04	1
C	11.52	4.82	3/04	1
Total	575.70			

Source: Bloomberg

The reserve fund target level is defined as a percentage of the outstanding balance and is usually 1% to 2%. As the collateral pays down after the target percentage is reached, any amounts in the reserve fund in excess of the required percentage will be released each month after principal to the noteholders is paid out. In the case of the OC, a portion of the principal collections may be allocated to reduce the OC to maintain the required percentage.

The reserve fund and OC will be subject to a floor amount or a nominal minimum amount at which they will be frozen for the remainder of the deal. This feature allows the credit enhancement to grow as a percentage of the deal and provides investors with significant amounts of enhancement in the late stages of a transaction's life. Performance triggers may also be incorporated to protect investors from collateral deterioration. The breach of a performance trigger causes the reserve account to either step up or become frozen to increase the credit enhancement as a percentage of the outstanding deal.

The CIT RV 1999-A deal (shown above) provides a good example of the reserve fund mechanics. In this structure, the reserve fund is initially 1.71% of the balance with a target balance set at 2% of the outstanding pool balance. Monthly deposits of excess spread will be deposited to the reserve fund until the target level is met. Amounts in excess of the required 2% level will be released each month until the reserve account reaches a floor amount of $5.7 million. After the floor is reached, no further funds will be released from the account and this nominal amount will be maintained over the remaining life of the deal. This issue also includes a delinquency and a loss trigger based on a schedule of performance levels that increase over time. If the trigger is hit, the required reserve account percentage is doubled from 2% to 4% and is funded out of future excess spread. The trigger is reversible in the CIT deal, so if the performance of the pool improves to within the prescribed levels, the required reserve account level returns to 2%.

Credit Enhancement Across Asset Classes

The rating agencies incorporate several factors into sizing the credit enhancement for a securitization, including historical loss and delinquency experience, recovery experience, underwriting and servicing quality, maturity of the assets and obligor quality. As a result, the level of credit enhancement from deal to deal will differ and will be roughly correlated with the loss experience of an issuer's portfolio. We compared the credit enhancement from three recent RV transactions, a prime auto deal and a manufactured housing deal by calculating an enhancement ratio for each deal at the triple-A level as of day one (this is not a stress test and is meant for comparative purposes only). We divided the initial amount of credit enhancement by an approximate cumulative loss number (the annual net loss amount of the issuer's managed portfolio multiplied by the average life of the assets). Our results are shown in Exhibit 7.

Compared to either prime auto loan ABS or manufactured housing issues, RV loan securitizations offer generous levels of credit enhancement. The credit enhancement levels are even stronger when one considers that the annual variation of loss rates is much lower for RV collateral than for either prime auto loans, or manufactured housing loans, as shown by the range of losses on these portfolios from 1994 to 1999. The main reason for the generous enhancement relative to MH and prime autos is the lack of sufficiently deep and consistent historical performance information. Therefore, the rating agencies apply haircuts to the RV performance data to compensate for this.

Given the strength of the borrower base, we feel that the credit enhancement levels for RV deals are more than adequate, and the possibility of subordinate tranche upgrades over time exists. In fact, Moody's Investors Service upgraded four subordinate tranches on Fleetwood transactions in November 1998, including series 1994-A, 1994-B, and 1995-A from A2 to Aaa and 1995-B from A2 to Aa1. The reason cited for the upgrades is the level and distribution of losses compared to the amount of credit enhancement on each of these transactions.

Exhibit 7: Credit Enhancement versus 1998 Managed Portfolio Performance

	CIT RV Trust 99-A	Dist Fin Svcs 99-3*	Fleetwood CC GT 97-B**	Premier Auto 1999-3	Green Tree MH 99-4
Collateral Type	RV	RV	RV	Auto	MH
1998 Managed Portfolio					
Ann Net Losses	0.86	0.39	0.31	1.39	1.06
5-yr Range of Net Losses	0.49–1.05	0.31–0.39	0.21–0.31	0.73–1.39	0.60–1.06
At Deal Closing					
Subordination	7.08	4.50	3.50	3.75	17.50
Reserve Fund	1.71	0.50	0.75	0.25	0.00
Over Collateralization	0.00	0.00	0.00	4.00	0.00
Total	8.79	5.00	4.25	8.00	17.50
Asset Pool WAL (yrs)	2.39	2.46	1.62	1.85	7.52
Enhancement Ratio***	4.3	5.2	8.5	3.1	2.2

* Distribution Financial Services, 1996 - 1998
** Through July 31, 1997
*** Credit Enhancement/(annual net losses × pool WAL)
Source: DB Global Markets Research and Deal Prospectuses

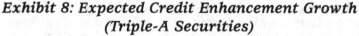

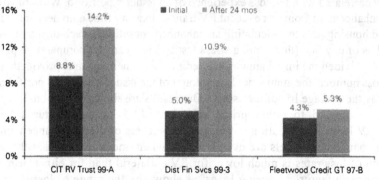

Exhibit 8: Expected Credit Enhancement Growth (Triple-A Securities)

Source: DB Global Markets Research

In the owner trust structures, the use of target levels and floors for the reserve funds and overcollateralization amounts along with the "locked-out" nature of the subordinated bonds means that credit enhancement will continue to grow over time. Exhibit 8 illustrates the growth of credit enhancement over two years. Investors should note that Fleetwood uses a grantor trust structure, which is a straight passthrough. This means that the subordinate bonds pay down simultaneously with the senior bonds, and therefore credit enhancement does not grow as quickly.

DELINQUENCY AND LOSS PERFORMANCE OF RV SECURITIZATIONS

How have RV loan securitizations performed historically? We analyzed the historical performance of RV loan securitizations compared to prime auto loan and manufactured housing ABS. With respect to both cumulative loss experience and delinquency experience, RV loan ABS compare well to auto and manufactured housing collateral. The Premier AutoTrust (PRAT) and the GreenTree (GT) deals experienced losses near 1.75% after 27 months, while Fleetwood and BankBoston RV losses over a comparable period were under 0.75% and CIT was barely above 1.00%. (See Exhibit 9.)

The 60+ day delinquency performance of RVs is also much better than Premier and Green Tree — with the exception of CIT. (See Exhibt 10.) CIT's poorer performance is explained by its more aggressive underwriting standards. In late 1994, CIT incorporated a risk-based pricing approach to its underwriting to allow origination of lower credit quality but higher yielding loans. This is reflected in a change in the pool weighted average coupon from 9.05% on the 1994-A issue to 10.96% on the 1995-A. In early 1997, CIT adjusted its marketing focus to target higher credit quality and larger balance borrowers, which is reflected in the larger average loan balance of recent issues. It is still too early to tell how this change will affect collateral performance on the post-1997 securitizations. Early indications show similar performance to past issues. While CIT's RV loan delinquency performance suffers relative to other RV securitizations, it remains better than many prime auto loan and MH pools on a cumulative loss basis.

Exhibit 9: Comparable Cumulative Losses for 1997 Securitizations (% of Original Balance)

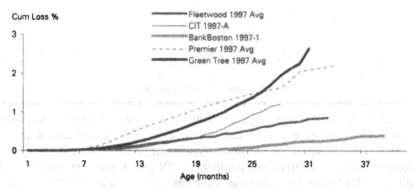

Note: Fleetwood includes Series 97A and 97B; Green Tree includes Series 97-1, 97-2, 97-3, 97-4, 97-5 and 97-7; Premier includes Series 97-1, 97-2, and 97-3. Information is through 9/30/99 except for Green Tree which is through 8/30/99

Source: Moody's Investors Service and DB Global Markets Research

Exhibit 10: Comparable 60 + Day Delinquencies for 1997 Securitizations (% of Current Balance)

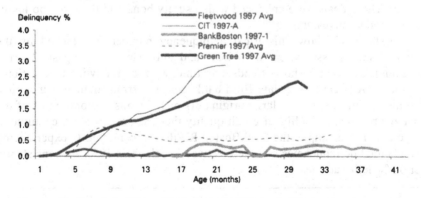

Note: Fleetwood includes Series 97A and 97B; Green Tree includes Series 97-1, 97-2, 97-3, 97-4, 97-5 and 97-7; Premier includes Series 97-1, 97-2, and 97-3. Information is through 9/30/99 except for Green Tree which is through 8/30/99

Source: Moody's Investors Service and DB Global Markets Research

Exhibit 11: Comparison of Cumulative Losses on Recession Tested RV ABS

Pricing date	Transaction	State exposure (%)	Cumulative losses (%)	Months seasoned at pricing
12/19/88	Fleetwood Credit Corp 1988-A	CA 92; AZ 6.2	0.82	5
9/28/89	Bank of the West 1989-1	CA 53.2; TX 13.4	3.41	9
10/18/89	CFC-7 Grantor Trust	CA 18.04; CO 15.09; FL 10.90; GA 6.08	4.76	16
10/26/89	Fleetwood Credit Corp 1989-A	CA 72; IL 4	1.46	11
3/14/90	Bank of the West 1990-1	CA 36.3; TX 15	2.12	7
7/17/90	Fleetwood Credit Corp 1990-A	CA 53.5; NC 6	1.55	18
2/6/91	Fleetwood Credit Corp 1991-A	CA 37; OR 7	1.35	5

Source: Moody's Investors Service

How do these securities perform during a recession? As with most ABS, there are a limited number of recession tested deals. There is sufficient data from the 1988 to 1991 period to demonstrate recessionary performance. In Exhibit 11 we show the final cumulative loss numbers on RV loan securitizations that withstood the 1991/92 recession. Even the worst case (CFC-7 with a 4.76% loss rate) is still well covered by the triple-A enhancement levels on current issues discussed above. At the triple-B level, recent RV transactions are able to withstand significant losses. For CIT RV Trust 1999-A the triple-B class can take up to a 4.3% cumulative loss before incurring a principal loss and the Distribution Financial Services RV Trust 1999-3 can take up to a 4.9% cumulative loss.[3] Furthermore, the performance of most of these issues is particularly impressive given the heavy exposure to California, one of the hardest hit states during the early 1990s recession. These deals were enhanced with a surety bond and therefore no losses were suffered by investors.

Exhibit 12 shows historical delinquency numbers as tracked by the American Bankers Association on RV loans and auto loans over the past 22 years. This graph is useful as it shows trends over time, with the following reservations. First, the ABA is capturing data from banks and not from finance companies, which historically have been large originators of RV loans. Second, most of the securitized pools are of a higher credit quality than the pool of loans captured in this average. For example, the BankBoston RV deal is consistently experiencing under 1% total delinquencies and the Fleetwood deals from 1997 are consistently under 0.5% delinquencies.[4]

---

[3] The cumulative loss amount equates to a 1.85% constant default rate (CDR) for CIT RV Trust 1999-A and 1.95% CDR for Distribution Financial Services RV Trust 1999-3 over the life of the transaction to maturity. Assumes a 1.4% ABS, zero recoveries and a zero lag time.

[4] Thirty-plus day delinquencies are used to compare against the ABA index and 60+ delinquencies are used in Exhibit 10 to compare against Green Tree and Premier.

Exhibit 12: American Bankers Association Delinquency Statistics (30+ Days, Seasonally Adjusted, %)

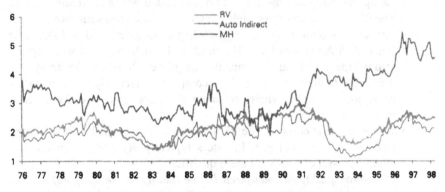

Source: American Bankers Association

Despite these shortcomings, there are several interesting observations. First, RV loan delinquency performance has closely tracked that of auto loans, and over the period 1992-1999, has been better than auto loans. Second, the performance of RV loans over the same seven years has been significantly better than manufactured housing loans. Third, the deterioration that was experienced across consumer lending sectors in the 1995 to 1997 period was also experienced by RV loans. But, the peak of this deterioration still fell short (albeit slightly) from the peak of the 1991-1992 recession. Lastly, current RV delinquency rates continue to decline.

FRAMEWORK FOR ANALYZING RELATIVE VALUE

When choosing benchmarks for comparison against RV loan ABS we took several factors into consideration, including the collateral, the structure, and the average lives of the securities being issued. Based on these factors we chose auto loan ABS and manufactured housing ABS as comparables. The sequential-pay structure of RV loan ABS with its relatively tight payment windows compares well to owner trust auto structures on the shorter average life securities (1- to 3-year classes). Manufactured housing securities are best for longer bond comparisons since auto ABS do not extend that far.

Several factors must be examined in assessing whether the spread give-up or pick-up, depending on the case, is enough to compensate an investor (see Exhibit 13 for a summary). Below are several of the factors that should be evaluated when determining relative value.

- *Credit strength of the issuer/servicer* — Since 1996 investors have started to value the credit strength of the servicer of an ABS transaction more than in the past. The root of these concerns is the increased risk of a financially constrained company cutting back staff or systems in its servicing operation and the uncertainty associated with a servicing transfer. The RV sector offers three highly-rated servicers. Banks run two of these servicers — Bank of America (Aa2/A+) owns Fleetwood and Deutsche Bank (Aa3/AA) owns DFS. The third, CIT (Aa3/A+),[5] is a well capitalized independent finance company. The prime auto sector also enjoys the benefits of high credit ratings. This compares attractively to the manufactured housing sector where the major servicers are barely if not below investment grade.

- *Size of the asset class* — The RV sector is relatively small and characterized by sporadic issuance. Investors typically demand a liquidity premium for asset classes with these qualities.
- *Collateral quality (as measured by the quality of the obligors)* — The market places a premium on securitizations backed by higher credit quality loans. The credit quality of RV collateral is excellent. While some differences exist between different issuers' pools of receivables, one thing stands out — over time this collateral has performed better than pools of securitized auto loans or manufactured housing product.
- *Prepayment optionality* — One of the least understood aspects of RV loan ABS is the prepayment characteristics of these securities. This is a main focus of the next section of this chapter. In short, we have found that prepayments on these assets are relatively insensitive to interest rate fluctuations. This contrasts with manufactured housing, where declining interest rates lead to higher prepayment rates, albeit less than in other mortgage related product such as home equity loans or residential mortgages.

Exhibit 13: Breakdown of Liquidity Factors and the Impact on Spreads

	Recreational Vehicles	Prime Autos	Manufactured Housing
Servicer Credit Strength	Strong ⇩	Strong ⇩	Medium to Weak ⇧
Asset Class Size	Small ⇧	Large ⇩	Medium ⇩
Collateral Quality	High ⇩	Medium to High ⇩	Low ⇧
Prepayment Optionality	Low ⇩	Low ⇩	Medium ⇧
Structural Complexity	Simple ⇩	Simple ⇩	Mild Complexity ⇧

⇧ Means that this factor should increase the spread
⇩ Means that this factor should decrease the spread

Source: DB Global Markets Research

[5] Moody's rating of Aa3 for The CIT Group, Inc. was placed on review for a possible downgrade as of March 8, 1999.

Exhibit 14: Relative Value Analysis (bp over Treasuries)
(a) Three-Year Issue Relative Value Analysis

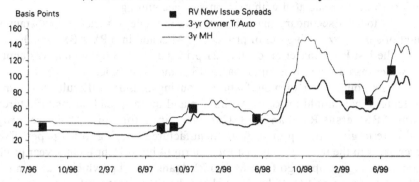

(b) Five-Year Issue Relative Value Analysis

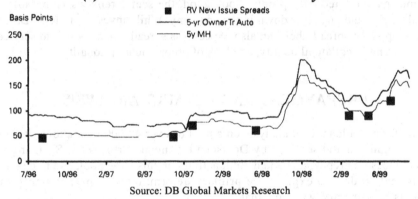

Source: DB Global Markets Research

- *Structural complexity* — Innovative structures often demand additional time and scrutiny on the part of investors, and until a new structure becomes well understood it will usually carry a liquidity premium. In the RV sector, structures used have been simple and straightforward, relying since 1998 solely on senior/subordinated, sequential-pay structures similar to the auto sector. The use of an easily recognizable and understood structure in the RV sector should help the liquidity of these securities. Manufactured housing issues have relied on a REMIC structure that incorporates crossover dates to prevent or allow paydown on the subordinate classes, subject to performance triggers.

We examined the historical pricing of new RV ABS issues compared to both auto ABS and MH ABS. As Exhibit 14 illustrates, RV ABS traditionally priced wide to the levels of auto loan ABS and tight to manufactured housing ABS. This should not be surprising. Prime auto loan ABS are one of the oldest and best understood of the frequently securitized asset classes and therefore offer significant liquidity. Manufactured housing ABS, on the other hand, have suffered from prepayment concerns as well as headline risk due to significant balance sheet write downs associated with gain-on-sale accounting.

In today's secondary market, investors are able to pick up a substantial amount of spread by trading out of prime auto ABS and into RV ABS. The 3-year class of the last RV transaction on July 21 priced at T+108 bp, which was about 19 bp wider than 3-year prime auto loan ABS at the same time.

The comparison to manufactured housing is more difficult. There are more factors that should make investors demand more spread on manufactured housing ABS versus RV loan ABS. Currently, investors on a 3-year security would have to give up 8 bp to go from manufactured housing to RV paper. This differential is in the middle of its historical norm (4 bp to 16 bp). On 5-year product, the current give-up to go from MH to RV loans is 12 bp, which is also in the middle of the range of 4 to 25 bp. We believe, however, that while the technicals for mortgage related ABS product look good, the sector remains vulnerable to headline risk and any slow down in the economy. While investors in RV ABS are giving up some spread, they can also expect less spread volatility due to servicer credit strength, collateral quality, and lack of prepayment optionality.

PREPAYMENT AND DEFAULT ANALYSIS

We performed a loan level analysis on a pool of over 42,000 recreational vehicle loans originated and serviced by Deutsche Financial Services (DFS). Our goal was to measure prepayment and default activity on this large pool, and to develop statistical models to explain the primary determinants of prepayments and defaults. In summary, we found that:

- Prepayment rates are insensitive to changes in interest rates, relative to residential mortgages. Prepayments on seasoned RV loans generally fall in the 18% to 25% conditional prepayment rate (CPR) range and are due mostly to demographic and turnover related factors such as trading up to a new RV.
- Defaults have been very low. Even though the borrower pool has a fairly homogenous credit profile, loans to borrowers with lower FICO scores and loans originated by dealers are more likely to default.

Collateral Characteristics

Loans in the pool were originated between April 1996 and August 1999. The origination data include borrower age, whether the collateral was new or used at origination, the age of the obligor, the origination channel (direct vs. dealer), FICO scores,[6] and the state where the obligor lives. We also have monthly payment information, prepayment, and, if applicable, default information for each loan.

The prepayment analysis was based on a set of 42,000 loans. These loans have an average loan size of approximately $45,000. Loan size ranges from $1,000 to almost $1,000,000. Most of the pool is made up of loans with 15-year original terms and is split 44/56% between new/used loans. More than 20% of the loans are from California and almost 10% are from Texas. Florida and Oregon follow with 8% and 5% of the pool, respectively.

Exhibit 15 gives a collateral summary by origination quarter along several dimensions such as average size, original loan term, and percent of loans made for the purchase of new RVs. Certain trends are apparent. The average borrower age has declined, coupon rates have been fairly stable, and loan terms have increased.

Until recently, the typical DFS RV loan has had a 15-year original term. For example, during 1996 nearly 80% (by balance) of all loans issued had an original term of 15 years. The remaining loans had 10-year and 5-year terms. Beginning in 1997, DFS began to issue 20-year RV loans. By the end of 1998, 20-year loans accounted for a 20% share, while 15-year issuance fell to a 65% share (also, by balance).

Exhibit 15: Issuance Trends, by Production Quarter

	Average loan size ($000s)	Loan term	Borrower age	% New	Number of loans	Total balance ($000s)	WAC (%)	Spread* (bp)
Q2-96	38	153	59	39	2,447	93,821	9.20	144
Q3-96	39	157	58	45	1,523	58,698	9.44	165
Q4-96	47	162	59	40	1,305	61,054	9.12	189
Q1-97	47	165	58	35	2,471	117,118	9.10	153
Q2-97	46	163	59	34	2,011	92,382	9.32	180
Q3-97	49	170	58	46	2,625	127,770	9.18	209
Q4-97	54	169	59	35	2,438	130,502	9.01	210
Q1-98	53	172	58	39	3,333	167,716	8.89	218
Q2-98	45	172	57	43	4,483	203,828	8.92	228
Q3-98	45	171	57	43	4,241	189,877	8.87	248
Q4-98	50	177	56	47	3,280	164,204	8.65	242
Q1-99	45	175	54	49	5,100	231,836	8.69	224
Q2-99	42	175	52	54	6,507	270,968	8.98	206
Q3-99	33	168	51	57	891	29,217	9.26	187
Total	45	168	57	43	42,655	1,938,990	9.03	202

* We define spread as the difference between the loan rate and the Freddie Mac 15-year, 30-day commitment rate at the time of loan origination. We use this definition of spread throughout the paper.

Source: DB Global Markets Research

[6] A FICO score is a measure developed by Fair Isaacs & Company to rank a person's credit worthiness. The score is calculated using 45 different criteria and ranges between 350 and 850 (a higher score is better). Factors such as the number of credit cards a person has, delinquency records, employment history and length of time at present residence affect one's FICO score. Fair Isaacs & Co. does not publish the exact formula.

Exhibit 16: Variation in Loan Characteristics

Attribute	Range	% of pool	Average size ($000s)	Term (mth)	WAC (%)	Spread (bps)	% New	Borrower age	FICO	% CA	% TX	% FL
FICO	<680	16	40	170	9.32	250	53	51	644	22	12	8
	680-719	20	44	169	9.00	214	43	54	701	22	11	9
	720-759	26	46	171	8.90	203	42	56	740	19	11	9
	760+	37	48	170	8.83	195	42	60	783	18	11	10
Borrower	<45	15	30	162	9.26	244	56	35	708	23	10	6
Age	45-54	22	45	172	9.03	216	48	50	719	21	10	8
	55-64	37	54	174	8.88	202	41	60	737	18	12	10
	65+	25	49	168	8.86	195	34	70	752	18	12	12
Loan	<100	6	15	76	9.87	294	34	55	730	22	10	8
Term	100-159	24	28	135	9.24	236	40	56	732	21	9	8
(months)	160-180	56	65	178	8.87	196	50	57	733	18	12	10
	240	13	158	240	8.50	182	79	55	732	19	14	9
Used		51	42	158	9.03	214	—	58	736	20	10	11
New		49	50	183	8.90	205	100	55	730	19	12	8
States	California	19	43	168	9.04	216	42	56	729	100	—	—
	Texas	11	54	175	8.94	208	45	57	732	—	100	—
	Florida	9	51	172	8.89	205	38	59	738	—	—	100
Loan	<15,000	5	10	101	10.60	376	54	48	716	20	8	7
Size	15,000-29,999	13	22	134	9.55	263	39	55	731	22	9	8
($)	30,000-44,999	15	37	158	9.09	214	30	58	737	21	9	9
	45,000-99,999	31	62	172	8.84	198	46	58	735	21	10	9
	100,000+	36	171	197	8.59	176	61	56	732	17	15	10

Source: DB Global Markets Research

Exhibit 16 displays loan attributes of the pool after grouping by key characteristics. There is some evidence that risk-based pricing takes place. For example, borrowers with the best FICO scores have loans with rates 49 bp lower than borrowers with the worst FICO scores. The 55–64 year old cohort is the largest, with the largest average loan size and longest loan term and as we shall see later, the best credit performance. This borrower group consists of new or near retirees who have both the income and physical vigor to pursue the upscale end of the RV lifestyle. There is also a marked link between loan size and pricing, with the largest loans receiving more favorable spreads. Since average borrower age and FICO scores are virtually the same across loan size groupings it may be that high-end motor homes are superior collateral (perhaps they maintain high resale value). (Surprisingly, there is only a slight relationship between loan size and FICO scores.) Typically people assume that larger loans are held by higher quality borrowers but here this does not appear to be the case.

PREPAYMENT BEHAVIOR

Investors analyzing mortgage prepayments accept that turnover-related prepayments are relatively low and stable. The bulk of prepayment behavior is due to refinancing activity, which is driven by changes in interest rates. In fact, correlating interest rate movements to CPR trends drives the bulk of the analytic effort in understanding mortgage prepayments. Quantitative analysts have attempted to associate demographic factors on mortgage loans to prepayment likelihood, but in the end, interest rates overwhelm all other factors.

Superficially, RV loans are very similar to certain mortgage loans. The balances are often relatively high, the terms are relatively long, and most loans qualify for the mortgage interest tax deduction. Notwithstanding this, we found that demographic characteristics and turnover-related factors play a larger role in determining RV prepayments relative to mortgage loans. Specifically, over the life of our pool, primary interest rates fell some 180 bp to 30-year lows and mortgage prepayments soared from less than 10% CPR to over 70% CPR. By contrast, prepayments for BBRV 97-1, which is backed by a pool of fully seasoned RV loans, start relatively high, but peaked at about 30.5% CPR when interest rates hit their lows. To the extent that interest rates affect prepayments, our analysis shows this effect to be relatively mild. For example, a 50 bp decrease in interest rates appears to cause prepayments to increase about 3.5% CPR. While some interest rate sensitivity exists, most of the prepayment patterns point, at least indirectly, to lifestyle-related motivations for prepayments.

Turnover refers to the sale of an RV unit and is due to a variety of factors, such as a desire to "trade-up" (which may be influenced by changes in household wealth) or to exit the RV lifestyle. For example, wealthier people usually have more disposable income with which to make discretionary purchases. Consistent with this, we observe that attributes like FICO score and loan size, which tend to increase with wealth, also tend to increase with the likelihood of prepayment. Also, obligor age is useful for predicting prepayments, since it acts as a proxy for the likelihood of a lifestyle change. Other factors, such as original term, loan size, and whether a borrower purchased a new or used RV sharpen the picture of a borrower's creditworthiness and tastes and thereby play a role in explaining turnover related prepayments. While we cannot know for certain why RV borrowers pre-pay, the data, and extensive discussions with industry professionals, lead us to believe that investors seeking to understand RV prepayments need to focus on demographic and turnover related factors rather than interest rates and refinancing.

The rest of this section examines in detail the relationship between prepayments and loan seasoning, interest rates, season of the year, loan size, original term to maturity, borrower age, loan origination channel, whether the RV is new or used, and changes in interest rates. All of the aforementioned loan and borrower characteristics are correlated with prepayments at a high level of statistical significance. In order to make comparisons between the effects of loan characteristics, the rest of this section will use a standard pool unless explicitly stated otherwise. This pool consists of loans that have seasoned for 30 months, with 180-month original terms, $35,000 original balances, and 9.5% coupons. The pool is split 35/65% between loans that were directly and indirectly originated and ⅓ of the indirectly originated loans are for used RVs making the new/used split 50/50 (all directly originated loans are used). The loan obligors are 65-years old and have a 730 FICO score.

In summary we found that:

- The sample pool experienced prepayments growing from 10% to 32% CPR in 25 months. Thereafter, prepayment rates decreased to the mid 20s. The effects of aging, seasonality, and refinancing are all driving the prepayments in Exhibit 17.
- For our standard pool, prepayments, solely due to aging, free of interest rate and seasonal effects, immediately start at 7% CPR and increase to 20% CPR when the loans become fully seasoned at approximately 30 months.
- Seasonal factors cause prepayments to increase by 3% CPR from winter to spring.
- Large loans experience higher prepayment rates.
- Loans with shorter original terms prepay faster than longer-term loans.
- Borrowers with high FICO scores prepay faster than borrowers with low FICO scores.
- Older borrowers prepay at higher rates than younger borrowers.
- Loans originated directly by DFS prepay more slowly than loans originated by dealers.
- Loans collateralized by new RVs prepay more slowly than loans collateralized by used RVs.

Exhibit 17: DFS RV Loan Pool Performance (Age in Months)

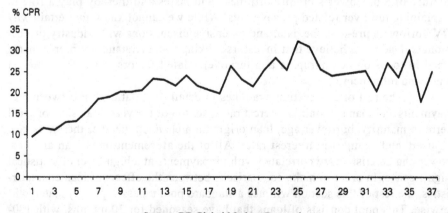

Source: DB Global Markets Research

Exhibit 18: Seasoning Curve for Recreational Vehicles (Age in Months)

Source: DB Global Markets Research

In conducting our statistical analysis, we employ a discrete choice methodology. In this framework a borrower has only two choices at any point in time. For example, when examining the effects of prepayments, a borrower can either prepay the whole loan balance or not. There are no other alternatives such as skipping a payment or curtailing the outstanding loan balance. This methodology allows us to examine the effect of various loan and borrower characteristics in isolation. In effect, we ask the question: holding all other factors constant, what is the impact on prepayments (or defaults) of changing a specific variable — e.g., FICO score.

One final point: similar to auto loans, the market convention for projecting and measuring RV prepayments is the absolute prepayment speed (ABS) assumption. In the analysis that follows, however, we measure prepayments using the conditional prepayment rate (CPR) method.

Seasoning

The aging curve is fairly flat as shown in Exhibit 18. Controlling for factors such as interest rates, FICO score, borrower age, and loan size, we constructed an aging curve for RV loans. We estimate that for our hypothetical pool prepayments immediately start at 7% CPR and steadily rise over the next 27 months to 20% CPR.

The rapid rate of initial prepayments on RV loans is different from most other asset classes, including home equity loans, and manufactured housing loans. In these asset classes, the seasoning process is rapid, but prepayments are low for at least the first few months.

The seasoning curve demonstrates the pattern of prepayments one can expect from RV loans in the absence of interest rate changes and seasonal effects. To predict how a pool of loans will prepay one must start with the seasoning curve and then adjust it for changes in interest rates and a given pool's characteristics, such as FICO scores, borrower ages, loan terms, and loan sizes. The rest of this section outlines the correct adjustments to make to this base curve of prepayments.

Exhibit 19: 1998 Prepayments versus 1997 Prepayments

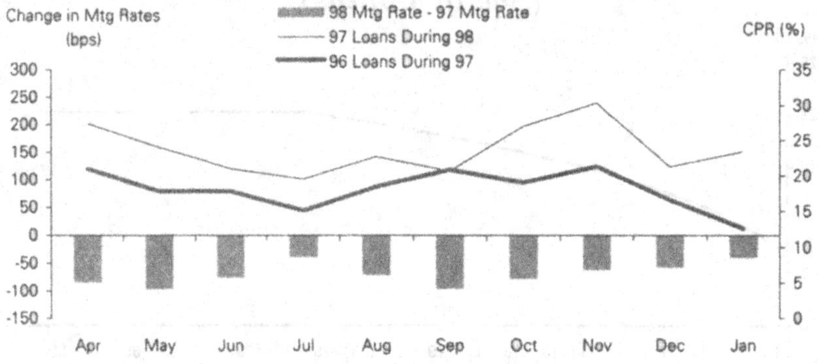

Source: DB Global Markets Research

Interest Rate Sensitivity

Our study suggests that some amount of refinancing-driven prepayments do occur. Accurately assessing the sensitivity of RV loans to interest rate changes is not straight-forward. Whereas in residential mortgages homeowners have only one source of funding, RV owners can choose from a variety of funding options. They can take out a RV loan, use equity built up in their homes, tap into unsecured lines of credit, or perhaps choose not to finance the RV at all. Despite these difficulties, we have found some patterns relating to interest rate movements.

For example, we compared the prepayment rates of two similar 1-year-old pools during 1997 and 1998. (See Exhibit 19.) The first pool, originated during 1996, had a WAC of 9.24% while the second pool, originated in 1997, had a 9.13% WAC. During 1998, when Freddie Mac 15-year mortgage rates were between 41 to 98 bp lower than levels a year earlier, the second pool prepaid an average of 5.7% CPR faster than the first pool had in 1997.

While prepayment rates are clearly higher during 1998 and mortgage rates are significantly lower, it seems unlikely that all the increase in prepayments is attributable to refinancing activity.

Several points should be noted. First, we analyze refinancing activity relative to primary mortgage rates rather than RV rates because there is little incentive for RV owners to refinance into new RV loans. RV loan rates do not seem to track downward with prevailing interest rates and have been much more stable throughout the sample period compared to other consumer loan rates. For example, as 15-year Freddie Mac rates dropped by 181 bp from 7.91% to 6.10% between 1996 and 1998, RV loan rates in the sample pool dropped by 58 bp from 9.42% to 8.84%. For a 15-year loan with a $50,000 original balance, 58 bp translates into $17 in savings each month. Therefore we assume that interest rate driven refinancing occurs when borrowers draw on other sources of credit — in particular home equity loans or cash out refinancings of their home mortgage to pay off an RV loan.

Second, the prepayment sensitivity to observed changes in mortgage rates is quite modest. Perhaps many people did not have enough equity in their homes to make cash-out refinancings feasible. Furthermore, it has been suggested that homeowners are reluctant to combine all personal debt into their mortgage.

Third, it is possible that what appears to be refinancing-driven prepayment activity was in some cases actually a move to trade up. Between 1997 and 1998 the economy continued to grow and some homeowners may have taken advantage of increases in household wealth to acquire a larger and more expensive RV. In these cases, wealth rather than interest rates was the driving factor and we consider this to be a turnover related rather than interest rate related prepayment. Unfortunately, it is difficult to isolate interest rate effects on prepayments from the effects of economic expansion.

As we observe prepayments under various interest rate and economic environments we can better isolate the relationship between interest rates and RV loan prepayments. For now, our model indicates that a 50 bp drop in interest rates causes RV prepayments to increase by 3.5% CPR.

Loan Term

Loan term has proven to be a statistically significant factor for explaining prepayment activity, with shorter loans prepaying substantially faster than loans with longer terms. A $35,000 loan that has seasoned for 30 months and has an original term less than 10 years can be expected to prepay at 25% CPR. A similarly seasoned 15-year loan will prepay at 20% CPR, while 20-year loans prepay at about 15%.

The most likely reason for the above pattern is that shorter loans are held by people sampling the RV lifestyle. Short loans are collateralized by smaller, used RVs, which tend to be used as samples. These borrowers have a relatively short horizon before they decide whether or not to purchase a vehicle for the long term. Eventually they will either buy a larger RV or choose to spend their recreation dollars elsewhere.

Additionally, longer-term loans tend to have both larger balances and lower rates. On average, borrowers have about the same FICO scores and are the same age, regardless of the maturity of the loan they hold. The main differences between these types of loans are the types of RVs behind them. Longer-term loans are more likely to be backed by more expensive RVs, and to be new rather than used. It therefore seems likely that DFS perceives larger loans to be better collateral and rewards these borrowers with longer loan terms and lower rates.

New versus Used

As previously stated, the pool is evenly split between loans backed by new and used RVs. Anecdotally, used RV loans are assumed to prepay faster because many of these buyers are trying out the product. After some time passes, they either decide to make a long-term commitment and buy a more expensive, new RV or sell their RV and spend their leisure dollars elsewhere. To the extent that owners of used RVs do have different horizons for the use of their RVs, new and used loans will exhibit different prepayment behavior. The statistical evidence bears this out. A fully seasoned pool (30 months) of indirectly originated used loans with a 15-year loan term will prepay more than 4% CPR faster than a similar pool of new, indirectly originated RV loans.

In this analysis, we distinguish between used RV loans that were directly originated by DFS and indirect originations (by a dealer). As we discussed earlier, DFS has developed a successful direct refinancing program aimed at RV owners with existing financing from another lender. For borrowers with good quality collateral and solid credit characteristics, DFS will refinance existing loans at lower rates than comparable financing available from dealers. Therefore, technically, a used RV backs almost every DFS directly originated loan even though many of the RVs may have been new when purchased. Since dealer originated used RV loans are actually backed by used RVs there is a clear difference between those loans and used RV loans directly financed by DFS.

The data show that a pool of used RV loans that have been indirectly originated will prepay as much as 7% CPR faster than a pool of directly originated used loans when fully seasoned. In other words, once an RV owner refinances a loan with DFS, the propensity to prepay falls sharply. Whether or not this difference in prepayments can be attributed to the lower loan rates offered by DFS or some other unobserved characteristic is unclear.

Loan Size

Loan size varies significantly in the pool. As loan size varies, so too does the type of borrower. Therefore, one can expect loan size to predict prepayment behavior. Unfortunately, the relationship between loan size and prepayments is somewhat muddled.

The smallest loans in the sample experience 22% CPR prepayment rates, probably due to turnover as borrowers trade-up or pay off small balances. Prepayment rates decrease for medium sized loans and increase again for large loans. Loans larger than $100,000 are 1.24 times more likely to prepay than $50,000 loans, all else being equal.

Despite the fact that these predictions are made in the context of a model that controls for the effects of interest rate movements (and other factors such as age, state, FICO score, etc.) the results are not always straightforward. One simple explanation is that the owners of small RVs have the most room to move up and large RV owners have the most resources to move up (or to obtain alternative sources of financing), although this seems more convenient than convincing. In this case, however, it seems unlikely that loans larger than $100,000 (roughly one in every ten) pay 4% CPR faster than $75,000 loans, due solely to turnover. It is more probable that some refinancing activity was captured for these large loans. At this point, we think higher prepayments on larger loans may reflect some refinancing activity.

Exhibit 20: FICO Score and Prepayments

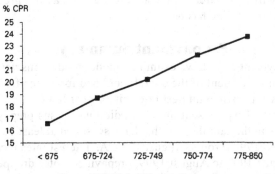

Source: DB Global Markets Research

Borrower Age

As borrowers age they are more likely to prepay. Since the typical RV owner is 55 years old, and people usually undergo life style changes at about this period of their lives (they begin the transition from work to retirement), one can expect RV owners' needs to change. Therefore, it is no surprise that obligor age has statistical power in explaining prepayments. Furthermore, as RV owners continue to age they may be forced to abandon using an RV due to illness or death. We find that a 75-year-old is 1.4 times as likely to prepay as an 45-year-old. Put another way, fully seasoned pools backed by 75-year-old borrowers would prepay at 22% CPR versus 17% CPR for pools backed by 45-year-old borrowers.

FICO Score

FICO scores are a proxy for borrower credit quality and we find that borrowers with higher FICO scores (i.e. better credit) prepay at higher rates than borrowers with lower FICO scores, other factors equal. A seasoned loan pool collateralized by loans with FICO scores lower than 675 is estimated to prepay at 17% CPR, while loans with FICO scores in the 750 – 775 range prepay at about 22% CPR. (See Exhibit 20.)

The differences in prepayment rates may be due to various factors. One possibility is that borrowers with good credit may be more likely to make a cash payoff. Another possibility is that these borrowers are more likely to "trade-up" than other borrowers. Finally, these borrowers will have more access to credit, and therefore may be able to refinance the loan with a home equity loan or line of credit.

Seasonality

Like many other durable goods, RV prepayments exhibit seasonal fluctuations. Prepayments are slowest in winter and fastest in spring, all else being equal.We believe prepayment seasonality is due to increased turnover as RV owners prepare for summer vacations. Controlling for other factors, we found that RV prepayments will experience an increase of almost 3% CPR from winter to spring, then decrease by about 1% in the summer and fall months. In fact, seasonal variations of prepayments will be greater than 3% CPR, but we can not precisely measure the variation until more time has passed.

Prepayment Summary

To test our prepayment model, we examined model predictions versus actual prepayments for a large segment of the overall pool and for a specific RV transaction that was fully seasoned when interest rates hit 30-year lows.

In Exhibit 21 we present model predictions versus prepayments experienced by all loans in the sample pool that have seasoned at least 15 months over a period from March 1998 through August 1999. As interest rates increased by over 100 bp from August 1998 to August 1999, prepayment rates dropped from 29.5% CPR to 20.5% CPR.

Turning to the individual transaction level, from April through July of 1998 BBRV 1997-1 experienced prepayment rates between 28% and 30.5% CPR. (See Exhibit 22.) Here we check those prepayments against our model. At that time the pool was 23 months seasoned so we adjust the base prepayment rate of 20.2% CPR down by 0.9% CPR. Then we adjust prepayment rates up by 8.1% CPR to reflect the fact that Freddie Mac rates were approximately 116 bp lower than at the time of loan issuance. Because the borrower age of BBRV 97-1 is 57 years old versus 65 years old for our hypothetical pool we adjust prepayments down by 1.5% CPR. Then, we increase our projected prepayment rate by 3.0% CPR to account for seasonality. Since other parameters such as loans terms, new/used mix, loan sizes, and FICO scores are not significantly different from the hypothetical pool we do not make any adjustments for them. We are left with a prepayment estimate of 28.9% CPR, which is close to the total prepayment rate of 29.5% CPR[7] (default rates are estimated at the end of the next section).

Exhibit 21: Prepayment Model Predictions

Source: DB Global Markets Research

---

[7] Prepayment rates on Bloomberg reflect involuntary as well as voluntary prepayments.

Exhibit 22: Decomposition of BBRV 97-1 Voluntary Prepayments (April 1998)

	Hypothetical Pool	BBRV 97-1	Prepayment Adjustment
Base Rate (Turnover)	Fully Seasoned	—	20.2
Months Seasoned	30 months	23 months**	−0.9
Interest Rates	Unchanged	−116	+8.1
Original Loan Term	180 months	155 months	+0.0
New/Used*	50/50	45/55	+0.0
Loan Size	$35,000	$38,000	+0.0
Borrower Age	65 years	57 years	−1.5
FICO	730	737	+0.0
Seasonality	Winter	Spring	+3.0
			28.9

* The same mix of direct/indirect is used for both pools
** Since the loans were seasoned 15 months on average when the deal settled
Source: DB Global Markets Research

In conclusion, this is a fairly robust model of RV prepayments. Furthermore, since the RV owner universe appears to be fairly homogeneous, we think that this model can be applied to the broader set of RV loans and transactions from other originators.

One important caveat is that falling rates and a growing economy characterized the sample period. This has made it difficult to fully isolate the impact of certain variables on RV prepayments, such as changes in interest rates and measures of borrower credit quality. We also cannot extrapolate with any level of confidence at this time how prepayments will behave if interest rates rise for a sustained period or the economy slows.

While more data for a longer period of time will allow us to fine tune our analysis, we conclude that voluntary prepayments for RV loans are driven more by lifestyle related turnover effects than by interest rate changes. This bodes well for ABS investors sensitive to convexity and drawn to products with inherent stability.

DEFAULTS AND LOSSES

The sample loan pool is experiencing low defaults and losses. Out of over 42,000 loans in the pool there have been 251 defaults over a 5-year period. Arranging the pool by age, defaults have steadily increased to 1.2% on a constant default rate (CDR) basis over 4½ years. (See Exhibit 23.) Similarly, two static pools comprised of loans originated during Q2 1997 and Q1 1998 experienced cumulative net losses of 35 bp over 28 months and 21 bp over 19 months, respectively. (See Exhibit 24.) Recoveries on the whole pool average 55% of the defaulted balance. The time to recovery has been short, with about one-third of all defaults recovered within one month.

Exhibit 23: Pool CDR Rates (Age in Months)

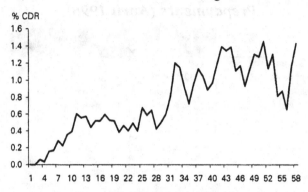

Source: DB Global Markets Research

Exhibit 24: Cumulative Net Losses for Two Static Pools* (Age in Months)

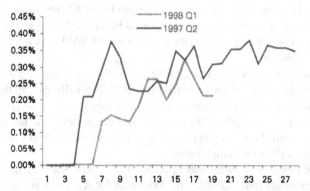

*The cumulative net loss curve for RV loans can decrease during certain months for three reasons. First, recoveries often occur one or more months after defaults; second, recoveries often return a large portion of the defaulted balance; and third, defaults are rare, meaning that there will be no defaults and only recoveries in certain months.

Source: DB Global Markets Research

Generally, the loan pool has good credit. The median FICO score is 730 and over seventy percent of the obligors have FICO scores above 700. The average borrower is 55 years old, has been in the same job for 13 years and has lived at the same address for 11 years. Over 90% of the borrowers in the pool are married. Insofar as DFS borrowers are typical RV owners, the above statistics bode well for all RV loan pools.

The lack of dramatic variation among borrower credit makes it difficult to determine which characteristics are most important for determining defaults. However, we do identify the following basic factors related to defaults:

- The likelihood of default increases as loans season.
- Borrowers with higher FICO scores are less likely to default.
- Holders of large loans are more likely to default than holders of small loans.
- Borrowers between the ages of 50 and 65 are the best credits.
- Owners of new RVs are less likely to default than owners of used RVs.
- Loans directly originated by DFS are less likely to default than dealer originated loans.
- Borrowers that are charged higher loan rates (after adjusting for credit differences) are more likely to default.
- Loans with longer terms are less likely to default.
- Typically, recovery of a charged-off balance occurs within three months and averages 55% of the defaulted balance.

The rest of this section examines the relationship between defaults and loan seasoning, FICO score, borrower age, and coupon spread and the time between loan default and loss recovery. All of the aforementioned loan and borrower characteristics are correlated with defaults at a high level of statistical significance.

In the sections that follow we compare default experience for different loan and pool characteristics to a standard pool unless explicitly stated otherwise. This standard pool is collateralized by loans that are seasoned for 20 months, have 180-month original terms, have $35,000 original balances, were dealer originated and are backed by used RVs. The loan obligors are 65-years old and have a 700 FICO score. Each loan has a coupon spread of 0 bp after credit adjustment (discussed later).

Seasoning

The likelihood of default increases with the passage of time. Assuming that a lender's underwriting process is reasonably capable of weeding out borrowers with impending credit problems, it will take time for a borrower's personal situation to deteriorate to the point where default is the only option. Furthermore, people typically do not buy RVs if they are not healthy enough to use them. Therefore, one would expect that a newly originated loan is less likely to default than a seasoned loan. The empirical evidence bears out this line of reasoning.

Over a 1-year period, defaults for our standard pool climb from near 0% to about a 1% CDR peak at about 22 months. The default rate subsequently declines and stabilizes near 0.6% CDR (see Exhibit 25).

FICO Score

Even though the range of FICO scores within the pool is fairly narrow, these scores still have great explanatory power. We examined a static pool comprised of 1997 production RV loans. Cumulative net losses after 30 months for loans held by borrowers with FICO scores in the lowest quartile were 62 bp versus 9 bp for loans held by borrowers with FICO scores in the highest quartile. (See Exhibit 26.)

Exhibit 25: Seasoning Effect on Defaults (Age in Months)

Source: DB Global Markets Research

Exhibit 26: Cumulative Net Losses for 1st and 3rd FICO Score Buckets (Age in Months)

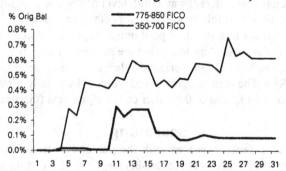

Source: DB Global Markets Research

Loans with low FICO scores account for more than their proportional share of defaults. For example, more than 70% of all loans in the pool have a FICO score greater than 700. By contrast, only 24% of the defaulted loans have FICO scores greater than 700. We estimate that loans seasoned for 20 months with FICO scores below 675 will peak at 1.4% CDR. (See Exhibit 27.) By contrast, comparable loans with FICO scores greater than 800 have a peak CDR of 0.2%, almost no chance of defaulting. Put another way, low FICO score loans are over 7 times more likely to default.

One of the features of the model is that the seasoning effect weakens as credit quality increases. For borrowers with FICO scores below 675, defaults peak near 2% CDR, and stabilize at about 1.5% CDR. For high credit quality borrowers with FICO scores over 800 the default rate peaks at about 0.20% CDR. (See Exhibit 28.)

Exhibit 27: Estimated Default Rate by FICO Bucket (20 Months Seasoning)

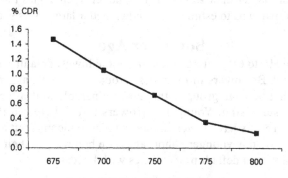

Source: DB Global Markets Research

Exhibit 28: Seasoning Effect for Different FICO Buckets

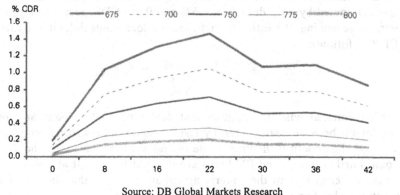

Source: DB Global Markets Research

Loan Size

After adjusting for credit considerations we find that borrowers holding larger loans are more likely to default. Loans in the $50,000-$100,000 range are the worst performers and are over three times as likely to default as the smallest loans in the pool. Performance improves for the very largest loans (greater than $100,000). The effect is that a pool of $75,000 loans will experience a peak CDR of 2.2% whereas a pool of $15,000 loans will peak at 0.6% CDR. The results are displayed in Exhibit 29.

This unexpected result demonstrates the power of the model to identify hidden trends. Generally, larger loans are associated with better credit characteristics and such loans undergo greater scrutiny at origination, which should result in superior default performance. For this reason we initially expected that loan size alone would have positive implications for default rates. In our pool, however, there are almost exactly the same number of large loans among the defaulted loans (in the pool 24.6% of the loans are larger than $50,000 whereas 24.8% of the defaulted loans are larger than $50,000). The model disentangles the effects of all loan attributes allowing us to estimate how much better large loans should perform.

Borrower Age

Borrowers in the 50- to 65-year age group have the lowest default rates, as shown in the chart below. Borrowers in the oldest group, 65+ years, are most likely to default. Given that this age group is the most vulnerable to death or serious illness, this is not surprising. Younger borrowers fall in between the other two groups. These borrowers have lower and more volatile income, but are not as vulnerable to illness. As this younger cohort ages, we believe that their incomes will become more stable and default probabilities will decrease.

New versus Used/Direct versus Indirect

Borrowers who own new RVs or have refinanced with DFS are less likely to default than owners of used RVs with dealer-originated loans. Loans for new RVs and those originated by DFS default at 0.6% and 0.7% CDR, respectively, after 20 months of seasoning. We estimate that used RV loan pools default at a rate of 1.0% CDR as follows:

DFS Originated Loans		Dealer Originated Loans	
New	Used	New	Used
N/A	0.7%	0.6%	1.0%

Conventional wisdom suggests that dealer originated loans are more likely to default because dealers employ less stringent underwriting procedures since they get the benefit of making a sale but do not bear the cost of holding a risky loan. Furthermore, used RV loans are thought to default at higher rates because the lower quality of the underlying collateral means that the owner has less incentive to hold on to his RV.

Exhibit 29: Effect of Loan Size on Defaults

Source: DB Global Markets Research

Exhibit 30: Effect of Loan Term on Defaults

Source: DB Global Markets Research

While conventional wisdom does seem to be borne out, there is a twist. It is not clear how many of the loans originated by DFS are collateralized by essentially new RVs. Since these loans are almost all refinancings it is possible that many of them are backed by RVs that were recently purchased. Therefore, the salient characteristic may simply be whether the RV was new or used when it was purchased and not who originates the loan.

Coupon Spread

Borrowers who pay higher rates on their RV loans (after adjusting for differences between available loan and borrower characteristics) are more likely to default. Because originators have a clearer picture of each borrower's credit profile they are able to make fine distinctions between borrowers whose credit profiles are otherwise identical and set loan rates accordingly. For example, borrowers with less stable jobs or a poor credit history will probably pay relatively higher loan rates. We attempt to capture distinctions that originators make between borrowers by adjusting individual loan rates according to demographic and loan characteristics.

A potential problem with this methodology is that some of the differences between loan rates are unrelated to relative credit strength. For example, a loan rate may be influenced by competition between lenders. Because of competition, two people with the exact same credit profiles may get different loan rates in different locations. Nevertheless, the residual spread serves as a powerful predictor of defaults.

Loan Term

Loans with longer terms tend to have fewer defaults (after controlling for other characteristics). A short-term loan (loan term less than 15 years) is 1.5 times more likely to default than a 15-year loan and almost 3 times as likely to default as a 20-year loan. On a CDR basis, a pool of short-term loans default at 1.0% CDR compared to pools of 15-year and 20-year loans that default at 0.6% and 0.3% CDR, respectively (see Exhibit 30). This is consistent with the theory that DFS only allows RV owners with the best credit (or collateral) to take out long term loans.

Recoveries

The percentage of defaulted balance recovered has been consistent across different RV loans. On average the recovery amount (net of expenses) has been approximately 55% of defaulted balance regardless of the borrower's FICO score, month of the year when the default occurs, loan age, time of the year when the default occurred or the loan size. Recovery levels drop only for loans with long times to recovery (over 10 months) or very low FICO scores.

Time to Recovery

We observed that just over one-third of the loans that default are recovered within one month. There are four possible reasons for this. First, because recreational vehicles are inherently mobile they can be transported to the best location for a quick sale. Second, there is a robust market for used RVs. Approximately 50% of RV sales nationwide are of used RVs. Third, it is common for RV borrowers who default to voluntarily release their vehicle to the lender for liquidation. Fourth, servicers can and do initiate repossession proceedings before an RV is charged off.

Unlike defaulted mortgages, which must typically go through a protracted foreclosure process before losses are recovered, RV defaults are often resolved within a few months after the initial delinquency. This is because RVs are considered personal rather than real property, and are subject to an accelerated repossession and recovery process.

Default is traditionally defined as 120 days past due. Notwithstanding this, the repossession process is usually initiated when the loan is 45 to 75 days past due. Furthermore for the purpose of this study we start counting the number of months between recovery and charge-off on the date that DFS actually charges off the loan, even when a RV has already been repossessed. This charge-off occurs at 120 days past due for securitized loans. It can occur sooner if the RV has been repossessed and sold.

Default Summary

Most characteristics associated with fewer defaults are also associated with lower loan rates and vice versa. For example, loans with higher FICO scores are less likely to default and have lower margins. This means that higher risk loans contribute more to excess spread and therefore credit enhancement at a deal level.

Furthermore, most of the results of this section were not surprising, with one exception. Because larger loans undergo greater scrutiny at origination and require higher standards (manifested in higher FICO scores, incomes, etc.) they should have lower default rates than smaller loans. We found the opposite to be true. Our finding does not mean that large loans are worse performers than small loans. It simply means that large loans perform worse than expected after consideration of all other credit characteristics.

Again we turn to the experience of BBRV 1997-1 during April 1998, this time to check the results of our default model. (See Exhibit 31.) At that time the pool was seasoned 23 months so we start with a default rate of 1.0% CDR. Then we adjust the default rate down by 0.3% CDR since the average FICO score for BBRV 97-1 is 737, not 700. Again we adjust the default rate down, now by 0.2% CDR, to reflect the new/used and direct/indirect loan mix of BBRV 97-1. Finally, we increase our default projection by 0.5% CDR because the weighted average original loan term is 155 months, a difference large enough to affect defaults. We make no adjustments for the other parameters since they are not significantly different from our standard pool. We are left with a default estimate of 1.0% CDR, giving us an estimate of 29.9% for total prepayments which compares well to the actual prepayment rate of 29.5% CPR.

The lack of recovery variability is striking and attests to the high quality of the collateral behind each loan. All loans but those held by RV owners with the lowest FICO scores have recovery rates in excess of 50%. Even loans that took over a year to recover the defaulted balance had low loss rates.

Finally, the absolute number of defaults is quite low. This may have played a role in recovery rates and length of time to recovery. For example, at least 4900 used RVs entered the loan pool during 1998 compared to 208 defaults during the same period. It seems unlikely that these loans presented an onerous resale burden.

Exhibit 31: Decomposition of BBRV 97-1 Defaults (April 1998)

	Hypothetical Pool	BBRV 97-1	Default Adjustment
Months Seasoned	20 months	23 months**	+1.0
FICO	730	737	−0.3
Loan Size	$35,000	$38,000	+0.0
Borrower Age	65 years	57 years	+0.0
New/Used	0/100	45/55*	−0.2
Coupon Spread	0	0	+0.0
Original Loan Term	180 months	155 months	+0.5
Defaults			+1.0
Voluntary Prepayments			+28.9
Total Prepayments			29.9

* The direct/indirect mix is 35/65
** Since the loans were seasoned 15 months on average when the deal settled
Source: DB Global Markets Research

Chapter 6

Equipment-Financed ABS

James S. Anderson
Managing Director
Asset-Backed Research
First Union Securities, Inc.

Scott H. Shannon
Managing Director
Asset-Securitization Division
First Union Securities, Inc.

Kristina L. Clark
Associate
Fixed-Income Research
First Union Securities, Inc.

INTRODUCTION

The securitization of equipment leases began in 1985, when Sperry Lease Finance Corp. issued two deals backed by leases on computer equipment. This makes lease-backed paper among the first non-mortgage assets to be securitized. Subsequent to the Sperry transactions, volume from equipment issuers was sporadic, with most of the notable transactions through 1992 being computer-related. The past several years have witnessed significant growth in the types of leased assets being securitized. Large- and small-ticket construction, medical, office, transportation, and essential-use industrial equipment are collateral types underlying asset-backed security transactions.

The asset class had a watershed year in 1996 as GPA securitized in excess of $4 billion of aircraft and AT&T Capital entered the ABS market with a $3 billion transaction. Liquidity and investor acceptance of the asset class dramatically improved, as numerous institutions became educated on the characteristics of equipment ABS. Nominal spreads, which provided a significant 10-15 basis point pickup over alternative asset classes such as automobile and credit card ABS, narrowed on a relative basis and trended down over the year to a point where the equipment ABS traded in line with automobile ABS.

139

Exhibit 1: Business Trends in Equipment Lending

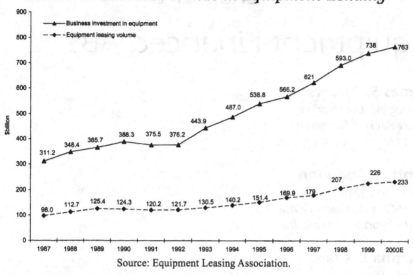

Source: Equipment Leasing Association.

This trend continued in 1997 as several well-known issuers accessed the equipment-backed ABS market for the first time and investors, concerned with a general decline in consumer credit quality, looked to diversify. Because the collateral underlying equipment ABS generally represents commercial obligors, investors further embraced the asset class. The diversification of issuers as well as investors has continued through the end of 1999.

This chapter explores the collateral underlying equipment ABS and the investment characteristics of the securities. It discusses the various types of originators and their motivation for issuance, as well as how investors should analyze particular structures. Finally, it discusses equipment ABS as a component of the broader ABS market.

THE EQUIPMENT LEASING INDUSTRY

Business investment in equipment has grown dramatically, with an estimated $763 billion coming into service in 2000.[1] Of this, approximately 31% was leased. An estimated 80% of corporations lease some or all of their equipment, either for cash flow reasons or in recognition that the productivity of equipment comes from use, not ownership. This represents a huge pool of potential collateral for securitization.

Exhibit 1 displays the trends in new business investment in equipment and equipment leasing. Note the explosive growth coming out of the 1991-1992 economic slowdown.

---

[1] Data in this section may be found on http://elaonline.com.

Exhibit 2: 1998 Equipment Leasing Volume by Type

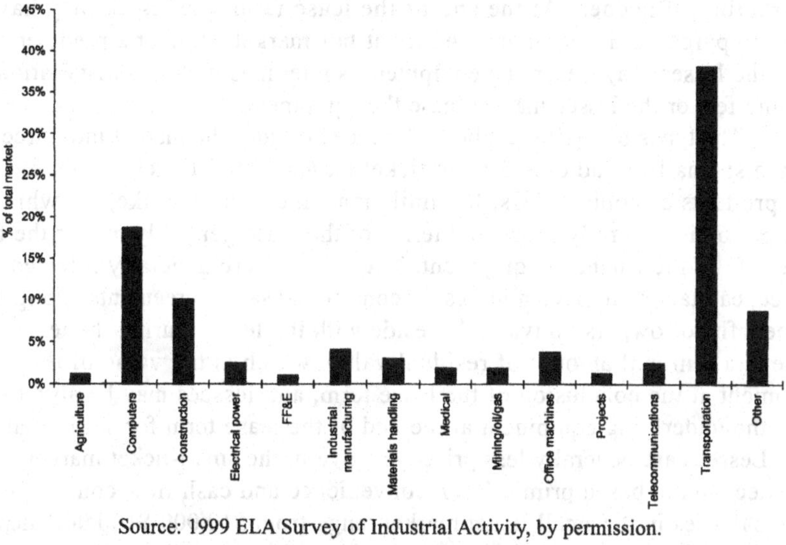

Source: 1999 ELA Survey of Industrial Activity, by permission.

Exhibit 2 breaks down the types of equipment by use. Various modes of transportation and computers are the two largest types of leased equipment. Within the computer group, the share of personal computers (PCs) and networks has been increasing vis-à-vis mainframes during the 1990s as lessees seek protection from technological obsolescence.

Lease originators fall into three basic categories: banks, financial service companies (e.g., GECC, Heller Financial, and CIT), and captive subsidiaries of equipment manufacturers (e.g., Case Credit Corporation). Each originator may have different reasons to securitize its lease streams, which are discussed below.

Leasing companies compete based on price, flexibility in structuring leases to customer requirements, relationship with equipment vendors (whom they represent to the market), product knowledge, and service. Individual companies tend to specialize, whether by industry focus or equipment, lease or lessee type. The industry is fragmented, with over 2,000 leasing companies. Fragmented industries often benefit from access to ABS markets.

LEASING BASICS

A lease is essentially an agreement between an equipment owner (the lessor) and the equipment user (the lessee).[2] The lessee remits to the lessor a periodic payment in return for use of the equipment. The lessor continues to own the equip-

---

[2] For further discussion, see Terry A Isom, *et al*, *The Handbook of Equipment Leasing* (Salt Lake City, UT: Amembal & Isom, 1988) or Peter K. Nevitt and Frank J. Fabozzi, *Equipment Leasing: Fourth Edition* (New Hope, PA: Frank J. Fabozzi Associates, 2000).

ment and may provide additional services such as routine maintenance or remarketing, if needed. At the end of the lease term, the lessee may have an option to purchase the equipment either at fair market value or a predetermined price; the lessee may return the equipment, sometimes with a deinstallation and shipping fee; or the lessee may re-lease the equipment.

The types of equipment being financed divides the market into three core segments: small-, middle- and large-ticket leases. Small-ticket lessors focus on such products as copiers, PCs, facsimile machines, and the like, for which the lease period is generally short, and terms of the lease generally mirror the functional life of the financed equipment. These leases are generally referred to as finance, capital or full payout leases, or conditional sales agreements. Obligations and benefits of ownership typically reside with the lessee during the lease term. There is a minimal amount of residual value, which is the value of the leased equipment at the conclusion of the lease term, and lessees may be able to purchase the underlying equipment at the end of the lease term for a minimal payment. Lessees are generally less price-sensitive in the small-ticket market, as the lease decision is based primarily on convenience and cash flow considerations. Lease balances in the small-ticket market range from $10,000-$100,000, depending on individual companies' interpretations.

The Large-Ticket Market

The large-ticket market is for capital equipment with an initial cost basis of at least $2 million. The underlying leases are generally operating leases, in which the lessee's payments do not cover the original equipment cost over the term of the lease. Thus, there is significant residual value in the underlying equipment, which is managed by the lessor. Additionally, obligations and benefits of ownership, including depreciation, stay with the lessor during the lease term. Operating leases are often thought of as usage leases, as opposed to finance leases, which are sometimes called ownership leases. An example of an operating lease would be one written on medical equipment such as magnetic resonance imaging (MRI) or CAT scan machines.

Economic Risks and Rewards

The primary distinction between finance and operating leases is which party, the lessee or the lessor, bears the economic risks and rewards of owning the underlying equipment. To be classified as a finance lease for financial reporting purposes, one of the following statements must be true:

- The lease transfers title and ownership of the leased equipment to the lessee at the end of the lease term.
- The lease contains a bargain price option (e.g., "$1 buyout").
- The lease term at inception is at least 75% of the estimated life of the equipment leased.
- The present value of the minimum lease payments is at least 90% of the fair market value of the equipment at lease inception.

Exhibit 3: Equipment Finance New Issue Volume

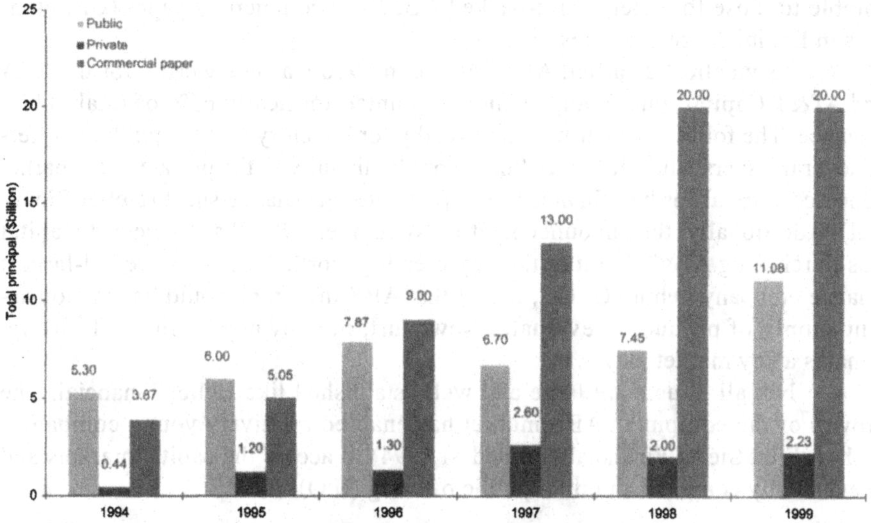

Note: Private and commercial paper numbers for 1998 and 1999 are estimates.
Source: First Union Securities, Securities Data Corp., and *Asset-Backed Alert*.

The Leveraged Lease

Another type of operating lease is the leveraged lease, in which the lessor borrows a significant portion of the equipment cost on a non-recourse basis and assigns the future lease payment stream to the lender. The lessor puts up a minimal amount of funds (the difference between the equipment cost and the present value of the lease stream), but the lessee is generally entitled to the full tax benefits of owning the equipment. Aircraft and railroad cars are usually leveraged leases.

The Middle Market

The middle market covers the ground between the aforementioned two groups. Lessors in this segment tailor lease terms to the needs of their customers, who may have specific tax considerations or cash flow needs that are addressed by the structure and terms of the lease. The equipment cost per item is higher than for small-ticket. Computer networking equipment, application licenses (billing and payroll systems), and printing presses are examples of middle market leased equipment or systems.

GROWTH OF THE ABS EQUIPMENT MARKET

Exhibit 3 chronicles the growth of the equipment ABS market. We have included ABS issued by captive finance companies such as Case Credit Corporation and Navistar Financial because we believe that although they are loans on agricultural and transportation equipment, the obligor profile and investor analysis are comparable to those for solely lease-backed ABS. The commercial paper (CP) numbers in Exhibit 3 are estimates.

As mentioned earlier, ABS volume in 1996 was noteworthy for the GPA and AT&T Capital transactions, which accounted for nearly 65% of total public issuance. The following year was noteworthy for the entry into the public markets of several issuers who had either funded predominantly in the private ABS market (Copelco Capital) or had financed their portfolio on-balance sheet (Heller Financial). Additionally, the announcement in November 1997 that Newcourt Capital was purchasing AT&T Capital, thereby creating North America's second-largest finance company behind GECC, meant that ABS investors would have a consistent supply of product to evaluate. Newcourt, now owned by the CIT Group, remains a key market player.

Not all issuers are large and well established like Heller Financial. The growth of the equipment ABS market has enabled relatively young companies such as First Sierra Financial (formed in 1994) to access the capital markets and to eventually complete an initial public offering (IPO).

Reasons for Issuing ABS

Equipment finance companies use securitization as a funding tool for three basic reasons:

- Cheaper cost of funds than traditional sources such as bank loans.
- Securitization structured to remove the assets from the balance sheet, thereby accelerating income and improving traditional capital efficiency ratios such as return on assets and return on equity.
- Increased liquidity by accessing an alternative funding source.

Depending on a company's access to varying funding sources, any or all of the above may be reasons to issue term ABS securities.

For a smaller company, securitization generally provides a cheaper cost of funds because the focus is on the asset quality of the underlying pool and not the investment ratings of the originator/seller-servicer. For established, investment-grade issuers such as Heller Financial, the maturation of the equipment ABS market with its more competitive spreads makes it a compelling alternative source of funding.

Balance Sheet Aspects

The off-balance-sheet aspect of securitization, along with the ability to manage the asset side of the balance sheet so as to recognize income from securitization, applies to large established companies as well as startups looking to achieve a history of profitability in preparation for an IPO. While gain-on-sale has been criticized, it remains a viable method for accounting, provided accurate discount rates are used and prepayment modelling is conservative.

Liquidity

The ability to increase corporate liquidity by accessing the equipment ABS market has been a significant contributor to the growth of the market. Although large originators may have multiple sources of funding — including corporate MTNs, CP, and bank lines — some at more attractive all-in levels than ABS, the rating agencies, in evaluating a corporation's liquidity, will likely look favorably on originators that have opened alternative funding sources by accessing the ABS market. When combined with the off-balance-sheet treatment noted above, and the conservative measurement of gain-on-sale, the equipment ABS market becomes a compelling financing tool for larger companies as well.

Securitization Alternatives for Issuers

Equipment finance companies have three basic securitization alternatives:

- Issuance of term securities in the public ABS market.
- Issuance of term securities in the private ABS market
- Issuance of CP through either a bank-sponsored multi-seller CP conduit or a single-seller conduit.

Public Market

The public market is the largest and most liquid and typically offers the best pricing execution. The global investor base includes insurance companies, money managers, domestic and foreign banks, and pension funds. Upfront issuance costs can be somewhat higher owing to Securities and Exchange Commission filing costs and increased legal fees resulting from the greater disclosure requirements needed for a public offering. Issue size is generally at least $200 million, as investors will not pay up for issues perceived as too small for a liquid secondary market.

Private Placement

The private market, while less liquid than the public market, is nonetheless attractive for many issuers because the investor base is still large and disclosure requirements are somewhat less. Transactions can range from small, negotiated transactions with a single investor (often the strategy with newly formed companies) to large underwritings in the 144A market that price and trade much like public ABS.

Commercial Paper

The CP market can be accessed for either permanent financing through interest rate swaps to lock in a fixed rate or for warehouse financing prior to arranging permanent financing via a public or private ABS. Because all commercial paper needs to be fully supported by bank liquidity lines, this type of financing is essentially bank financing in another form. From an all-in cost perspective, CP can be extremely competitive. Although price competitive and flexible, CP execution does not broaden a company's investor base because the conduits are bank sponsored and the underlying collateral is transparent to the CP buyer.

Active on All Fronts

Equipment is unique in that significant activity occurs in all three of these markets. Companies often use the asset-backed CP market to warehouse their originations prior to coming to market with a public term ABS. A recent trend is to access both the public and private markets simultaneously by issuing senior securities in the public market and subordinate securities in the private market.

STRUCTURE OF EQUIPMENT-BACKED ABS

Lease- and equipment-backed ABS differ somewhat from generic consumer loans in that the former do not have a specified loan balance and contract interest rate. Thus, they do not have a weighted-average coupon (WAC) and the concept of loan-to-value (LTV) does not apply. Instead, the lease contract between a lessor and lessee calls for a specified stream of payments over the life of the lease. Presumably, these payments adequately compensate the lessor, and it is this stream of payments that underlies the ABS.

Valuation

Valuation in equipment ABS is done by taking this stream of payments and discounting them at a rate equal to the weighted-average coupon of the securities plus ongoing expenses, which typically are servicing and trustee fees, as well as credit-enhancement fees, for which the transaction is "wrapped" (or insured by a third-party surety). Therefore, only after an issue's nominal spread is set can an exact principal amount of bonds be determined. This is why par amounts on a preliminary prospectus ("red herring") are approximate.

Allocation of Payments

Payments are allocated between principal and interest so that the remaining notional balance of the leases equals the net present value of the remaining stream of lease payments. To the extent that all leases in a pool are level pay throughout the term of the loan, the amortization of equipment ABS is similar to that of a pool of fixed-rate loans. Any particular securitization may contain cash flow variability owing to the presence of pre-funding or revolving accounts, irregular (i.e., non-monthly) lease payments or other variable cash flow features. The rating agencies evaluating the transaction structure perform analyses to ensure cash flow sufficiently supports monthly payments to bondholders. Because lease prepayments are infrequent (discussed in detail later), the cash flow characteristics of equipment ABS tend to be fairly stable and most closely resemble a generic amortizing security.

FRAMEWORK FOR EVALUATING EQUIPMENT ABS

For an investor in any type of asset- or mortgage-backed security, the first "law" should be to understand thoroughly the underlying collateral.[3] Whether evaluating the prepayment characteristics of agency MBS or assessing credit risk on a pool of subprime automobile loans, an understanding of the factors influencing the cash flows of the underlying collateral is paramount.

Primary Credit Risks

As in all classes of ABS, obligor (the lessee) delinquencies and defaults are the primary credit risks of equipment-backed deals. These can result in the disruption of anticipated cash flows. Structuring tools such as excess spread, subordination, third-party surety guarantees, and trigger events are used to hedge against such disruptions. An originator's ability to demonstrate consistent realization of residual values is an additional source of credit enhancement for equipment ABS.

Market Insights

An understanding of the market niche the originator serves gives insight into the credit quality of the lessees and their susceptibility to cyclical economic conditions. Qualitative areas of focus for the rating agencies are management's experience, competitive strategies, financial resources, market segments served, and the types of leases/loans originated.

Analysis and Evaluation

To the extent that a pool of leases is originated via a vendor program in which the lease originator acts as a financing source for the manufacturer, an analysis is conducted by the rating agencies to evaluate the vendor's ability to service and maintain the equipment. This service ensures the lessee remains willing to continue making payments on the lease. Many third-party originators have remarketing agreements with their vendors so that after termination of the lease, or repossession of the equipment in the event of lessee default, the anticipated residual value may be realized or the net loss (also known as loss-to-liquidation) will be minimized.

Concentration Risk

Concentration risk is also addressed during the structuring process. To the extent a particular pool has exposure to an industry or obligor, various structural requirements may be put into the transaction. For example, we have seen an originator agree to forego its servicing fee in the event any one of the three largest obligors in the pool defaults prior to credit enhancement reaching certain levels. This is generally more of an issue in the middle- and large-ticket market because most small-ticket securitizations have a large number of obligors and sufficient diversification. When analyzing pool composition and concentrations, it is helpful to

---

[3] The basics for this analysis come from *Standard & Poor's Equipment Leasing Criteria* (New York, NY, May 1996).

ascertain if the leased equipment is integral to the lessee's business. Lease payments are more likely to remain current for essential use equipment.

Rating agencies will evaluate a lessor's historical portfolio chargeoffs, preferably on a static pool basis. This shows likely performance over the life of the pool and may provide insight into crucial elements affecting portfolio performance, such as changes in underwriting guidelines and collections procedures. Static pool data are preferable to dynamic, or gross, portfolio data because growth can mask and dampen the true effects of defaults and losses. Static pool data may or may not be available in a prospectus supplement. If it is not available, investors should ascertain the expected default and net loss curve used in structuring the transaction. A related question investors should ask is what charge-off policy applies to the pool. The timing of the recognition of defaults and subsequent recoveries affects cash flow to the pool. Recoveries in lease-backed transactions can be significant owing to the secured nature of the obligations. The nature of the equipment being financed is a factor in determining the amount and timing of recovery recognition. For example, a copier is easier to repossess and re-lease or sell than is a medical diagnostic center.

Residual Analysis

As mentioned earlier, residual values are unique to equipment transactions. When the lease is originated, the lessor books a residual value for the equipment. The amount is the lessor's estimate of the equipment's future value at the end of the lease. For finance leases with a nominal buy-out at the end of the lease, residual values are low. For operating leases, the amount can be significant.

If recognized residual cash flow is to be used as a credit enhancement to cover periodic losses or, more important, if some portion of the residual value is being financed through the issuance of ABS, it is essential that anticipated residual realizations meet or exceed the credit given them by the rating agencies. Generally, residual realization exceeds the booked value. In fact, leasing companies are generally very conservative in booking their residuals and have historically realized 1.1 to 1.5 times book value.

Rating agencies conservatively evaluate what credit should be given to residuals. Typically, no more than 50% of book value is given credit in an ABS structure. The agencies require seven to 10 years of historical residual realization data to evaluate how an originator has performed over an extended economic cycle. Obviously, to the extent historical residual realizations exceed the credit given by the rating agencies, investor credit support is enhanced. The more experience a lessor has with the particular industry, as well as any remarketing support from vendor affiliations, the greater the likelihood of adequate residual realization. The type of equipment being financed also has an impact on residual analysis. Shifts in demand for particular types of equipment, as well as the risk of technological obsolescence, may have an impact on residual realizations, so any concentrations in equipment types or industries serviced are part of a residual analysis.

Residuals by definition are back-end loaded, that is, they occur at the end of the lease. Typically, residuals flow through the deal structure in the month they are realized and are used to cover any shortfalls in cash. If no trigger events have occurred, which would require capturing excess cash or residual realizations, then the unused portion of the residual realized is released to the originator/issuer. Therefore, an analysis of the pool by lease expiration and amount of residual can provide insight into the timing of potential cash flow or credit support.

Prepayment Characteristics

Equipment ABS are much less negatively convex than other asset types in that little prepayment activity is rate-driven in this asset class. Also, structural considerations exist within most leases that mute prepayments.

Leases are generally written without a prepayment option and most contain a "hell or high water" provision whereby a lessee, if it chooses to make a prepayment, is obligated to make all contractual payments at the early termination of the lease. This provision is in effect to protect the lessor and by extension the investor. The lessee must unconditionally make all payments as specified in the lease contract. If the equipment fails, the lessee's claim is with the manufacturer, not the lessor. This is a powerful disincentive to prepay a lease.

There are still events in which lease prepayments occur and cash flow to the ABS is affected. The two primary sources of prepayments of equipment ABS are lessee defaults and equipment upgrades, under which the lessor allows a lessee to prepay one lease to upgrade to new equipment through a new lease. For example, if an owner-operator of a semitrailer upgrades to a larger and more powerful over-road system, it is not unusual for a lessor to allow an existing lease to be prepaid to facilitate the equipment swap. Our experience suggests that most lessees do not prepay early in the lease term (because they are still happy with their purchase) or late in the lease term (because the lease is almost paid off).

Pricing Speed

Issuers can substitute new lease collateral in the event the pool experiences prepayments. Copelco Capital is notable in that it has historically substituted new collateral in the event of a prepayment. From an investor's perspective, the substitution of new leases for prepaid leases ensures the pool's stability and the realization of the average life expected at the ABS pricing. Other issuers take the attitude that prepayments are a normal part of their business and are minimal in any event. An investor should seek historical prepayment information to verify whatever pricing speed is used.

Average Life

In that the final maturity of loans and leases in equipment pools are usually five to seven years, the average lives of ABS structured from these pools are generally two to three years. An investor should look at the declination tables in the prospectus supplement to evaluate the average life stability of any particular ABS under varying prepayment scenarios. It will become apparent that the average life sensitivity to a change in CPR assumption is minimal, generally measured in fractions of a year. In addition, with the average deal size for equipment ABS increasing, the market has seen a move toward multiple tranches of pools, which further mitigates duration drift.

RELATIVE VALUE

Exhibit 4 shows the nominal spreads of equipment ABS vis-à-vis other ABS classes from 7/98 to 2/00. Equipment spreads peaked in the third quarter of 1998 owing to the liquidity crisis that plagued the bond market. Spreads have since come in as of this writing under 80 bps. Along with this tightening has come a closer margin when compared to credit cards and automobile ABS.

As discussed throughout this chapter, many product attributes make equipment paper attractive for investors. Benign prepayment characteristics and a collateral base of commercial obligations make this asset class attractive for an investor seeking diversification from prepayment risk and consumer credit. That the collateral underlying equipment ABS is so stable makes it particularly attractive to investors looking to swap into LIBOR-based assets.

We believe that equipment ABS exhibit many of the characteristics of amortizing automobile ABS and should trade on top of, if not through, this competing asset class. Furthermore, we believe that this will be the case as the market evolves in size and number of issuers.

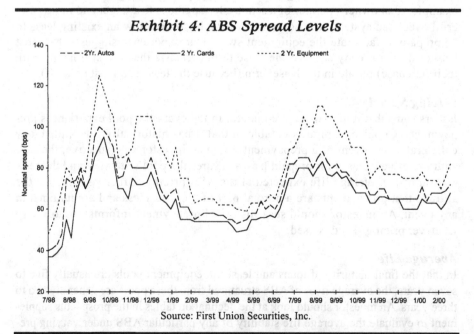

Exhibit 4: ABS Spread Levels

Source: First Union Securities, Inc.

Chapter 7

Aircraft Asset-Backed Securities

Joseph Philips
Morgan Stanley Dean Witter

Oliver Hsiang
Morgan Stanley Dean Witter

INTRODUCTION

Through the year 2010, an estimated $330 billion of external capital will be required to finance the growth in the aircraft industry. Consistent with their role in many capital-intensive sectors, the public capital markets are expected to provide much of this capital, having significantly disintermediated commercial banks since the mid-1990s. In this chapter we will discuss aircraft asset-backed securities These securities offer investors the opportunity to gain diversified exposure to this projected growth in the commercial aircraft industry without making a credit decision on a specific airline, region or aircraft type and, most critically, while limiting investors' exposure to the industry cycle.

The Aircraft ABS market was initially restricted to a single issuer, GPA Group PLC, but has matured to include highly rated participants such as ILFC and GE Capital. In 1998, Morgan Stanley underwrote two refinancings and one new issue totaling $4.3 billion. In 1999, we expect a total of $2.5-$3.5 billion of Aircraft ABS to come to market with at least that much in subsequent years (independent of refinancings). Since the first Aircraft ABS deal in 1992, this sector has evolved to include features such as a master trust structure, debt reduction from operating cash flow rather than asset liquidation, a combination of fixed and floating rate tranches and periodic refinancing of soft bullet tranches. Recent new issues indicate a slowdown in the rate of structural innovation and a degree of standardization is beginning to appear.

HISTORY OF AIRCRAFT ABS

Aircraft Lease Portfolio Securitization (ALPS) 1992-1 was the first Aircraft ABS transaction (see the timeline in Exhibit 1). This issue relied on aircraft sales to pay principal on the debt. The next transaction, ALPS 1994-1, differed fundamentally from the 92-1 transaction in that principal payments to bondholders were allowed to be deferred to avoid aircraft sales in a depressed environment (although sales were eventually required to retire the bonds).

Airplanes Pass Through Trust (AIRPT), issued in the first quarter of 1996, added two wrinkles: (1) outstanding debt was expected to be retired entirely from lease revenues and not sales, and (2) several of the senior tranches in the structure were structured as soft bullets, with refinancing of those tranches expected to occur on or before their respective bullet dates. Four classes of this particular transaction were refinanced in early 1998.

With the general structure of Aircraft ABS becoming more and more standardized, two more large transactions were completed in 1998 — Morgan Stanley Aircraft Finance (MSAF) and AerCo Limited. The MSAF transaction was unique in that it was not a liquidating trust, but allowed for the addition of aircraft. AerCo also has this feature. Similar to credit card master trusts, all transactions issued from the trust are backed by all leases in the master trust. However, the oldest issued classes in a trust have some form of cash flow priority over newer classes.

The evolution of Aircraft ABS from the original ALPS 1992-1 deal has left us with the following typical characteristics to be expected in a new deal:

- A master trust structure, i.e. aircraft additions are allowed.
- Debt reduction entirely from lease revenues, although sales are permitted.
- Credit tranching resulting in AA through BB rated classes.
- Floating rate AA seniors. The single-A and BBB tranches may also be floating rate.
- One or more of the AA seniors is a soft bullet, i.e. a refinancing tranche.
- Junior classes, which are typically long amortizers that pay simultaneously with the seniors and are rated from single-A through BB.

Exhibit 1: Aircraft ABS Issuance Timeline
(Includes Most Major Transactions)

Date	Deal	Size ($bil)	Comment
6/92	ALPS 1992-1	0.521	Structure forced aircraft sales to repay debt
8/94	ALPS 1994-1	0.998	Deferral of aircraft sales introduced
3/96	Airplanes Pass Through Trust	4.048	Soft bullets and debt repayment from lease revenues introduced
6/96	ALPS 1996-1	0.394	Refinancing of ALPS 1992-1
2/98	Morgan Stanley Aircraft Finance	1.050	Master trust structure introduced, i.e. aircraft additions allowed
3/98	Airplanes Pass Through Trust (Refinancing)	2.437	Refinancing of original Airplanes Pass Through Trust
6/98	AerCo Limited	0.800	Refinancing of ALPS 1994-1
4/99	Aircraft Finance Trust 1999-1	1.205	Similar to structures done in 1998

Source: Morgan Stanley

Exhibit 2: Comparison of Major Aircraft ABS Transactions as of New Issue

Feature	Airplanes Pass Through Trust	Morgan Stanley Aircraft Finance	AerCo Limited
Original Issue Date	March 1996	February 1998	June 1998
Original Size	$4,048 mm	$1,050 mm	$800 mm
Initial Aircraft Pool	229	33 + 1 spare engine	35
Initial Appraised Value	$4,527 mm	$1,115 mm	$952 mm
Depreciation Assumption*	4/3	4/2	4/2
Stage III compliance	93.4%	100.0%	100.0%
Number of Lessees	83	27	25
Number of Countries	40	19	18
Largest Country Exposures	USA 12.05% Mexico 9.82% Turkey 8.48%	UK 12.65% USA 10.95% Brazil 9.01%	UK 17.12% Spain 11.05% Turkey 10.88%
Largest Lessee Exposures	Garuda 5.86% Aeromexico 5.41% Canadian 5.22%	Air Pacific 6.43% Unijet 6.26% Varig 6.09%	Spanair 11.05% Airtours 6.60% Lan Chile 6.56%
Manufacturer Exposure	Boeing 42.2% McDon. Douglas 34.8% Airbus 10.7% Fokker 7.4% Bomb. De Hav. 4.2% Other 0.8%	Boeing 63.7% Airbus 25.4% McDon. Douglas 5.4% Fokker 4.9% GE (engine) 0.5%	Boeing 63.8% Airbus 17.6% McDon. Douglas 10.2% Fokker 8.4%
Master Trust	No (Liquidating Trust)	Yes	Yes
Public	Yes	Yes (144A initially)	No (Exchange offer in progress)
ERISA Eligible	Yes	Yes	Yes
Servicer	GECAS	ILFC	Babcock & Brown

* See Glossary

Source: Prospectus, Morgan Stanley

Exhibit 2 is a summary comparison of the major Aircraft ABS transactions as of new issue.

AIRCRAFT ABS AND EETCS

The choice of securitization vehicle — Aircraft ABS or Enhanced Equipment Trust Certificates (EETC) — is more a function of the issuer than anything else. Nevertheless, it is instructive to discuss the differences between EETCs and Aircraft ABS. EETCs are issued by individual airlines looking to finance their aircraft via the capital markets. In essence, there is only one lessee, the airline, and that lessee makes monthly payments out of general corporate revenues, which are passed through to bond investors.

Exhibit 3: Comparison of Aircraft ABS and EETCs

	Aircraft ABS	EETC
Security type	Asset-backed security	Corporate bond
Issuer	Leasing company/Servicer	Airline
Nature of default	Partial	All or none (binary)[3]
Forced sale on default	No	Yes
Bond type	Soft bullets and amortizers	Typically amortizers
Number of aircraft	30+	5-30
Number of lessees	25+	1
Geographic diversification	Global	US
Re-leasing risk	Yes (approximately every 5 years)	No
Default remedies	1948 Geneva Convention	Section 1110

Source: Morgan Stanley

An EETC is rated higher, on average, than the airline itself because of the security provided by the underlying aircraft (via Section 1110) over and above the general creditworthiness of the airline. For example, the combination of Section 1110 protection and subordination means that a BB rated airline could issue an EETC structure with tranches rated AAA through BBB. Since an EETC is a corporate bond, even the lowest rated tranche does *not* have a rating less than that of the issuing airline. In addition, like a corporate bond, an EETC defaults in a binary fashion (all or none).[1] In the event of default, investors have Section 1110 protection, which permits the sale of the aircraft to redeem bondholders.

In contrast to EETCs, Aircraft ABS have been issued exclusively by aircraft leasing companies/servicers.[2] This automatically implies that an Aircraft ABS transaction is likely to be backed by several lessees in geographically diverse areas. The size of the portfolio of aircraft is also usually bigger than with EETCs. Newer Aircraft ABS are typically issued as a mixture of soft bullets and amortizing notes, unlike EETCs, which generally amortize. In the event of lessee default, the aircraft is recovered and re-leased. If the lessee contests the repossession, the matter usually goes to a court in the jurisdiction chosen at the time the lease was written (under the guiding principles of the 1948 Geneva Convention on the International Recognition of Rights in Aircraft).

Overall, unlike EETCs, Aircraft ABS allow investors to gain diversified exposure to the airline industry without making a credit decision on a specific airline, region or aircraft type. Exhibit 3 summarizes the differences and similarities between EETCs and Aircraft ABS.

STRUCTURE OF AIRCRAFT ABS

The general structure of Aircraft ABS is such that cash generated from the aircraft collateral is allocated to the deal in a waterfall fashion. In the following sections,

[1] Strictly speaking, there could be several leveraged leases underlying an EETC deal and the issuer could potentially choose to reaffirm only some of those leases and not others, i.e. defaults may not be binary.
[2] The MSAF transaction used planes sold by ILFC.

we will first discuss the sources of cash flow in an Aircraft ABS transaction followed by allocation of that cash flow to the bonds. We will then discuss the unique refinancing feature introduced in the AIRPT transaction and end with a summary of built-in features that make Aircraft ABS conservatively structured securities.

Sources of Cash Flow

There are several sources of cash flow in an Aircraft ABS transaction. These include:[3]

- lease revenues
- aircraft sales
- maintenance receipts
- non-delivery of aircraft
- insurance proceeds
- swap adjustments

Lease Revenues

Under normal circumstances, the largest component of the cash flow comes from lease revenues, which, on a monthly basis, are approximately 1% of the appraised value of the aircraft. The prospectus typically assumes that lease rates remain constant at the originally contracted lease rates for the first 60% of an aircraft's assumed life of 25 years, and then linearly decline to 40% of that value over the remaining life. Greater-than-expected lease revenues put all amortizing bonds ahead of the prospectus assumed paydown schedule and vice versa.

The leases backing Aircraft ABS tend to be fixed-rate *operating* leases with terms of approximately five years. The occasional *finance* lease — with a term of up to 15 years — can also back such transactions. A fundamental advantage of the operating lease business is that aircraft can be moved from areas of poor demand to areas of robust demand. In addition, leases are almost always denominated in U.S. dollars, mitigating the risk to the transaction of currency devaluations, like the recent one in Brazil. A devaluation, however, *can* increase the risk of lessee default, since substantially more revenues than costs of the lessee may be denominated in the local currency.

Lease revenues from the pool of aircraft tend not to change dramatically from month to month because the lease rolls are staggered.[4] However, a prolonged downturn/upturn in the aircraft leasing markets will eventually result in all the lease rates resetting to lower/higher levels. Lease revenues will also suffer to the extent that lessees default and/or there are aircraft on the ground (AOG), i.e. not leased out.

---

[3] In addition to the major sources of cash flow, there are small amounts of interest on funds in the collection account.
[4] However, having a mixture of quarterly and monthly pay leases could cause some variability.

Aircraft Sales

The sale of aircraft backing a modern Aircraft ABS transaction is not mandatory for payment of principal to bondholders (unlike the ALPS 1992-1 issue, where it was). Sales can occur for several reasons. First, lessees may exercise purchase options that they hold. Relatively few aircraft are subject to such options. More likely, the servicer will sell aircraft on an opportunistic basis when the market for a particular aircraft is well bid. The servicer is more likely to sell aircraft that do not do well in business downturns, such as freighters or widebodies, essentially improving the portfolio composition over time. AIRPT has, in fact, sold 25 out of 229 aircraft over the past three years.

In order to protect bondholders from a par call and from adverse aircraft selection, there are several conditions that a sale must satisfy. For example, AIRPT generally requires aircraft to be sold at over 105% of their representation in the deal. If the sale price is not at least this level, not more than $50 million of Initial Appraised Value (IAV) of aircraft can be sold each year, and not more than $500 million of IAV can be sold over the life of the deal. In addition, the sale must not violate concentration limits specified in the prospectus. Finally, bonds redeemed in excess of the *Supplemental Principal Amount* (discussed later) have to be paid their respective call premiums. Prospectus cash flows assume no aircraft sales.

In months where aircraft are sold, cash flow from aircraft sales can be far in excess of those from lease revenues. The "excess" cash flows are added to the collection account and paid to the transaction, typically putting the bonds ahead of their assumed paydown schedule. Note, however, that sales automatically reduce future lease revenues, implying an offsetting slowdown in debt reduction later on.

Maintenance Receipts

Maintenance of the aircraft is the responsibility of the airline operator. Operators perform a series of periodic maintenance checks on the engines and the airframe. The airframe checks can be roughly divided into four categories, which, in increasing order of complexity and expense, are referred to as "A", "B", "C", and "D" checks. Generally speaking, one can assume that A, B, and C checks occur at weekly, monthly and annual frequencies, while D checks occur every eight years or so. The D check is the most expensive and more or less requires the aircraft to be stripped down and rebuilt. For a 15-year old Boeing 737-300, a D check would likely cost $1.25-$1.5 million, representing about 8-10% of the cost of the aircraft.

Given the expense and importance of D checks, lessors typically require airlines to accrue for the cost in advance through the payment of maintenance reserves. If the check is performed, and the appropriate work packages are completed, the airline then seeks reimbursement from the lessor to the extent only of the amount paid in. If the check costs are lower than the accrued maintenance, the bondholders get to keep the excess; however, if higher, the lessee has to pay, i.e. the airline bears the entire risk of the check.

In addition to having certain time-related check costs, modern engines are typically maintained "on condition," which means that they are monitored continually to check for performance characteristics. When those characteristics fall outside a certain tolerance, the engine is removed and overhauled. These overhauls, while difficult to predict, are typically more frequent than airframe D checks, and are usually accrued for by the lessee.

Maintenance accruals add to the cashflow available to bondholders but are not expected to produce any positive cash flow over time.[5] As the flows are cyclical, they can represent a substantial source of cash flow — as MSAF has recently experienced — or a use of cashflow, as AIRPT has recently experienced.

Non-Delivery of Aircraft

The MSAF transaction was issued in February 1998, raising capital for a total of 33 aircraft and one spare engine. MSAF had contracted to purchase an aircraft on lease to the Turkish airline, THY, from ILFC by a deadline of May 31, 1998. Since ILFC was unable to complete the legal assignment of the lease to MSAF, this "non-delivery" of one aircraft meant that excess capital, which had been raised at new-issue, had to be redistributed to bondholders. Consequently, in June 1998 approximately $27 million was added to the cash flow available to be paid to bondholders. This source of cash flow is a one-time event and tends to occur soon after issuance.

Insurance Proceeds

Lessees are responsible for maintaining proper insurance on their aircraft. When an insurance "event" occurs, the proceeds from the insurance are passed through to bondholders. For example, when TWA flight 800 was destroyed mid-air over Long Island, the insurance company would have paid out the insured value of the aircraft, which is typically higher than the depreciated value.

There are several kinds of insurance including passenger liability, third party liability, hull insurance and hull war insurance. Only hull insurance and hull war insurance are relevant to Aircraft ABS. Hull insurance protects the insured against accidents during flight, while on the ground or while taxiing. Hull war insurance — also known as insurance against "war risks and allied perils" — pays for damage to aircraft resulting from acts of war or terrorism. If the aircraft are to be operated in politically unstable jurisdictions, there may also be a requirement for Political Risk and Contingent Hull War insurance. Importantly, all operating jurisdictions are legally vetted before aircraft are leased out, and jurisdictions with a material risk of loss are excluded.

Swap Adjustments

Aircraft ABS typically have a combination of fixed- and floating-rate tranches. The underlying leases are also a mixture of fixed and floating, with the proportion

---

[5] The prospectus typically assumes that net maintenance receipts are zero.

varying by servicer. For example, AerFi (formerly known as GPA) has histori-cally originated a larger proportion of floating-rate leases than has GECAS or ILFC. To ensure that cash inflows on the leases equate to cash outflows on the bonds under all interest rate environments, an interest rate swap is employed. As interest rates change and the bonds pay down faster or slower than expected, pos-itive or negative cash flows may result from these swap positions.

Uses of Cash Flows

Of the six sources of cash flow discussed in the previous section, gross lease rev-enues are the largest component and are likely to be reduced by several factors. The standard prospectus assumption is an 8% revenue haircut to the gross reve-nue line[6] from several assumed stresses, broken down as follows for the MSAF transaction:

- (3.0%)   Aircraft on ground (AOG)
- (0.5%)   Aircraft repossessions
- (1.0%)   Bad debts, and
- (3.5%)   Operating costs including insurance, leasing and aircraft related costs

It is normal to have *some* AOG due to expiring leases on aircraft that have then to be re-marketed. Lessee defaults also typically generate some AOG, and, in addi-tion, introduce repossession costs. Several types of repossession costs could be incurred, including legal costs to retrieve an aircraft in a foreign jurisdiction, or maintenance costs required to bring a retrieved aircraft into a condition satisfac-tory for re-leasing. It is important to note that these stresses are variable, but an 8% revenue haircut is considered to be conservative. In the recession of the early 90s, which was the worst 3-year experience lessors have had to date, GPA Group lost, on average, 8% of gross revenues annually. We believe that ILFC's experi-ence was considerably better during that period. If the stresses are less than 8%, the bonds will be paid down quicker than assumed in the prospectus base case. Current AOG for APPT is only one out of 204 aircraft.

After the stress-related items are subtracted from the gross revenue line, the net revenue is then fed into a waterfall such as the one shown for AIRPT in Exhibit 4 (and depicted graphically in Exhibit 5). In broad terms, after the operat-ing expenses have been paid (Required Expense Amount), the A and B tranches are paid interest and the Minimum Principal Amount, which is intended to keep their balances at a certain *declining* percentage of the *expected*[7] value of the air-craft portfolio. Classes C and D then receive their interest, following which, the A class receives a Principal Adjustment Amount.

---

[6] An 8% haircut means that only 92% of gross revenues are assumed to come in each month.

[7] The expected portfolio value at any time represents the aggregate value of the remaining aircraft using the prospectus depreciation schedule.

Exhibit 4: Cash Flow Waterfall for Airplanes Pass Through Trust

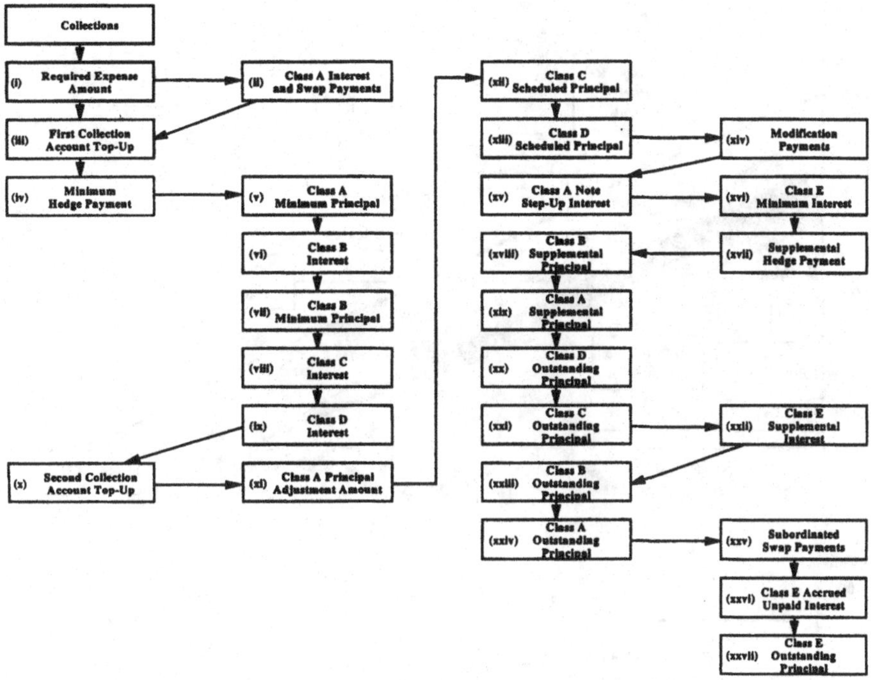

Collections

(i) Required Expense Amount

(ii) Class A Interest and Swap Payments

(iii) First Collection Account Top-Up

(iv) Minimum Hedge Payment

(v) Class A Minimum Principal

(vi) Class B Interest

(vii) Class B Minimum Principal

(viii) Class C Interest

(ix) Class D Interest

(x) Second Collection Account Top-Up

(xi) Class A Principal Adjustment Amount

(xii) Class C Scheduled Principal

(xiii) Class D Scheduled Principal

(xiv) Modification Payments

(xv) Class A Note Step-Up Interest

(xvi) Class E Minimum Interest

(xvii) Supplemental Hedge Payment

(xviii) Class B Supplemental Principal

(xix) Class A Supplemental Principal

(xx) Class D Outstanding Principal

(xxi) Class C Outstanding Principal

(xxii) Class E Supplemental Interest

(xxiii) Class B Outstanding Principal

(xxiv) Class A Outstanding Principal

(xxv) Subordinated Swap Payments

(xxvi) Class E Accrued Unpaid Interest

(xxvii) Class E Outstanding Principal

Source: 1998 Prospectus

Under normal circumstances, the Principal Adjustment Amount is zero. However, if the ratio of the A outstanding amount to the appraised aircraft value, i.e. the LTV, is lower than expected, the Principal Adjustment amount will "turbo" cash flows to the A class. The turbo ensures that the A class has at least a certain appraisal-based LTV. This feature is unique to Aircraft ABS and protects the senior class from deteriorating aircraft valuations. The appraisal is performed annually by independent experts.

The C and D classes are then paid down to their scheduled balances, after which the A and B classes get another round of principal known as Supplemental Principal. The base case prospectus assumption of an 8% revenue haircut is designed to pay the entire Minimum Principal Amount, the Scheduled Principal Amount on the C and D classes and some of the Supplemental Principal Amount on the A class.

Assuming that there is some cash flow left at this point — due to aircraft sales or positive maintenance receipts, for example — it is applied to the structure in reverse alphabetical order so as to pay off the D class entirely, followed by the C, B and A classes. Note that at this level in the cash flow priority, payments to the bonds are considered to be calls, and, therefore, the call premium, if any, must be paid.

Exhibit 5: Projected Principal Balance of All Classes in Airplanes Pass Through Trust (Pre- and Post-Refinancing)

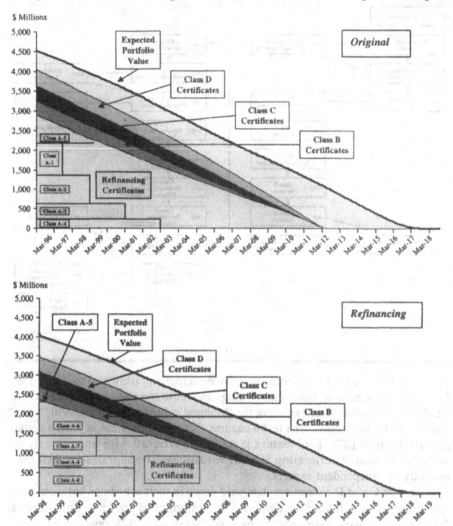

Source: Airplanes Pass Through Trust Prospectus (1996 and 1998)

The E class represents the equity in the transaction and its rights are heavily subordinated to more senior note holders. This is another unique feature of Aircraft ABS transactions. In essence, only a small amount of class E interest is paid out of cash flow. The "excess" cash flow is captured each month and applied towards debt reduction rather than released to the "residual holder" (as in credit card and home equity loan transactions).

Other Structural Considerations — Refinancing

So far, we have discussed the A class only in its entirety. In reality, however, the senior class of a modern Aircraft ABS transaction consists of two or more tranches, which are a combination of soft bullets and amortizers. Soft bullets were introduced to broaden the investor appeal of these securities and are expected to be refinanced on their bullet dates.

Exhibit 5 shows the original paydown structure of AIRPT in March 1996, as well as the refinanced structure in March 1998. The original structure consisted of four soft bullets, A1 through A4, and an amortizer, the A5. In March 1998, the A1 through A3 classes were all refinanced and the B class was called, resulting in the new structure shown at the bottom of Exhibit 5.

In this case, the board of Airplanes chose to call the A-2 and A-3 *prior* to their soft bullet dates. The new structure introduced two soft bullets — the A-7 and A-8 classes — and one amortizer (the A-6). The A-7 and A-8, in turn, are expected to be refinanced on their respective bullet dates (as will the A-4 from the original transaction). The new B tranche completely replaced the original one and has a lower coupon (but confusingly has the same name!).

If the issuer fails to refinance a soft bullet, that will not constitute an event of default. Rather, the coupon of the tranche in question will step up by 50 bp until such time as it is refinanced. Payment of the step-up interest comes ahead of Supplemental Principal Payments (see Exhibit 4). Clearly, the issuer is unlikely to refinance if the market spread of the tranche in question is more than the coupon plus 50 bp. However, lack of refinancing does not automatically imply extension to maturity, i.e. the issuer will assess the attractiveness of refinancing each month.

A soft bullet that is not refinanced effectively becomes an amortizer until such time that it is refinanced. The amortization schedule of a soft bullet that has not been refinanced is designed to pay off the bonds by their final maturity date.

Conservatism Built into Aircraft ABS Structures

Aircraft ABS are structured in an inherently conservative manner. This conservatism is derived from several sources:

- *Actual aircraft life is longer than the prospectus assumption.* Passenger aircraft in Aircraft ABS pools are assumed to produce cash flow over useful lives of 25 years, while the assumption for freighters is 20 years from the date of their conversion. In reality, passenger aircraft can have residual value after 25 years and are sometimes modified for use as freighters at that point in time.
- *Prospectus cash flows have a conservative haircut.* The prospectus base case conservatively assumes that 8% of gross revenues are lost due to various stresses. In the early 90s recession, the worst average annual revenue loss over a 3-year period was 8% and the worst in any one year was 12%.

- *Annual appraisals cross-check the prospectus depreciation assumption.* A desktop appraisal is performed annually by three appraisers, revalidating the value of the aircraft portfolio. If the value is less than suggested by the prospectus depreciation schedule, the senior class is accelerated. Other ABS do not check for declines in the value of the underlying collateral.
- *Losses are not monetized like they are in other ABS.* Most leases backing Aircraft ABS are operating leases and, in the event of lessee default, the aircraft is leased out to a new lessee, i.e. there is no forced sale of the aircraft. Effectively, this implies that declines in the market value of aircraft in economically depressed environments are not "marked to market". It is therefore possible for the transaction to "earn" its way out of revenue declines in one period through excess revenues in some future, presumably more positive, environment.
- *Overcollateralization tends to grow over time.* Aircraft ABS are designed to pay down well in advance of the 25-year assumption of aircraft life. This creates a natural tendency for the overcollateralization to grow as a percentage of the outstanding debt. In addition, the prospectus depreciation curve understates an aircraft's value as it ages (since a zero value is assumed in 25 years and an appraiser would place a positive value on the aircraft at that point).
- *Excess cash flow captured each month.* In an ABS structure, excess cash is normally released to the residual holder each month. However, in Aircraft ABS, any excess is used for debt reduction and the "residual holder" only gets paid after all outstanding bonds are repaid.[8] This offers fundamental protection against whipsaw scenarios, i.e., good followed by bad environments.
- *Liquidating aircraft portfolios typically improve in composition.* The MSAF and AerCo transactions are master trusts that allow the addition of aircraft post-issuance. The AIRPT transaction, on the other hand, is a liquidating trust whose composition has arguably improved over time. This occurs because the servicer is likely, but is not required, to sell aircraft that do poorly in downturns, such as freighters and widebodies.

STRESSING THE STRUCTURE OF AIRCRAFT ABS

Although we believe that Aircraft ABS are structured conservatively, it is important to assess the impact of fluctuations in lease revenues on various bonds in the structure. Exhibit 6 shows the volatility of aircraft lease rates for the past ten years. After the peak of 113% in 1989 (1987 = 100%), lease rates declined for four years before bottoming out at 84% in 1993.[9] Since then, lease rates have recovered but, more recently, have begun to show some weakness.

---

[8] Note, however, that the servicer's performance based incentive is paid prior to bondholders. In addition, the "residual holder" does get some interest.

[9] It is easier to think of cumulative lease rates in dollar terms, i.e. $100 in 1987, $113 in 1989, etc.

Exhibit 6: Cumulative Aircraft Lease Rates Indexed to 1987

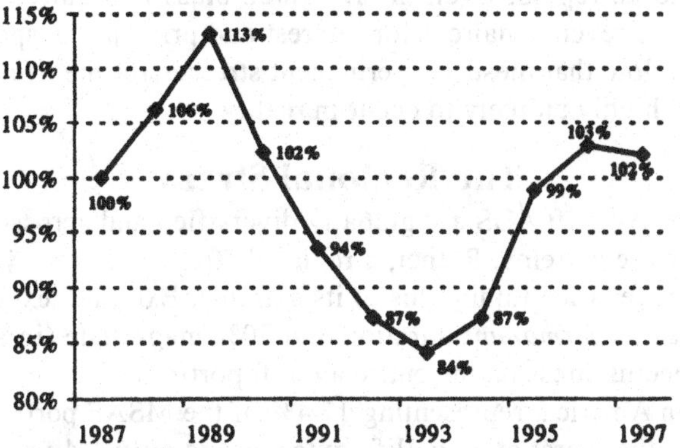

Source: Airclaims

The widebody market, in particular, has seen significantly lower lease rates due to the Asian crisis. Asian carriers typically have long-haul routes and tend to be among the biggest purchasers of widebody aircraft. Relative to 1987, the range of aircraft lease rates appears to be in the +13% to −16% range.

The 1990-1993 Stress

Using the above lease rate volatilities as a guide, Exhibit 7 demonstrates the robustness of the MSAF structure. Let us assume that the MSAF transaction was issued under a lease rate assumption of the 1989 peak. Further assume that lease rates followed the pattern in Exhibit 6, dropping from 113% in 1989 to 84% in 1993 before rising and flattening out at 102% in 1997 (in total the "1990-1993" stress). Note that this is still down from the 113% on which the transaction cash flows were based. Finally, assume that *in addition to the above-mentioned stress*, 6% of lease revenues are lost in the worst years (1992, 1993 and 1994) to various stresses including defaults, repossessions and AOG.

Relative to our base of 113%, the total annual revenue loss in each year for our hypothetical projection is therefore 9.73%, 16.81%, 29.01%, 31.66%, 29.01%, 12.39%, and 8.85% followed by 9.73% for the remaining life of the transaction.[10] Even under this severe stress assumption, the outstanding principal balances of all the bonds — down to the BB tranche — are repaid in full and not a single interest payment is missed (although, as Exhibit 7 shows, the bonds do extend).

The Principal and Interest "Money-Good" Stresses

The conservative structure of Aircraft ABS is further demonstrated by the permanent stresses shown in Exhibit 7. For example, for class C-1 to miss an interest payment, 23.1% of gross revenues would have to be lost in each and every year.

---

[10] The first year's stress, for example would be (113 − 102)/113=9.73%.

In addition, 26.6% of gross revenues would have to be lost for the principal of this class not to be repaid. Even the BB rated class D requires greater than a 17.7% and 17.9% revenue haircut for interest and principal, respectively, not to be paid in full. Note that these are permanent stresses for the life of the transaction, a situation highly unlikely to occur in reality.

The Regional Stress

As noted above, Aircraft ABS are globally diversified and across-the-board permanent stresses are extreme. Rather, a regional stress of 2- to 4-year duration is the more likely scenario. Taking this to its extreme, Exhibit 7 examines regional revenue stresses of *permanent* duration and 30% magnitude (in addition to the basic 8% prospectus stress on the entire aircraft portfolio).

If Latin America, representing 17.4% of the MSAF portfolio, is stressed in this manner, the worst average life extension is only 1.4 years (class D-1). Adding Asia to the stress (another 13% of the portfolio) extends average lives by a maximum of 4.5 years (class D-1).

In none of these severe and permanent regional stresses is there an interruption of interest, and principal is always eventually paid in full.

RATING AGENCY METHODOLOGY

Investors should get some comfort from the fact that every tranche of an Aircraft ABS is rated by three major rating agencies, namely Standard & Poor's, Moody's Investors Service and Duff & Phelps Credit Rating Co. Below, we describe the approach taken by Standard & Poor's as a representative example of the rating methodology for the sector.

Exhibit 7: Performance Under Stress Scenarios for Morgan Stanley Aircraft Finance (as of April 15, 1999 Remittance Date)

Tranche	WAL Under Base Case	Money-Good Revenue Decline 1990-93 Stress	WAL Under Regional Stress of −30% Interest
A-1	0.9 Yrs.	0.9 Yrs.	46.6%
A-2	2.9	4.0	46.6
B-1	7.8	8.4	26.3
C-1	9.5	13.2	23.1
D-1	11.0	15.7	17.7

Note: The average life of the A-1 does not change because it is always assumed to be refinanced.
The Base Case stress assumes that 8% of gross revenues are lost each year.
The 1990-1993 Stress assumes a lease revenue stress that approximates the worst recession in the airline/aircraft industry (see text).
The Money-Good Revenue Decline shows the maximum permanent revenue decline under which each tranche is either made whole on its outstanding principal balance or never misses an interest payment.
The Regional Stress assumes, in addition to the 8% Base Case Stress, an additional 30% of lease revenues are permanently lost in each region specified. LA = Latin America, AS = Asia.
Source: Morgan Stanley

Exhibit 8: Typical Cash Flow Stress Tests

Test	"AA" Scenario	"A" Scenario	"BBB" Scenario	"BB" Scenario
Depression 1 Start	Month 24	Month 24	Month 36	Month 48
Depression 2 Start	Month 132	Month 132	Month 144	Month 168
Length of Depression	3 Years	3 Years	3 Years	3 Years
Annual Lessee Defaults (Depression 1)	25%	20%	15%	8%
Annual Lessee Defaults (Depression 2)	30%	25%	20%	10%
Lease Rate Decline (Depression 1)	58%	45%	32%	21%
Lease Rate Decline (Depression 2)	85%	70%	55%	40%
Repossession Time (Outside Depression)	3 mo.	3 mo.	2 mo.	1 mo.
Repossession Time (Inside Depression)	3 mo.	3 mo.	3 mo.	2 mo.
Remarketing Time (Outside Depression)	3 mo.	3 mo.	2 mo.	1 mo.
Remarketing Time (Inside Depression)	9 mo.	8 mo.	7 mo.	6 mo.
Lease Term (Depression 1)	4 years	4 years	4 years	3 years
Lease Term (Depression 2)	3 years	3 years	3 years	3 years
Lease Term (Outside Depression)	5 years	5 years	5 years	5 years
Repossession Costs	$750k	$500k	$500k	$250k-$500k
Airplanes on Ground	5%	5%	5%	5%

Source: Standard & Poor's

Standard & Poor's looks at transactions backed by aircraft in a spectrum that ranges from ETCs to Aircraft ABS. At one end of the spectrum, ETCs and EETCs are rated using a corporate bond approach given the reliance on a single airline and relatively few aircraft. At the other end, Aircraft ABS, typically consisting of portfolios with 25+ lessees and aircraft, are rated using a structured finance approach, where default risk is driven by both the airline risk as well as the value of the aircraft.

Standard & Poor's judges aircraft asset value risk by analyzing the technological risk of the aircraft, the diversification by aircraft type, an evaluation of the manufacturer and other factors. Technological risk assesses the risk of asset value and lease rate fluctuations due to obsolescence of the aircraft. Older aircraft, by definition, score worse on this measure than new aircraft. The term of the transaction is also important. Diversification by aircraft type measures how closely the Aircraft ABS fleet resembles the world fleet, i.e. what are the planes' sizes and mission capabilities? An evaluation of the manufacturer measures the distribution of the airframe manufacturers in the fleet to the world fleet. Finally, other factors that S&P looks at include the expected customer base and usage conditions of the aircraft, and the evaluation of the servicer.

The above-mentioned analysis, along with an assessment of the airline risk, feeds into cash flow modeling of the aircraft portfolio. For operating lease portfolios, lease rates are modeled as a function of depreciated aircraft values and the historical yields on operating leases. A further lease value decline is assumed during recessions. S&P then stresses these cash flows by using different combinations of lessee default rates, timing of depressions, repossession and re-marketing periods, repossession costs and increasing asset risk as the portfolio ages. Example scenarios for each rating category are shown in Exhibit 8.

Exhibit 9: Aircraft ABS versus Competing Asset Classes, April 29, 1999

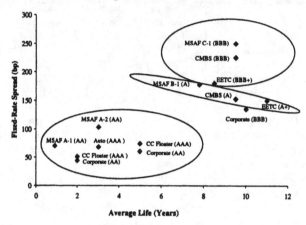

Note: Floating-rate securities swapped to fixed for comparison.
Source: Morgan Stanley

Standard & Poor's also takes other factors into account including adequacy of the maintenance reserve (to absorb fluctuations in maintenance events), legal issues and the dynamic hedging strategy for the trust. Finally, the ability of the servicer is a key element in the rating.

RELATIVE VALUE

Aircraft ABS bear similarities to a variety of fixed-income instruments including EETCs, CMBS, corporates, credit card ABS and auto loan ABS. Given that their spreads have not fully recovered from 1998's debacle, they should appeal to a wide cross-section of portfolio managers. Using Exhibit 9 as a guide, we compare Aircraft ABS to each of these asset classes.

Aircraft ABS versus EETCs

EETCs are the natural comparison to Aircraft ABS because they have similar underlying risks relating to the aircraft/airline industry. Since most EETCs are amortizers with average lives of 8-14 years, the appropriate comparison is the BBB tranche of Aircraft ABS. BBB-rated Aircraft ABS currently have a 70 bp spread advantage over a comparable EETC class (see Exhibit 9). In addition, single-A Aircraft ABS have a shorter maturity and wider spread than some A+ rated EETCs. Even at similar spreads, we would prefer Aircraft ABS over EETCs given that Aircraft ABS expose the investor to a larger and more diversified pool of aircraft and investors are not subject to the default/no default decision of a single issuer.

Aircraft ABS versus Corporates

Aircraft ABS have spreads that are 25-50 bp wider than short corporate bonds. Since most corporates are bullets, the AA-rated refinancing tranches of Aircraft ABS are the closest comparison. However, investors willing to buy amortizing classes would do well to move down in credit quality to single-A or BBB-rated Aircraft ABS, where the advantage over corporates is a heftier 80-115 bp. There should also be some added benefit to a corporate portfolio from asset class diversification, i.e., corporate spreads and Aircraft ABS spreads do not move in lockstep.

Aircraft ABS versus Credit Card ABS

AA-rated refinancing tranches of Aircraft ABS have a 20-25 bp advantage over AAA-rated credit card floaters. Both are soft bullets with some extension risk — the Aircraft ABS due to a failure to refinance and the credit cards due to an inadequate monthly payment rate. Credit cards are also subject to early amortization. However, the average life of a refinancing Aircraft ABS issue can contract only if a substantial number of aircraft are sold and the amortizing senior pays down completely.

Aircraft ABS versus Auto Loan ABS

Amortizing auto loan ABS are best compared to the amortizing senior of an Aircraft ABS transaction. The Aircraft ABS spread advantage is on the order of 35 bp, although auto loan ABS are rated AAA, while the highest Aircraft ABS rating is generally AA. Both classes are subject to some average life variability, but not significantly so.

Aircraft ABS versus CMBS

Spreads of BBB-rated CMBS tranches are about 25 bp tighter than those of comparably rated Aircraft ABS. Both asset classes provided diversified exposure — CMBS to real estate and Aircraft ABS to the aircraft/airline industry — but the diversification of aircraft ABS is global rather than domestic. Aircraft on operating base can also be moved to regions of high demand (unlike buildings!).

AVAILABILITY OF INFORMATION

Information on Aircraft ABS can be obtained from a variety of sources. Each transaction has a monthly remittance report, which lists total available cash and its allocation within the waterfall. The remittance reports will also usually note the type and number of aircraft, if any, that were sold during the month.

The transactions mentioned in this report are also modeled on Bloomberg. Investors can also read more about Airplanes Group and access AIRPT's SEC filings at http://www.airplanes-group.com. Furthermore, SEC filings every quarter (available through Free Edgar) update the status of the lessees and the cash flow performance of the transaction. Every year, the appraised value of the portfolio, along with the composition of the fleet, is also released in an SEC filing.

CONCLUSION

The Aircraft ABS sector provides investors with diversified exposure to the aircraft/airline industry. Modern deals are well structured and have several unique features not found in other ABS. Investors who buy EETCs, CMBS, corporates, credit card ABS and auto loan ABS should seriously consider this sector as an alternative.

Chapter 8

SBA Development Company Participation Certificates

Christopher Flanagan*

Weisi Tan*

INTRODUCTION

The Small Business Administration (SBA) is a regular issuer of 10-year and 20-year Development Company Participation Certificates (DCPC's). Under the auspices of Section 504 of the Small Business Investment Act (the "504 Program"), issuance of DCPC's began in 1986. Since then, annual issuance volume has been steadily increasing. The 20-year program is the dominant program. The 10-year program typically is used to finance equipment and machinery, while the 20-year program is used to finance real estate.

The SBA guarantees timely payment of principal and interest on DCPC's, which are collateralized by Debentures issued by state and local development companies. A detailed description of the 504 Program is provided in the final section. The Debentures represent loans to small business borrowers. These borrowers have the option to prepay the loan but must do so in accordance with a prepayment penalty schedule. These prepayments are often referred to as "voluntary" prepayments. In the event of a voluntary prepayment, the DCPC investor will receive the principal amount outstanding on the loan, along with the prepayment penalties.

The early prepayment option is one source of prepayment risk for DCPC's. The other source is related to "accelerations", or "non-voluntary" prepayments. This prepayment occurs when the borrower defaults on the underlying

---

* Messrs. Flanagan and Tan were employed at Merrill Lynch at the time they wrote this chapter.

The authors thank Roland Cook, Development Company Funding Corporation's Fiscal Agent, for his ongoing support of our efforts; Scott Wagman and Vitaliy Shor for their implementation of the Model on Bloomberg; John Winchester, Ted Bouloukos, Frank Keane, Ken Hackel, and Ryan Asato for their input into the development of the model and the preparation of this chapter; and Albert Zeigerson for his assistance in the production of this chapter.

loan. As with other government-guaranteed securities, such as GNMA mortgage-backed securities, the guarantee of the timely receipt of all principal and interest means that a default event results in the early, or accelerated, return of principal to the holder of the DCPC. However, in this instance, there are no prepayment penalties to be passed through to the investor.

Merrill Lynch has developed a model of voluntary prepayment and default for SBA 504 DCPC's. The purpose of this chapter is to present this model and use it to explain the key determinants of voluntary prepayment and default. Model fit and projections are provided.

The primary application of the Model is to assist in the valuation process for DCPC's. Merrill Lynch has integrated the SBA Prepayment and Default Model into a price-yield calculator which is currently available on Bloomberg. A description of how to use the calculator for valuation purposes is provided at the end of this chapter.

THE SBA 504 PROGRAM DESCRIPTION[1]

The U.S. Government Guaranteed Development Company Participation Certificates (DCPC's) are issued by Harris Trust Company of New York as agent for the U.S. Small Business Administration (SBA). DCPC's are passthrough certificates representing fractional undivided ownership interests in pools of Debentures issued by state and local development companies (Development Companies). The Debentures, which are guaranteed by the SBA, represent loans to small business concerns nationwide. DCPC's are guaranteed by the SBA and are backed by the full faith and credit of the United States.

The SBA DCPC Program was created to better enable small businesses to create new jobs, primarily through physical plant expansions, and to increase community or area development. The Program provides funding to small businesses at attractive rates by creating access to the long-term capital markets, as well as creating a vehicle to supplement financing from conventional lending sources in the private sector.

The Debentures

Section 503 of the Small Business Investment Act authorizes SBA to guarantee the Debentures issued by Development Companies certified by the SBA. The proceeds raised by the Development Company-issued Debentures are used to fund loans to small business concerns for the construction or acquisition of new plants, machinery or equipment. The small business concern provides an executed promissory note or lease agreement to the Development Company.

---

[1] This description is an excerpt from Gary Isaacs and John Winchester, "U.S. Government Guaranteed Development Company Participation Certificates," July 1995.

The SBA Development Company Program operates in conjunction with non-federally funded sources. A minimum of 50% of the financing for any development company project must be provided by a non-federal source, typically a conventional bank loan secured by a first lien. This loan is not guaranteed by the SBA. As much as 40% of the project costs, up to $1 million, may be funded by SBA guaranteed Debentures. The Debentures provide for semiannual level payments of principal and interest and are fully amortizing on a level yield basis over their terms of either 10 or 20 years. Generally, 10-year maturities are for equipment and machinery loans and 20-year maturities are for real estate loans. These loans are made at rates typically below the market for such loans and are secured by second liens. The small business concern (the borrower) is required to commit a minimum of 10% in equity. This is advantageous relative to the 20% minimum equity typically required for conventional financing.

The first Development Company Debenture was issued in 1981. From 1981 to October 1986, all Debentures issued pursuant to Section 503 were sold to the Federal Financing Bank (FFB), an instrumentality of the United States supervised by the Secretary of the Treasury.

The Certificates

In 1986, Sections 504 and 505 were enacted under the Small Business Investment Act. Section 504 required SBA to conduct a 2-year pilot program selling Section 503 Debentures to investors as an alternative to the sales to FFB. Section 505 authorized the formation of pools of Debentures and the issuance of certificates representing ownership interests in the pools. In turn, the SBA guaranteed timely principal and interest payments to Certificateholders.

After the 2-year period, the 504 Program was made a permanent part of the law and the FFB was prohibited from future Debenture purchases. Pursuant to a Trust Agreement dated as of December 1, 1986, as amended, Harris Trust Company was appointed trustee and the Development Company Funding Corporation was appointed Fiscal Agent for the SBA.

DCPC's are offered on the Tuesday after the first Sunday of each month through a negotiated underwriting. The offering is priced on that day and the coupon assigned to the DCPC's is also assigned to the underlying Debentures in the related pool. Each of the Debentures in a pool carries the same issue, maturity and payment dates as the corresponding DCPC's. Since 1986, Debentures with a 20-year final maturity have been offered each month while Debentures with a 10-year final maturity were offered on a quarterly basis. Beginning in March 1995, 10-year pools have been offered every other month. The underwriters make secondary markets in the Certificates.

The small business projects associated with the underlying Debentures are typically funded, guaranteed by the SBA and then sold to investors as shown in Exhibit 1.

Exhibit 1: 504 Program
Debentures, Certificates, and Funds Flow

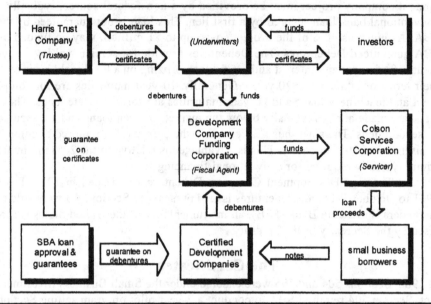

Full Faith and Credit Guarantee

As stated above, the timely payment of all principal and interest due on the Debentures is guaranteed by the SBA. The full faith and credit of the United States is pledged to this guarantee, the highest credit quality available. Additionally, the SBA guarantees the timely distribution of all payments due on the Debentures to the Certificateholders. The full faith and credit of the United States is also pledged to this guarantee. Collectively, these guarantees form SBA's guarantee to the Certificateholders of timely distribution of all payments of principal and interest due on the Debentures.

SOURCES OF PREPAYMENT RISK

Voluntary Prepayments

Under the 504 program, a voluntary prepayment by a small business borrower is subject to a prepayment penalty equal, in the first year, to the Debenture rate of interest and then declining annually and ratably to zero over the first half of the Debenture's life. For example, a 20-year DCPC with a 6.00% coupon has a prepayment penalty of 6.00% during its first year. The prepayment penalty declines annually and ratably from 6.00% in year 1 to zero in year 11. In the event that a borrower chooses to prepay during the first year, the amount required would be 106% of the then current principal balance of the loan (see Exhibit 2).

Exhibit 2: Prepayment Penalty Schedule for a 6% 20-Year DCPC

Year	Prepayment Price (% of current balance)
1	106.00
2	105.40
3	104.80
.	.
.	.
10	100.60
11	100.00

It is also important to note that voluntary prepayments can only be made on the related borrower's semiannual payment date. Voluntary prepayments, including the prepayment penalty amounts and applicable interest, are distributed pro rata to the Certificateholders on the semiannual payment date on which such prepayments are made.

In the discussion which follows, we refer to this source of prepayment risk as either voluntary prepayments or, simply, prepayments.

Non-Voluntary Prepayments

The Debentures underlying the DCPC's are subject to prepayments through the SBA's acceleration of defaulted loans. In the event of a default, the SBA may, and in certain instances shall, accelerate the maturity of a Debenture. Pursuant to its guarantee, the SBA makes payment of 100% of the then outstanding principal amount and distributes such payment pro rata, with applicable interest, to the Certificateholders. In the event that a borrower has ceased making payments but the SBA has not exercised its option to accelerate the loan, the SBA will, pursuant to its guarantee, make the semiannual payment for such loan to the related pool. Acceleration amounts, or non-voluntary prepayments, are distributed to Certificateholders pro rata on the semiannual payment date on which such prepayments are made.

In the discussion which follows, we refer to this source of prepayment risk as either non-voluntary prepayments or, simply, defaults.

MODELS OF PREPAYMENT AND DEFAULT

The Data Set

The prepayment and default analysis was based on $7.6 billion of DCPC's originated between 1986 and 1997. The prepayment and default performance was measured through April 1998. The data incorporate many of the same exogenous trends which have influenced the performance of other assets such as mortgages, home equity loans, and manufactured housing loans. These include the economic downturn in the early 1990s, the precipitous drop in interest rates in 1993, 1994's rising rate environment, and the credit expansion of 1995-1998. The opportunity to observe data throughout these various economic environments provides for a robust model of prepayment and default.

It is particularly useful to examine two views of historical prepayment and default data. In the first view, aggregate performance data are observed over time and as a function of some exogenous economic data. This view provides intuition regarding the exogenous determinants of either prepayment or default. In the second view, all "current coupon" loans are aggregated according to loan age and the prepayment or default rate for each age aggregate is measured. This view provides insight into the normal "aging pattern" for a given collateral type.

Aggregate Prepayments and Defaults

Exhibit 3 shows aggregate prepayment rates for the 20-year DCPC's from January 1988 through April 1998. As an indicator of the interest rate environment during this period, the yield on the 10-year Treasury is also shown. The data indicate that prepayment rates for the DCPC's exhibit a dependency on interest rates. Two periods are particularly noteworthy. In 1993, when the yield on the 10-year Treasury hit a historic low, prepayment rates accelerated, moving from about 1% CPR to 3% CPR. In early 1998, when interest rates approached the historic lows yet again, aggregate prepayment rates jumped from about 2% CPR to 3.5% CPR.

Exhibit 3: 20-Year Voluntary Prepayments versus Interest Rates

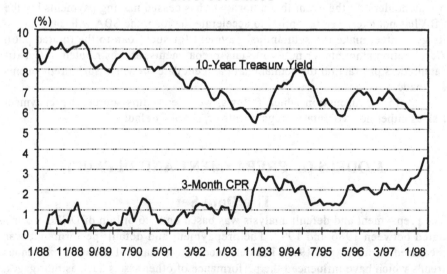

Exhibit 4: 20-Year Non-Voluntary Prepayments versus Unemployment Rate

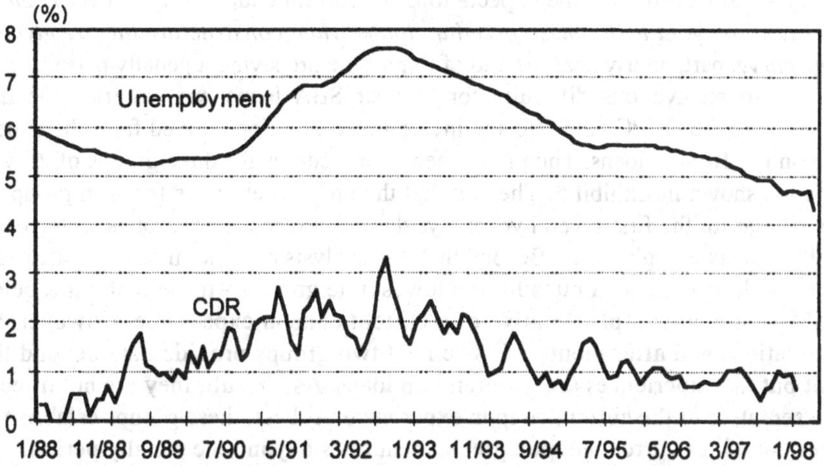

Before considering these prepayment responses, it is useful to first consider why the prepayment rates in Exhibit 3 are so low. There are two reasons. First, since the program has experienced steady growth since 1988, large pools of unseasoned loans are constantly entering the aggregate. This biases down the aggregate prepayment rate. Second, this effect is compounded by the impact of prepayment penalties on the prepayment aging curve. As will be discussed in a shortly, the presence of penalties results in a particularly long prepayment aging ramp for the DCPC's — roughly 10 years on the 20-year program!

With this perspective, the prepayment increases in 1993 and 1998 take on more meaning. The 1993 experience showed that, in their own way, the SBA DCPC's were quite responsive to the rate environment. The increases came in spite of the fact that, on average, the loans were still very new and, as a result, faced steep prepayment penalties. The 1998 jump is important because it incorporates some prepayment rates after the penalty period has ended.

The aggregate view of default rates on the 20-year DCPC's is shown in Exhibit 4 ("CDR" is conditional default rate). By lagging the default data three months relative to unemployment rates, the exhibit shows a strong correlation between the health of the economy and default likelihood. The lagged default rates show that a weakening employment environment is ultimately followed by a rise in business failures. Currently, with unemployment rates at historic lows as of this writing, default rates for SBA loans should remain subdued over the next few years.

Prepayment and Default Aging Curves

One of the challenges faced when constructing prepayment aging curves for 20-year SBA loans is the lack of data for seasoned, current coupon loans. The only loans that are out of, or near the end of, the penalty period are the premiums that were originated in the high interest rate environment of the late 1980s. Since a prepayment aging curve typically represents the expectations for current coupon loans, *it is extremely important to avoid using these premium loans when constructing the prepayment aging curve*, particularly near the end of or past the prepayment penalty period.

To resolve this difficulty for 20-year SBA loans, we stratified the data according to the DCPC note rate and incorporated intuition derived from the experience on the 10-year loans. The prepayment aging curves for three groups of 20-year loans are shown in Exhibit 5. The fact that the prepayment rates for each group are very similar for the first several years says that we can construct a robust aging curve for the first six to eight years. Beyond that, the analysis becomes more complicated.

The prepayment rates for the lowest rate group — those with rates below 6.85% — are most representative of a current coupon experience. However, the observations end after month 66. The next two groups provide data beyond this point but the experiences are for premium loans. As a result, they are not directly representative of the current coupon experience. At best, these groups establish an upper bound for current coupon prepayment rates beyond the penalty period.

Additional information can be gleaned from the 10-year DCPC program, which has both current coupon and premium data beyond the penalty period. The data in Exhibit 6 show that there is a modest acceleration in prepayment rates at the end of the 5-year penalty period, for both the premium and the current coupon groups. Prepayment rates peak shortly after the end of the penalty period and decline thereafter. These data can be extrapolated to help shape the 20-year current coupon prepayment aging curves beyond the penalty period.

Exhibit 5: 20-Year Voluntary Prepayment Aging Curve by Coupon Bucket — Historical Experience

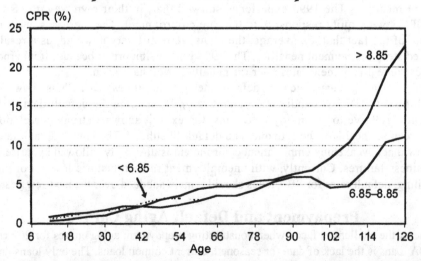

Exhibit 6: 10-Year Voluntary Prepayment Aging Curve by Coupon Bucket —Historical Experience

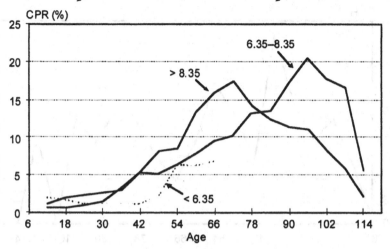

Exhibit 7: 20-Year Non-Voluntary Prepayment Aging Curve — Historical Experience

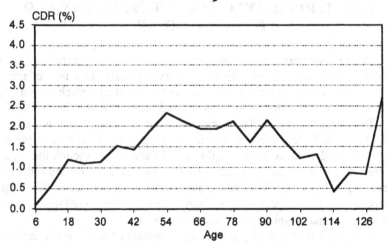

The aging curves for defaults (Exhibits 7 and 8) show that the aging period depends on the loan term. The 20-year loans ramp up to a peak default level after about four years while 10-year loans peak after about two years. Also, the peak is higher for the 10-year loans. Given the superior collateral quality of the 20-year program (real estate) relative to the 10-year program (equipment), these results are not surprising.

Exhibit 8: 10-Year Non-Voluntary Prepayment Aging Curve — Historical Experience

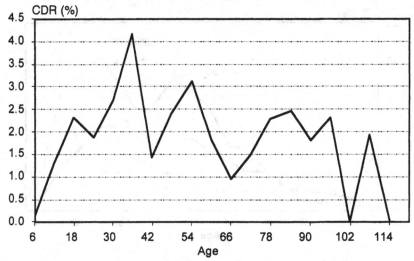

THE MERRILL LYNCH SBA PREPAYMENT AND DEFAULT MODEL

The only loan parameters that are transparent under the 504 program are the coupon, the loan term, and the prepayment penalty schedule. This lack of transparency translates into a necessarily simple model structure which captures pool level performance and which reflects the limited set of available loan parameters.

The Merrill Lynch SBA Prepayment and Default Model can be understood as follows. Prepayment and default aging curves for a baseline set of parameters were developed based on the actual data. In our model, these curves, which are referred to as the *baseline curves*, incorporate the intuition developed in the preceding discussion. The model specification also includes risk multipliers associated with the baseline parameters and which explain deviations in the actual experience from that defined by the baseline curves.

Under our simple model structure, the impact of loan term is captured by using different baseline curves and risk multipliers for the 10-year and 20-year programs for both prepayments and defaults. Dynamic parameters for prepayments include the pool age and the change in the 10-year Treasury yield since the DCPC origination date.[2] The pool age implicitly accounts for changes in prepay-

---

[2] The impact of variations in the gross spread (loan rate – DCPC rate) within pools and between pools was ignored. Given the significance of prepayment penalties in determining prepayments, we do not believe this creates significant model error.

ment penalties as defined by the prepayment penalty schedule. The one dynamic parameter for defaults is the national unemployment rate.

Baseline Characteristics and Curves

The baseline characteristics for the model are shown in Exhibit 9. The baseline prepayment and default curves associated with these baseline characteristics are shown in Exhibits 10 and 11. Effectively, these curves show the prepayment and default expectations — in CPR and CDR terms — for pools of newly originated, current coupon loans. Note that the long, slow aging period of the baseline prepayment curve implicitly captures the impact of prepayment penalties.

Exhibit 9: Baseline Characteristics

Characteristic	Value	Comment
Loan Term	10-Year Model: 10 years 20-year Model: 20 years	Separate baseline prepayment and default curves are used for the 10-year and 20-year programs.
Change in 10-year Treasury Yield since DCPC Origination Date	0	Baseline interest rate environment is unchanged
Pool Age	0	Baseline pool age is 0
Change in Unemployment Rate Relative to Long Term Moving Average	0	Baseline Unemployment Rate equals Long Term Moving Average

Exhibit 10: 20-Year Voluntary Prepayment Baseline Aging Curve

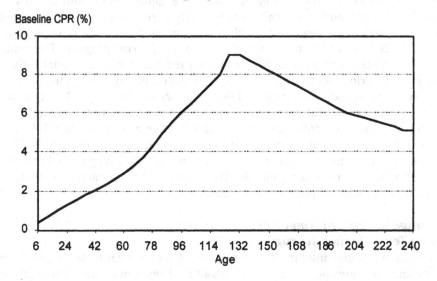

Exhibit 11: 20-Year Non-Voluntary Prepayment Baseline Aging Curve

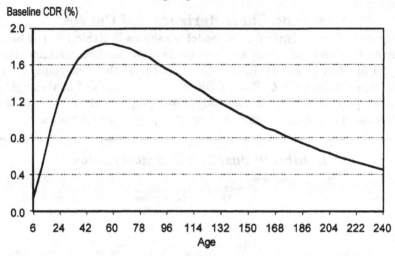

Risk Multipliers

The parameters and risk multipliers for the model are shown in Exhibit 12. The key model findings are explained below.

Interest Rate Spread and Pool Age

The interest rate spread and age pool parameter measures the sensitivity of voluntary prepayments to changes in interest rates. The multipliers for both the 10-year and 20-year programs show that as the penalty period nears an end, the loans become increasingly responsive to changes in interest rates. For example, consider the 200 basis point incentive scenario for the 20-year program. The multiplier of 1.00 at the pool age of 30 months says there is no rate sensitivity early in the penalty period; the multiplier of 1.25 at age 60 (midway through the penalty) shows increasing rate sensitivity; and the multiplier of 1.56 at age 120 (at the end of the period) shows full rate sensitivity. The interpretation of the multiplier of 1.56 is that there is a 56% increase from the baseline expectation in a 200 basis point rally scenario. For example, if the peak baseline expectation is 9.0% CPR, in the 200 basis point rally scenario, that expectation is scaled up to 14.04% CPR. For rising interest rates, the multiplicative inverse of the risk multiplier would be used to scale down the prepayment expectation.

Change in Unemployment Rate Relative to Long-Term Moving Average

The change in unemployment rate relative to the long-term moving average parameter measures the sensitivity of default to changes in economic strength. In this case, economic strength is gauged by the unemployment rate. Using the 20-year program as an example, if the peak baseline default rate expectation is 1.85% CDR, a 10% increase in the unemployment rate from the 5-year moving average would cause that expectation to go to 2.52% CDR (1.36 × 1.85% CDR).

Model Error

One test of the model's efficacy is to compare actual pool factors with in-sample projections of the pool factors. This allows for joint testing of the model's ability to project voluntary and non-voluntary prepayments. Exhibit 13 shows actual and projected pool factors for the 20-year program at various points in time, where individual pool factors are weighted by pool balance and then on a simple arithmetic basis. The in-sample data show minimal differences between the average actual and projected pool factors, as well as small standard deviations between the factors. This holds true even for the 10-year horizon period which, given that the observations for this period are primarily for high premiums, indicates an increased level of robustness for the model.

Exhibit 12: Model Parameters and Multipliers

SBA Voluntary Prepayment Model

Parameter	Risk Pattern	Prepayment Risk Multiplier	
		10-Year Program	20-Year Program
Change in 10-Year	*−100 Basis Points:*		
Treasury Yield since	Pool Age: 30	1.09	1.00
DCPC Origination Date	Pool Age: 60	1.19	1.03
	Pool Age: 120	1.19	1.07
	−200 Basis Points:		
	Pool Age: 30	1.17	1.00
	Pool Age: 60	1.37	1.25
	Pool Age: 120	1.37	1.56
	−300 Basis Points:		
	Pool Age: 30	1.27	1.00
	Pool Age: 60	1.60	1.40
	Pool Age: 120	1.60	1.96
	−400 Basis Points:		
	Pool Age: 30	1.42	1.00
	Pool Age: 60	2.02	1.52
	Pool Age: 120	2.02	2.29

SBA Default Model

Parameter	Risk Pattern	Default Risk Multiplier	
		10-Year Program	20-Year Program
Change in Unemployment Rate Relative to Long Term Average	+10%	1.20	1.36

Exhibit 13: Actual versus Projected Pool Factors for 20-Year SBA Program

Horizon	3 Years	5 Years	10 Years
Weighted Average Actual Factor	0.905	0.788	0.419
Weighted Average Projected Factor	0.902	0.786	0.397
Difference	0.003	0.002	0.022
Standard Deviation	0.024	0.045	0.055
Arithmetic Average Actual Factor	0.906	0.780	0.416
Arithmetic Average Projected Factor	0.902	0.786	0.399
Difference	0.004	−0.006	0.017
Standard Deviation	0.026	0.048	0.055
Amount Outstanding at Horizon ($MM)	3,184.8	1,539.7	1,163.6
Number of Deals	102	78	18

THE BLOOMBERG SBA PRICE/YIELD CALCULATOR: ACCESSING THE MODEL

We conclude this chapter with an illustration how the Merrill Lynch SBA Prepayment and Default Model availability through the SBA Price/Yield calculator on Bloomberg. The screen, shown in Exhibit 14, can be accessed by typing "SBYA Govt Go". This brings up the Price/Yield Calculator where the prepayment and default expectations (vol. CPR and non-vol. CPR, respectively) are provided by the Merrill Lynch SBA Prepayment and Default Model. The user can recognize that the model is being used by the fact that the "Prepay Rate" inputs on the lower left part of the screen are set to zero. The "Aggregate" numbers below these inputs represent the weighted average life equivalents of the vectors of voluntary and non-voluntary prepayment rates projected by the Model. Note that the yield calculation correctly accounts for the passthrough of prepayment penalties to the Certificateholder.

   Exhibit 15 shows the times series of projected prepayments and defaults for the bond shown in Exhibit 14. The model projections are made using the DCPC indicatives and the current economic environment (interest rates and unemployment rates) as inputs. Note that since the DCPC shown is a new issue, there is no prepayment and default history to date. (The prepayment and default history for seasoned bonds are shown in this screen when some history exists.)

   Note that the "Aggregate" numbers in Exhibit 14 provide the weighted average life equivalents of the vectors of voluntary ("vol.") and non-voluntary ("non-vol.") CPRs. In Exhibit 16, we provide these equivalents for a broad range of DCPC's. These equivalents provide insight into the impact of seasoning, prepayment penalties and coupon in determining the aggregate prepayment expectation.

Exhibit 14: Bloomberg SBA Price/Yield Calculator with Merrill Lynch SBA Prepayment and Default Model Inputs

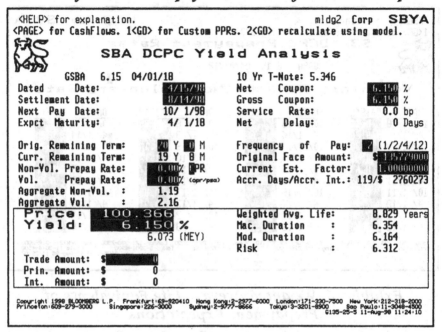

Exhibit 15: Merrill Lynch SBA Model Projections of Voluntary and Non-Voluntary Prepayment Rates
(Page 1)

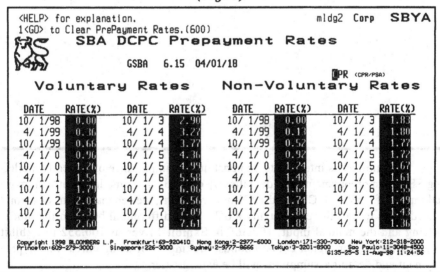

Exhibit 15 (Continued)
(Page 2)

```
<HELP> for explanation.                                mldg2  Corp   SBYA
1<GO> to Clear PrePayment Rates.(600)
            SBA DCPC Prepayment Rates

               GSBA   6.15  04/01/18
                                                   CPR  (CPR/PSA)
   Voluntary  Rates            Non-Voluntary  Rates

  DATE   RATE(%)   DATE   RATE(%)     DATE   RATE(%)   DATE   RATE(%)
 10/ 1/ 8  8.13   10/ 1/13  6.94     10/ 1/ 8  1.30   10/ 1/13  0.78
  4/ 1/ 9  9.20    4/ 1/14  6.66      4/ 1/ 9  1.24    4/ 1/14  0.74
 10/ 1/ 9  9.20   10/ 1/14  6.38     10/ 1/ 9  1.18   10/ 1/14  0.70
  4/ 1/10  8.91    4/ 1/15  6.09      4/ 1/10  1.12    4/ 1/15  0.66
 10/ 1/10  8.63   10/ 1/15  5.95     10/ 1/10  1.07   10/ 1/15  0.63
  4/ 1/11  8.35    4/ 1/16  5.81      4/ 1/11  1.02    4/ 1/16  0.59
 10/ 1/11  8.07   10/ 1/16  5.66     10/ 1/11  0.96   10/ 1/16  0.56
  4/ 1/12  7.79    4/ 1/17  5.52      4/ 1/12  0.91    4/ 1/17  0.53
 10/ 1/12  7.50   10/ 1/17  5.38     10/ 1/12  0.87   10/ 1/17  0.50
  4/ 1/13  7.22    4/ 1/18  5.24      4/ 1/13  0.82    4/ 1/18  0.48

Copyright 1998 BLOOMBERG L.P.  Frankfurt:69-920410  Hong Kong:2-2977-6000  London:171-330-7500  New York:212-318-2000
Princeton:609-279-3000  Singapore:226-3000   Sydney:2-9777-8666   Tokyo:3-3201-8900   Sao Paulo:11-3048-4500
                                                             G135-25-5 11-Aug-98 11:25:07
```

Exhibit 16: Weighted Average Life Equivalents of Prepayment Expectations

DCPC	Program	June 1998 Factor	Voluntary CPR	Non-Voluntary CPR	WAL
5.85 04/03	10-year	0.487	10.18	2.07	2.114
6.20 11/05	10-year	0.745	4.78	2.49	3.325
6.80 03/07	10-year	0.902	2.94	2.27	3.931
7.50 07/04	10-year	0.612	9.70	2.27	2.721
5.90 09/13	20-year	0.761	4.74	1.69	6.104
6.10 07/18	20-year	1.000	2.15	1.19	9.160
6.80 06/15	20-year	0.862	3.92	1.71	7.140
7.50 04/17	20-year	0.970	2.86	1.46	8.254
8.00 07/14	20-year	0.798	6.07	1.70	6.250
8.75 11/06	20-year	0.262	15.38	1.04	3.088
9.75 06/07	20-year	0.332	19.54	1.09	2.858
10.00 05/09	20-year	0.395	17.80	1.28	3.232

Exhibit 17 is intended to demonstrate the importance of correctly modeling SBA loan prepayments and defaults. By overriding the model input with manual inputs of 2.5% vol. CPR and 1.5% non-vol. CPR, we see that, even for a bond priced close to par, there is roughly a 6/32 price differential between the model pricing and the manual input (100.366 in Exhibit 14 versus 100.552 in Exhibit 17). Obviously, for higher coupon bonds, the impact of using unreasonable prepayment and default assumptions will be even greater.

Exhibit 17: Bloomberg SBA Price/Yield Calculator with Manual Inputs

```
<HELP> for explanation.                                    mldg2  Corp   SBYA
<PAGE> for CashFlows. 1<GO> for Custom PPRs. 2<GO> recalculate using model.

            SBA  DCPC  Yield  Analysis

       GSBA   6.15  04/01/18        10 Yr T-Note: 5.346
  Dated      Date:        4/15/98    Net    Coupon:        6.150 %
  Settlement Date:        8/14/98    Gross  Coupon:        6.150 %
  Next Pay Date:         10/ 1/98    Service  Rate:         0.0 bp
  Expct Maturity:         4/ 1/18    Net    Delay:           0 Days

  Orig. Remaining Term:   20 Y  0 M  Frequency   of   Pay:  2 (1/2/4/12)
  Curr. Remaining Term:   19 Y  8 M  Original Face Amount:  $ 135779000
  Non-Vol. Prepay Rate:   1.50% CPR  Current  Est.  Factor:    1.00000000
  Vol.     Prepay Rate:   2.50% (cpr/psa)  Accr. Days/Accr. Int.: 119/$  2760273
  Aggregate Non-Vol.  :    1.50
  Aggregate Vol.      :    2.50

    Price:  100.552            Weighted Avg. Life:      8.947 Years
    Yield:    6.150 %          Mac. Duration     :      6.263
              6.073 (MEY)      Mod. Duration     :      6.076
                               Risk              :      6.233
  Trade Amount:  $         0
  Prin. Amount:  $         0
  Int.  Amount:  $         0

Copyright 1998 BLOOMBERG L.P.  Frankfurt:69-920410  Hong Kong:2-2977-6000  London:171-330-7500  New York:212-318-2000
Princeton:609-279-3000    Singapore:226-3000    Sydney:2-9777-8666    Tokyo:3-3201-8900    Sao Paulo:11-3048-4500
                                                                      G135-25-5 11-Aug-98 11:25:36
```

Chapter 9

Franchise Loan Securitization

James S. Anderson
Managing Director
Asset-Backed Research
First Union Securities, Inc.

Kristina L. Clark
Associate
Fixed-Income Research
First Union Securities, Inc.

INTRODUCTION

It is impossible to drive down any major thoroughfare and not see a multitude of retail franchises. One-stop convenience shopping has society addicted to and dependent on fast and reliable products and services. Franchise industry sales are expected to account for about $1 trillion by 2000. Exponential growth of this industry has fueled increasing capital needs. Originally, small banks and thrift institutions dominated the franchise lending industry by capitalizing on their knowledge of local economies and preexisting relationships. However, throughout the 1980s and early 1990s, as banks and thrifts began merging into larger entities, lending to smaller obligors became a less important business; franchise lending fell below their radar. The increasing need for capital by franchise operators and the withdrawal of larger lending institutions opened the door for specialty finance companies to supply funding to this industry.

The growth of the franchise industry and the increasing number of loans made to franchisees created pools of collateralized loans prime for securitization. Growing investor awareness and demand support the success and rising popularity of franchise loan securitization in today's markets. As an asset class, franchise loans exhibit stable average lives, predictable cash flows, and low prepayments. Yield maintenance and significant prepayment penalties are structural features that enhance the securities created from this collateral. Securitizations are structured with average lives of 5, 7, and 10 years or longer for subordinated pieces. Indeed, it may appear franchise loan securities are similar to commercial mortgage-backed securities (CMBS) and in many ways this is true. However, the underlying collateral differs. The collateral supporting CMBS is typically a first lien mortgage, whereas the underlying collateral for a franchise loan security is a combination of the property value (land, buildings, and equipment) and the value of the underlying business — the value of the cash flow.

187

The concept of franchising emerged out of a need to grow a retail network in an affordable way while mitigating risk through economies of scale. The first franchises were quick-service restaurants (QSRs), fast-food eateries that provided convenience, variety, and reliability. Consumer demand for uniform stores and quick service soon flowed into other retail segments, and the industry expanded to include gas stations, auto service centers, video rental stores, convenience stores, car washes, golf-related businesses, and funeral homes. Within the various franchise business segments, there are two primary franchise templates:

- Business format franchising: The franchisee assumes the franchisor's names and logos as well as its preset processes and methodologies.

- Product/name franchising: The franchisee assumes the franchisor's names and logos but is free to run the unit or units.

At business format franchises, customers can expect the same products, services, and management styles. The most obvious example is a QSR. For example, at any Burger King, customers are certain they will receive basically the same hamburger and services in a consistent environment.

Product/name franchises differ from each other because owners have the right to run the business according to personal preferences. An owner typically purchases this kind of franchise for brand recognition, product continuity, and the freedom to operate outside of the franchisor's control. Common examples are service stations and car dealerships. Customers entering any Cadillac dealership can find or order the same car. Prices, facility layout, style and ancillary services, however, may vary from dealership to dealership.

Given the business enterprise valuation associated with franchise loans, the most important factor to consider is the obligor's ability to generate sufficient cash flow to meet the loan obligations. Supporting the obligor's effort is the strength of the concept (i.e., a strong obligor implies both strong cash flows and a strong brand). After a loan is initiated and placed in a pool, the investor is concerned with the cash flow and security of the loan. Underwriters use multiple tools to gauge an obligor, and investors should be familiar with these measurements when analyzing potential franchise loan investments.

FRAMEWORK FOR RISK ASSESSMENT

Multiple levels of analysis are associated with franchise loans: analysis of the strength of the brand or concept; analysis of the franchise owner on multiple levels, both consolidated and at the unit level; and analysis of the franchisor. An obligor managing multiple units usually has an established credit history and an easily tracked record of performance. The obligor/franchisee is judged based on individual unit(s) performance, ability to repay the loan and the collateral supporting the loan. This obligor may not have publicly documented historical performance and is almost always unrated, so analysis requires more in-depth research for accurate credit profiling.

As with any investment, the specific risks associated with the issue and the characteristics of the cash flow are key analytical components when determining investor suitability. There is always a certain amount of risk inherent in using historical information to predict future probabilities. This risk is not unique to franchise lending. The concepts characteristic of franchise lending discussed in this chapter are as follows:

- concept strength
- obligor experience
- fixed-charge coverage ratio (FCCR)
- loan-to-value (LTV) ratio
- servicing capabilities of the underwriter (or outside servicing firm)

Although the obligor, as the recipient of the loan and the party ultimately responsible for repayment, is the focal point in rating an issue, the credit criteria and reputation of the lender must also be considered. Because the lender actually assesses the obligor and the associated collateral, the lender's processes, formulas and methodologies should be reviewed. This party has the responsibility to properly underwrite the loan and, in many cases, to service it. The ability to accurately monitor the loan's progress and to solve distressed situations contribute to a securitization's success.

CONCEPT STRENGTH

Part of what makes a Burger King franchise so marketable is the recognition of its name. Consumers appreciate the consistency of the brand, products, and atmosphere. Brand-name recognition and associated customer loyalty affect the viability of a franchise, and this is reflected in store performance. A strong concept has extensive geographic presence, a history of profitability, extensive advertising, and is well situated for continuing success. Maintaining 500 units or generating $500 million in annual sales are general guidelines for designating a strong concept in the quick-service sector. Such franchises benefit from established brand names, logos, products, supplier relationships, and other economies of scale. As long as the brand maintains a solid reputation and the location of the franchise unit is in a medium to high traffic area with easy access, the cash flow of the franchise unit is somewhat sheltered from volatility.

Having a strong concept helps to ensure that an operator will follow the accepted way of doing business. In addition to franchisor intervention, other franchisees associated with the same brand name (and located within the same area) will act as a secondary check if one operator's business is not up to concept standards. For instance, if service is poor at one of four Burger Kings run by different operators, the other three franchisees have a vested interest in pressuring the faltering operator to improve. If customers boycott the subpar Burger King, they may boycott the others, and this possibility is enough to prompt franchisees to set up checks and balances in tandem with those established by Burger King Corp.

National marketing and advertising are functions of the franchisor. The higher the sales in the concept the more the franchisor can spend on these functions. A strong concept can introduce new products with greater ease. The franchise operator does not have to shoulder this part of the business and can instead spend more of its effort on local advertising, streamlining operations and maximizing cash flow.

Concept tiering, a method of segregating brands by concept strength, is used by underwriters and rating agencies. Concept revenue, market share, geographic dominance, advertising, and market penetration are all important in judging the strength of a concept. A franchisee in a strong concept will typically generate significant cash flow during a strong as well as a weak economy. Because this asset class is not as prone to a recessionary environment as consumer products, franchise loans provide investors a good portfolio hedge. Examples of the top three tiers within the restaurant are shown in Exhibit 1 and within energy concepts in Exhibit 2.

OBLIGOR EXPERIENCE

Operational experience is a leading indicator of the ability to run units and generate sufficient cash flow to repay indebtedness. The obligor helps sustain the strength of the concept by providing fast service and quality products and by maintaining efficient operations. To ensure the obligor is creditworthy, the underwriters will conduct site visits and perform extensive financial due diligence.

Exhibit 1: Restaurant Concept Tiers

Tier 1	Tier 2	Tier 3	
McDonald's	TGI Friday's	Dairy Queen	Domino's
Burger King	Hardee's	Jack in the Box	Perkins
Wendy's	Golden Corral	Long John Silver's	IHOP
Pizza Hut	Denny's	Arby's	Taco Cabana
Taco Bell	Carl's Jr.	Sonic	Tony Roma's
KFC	Dunkin' Donuts	Bojangles'	Papa John's
Applebee's		Houlihan's	Ruby Tuesday
		Little Caesar's	Popeye's/Church's

Source: Fitch IBCA and First Union Securities, Inc.

Exhibit 2: Energy Concept Tiers

Tier 1	Tier 2	Tier 3
Exxon	Coastal	Quaker
Mobil	Diamond/Ultramar	Sinclair
Texaco	Tosco	USA Petroleum
Chevron	Sun	Beacon
Amoco	Amerada Hess	Independent/Private Label
Shell	Unocal	
Conoco	FINA	
Arco	MAPCO	
Phillips/Phillips 66	Total	
Marathon	Pennzoil	
Ashland	Murphy's	
Citgo	Kerr McGee	
Sunoco		
Gulf		

Source: Fitch IBCA and First Union Securities, Inc.

Site visits are made to assess the property value as well as the capital expenditures necessary over the next several years. Location plays an important role in determining customer flow and profitability. If the unit is not easily accessible to the public, customers will switch to a more convenient franchise and the cash flow underlying the loan will tend to decrease. Quality and age of equipment and facility maintenance must be assessed. If a building or property is outdated or not well maintained, a perceived decrease in quality may be associated with the operation, and customers may choose a competitor's franchise.

Financial due diligence is important in determining the obligor's ability to repay the loan obligations. This profiling incorporates earnings analysis, credit history checks, and assessing collateral offered as security for the loan. It is industry standard to obtain earnings statements reflecting the three years of historical unit/obligor performance. Outside debt obligations and lien positions on the collateral are further components determining the obligor's financial strength. In addition to lender due diligence, a third-party valuation firm is typically introduced to verify unit level cash flow and provide a valuation for the units offered as collateral for the loan request.

FIXED-CHARGE COVERAGE RATIO (FCCR)

FCCR is a formula designed to measure the leverage at a unit and company level by comparing pre-occupancy cash flow to debt service plus fixed occupancy costs. Because it is essentially a debt-service ratio, it is a main component in the financial due diligence. FCCR measures the obligor's ability to handle disruptions in cash flow based on its leverage position and occupancy costs.

Exhibit 3: FCCR Example

A higher volume unit typically has a higher POCF.
In this example, it is 24% for the higher compared with 20% for the lower.

	High Volume		Low Volume	
Unit Sales	1,000,000	900,000	700,000	600,000
POCF	240,000	216,000	140,000	120,000
Fixed Charges	120,000	120,000	70,000	70,000
	↓	↓	↓	↓
	(2:1)	(1.8:1)	(2:1)	(1.7:1)

POCF: Pre-occupancy cash flow.

Source: First Union Securities, Inc.

Lenders generally calculate FCCRs from income statements prepared according to generally accepted accounting principles (GAAP). The actual ratio compares an entity's historical pre-occupancy cash flow (POCF) to its historical fixed occupancy costs and debt service. The result is a measure of the cushion between operating cash flow and cost structure. This is important in determining default potential and, as such, is a quantitative indication of a borrower's ability to repay the loan.

The calculation of FCCR from lender to lender is relatively standard, however, there is the opportunity for subjectivity when allocating overhead addbacks and nonrecurring expenses. Typical nonrecurring expenses include those associated with expensing capital equipment, start-up costs, and nonrecurring fees. FCCR is the most important factor in projecting a borrower's ability to repay a loan. A common definition is as follows:

$$\frac{\text{Pretax operating income + Interest expense + Depreciation + Amortization + Rent + Nonrecurring expenses}}{\text{Fixed costs(i.e., Rent + Fixed lease obligations + Principal + Interest payments)}}$$

FCCR is calculated on multiple levels and generally appears as consolidated and unit FCCR. Both are used in assessing the default probability of the subject entity. A company may have multiple franchise lending relationships, and a combination of the aggregate default risks is measured using a consolidated FCCR. Unit FCCR is derived from the operations of a single store and is calculated for each loan in a securitized pool.

FCCR measures the ability to withstand volatility of the underlying cash flow and the ability to continue to service outstanding debt obligations. It is not enough to base a loan solely on FCCR because a strong and a weak obligor can have the same FCCR, but their ability to tolerate earnings volatility differs. For example, even if a franchise with average annual sales of $1 million and a franchise with average annual sales of $700,000 have the same unit level FCCR, they will be affected differently by a $100,000 decrease in sales. Keeping in mind that their respective fixed costs remain the same, the lower volume unit's FCCR will decrease by more than the higher volume unit's FCCR (see Exhibit 3).

LOAN-TO-VALUE (LTV) RATIO

LTV is one of the key tools used by lenders to evaluate and underwrite franchise loans. The ratio helps investors quantify the value of a unit as a going concern if a willing buyer and seller came to terms on a certain date. LTVs of franchise loans are formulated based on real estate value and business enterprise value. Real estate value is the market value of the property, utilizing the income approach to valuation, used to partially collateralize the loan. The business enterprise value is the value of cash flow from operations. Total value of a property is the combination of the two.

The type of collateral supporting a franchise loan determines the loan amount and the LTV. The more collateral associated with a transaction leads to a higher appraised value, which allows a borrower to request a higher loan amount. Franchise loan collateral appears as either a fee-simple, ground lease or enterprise loan.

- *Fee-simple loans:* These real estate-based loans require a first mortgage on the property; a first lien position on furniture, fixtures, and equipment (FF&E); and title insurance. A fee property includes real estate value (both the land and the building) that can be remarketed apart from the value of the underlying business. Should a default occur, this collateral holds the greatest recovery potential and, as a result, LTVs for loans backed by this collateral are generally around 70%.

- *Ground lease loans:* These loans involve ownership of the improvements on leased land and require assignment of that land lease. A first lien position on the building, the FF&E, and title insurance are required. Similar to a fee-simple collateral loan, this loan includes the value of the building, which can be remarketed apart from the value of the underlying business. LTVs for loans backed by this collateral are generally 65%–70%.

- *Enterprise loans:* These loans are typically divided into two types:
  - *Enterprise:* Collateral includes a first lien position on the FF&E, an estoppel that allows for filing a leasehold mortgage, and a loan term equal to or less than the term of the remaining lease. The lender typically has notice of default and right-to-cure provisions allowing for some control of the property in a default situation. LTV for loans backed by enterprise are typically 65%.
  - *Equipment/space lease:* Full estoppel and leasehold mortgage are unattainable and result in less than full control of the property. The collateral is limited to UCC-1 financing statements on the FF&E, cross-security, and personal guarantees. In these cases, maximum LTV is generally 50%.

If a franchisee becomes distressed, there are a multitude of options to work out the situation. Because the franchisor has a vested interest in maintaining the location, it will usually work with the lender or servicer to remedy the situation. If a lender holds tangible collateral, it has the option to liquidate the property, sell the property to another franchisee or reconstruct the property for alternative use. In addition, the lender has the option, with the approval of the franchisor, to replace the obligor with another approved franchisee willing to assume the loan.

A lender who holds collateral only in the form of business value is limited to remedying a default situation by finding another operator to fill the defaulting operator's position. The lender would prefer that the obligor be a part of a strong concept because it becomes easier to find another operator willing to assume the loan.

In a distressed situation, real estate and business values are not affected simultaneously or to the same degree. A holder of soft collateral will find it more difficult to recover full loan value than would a holder of hard real estate collateral. If sales begin to deteriorate, an operation's cash flow decreases; less money is coming in but the same amount of money is allocated to fixed costs. Business value tends to erode before real estate value. Following this logic, loans backed primarily by business value, such as enterprise and equipment/space lease loans, typically are underwritten to a lower LTV than fee-simple or ground lease loans.

SERVICING

After gaining confidence in the lender's ability to properly underwrite a franchise loan, investors must analyze the lender's, or outside servicing firm's, ability to service it. While the franchisee is making payments on a current basis, servicing functions are not different from those of other asset classes. When a default or distressed situation occurs, however, the servicer takes on an increased role — that of facilitator. Because franchise loans are underwritten based on the cash flow of the business, liquidation is rarely the optimal solution to a default situation. A servicer has the option to require additional collateral or to restructure the loan so the obligor has less trouble meeting the obligation. As mentioned previously, the servicer, realizing the value of the operation, has the option to continue to capitalize on the cash flow of the franchise by bringing in a new operator to assume the loan and the business.

Servicing functions inherent in franchise loans include collecting timely payments, making sure collateral is insured, reporting periodically on pool performance, advancing principal and interest and working out potential and existing default situations. If a servicer does not properly monitor its post-underwriting duties, the integrity of the loan and the associated securitization could be compromised. Accurate, up-to-date computing capabilities, experienced and knowledgeable employees, and a procedure for pursuing delinquent accounts are also important for successful servicing.

FRANCHISE LOAN SECURITIZATION VOLUME

Franchise securitization volume has grown tremendously from $175 million in 1995 to $3.1 billion in 1998. Franchise loan securitization is a growing segment of the ABS market. The securitization of franchise loans has evolved into a viable part of the fixed-income market. Franchise loan securitization began in 1991 with Franchise Mortgage Acceptance Corp.'s (FMAC) FLRT 1991-A transaction. From 1991 through 1998, there were 36 franchise loan securitizations.

As franchise securitization volume has grown, its percentage of the *private* ABS industry has also increased. Franchise securitizations accounted for about 7% of total private ABS issuance in 1998 compared with only about 1% in 1993.

INDUSTRY OVERVIEWS

The key drivers of the franchise loan industry are the trends toward convenience, consolidation, diversification, and strategic positioning at the borrower level. Consumers are demanding quicker service, geographic proximity, and variety as lifestyles in the United States become faster paced. Operating efficiencies and cost pressures have led to market consolidation and an increase in multiunit operators. The two most prominent industries are the food service industry and the convenience store and petroleum marketing industry, both significant to gross domestic product (GDP).

Food Service Industry

According to the U.S. Department of Commerce, the food service industry is one of the largest sectors of the nation's economy. The industry generated an estimated $321 billion of revenue in 1997, representing more than 4% of GDP. The industry grew at an inflation-adjusted rate of 1.7% during 1997 versus a 2.5% increase in GDP. According to the National Restaurant Association (NRA), continued sales growth in the food service industry is driven by new development propelled, in part, by consumers' sustained appreciation for convenient, reasonably priced, and good-tasting food.

The food service industry is divided into three major segments: commercial, industrial, and military. The commercial segment includes full-service (i.e., casual dining) and fast-food restaurants, cafeteria/buffet restaurants, social caterers, ice-cream/yogurt stores, food contractors, and hotel/motel restaurants. The institutional segment includes colleges, universities, and hospitals, and the military segment includes the armed services.

Convenience Store and Petroleum Marketing Industry

The convenience store (c-store) and petroleum marketing industry can be defined as those retailers primarily engaged in the retail sale of motor fuel (gasoline) and/or convenience products. This industry is estimated to be $215 billion in size, which is 2.7% of GDP. The industry total includes c-store merchandise, c-stores selling gasoline, gasoline sold apart from c-stores, and automotive services sold at gasoline stations. Five factors have driven the growth of the c-store and petroleum marketing industry: (1) higher disposable personal income, (2) greater desire for convenience, (3) increased travel, (4) more vehicles on the road, and (5) industry trends designed to boost c-store demand.

The c-store and petroleum marketing industry has gone through several recent changes, including image improvements, the emergence of new brand names, a wider variety of ancillary services, and technology improvements to enhance service. Changing oil prices, new facility layouts, and consolidation among major oil companies are evolving factors affecting this industry.

MAJOR FRANCHISE SECURITIZATION PARTICIPANTS

The national lenders originating and securitizing in the franchise lending industry include AMRESCO Commercial Lending Corp. (ACLC), Atherton Group Inc., CNL Group, Inc., Franchise Finance Corp. of America (FFCA), Franchise Mortgage Acceptance Corp. (FMAC), and Peachtree Franchise Finance LLC (PFF).

AMRESCO Commercial Lending Corp. (ACLC)

Following the acquisition of Commercial Lending Corp. in 1997, ACLC became the franchise finance unit of AMRESCO, Inc. ACLC provides long-term, fixed- and floating-rate financing to franchisees, small businesses, equipment owners, and small commercial real estate owners. ACLC also originates, securitizes, and services cash-flow-based loans to franchise and small business owners. At the time of acquisition, ACLC was focused on lending to fast-food restaurants, casual dining restaurants, and automotive service providers. Since the acquisition, ACLC has approved a number of new restaurant concepts for its lending program as well as hotels, motels, and truck stops. ACLC has completed three securitizations totaling approximately $395 million. Volume for AMRESCO reached a record level in 1998 with $400 million in franchise and business lending, up 43% over 1997.

Atherton Group Inc.

Based in San Francisco, Atherton Group is a specialty commercial finance company that provides loans to experienced multistore operators of established national and regional franchises. Among the 50 franchises the lender accepts into its programs are fast-food restaurants (Burger King and Taco Bell), casual dining restaurants (Denny's), specialty retail companies (Blockbuster and Jiffy Lube), and retail gas stations (Amoco). Atherton originates loan products through 12 locations serving eight regions, including Atlanta, Chicago, Denver, Greenwich, Los Angeles, Minneapolis, San Francisco, and Seattle. Financing programs include debt refinancing, acquisition of existing units, new store construction, real estate acquisitions, equipment purchases, and store improvements.

CNL Group, Inc.

CNL Group is a privately held real estate investment, finance, advisory, and development company with headquarters in Florida. Founded in 1973, CNL owns and manages more than $2.8 billion in commercial real estate properties, primarily composed of more than 1,800 freestanding, net lease properties in 48 states (as of December 1998). CNL provides full-service financing to franchisors and franchisees through sale/leaseback transactions, permanent and construction lending, and advisory services. CNL's restaurant properties consist of sale/leaseback transactions and debt obligations. In sale/leaseback transactions, CNL buys the property, building, and equipment and leases the assets to a franchisor (who may sublease to a franchisee) or a franchisee. Through its Restaurant and Financial Services Group, CNL is one of the largest providers of sale/leaseback financing, construction and permanent debt, and venture capital to the franchise restaurant industry. In 1998, CNL originated in excess of $275 million of restaurant loans and completed its first securitization. CNL is expected to come to market with its second securitization in mid-1999.

Exhibit 4 summarizes a 1998 deal by CNL.

Franchise Finance Corp. of America (FFCA)

Based in Scottsdale, Ariz., FFCA is one of the nation's leading financing sources for chain restaurants, convenience stores, and automotive parts retailers. FFCA provides mortgage and equipment loans, long-term real estate leases, construction and acquisition financing, and other custom financing solutions to multiunit operators. As of Sept. 30, 1998, FFCA had investments in more than 3,300 properties (including interests in securitized loans) throughout North America. The company's portfolio includes some of the nation's leading chains, including Applebee's, Burger King, Checker Auto Parts, Circle K, Citgo, Taco Bell, Texaco, Valvoline Instant Oil Change, and Wendy's. Loan volume at year-end 1998 reached $272 million compared with $191 million in 1997.

Exhibit 5 summarizes a 1998 deal by FFCA.

Franchise Mortgage Acceptance Corp. (FMAC)

Based in Los Angeles, FMAC, a leading provider of specialty financing, pioneered the market of franchise restaurant lending through its restaurant and equipment finance groups. In 1996, the company formed the Golf Finance Group, expanding its lending activities to include golf-related businesses. In 1997, FMAC added the Energy Finance Group to fund service stations, truck stops, convenience stores, lube centers, car washes, golf courses, and automotive service retailers. That same year, it formed the Funeral Finance Group to service funeral home and cemetery owners. FMAC has participated in 13 securitizations of pooled loans totaling more than $2.1 billion. Loan origination volume reached $2.14 billion by the end of 1998.

Exhibits 6 and 7 show two deals issued in 1998 by FMAC.

Exhibit 4: Notable Franchise Securitization Deal — CNL 1998-1

Public ABS Issuances: 1

Lead Manager: Merrill Lynch

Date of Issuance: Aug. 7, 1998

Pricing Speed (CPR): 0%

Issuance Amount: $245.19 million

Rating Agencies: DCR/Fitch/Moody's

Collateral Summary

Loan Type	FS	51.2%
	GL	25.5%
	Ent	23.3%
Industry Type	Rest	100.0%
State Concentration	FL	13.7%
	PA	12.2%
	CA	8.9%
Wt. Avg. Orig. Term		183 months
Wt. Avg. Rem. Term		176 months
Avg. Contract Balance		1,716,209
Wt. Avg. Unit FCCR		1.57×
Wt. Avg. Business FCCR		NA

Securities Summary	A-1a	A-1b	A-2a	A-2b	IO-1	IO-2	B-1	B-2	C-1
Size ($ million)	73.23	43.25	54.00	28.91	143.24	101.96	7.87	5.60	9.44
WAL (years)	5.0	10.5	4.5	10.1	8.2	7.6	12.4	12.1	13.0
Window (months)	104	144	99	141	168	164	151	148	159
Rating	AAA	AAA	AAA	AAA	AAA	AAA	AA	AA	A
Spread (bps)	80	110	61	64	530	10,161	125	89	145
Enhancement	26.0%	26.0%	26.0%	26.0%	26.0%	26.0%	21.0%	21.0%	15.0%

Securities Summary	C-2	D-1	D-2	E-1	E-2	F-1	F-2	G-1	G-2	H-1	H-2
Size ($ million)	6.72	6.30	4.48	3.15	2.24	2.24	2.24	2.24	2.24	2.24	2.24
WAL (years)	12.8	13.6	13.3	14.0	13.7	14.2	13.9	14.5	14.3	16.3	16.4
Window (months)	156	164	161	168	164	171	166	175	176	225	222
Rating	A	BBB+	BBB+	BBB-	BBB-	BB	BB	B	B	NR	NR
Spread (bps)	110	180	146	220	187	325	295	550	529	937	936
Enhancement	15.0%	11.0%	11.0%	9.0%	9.0%	7.5%	7.5%	5.5%	5.5%	NA	NA

Note: Shading denotes floating-rate tranches for the CNL 1998-1 transaction.

CPR: Constant prepayment rate; FCCR: Fixed-charge coverage ratio; WAL: Weighted average life.

Source: First Union Securities, Inc.

Exhibit 5: Notable Franchise Securitization Deal— FFCA 1998-1

Public ABS Issuances: 3   Date of Issuance: May 7, 1998
Lead Manager: MSDW   Pricing Speed (CPR): 5%

Issuance Amount: $335.33 million
Rating Agencies: Moody's/Fitch/DCR

Collateral Summary

Loan Type		NA
Industry Type	Rest	51.8%
	C&G	44.8%
	Auto	3.4%
State Concentration	TX	17.9%
	NC	9.7%
	IL	7.9%
Wt. Avg. Orig. Term		231 months
Wt. Avg. Rem. Term		227 months
Avg. Contract Balance		600,956
Wt. Avg. Unit FCCR		1.94×
Wt. Avg. Business FCCR		NA

Securities Summary	A-1A	A-1B	A-2A	A-2B	B-1	B-2	C-1	C-2	D-1	D-2	IO
Size ($ million)	51.00	151.90	32.00	19.96	16.02	4.10	9.34	2.39	14.68	3.76	242.94
WAL (years)	2.9	10.0	3.0	9.5	15.9	13.8	17.0	15.1	18.0	16.3	9.6
Window (months)											
Rating	AAA	AAA	AAA	AAA	AA	AA	A	A	BBB	BBB	AAA
Spread (bps)											
Enhancement	24.0%	24.0%	24.0%	24.0%	18.0%	18.0%	14.5%	14.5%	9.0%	9.0%	NA

CPR: Constant prepayment rate; FCCR: Fixed-charge coverage ratio; WAL: Weighted average life.
Source: First Union Securities, Inc.

Peachtree Franchise Finance LLC (PFF)

Based in Atlanta, Ga., PFF began operations in April 1998 as a specialty commercial finance company engaged in originating, securitizing, and servicing franchise restaurant loans. To date, the company has funded almost $200 million in this sector. PFF has already funded loans in 12 concepts. The company has origination offices in New York and Chicago and plans to add origination capacity in the coming year. Senior management has more than 30 years direct experience in the franchise lending arena. The company also has a capital markets team with Wall Street experience. PFF plans to complete its first securitization in the spring of 1999.

Exhibit 6: Notable Franchise Securitization Deal—
FMAC 1998-A

Public ABS Issuances: 4   Date of Issuance: March 13, 1998
Lead Manager: Morgan Stanley   Pricing Speed (CPR): 0%

Issuance Amount: $201.75 million
Rating Agencies: DCR/Fitch/S& P

Collateral Summary

Loan Type	FS	45.5%
	GL	8.5%
	Ent	46.0%
Industry Type	Rest	56%
	Energy	44%
State Concentration	NC	20%
	TN	12%
Wt. Avg. Orig. Term		200 months
Wt. Avg. Rem. Term		199 months
Avg. Contract Balance		752,795
Wt. Avg. Unit FCCR		1.40×
Wt. Avg. Business FCCR		NA

Securities Summary	A-1	B	C	D	E	F	Certs.	Reserve
Size ($ million)	137.19	14.12	14.12	12.11	10.09	4.04	10.09	1.01
WAL (years)	7.8	13.7	14.5	15.9	17.5	18.5	19.4	
Window (months)	160	170	180	202	219	225	240	
Rating	AAA	AA	A	BBB	BB	B	NR	
Spread (bps)	85	115	140	185	325	590	0	
Enhancement	32.0%	25.0%	18.0%	12.0%	7.0%	5.0%	0.0%	

CPR: Constant prepayment rate; FCCR: Fixed-charge coverage ratio; WAL: Weighted average life.
Source: First Union Securities, Inc.

CONCLUSION

The strength of the franchise industry in the United States and globally is evidenced by growing sales, concept expansion, and low default rates. This growth, coupled with investor demand, will continue to fuel the franchise loan securitization market. Although franchise loan ABS have been in existence since 1991, the asset class has grown significantly in the past three years. At year-end 1998, franchise loan securitization volume topped $3 billion, a 1,657% increase over year-end 1995. Low prepayments, low defaults, and attractive spreads support this growth and make franchise loans attractive to investors looking for an alternative to investing in more traditional investment vehicles such as corporate issues or CMBS.

Exhibit 7: Notable Franchise Securitization Deal— FMAC 1998-D

Public ABS Issuances: 7   Date of Issuance: Dec. 7, 1998
Lead Manager: CSFB   Pricing Speed (CPR): 0%

Issuance Amount: $275. 84 million
Rating Agencies: DCR/S&P/Moody's/Fitch

Collateral Summary

Loan Type	FS	80.5%
	Ent	11.4%
	GL	8.2%
Industry Type	Rest	52.5%
	Energy	32.6%
	Funeral	14.9%
State Concentration	TX	18.6%
	GA	6. 7%
Wt. Avg. Orig. Term		
Wt. Avg. Rem. Term		196 months
Avg. Contract Balance		916,401
Wt. Avg. Unit FCCR		1. 42×
Wt. Avg. Business FCCR		1. 59×

Security Summary	A-1	A-2	A-3	Certs.
Size ($ million)	71.49	65.49	134.72	4.14
WAL (years)	3.0	6.9	11.3	14.1
Window (months)	1/99-3/04	3/04-7/07	7/07-1/13	1/13-2/13
Rating	AAA/Aaa	AAA/Aaa	AAA/Aaa	NR
Spread (bps)	135	160	190	0

Enhancement by Financial Securities Assurance, Inc. (FSA)

CPR: Constant prepayment rate; FCCR: Fixed-charge coverage ratio; WAL: Weighted average life.
Source: First Union Securities, Inc.

Chapter 10

Student Loan Floaters

Thomas Zimmerman
Senior Vice President
Mortgage Strategy Group
PaineWebber

INTRODUCTION

Structures on student loan floaters have experienced more than the usual amount of change over the past several years. The reason for this is quite simple. The underlying collateral — student loans — is exclusively indexed to 3-month Treasury-bills, while a large percentage of securities are issued as LIBOR floaters. This creates an inherent mismatch between the collateral and the securities. (Recently, the index for special allowance payments (SAP) to lenders was changed from T-bills to commercial paper (CP), but it will be several years before that significantly impacts student loan securities.)

Issuers have dealt with the mismatch in a variety of ways. Some issued T-bill floaters which eliminates the mismatch, others issued hedged or unhedged LIBOR floaters, while others switched back and forth between the two. Recently, some have issued both Treasury and LIBOR floaters in the same transaction. Also in conjunction with the choice of index, issuers have incorporated a variety of basis swaps and/or have bought cap protection from third parties, while some have used internal structures to deal with the risk.

The need to deal with the mismatch and cap risk in student loan securitizations has escalated in recent years with the increased volatility in the Treasury and swap markets. Because of this, several issuers have once again modified their structures. In this chapter we review some of these recent innovations.

BASIC CHOICES

Exhibit 1 lists the main structural permutations from which issuers can chose. They can issue securities linked to T-bills. If they chose this route, there is minimal mismatch risk because the coupon on the bonds will rise and fall in line with the index on the collateral. Such floaters are essentially capless, although typically they do contain a "student loan rate" cap for liquidity management purposes. Investors who prefer LIBOR-indexed assets, and who want to invest in student loan floaters from such an issuer, are forced to purchase an asset swap outside the deal.

Exhibit 1: Alternative Structures for Student Loan ABS

Collateral Index	Internal to the Deal From Third Party		Security Issued
	Swap	Cap	
3-mo T-bill	No	No	T-Bill/student loan rate cap
	No	No	3-mo LIBOR/student loan rate cap
	No	Yes	3-mo LIBOR/capless
	3-mo T-Bill/ 3-mo LIBOR	No	3-mo LIBOR/capless

The other issuance selection is to issue LIBOR floaters. When no cap protection is provided, the bonds have an available funds cap, i.e., a student loan rate cap. This cap is generally defined as the monthly or quarterly cash flow from the student loan rate, less servicing and administration fees. The student loan rate is a weighted average of the various types of loans in a particular deal plus the rates on the SAP payments. If LIBOR spiked relative to the 3-month T-bill rate, or if bills dropped in a flight to quality, it is possible there would be insufficient funds available to meet bond interest payments.

In such structures, it is typical to have a make-up or carryover provision. Once the index on the collateral rises (or the coupon on the bonds falls) sufficiently, the increased cash flow is used to make up the interest carryover amount. While it is conceivable that the TED spread could widen and stay permanently at a level that the shortfall might never be recouped, this is a highly unlikely event based on historical experience.

When issuing LIBOR securities, it is possible to reduce or virtually eliminate the cap risk by buying cap protection for the deal. Generally within these agreements, if the coupon on the bonds is greater than the student loan rate, then the cap provider pays the difference to the trust.

A second approach is to provide a basis swap within the deal, where the issuer pays a fixed spread to T-bills. As LIBOR increases, the swap provider implicitly meets the increasing coupon on the bonds by payments on the LIBOR leg of the swap. A variation on this theme is the partially hedged structure, in which the percentage of protection can range from 0-100%. For example, in some USA Group Secondary Market Services (SMS) deals, a portion of the notional bond amount is protected by a swap. This is a cost-effective approach, since eliminating all mismatch risk would be expensive relative to the range of expected values for T-bills and LIBOR.

ILLIQUID SWAP MARKET

One of the reasons that many LIBOR investors are not inclined to purchase T-bill floaters and then swap them is that the 3-month T-bill/3-month LIBOR component of the swap market is relatively small and illiquid, with swap spreads considerably wider than spot levels. Often the swap widens sharply when a large student loan deal comes to market, which makes it expensive to swap out of T-bills into LIBOR. This is the same reason why issuers may decide not to hedge a LIBOR indexed transaction with a swap — it locks in a high T-bill cost of funds.

WHOSE RISK — ISSUER OR INVESTOR?

It is important to bear in mind that when an ABS structure contains a basis mismatch, it is not only the investor, but the issuer that bears a risk. Student loan deals (like deals in many other ABS classes) have excess spread, i.e., roughly the difference between the net coupon on the collateral and the coupon on the bonds.

In mortgage-related ABS, the excess spread is much larger than in the student loan sector, and is used to absorb monthly losses. Since losses in federally guaranteed student loans are relatively small, the vast majority of the excess spread flows back to the issuer. Hence, the T-bill/LIBOR basis risk is of major concern to issuers. When an issuer incorporates a swap in the deal, it not only reduces the risk to the investor (by eliminating the effect of an available funds cap) but reduces risk to the issuer, as well, by protecting a level of excess spread. When a cap is purchased, it is primarily for the benefit of the investor, because the cap only comes into play once the excess spread in the deal has been effectively reduced to zero. (Of course, with cap protection the issuer should also benefit by being able to price their bonds at a tighter spread.)

CHOICE OF INDEX

Exhibit 2 shows the indices used on private and public student loan ABS transactions since the earliest deals in 1993. It illustrates how the underlying index has shifted over time (even though throughout this period the index on the underlying loans was always 3-month bills).

Exhibit 2: Public and Private ABS Transactions

Year	3-mo LIBOR	3-mo T-Bills	1-mo LIBOR	Auction Rate	Fixed
2000*	4	2	0	0	0
1999	8	2	2	9	0
1998	1	3	4	6	3
1997	0	11	5	5	1
1996	0	11	11	5	1
1995	0	2	7	2	0
1994	0	0	10	3	0
1993	0	0	4	1	0

* Through March 2000.

During 1993-1995, most issuers, with the notable exception of Sallie Mae, used 1-month LIBOR, which indicated strong investor preference for LIBOR floaters. By contrast, from Sallie Mae's first deal in late 1995-on, that issuer chose to issue T-bill floaters to minimize interest rate mismatch. The company worked hard to develop an investor base that could use T-bill floaters. As Sallie Mae became the largest issuer and the dominant force in the market, its preference for a T-bill index persuaded other issuers to use the same. While Sallie Mae championed T-bills, some other issuers stayed with 1-month LIBOR, choosing a wider and deeper investor base to the cost of dealing with the index mismatch. Hence, during 1996-1998, a mixture of T-bill and LIBOR floaters were issued by a variety of companies.

However, beginning in late 1998 most issuers began to turn to 3-month LIBOR. With the decision by Sallie Mae to use a mix of T-bill and 3-month LIBOR securities in their recent deals, the cycle has come full circle. Almost all new issues are LIBOR-based. (The large number of auction rate deals shown in Exhibit 2 are mainly from not-for-profit issuers.)

HOW MUCH RISK?

When considering the various choices issuers have for structuring student loan ABS, it is useful to get some idea of just how big the mismatch is between 3-month T-bills and 3-month LIBOR. More importantly, how likely is it that a spike in 3-month LIBOR would hit the available funds cap on a 3-month LIBOR student loan deal?

Exhibit 3 shows the excess margin on a typical 7-year, 3-month LIBOR floater using T-bill and LIBOR rates from January 1997 to March 2000. Assumptions for calculating the excess spread include the following. For the collateral, we assumed an average student loan payment rate of 3-month T-bills + 270 basis points, which is the average of pre- and post-1998 margins on Stafford loans. We also used a combined servicing and administration fee of 100 basis points. For the coupon we assumed 3-month LIBOR + 18 basis points. As the exhibit shows, with our assumptions it was only during the most volatile period (of fall 1998) that excess margin turned negative (and that was only for one day). As the exhibit also indicates, when there are spikes in LIBOR versus T-bills, the extreme distortions only last a few days. Given this historical relationship, it seems unlikely that in the future there will be many instances of available funds student loan floaters getting capped out, or of investors getting delayed interest payments.

A SHRINKING TREASURY MARKET

While the volatility of the TED spread has always been a factor in determining the relative attractiveness of LIBOR and T-bill floaters, we have entered a new era of fixed income markets. Among other things, the relationship between T-bills and LIBOR is more tenuous than ever. Mounting government surpluses are reducing U.S. government debt and shrinking the available supply of Treasuries, including T-bills. As this continues, the Treasury market will become ever more disconnected from other domestic and global markets. Accordingly, demand for T-bill based floaters is also shrinking. And the TED spread is becoming more volatile.

Responding to these trends, Sallie Mae began to issue both LIBOR and T-Bill floaters. The percentage of each in a deal is determined by the demand for the two types of securities. Exhibit 4 shows each Sallie Mae deal that contains a mix of T-bills and LIBOR floaters, plus the percentage of each. In SLMA 1999-1, the split was 16% T-bill and 84% LIBOR. In SLMA 2000-2, it was 8.8% T-bill and 91.2% LIBOR. We expect the percentage of T-bill securities in Sallie Mae deals to remain low. At some point in the near future, student loan ABS securities will become almost exclusively LIBOR based.

Exhibit 3: Excess Spread on 7-Year Student Loan Floater

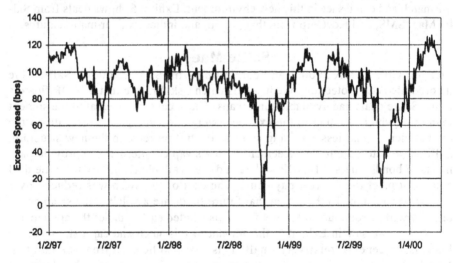

Exhibit 4: Distribution of T-Bill and LIBOR Securities in Sallie Mae Deals

Deal	T-Bill (%)	LIBOR (%)
1999-1	16.0	84.0
1999-2	14.6	85.4
2000-1	7.3	92.7
2000-2	8.8	91.2

Exhibit 5: Student Loan Deal Structures in Late 1999/Early 2000

Issuer/Issue	Bond Indices	Internal to Deal		Shortfall Payments From Reserve Account
		Swap	Cap	
Sallie Mae 2000-1	3-mo T-Bill & 3-mo LIBOR	No	Yes	No
Sallie Mae 2000-2	3-mo T-Bill & 3-mo LIBOR	No	Yes	No
KeyCorp 1999-B	3-mo LIBOR	No	Yes	No
SMS 2000-A	3-mo LIBOR	No	No	Yes

DIFFERENCE OF OPINION

We only have to look at deals from three leading student loan issuers from late 1999 and early 2000 to see that there is no consensus on how best to deal with mismatch and cap issues in this new environment. Exhibit 5 shows deals from Sallie Mae, SMS, and KeyCorp from that period, and indicates their main features.

Sallie Mae

Starting with SLMA 2000-1 and continuing with SLMA 2000-2, Sallie Mae incorporated cap protection to reduce mismatch risk. Prior to that, LIBOR floaters in the Sallie deals had available funds caps. Those caps were equal to the student loan rate (which is equal to the expected weighted average interest rate on the trust student loans) less servicing and administration fees. In the new structure, Sallie Mae entered into an agreement with a swap counterparty to provide payments to bondholders if LIBOR spiked and the available cash flow from the deal could not meet the interest payments. The cost of the swap was reduced by a make-up provision. To the extent that future funds are available, the swap counterparty will be reimbursed for any funds distributed earlier under the agreement.

As we saw in Exhibit 3, the amount of mismatch and cap risk in student loans is, in general, relatively small. This can also be seen from the fact that Moody's did not need to consider the swap when rating the senior bonds on the SLMA 2000-1 deal. It was used, however, in rating the subordinated certificates, which received an A2 rating. Hence, even if the swap counterparty is downgraded, it may not impact the rating of the senior bonds. In SLMA 2000-1 the swap counterparty was rated Aaa, in SLMA 2000-2 the two counterparties are rated Aa2 and Aa3.

KeyCorp

Historically, KeyCorp issued both T-bill and LIBOR-based floaters, but never both in the same deal. Their two 1999 deals were both LIBOR. The first, 1999-A, was an available funds floater without cap protection. However, their 1999-B deal contained cap protection similar to that found in Sallie Mae 2000-1 and 2000-2. (We should note that KeyCorp was the first to use this structure.) The cap provider is reimbursed any interest payments once the available funds become sufficient to cover all other payments in the deal.

USA Group SMS

Since 1998, SMS issued only LIBOR-based student loan securities. SMS deals 1998-A through 1999-B had an available funds cap, but the cap and mismatch risk were mitigated by the purchase of an interest rate swap on 60% of the deal. On any sharp increase in LIBOR, the swap counterparty would match those increases on 60% of the amount outstanding in the deal.

In SMS 2000-A, the company eliminated both the swap and the available funds cap. In their place they introduced a reserve account which will be used to cover any interest shortfall if LIBOR spikes. The deal has a reserve account trigger which captures excess spread into the reserve account whenever 3-month LIBOR exceeds the related T-bill rate by 125 basis points. As a further protection (for investors and for SMS), the company reserved the right to enter into a swap to convert a portion of the T-bill based cash flows to LIBOR.

NEW SAP INDEX

The entire question of which index to use for student loan floaters will become much simpler in a few years. In 1999, Congress changed the formula for calculating SAP payments made to lenders. (Federal student loans are capped. The SAP provides interest payments to lenders when student loan borrower rates get capped out.) In the new formula, the SAP is linked to 3-month financial CP, rather than 3-month T-bills. At the same time, the yield was reduced from 3-month T-bills + 2.80% to 3 month CP + 2.34%. The new payment formula will be in effect from January 1, 2000 through July 2003, which is the date for the next reauthorization of the Higher Education Act.

Since most originators keep student loans on their books until the loans go into repayment, the large purchasers/issuers of student loan ABS will not see a large flow of CP-backed paper for several years. However, ultimately there will be a large amount of student loan paper linked to CP. At that point the mismatch problem will be greatly reduced, since CP and LIBOR are quite closely correlated.

We expect the new CP index will make it easier for lenders to fund their business, and that this will increase the volume of student loan ABS securities. However, for the next several years, issuers and investors of ABS student loans will have to deal with the mismatch problems addressed in this chapter.

Chapter 11

Healthcare Receivable Backed ABS

Neil McPherson
Head of ABS Research
Credit Suisse First Boston

with assistance from

Todd Fasanella
Asset Finance
Credit Suisse First Boston

INTRODUCTION

Healthcare receivable ABS (HCABS) deals have been around since the early 1990s yet remain the province of a growing, but still relatively small, group of ABS investors. Issuance has been dominated by a few finance companies that specialize in financing receivables for small- to medium-sized healthcare providers. A review of several deals outstanding indicates the performance of the collateral has been strong. In this chapter we'll describe the structure of HCABS and the collateral behind them. We'll also address the risks in the transactions to investors and their mitigants, and we'll highlight performance metrics that investors can use to monitor deal progress.

HOW HCABS RESEMBLE CREDIT CARD ABS IN STRUCTURE

HCABS resemble credit card ABS because they are backed by a revolving pool of assets (usually with a 3- to 5-year revolving period), followed by an amortization period. Both senior and subordinate tranches in a series can be issued in a form resembling a master trust — one or more series being issued from a larger revolving asset pool. HCABS structures come in two forms: (1) those backed directly by pools of receivables from various healthcare providers and (2) those backed by revolving loans to healthcare providers (with these loans in turn secured by the receivables). This chapter will focus on the former, as they have accounted for most of the HCABS deals, at more than 90% of the $2.4 billion issued since 1995. In both types of deals, however, the amount advanced to the providers by the finance companies is a critical aspect of controlling risk in HCABS, as we'll discuss later in this chapter.

Similar to credit card ABS, HCABS are structured with early amortization events and triggers, such as rising losses/dilution,[1] inadequate levels of overcollateralization, servicer bankruptcy or events of default, etc. Unlike credit cards, however, HCABS typically use dynamic credit enhancement: in addition to subordination, HCABS have overcollateralization and cash reserves that may be resized depending on collateral pool performance.[2] A structural diagram of a typical HCABS transaction backed by healthcare receivables (not loans) is shown in Exhibit 1.

Exhibit 1: Healthcare Receivables Securitization Structure

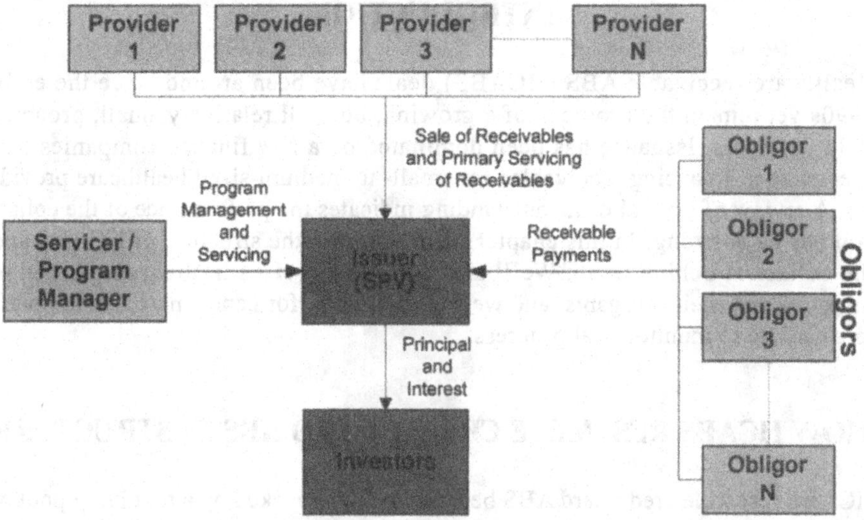

Source: Credit Suisse First Boston

---

[1] Dilution refers to receivables that will be uncollectible for some reason. In credit cards, sources of dilution are merchandise returns, and investors are protected against dilution by excess spread and the seller's interest. In HCABS, dilutions typically arise from rejected or aged claims due from healthcare insurers and investors are protected against dilution by overcollateralization and reserve funds.

[2] In a similar vein, in many credit card deals, the C-pieces are often structured with dedicated reserve funds that can rise and fall with the level of available excess spread.

In short, the issuer (a bankruptcy remote SPV) sells notes to investors, and, with the proceeds from the sale, purchases receivables from healthcare providers on an ongoing basis. The receivables are typically serviced by the providers (technically sub-serviced) and collections from the obligors (mostly healthcare insurers) are sent to the trustee via a lockbox arrangement. The lockbox arrangement[3] ensures that the collected funds do not pass through the provider's hands, where they would be subject to the healthcare provider's credit risk. The program manager oversees the activities of the SPV and ensures that receivables are eligible, that concentration limits with respect to obligors and providers are followed, and that credit enhancement levels and receivables valuations are sufficient to maintain the bonds' credit ratings. The deal's fixed or floating coupon payments come from payments made by providers. These payments are billed monthly to sellers, netted from the collection proceeds due to the healthcare providers, and are sized to cover bond coupons plus a servicing fee, usually between 1% and 3% per annum.

DIFFERENCES IN COLLATERAL RISKS FOR HCABS VERSUS CREDIT CARD ABS

The collateral in HCABS consists of the insured portion only of healthcare receivables, generally obligations payable by:

- commercial insurers
- Blue Cross/Blue Shield plans
- a federal or state government agent (such as Medicare or Medicaid plans)
- a health maintenance organization (HMO) or Preferred Provider Organization (PPO), or
- medical services providers reimbursed by any of the above[4]

Hence, HCABS are non-consumer credit backed ABS because the collateral performance depends solely upon repayment by the aforementioned commercial obligors (referred to as "payors"). Importantly, the portion of the healthcare receivable that may be owed by the patients themselves (usually called the "self-pay" or "co-pay" portion) is not part of the transaction.

Most payors do not pay the full billed amount for healthcare services but instead pay a standard amount based upon the procedure involved, geography, the patient's coverage, contracts between payors and providers, etc. Some definitions: first, the co-payment is deducted, leaving the *gross amount*. The difference between the gross amount billed and the amount the insurer will reimburse is termed the *contractual allowance*. The amount the payor will reimburse is referred to as the *net eligible receivable*. Estimating, *a priori*, the amount of the contractual

---

[3] Government obligors may require disbursement first to a lockbox in the name of providers; these funds are swept daily from the providers' lockbox to the issuer's lockbox.

[4] Provider payors are only allowed subject to prior approval by the rating agencies.

allowance is the key to healthcare receivables lending, as any underestimation may lead to losses. Providers are paid cash for their receivables based upon an advance rate or haircut applied against the net eligible receivable, thus creating either cash reserves or overcollateralization in HCABS deals. These haircuts are repayable to the healthcare providers when the receivables' full value is collected. In fact, for each $100 of receivables deposited by the seller, they may receive only $80, depending on the various reserve amounts specified in the arrangement between the providers and the issuer of a HCABS deal. Exhibit 2 shows conceptually how a receivable may be divided into its components for securitization.

The advance rate on each net eligible receivable is a function of the structure's required reserves, and there may be separate reserve amounts required for (typically government) obligor offset, a seller's rejected receivables, and defaulted receivables. Defaulted receivables are typically defined as those receivables uncollected after 180 days, but can also include those deemed uncollectible by the program manager, as with obligations of an insolvent or bankrupt insurer. Generally speaking, the credit quality of the insurers or other payors is very high, and there are strict limits on concentrations of receivables payable by lower and/ or unrated payors. The seller (medical provider) is obligated to repurchase any receivables where there is a breach of the seller's representations and warranties.[5] Offset amounts can arise when a payor, usually a Medicare/Medicaid program, after reviewing past payments made to providers, determines an overpayment was made, and decides to hold back some portion of future reimbursements.

Exhibit 2: Only Commercially Obligated Portion of Healthcare Receivables is Securitized

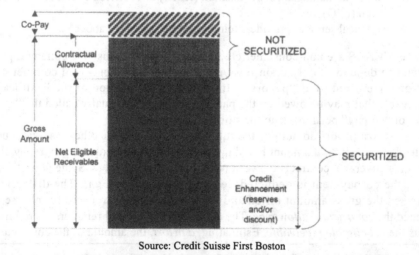

Source: Credit Suisse First Boston

---

[5] Examples include submitting a receivable that is aged more than 150 days past the billing date, or a receivable that has incorrect obligor information. Many other breaches are defined in a deal's documentation.

Exhibit 3: Representative HCABS Capital Structure

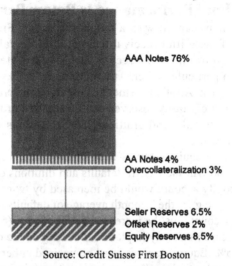

AAA Notes 76%

AA Notes 4%
Overcollateralization 3%

Seller Reserves 6.5%
Offset Reserves 2%
Equity Reserves 8.5%

Source: Credit Suisse First Boston

CREDIT ENHANCEMENT

Sources of credit enhancement in a typical HCABS deal include subordination, overcollateralization, and cash reserves. A recent deal in which AAA senior tranches were created was enhanced with a 4% subordinate AA-rated tranche, overcollateralization of 3%, and reserve accounts totaling 17%, for a combined senior credit enhancement level of 24%.

The reserve accounts in the deal included seller-specific reserves of 6.5%, offset reserves of 2%, and equity reserves of 8.5%. Seller-specific reserves protect against dilutions from rejected receivables and losses from defaulted receivables. Any draws against a seller's reserve must be replenished from the seller, out of future proceeds from collections, or the seller will be terminated from the program. Offset reserves of 2% minimum were also in place in this particular HCABS. These reserves are available to cushion against any offsets (usually from government payors) that may arise in the pool. Unlike seller reserves, offset reserves and overcollateralization are not seller-specific, but rather cross-collateralize the entire master trust's receivables pool, because they are generally available to cover *any* undercollections due to offset in the receivables pool.

Equity reserves are available to cover shortfalls *only within each series of notes issued by the master trust*. In the event of early amortization, equity reserves are first used to create an interest reserve (equivalent to three months interest on the outstanding notes) while the amortization process is underway, to ensure timely interest payments.

A representative capital structure for HCABS is shown in Exhibit 3.

Offset And Equity Reserves Can Increase If Pool Performance Is Below Par

The credit enhancement can grow in a number of ways. First, offset reserves, while sized at 2% of the initial receivables' net eligible value, can grow to an amount equal to 1.5 times the most recent year's aggregate audited Medicare/Medicaid offset for a particular seller. Any increase is "sticky" — that is, it stays around until the next year. Another element of the dynamic credit enhancement in HCABS is that amount of equity reserves can increase to protect investors when higher-than-expected defaults and dilutions from rejections occur in the overall pool over a 3-month period.

In a recent deal, equity reserves were initially sized at 8.5% of the eligible receivables amount, and will increase if defaults and dilutions exceed 5.75% in a 3-month period. The equity account would be increased by twice the amount that the losses exceed 5.75% — e.g., if the 3-month average of defaults and rejections is, say, 6%, then the equity account must be increased by 50 bp ($2 \times (6.00\% - 5.75\%) = 50$ bp), to 9%. This increase must stay in place for as long as the default and rejection rate stays above 5.75%. Equity reserves must be upsized either through further discounting of the receivables to the sellers or through a cash infusion from the issuer.

How Credit Enhancement Is Sized By The Rating Agencies

When sizing credit enhancement levels, the ratings agencies look to the largest of three requirements based upon (1) historical rejection and dilution experience, (2) payor concentrations, and (3) seller (healthcare provider) concentrations (in the case of HCABS backed by loans). Static pool analysis by one rating agency indicates that the AAA enhancement level for a deal with a 36-month revolving period and a 12-month amortization period (about a 3-year average life) is about six times expected lifetime losses.

Other Structural Elements Protecting Investors

Other structural aspects present in HCABS to protect investors include payor concentration limits and collateral coverage tests, which ensure an adequate ratio of trust assets to liabilities. There may also be a *"seller's defaulted receivable test"* that will eliminate a seller from the issuer's finance program if defaults and rejections in a specified period exceed a certain percentage, for example 10% over a 3-month period. There may also be a *"program defaulted receivables test"* under which the program would be placed into early amortization should total defaulted receivables for a given series exceed a certain percentage over a specified period.

Obligor Concentration Limits

Payor concentration limits are important since a well-diversified pool of payors reduces the risk to the trust in the event of a payor bankruptcy. To the extent that a subset of the receivables pool exceeds the concentration limits, the amount of the excess is subtracted from the eligible receivables pool for the purposes of calculating collateral coverage and credit enhancement requirements. In this way, the issuer/servicer has the incentive to adhere to the concentration limits, because purchased receivables in excess of the concentration limits are not *funded* by the trust. Concentration limits are essentially set up by type of obligor (government versus commercial insurer, etc.) and by rating category: for example, no more than X% of eligible receivables payable by any single commercial insurer/HMO rated BBB or better, etc. As would be expected, the lower the rating, the lower the allowable concentration for those payors.

Provider Concentration Limits

Provider concentration limits are somewhat simpler. In the case of HCABS backed by receivables (as opposed to HCABS backed by loans to providers), the provider limits are really designed to maintain diversification amongst the providers and thus prevent the occurrence of an early amortization event. Said another way, the risk of provider bankruptcy causes credit concerns in loan-backed HCABS, but only causes early amortization concerns in receivables-backed HCABS. If a large provider of healthcare receivables can no longer generate receivables for the trust during the revolving period, and cannot be replaced quickly by other sellers, collateral coverage tests may fail and the deal could go into early amortization.

In a recent transaction, the provider (seller) limits in a receivables backed deal we reviewed were 24% maximum for the single largest provider, and 20% maximum for the second largest provider. Again, deal documents specify that any receivables in excess of the provider limits will not be included as eligible receivables for the purpose of calculating credit enhancement levels.

Collateral Coverage Tests

As stated earlier, a collateral coverage test exists in HCABS to ensure that there is an adequate ratio of assets to liabilities in the trust in the event of an early amortization. If the coverage test is violated, a servicer event of default is declared and the deal may be forced into early amortization. In essence, the collateral coverage test ensures that the amount of eligible receivables plus overcollateralization and cash reserves (excluding equity reserves) exceeds the amount of the notes by a specified percentage. This test serves to limit the amount of allowable variance in cash reserves and overcollateralization.

MONITORING HCABS PERFORMANCE

As expected, the servicer reports for a given HCABS trust backed by receivables contain the details necessary for monitoring deal performance. An investigation of various deal reports indicates some common performance metrics for investors. First, let's review the collateral aging. This is shown in Exhibit 4 for a trust with some $770 million in bonds outstanding over five different series issued since May 1998.

Exhibit 4: Receivable Aging Distribution Should be Stable Over Time

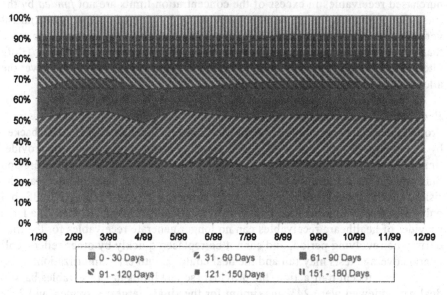

Sources: Credit Suisse First Boston, Servicer Reports

As Exhibit 4 displays, for the 5-month period July 1999 to December 1999, the percentage of receivables in each aging bucket has remained very stable. Three series, totaling $590 million in bonds, were added to the portfolio in 1998, and an additional series was added to this trust in March of 1999. Within a few months the portfolio seems to have reached a "steady state" with no signs of increases in the older (150+ days) aging buckets. An increasing proportion of aged receivables would be of concern, since receivables are deemed defaulted after 180 days.

With respect to payor limits and the ability of the issuer to generate enough receivables of various types, and hence mitigate payor concentration risk, investors can compare each category's respective limit with the average actual concentrations in each category over time. We took the average actual concentration over a year and a half and compared it to its respective category limits. In each category, there was excess capacity. This issuer seemed to have no trouble meeting the rating agency concentration limits as specified in the deal documents. Moreover, since we were considering averages, it was also useful to consider how many incidents of exceeding a payor concentration limit occurred. Only two such incidents occurred in this portfolio, at the inception of the program, in the single A rated payor limit category and in the below single A category, and by fairly small amounts. Recall also that the issuer gets no credit for receivables in excess of a concentration limit.

Exhibit 5: Provider Concentration Limits Should Also Be Met

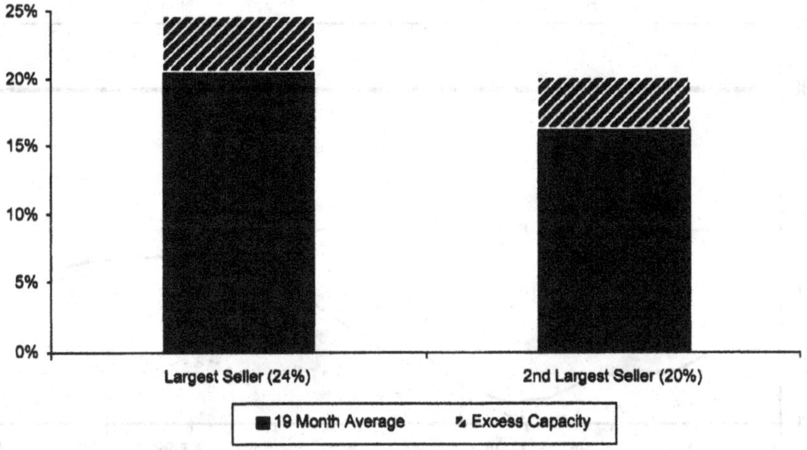

Sources: Credit Suisse First Boston, Servicer Reports

Provider limits indicate the ability of the issuer to generate enough receivables from various sellers and avoid over-dependence on a single seller. As can be seen in Exhibit 5, since the inception of the program, the average provider limit has been met. In early 1999, however, the data indicate that the portfolio is bumping up against these constraints. Moreover, for a few months in late 1999, the second largest seller concentration was exceeded slightly. However, again, *the issuer gets no credit for receivables in excess of provider limits*. As we discussed earlier, this is more of an early amortization concern, and should be monitored by those holders for whom early amortization would be disadvantageous.

As stated earlier, defaulted and defaulted/rejected receivables are important indicators of the issuer's ability to effectively estimate contractual allowances, price receivables from sellers and manage the program overall. In addition, sellers can be terminated from the finance program for having high rates of defaulted receivables and equity reserve requirements in HCABS deals can be increased. Exhibit 6 graphs 1-month defaulted receivables as well as 3-month average defaulted and rejected receivables, in both cases as a percentage of net eligible receivables. Defaulted and rejected receivables in excess of 5.75% can cause an increase in required equity, and the overall program can be wound down if the total of defaulted and rejected receivables exceed 10% in a 3-month period.

Exhibit 6 shows that the 1-month rate of defaulted receivables is stable to declining, and the 3-month average of defaulted and rejected receivables has always been below the 5.75% threshold, and, while rising in mid 1999, began declining in late 1999. The increase in 3-month average of defaulted and rejected receivables coincided with the issuance of a new series of notes, and the addition of several new providers to the pool. Recall also that every month defaulted and rejected receivables are charged back to the seller, out of proceeds from collections.

Exhibit 6: Defaulted and Defaulted/Rejected Receivables

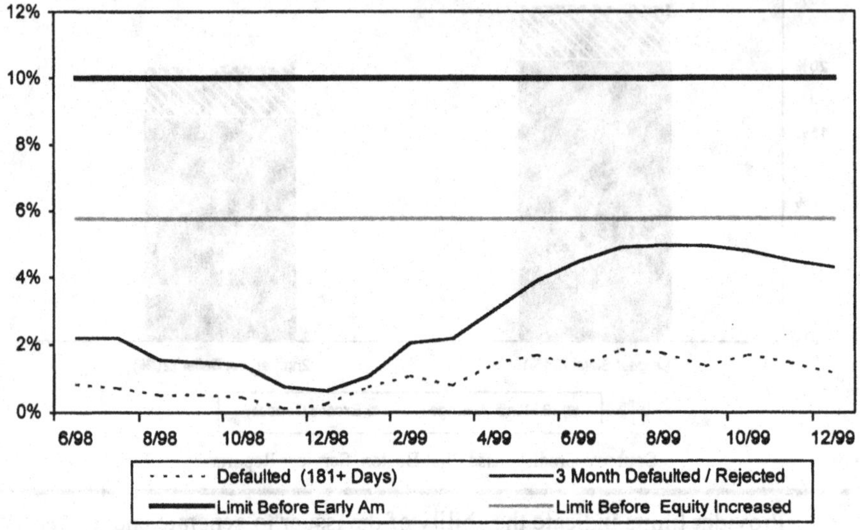

Sources: Credit Suisse First Boston, Servicer Reports

The collateral coverage test must always be met for the deal to be in compliance with early amortization triggers. Deal documents typically specify a certain time period, usually seven days, during which the issuer can act to remedy the inadequate collateral coverage because of anticipated timing delays between posting collections and purchasing new receivables from sellers.

SUMMARY

HCABS backed directly by receivables pools are a growing asset class. While they share some of the simple characteristics of credit card ABS, they have structural and collateral characteristics that are very different. Many forms of investor protections exist in these deals, and monitoring performance can be easily done through careful analysis of servicer reports. Investors can review collateral aging and compliance with obligor and provider concentration limits. Default and rejection rates can be examined and collateral coverage tests and adequate reserves can be verified. Exhibit 7 provides a listing of deals issued since 1995.

Exhibit 7: HCABS Issuance Since 1995

Deal	Date	Amount	Ratings	Rated By	Pricing
NPF V (Series 2)	15-Mar-95	$20.00	AA	S&P	NA
NPF VI (Series 1)	15-May-95	73.00	AAA	DCR	NA
NPF VI (Series 2)	4-Jan-96	50.00	AAA	DCR	NA
NPF VIII	30-May-96	50.00	A	DCR	NA
NPF IX	27-Jun-96	125.00	AAA/AA	DCR, Fitch	NA
NPF XI	6-Jun-97	112.10	AAA/AA/A	DCR, Fitch	NA
NPF IX (Series 2)	29-Jul-97	85.00	N/A	DCR	NA
NPF VIII (Series 2)	23-Dec-97	25.00	N/A	DCR	NA
DVI Business Credit Receivables Corp. III	12-Feb-98	75.00	AAA/A/BBB-	DCR, Fitch	1ML +35/70/150
Daiwa Healthco-3 LLC	1-Mar-98	105.00	AA/BBB	DCR/Fitch	NA
NPF VI (Series 3)	31-Mar-98	77.00	N/A	DCR	NA
NPF VI 1998-1	1-Jun-98	300.00	AAA/AA-	DCR	3yr +73/88
NPF VI Series 1998-2	14-Aug-98	125.00	AAA/AA-	DCR	5yr +85/+92
NPF VI Series 1998-4	4-Nov-98	50.00	AAA/AA-	DCR/Fitch	5yr +200/260
NPF VI Series 1998-3	4-Nov-98	114.60	AAA/AA-	DCR/Fitch	3yr +175/230
NPF XII Series 1999-1	10-Mar-99	100.00	AAA/AA-	DCR	5yr +120/150
NPF VI Series 1999-1	25-Mar-99	180.00	AAA/AA-	DCR/Fitch	3yr +125/ 1ML + 90
NPF XII Series 1999-2	28-Jun-99	350.00	AAA/AA-	DCR	3yr +147/167
DVI Business Credit Receivables Corp. III	10-Nov-99	88.00	AAA/AA/A/BBB	DCR/Fitch	1ML +68/130/180/295
NPF-XII Series 1999-3	23-Nov-99	200.00	AAA/AA-	DCR	1ML +65/95
NPF-XII Series 2000-1	29-Mar-00	125.00	AAA/AA-	DCR	1ML +48/90

Source: Credit Suisse First Boston

Chapter 12

Dealer Floorplan ABS

Karen Weaver, CFA
Managing Director
Global Head of Securitization Research
Deutsche Banc Alex. Brown

Nichol Bakalar
Vice President
ABS Research
Deutsche Banc Alex. Brown

INTRODUCTION

Floorplan securitizations are a well-established niche ABS asset class, with a 10-year history and outstandings at year end 1999 of roughly $15 billion (see Exhibit 1). Floorplan ABS offer ABS investors an opportunity to diversify away from exposure to consumer credit, yet have many of the attractive structural protections found in credit card ABS, in that early payout triggers reduce investors' exposure to underperforming collateral. Unlike other non-consumer ABS such as trade receivables, floorplan ABS benefit from first lien security interests in hard assets. Unlike equipment ABS, most floorplan deals have very straightforward, easily-swapped cash flows due to their bullet structure.

Exhibit 1: Historical Floorplan Issuance

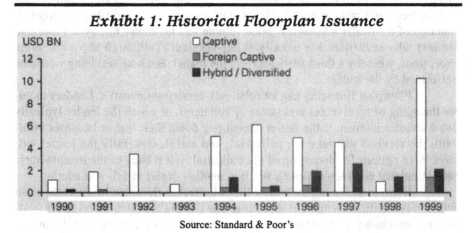

Source: Standard & Poor's

223

In this chapter we present: (1) an overview of this lending industry and the participants in it; (2) the structural characteristics of floorplan ABS, including cash flow characteristics and the sizing and form of credit enhancement; and, (3) a summary of the floorplan securitization market.

THE FLOORPLAN LENDING INDUSTRY

Floorplan lending (commonly referred to as "inventory finance") is a specialized type of working capital financing that is particularly prevalent in high-ticket industries, most notably automobiles. Floorplan lending finances a dealer's inventory (the inventory that is "on the floor") pending the product's retail sale. Broadly speaking, there are two types of floorplan lenders: captive and independent.

Captive floorplan lenders are affiliates of a manufacturer that are created, among other things, to offer financing to a manufacturer's dealer network. Examples of captives that are active in the floorplan ABS market include: for autos, Chrysler Financial Company (CARCO), Ford Motor Credit Company, General Motors Acceptance Corp. (SWIFT), Volkswagen Credit Corp, World Omni Financial (a major US distributor for Toyota), and in trucks, Navistar Financial and in motorcycles, Yamaha Motor Corp.

Independent (or "diversified") floorplan finance companies finance various unrelated dealers, often covering different products from multiple manufacturers. Examples of independent floorplan companies active in the ABS market include GreenTree, TransAmerica, Deutsche Financial Services (DFS), and Bombardier (which is in fact a hybrid, as Bombardier issues ABS that include some financing of products which they also manufacture). Captives dominate the dealer floorplan securitized market with about 80% share of cumulative U.S. dollar public floorplan ABS issuances as of March 31, 2000.

Floorplan lenders generally underwrite, service, and monitor loans. In underwriting loans to dealers, lenders examine bank references and credit reports and do trend and ratio analysis. The size of an approved credit line is largely a function of the dealer's historical sales volume and inventory turnover. Floorplan lenders who securitize are usually seller-servicers (although there are some exceptions, whereby a third party services the loans). Back-up servicing would be performed by the trustee.

Floorplan financing can be relatively servicing intensive. Lenders monitor the aging of receivables and status of collateral, in which the lender typically has a security interest. If the dealer cannot pay down their line or becomes insolvent, the servicer can take the collateral, and sell it. Generally the lender will have three options for disposing of the collateral: sell it back to the manufacturer (at a stipulated contractual price), sell it to another dealer or sell it at auction.

Because of the importance of the collateral in floorplan lending, the audit function is a critical element of servicing. The lenders' auditors travel to the dealers and reconcile the physical inventory on the dealer's premises with the inventory the lender has financed. Generally these audits are monthly (more often if problems are detected) and occur without prior notice. It is not uncommon for lenders to require that no auditor audit the same dealer twice in a row, to reduce the likelihood of auditor collusion in any possible dealer fraud. For automobiles, "VINs" or vehicle identification numbers make the auditing process easier. Standard and Poor's points out that auditing can be more complex for assets that do not have unique identifiers (for example, floorplan financing of furniture) or, in the unusual case of marine lending, where customers purchase boats from a dealer but leave them at the dealer's dock.

Auditing is integral to reducing "SOT" risk, or the risk that assets are "sold out of trust." If a dealer sells a unit that was financed by a floorplan lender, but fails to forward the associated sale proceeds to the floorplan lender, the lender is at risk. There is no asset to sell, and no manufacturer buy-back to enforce. The only source of recovery for equipment sold out of trust is the dealer, who, if he is willfully selling out of trust, is probably experiencing financial difficulty.

The Lending Relationship

Lending arrangements in floorplan financing are typically a three-party affair. At the time the dealer places an order with the manufacturer, the manufacturer contacts the lender to confirm the dealer's financing capacity. The manufacturer will issue an invoice to be paid by the lender, and send the unit to the dealer. The dealer has an obligation to repay the lender, generally as soon as the unit is sold. Until the unit is sold, the dealer pays the lender monthly interest and the lender holds a security interest in the unit. The manufacturer usually adds support to the transaction, most notably by contractually committing to repurchase the unit if the dealer defaults, at a stipulated price and assuming satisfactory condition. Exhibit 2 lays out a lending arrangement between dealer, manufacturer and floorplan lender.

Exhibit 2: How Inventory Financing Works

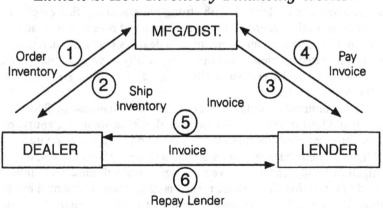

Source: DB Global Markets Research

Typical Loan Terms

The loans made to dealers are almost always secured by the equipment, and to a far lesser extent, by other dealership assets (parts, fixtures, real estate, etc.). Floorplan issuers have different mixes of asset types in their portfolios, but some of the most common types of equipment are: automobiles, boats ("marine"), manufactured housing, trucks, agricultural equipment, construction equipment, computer equipment, recreational vehicles, motorcycles, snowmobiles, and pianos.

The loans require monthly interest payments from the dealer to the lender, usually at a margin over Prime or LIBOR. The margin can range from under 25 bp to 125 bp and more. The principal is usually due at the earlier of a specified period or the date of the sale of the equipment. In some cases principal is due back over a scheduled period (most often in the case of lower-ticket, faster-moving items). In some cases, a dealer can extend the term by paying down a portion of the balance (curtailing). In a securitization, the rating agencies would adjust credit enhancement requirements to account for such features.

The amount of the equipment's purchase price that is financed ("the advance rate") can vary. For example, in autos, a dealer would usually be advanced a 60-day supply of new cars at 100% of the invoice price (plus add-ons). However, for used cars, the lender would finance only a 30-day supply at a 90% advance rate. In some asset types floorplan lenders do not finance used equipment at all. The rating agencies take into account used equipment exposure in sizing credit enhancement.

Dealer/Manufacturer Relationships

The dealer community is generally comprised of small, privately held companies. For example, in one large independent floorplan finance company portfolio, 93% of the dealers have outstanding balances of under $1 million. While this reduces risk at the security level by providing diversification, the dealers' small size and low level of sophistication generally indicates more credit risk at the dealer level. The lender addresses dealer risk with strong underwriting, that emphasizes the dealer's historical sales record, net worth, diversity of revenues (e.g. across products or from other services) and sometimes, a dealer's personal guarantee. Dealer risk is also mitigated by close monitoring, especially auditing. Within the collateral pool, limits on dealer exposures (including dealer affiliates) mitigates exposure to the dealer as well.

The equipment manufacturer is critical to the success of floorplan lending. This is obvious in the case of a captive floorplan financing entity, but also holds true for diversified floorplan lenders. Most directly, manufacturers are typically obligated to buy back inventory should a dealer default. This is, of course, a key mitigator of risk, especially given the size, financial muscle and investment-grade credit ratings that characterize many manufacturers represented in floorplan portfolios. There are, however, many forms of financial support that flow from manufacturers to their dealers, including reimbursement of interest during transit of the equipment, volume rebates, deferred billing, capital loans, assistance in locating buyers of terminated franchises, repurchase agreements, and floorplan assistance on certain models. Of course, should a manufacturer falter, the withdrawal of some of these supports would exacerbate the impact of the manufacturer's woes on their dealers. Inventory turnover would likely be weak in such a scenario, as buyers will be less willing to purchase items (especially high-ticket durable goods) from an ailing or, worse yet, defunct manufacturer.Rating agencies explicitly model stress scenarios for the manufacturer(s) when analyzing floorplan ABS.

While the health of the manufacturer and the quality of the servicing are probably most important in floorplan ABS, the industries represented also impact risk. For example, heavy trucks are more cyclical than automobiles. Automobiles may have more stable valuations than, for example, pianos, which are more of a discretionary item. The various industries represented have different historical performance and different volatility of results. These factors are taken into account in sizing credit enhancement for floorplan securitizations. Exhibit 3 shows the collateral composition of several dealer floorplan trusts.

Exhibit 3: Master Trusts Asset Type Composition

	Percentage of Receivables
Green Tree Master Trust (Servicing Portfolio 8/31/99)	
Manufactured Housing Floorplan Receivables	63.75%
Asset-Based Receivables	17.62%
Recreational Vehicle Floorplan Receivables	8.14%
DFS (trust portfolio 2/29/00)	
Boats and Boat Motors	19.00%
Accounts Receivable	15.50%
Recreational Vehicles	15.30%
Navistar	
Medium and Heavy Duty Trucks and Trailers	100%
Bombardier (as of 3/31/00)	
Marine[1]	32.06%
Manufactured Housing	28.87%
Bombardier[2]	22.18%
Recreational Vehicles	13.18%
CARCO (Chrysler Credit)/Ford Master Trust (Ford Motor Credit)/SWIFT (GMAC)	
Auto	100%

[1] Non-Bombardier boats (less than 25 feet), motors and trailers
[2] Ski-Doo® snowmobiles, Sea-Doo® personal watercraft and jet boats and Celebrity® boats and related parts and accessories

Source: Prospectuses

Exhibit 4: Floorplan ABS Principal Allocations*

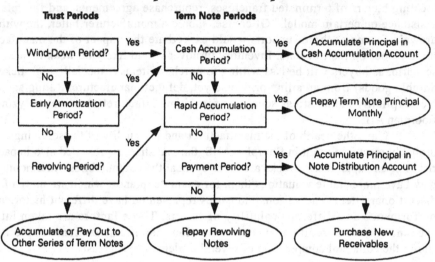

* "Triggers" are discussed later in this chapter.
Source: Source: *Fitch Asset-Backed New Issue Report*, "Superior Wholesale Inventory Financing Trust V," January 6, 2000.

FLOORPLAN SECURITIZATION STRUCTURES

With short-lived assets, revolving master trusts are a good fit for floorplan ABS. Because floorplan financing is short-term in nature, a revolving structure is used to create term ABS. (For a complete diagram of the payment structure, see Exhibit 4.) The approach mirrors that used to securitize credit cards and trade receivables. The transaction is initially in a "revolving period," whereby principal collections are reinvested in new, eligible receivables and bond investors receive interest only. "Eligible" receivables are defined for each floorplan ABS by the rating agencies. Generally, eligible receivables must be from solvent parties, who cannot be affiliated with the lender, and must meet certain minimum quality designations used by the lender in their underwriting process. Further, to be eligible, a receivable cannot cause the collateral pool to breach concentration limits with regard to dealers, manufacturers, product types (including new versus used) and geographic areas.

After the revolving period, the transaction enters the "wind down period." During the wind down period, principal collections are deposited in a "note distribution account" (also known as a principal funding account), for distribution on the expected final maturity date. During the wind-down, funds are invested in "eligible investments," generally A1/P1 money market instruments. The servicer determines the duration of the wind-down period formulaically. In general, the servicer takes the reciprocal of the collateral's monthly payment rate and rounds it to the nearest whole number, to determine the length of time needed to repay the principal out of monthly collections. For conservatism, the lowest monthly payment rate observed in the trailing 12-month period is used. An example of the calculation is as follows.

> Lowest Monthly Payment Rate (trailing 12 months) = 33% MPR
> 1/33% = 3-month wind-down period

After the "wind-down period" is the "payment period." Typically, floorplan ABS are "soft bullet" and so the payment period is a single payment date. The term "soft bullet" is common throughout ABS and refers to the expected maturity of the ABS, used for pricing. The "legal final maturity" can be two years or more beyond the expected final maturity. The rating agencies rate the certainty of investors being fully repaid on or before the legal final maturity. In practice, the market trades on the basis of expected final maturities, and we know of no instance in a floorplan ABS where a bond's life extended beyond the expected final maturity.

Many floorplan ABS issuers have used a master trust structure. The master trust is the issuing entity, and is established to purchase receivables (the loans made to dealers to finance their inventory, secured by that inventory) from the seller-servicer, in what constitutes a true sale. The master trust then issues investor and seller certificates. Multiple series are issued, backed by the same master trust collateral. During accumulation, the series may be able to share principal collections among all of the series in the trust.

Over the last several years, a new structural alternative has been developed in the revolving ABS marketplace — the owner trust as a substitute for the master trust. This technology developed in the credit card market facilitates the placement of subordinate tranches and thus maximizes the benefits of securitization.

Owner trusts and master trusts are substantially similar in their mechanics: the cash flows are parallel and many of the documents contain the same provisions. However, the owner trust structure allows a "clean" debt opinion, which makes all investment grade securities issued in an owner trust transaction ERISA-eligible. Other benefits of the owner trust structure include the ability to sell notes to non-US investors and the elimination of transfer restrictions on lower-rated classes.

Citibank and Chase have converted their credit card programs to owner trusts and WorldOmni issued their 2000-1 floorplan transaction from an owner trust. We believe that more issuers will convert their floorplan programs to owner trust issuance.

It is common for floorplan ABS to contain an available funds cap. The coupon paid to investors is the lesser of the index plus the pricing spread, and the net receivables rate. The net receivables rate is the gross rate earned on the receivables, less the servicing fee. Some of the large, captive auto floorplan lenders charge a 100 bp servicing fee. For diversified lenders, servicing fees are usually 200 bp. Some servicers subordinate their servicing fee (with the fee becoming senior in the event of a servicing transfer). In some portfolios, yields are such that there is a meaningful level of excess spread, as a "first-line-of-defense" against losses. In other portfolios, especially those of captive floorplan lenders, lending may be subvented and yields low. In such cases, receivables may be sold to the trust at a discount in order to boost the yield.

Triggers

Triggers are mechanisms that primarily exist to protect investors when collateral performs below expectations, and/or in the event of a seller/servicer bankruptcy. In revolving structures, triggers allow principal to be trapped and held in cash (or cash substitutes) or paid out to investors ahead of schedule. Triggers stop seller-services from reinvesting principal collections in (poorly performing) assets. In this sense, pay-out triggers are much like a "put option" for the ABS investor.

Floorplan ABS typically feature two types of triggers, cash accumulation and rapid amortization. A cash accumulation trigger protects investors but does not lead to an early prepayment of principal. Instead, the noteholders' pro rata share of principal collections is deposited into a cash accumulation account, which is then used to pay principal as due (at the expected final maturity). The cash is invested in high-quality money market securities ("eligible investments"). A cash accumulation reserve fund is created at the beginning of the deal, which is sized to cover any negative carry arising from reinvestment of the principal collections into "eligible investments" under a cash accumulation trigger event.

By contrast, with a rapid amortization trigger, both the noteholders' pro rata share of principal collections and any moneys in the cash accumulation account are paid out to investors, shortening the life of their investment.

Most floorplan ABS feature both types of triggers, based on the triggering event. For example, the insolvency of the seller-servicer might trigger a rapid amortization, while a monthly payment rate that falls below a threshold level or a decline in new account originations that leads to a below required minimum seller's interest might trigger a cash accumulation period. In some instances, the issuer has the ability to "cure" and thus prevent triggers from taking effect. We outline various factors used in triggers below.

The Monthly Payment Rate Trigger

The monthly payment rate (MPR) is the best barometer of health because it indicates how rapidly inventory is being sold. Quite simply, the MPR is the percentage of outstandings that is paid down every month. If the MPR is falling, that indicates either that sales are falling or that inventory is too high. Like most variables in securitizations, consistency is most important. As long as a variable is consistent, risks can be covered in the structure.

The MPR can range quite a bit from pool to pool (see Exhibit 5). For the auto captives, MPRs are typically 30 to 50%. In diversified portfolios, they can be as low as 10% for some product types and are generally below 40%. Usually

MPR triggers are set substantially below recent experience for the portfolio. There is a trade-off whereby, if an issuer chooses, they can set a more aggressive MPR trigger (read as lower) in exchange for providing more credit enhancement.

Loss Triggers

Loss triggers are common throughout ABS. In floorplan financing, losses have been very low historically. As a general rule, they average approximately 50 bp per annum. Several portfolios post single-digit basis point losses, and the most aggressive portfolios might have annual losses in the 2% range. Loss triggers are usually a multiple of historical experience.

Other Common Triggers

Other common triggers include breach of any concentration limits on eligible receivables, a decline in receivables balances, breach of representations and warranties, failure to perform on the part of the seller-servicer, monetary default, seller-servicer bankruptcy, termination of any basis swap, and inadequate reserve fund balances.

Credit Enhancement

Floorplan finance receivables are credit-enhanced by the use of excess spread, subordinated and/or mezzanine tranches, and reserve funds. Generally only internal sources of credit enhancement are used. In some cases the servicing fee is subordinated to supplement excess spread. Often, credit enhancement requirements are dynamic, and incremental subordination must be provided based upon changes in the collateral pool's characteristics. The liquidity needs of a transaction can be met with the use of reserve funds and/or servicer advances (depending upon the servicer's credit quality).

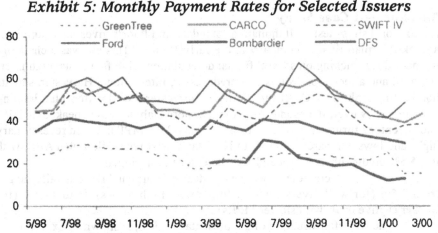

Exhibit 5: Monthly Payment Rates for Selected Issuers

The data for constructing the graphs in this exhibit were obtained from Moody's Investors Service and Fitch.

The sizing of loss protection is similar to credit card ABS, where a base case is established for certain key variables; namely MPR, losses, and yield. These variables are stressed in accordance with the rating of any given class. As mentioned previously, the rating agencies focus heavily on dealer concentrations when sizing credit enhancement. Floorplan ABS have an additional element, however, that must be modelled in the determination of credit enhancement levels. That is, floorplan ABS have credit exposure to the equipment manufacturers that is not always assessed actuarially.

First we will discuss stressing portfolio performance (MPR, losses, yield). A faltering economy could slow sales (payment rates) and lead to higher losses. The extent to which a portfolio is vulnerable will depend upon the nature of the equipment, and the nature of the economic downturn including the geographic area impacted. Because most floorplan portfolios are Prime-based, there is often basis risk, because the issuers typically create either LIBOR floaters or fixed-rate ABS. If there is no basis swap in the deal, the agencies stress the basis risk and size the credit enhancement accordingly, or the issuer incorporates a yield supplement account or net receivables cap.

In addition to this modeling exercise, rating agencies explicitly model the exposure to the equipment manufacturer(s). This is especially true of captive deals, but it also applies to other deals where large manufacturer concentrations exist and the lender is relying on manufacturer buybacks. If the manufacturer were to file bankruptcy, receivables would likely drop. The rating agencies examine the joint probability of a dealer and a manufacturer default. For example, in Standard and Poor's AAA scenario, they assume that once a manufacturer defaults, between 30 to 50% of the dealers will default (depending on the product type and other factors). The probability of a given manufacturer defaulting is a "traditional" credit risk, not an actuarial credit risk.

Navistar — A Case Study

A real-world stress test is illuminating. Standard and Poor's gives the example of a truck floorplan finance company in the early 1980's.[1] This era was a challenging period for trucking on several fronts: deregulation, high fuel costs, high interest rates, and a recession. Navistar's predecessor, International Harvester, saw its bond rating sink to CCC. At International Harvester's dealer floorplan lending operation, however, the scenario was much more stable. Losses peaked at 1.1% and inventory turnover was 2.6× to 2.9× (21%-24% MPR). These recessionary highs and lows compare favorably to Navistar's most recent floorplan ABS, with its 15.5% credit enhancement and 1.7× inventory turn trigger.

Total AAA credit enhancement in dealer floorplan ABS generally ranges from 8.5% (for well diversified portfolios with high MPRs) up to 14.5% (for weaker captive deals with slower MPRs).

The waterfall structure of a representative deal, is shown in Exhibit 6.

---

[1] Standard and Poor's, *Structured Finance*, August 1995.

Exhibit 6: Representative Cash Flow Waterfall: GMAC SWIFT V

- Servicing fee
- Notes basis swap
- Noteholders' interest
- Balance of noteholders' interest
- Certificate's basis swap
- Servicer advances
    (If available funds are insufficient to meet the expenses above, GMAC is required to make a servicer advance to cover the deficiency)
- Reserve fund replenishment
- Cash accumulation reserve fund replenishment
- Aggregate certificate interest
- Trust defaulted amount
- Trust chargeoffs
- Certificate reserve fund
- Release to seller

Note: this transaction included a basis swap for both noteholders and certificate holders.
Source: *Moody's Investors Service New Issue Report*, "Superior Wholesale Inventory Financing Trust V (SWIFT V)," June 25, 1999. Reprinted with permission from Moody's Investors Service.

Exhibit 7: Floating-Rate Dealer Floorplan ABS Trade Off of Credit Card Spreads

Source: DB Global Markets Research

THE FLOORPLAN ABS MARKET AND RELATIVE VALUE

Historically, dealer floorplan securitizations have priced in the new issue market and traded in the secondary market at spreads that are close to top tier credit card ABS (see Exhibit 7). Though not consumer receivables, floorplan ABS trade off of credit card ABS because of the similarity in structures and maturities offered.

Exhibit 8: Factors Driving Relative Spread Between Floorplan and Credit Card ABS

	Dealer Floorplans		CreditCards	
Servicer Credit Strength	Generally Strong	⇩	Mixed	⇩ ⇧
Asset Class Size	Small	⇧	Large	⇩
Deal Sizes	Large	⇩	Large	⇩
Collateral Quality	Strong	⇩	Mixed	⇩ ⇧
Prepayment Optionality/Early Amortization	Low	⇩	Low	⇩
Structural Complexity	Simple	⇩	Simple	⇩

⇧ Spread should be wider, all else equal
⇩ Spread should be tighter, all else equal

Source: DB Global Markets Research

Below we present a general framework for the factors that an investor should analyze when considering the purchase of a dealer floorplan issue. We also compare and contrast dealer floorplan and credit card ABS as pertains to these factors. Exhibit 8 is a summary of the impact these factors might have on the relative spread of a dealer floorplan issue. As shown in the exhibit, compared to a top tier credit card issuer (such as Citibank or MBNA) the only aspect that might support a wider spread on the dealer floorplan paper is the smaller size of the asset class. Because floorplan ABS is a relatively small subset of the ABS market, it is less liquid then top tier credit card ABS. The appropriate spread pick-up for this liquidity difference varies over time and from investor to investor.

Credit Strength of the Issuer/Servicer

Over the past few years, ABS analysis has increasingly included some focus on the credit quality of the servicer. The root of the concern is both the risk to a financially constrained company's servicing operation and the mark-to-market implications of a poorly regarded issuer (even given strong collateral performance).

The headline risk that has rippled through the home equity loan sector and the subprime auto sector over the past few years has not been a feature of dealer floorplan securitizations. Most floorplan issues are serviced by a well-capitalized captive or independent finance company and the industry has not been characterized by the rapid growth and loosening of lending standards that has been common in consumer lending. Moreover, with a floorplan securitization, the more relevant risk is the exposure to the manufacturer of the collateral. Diversified floorplan issues use industry and obligor concentration limits to mitigate these risks.

Size of the Asset Class

The dealer floorplan sector is relatively small and is characterized by somewhat sporadic issuance. Investors typically demand a liquidity premium for asset classes with these qualities. This premium is usually less for large issues and where the underlying assets are more broadly understood.

Exhibit 9: U.S. Bankruptcy Filings for Non-Businesses (Consumers) and Businesses

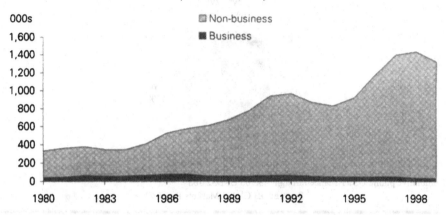

Reprinted with permission from the American Bankruptcy Institute. For regular updates of bankruptcy legislative activity and other insolvency news, as well as ABI membership information, visit ABI World at http://www.abiworld.org.

Quality of the Obligors and Collateral

All else equal, the market places a premium on securitizations backed by higher credit quality loans.The collateral quality of dealer floorplan securitizations is uniquely attractive in this respect because the receivables are secured and are obligations of business concerns (dealers) rather than consumers. Over time, this combination has resulted in low and stable losses on these securitizations. This is particularly attractive when compared to the credit card sector, where performance over the past few years has been volatile due to higher consumer bankruptcy filings and in some cases the extension of credit to lower quality borrowers. Exhibit 9 contrasts the jump in household bankruptcies in the 1990s with the stability of business filings.

Prepayment Optionality

The revolving collateral allows dealer floorplan securitizations to be structured as soft bullets with virtually no variation in principal repayments. Though early amortization remains a potential risk, no dealer floorplan issue has failed to mature as expected in this product's 10-year history.

Structural Complexity

The general structure of a dealer floorplan ABS, soft bullet issued from a master trust, is easily recognizable and well understood by investors. The fact that credit card ABS, arguably the largest and most liquid of the ABS asset classes, use a similar structure lends liquidity to this asset class.

Exhibit 10: Dealer Floorplan Issuance by Maturity

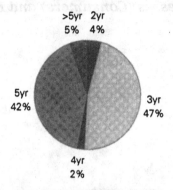

Cumulative public US$ issuance through 3/30/00 USD32.5bn
Source: DB Global Markets Research

Dealer floorplan issues are primarily floating-rate (72% floating versus 28% fixed as of March 30, 2000). Exhibits 10 and 11 describe the floorplan ABS market.

CONCLUSION

With a 10-year track record of performance, large and strong seller-servicers, and simple, soft bullet cash flows, dealer floorplan ABS have much in common with better-known asset types, such as credit cards and autos. Though the floorplan ABS market is not nearly as sizable as credit cards, floorplan deals are single-tranche offerings, and are as large or larger than the typical credit card ABS. Collateral performance to date has been very strong, especially relative to credit enhancement requirements. The floorplan loan portfolios benefit from the support of equipment manufacturers (often highly rated entities), the loan collateral, and, for independent floorplan lenders, diversification across industries and/or manufacturers. At a pickup to the most liquid asset types, which varies based upon market demand for liquidity and other factors, floorplan ABS offer an attractive diversification move in a tried-and-true asset type.

Exhibit 11: Outstanding Floorplan Issues (Public Only, USD Millions)

Pricing Date	Issuer	Seller	Collateral	Deal Size
5/25/1995	Navistar Financial Dealer Note MT 1995-1	Navistar Financial	Eqp	200.00
8/1/1995	Ford Credit Auto Loan MT 1995-1	Ford Motor Credit	Auto	1,000.00
10/20/1995	Yamaha Motor MT 1995-1	Yamaha Motor Credit	Eqp	100.00
2/12/1996	Ford Credit Auto Loan MT 1996-1	Ford Motor Credit	Auto	800.00
2/12/1996	Ford Credit Auto Loan MT 1996-2	Ford Motor Credit	Auto	960.00
3/14/1996	Volkswagen Credit Auto MT 1996-1	Volkswagen	Auto	375.00
10/25/1996	CARCO Auto Loan MT 1996-1	Chrysler Financial Corporation	Auto	500.00
12/11/1996	Green Tree Floorplan Receivables MT 1996-2	Green Tree Financial Corp.	MH	500.30
12/16/1996	CARCO Auto Loan MT 1996-2	Chrysler Financial Corporation	Auto	500.00
1/15/1997	Bombardier Receivables MT 1 1997-1	Bombardier Capital Inc.	Eqp	427.13
7/24/1997	CARCO Auto Loan MT 1997-1	Chrysler Financial Corporation	Auto	700.00
8/5/1997	Navistar Financial Dealer Note MT 1997-1	Navistar Financial	Eqp	200.00
4/9/1998	Green Tree Floorplan Receivables MT 1998-1	Green Tree Financial Corp.	MH	420.88
6/16/1998	CARCO Auto Loan MT 1998-1	Chrysler Financial Corporation	Auto	1,000.00
8/20/1998	Green Tree Floorplan Receivables MT 1998-2	Green Tree Financial Corp.	MH	462.50
3/1/1999	CARCO Auto Loan MT 1999-1	Chrysler Financial Corporation	Auto	1,000.00
5/6/1999	Superior Wholesale Inventory Fin Trust V 1999-A	GMAC	Auto	750.00
5/13/1999	CARCO Auto Loan MT 1999-2	Chrysler Financial Corporation	Auto	1,350.00
5/20/1999	Yamaha Motor MT 1999-1	Yamaha Motor Credit	Eqp	214.04
7/13/1999	CARCO Auto Loan MT 1999-3	Chrysler Financial Corporation	Auto	1,000.00
9/30/1999	Green Tree Floorplan Receivables MT 1999-1	Green Tree Financial Corp.	MH	637.00
11/4/1999	CARCO Auto Loan MT 1999-4	Chrysler Financial Corporation	Auto	500.00
3/22/2000	World Omni Wholesale MT 2000-1	World Omni	Auto	700.00
3/24/2000	CARCO Auto Loan MT 2000-1	Chrysler Financial Corporation	Auto	750.00
4/20/2000	Deutsche Floorplan Receivables MT 2000-1	Deutsche Financial Services	Various	1,232.00
4/20/2000	Deutsche Floorplan Receivables MT 2000-2	Deutsche Financial Services	Various	492.50
Total				16,771.34

Source: DB Global Markets Research

Collateralized Debt
Obligations

Chapter 13

Collateralized Debt Obligations

Charles Schorin
Principal
Director of ABS Research
Morgan Stanley Dean Witter

Steven Weinreich
Associate
Morgan Stanley Dean Witter

INTRODUCTION

The market for *collateralized debt obligations* (CDOs) is the fastest growing sector of the asset-backed securities market. From less than $3 billion originated as recently as 1995, the market for CDOs reached $57 billion in 1997 and another $30 billion in the first half of 1998. Though it is not the newest asset class — the first CDO was created in 1988 — it has become both an extremely popular instrument for investors and a very attractive vehicle for issuers. Investors have been attracted to the sector because of the relatively high yield for the highly rated paper, while issuers' motivations — among others — have been to maximize return on equity and increase assets under management.

CDOs are special purpose vehicles investing in a diversified pool of assets. The investments in the CDO are funded through the issuance of several classes of securities, the repayment of which is linked to the performance of the underlying securities that serve as collateral for the CDO liabilities. The investments are managed/serviced by an experienced investment manager/servicer, sometimes referred to as the *collateral manager*.

The securities issued by the CDO are tranched into rated and unrated classes. The rating of each class is primarily determined through the priority of interest in the cash flows generated by the collateral. The senior notes are typically rated AAA to A, may pay a fixed or floating rate coupon and have the highest priority on cash flows. The mezzanine classes are typically rated BBB to B, may pay either a fixed or floating rate coupon and have a claim on cash flows that is subordinate to the senior notes.

The subordinated notes/equity of the CDO are generally unrated and are the residual of the transaction. Subordinated noteholders receive a current coupon out of the residual interest proceeds generated by the collateral, after payment of expenses and debt service on the securities that rank senior to the subordinated notes. The coupon may be deferred or eliminated depending upon available cash flow. The subordinated notes are in a first loss position; because they represent a leveraged investment in the underlying collateral, they have a higher expected return — although with a higher volatility of return — than the underlying collateral pool.

CDOs may be characterized as *collateralized bond obligations* (CBOs), *collateralized loan obligations* (CLOs) or both. These instruments are analogous to other collateralized securities, with the collateral for a CBO being a pool of outstanding bonds or bond-like securities, while that for a CLO is a pool of loans. The collateral also may contain various types of credit derivatives, including credit linked notes (CLNs).

CDOs can further be categorized into two types: arbitrage or balance sheet transactions. In an *arbitrage transaction*, the equity investor is capturing the spread difference between the relatively high yielding collateral and the yields at which the senior liabilities of the CDO are issued. A *balance sheet transaction*, in contrast, is intended to remove loans, or in some cases, bonds, from the balance sheet of a financial institution so that it achieves capital relief, improved liquidity or a higher return on assets through redeployment of capital.

Arbitrage transactions can be divided into *cash flow transactions* or *market value transactions*. Balance sheet deals are all cash flow transactions. Cash flow deals are those that are based on the ability of the collateral to generate sufficient cash to pay interest and principal on the rated classes of securities issued by the CDO. Market value transactions, in contrast, depend upon the ability of the fund manager to maintain a collateral market value, potentially through actively trading the portfolio subject to various constraints, sufficient to generate cash upon the sale of such collateral in the collateral pool to pay the CDO securities.

The collateral manager of a CDO monitors the pool and makes ongoing trading decisions within parameters established prior to closing and defined in the transaction indenture. In fact, a trustee is hired to ensure that these covenants of the CDO are followed. The trustee assumes complete control of the release of any cash and/or securities of the transaction, and pre-approves all trading decisions.

Investors in CDO senior notes are attracted to the sector because it enables them to achieve high yields relative to other asset-backed securities for a given bond rating category.

The collateral manager/sponsor may have several motivations for the creation of a CDO. For balance sheet CLOs, sponsors can achieve capital relief by removing assets from their balance sheet. In addition, to the extent that these assets are relatively high quality and therefore low yielding, the sponsor can redeploy capital to higher yielding investments, as well as tap a relatively inexpensive or new funding source.

Sponsors of arbitrage transactions are motivated by the ability to increase assets under management in order to increase management fees. Equity investors are motivated by the ability to realize leveraged returns on the underlying assets, while achieving funding that is attractive relative to alternatives, such as repo financing.

Exhibit 1: Generic CDO Structure

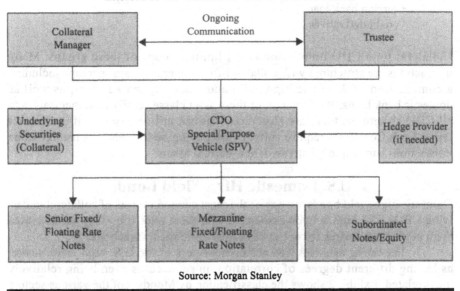

Source: Morgan Stanley

This chapter begins with a description of the collateral types employed in CDO transactions and then moves to a discussion of the various CDO structures and mechanics. We include discussions of credit enhancement and coverage and quality tests, as well as present sample transactions. We next turn to the manner in which ratings agencies analyze CDO structures in terms of credit, followed by a framework in which investors should analyze the senior notes and mezzanine classes in terms of relative value. In Chapter 14 we introduce a new method to better analyze defaults and the credit protection of CDO transactions. The Appendix to this chapter contains details on the calculations behind Moody's diversity score and binomial expansion methodology and a description of Standard & Poor's CBO/CLO model.

COLLATERAL

Investors in a CDO have a perfected security interest in the underlying collateral, which may consist of a multitude of asset types. This diversity of collateral types can make the sector as a whole quite challenging to understand.

In this section we consider the most common types of assets utilized to date. These asset classes are:

- U.S. domestic high yield bonds
- emerging market debt
- U.S. domestic bank loans

- special situation loans and distressed debt
- foreign bank loans
- credit derivatives

Collateral for a CDO transaction is not limited to one of these groups. Many transactions are structured with collateral from several groups, perhaps including a combination of domestic high yield and emerging market debt, as well as domestic bank loans. While not all of these asset classes easily lend themselves to all CDO structures, there are structures that can utilize any one of these asset types. Cash flow deals require current cash paying assets, whereas market value transactions can employ distressed, non-current assets.

U.S. Domestic High Yield Bonds

Domestic high yield bonds are one of the most common forms of collateral underlying CBOs. The high coupon associated with these relatively risky assets makes them perfect candidates for use in cash flow arbitrage transactions.

The rating agencies treat different sectors of the U.S. high yield market as having different degrees of correlation, in some cases even being relatively uncorrelated. Exhibit 2 shows the classification by Moody's of the various sectors of the high yield market. The rating agencies tend to give diversity credit for multiple industrial sectors within developed economies, but group together various sectors within single countries or regions of emerging markets.

Exhibit 2: Domestic High Yield Sectors

	Industry		Industry
1	Aerospace and Defense	18	Grocery
2	Automobile	19	Healthcare, Education and Childcare
3	Banking	20	Hotels, Motels, Inns and Gaming
4	Beverage, Food and Tobacco	21	Insurance
5	Broadcasting	22	Leisure and Entertainment
6	Buildings and Real Estate	23	Machinery
7	Cargo Transport	24	Mining and Non-precious Metals
8	Chemicals, Plastics and Rubber	25	Oil and Gas
9	Containers, Packaging and Glass	26	Personal and Non-durable Consumer Prod
10	Div. Nat. Resources, Precious Metals	27	Personal Transportation
11	Diversified/Conglomerate Manufacturing	28	Personal, Food and Miscellaneous Services
12	Diversified/Conglomerate Service	29	Printing, Publishing
13	Durable Consumer Products	30	Retail Stores
14	Ecological	31	Telecommunications
15	Electronics	32	Textiles and Leather
16	Farming and Agricultural	33	Utilities
17	Finance		

Source: Moody's Investors Service

Emerging Market Debt

Emerging market collateral has been used frequently in cash flow arbitrage transactions. The relatively large yield spread between these securities and the higher rated bonds sold out of the special purpose CDO vehicle allow these bonds to be used in cash flow transactions. Their high price volatility has prevented them from being employed very often in market value transactions.

In emerging market regions, the rating agencies generally do not grant credit for sector diversification within a country. The reason for this is that the perceived high correlation between the overall emerging economy and an individual sector within that market is high enough not to warrant diversification credit in the analysis. In fact, for purposes of measuring portfolio diversification, Moody's, for instance, groups all emerging market countries into five regions, and further penalizes Latin America with a higher correlation of bonds defaulting.

When emerging market securities are used as collateral, rating agencies tend to place restrictions on the concentration a portfolio can maintain in any one geographic region. These restriction levels have typically been somewhat higher than the percentages in the actual collateral portfolios at time of origination. A large percentage of CDOs structured in the past few years have used at least some portion of emerging market debt in the collateral pool. The ratings analysis for emerging market backed CDOs is similar to that of domestic high yield CDOs.

U.S. Domestic Bank Loans

Higher quality domestic bank loans have typically been employed as collateral in balance sheet CLOs. As mentioned above, the relatively low yield of higher quality domestic bank commercial and industrial (C&I) loans makes their use impractical in arbitrage or market value CBOs. For instance, the NationsBank Commercial Loan Master Trust balance sheet CLO transaction is backed by higher quality bank loans; the objective of NationsBank was to remove these assets from its balance sheet and achieve a higher return on the assets that remained on balance sheet. The NationsBank transaction is said to be de-linked from the issuer, in that investors face credit exposure only to the assets in the trust and not to the sponsor. Similar to traditional asset-backed transactions for which the collateral was transferred to the trust in a true sale, a downgrade of the sponsor would not in and of itself result in a downgrade of the transaction.

High yield loans have also been employed in CDO collateral pools. Also referred to as HLT loans — loans from highly leveraged transactions — these high yield loans contain certain covenants that provide additional protection. This protection frequently includes a security interest. High yield loans have been used extensively as collateral for cash flow arbitrage CLOs.

Special Situation Loans and Distressed Debt

In addition to high quality C&I loans, more risky types of bank loans have also been employed as CDO collateral. These include special situation loans and distressed debt. Special situation loans are those that involve unique, individually negotiated terms, such as workout loans. Distressed debt represents loans to borrowers that already have experienced some economic difficulty and may be expected to have a higher likelihood of default. These more risky types of bank loans have been in pools backing market value arbitrage transactions.

Foreign Bank Loans

Foreign bank loans have also been used as CDO collateral. These generally have been relatively high quality loans backing balance sheet CLOs. The loans themselves may be dollar or non-dollar denominated. Examples of non-dollar loans include the British pound loans behind ROSE Funding and the French franc loans backing Credit Lyonnais Cyber Val. Foreign loans introduce special considerations for perfection of security interests owing to the differential development of the legal infrastructure pertaining to securitization in various countries.

Credit Derivatives

Credit derivatives, including credit linked swaps and linked notes (CLNs), have also been used as collateral in various CDOs. Credit derivatives have typically been used to tailor exposure to a specific credit or efficiently transfer credit risk.

The cash flows from credit derivatives are tied to the performance of anything from a single credit to a basket of corporate or sovereign credits. Investors in credit derivatives, then, achieve exposure to defined credit instruments of potentially varying credit ratings by holding a single instrument. Ratings of CLNs or credit swaps are linked not only to that of the underlying credits, but also to that of the issuing entity or swap counterparty. For example, ratings of the SBC Glacier transaction are linked to those of Swiss Bank Corporation. This is in contrast to de-linked structures, for which the assets have been sold or assigned directly into the issuing vehicle and the investor has no exposure to the issuer/sponsor, per se.

TRANSACTION STRUCTURES AND MECHANICS

Most collateralized debt obligations can be placed into either of two main groups, arbitrage or balance sheet transactions. Within the arbitrage heading, there are cash flow and market value transactions. For the most part, balance sheet transactions utilize the cash flow structure. Exhibit 3 diagrams the conceptual breakdown between arbitrage and balance sheet transactions, while Exhibit 4 shows their relative market composition over the past few years. In this section we will explore the structural nuances of these types of deals.

Arbitrage Transactions

Arbitrage transactions can be classified into cash flow and market value transactions. In this section we discuss their structural and practical differences. The primary difference relates to the manner in which the collateral asset pool generates cash to pay the transaction liabilities. Whereas cash flow transactions focus on the ability of a collateral pool to generate interest and principal sufficient to pay the CDO's liabilities with a substantial cushion to protect against defaults, market value transactions rely on the value of the underlying collateral. The collateral in a market value deal is marked to market on an ongoing basis and must maintain enough market value to pay off the fund's liabilities with substantial cushion to protect against market declines. This is the primary distinction between the two structures, although there are other differences that cause the two structures to behave and trade quite differently. Arbitrage transactions generally range in size from $100 million to as much as $1 billion or more.

Cash Flow Transactions

Cash flow arbitrage deals attempt to extract the difference between the relatively higher yield on the speculative grade and/or emerging market debt assets of the CDO and the lower cost of the relatively higher rated securities issued by the CDO structure. These transactions employ a collateral pool with a given expected loss and prioritize the underlying pool's credit exposure into several classes which, in aggregate, have credit exposure identical to the pool's, but individually have either greater or lesser risk. This differential credit exposure is achieved primarily via subordination. Added credit enhancement in the form of excess spread, overcollateralization, structural triggers, reserve accounts or insurance wraps may also be utilized.

Exhibit 3: CDO Market

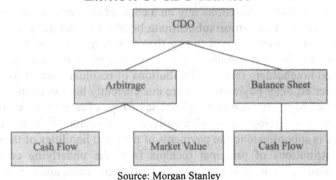

Source: Morgan Stanley

Exhibit 4: CDO Market Composition: Arbitrage versus Balance Sheet (1996, 1997, 1998 through July)

	Volume (Billions of $)		No. of Transactions	
	Arbitrage	Balance Sheet	Arbitrage	Balance Sheet
1998	10.9	19.3	27	20
1997	22.2	34.9	68	18
1996	12.7	5.0	36	1

Source: Morgan Stanley

Ratings on the liabilities of cash flow CDOs are dependent upon cash flow generation and portfolio characteristics. There are no requirements to buy or sell securities of the underlying collateral pool due to adverse market value movements. The primary consideration is the default risk of the underlying collateral.

A benchmark cash flow arbitrage transaction is the $1.276 billion Van Kampen CLO I, Ltd. structure. This is backed entirely by U.S. domestic bank loans, with neither high yield bond nor emerging market collateral. It consists of an Aa2/AA rated senior secured floating rate class totaling $375 million; an Aa2/AA rated revolving credit facility that may be drawn up to $625 million; a Baa3 rated second priority senior secured note class totaling $130 million; and unrated subordinated notes of $146 million.

Collateral Because the rating of cash flow CDOs is supported by projected cash flows of the underlying collateral, the collateral pool tends to consist more of conventional debt instruments with defined principal and interest schedules than is the case with market value transactions. Securities backing cash flow CDOs may consist of a variety of assets types, such as bank loans, high yield bonds, emerging market debt (both sovereign and corporate), and securities from other structured transactions.

Generally bank loans included in such arbitrage structures would consist of sub-investment grade loans, whereas higher quality commercial and industrial loans would more likely be included in balance sheet transactions.

Structure Cash flow transactions rely on a concept similar to most asset-backed securities structured as senior/subordinate bonds. Income generated from the underlying pool of assets is used to pay first servicing and other trust fees, then interest to the senior most bondholders and then interest to the mezzanine holders. Subordinated noteholders receive distributions of residual interest by the collateral only after all other payments that are due currently have been made.

Principal payments go through the same type of cash flow waterfall after a reinvestment or revolving period. Generally, a large portion of the servicing/management fee is subordinate to the payments of the rated liabilities of the CDO.

Distributions of principal receipts from the underlying collateral are made to subordinated noteholders only after all of the senior and mezzanine securities have been paid in full.

Cash flow CDOs typically have a 3- to 6-year period — referred to as the *reinvestment period* or *revolving period* — during which principal cash flows from the collateral pool may be reinvested in new collateral, subject to certain predefined constraints. After the reinvestment period, only unscheduled principal, such as that from calls, tenders or collateral sales, may be reinvested. All other principal collections from the collateral are used first to repay the senior notes until they are retired. The basic structure and cash flow waterfall for an arbitrage CDO transaction are diagrammed in Exhibits 5 and 6.

Exhibit 5: Interest Cash Flow Waterfall of Cash Flow CDO

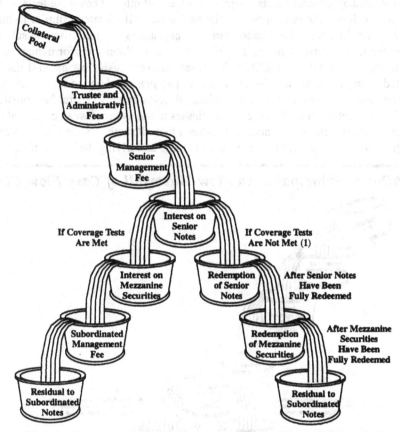

Note: (1) If Coverage Tests are not met, and to the extent not corrected with principal proceeds, the remaining interest proceeds will be used to redeem the most senior notes to bring the structure back into compliance with the Coverage Tests. Interest on the Mezzanine Securities may be deferred and compounded if cash flow is not available to pay current interest due.

Source: Morgan Stanley

In general, a certain percentage of the pool can be traded at the portfolio manager's discretion in order to take advantage of relative value opportunities that may become apparent after the transaction has been issued. To ensure that the collateral pool maintains a resemblance to its composition at issuance, the transaction's indenture will stipulate restrictions and diversification requirements that will be maintained throughout the transaction's life. These are referred to as *quality tests* and will be explained below.

Credit Enhancement Senior notes in cash flow transactions are protected by subordination and overcollateralization. The senior notes have a priority claim on all cash flows generated on the underlying collateral pool. The senior notes are further protected by coverage tests — generally par and interest coverage tests — that serve to accelerate the redemption of the senior notes if violated. Similar to home equity loan ABS senior/subordinate transactions, cash is diverted from the subordinate notes to the senior notes in the event of poor collateral performance. In the case of cash flow arbitrage CDOs, however, *interest* cash flow as well may be diverted from the more subordinate classes to pay *principal* on the senior classes if coverage tests are breached. The subordinated notes being in a first loss position, plus this redirection of cash to the senior classes in the event of weak collateral performance, are the credit enhancement features that allow the senior notes to obtain ratings significantly higher than the pool of assets underlying the transaction.

Exhibit 6: Principal Cash Flow Waterfall of Cash Flow CDO

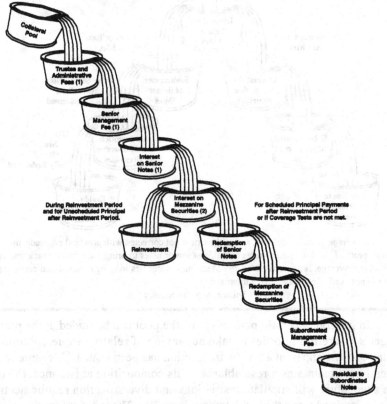

Note: (1) To the extent not paid by Interest Proceeds.
(2) To the extent Senior Note Coverage Tests are met and to the extent not already paid by Interest Proceeds. If Coverage Tests are not met, the remaining Principal Proceeds will be used to redeem the most senior notes to bring the structure back into compliance with the Coverage Tests. Interest on the Mezzanine Securities may be deferred and compounded if cash flow is not available to pay current interest due.

Source: Morgan Stanley

There are two scenarios where the senior notes may receive accelerated principal payments, other than those applied after the reinvestment period due to principal payments generated by the underlying collateral pool. One scenario would be if the senior notes are called. Cash flow CDOs usually provide for the senior notes to be callable at par or at a make-whole premium by the subordinated note holders after a stated non-call period, which usually is 2 to 5 years. The second scenario is if the interest or par value coverage tests are breached. This may occur, for instance, due to defaults within the underlying collateral portfolio. In this case, cash flow that would otherwise go to holders of the subordinate classes, and even mezzanine classes, if necessary, would be used to pay down the senior notes until coverage levels are restored. After this point, cash flow would be resumed to the mezzanine and subordinate classes, respectively.

Besides coverage tests, cash flow transactions also provide for quality tests. While the violation of a coverage test leads to the redirection of cash flows, the quality tests are put in place to ensure that the portfolio maintains similar characteristics as those at issuance.

Coverage Tests There are two types of coverage tests — par value test and interest coverage test.

1. *Par value test:* For cash flow CDOs, the *par value test* requires that rated bonds have at least a given stated percentage of collateral supporting it. This is analogous to the overcollateralization trigger in the home equity loan ABS arena. For example, if the trigger is set at 115% on a $100 million senior bond, then if at any time the par value of the assets in the collateral portfolio decreases below $115 million, the senior bonds will receive principal payments until the trigger is cured.

Lower rated CDO bonds will have lower percentage par value hurdles. For example, if the senior par value percentage were set at 115%, the mezzanine securities may have a par value test of 105%. However, in the calculation of the par coverage test for mezzanine classes, the amount of the senior bonds is included in the analysis. Consider a $20 million mezzanine class with $100 million in senior bonds above it. If the minimum par coverage level were set at 105% for the mezzanine bond, the collateral must maintain a minimum level of 105% of $120 million, or $126 million. Again, if the test were breached, the most senior notes would be redeemed until the test came back into compliance.

2. *Interest coverage test:* For cash flow CDOs, the *interest coverage test* is applied to ensure that the interest cash flow on the underlying collateral has sufficient cushion to absorb losses and still make interest payments to the rated CDO securities. This test is analogous to the debt service coverage ratio analyzed in the commercial mortgage backed securities (CMBS) market, although in the CMBS market, a decline in the debt service coverage ratio would not trigger a reprioritization of cash flow. The debt service coverage ratio in CMBS analysis is purely a

descriptive statistic. With cash flow CDOs, however, should the interest coverage test be breached, payments will be redirected to the senior bonds until the trigger is cured. An interest coverage level is generally set for each rated security at time of issuance.

Quality Tests Examples of quality tests within other sectors of the ABS market are difficult to find. The reason is due to the difference in the collateral pool composition of CDOs versus other ABS. CDO collateral pools are actively traded, in contrast to the static nature of ABS pools. In addition, ABS pools typically comprise thousands, and perhaps tens of thousands of individual loans, so that the performance of any one loan would generally not affect the transaction performance. In contrast, there are fewer loans or bonds in CDO collateral pools, so the risks are more lumpy. Poor performance of a single component of a CDO collateral pool could have a marked affect on deal performance.

The basic purpose of quality tests in CDOs is to ensure that the collateral pool does not become under-diversified or have its composition change dramatically through the normal trading activities of the manager. When quality tests are breached, there is no change to the cash flows directed to bond holders, but trading is restricted to actions that improve the collateral composition in relation to the breached quality measure. The four primary quality tests focus on diversity scores, concentrations in certain regions, the weighted average rating of the underlying collateral pool, and maturity restrictions.

1. *Minimum diversity score:* The diversity score developed by Moody's is probably the single statistic in the CDO market that is most associated with a rating agency. We discuss the methodology for calculating diversity scores more fully in the Appendix.

A diversity score is a statistic indicating the degree of variability — or diversity — in the CDO collateral pool. It is recalculated each time the bonds in the collateral pool change. The collateral pool may change for any of several reasons, including:

- bond in the collateral pool being sold
- bond being purchased into the collateral pool
- scheduled repayment changing the percentage composition of the pool
- unscheduled payments (e.g., calls or tenders) of underlying assets
- defaults.

A portfolio manager may not execute a trade that would result in this test being breached, i.e., that would result in a diversity score below the stated minimum. If an event happens outside the control of the portfolio manager that causes the diversity score to fall below the stated minimum — for example, a bond paying down — then future trades would be restricted to actions that would improve the diversity score.

2. *Concentrations in emerging market regions:* The indenture will also formally describe certain restrictions as to the exposure of the portfolio to certain sectors and/or regions. During the ratings process, the agencies place levels on the securities based on certain assumptions as to the composition of the portfolio once the collateral pool is completely populated. For example, consider a portfolio that, when fully populated, will contain 80% domestic high yield bonds and 20% emerging markets debt, with the emerging market composition being 3% Latin America, 5% Russia, 8% non-Japan Asia and 4% Eastern Europe. The rating agencies will assign ratings based on this portfolio composition. They will, however, run stress scenarios to ensure that the rating is applicable given even higher concentrations in these emerging market regions. As such, the indenture may stipulate that the portfolio may have no more than 5% in Latin America, 8% in Russia, 10% in non-Japan Asia, and 5% in Eastern Europe. These levels would constitute the maximum representation of the given regions in the portfolio.

Defaults, amortization and call provisions may result in the maximum concentration percentages being breached. The portfolio manager is prohibited from executing a trade that would breach these levels. If these levels are breached, once again there are no implications on cash flows to the CDO noteholders. The portfolio manager's trading ability, however, would be limited to actions that would improve the representation of these regions in the underlying collateral pool.

3. *Minimum weighted average rating:* The indenture will require that the collateral pool underlying the transaction maintains a minimum average rating. The balances of the securities in the pool as well as the non-linear expected default rate of different ratings categories, derive the weighted average rating. Moody's, Fitch, and DCR assign a numerical measure to each rating category, incorporating the expected default for that category. Since expected default is non-linear in the ratings categories, the numerical progression of this measure does not move one-for-one along the ratings spectrum. While S&P does not specifically employ a numerical average rating concept, its trading model does factor in the expected defaults based upon the ratings distribution of the collateral.

Exhibit 7 shows the integer value that Moody's, Fitch and DCR equate to each rating level. Averaging these values across the collateral pool, weighted by the balance of the respective security in the pool, will result in the weighted average rating. Typically the minimum average rating will be set initially at a level somewhat lower than the actual rating of the existing pool to allow for some trading flexibility after issuance.

Similar to the diversity score test described above, a portfolio manager cannot add or remove a bond from the portfolio if the resultant portfolio violates the minimum weighted average rating test. This test may be breached if assets within the portfolio are downgraded. On an ongoing basis, the trustee calculates the average rating on each remittance date. Breaches of this trigger result in similar trading restrictions as discussed above. Trading would be limited to actions that improve the collateral pool relative to this test.

Exhibit 7: Rating Factors Used to Derive Weighted Average Ratings

	Moody's	Fitch	DCR
Aaa/AAA	1	1	0.001
Aa1/AA+	10	8	0.010
Aa2/AA	20	10	0.030
Aa3/AA-	40	14	0.050
A1/A+	70	18	0.100
A2/A	120	23	0.150
A3/A-	180	36	0.200
Baa1/BBB+	260	48	0.250
Baa2/BBB	360	61	0.350
Baa3/BBB-	610	94	0.500
Ba1/BB+	940	129	0.750
Ba2/BB	1,350	165	1.000
Ba3/BB-	1,780	210	1.250
B1/B+	2,220	260	1.600
B2/B	2,720	308	2.000
B3/B-	3,490	356	2.700
CCC+	NA	463	NA
Caa/CCC	6,500	603	3.750
CCC-	NA	782	NA
< Ca/ <CCC-	10,000	1,555	NA

Source: Moody's Investors Service, Fitch Investors Service, Duff & Phelps Credit Rating

4. *Maturity restrictions:* In older cash flow transactions, maturity restrictions stipulated that if the collateral manager were to sell a security, he would be constrained to purchasing another security with a maturity no longer than the security that was sold. For more recent transactions, the manager trades the portfolio within maturity buckets, so that the sale of one security could be followed by the purchase of a longer dated security, so long as there is room in the maturity bucket into which the purchased security will be placed. Maturity restrictions are used to ensure that when rated securities are scheduled to be redeemed, a large enough portion of the collateral is scheduled to mature to pay the issuing vehicle's liabilities.

Sample Transaction: Calhoun CBO, Ltd. Calhoun CBO, Ltd. is a representative cash flow arbitrage transaction. It is collateralized by a high yield/emerging market breakdown of approximately 80%/20%. The deal is summarized in Exhibit 8.

The Calhoun CBO contains the features discussed here: non-call and reinvestment periods, minimum collateral diversity score and average rating requirements. The capital structure consists of Aa2 rated senior notes, Baa3 rated second priority senior notes and unrated subordinated classes.

Exhibit 8: Representative Cash Flow Arbitrage Transaction: Calhoun CBO, Ltd.

- Manager: American Express Asset Management
- 82.2% U.S. high yield bonds, 17.8% emerging market bonds
- Fixed rate: 91.4%
- Interest rate hedge: $180 million notional
- Minimum average rating: B2
- Minimum diversity score: 40
- Reinvestment period: 5 years
- Non-call period: 3 years
- 12-year final maturity
- Aa2 rated Senior Notes, 7.7 yr AL (70.18% of transaction)
- Baa3 rated Second Priority Senior Notes, 11.0 yr AL (15.79%)
- Senior Subordinated Notes (7.02%)
- Junior Subordinated Notes (7.02%)

Source: Morgan Stanley

Rating Cash Flow Arbitrage Transactions The approach to rating cash flow arbitrage transactions differs in specifics among the four major rating agencies, but the basic methodology is essentially the same. The most important aspect of cash flow transactions in terms of rating analysis is expected loss.

Rating agencies analyze three main aspects of a cash flow CDO transaction: collateral, structure and manager. The net result is an expected loss level for each rated security. Once this expected loss level is derived, and stressed, the agencies can apply ratings to the securities based on the results of the analysis.

1. *Collateral:* The collateral underlying CDO transactions can vary across rating, industry, maturity, pay type and geographic region. As such, the analysis of this collateral is a complex and potentially arduous process. The rating agencies examine the underlying assets in terms of:

- diversity of the assets in the pool
- ratings of the underlying assets
- recovery rates associated with different asset classes
- asset/liability characteristics.

The rating agencies analyze each of these factors under various default and interest rate scenarios in order to determine the impact of each factor on the rated debt.

Diversity: The rating agencies view diversity as a positive factor. Moody's has developed a quantitative method for calculating the level of diversity within a pool of assets but each rating agency gives credit to the level of diversification in the collateral pool. The concept is analogous to the benefit — in terms of credit enhancement levels — granted securities in the CMBS market, which have a wide variety of collateral types ranging from mortgages on office buildings to retail space. In the CDO market, the rating agencies grant credit for diversity of industry, region and absolute number of issuers within an industry or region. Clearly, the marginal benefit afforded the collateral pool by including an additional issuer should decrease as the number of issuers within the sector increases. Exhibit 9 is a sample of the diversity credit granted by Moody's for various numbers of issuers within an industry.

Lack of correlation must be exhibited between sectors in order for the rating agencies to grant credit for diversity. Including two five dollar positions that exhibit 100% correlation in a pool is essentially the same as including one security representing 10 dollars in the same pool. Clearly, if the securities are 100% correlated, there should be no benefit due to diversity for including these two assets in the pool. It is not necessarily the case that two issuers within the same industry/ region will exhibit 100% correlation. We will explore the calculation of diversity in more detail below. While Moody's is the only agency to publish a quantitative method for calculating the diversity of a portfolio of securities, each rating agency examines the diversity characteristics of a pool when rating a CDO.

Ratings: Each of the assets in the collateral pool must be rated, either publicly or privately, by the rating agency analyzing the pool. In the absence of such a rating, the agency may apply a shadow rating, or may take the level assigned by a different established agency and imply a rating, sometimes haircut by one or two notches. Moody's, Fitch and DCR calculate a weighted average rating on the collateral. This was discussed above in the section on Quality Tests. Ratings factors were displayed in Exhibit 7.

Exhibit 9: Moody's Diversity Scores for Firms within an Industry

Number of Firms in Same Industry	Diversity Score
1	1.00
2	1.50
3	2.00
4	2.33
5	2.67
6	3.00
7	3.25
8	3.50
9	3.75
10	4.00
>10	Evaluated on a case-by-case basis

Source: Moody's Investors Service

Exhibit 10: Sample Calculation of Weighted Average Collateral Rating

A	B	C	D	E	F
Security	% of Pool	Moody's Rating	Rating Factor	Weighting * Rating Factor (B * D)	Portfolio Average Rating
1	15	Ba1	940	141.0	
2	15	Ba3	1,780	267.0	
3	20	B1	2,220	444.0	
4	50	B3	3,490	1,745.0	
Portfolio				2,597.0	B2

Source: Moody's Investors Service, Morgan Stanley

Exhibit 11: Base Case Recovery Rate Assumptions for Various Rating Agencies

US Debt	Base Recovery Assumptions (%)			
	Moody's	S&P	DCR	Fitch
Senior Secured Bank Loans	50	50-60	60	60
Senior Secured Bonds	30	40-55	50	50
Senior Unsecured Debt	30	25-50	40	45
Subordinated Debt	30	15-28	30	25
Emerging Markets	Moody's	S&P	DCR	
Sovereign Bonds	25	25	25	
Corporate Bonds	10	15	20	

Source: Moody's Investors Service, Standard & Poor's, Duff & Phelps Credit Rating and Fitch Investors Service

Exhibit 10 works through a sample calculation based on a pool containing four rated securities. Clearly the portfolio's overall rating is skewed downward by the 50% weighting in the B3 rated asset. The non-linear relationship between ratings and expected defaults skews the aggregate rating towards the lowest rated asset in the pool. The exact rating factors used by Moody's, Fitch and DCR are different due to varying experience and data sources, but the overall methodology is essentially the same.

Recovery assumptions: The recovery rate assumed for different asset types varies across rating agencies as well as across collateral types. Exhibit 11 shows base case recovery assumptions for the four major rating agencies across various asset classes. These assumptions are intended to be conservative relative to historical recovery rates computed by the agencies. Preference in the form of higher recovery rates is awarded to more senior liens in the issuing entities' capital structure. For example, senior secured loans will exhibit higher recovery rates than unsecured senior debt.

Asset/liability characteristics: Another issue more specific to cash flow transactions is the maturity profile of the underlying collateral relative to the CDO securities. The rating agencies prefer to include securities with expected maturity dates prior to the maturity dates of the rated debt. Securities that are scheduled to mature after the rated debt may have to be liquidated in order to retire the CDO. Cash flow transactions are not based upon the actual market value of an asset, however the rating agencies will severely haircut the amount of par credit given longer dated assets in a cash flow pool.

The fixed/floating composition of the pool also becomes an issue when analyzing cash flow transactions. If the rated securities issued out of the SPV are predominantly floating rate, yet the collateral underlying the transaction is mostly fixed rate, investors would be taking on interest rate risk on top of the credit risk inherent to the CDO market. In order to achieve the desired ratings, interest rate hedges are frequently incorporated at issuance in order to mitigate this interest rate risk. These hedges may be in the form of cap or swap instruments.

2. *Structure:* Rating agencies analyze the structure of a given cash flow CDO during the ratings process. Various aspects of structure that affect the CDO ratings are:

- coverage (early-amortization) tests
- internal credit enhancement, and
- legal soundness of securitization structure.

We address the first two of these below. The target ratings of the issued debt will affect the stress levels applied on the collateral pool during the process. The higher the desired rating for a given tranche, the more rigorous the stress that has to be withstood.

Coverage and quality tests: During the rating process, the agencies evaluate the coverage and quality tests that were discussed in detail above. The levels are designed to give the CDO noteholders the necessary protection to achieve the desired rating, given the composition of the collateral pool.

Should a coverage test be breached, interest and principal proceeds are directed from the more subordinated bonds and redirected to retire the senior bonds ahead of schedule. This redirection continues until the senior bonds are retired, or the performance level is brought back into alignment. The main difference between these triggers and those often found in home equity loan ABS is that in CDOs, the subordinate bonds are completely locked out from cash flow until the trigger is cured. In home equities, the subordinate bonds do not receive principal, but do continue to receive interest. Most cash flow CDOs pay sequentially down the ratings spectrum, as opposed to pro-rata (after a stepdown date) in the HEL sector. Subordinate CDO classes are generally not scheduled to receive principal until the more senior classes are retired.[1]

Should a quality test be breached no redirection of cash flow is required, however the collateral manager's trading flexibility would be curtailed. Trading would then be restricted to actions improving the collateral pool relative to the breached test.

Internal credit enhancements: Internal credit enhancements can be provided to a CDO through methods similar to those of more traditional asset backed securities. The most common form of enhancement is provided through excess spread: the yield on the collateral is higher than the yield on the CDO securities, otherwise there would be a negative carry situation and it is unlikely that the transaction would be economically feasible for the issuer. Just as in the home equity loan, credit card, auto and manufactured housing sectors of the ABS market, excess spread in CDOs represents the first loss position in the structure. Somewhat lower than the better performing master trusts in the credit card arena, it is not uncommon to see excess spread values near 200 basis points.

The rating agencies tend to shock interest rates substantially during the rating process. As a result, it is often the case that some form of interest rate hedge is employed in the CDO structure at issuance. This hedge may be in the form of caps or swaps and would depend on the performance of the specific collateral pool in various environments.

3. *Manager:* One of the fundamental manners in which CDOs differ from other asset backed transactions is the active trading of the CDO collateral pool, in contrast to the static nature of asset backed collateral pools. As such, the primary responsibility of the portfolio manager in a cash flow CDO is to minimize defaults in the collateral pool. As part of the ratings process, the agencies will perform due diligence on the manager's performance history as well as back office capabilities. An adequate infrastructure is required by the rating agencies and can greatly affect ratings. The track record of the manager, specifically a proven ability to perform well in adverse market conditions, is also considered important. Clearly, the CDO structure is not suited to all managers.

The manager of a cash flow transaction is typically permitted to actively trade a percentage of the portfolio per year, in what is called a "discretionary trading basket." The manager is always permitted to sell defaulted, equity or perceived credit risk securities. Securities that have been upgraded, or are on watch to be upgraded, can also be sold subject to certain constraints. In no case may a portfolio manager exercise a transaction resulting in a portfolio that violates any of the coverage or quality tests as specified in the transaction's indenture.

---

[1] To be technical, deferred interest on mezzanine tranches added to principal can be paid down early.

Exhibit 12: Capital Structure of a Market Value Arbitrage Transaction

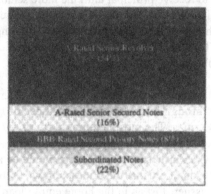

Source: Morgan Stanley

Market Value Transactions

Market value transactions actually predated cash flow structures, and after a bit of a lull, have made a major resurgence recently. It has become an attractive capital structure due to the greater flexibility afforded the portfolio manager in terms of trading ability, and the types of collateral that can be included in the asset pool. Because the actual cash flows provided by the collateral pool do not necessarily affect the rated securities, a portfolio manager can include a wider selection of asset types in the pool.

Market value transactions require that the securities in the collateral pool be marked to market by the collateral manager on a frequent basis. Therefore, investors who prefer a marked-to-market discipline may be more comfortable with this type of structure. Further, the expertise of the portfolio manager can be maximized because the capital structure can be changed post-securitization and additional leverage can be employed to invest in perceived relative value opportunities. Exhibit 12 diagrams the basic structure of a market value arbitrage transaction.

In a market value transaction, the bond classes are paid down from the sale — as opposed to the maturity — of underlying collateral, based upon either a soft bullet or controlled amortization payment schedule. The frequent marking to market of the collateral pool, mentioned above, is necessary to ensure the ability of the CDO to pay down the rated debt on schedule. As such, the primary considerations in evaluating a market value transaction are the price volatility and liquidity of the underlying assets.

Collateral The primary consideration in a market value CDO is the price volatility of the underlying collateral. Price volatility, as measured by the rating agencies, dictates an advance rate for each pre-approved category of collateral. Since the rating of the bond classes is based upon market value overcollateralization, market value CDOs lend themselves to a wider array of collateral types than cash flow CDOs. Virtually any security that can be valued in the capital markets and have its price volatility estimated may be employed in these structures. The collateral pool for a market value CDO may consist of securities includable in cash flow CDOs, mezzanine debt, convertible debt, preferreds/convertible preferreds, distressed debt, and equities.

Large percentages of emerging market debt tend to be difficult to manage in the collateral pool. The high price volatility of these asset classes results in low advance rates, making them somewhat unruly in a market value transaction. Advance rates will be discussed more completely in the credit enhancement section.

Structure Market value transactions generally include a revolver in the capital structure. This revolver is obtained by the CDO to allow the portfolio manager to increase or decrease the amount of funding in order to adjust the leverage as investments are shifted among asset classes with different advances rates and/or as the market value of the collateral changes. Additionally, to the extent that the revolver is not fully funded, payments to the liabilities may be paid by drawing down on the revolver. Market value deals tend to be more actively managed — subject to predefined constraints — than cash flow transactions. These constraints would include:

- concentration limits based on issuer, industry, geography and asset quality, and
- minimum market value of the asset pool relative to the face amount of outstanding bonds.

Exhibit 13 is a time line of the phases through which a typical market value transaction will go during its life. The transaction generally begins with a ramp-up phase, during which the manager fills the collateral pool by purchasing assets in the capital markets. This phase can last as long as six months to a year.

Exhibit 13: Time Line of Events of a Typical Market Value Arbitrage Transaction

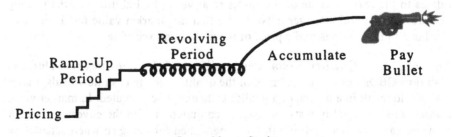

Source: Morgan Stanley

Similar to credit card ABS, there is an extensive revolving or reinvestment period during which cash flow from the underlying collateral due to maturities, whole or partial calls, amortization or any other cash flow or sale proceeds are reinvested. During the reinvestment period, the collateral manager has the ability to increase the debt exposure of the trust through the bank line established at issuance. The manager can also decrease debt exposure through the same means. Following the reinvestment period, principal collections from the collateral would be either accumulated to pay out a bullet payment, used to delever the deal and pay down the revolving line of credit or passed through to bond or equity holders, depending on the details of the structure.

Price volatility and asset liquidity are of primary importance in market value transactions. The actual weighted average rating of the underlying collateral is not important in market value structures, but a lower rating of a specific asset may result in a lower advance rate. Managers of market value transactions attempt to maximize the total value of the underlying portfolio while minimizing the volatility in that value.

Credit Enhancement The rating agencies assign advance rates to different types of collateral. This advance rate is the percentage of the market value of a particular asset that is allowed to be issued as rated debt. Analogous to net interest margin transactions in the home equity and manufactured housing ABS sectors, this percentage would be less than 100% and would move inversely with the perceived riskiness of the asset. Advance rates depend upon the return volatility of the assets, availability and quality of price/return data and liquidity of assets. The higher volatility of lower rated securities will result in generally lower advance rates. For example, equity-type securities would have a lower advance rate than high yield domestic bank loans. Additionally, this percentage will move with the target rating of the security being analyzed.

Exhibit 14 shows a sample table of advance rates that Fitch would apply to several types of collateral and target ratings. While specific levels will differ based on the actual pool of collateral, the relative difference in the levels for a given asset's expected losses, and a particular bond's target rating, can be seen.

These advance rates represent the primary form of credit enhancement employed in the structure. Therefore, the coverage test utilized in these structures relates to the market value of the assets relative to the liabilities of the issuing vehicle. A collateral manager must ensure that this market value test is not violated due to fluctuations in the price of the underlying securities.

Coverage and Quality Tests A major difference between market value and cash flow CBOs lies in the treatment of the quality tests. In cash flow deals, trades that would result in a breach of a quality test *cannot* be executed. In market value transactions, the quality tests are used in conjunction with the coverage tests. A manager can breach a quality test, but is penalized for doing so when calculating coverage tests. An example of this is provided below.

Exhibit 14: Sample Advance Rates for Indicated Asset Type and Liabilities

Asset Category	AA	A	BBB	BB	B
Cash and Equivalents	100%	100%	100%	100%	100%
Certificates of Deposit, Commercial Paper	95	95	95	100	100
Senior Secured Bank Loans	85	90	91	93	96
BB- High Yield Debt	71	80	87	90	92
<BB- High Yield Debt	69	75	85	87	89
Convertible Bonds	64	70	81	85	87
Convertible Preferred Stock	59	65	77	83	86
Mezzanine Debt, Distressed, Emerging Market	55	60	73	80	85
Equity, Illiquid Debt	40	50	73	80	85

Source: Fitch Investors Service

1. *Market value test:* A common trigger found in market value deals is that the collateral must be valued at some multiple of the outstanding bond balance. For example, a $400 million collateral pool may support $320 million of rated debt. If the indenture stipulated that the market value of the collateral, haircut by the appropriate advance rate, must represent 125% of the par value of the outstanding debt, then this transaction would pass this test. If, however, the market value were later reported to be only $380 million, the portfolio manager must cure the situation either by trading collateral to improve quality and thereby advance rates or by liquidating collateral in order to reduce the outstanding debt, de-lever the transaction, and raise the collateral-to-bond ratio.

2. *Minimum net worth test:* Another common trigger found in market value transactions is a minimum net worth test. This test is designed to ensure that a minimum amount of equity is maintained in the structure. It is calculated as the market value of the collateral minus the sum of the par value of all the rated debt, as a share of the subordinated debt. Breaching the minimum net worth test is considered an event of default. Control of the transaction is passed from the equity holders to senior bondholders. The senior bondholders then can decide whether to continue the transaction or liquidate collateral and early amortize the deal.

Trading Constraints Market value transactions do not contain a minimum weighted average rating condition at all, and the concentration limits that are employed behave differently. Portfolio managers are allowed to exceed concentration requirements in issuers, industries or regions, but they are penalized in the calculation of coverage tests if they violate the quality limits.

As an example, consider a manager with a maximum concentration of $25 million permitted in the telecom industry. The manager currently holds a $15 million position in that sector, but wants to purchase an additional $15 million. The manager of a cash flow transaction would be allowed to purchase only $10 million, but a market value manager can execute the entire $15 million order. For the purposes of calculating the overcollateralization of the rated debt in the market value structure, only $25 million of collateral can be considered. If the advance rate for the particular security were 0.80, then this position would represent only 0.80 times $25 million, or $20 million for the purposes of calculating overcollateralization. Without the concentration constraint, the same $30 million security would provide 0.80 times $30 million, or $24 million, of market value.

If there is a breach of a performance trigger, the manager has a period of time, generally two weeks, to cure the breach, either by trading collateral to improve quality or by liquidating collateral from the pool in order to redeem senior bonds and bring the structure back into compliance with the coverage test. The possible need to liquidate collateral subjects market value transactions to liquidity risk. Exhibit 15 details the generic trading constraints, i.e., quality and coverage tests, for market value transactions.

Sample Transaction: AG Capital Funding Partners, L.P. The AG Capital Funding transaction is actually a hybrid cash flow/market value transaction, but the market value aspect is representative of the sector. It is summarized in Exhibit 16.

The transaction is backed by HLT and special situation loans. While the HLT portion is subject to cash flow transaction standards, the special situation basket follows market value transaction rules. The market value aspects are necessary because the special situation loans do not generate predictable cash flows.

Exhibit 15: Generalized Trading Restrictions

Issuer Diversification	
• Up to Three Issuers May Each Have	7%
• Subsequent Issuers	4%
Industry Diversification	
• Single Industry	15%
• Any Three Industries	40%
Other Parameters	
• Emerging Markets Investments	5%
• Unquoted Investments	5%

Source: Morgan Stanley

Exhibit 16: Representative Market Value Transaction: AG Capital Funding Partners

- Manager: Angelo Gordon
- 60% HLT loans, 40% special situations
- A rated senior notes, revolver, 6.7 yr maturity, extendible to 9.7 yr (69% of transaction)
- BBB rated second priority senior notes, 7.0 yr, extendible to 10.0 yr (9%)
- Subordinates notes, 7.0 yr extendible to 10.0 yr (22%)
- Rated by Fitch Investors Service.

Source: Morgan Stanley

Rating Market Value Arbitrage Transactions Market value transactions are analyzed much the same way as cash flow transactions. The fundamental difference in the rating process is the need to analyze price volatilities and liquidity when rating a market value transaction. Principal payments to CDO securities are funded primarily through the liquidation of assets. Therefore, steep decreases in the value of the underlying collateral can result in losses to the rated CDO securities.

The primary means by which rating agencies establish acceptable over-collateralization levels is through the use of advance rates. Exhibit 14 is a sample table of advance rates applied by Fitch to various collateral type and target rating combinations. Clearly, the higher the target rating on a security, the larger the cushion required to satisfy the rating agencies, and the lower the advance rate. Similarly, the perceived riskiness or volatility of the underlying asset is inversely proportional to the advance rate, i.e., higher risk assets will be given lower advance rates.

The main difference in the performance triggers associated with market value versus cash flow transactions is in the reliance on the marked-to-market value of the underlying assets. Cash flow transactions focus on the par amount of underlying assets, whereas market value transactions rely on just that, the market value. Estimates of price volatility have been calculated by each rating agency individually. The results of these analyses are, not surprisingly, somewhat different, resulting in somewhat different advance rates across agencies. In principal, however, the methodology is similar.

The role of the manager in market value transactions is somewhat different than in cash flow deals. A market value manager attempts to maximize total returns while minimizing portfolio price fluctuations. The agencies consider the resources, as well as analyze the investment style, of the manager. Greater emphasis is placed on the infrastructure the manager has in place, as well as historical performance. In evaluating managers, the agencies will place particular emphasis on the amount of assets under management and the number of years managing the major asset classes included in market value CDOs, as well as historical performance and experience during market downturns. Both credit and trading expertise are vital, because poor credit decisions can lead to spread widening, price depreciation and defaults, and will result in overall poor performance. Clearly, a market value transaction is not designed to be issued by every portfolio manager.

The analysis of the manager is a somewhat subjective process relative to the analytic approach to quantifying price volatility, advance rates, and diversity scores.

Cash Flow and Market Value Arbitrage Transactions Comparison

Exhibit 17 summarizes the primary differences and similarities between cash flow and market value arbitrage CDOs, for each of several criteria.

Exhibit 17: Summary Comparison of Cash Flow and Market Value Arbitrage Transactions

	Cash Flow	Market Value
General Features		
Security	Secured by collateral portfolio cash flow generation	Secured by collateral portfolio market value
Rating Criteria	Based upon stressed default scenarios and expected recovery of the collateral	Based upon stressed price volatility assumptions of the collateral
Collateral Manager	Attempts to minimize defaults	Attempts to maximize total return and minimize portfolio price volatility
Credit Protection	If coverage tests are failed, cash flow is diverted from mezzanine and subordinate classes to senior notes. There are no forced liquidations	If overcollateralization tests are failed, liquidations of collateral may be required to pay down senior classes and bring overcollateralization levels back into line
Funding	Generally term floating rate note; but may be fixed. Could have revolver	Some portion of senior notes in the form of revolving credit facility or commercial paper conduit program
Maturity and Amortization	• 10- to 15-year final maturity • Average life expected to be 6 to 8 years for senior-most class; other classes longer • Amortizations usually begin in years 3 to 5, after the reinvestment period, as underlying collateral amortizes or is redeemed	• 5- to 8-year final maturity • Drawn amount of credit facility varies based on portfolio market value • Amortizations of term notes not very likely
Leverage	Generally 10-20% subordination below investment grade classes	Generally 20-25% subordination below investment grade classes
Structural Credit Protection		
Overcollateralization	• Measured on basis of portfolio par value and contractual interest payments to be received • Monitored at least monthly	• Measured on basis of portfolio market value adjusted by advance rates • Monitored weekly or bi-weekly using third party valuations from independent sources
Key Ratios	• Par value ratio • Interest coverage ratio	• Market value overcollateralization • Minimum net worth of equity
Remedies	• Collateral interest and principal diverted to redeem senior debt. No portfolio liquidations are ever required. • No stated cure period	• Ratios must be restored with two-week cure period via portfolio trading and/or liquidations

Exhibit 17 (Continued)

	Cash Flow	Market Value
	Restrictions on Underlying Portfolio	
Ratings	• All collateral securities must be rated, but may be public or private • Minimum rating should be maintained • If breached, future portfolio switches must maintain or improve average rating	• Ratings not essential for all assets, but may affect advance rates • No minimum average rating required
Diversity	• Industry and geographic concentrations are monitored and must be maintained by issuer • Breaches remedied through restrictions on future trading	• Industry and geographic concentrations are monitored and must be maintained by issuer • Breaches not included in overcollateralization calculations
Type of Securities	• Limited to mostly current pay debt instruments	• May include distressed debt, preferred stock, equity and other "special situation" assets
Liquidity	• No specific requirements	• Majority of securities must be readily marketable, with easily available objective valuations • Price volatility data on target portfolio assets must be available
Trading Constraints		
Management Restrictions	• Maximum or minimum asset composition limits (e.g., bank loans, high yield bonds, emerging market debt) • Maximum or minimum limits on floating rate and fixed rate securities • Maximum fixed maturities of assets • Minimum asset ratings • Minimum average portfolio rating • Diversification requirements • Maintenance of portfolio par value and interest coverage • Reinvestments restricted after stated reinvestment period (usually 3 to 5 years) • Interest rate hedges established upfront; generally cannot be actively managed	• Maintenance of market value overcollateralization • Diversification requirements • Asset liquidity requirements • Maximum or minimum asset composition limits • No maturity restrictions

Source: Morgan Stanley

Balance Sheet Transactions

Balance sheet deals are generally the securitization of lower yielding, borderline investment grade loans, for the purpose of gaining capital relief, obtaining alternative funding or increasing the issuing entity's return on equity by removing lower yielding assets from its balance sheet. In the past year, many Japanese banks have structured balance sheet transactions to improve their capital usage, gain off-balance sheet treatment of assets and obtain term funding. In general, the Japanese banks have securitized dollar-, rather than yen-, denominated loans, although there have been some yen-based transactions. Concerns about Asian credit, as well as the lack of a financial and legal structure in Japan defining terms crucial to securitization, have thus far prevented wholesale securitization of yen-based loans.[2] Balance sheet transactions generally range in size from $1 billion to as much as $5 billion.

From an investor's point of view, balance sheet CLOs have begun to be viewed as credit card substitutes, and this trend is likely to continue. Balance sheet CLOs offer investors in credit card ABS diversification away from consumer credit into heavily diversified corporate credit with similar structure.

Collateral

Cash flow balance sheet transactions rely on the ability of the collateral to generate sufficient principal and interest to redeem the structured notes. CLOs of this type would generally contain high grade C&I loans. The relatively low coupon on these assets versus typical high yield and emerging market securities results in a much smaller excess spread cushion than in most arbitrage deals. However, the higher quality of the balance sheet CLOs requires less subordination than in arbitrage deals.

Structure

Balance sheet transactions are structured very similarly to credit card ABS, even employing the master trust structure as the primary vehicle for securitization. Loans, and from time to time bonds, are sold into a trust as collateral to support the issuance of credit- and time-tranched securities. In the credit card arena, issuers that themselves are rated BBB at best are able to remove receivables from their balance sheet and finance their assets at near AAA levels. The need to tranche credit exposure among different rating levels within a senior/subordinate structure, or purchase an insurance wrap, prevents the issuing entity from obtaining completely AAA rated all-in funding levels.

Balance sheet CLOs work in a similar manner. The trust will issue several securities prioritizing payments sufficiently to garner the desired rating. The most subordinate piece of the structure is the unrated equity piece, which would

---

[2] For example, the concepts of bankruptcy remoteness, true sale and perfected security interest had not been addressed in the Japanese legal system. More recently, however, steps have been taken to facilitate securitization. Recent legislation in Japan provides for perfecting assignment of certain assets without notifying the obligors.

be exposed to the greatest amount of risk, with the highest potential returns. The senior and mezzanine tranches are generally structured with soft bullet maturities. The basic structure of a cash flow balance sheet transaction is as follows

AAA rated senior class (95%)
A rated class   2%
BBB rated class   3%

Similar to arbitrage cash flow deals, the indenture would specify a formal cash flow waterfall defining the priority of cash flows to the respective bond classes.[3] The documents would also stipulate trigger events that would cause changes in the waterfall should the triggers be breached. Common triggers will be described in more detail below. These may include, but are not limited to, an interest coverage ratio test and a par value ratio test for each rated security. The payment waterfalls are similar to those found in arbitrage cash flow transactions, which were diagrammed in Exhibits 5 and 6. The effect on the cash flow of breaching the performance triggers is indicated.

Unlike arbitrage CDOs, where there can be extensive trading by the collateral manager, with balance sheet CLOs, there is no active trading of loans already in the portfolio. Active trading or control over the portfolio would imply that the sponsor has recourse to the pool and thus violate true sale provisions. If so, the assets would have to go back on the sponsor's balance sheet and negate any capital advantage from the transaction.

The master trust structure allows portfolio managers to add newly originated loans, or loans purchased in the secondary market, to the trust for the purpose of issuing future debt. Similar to credit card ABS, transactions are most commonly structured as soft bullets with an accumulation period, in addition to credit and time tranching.

Linked versus De-linked If the loans are transferred into the issuing trust in a true sale, then the investor's exposure is limited to that of the performance of the assets and is divorced — or de-linked — from the fortunes of the sponsor. On the other hand, if the assets have not been sold, the investor retains exposure to the sponsor. A downgrade of the sponsor, or poor performance of the portion of its loan portfolio that is not included in the particular transaction, could result in a ratings action against the CLO owing to its relationship to the sponsoring institution. This is referred to as a linked transaction.

---

[3] Some earlier transactions, for example, the NationsBank CLO, issued certificates through a master trust structure, the cash flows of which are typically governed by a pooling and servicing agreement.

The benchmark transactions in the bank balance sheet CLO sector are those from the NationsBank Commercial Loan Master Trust for de-linked structures and SBC Glacier Finance for linked transactions. The NationsBank de-linked transaction was priced at a spread that was only 6 bp wider than credit card ABS and currently trades about 10 bp behind credit cards.

Credit Enhancement

Credit enhancement in the form of overcollateralization and subordination is employed in order to attain the high rating on senior notes. Similar to other ABS sectors, cash flows from the underlying collateral are prioritized to protect the higher rated bonds in the capital structure. This tranching of cash flows effectively distributes the credit exposure unevenly across the rated and unrated securities.

Early Amortization Triggers: Coverage Tests

The balance sheet CLO sector has two primary coverage tests, the failure of which would trigger an early amortization of the transaction. These are similar to early amortization triggers pertaining to excess spread and minimum seller's interest in credit card ABS transactions. In the CLO sector, these are the par value test and interest coverage test.

The early amortization concept in the balance sheet CLO sector is similar to that in the credit card ABS arena, in that it provides a credit put from the investor back to the issuer in the event that a transaction performs poorly. Unlike in the credit card sector, however, if a trigger is breached, there is a cure period during which the trust can attempt to rectify the performance problem. If the breach is not cured, principal payments will be directed to bond holders in order of seniority until either the bonds are fully redeemed or the trigger is cured.

The difference in early amortization between balance sheet CLOs and credit cards lies in the treatment of interest and the extent of the amortization. With balance sheet CLOs, subordinate bonds are completely locked out from receiving both principal and interest payments until either the trigger is cured or the senior bonds are fully paid down. Interest is used to turbo the senior bonds to speed their paydown. In contrast, in the credit card sector, only principal payments are directed to the senior bonds, while subordinate classes continue to receive interest to the extent that funds are available.

In addition, in CLOs, a partial early amortization is possible if the trigger is cured through the early amortization process, whereas credit card securities do not allow for partial early amortization.

The par value test and interest coverage tests were discussed above in the analogous section on cash flow arbitrage transactions. The function of these tests is the same for balance sheet transactions as for cash flow arbitrage deals.

Quality Tests

Balance sheet transactions employ quality tests similar to those of the cash flow arbitrage deals. These tests would include, but are not limited to:

- minimum diversity score
- minimum weighted average rating
- concentration limits in regions and industries.

These tests were discussed above in the section on quality tests for cash flow arbitrage transactions and function similarly. Rather than redirecting the cash flow in the event that a quality test is failed, the activities of the collateral manager are restricted to trading activities that would enhance the quality of the portfolio with respect to the violated trigger.

Rating Balance Sheet Transactions
The discussion in the section on rating agency approaches to cash flow arbitrage transactions is directly applicable to balance sheet deals.

RATING AGENCY APPROACHES TO EVALUATING CDOS

The basic difference in rating approaches lies in the probability weighted analysis Moody's employs with its binomial expansion method versus the absolute threshold of losses utilized by S&P, Fitch and DCR. The manner by which the absolute threshold is computed differs across the three rating agencies. If a CDO security survives the loss level associated with a given rating level applied with varied timing of losses, the rating is applied.

The other difference is in the calculation of diversity. Fitch divides the domestic high yield arena into fewer sectors, 25, than Moody's and S&P, which consider 33 and 39 sectors, respectively. Fitch, then, has a somewhat more conservative approach to diversity and allows for a more limited amount of total diversity between industries.

Moody's Investors Service[4]
For cash flow deals, Moody's analysis is based primarily on two concepts: the diversity score and the binomial expansion method. These concepts are used to evaluate expected losses on a transaction and the manner in which these losses affect the rated securities. We will explain these two concepts briefly here and then work through a mathematical example in the appendix to this chapter.

The diversity score explains with some level of confidence the variability, or diversity, of the portfolio underlying the structure. Small investments in a wide variety of relatively uncorrelated domestic high yield and emerging market sectors will result in a better (higher) diversity score than larger investments in a smaller number of sectors. The reason for this is clearly to ensure that a concen-

---

[4] Moody's Investors Service, Structured Finance Special Report, "Rating Cash Flow Transactions Backed by Corporate Debt: 1995 Update," April 7, 1995.

tration in a particular industry or sector is either prevented or compensated for by larger credit enhancement levels or more stringent performance triggers. The diversity score is used as a proxy for an equivalent number of uncorrelated securities in the portfolio.

The binomial expansion method is used instead of the more computationally intensive Monte Carlo simulation technique to simplify the analysis. The premise is based on a few key assumptions, namely that all of the equivalent uncorrelated securities in the collateral pool:

- have an equal probability of default,
- are of equal size
- will continue to be statistically uncorrelated.

These assumptions make the calculations straightforward. Each bucket has two possible outcomes: default or not default. Therefore, the number of potential default outcomes (one default, two defaults, ..., n defaults) equals the number of equivalent bonds in the portfolio. Because the probability of default is assumed to be constant for all securities, these possible outcomes expand into a binomial tree, and the probability of each event occurring is easily computed. These two concepts in tandem are used to estimate losses on a portfolio, giving credit for diversity and penalizing for potentially devastating, but low probability events. The calculation of the diversity score accounts for correlation among securities in the asset pool by grouping correlated assets into a single entity in the binomial expansion analysis.

Standard & Poor's[5]

For cash flow transactions, Standard & Poor's uses an internally developed default model that analyzes the effect of asset substitution and credits the shortening of an asset pool's life and default expectation as time passes. Using similar inputs as the other agencies, including obligor rating, concentration, representation in the pool, amortization schedule and number of assets, the S&P model analyzes all possible default scenarios and the probability associated with each event. An absolute threshold of losses is determined from the average life and target rating of the CDO security. The results of the S&P default model are then compared to the loss threshold before assigning ratings.

Fitch IBCA[6]

Fitch IBCA has generally focused on market value transactions. Its approach is similar to that described in the section Rating Market Value Arbitrage Transac-

---

[5] Standard & Poor's, Structured Finance Ratings, *CBO/CLO Criteria Update: Market Innovations*, February 1998.
[6] Fitch Investors Service, Structured Finance Special Report, "CBO/CLO Rating Criteria," March 17, 1997. In April 2000, Fitch IBCA merged with Duff & Phelps Credit Rating Company to form Fitch.

tions, with some exceptions. Fitch tends to place more emphasis on the ramp up period associated with CDOs. Somewhat like the concept of prefunding in the home equity sector, CDOs are often issued without a full collateral pool. It is the intention that the pool will be filled with securities purchased in the capital markets with the proceeds from the sale of the CDO. As such, there is the potential for interest shortfalls in the early months of the transaction if the manager cannot adequately fill the pool with sufficient high yielding assets. Fitch often requires surplus equity to protect against such shortfalls. Fitch also sets concentration restrictions in terms of dollars, as opposed to percentages, to protect investors from a manager overweighting a particular sector by drawing more funding from the revolving line of credit or commercial paper vehicle.

Fitch heavily and repeatedly shocks interest rates and decreases the value of the collateral over an extended period of time to identify weaknesses in the structure. It penalizes the inclusion of illiquid assets in the collateral pool by decreasing the advance rates assigned such assets.

DCR[7]

Duff's rating approach for cash flow transactions is similar to that of the other agencies. Duff's analysis is based on an absolute sustainable level of defaults. Exhibit 18 is a sample table of thresholds Duff requires for various rating targets and a given weighted average collateral rating. If Duff has not rated an asset in the pool, but two or more major rating agencies have, Duff will use that level, rounding down in the case of a split rating. The other agencies tend to use more conservative assumptions in these situations.

Exhibit 18: Sample Table of Threshold Loss Levels used by DCR Assuming Weighted Average Collateral Rating of B

Target Rating of CDO Note	Average Life of CDO Note	
	5-yr	7-yr
AAA	49.1%	57.1%
AA+	44.9	52.6
AA	43.4	51.1
AA–	41.9	49.6
A+	37.2	44.9
A	35.8	43.5
A–	34.5	42.2
BBB+	31.9	39.6
BBB	30.5	38.2
BBB–	29.2	36.9

Source: Duff & Phelps Credit Rating Co.

---

[7] Duff & Phelps Credit Rating Co., Special Report, "DCR Criteria for Rating Cash Flow and Market Value CBOs/CLOs," September 1997. In April 2000, DCR merged with Fitch IBCA to form Fitch.

CONCLUSION

Collateralized debt obligations comprise the fastest growing sector of the asset backed securities market. Because the potential collateral for these transactions runs the gamut from unsecured corporate loans and high yield bonds to distressed loans and emerging market debt, analysis of these transactions can be extremely complicated and somewhat forbidding. To compensate for this, CDOs offer wider spreads than comparably rated paper from other ABS sectors. In this chapter we discussed the differences between the various structures and the manner in which rating agencies evaluate the credit.

APPENDIX

MOODY'S DIVERSITY SCORE AND BINOMIAL EXPANSION METHOD[8]

Sample Calculation of Moody's Diversity Score

Portfolio

Issuer of Bond	Industry	Par Amount
A	Farming and Agriculture	6.0
B	Machinery	1.0
C	Utilities	2.0
A	Farming and Agriculture	3.0
D	Farming and Agriculture	2.0
E	Utilities	4.0
B	Machinery	9.0
C	Utilities	2.0
A	Farming and Agriculture	7.0
D	Farming and Agriculture	8.0

The first step in calculating diversity score involves calculating the total par value of the bonds and the average par value per issuer in the collateral pool. We aggregate the par value of bonds for each issuer and divide by the average par value per issuer, restricting this unit score to a maximum value of 1.0.

Issuer Composition

Issuer	Par Amount	Unit Score Per Issuer
A	6.0 + 3.0 + 7.0 = 16.0	16.0/8.8 = 1.81 → 1.0
B	1.0 + 9.0 = 10.0	10.0/8.8 = 1.14 → 1.0
C	2.0 + 2.0 = 4.0	4.0/8.8 = 0.45
D	2.0 + 8.0 = 10.0	10.0/8.8 = 1.14 → 1.0
E	4.0	4.0/8.8 = 0.45
Total Par Amount	= 16.0 + 10.0 + 4.0 + 10.0 + 4.0 = 44.0	
Average Par Amount Per Issuer	= 44.0 / 5.0 = 8.8	

We then aggregate across industries by summing the unit score from the previous steps for all issuers within the same sector. In this case, both issuer A and D are in the Farming and Agriculture section, so we add their unit scores of 1.0 and 1.0, respectively, to obtain the value 2.0. This represents the unit score for the Farming and Agriculture industry. This value is then matched against the diversity score table (summarized in Exhibit 9 in the text) to obtain the diversity credit. The sum of the diversity credit across all issuers is the diversity score for the transaction.

[8] Moody's Investors Service, Structured Finance Special Report, "Rating Cash Flow Transactions Backed by Corporate Debt: 1995 Update," April 7, 1995, and "The Binomial Expansion Method Applied to CBO/CLO Analysis," December 13, 1996.

Total Unit Score

Industry	Issuers in Industry	Total Unit Score per Industry	Diversity Credit
Farming and Agriculture	A, D	$1.0 + 1.0 = 2.0$	1.5
Machinery	B	1.0	1.0
Utilities	C, E	$0.45 + 0.45 = 0.9$	0.9
		Diversity Score =	3.4

Binomial Expansion

Binomial expansion is a computationally efficient method for calculating the probability associated with a variety of outcomes, given an equal probability of default across all securities. Here, securities mean diversity score units. If a portfolio of bonds has a diversity score of 30, Moody's would treat that portfolio as having 30 uncorrelated bonds. The expansion of the two possible outcomes (default or not default) for each of the 30 bonds would result in a binomial tree with 30 possible outcomes. Either one bond defaults, two default and so on, to the extreme of the entire portfolio defaulting. The probability of each of these outcomes is calculated using the following formula. Let j equal the number of defaults, p define the probability that any one bond defaults, P_j represent the probability that j bonds default, and D equal the total number of bonds or the diversity score. Then the probability of any event is calculated with the binomial formula:

$$P_j = [D!/(j!(D-j)!)] \times p^j \times (1-p)^{D-j}$$

The sum of P_j for all values of $j \leq D$ equals 1, and the expected loss for the transaction is the sum of the probability of any event happening, multiplied by the loss to the note — calculated in a CDO cash flow model — being rated under that scenario.

The benefit of this analysis is the computational ease by which one can calculate an expected loss for the rated note. A potential weakness in the method is the assumption of an equal probability of any one bond default.

STANDARD & POOR'S CBO/CLO MODEL[9]

Standard and Poor's has developed a default model that requires the input of characteristics about a portfolio of bonds or loans. These characteristics include maturity, rating and amount of each asset. The goal of the model is to answer the question, "At a given rating level, how much collateral in a specific pool of rated obligors would we assume defaulted?" S&P assigns a probability of default to each bond based on the credit rating on the underlying asset's obligor and remaining term of each obligation. The S&P model calculates the exact distribution of all potential loss outcomes and their respective probability of occurrence.

---

[9] Standard & Poor's, Structured Finance, "Using Standard & Poor's CBO/CLO Model" (February 1998).

To account for correlation among obligors in the collateral pool, S&P groups affiliated obligors together in the model. Industry diversification is accounted for by using a haircut of the ratings of each obligor within an over-represented industry in the same transaction. For concentrations greater than 8% in one industry, S&P will haircut from one to three rating notches, and potentially even more.

The model's inputs may require modification if, for example, a pool contains unrated obligors. In this case, proxy ratings or rating estimates would be needed. If a large amount of unrated debt is included in the pool, S&P may turn to an alternate rating methodology to assess the default risk.

For emerging market CBOs, S&P relies on the foreign currency issuer rating, rather than the local currency ratings. For a small amount of nonsovereign credits, S&P would modify the output of the model for analytical purposes; the model was not intended to measure default risk when a large portion of the pool contains nonsovereign credits whose local currency is not that of the CBO transaction.

Chapter 14

Relative Value Framework for Collateralized Debt Obligations

Charles Schorin
Principal
Director of ABS Research
Morgan Stanley Dean Witter

Steven Weinreich
Associate
Morgan Stanley Dean Witter

INTRODUCTION

In this chapter, we develop a framework for analyzing relative value both within the collateralized debt obligation (CDO) sector and between CDOs and other asset-backed securities. We discussed the collateral, structures, and ratings of CDOs in Chapter 13.

In analyzing CDOs, we first attempt to genericize the sector by differentiating between balance sheet CLOs on the one hand and arbitrage CDOs on the other. After this initial cut, we can further categorize CDOs as generally belonging to one of the following:

- 100% domestic high yield loans
- 100% domestic high yield bonds
- 80% domestic high yield/20% emerging markets
- 60% domestic high yield/40% emerging markets
- > 80% emerging markets.

The composition of the underlying collateral pool, and its breakdown into high yield and emerging market debt, provide the initial pass at valuing the transaction. Morgan Stanley monitors yield spreads of arbitrage CDOs on a generic basis, with the collateral breakdowns listed above. We also track yield spreads on balance sheet CLOs on a generic basis. (See Exhibit 1.)

Any individual transaction, of course, could deviate from the benchmark in terms of the collateral, manager or structure. These differences would be reflected in the pricing of the tranches. The previous sections describing the various transaction structures reported representative transactions corresponding to some of the respective generic deal types.

279

Exhibit 1: Generic CDO Yield Spreads by Collateral Composition

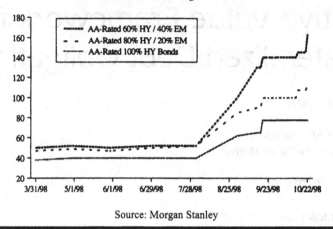

Source: Morgan Stanley

COMPARISON WITH ABS PRODUCT

In comparing CDOs to other asset backed product, investors should

1. first consider the asset backed collateral,
2. then examine the structural overlay and resultant average life and rating, and
3. finally, compare the cash flow similarity.

It sometimes may be difficult to make a direct comparison, owing to the CDO collateral mix, its various restrictions and the trading that may occur within the CDO collateral pool. Analyzing a static pool of collateral is not necessarily appropriate, because the composition can, and generally does, change over time. Nevertheless, there are similarities to other ABS sectors. For example, home equity loan collateral itself is low investment grade, at best; it is only the structural overlay and credit enhancement that provides for the highly rated ABS classes. Also, note that the mechanics of the home equity senior/subordinate structure, with the diversion of cash flow away from the mezzanine and subordinate classes in the event that collateral performance triggers are failed is not dissimilar from the various collateral tests and constraints on CDO collateral. The triggers may actually be more conservative in CDOs because they allow for the redirection of interest to pay principal, in addition to redirecting principal to pay principal. Manufactured housing ABS also could be compared to CDOs, although we would have to make the comparison on a swapped to LIBOR basis, because manufactured housing paper has been almost exclusively fixed rate.

Exhibit 2: Yield Spread Comparison: 80% Domestic High Yield / 20% Emerging Market CDO versus HEL ABS

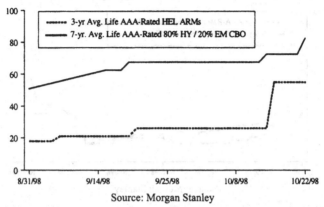

Source: Morgan Stanley

Exhibit 2 compares spreads on AAA-rated CDOs with a collateral mix of 80% domestic high yield/20% emerging markets to those on AAA rated 3-yr HEL ABS. In both cases, the bonds are floating rate.[1]

The asset class most similar to any type of CDO is the credit card ABS sector, which closely resembles balance sheet CLOs. Whereas credit card asset backeds are secured by a multitude of consumer credit lines, balance sheet CLOs are backed by large numbers of commercial and industrial loans. Generally, the credit quality of the C&I loans is superior to that of the consumer credit cards, with higher expected recovery rates. Structurally, however, the two types of securities look very similar. The extent to which yield spreads deviate significantly between the two sectors would be the extent of a relative value opportunity. Exhibit 3 shows the historical relationship between credit card ABS and balance sheet CLOs.

We also can compare mezzanine classes of CDOs to similarly rated asset backed securities. Exhibit 4 compares the spreads of a generic BBB rated CDO with a collateral mix of 80% domestic high yield/20% emerging markets to BBB rated floating rate HEL ABS. The average lives are on the order of 12 and 6 years, respectively.

COMPARISON WITH UNSECURED CORPORATE DEBT

CDOs also can be compared with unsecured corporate debt. Most domestic unsecured corporates are fixed rate, but still can be compared to floating rate CDOs by incorporating swap rates.

---

[1] Historical generic yield spreads on ABS products are reported regularly in the Morgan Stanley *ABS Research Weekly.*

Exhibit 3: Yield Spread Comparison: Credit Card ABS and Balance Sheet CLOs

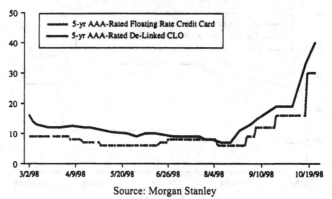

Source: Morgan Stanley

Exhibit 4: Yield Spread Comparison: Mezzanine CDO Class and BBB Floating Rate HEL ABS

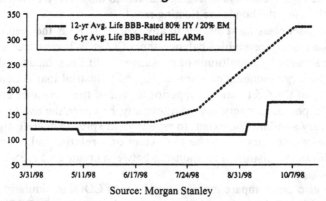

Source: Morgan Stanley

For a given rating category assigned by a rating agency, the risk of loss is normalized across the various bond products. Therefore, the expected loss should be the same on an A rated unsecured corporate bond, an A rated asset backed security and an A rated CDO class. This makes them directly comparable.

Exhibit 5 shows yield spreads from our generic series of AA-rated CDOs, with collateral comprised of 100% domestic high yield bonds. This series is compared to that of an index of A2-rated fixed rate unsecured corporate debt, swapped to LIBOR. Note the spread advantage of the CDO despite its higher rating.

Some of the spread differential clearly is related to technicals, such as the relatively wide sponsorship of the domestic corporate debt market and the relative lack of transparency of CDOs. Nonetheless, the differential in spreads — when put on a common benchmark — makes the CDOs look very compelling.

Exhibit 5: Yield Spread Comparison: AA-Rated High Yield CDO versus A-Rated Unsecured Corporate Debt

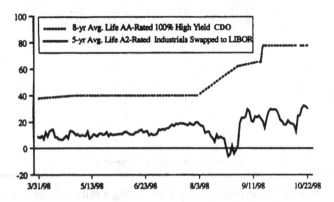

Source: Morgan Stanley, Bloomberg Financial Markets

DEFAULT ANALYSIS

Determining value in the CDO sector requires understanding and analyzing both credit and structure. Here we present a framework for examining defaults and their impact on the rated notes of a CDO transaction.

One cannot simply examine the maximum amount of defaults a particular structure can withstand before taking a loss, and then determine value through this absolute threshold approach. The timing of defaults and recoveries, along with the probability associated with different default events, must be examined in order to differentiate transactions.

Morgan Stanley has developed a methodology drawing from Moody's default and ratings migration studies.[2] The premise of the analysis is that examining an actively managed portfolio while holding ratings and expected defaults constant over time is inherently a flawed approach. Over time, the ratings, and expected default risk, of the underlying collateral change.

Morgan Stanley's approach is based on the probability distribution of ratings migration over a 1-year period. Ratings migration is characterized by a transition probability matrix. This transition matrix is then applied for successive years, using the resultant ratings composition of the pool from each respective prior period. This methodology is then repeated numerous times by generating multiple default paths in a Monte Carlo simulation. Exhibit 6 shows the probability distribution for the ending rating after a one year period of a bond rated Ba by Moody's at the beginning of the year.

---

[2] Moody's Investors Service, Global Credit Research, *Moody's Ratings Migration and Credit Quality Correlations, 1920-1996,* July 1997.

Exhibit 6: Probability Distribution of Rating After One Year for Ba-Rated Security

Rating at End of Year	Probability of this Event (%)
Aaa	0.01
Aa	0.08
A	0.39
Baa	4.61
Ba	79.03
B	4.96
Caa-C	0.41
Default	1.11
Rating Withdrawn	9.39

Source: Moody's Investors Service

This approach has multiple benefits. Using a rating transition matrix captures the ratings dynamics and allows investors to explore potential scenarios of both default and rating changes over time, and most important, the distribution of a given amount of loss on a pool through time. While a CDO class may be able to withstand a certain level of defaults over its life if defaults were evenly distributed through time, the performance may be weaker if defaults were applied more realistically — i.e., with spikes and drop-offs in default rates. A static pool approach holding ratings — and therefore expected defaults — constant through the life of the transaction fails to account for the potential change in the distribution of ratings within a portfolio.

As an example, consider a portfolio with two bonds, one rated B and the other rated Baa. Moody's transition matrix implies a probability of 3.49% and 0.28%, respectively, that these bonds will default by the end of one year. Examining the possibility of rating migration, however, adds a layer of realism to the analysis. Moody's one-year ratings transition matrix implies a 4.68% chance of the Baa rated bond being downgraded to Ba over a one-year time horizon. If this event occurs, the probability that the now Ba rated bond will move into default in one year is 1.11%, nearly four times as likely. With a probability of 3.08%, the B-rated bond will be downgraded to Caa. At this rating, the probability of defaulting at the end of year 2 is now 12.41%, more than three times that of a B-rated security.

This analysis attempts to answer the basic questions which investors should ask:

- What are realistic default expectations over time?
- How much variance from this expected default curve can the structure absorb?

Step 1 — Condense a large portfolio of correlated bonds to a smaller portfolio of representative, uncorrelated bonds. Examining each issue in the collateral pool independently ignores the correlation of bonds within the pool. To account for this without calculating correlations, we create a portfolio with the number of equal par value bonds equal to its diversity score. The initial rating applied to each of these bonds is determined by the representation of each rating in the underlying pool. Exhibit 7 works through this methodology for a collateral pool with a diversity score of 8.

Step 2 — Generate Ratings Migrations Matrix We next use the cumulative probability distribution in conjunction with a uniform random number generator to create a timeline of events for each representative bond in our portfolio. The random number is matched against the cumulative distribution to determine the rating at the end of a year. Another random number is then drawn from the cumulative distribution of the resultant rating, resulting in a rating at the end of year 2. This process is repeated for each year, for each representative bond in the portfolio. The probability that a bond with a given rating defaults is included in the transition matrix. Exhibit 8 steps through this process for a single bond in the portfolio over a 12-year period.

Exhibit 7: Creating a Representative Portfolio: Diversity Score of 8

Rating	Percent of Total Portfolio Par Value	Number of Bonds in Condensed Portfolio
Baa	12.5	$0.125 \times 8 = 1$
Ba	25.0	$0.250 \times 8 = 2$
B	62.5	$0.625 \times 8 = 5$

Source: Morgan Stanley

Exhibit 8: Ratings Migration of a Single Ba-Rated Bond, 1 Path

Year	Rating at End of Year	Par Value
1	Ba	$100
2	Ba	100
3	Ba	100
4	Ba	100
5	B	100
6	Default	0
7	Ba	40
8	Ba	40
9	Baa	40
10	Baa	40
11	Baa	40
12	Baa	40

Note: Assumes 40% recovery rate for a bond with original par value equal to $100.
Source: Morgan Stanley, Moody's Investors Service

Step 3 — Simulation Step 2 above is repeated multiple times generating a new random number for each iteration. We can then calculate the mean expected default over several paths and apply it to the rated debt. If the rated bonds survive the base case level of defaults, then we can apply stress scenarios next. The stress scenarios we have chosen are based upon examining the distribution of the default observations in each year over the numerous paths. We calculate the level below which a target percentage of observations fall. This target percentage — analogous to a confidence interval — should change relative to the rating of the bond, as well as the spread versus competing products. All else equal, a more highly rated bond must sustain a higher target percentage than a lower rated bond, i.e., survive the level below which a larger percentage of observations fall.

DEFAULT FRAMEWORK APPLIED TO CALHOUN CBO

Exhibit 9 applies this analytical technique to Calhoun CBO, Ltd., the representative cash flow arbitrage transaction that was displayed in Exhibit 8 in Chapter 13. Exhibit 9 works through the steps listed above beginning at the closing date of the transaction.

Exhibit 9: Default Analysis of Calhoun CBO

Step 1 — Condense the Portfolio

The diversity score for the collateral pool at time of closing was calculated to be 46. As such, the 113 bonds in the original portfolio are condensed into 46 representative securities. The composition of the original pool in terms of rating breakdown is listed below.

Moody's Rating	% of Par Value in Rating Bucket	Number of Diversified Bonds in Portfolio
A	0.61%	0
Baa	1.21%	1
Ba	18.98%	9
B	79.20%	36
Total Portfolio	100.00%	46

Step 2 — Generate Ratings Migration Matrix

We generate a transition for each of these 46 representative buckets for a 12 year time horizon. Defaulted bonds are added back into the analysis at the original rating, but with a smaller balance based on the recovery rate assumption. For example, consider a Ba-rated bond migrating to a B rating in year 3 and defaulting in year 4. If this bond represented 2% of the par value of the collateral, then in year 5 the bond would be reintroduced into the pool with a Ba initial rating and a par value equal to the recovery rate times the original par value. Subsequent defaults of this bond would further reduce the balance. All defaults are calculated as a percent of outstanding balance, analogous to a percent CDR (conditional default rate) for use with the cash flow model for the particular transaction.

Exhibit 9 (Continued)

Step 3 — Simulate Defaults

We simulate 10,000 paths and aggregate the defaults in each period to come up with a mean expected default curve. Below are the mean and median default schedules along with the levels below which 80%, 90% and 95% of simulated observations occurred for the Calhoun transaction for each year, assuming a 40% recovery rate on all defaulted securities.

Year	Mean	Median	80% Target Level	90% Target Level	95% Target Level
1	2.90%	2.17%	4.35%	6.52%	6.52%
2	2.70	2.20	4.46	6.52	6.70
3	2.79	2.26	4.53	6.61	6.88
4	2.82	2.29	4.59	6.70	7.02
5	2.79	2.33	4.69	6.71	7.08
6	2.77	2.36	4.75	6.79	7.29
7	2.76	2.39	4.81	6.70	7.39
8	2.77	2.44	4.89	6.04	7.40
9	2.64	2.46	4.89	5.83	7.39
10	2.66	2.49	4.93	6.00	7.48
11	2.66	2.53	5.00	5.90	7.55
12	2.62	2.55	4.98	5.92	7.60

Results

Scenario	Results for Senior Bond	Results for Mezzanine Bond
Mean Defaults	• No coverage tests are breached • No losses	• No coverage tests are breached • No losses
Median Levels	• No coverage tests are breached • No losses	• No coverage tests are breached • No losses
80% Target Level	• No coverage tests are breached • No losses	• No coverage tests are breached • No losses
90% Target Level	• No senior coverage tests are breached • No losses	• Par value test breached in period 5 and recovers in period 18. • No losses
95% Target Level	• No senior coverage tests are breached • No losses	• Second priority par value coverage test is breached in period 5 and does not recover • Incurs $500,000 interest shortfall and $3.4 million principal loss. IRR is reduced 36 bp to 6.85%.

Source: Morgan Stanley

The Morgan Stanley default model predicts that even with 95% confidence, the senior notes from the Calhoun transaction continue to perform extremely well, and the second priority notes are only marginally affected, with a 36 bp reduction in IRR. In fact, the senior notes are unaffected at the 99% confidence level as well; however, the mezzanine securities are detrimentally affected and incur significant losses at this level. Consider, however, the absolute level of losses implied by the 99% confidence level: consistent annual defaults ranging from 9.5% to nearly 11.0% for 12 consecutive years. This is an extremely high level of losses to apply for such an extended period of time.

Also, note that this is a conservative analysis, because it ignores any active role of the collateral manager. In reality, the professional collateral manager is hired to improve upon these simulated results. To the extent that a bond performs well in this default analysis methodology, it should perform even better when the collateral pool is actively managed.

CONCLUSION

In this chapter we present a new methodology for analyzing defaults and their impact on CDO transactions. Rather than simply examine the amount of defaults that a transaction can withstand over its life, we calculate ratings transitions — including defaults — probabilistically on an interim basis and apply these to the transaction. This methodology dynamically updates the ratings distribution of the collateral pool on a probabilistic basis and accounts for changing risk, and therefore, changing default likelihood, on an ongoing basis.

Chapter 15

Analyzing Mezzanine Tranches of CBOs

Laurie Goodman, Ph.D.
Managing Director
Mortgage Strategy Group
PaineWebber

Jeffrey Ho
Senior Vice President
Mortgage Strategy Group
PaineWebber

INTRODUCTION

Fixed-income investors are often rewarded, through higher yields, for taking advantage of new asset types. For example, in 1993 spreads on AAA commercial mortgage-backed securities (CMBS) were 70 basis points wider than on agency current coupon passthroughs, by February 2000 they were 30 bp tighter. Similarly, short AAA home equities initially traded 50 bp wider than CMOs, two years later they were trading 20 bp tighter. Collateralized bond obligations (CBOs) are one new, and rapidly growing, type of fixed income product. The first year of significant CBO issuance was 1996. Since then, the growth of CBO issuance has been dramatic; in 1996 Moody's rated $20 billion in CBOs, in 1999 it rated $92 billion. (We use the term CBOs throughout the course of this chapter to refer both to collateralized bond obligations and to collateralized loan obligations.)

In dealing with CBOs, as with any asset, investors need to evaluate whether or not they will be rewarded sufficiently for the risks entailed. Part of that process entails developing a comfort level about investing in CBO paper, via relative value comparison to other products. However, the risk-return profile of CBOs is very different from that on a typical corporate bond. Moreover, the collateral behind the CBO is often different from a corporate bond of the same rating. In this chapter, we focus on the methodology to determine value in the mezzanine tranches. We discuss the risk-return profile on the mezzanine tranches of CBOs, and focus on comparing the mezzanine tranche to corporate alternatives.

This topic is particularly important, as the mezzanine tranches of CBOs appeal to many different types of investors. The fixed-rate cash flows of the mezzanine tranches are an ideal fit for insurance companies, which seek to manage portfolio assets against their long-term, fixed-rate liabilities. The floating-rate coupons of CBO tranches fit quite well into LIBOR-plus portfolios. In all cases, investors need to be able to make relative value comparisons.

METHODOLOGY

We begin our demonstration by looking at risk-return profiles of a BBB rated CBO mezzanine tranche versus a BBB rated corporate bond. Comparing yields on representative bonds as a function of defaults readily shows the difference in the yield profiles between the two types of securities. We then tested to determine the better yielding bond at the same level of risk, by calculating breakeven default rates necessary to produce the same yield on the two securities. These default rates are then evaluated relative to historical experience.

Our analysis shows that given the spread configuration typical of December 1999 deals, BBB rated CBOs yield considerably more than do typical corporate bonds, even at the highest default levels the underlying collateral ever experienced over the past three decades. This indicates that there is definitely relative value within CBOs. *While this conclusion of relative investment value is dependent on the present spread configuration, our methodology is more general.*

INTRODUCING THE SECURITIES

There is no standard, generic, or "plain vanilla" CBO deal. Each has slightly different collateral, and a slightly different structure. The representative CBO we used for this comparison is a cash flow structure deal. For pricing purposes, we assumed that the deal is backed by collateral consisting of 80% bank loans and 20% high yield bonds. Funding has been divided into three classes:

1. 74% AAA rated senior floating rate notes
2. 16% BBB+ rated subordinated floating rate notes
3. a 10% unrated equity tranche

Our test case CBO deal has a 7.25-year expected maturity and a 12-year legal maturity. In this chapter, we focus on the BBB+ tranche, which is commonly called the "mezzanine" tranche, and compare it to 10-year BBB corporate securities.

We assumed a coupon on our representative Baa1/BBB+ rated CBO of LIBOR + 225. The bond was also issued at a slight discount, which produced a yield of roughly LIBOR + 230. To compare yield on the CBO to yield on an equivalently rated, fixed-rate corporate bond, we used the swap curve to convert the floating-rate LIBOR-based yield into a fixed-rate security. With 10-year swap yields at 6.78%, the equivalent fixed-rate yield on the CBO is 9.08% (6.78% + 2.30%).

As a proxy for a fixed-rate BBB security, we used the Merrill Lynch BBB rated corporate index (C0A4). We assumed that our representative corporate bond has the same coupon as the index's weighted average coupon — 7.356%, and same yield as the index — 7.76%. This corresponds to a spread of 180 basis points over the 10-year Treasury note. (The then-prevailing 10-year Treasury note was 5.96%, which equates to the 10-year swap yield of 6.78%, less the 82 basis points swap spread.) Assuming a 10.0-year average life, then the dollar price of the representative corporate bond is $97.32.

COMPARING DEFAULTS

It is a challenge to compare defaults on CBO collateral to those on a BBB corporate bond, as the underlying assets are so different. The CBO consists of both high yield and bank loan collateral, while our straw dog is a portfolio of BBB corporate bonds. We set up two alternative scenarios, which represent the upper and lower default bounds. We first assumed that the BBB corporate never defaults, while the collateral for the BBB CBO defaulted at rates assumed at the bottom of Exhibits 1 and 2. In our second iteration, we assumed that the two securities defaulted at the same rate. Both of these are obviously wrong. We know that BBB corporate bonds do default (although at a much lower rate than high-yield bonds, and they are usually downgraded first). Still, our assumptions provide bounds, albeit very wide bounds, for our analysis.

Exhibit 1: BBB CBO versus BBB Corporate with Base Case Recoveries

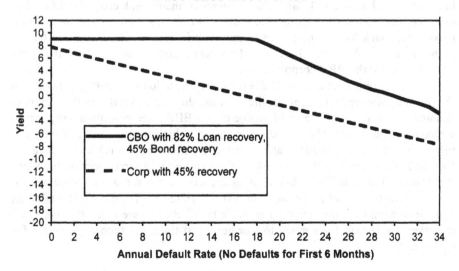

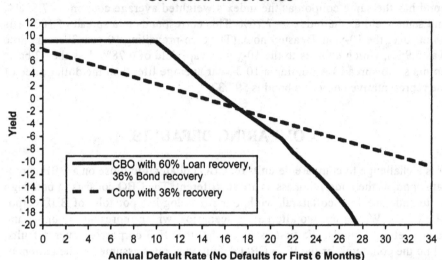

Exhibit 2: BBB CBO versus BBB Corporate with Stressed Recoveries

Exhibits 1 and 2 compare the yield profile on our representative BBB rated CBO tranche to that on a BBB rated corporate bond. We assume zero defaults for the first six months, then the annual default rate depicted on the horizontal axis of the two exhibits for the remainder of the term. Note that recovery rates on bank loans have typically been much higher than on unsecured bonds because of the built-in, risk-mitigating features of many bank credit facilities. For instance, bank lenders often require collateral before a loan is extended, which makes most bank loans senior to unsecured bonds, and therefore, likely to have a higher recovery. Accordingly, we used a lower recovery rate for both the high-yield bonds and the BBB corporate issue.

In Exhibit 1 we assumed 82% recovery on the loans, and 45% recovery on the unsecured corporate debt. In the exhibit, the yield profile on the CBOs is denoted by a solid line, The yield profile on the BBB rated corporate bond is presented as a dotted line. These levels correspond to historical evidence of recovery rates, sourced from Moody's and internally generated PaineWebber data. In Exhibit 2 we assumed 60% recovery on the loans and 36% recovery on the high-yield bonds. This is in line with the rating agencies' stress scenarios for recoveries.

Exhibits 1 and 2 demonstrate that the yield profile on the CBO is much more leveraged than that for the corporate bond. By this we mean that the CBO maintains its spread for a much longer period of time, but then deteriorates far more quickly.

RISK REWARD PROFILES

Look at risk-return profiles using the historical recovery rates in Exhibit 1. If we assume that the BBB corporate bond never defaults, and that all the collateral backing the CBO defaults at the annual rates shown on the horizontal axis of Figure 1, then the "breakeven default rate" is 19.4%. That is, at a 19.4% default rate on the CBO collateral, the post-default CBO yields the same 7.76% as does the zero-default corporate bond. (To replicate: find the point on the CBO curve in Exhibit 1 where the yield is 7.76%, and observe the corresponding default rate.) In fact, as will be shown in the next section, this 19.4% default figure is nearly double the highest level of high-yield default rates ever experienced over the last three decades. If we assume that annual default rates on the CBO and the BBB corporate bond are the same, then the CBO outperforms the corporate bond in all default scenarios. The exhibit shows results as high as a 34% annual default rate, which is the highest we tested.

We repeated the same analysis in Exhibit 2, using a rating agency stress scenario for recoveries. Assuming zero defaults for the BBB rated corporate bond, the collateral on the CBO can default at close to 11% and the CBO will still outperform on a yield basis. This is higher than the highest default rates experienced by high yield bonds in the early 1990s. Assuming the BBB corporate defaults at the same rate as does the high-yield bonds, then the breakeven default rate is even higher — at 17%. We now show that this number is well outside the range of historical experience. [1]

HISTORICAL DEFAULT RATES

Exhibit 3 shows Moody's compilation of historical default rates for the high-yield market since 1971. These are trailing 12-month default rates, and are expressed as the percentage of defaults per annum. The statistics are tallied both by the number of issuers and by outstanding balance. The latter understandably tilts the average towards the results of larger issuers, while the former gives equal weighting to all issuers.

Note that default rates historically have been quite low. In fact, as measured by percent of balance, the average default rate over the 1971-1999 period has been just 3.24% (with a standard deviation of 2.49%). As a percent of the total number of issuers, the historical default rate was 3.37% (standard deviation of 2.22%).

---

[1] Clearly, these results are dependent on our assumptions. We have assumed equal annual default rates after the first 6 months. Changing the default timing will make a difference. In particular, defaults early in the life of the CBO/CLO have a larger negative impact. Changing the recovery assumptions will also have an impact. In addition, we have assumed a stable interest rate environment. Changing this assumption will alter reinvestment rates and could trigger call provisions on the corporate bond, the collateral underlying the CBO, or the CBO structure.

Exhibit 3: Historical Annual Default Rates

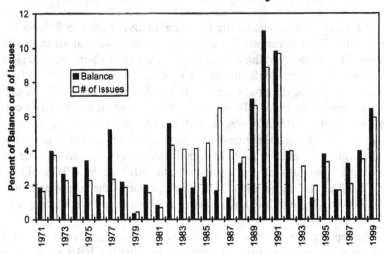

Exhibit 4: The Distribution of Annual Defaults

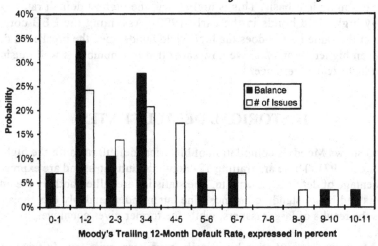

However, it's readily observable from Exhibit 3 that the "average" is heavily skewed by several very high default years during 1989-1991. Peak bond defaults typically occur 2-3 years after issuance. During the leveraged buy-out mania of 1987-1989, quite a few marginal deals were brought to market. Fall-out from that was reflected in the high default rates during the 1989-1991 period.

This skewness is also easily seen by looking at the frequency distribution of defaults, which is shown in Exhibit 4. The data in Exhibit 3 are regrouped into buckets to show the distribution more easily. Measured by outstanding loan balance, in fewer than 15% of the years were defaults greater than 4%.

BOTTOM LINE

Even though "average" numbers are skewed by the high default years of 1989-1991, we can still use these actual results to compare performance of our representative BBB+ CBO to a traditional BBB bond. We did so by interpolating data from Exhibit 1. (We looked up the yield for each of the two securities that corresponded to the average default rate of 3.24%.) It is clear that the CBO delivers its promised yield of 9.08%, while the BBB index is impacted by any defaults that occur. Assuming the BBB corporate bond never defaults, its base case yield is 7.76% — which the CBO outperforms by 132 basis points. Assuming the bonds both default at the 3.24% annual average for high-yield bonds — then the yield on the CBO is 9.08% versus the 6.25% for the BBB corporate bond — which is a 283 basis point difference. Using this market pricing, the CBO is expected to outperform by 132-283 basis points, and is hence, the more attractive opportunity.

The case for CBOs as of this writing is even stronger than indicated above. Even gilding the lily of the BBB corporate by assuming it never defaults, the CBO can still sustain default rates higher than ever been experienced over the last three decades — and still outperform.

STRESS TESTING

In performing any analyses, results are only as robust as the assumptions upon which they stand. The two we have made are that (1) recovery rates are higher on bank loans than on bonds; and (2) the BBB corporate bond either doesn't default at all, or defaults at the same rate as high-yield bonds. While we believe that our first assumption is fair, and our second provides fair bounds, it is certainly prudent to stress our assumptions.

Historically, recovery rates have been far higher on bank loans than on bonds. Nonetheless, we can test our comparison by assuming identical recovery rates and look at the results. Exhibit 5 shows the results of a single 36% recovery rate on both the loans and the bonds. Remember, this is the stress scenario. As can be seen, the breakeven default rate (the default rate at which the two securities yield the same) is 7%, assuming no defaults on the BBB corporate. That breakeven default rate is 10% if we assume equal defaults on the BBB corporate and the high-yield debt. These numbers are at the very higher end of historical experience (those high-default years following LBO issuance mania). Thus, even in the stressed scenario, the CBO holds up very well relative to the BBB corporate bond.

Defaults on BBB securities are certainly lower than defaults on a portfolio of high-yield securities, but it is not clear how best to make the comparison. Annual default numbers are unfair, as the BBB bond will need much more time to default than a high-yield bond. It is even more difficult to compare BBB rated bonds to a portfolio of 80% bank loans, 20% high yield bonds, as the default patterns on bank loans are not that widely studied. Thus, it really is not crystal clear how to best set up and make a comparison between the BBB corporate and the BBB+ rated CBO.

We essentially set an upper and lower band on the breakeven default rates by assuming that the BBB corporates either (a) do not default at all, or (b) default at the same rate as high-yield bonds. We can try to place a more reasonable number on the breakeven, by juxtaposing actual cumulative default rates over a 10- to 12-year period. Moody's data indicate that the cumulative losses on Baa securities are 4.39% after 10 years, 5.04% after 11 years, and 5.71% after 12 years. By contrast, high-yield bonds (all speculative grades combined) have a cumulative default rate of 28.32%, 30.16%, and 31.96%. Hence it seems reasonable to assume that default rates on the BBB corporate bond are approximately ⅙ as high as those on the CBO. Thus, a 12% default rate on the CBO corresponds to a 2% default rate on the BBBs. The results of this analysis are shown in Exhibit 6. At close to a 21% default rate on the BBB rated CBO and a 3.5% default rate on the BBB-rated corporate bond, the yields on the two securities are nearly identical. (Column 1 shows the default rates on the CBO; Column 4 shows the default rates on the BBB rated security and the horizontal line denotes the approximate crossover point.) At default rates above the crossover (lower default rates), the CBO represents the higher-yielding alternative. Clearly, for all default rates over the past three decades (even assuming that the default rate on the CBO is six times as high as on a BBB rated corporate bond) — the CBO represents the better relative value.

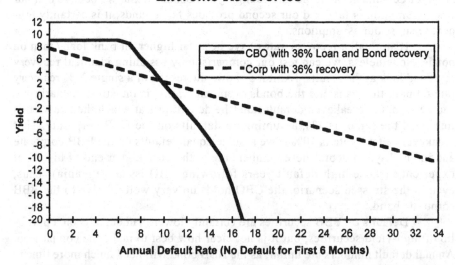

Exhibit 5: BBB CBO versus BBB Corporate with Extreme Recoveries

Exhibit 6: BBB CBO versus BBB Corporate Yields

BBB CBO Default*	CBO Yield with 82% Loan Recovery and 45% Bond Recovery	Corp Yield with 45% Recovery	BBB Corp Default*	Which Yields More?
0	9.08	7.76	0.00	CBO
1	9.08	7.68	0.17	CBO
2	9.08	7.60	0.33	CBO
3	9.08	7.53	0.50	CBO
4	9.08	7.45	0.67	CBO
5	9.08	7.37	0.83	CBO
6	9.07	7.29	1.00	CBO
7	9.07	7.21	1.17	CBO
8	9.07	7.14	1.33	CBO
9	9.07	7.06	1.50	CBO
10	9.07	6.98	1.67	CBO
11	9.07	6.90	1.83	CBO
12	9.07	6.83	2.00	CBO
13	9.07	6.75	2.17	CBO
14	9.07	6.67	2.33	CBO
15	9.07	6.59	2.50	CBO
16	9.07	6.51	2.67	CBO
17	9.07	6.44	2.83	CBO
18	8.88	6.36	3.00	CBO
19	8.11	6.28	3.17	CBO
20	7.23	6.20	3.33	CBO
21	6.33	6.12	3.50	CBO
22	5.50	6.05	3.67	Corp
23	4.65	5.97	3.83	Corp
24	3.82	5.89	4.00	Corp
25	3.06	5.81	4.17	Corp
26	2.25	5.73	4.33	Corp
27	1.55	5.66	4.50	Corp
28	0.88	5.58	4.67	Corp
29	0.41	5.50	4.83	Corp
30	−0.20	5.42	5.00	Corp
31	−0.83	5.34	5.17	Corp
32	−1.27	5.27	5.33	Corp
33	−1.87	5.19	5.50	Corp

* Annual Default Rate Expressed as a Percent.

CONCLUSION

The risk-return profile on the mezzanine tranche of a CBO is much more lever-aged than that on the corporate bond. Moreover, the collateral behind a CBO will often be different than on a corporate bond of the same credit rating.

In this chapter, we showed how to make relative value comparisons between CBOs and corporate bonds. We held that the correct approach is to compare "breakeven" default rates on CBO tranches versus corporate alternatives under a range of assumptions. This allows an investor to gauge under what scenarios the CBO tranche will outperform, and determine if those scenarios are likely, particularly given the range of historical experience.

Our results demonstrate that under all default scenarios experienced over the past three decades — the CBO represents better relative value than equivalent-rated corporate bonds. Of course, this will change if CBO spreads tighten relative to equivalently-rated corporate paper.

There is no question that some of the incremental yield on the BBB rated CBO is a function of liquidity. CBO tranches are smaller, and are clearly less liquid than equivalently-rated corporate bonds. The incremental yield is also a function of the fact that the CBO market is relatively new, and investors are usually compensated well for entering a market at the early stages. Indeed, as the CBO market matures, we expect liquidity to improve, and the new product yield premium should erode.

Chapter 16

Emerging Market CBOs

Laurie Goodman, Ph.D.
Managing Director
Mortgage Strategy Group
PaineWebber

INTRODUCTION

Many portfolio managers have invested a substantial amount of time and energy in understanding CBO structures. Most have become comfortable with CBO deals backed by both high-yield bonds and bank loans. However, these same portfolio managers are still quite uneasy about any CBO backed primarily by sovereign emerging markets bonds, as they believe that all emerging market debt is tainted by high default experience.

In this chapter, we shed some light on the differences (that matter) between emerging markets and high-yield deals. The picture that "emerges' (pun intended!) may surprise you — positively, that is — for the following reasons:

- There have actually been few defaults on U.S. dollar denominated sovereign Emerging Market (EM) bonds. The negative bias of many investors against EM CBOs is because they do not fully appreciate the differences between EM sovereign bank loans and EM sovereign bonds.

- Rating agencies are far more conservative in their assumptions when rating emerging markets deals than in rating high-yield deals, as performance data on EM bonds is far more limited. So there's an extra credit cushion already built into comparable credit levels.

- EM CBOs generally provide much greater structural protection, as the average portfolio credit quality is higher, resulting in a lower probability of default on the underlying portfolio. Subordination on EM deals is also much higher, hence the equity itself is much less leveraged.

We discuss each of these points in turn. Indeed, we believe that EM CBOs are no more risky than high-yield CBOs, and the rated debt often yields much more.

EM SOVEREIGN BOND DEFAULTS

EM debt has developed a bad rap. This tainted reputation stems from the fact that many potential investors do not distinguish between EM sovereign foreign currency bank loans and sovereign foreign currency bonds. In fact, the historical record on EM sovereign foreign currency bonds is very favorable. Sovereigns are far more likely to default on foreign currency bank loans than on foreign currency bond debt.

Let's look at the asset record, recently compiled in a Standard and Poor's study released in December 1999, which covers both public and private debt.[1] Exhibit 1 shows that out of a universe of 201 sovereign issuers, 13.9% of the issuers are currently in default. This includes defaults on foreign currency debt (both bank loans and bonds) as well as in local currency debt. Note that 11.9% of the issuers are in default within the category of total foreign currency debt (which includes both bank loans and bonds). But a separate break-out of just the sovereign foreign currency bonds indicates that most of these issuers are in default only on their bank loans. In fact, Column (6) of Exhibit 1 shows that in 1999 only 2.5% of the issuers were in default on their foreign currency bonds! Note that the 2.5% default on foreign currency bonds is even lower than the 3.5% default on local currency debt.

This 2.5% default rate amounts to only five issuers out of 201 issuers (sovereign borrowers). They consist of Ecuador, Ukraine, the former Yugoslavia, Pakistan, and Russia.[2] Ecuador was the only new issuer to default in 1999. That country first blew the whistle that it might not meet payments on its Brady debt during the summer, and then proceeded to default on the bonds. This shook the markets, since it was the first time that Brady debt had defaulted. However, realize that there was no contagion — other Latin American countries continued to make timely payments on their Brady bonds. Investors should realize that a sovereign can default on some bonds, while remaining timely on others. This would be reflected in Exhibit 1 as a default. For example, while Russia has defaulted on some of its bonds, it has continued to service on a timely basis its large public issues, including the Russian Federation's 'CCC' rated Eurobonds. It is also keeping current four other Ministry of Finance foreign currency bonds.

Cumulatively, since 1975, Standard and Poor's has identified a total of 78 issuers (38.8% of all sovereigns) that defaulted on their foreign currency bond and bank loans since 1975. (This constitutes a much smaller percent of all foreign currency debt in default.) Defaults usually took the form of late payments of principal and/or interest on bank loans. In fact, there were 75 bank debt defaults since

---

[1] See David T. Beers and Ashok Bhatia, "Sovereign Defaults: Hiatus in 2000?" *Standard & Poor's Credit Week* (December 22, 1999).

[2] On January 6, 2000, after the S&P study was published, the Ivory Coast announced it was suspended foreign currency debt payments indefinitely. It is clear that the country's bank loans will be impacted. It is unclear if their Eurobonds would be affected as well.

1975, and some sovereigns defaulted more than once. By contrast, only 14 issuers defaulted on foreign currency bonds in that same period. In most of these cases, the defaulted bonds had been issued by smaller countries which had little total debt outstanding. The bonds that the countries defaulted on tended to be held by banks, rather than being public issues held by a broad cross sector of investors.

This has been independently confirmed in a 1995 study by Moody's rating service. The Moody's study noted that "a review of worldwide sovereign default experience since World War II shows that when sovereign nations have defaulted on any of their foreign currency obligations…they have been more likely to default on bank loans than on sovereign bonds or notes."[3]

Exhibit 1: Sovereign Default Rates

(%of all sovereign issuers)	Number of issuers	All issuers in default (%)	New Issuers in default (%)	All foreign currency debt* (%)	Foreign currency bonds (%)	Local currency (%)
1975	164	2.4	N.A.	1.2	0.6	1.2
1976	165	2.4	0.6	2.4	0.6	0.6
1977	166	2.4	0.0	1.8	0.6	0.6
1978	169	4.7	2.3	4.1	0.6	0.6
1979	173	6.4	2.3	5.8	0.6	1.2
1980	174	6.3	1.7	5.7	0.6	0.6
1981	176	10.2	6.3	9.1	0.0	1.1
1982	176	15.9	5.7	15.3	0.0	1.7
1983	177	24.9	10.2	23.7	0.0	1.1
1984	178	25.3	1.1	23.6	0.6	1.7
1985	178	24.7	2.8	24.2	0.6	1.1
1986	179	28.5	5.6	27.9	0.6	1.7
1987	179	30.7	3.3	29.1	1.1	2.2
1988	179	30.2	1.7	29.6	1.1	1.1
1989	179	30.2	1.7	29.1	2.2	1.7
1990	178	30.9	4.2	29.8	1.1	2.8
1991	198	27.3	3.0	26.8	1.0	1.5
1992	198	29.3	3.5	28.8	2.0	1.5
1993	200	27.0	0.5	26.5	1.5	2.0
1994	201	24.4	0.0	23.9	1.5	2.0
1995	201	22.9	1.5	21.9	1.5	3.0
1996	201	21.4	0.5	19.9	1.5	3.5
1997	201	15.9	0.0	14.9	1.5	2.0
1998	201	15.9	2.5	13.9	2.5	3.5
1999	201	13.9	0.5	11.9	2.5	3.5

N.A. = Not available.
* Bonds and bank debt.

Source: Standard & Poor's

[3] Vincent Truglia, David Levey and Christopher Mahoney, "Sovereign Risk: Bank Deposits Versus Bonds," Moody's Investor Service, Global Credit Research, October 1995.

WHY THE BETTER TRACK RECORD?

There are four reasons that EM sovereign bonds have a better track record than sovereign bank loans. First, there is a strong disincentive for a sovereign to default on foreign currency bonds; it will restrict capital market access going forward. The consequences of defaulting on (or rescheduling) bank loans has been more predictable, and far less detrimental to a nation's interest than defaulting on its bonds. Defaulting on bonds could essentially bar a country from the international capital markets for a considerable period of time, and will result in much higher borrowing costs when the country is finally able to enter. Most of the developing nations depend on external financing for their growth, and hampering access to capital markets could sacrifice medium-term growth.

Second, more sovereigns have access to cross-border bank financing than have access to bond issuance in the international capital markets. International bond markets have been receptive to issuance by speculative grade rated sovereign credits since the early 1990s. But relative credit sanity has prevailed, as there have been barriers to entry by sovereigns of less credit quality, notably those from sub-Saharan Africa.

Third, it is far easier to renegotiate debt held by a few banking institutions rather than a bond issuance held by large numbers of international investors. For one, identification of creditors in advance is not always easy. By definition, there are a large number of creditors, some of which may have relatively small holdings. All of which makes restructuring more complex. Also, any one of even the smallest creditors can potentially bring legal proceedings against an issuer in a number of jurisdictions, depending on the security's documentation. The possibility of asset attachments is greater, simply because of the number of potential court cases.

The fourth and final major difference between bank loans and bond debt is that banks have multi-faceted relationships with borrowers, and usually receive sizeable fees for a variety of services. Banks often keep their long-term relationship with the borrower in perspective when agreeing to reschedule. Bondholders are not relationship-driven, and there are no business consequences for the bondholders in trying to extract the last possible dollar. The net result: sovereign default rates on bonds are much lower than on bank loans. Unfortunately, many investors do not distinguish between the two, and keep looking at sovereign debt as a homogeneous category, which clearly, it is not.

CBO RATING DIFFERENCES: EM VERSUS HIGH YIELD

The rating methodology for cash flow CBOs involves looking at the expected loss on the various tranches under various default scenarios, and probability weighting the results. This in turn requires making assumptions on how diversified the collateral is, how likely it is to default, and how much will be recovered if any default occurs. It is much harder for the rating agencies to feel comfortable with the parameters that they are using for EM bonds than U.S. high-yield bonds. Lets look at why.

First, consider EM sovereign debt. Default rate statistics on EM sovereign bonds are very limited. Moreover, EM economies are subject to greater economic instability than those of more developed countries. Corporate debt in EM countries is even more problematic for the rating agencies. Clearly, there's generally less publicly available information about companies in EM countries than about issuers in developed countries. Moreover, financial reporting in many foreign countries is often not subject to uniform reporting and disclosure requirements. Finally and most importantly, the actions of local governments are far more likely to affect the ability or willingness of EM corporates to service their debt.

Given the issues that were mentioned above, the rating agencies react by rating EM assets in a more conservative manner than other collateral. As a result, additional levels of credit protection are built into EM CBOs beyond that which is structured into high-yield CBOs. We now review some major differences in those assumptions.

Recovery Rates

The rating agencies typically assume 30% recovery rates for high-yield debt and 50% on bank loans. For sovereign debt, Moody's assumes that base case recovery rates are 30% of the market value, or 25% of par, whichever is lower. For EM corporate debt, Moody's assumes that recovery rates are 20% of market value (15% of par value) if the issuer is domiciled in an investment grade country, and 15% of market value (10% of par value) if the issuer is domiciled in a non-investment grade country. Bonds of countries that face unusually adverse political or economic conditions are treated as having a lower recovery rate, which in some cases, can be as low as zero.

In point of fact, historical recovery rates on sovereign bonds have proved far more favorable. A September 1998 Standard and Poor's study showed that since 1975, the recovery rate on foreign currency bonds has been around 75%.[4] It was higher in the majority of cases in which the defaults were cured quickly though the issuance of new debt. It was lower on bonds that remained in default for longer periods of time. Even for bonds that remained in default for longer periods, most of the recovery rates were just under 50% — far higher than the recovery assumptions made by the rating agencies. And the 75% overall recovery rate on sovereign foreign currency bonds is well above the 60% recovery rate on foreign currency bank loans.

Moreover, even though the rating agencies are more generous in the recovery rates they assume for U.S. high-yield borrowers than for sovereign borrowers, actual recovery rates for sovereign borrowers have been higher. A Moody's study showed that the recovery rates on senior unsecured U.S. corporate debt in the 1977-1988 period average 51.31%.[5] Compare this with the 75% recovery rate on the sovereign bonds.

---

[4] See David T. Beers, "Sovereign Defaults Continue to Decline," Standard and Poor's, September 1998.

[5] C. Keenan, Igor Shtogrin, and Jorge Sobehart, "Historical Default Rates of Corporate Bond Issuers, 1920-1998," Moody's Investors Service, January 1999.

Exhibit 2: Moody's Diversity Score Table for CBOs

No. of Companies (Regions)	Diversity Score	Diversity Score for Latin America*
1.0	1.00	1.00
1.5	1.20	1.10
2.0	1.50	1.25
2.5	1.80	1.40
3.0	2.00	1.50
3.5	2.20	1.60
4.0	2.30	1.65
4.5	2.50	1.75
5.0	2.70	1.85
5.5	2.80	1.90
6.0	3.00	2.00

*Diversity = 1+ (Standard Diversity Score − 1) × 0.5

Diversity Scores

Each rating agency has its own set of tools for measuring the diversity of underlying collateral. Moody's methodology has become the industry standard. This treatment reduces the pool of assets to a set of homogenous, uncorrelated assets. For CBOs backed by high-yield or bank loans, a diversity score is calculated by dividing the bonds into 1 of 33 industry groupings, and each industry group is assumed to be uncorrelated. (See Exhibit 2.)

Assumptions are more conservative for EM bonds, reflecting rating agency fears of "contagion." Countries that carry an investment-grade sovereign rating from Moody's are each treated as a separate industry. Bonds from non-investment grade EM issuers are grouped into six geographic regions. These are Latin America, The Caribbean, Eastern Europe, Africa, East Asia, and West Asia. The latter includes the Middle East. Each region constitutes a single "industry." All bonds from a region, regardless of the industry they represent, are taken as part of the same group. Thus, the value of including corporate EM borrowers, which would customarily be seen as providing greater diversity and reduced risk from that diversification, is discounted entirely. In point of fact, many EM deals include up to 20% of the portfolio in corporate form.

For all regions except Latin America, the diversity score is the standard table used by Moody's, which relies on the assumption that defaults on bonds in the same region or industry have a correlation coefficient of approximately 30%. This is shown in the first two columns of Exhibit 2. For example, if there were equal amounts of debt from each of four Caribbean countries, the diversity score is 2.3. That is, the deal would be credited as if there were 2.3 uncorrelated assets. For Latin American it is assumed the correlation is about 60%, and the diversity score is shown in the third column of Exhibit 2. If there were four Latin American issuers, the diversity score would be 1.65. Thus, combining four Caribbean issuers and four Latin American issuers in equal amounts would "count" as 3.95 uncorrelated issuers.

*Exhibit 3: Cumulative Default Rates After 10 Years as a
Function of Credit Quality*

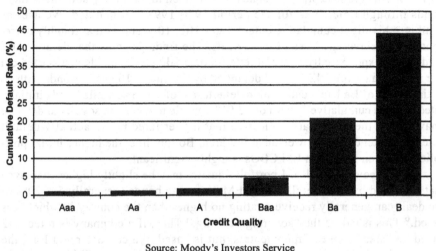

Source: Moody's Investors Service

To be even more conservative, all bonds from a particular EM country are taken as constituting one issue. Essentially, 100% correlation is assumed within each country. In effect, EM collateral does not receive diversity score "credit" for having multiple corporate issuers or industries. Thus, if one compares the diversity score on a pool of 100% emerging markets collateral with a pool of U.S. high-yield assets with similar industry diversification, the EM collateral would have a substantially lower diversity score.

Structural Protections

We have thus far focused on how Moody's deals with limited historical experience (by making more conservative assumptions). In practice, these more conservative assumptions mean several forms of additional built-in protection for the CBO buyer. First, the average credit quality is higher on a EM CBO than on a high-yield CBO. Second, subordination levels are also generally higher on an EM CBO than on a high-yield CBO.

Higher Average Credit Quality

The conservative approach used by Moody's means that average credit quality of an EM CBO deal is much higher than on a high-yield CBO. That is, CBO managers will generally choose to include higher credit quality bonds to compensate for the lower diversity scores and the more stringent recovery assumptions. Most EM deals have average credit qualities of Ba2 or Ba3. By contrast, most high-yield deals have an average credit quality of B1 or B2.

This difference is highly significant, as shown in Exhibit 3. The exhibit shows Moody's data for the average cumulative default rates by letter rating after 10 years. This groups corporate bonds with a given initial rating, and tracks those bonds through time. Data for the period 1970-1998 are included. We use the exhibit to highlight cumulative default rates after 10 years, as that roughly corresponds to the average lives of CBO deals. The findings show that default rates tend to rise exponentially as credit letter ratings fall. Of the bonds that started out life with a Baa rating, 4.39% had defaulted by the end of 10 years. Bonds with an initial rating of Ba had a cumulative default rate of 20.63%, while bonds initially rated B had a cumulative default of 43.91%. While numbers on sovereign debt are unavailable, the results are indicative that higher rated bonds actually default much less than do their lower-rated brethren. Bottom line: the higher initial portfolio quality on sovereign EM CBOs is highly significant.

Moreover, actual EM portfolio quality may be slightly higher than even that indicated by the overall rating. EM corporate bonds (generally 5%-20% of the deal) can generally receive a rating no higher than the country in which it is based.[6] This is called the "sovereign ceiling." Thus, if a company is rated Aa2 based on "stand-alone" fundamentals, but is based in a country rated Ba2, the company itself can generally only receive that same Ba2 rating. This same methodology and rating effect is reflected throughout the overall portfolio.

More Subordination

The more conservative rating methodology also means that the rating agencies require higher subordination levels. In particular, equity tranches are usually much larger on EM deals than in high-yield deals. Exhibit 4 shows a representative high-yield deal versus a representative sovereign EM deal, both brought to market at approximately the same time. Note that the equity tranche is 7.9% on the high-yield deal versus 18% on the EM deal. More generally, the investment grade bonds receive much more protection on the EM deal than they do on the high yield deal. In the EM deal, 22.2% of the deal is subordinated to the investment grade bonds, on the high-yield deal only 11.9% is subordinated.

The yields for each tranche are higher on the EM CBO than for the corresponding tranche on the high yield CBO, in spite of the fact that the rating is as high or higher on the EM debt. The AAA rated bond on the EM deal is priced at 68 discounted margin (DM), versus 57 DM on the high yield deal. The A rated EM tranche is priced at +250/10-year Treasury, versus +225/10-year Treasury for a lower rated (A-) tranche of the high yield deal. This translates into roughly a 50 b.p. differential, as the credit quality differential is worth 25 b.p. The Ba1 mezzanine bond in the EM deal is priced at +800/10-year, versus +700/10-year for the

---

[6] There have been a few CBOs backed primarily by Asian corporate bonds. These CBOs are "story bonds" driven by local investors, and have take advantage of brief "windows of opportunity." This chapter focuses on CBOs backed by diversified sovereign EM bonds. In practice, the rating agencies criteria is such that it has never been economic to include more than 20% EM corporate bonds in a sovereign EM deal.

BB- tranche of the high yield deal. Here the EM investor is receiving a 100 b.p. higher spread, as well as higher credit quality. The equity on the EM deal is the only exception to this. It may yield slightly less than on high-yield deals, as the equity is far less leveraged. The difference in the leverage can be seen by the fact that the EM equity is 18% of the deal versus 7.9% of the high-yield deal.

CONCLUSION

It is unfortunate that many investors may be reluctant to look at CBOs backed by EM collateral because of general misimpressions about the collateral. In this chapter, we have shown that there have been few actual defaults on sovereign EM bonds, which is the collateral used to back many EM CBOs. Many investors do not realize this, as they tend to clump together the experiences of both sovereign bank loans and sovereign bonds. Sovereign bank loans have clearly experienced more significant level of defaults. Moreover, when there is a default, the recovery rates are higher on the sovereign bonds than on the bank loans.

Moreover, because of the limited history of sovereign bonds, the rating agencies are far more conservative in their ratings. They are particularly harsh in the assumptions they make about recoveries and on diversity characteristics. This more conservative rating methodology means that the average credit quality of bonds is higher in the EM deal. Finally, EM CBOs have more subordination. This extra structural protection is clearly not priced in. EM CBOs trade wider than high-yield CBOs for every rated tranche.

Exhibit 4: Comparison of Emerging Market and High Yield Deal Structure

Class	Ratings Moody's/S&P/D&P	Amount ($M)	% of Deal	% Sub	Current Pricing Info
Representative Emerging Market Deal					
A1	Aaa/AAA/NR	163.00	68.6%	31.4%	+68 DM*
A2	A2/A/NR	22.00	9.3%	22.2%	+250/10yr Tsy
Mezz	Ba1/NR/NR	10.00	4.2%	18.0%	+800/10yr Tsy
Equity	NR	42.74	18.0%	—	—
Total		237.74			
Representative High Yield Deal					
A1	Aaa/AAA/AAA	344.50	68.2%	31.8%	+57 DM*
A2	NR/A-/A-	79.00	15.6%	16.2%	+225/10yr Tsy
Mezz 1	NR/NR/BBB-	22.00	4.4%	11.8%	+360/10yr Tsy
Mezz 2	NR/NR/BB-	20.00	4.0%	7.9%	+700/10yr Tsy
Equity	NR	39.79	7.9%	—	—
Total		505.29			

* DM = discounted margin

Chapter 17

Market Value CBOs

Laurie Goodman, Ph.D.
Managing Director
Mortgage Strategy Group
PaineWebber

INTRODUCTION

As explained in Chapter 13, there are cash flow and market value collateralized bond obligations (CBOs). Many investors look suspiciously at the senior and mezzanine tranches of market value CBOs. Their concern is that this deal structure gives the manager carte blanche to play the all but discredited "hedge fund" game. That view is wrong. It is based on a misconception about how market value CBOs are really structured and the protection they provide investors.

In this chapter, we provide an overview on the differences between cash flow and market value structures. We next examine the mechanics of market value CBOs, focusing on the advance rates (i.e., the percentage of a particular asset that may be issued as rated debt) — the key to protecting the debt holders. We then look at some volatility numbers, which indicate how conservative the advance rates used by the rating agencies really are. Finally, we conclude that the senior and mezzanine tranches of market value CDOs are very well protected.

CASH FLOW VERSUS MARKET VALUE DEALS

Cash flow deals are dependent on the ability of the collateral to generate sufficient current cash flow to pay interest and principal on rated notes issued by the CBO. The ratings are based on the effect of collateral defaults and recoveries on the receipt of timely interest and principal payments from the collateral. The manager focuses on controlling defaults and recoveries. Overcollateralization, as measured on the basis of the par value of the portfolio, provides important structural protection for the bondholders. If overcollateralization tests are not met, then cash flow is diverted from mezzanine and subordinated classes to pay down senior notes, or cash flow is trapped in a reserve account. There are no forced collateral liquidations.

Market value transactions depend upon the ability of the fund manager to maintain and improve the market value of the collateral. Funds to be used for liability principal payments are obtained from liquidating the collateral. Liability interest payments can be made from collateral interest receipts, as well as collateral liquidation proceeds. Ratings are based on collateral price volatility, liquidity, and market value. The manager focuses on maximizing total return while minimizing volatility.

Market overcollateralization tests are conducted regularly. These require that the market value of assets multiplied by the advance rates must be greater than or equal to debt outstanding. If that is not the case, collateral sales and liability redemptions may be required to bring overcollateralization ratios back into compliance.[1] Contrary to some investors' beliefs, market value deals do have diversity, concentration and other portfolio constraints, albeit less than cash flow transactions.

Exhibit 1 summarizes the salient features of cash flow versus market value deals.

WHY USE A MARKET VALUE STRUCTURE?

While market value deals are a distinct minority of CBOs, they are the structure of choice for certain types of collateral (such as distressed debt), where the cash flows are not predictable. It is very difficult to use unpredictable cash flows within the confines of a cash flow structure. Moreover, market value structures may also appeal to managers and equity buyers who like the greater trading flexibility inherent in these deals. Finally, market value transactions also facilitate the purchase of assets that mature beyond the life of the transaction, because the price volatility associated with the forced sale of these assets is explicitly considered.

THE RATING PROCESS

The credit enhancement for a market value deal is the cushion between the current market value of the collateral and the face value of the structure's obligations. Within this framework, the collateral must normally be liquidated (either in whole or in part) if the ratio of the market value of the collateral to the debt obligations falls below a predetermined threshold. The liquidated collateral is used to pay down debt obligations, which brings the structure back into compliance.

The biggest risk in a market value transaction is a sudden decline in the value of the collateral pool. Thus, the rating agencies focus on the price volatility and liquidity of the assets that may be incorporated into these structures. Volatility and liquidity are assumed to be reflected in a set of advance rates that are designed to provide a cushion against market risk, and represent adjustments to the value of each asset.

---

[1] There are other alternatives to bring the portfolio into compliance: higher quality securities with higher advance rates can be substituted for lower quality securities with lower advance rates. The point is that action must be taken to safeguard the interest of the bondholders.

Exhibit 1: Overview of CBOs/CLOs
(Cash Flow versus Market Value)

	Cash Flow Deal	Market Value Deal
Objective	Cash Flow deals depend on the ability of the collateral to generate sufficient current cash to pay interest and principal on rated notes issued by the CBO/CLO.	Market Value transactions depend on the ability of the fund manager to maintain and improve the market value of the collateral.
Rating Focus	The ratings are based on the effect of collateral defaults and recoveries on the timely payment of interest and principal from the collateral	Ratings are based on collateral price volatility, liquidity, and market value.
Manager Focus	Manager focuses on controlling defaults and recoveries.	Manager focuses on maximizing total return while minimizing volatility.
Structural Protection	Overcollateralization is measured on the basis of the portfolio's par value. If overcollateralization tests are failed, then cash flow is diverted from the mezzanine and subordinated classes to pay down senior notes, or cash flow is trapped in a reserve account. There are no forced collateral liquidations.	Market Value overcollateralization tests are conducted regularly. The market value of assets multiplied by the advance rates* must be greater than or equal to the debt outstanding; otherwise collateral sales and liability redemptions may be required to bring overcollateralization ratios back into compliance.
Diversity and Concentration Limits	Very strict.	Substantial diversification is required. More is "encouraged" by the structure of advance rates.
Trading Limitations	There are limitations on portfolio trading.	There is greater portfolio trading flexibility.
Collateral	Typical Cash Flow assets include bank loans, high yield bonds, emerging market bonds/loans, and project finance.	Typical Market Value assets include assets eligible for inclusion in Cash Flow CBOs/CLOs as well as distressed debt, equities, and convertibles

* Advance rate is the percentage of the market value of a particular asset that may be issued as rated debt. Advance rates depend upon the price volatility and quality of price/return data and the liquidity of the assets. Assets with lower price volatility and greater liquidity are typically assigned higher advance rates.

Let's first look at how a market value deal really works. We then take up the methodology used by rating agencies to determine the advance rate. Finally, we look at how conservative those advance rates are relative to the actual price volatility of these instruments.

Building Blocks

A market value deal simply requires that the market value of the collateral times the advance rate (the adjustment to the value of the assets to provide a cushion against market risk) be greater than the book value of the liabilities. Moody's and Fitch IBCA, the rating agencies that have rated the majority of market value deals thus far, both use a set of advance rates to determine how much rated debt can be issued against the market value of an asset.

Exhibit 2: Advance Rates for Different Asset Types and Rating Levels
(20 issuers, 5 industries, 100% investment in one asset type, 5-year maturity)

Asset Type	Aaa	Aa1	Aa2	Aa3	A1	A2	A3	Baa1	Baa2	Baa3
Performing Bank Loans Valued $0.90 and above	0.870	0.890	0.895	0.900	0.905	0.910	0.915	0.930	0.935	9.400
Distressed Bank Loans Valued $0.85 and above	0.760	0.780	0.790	0.795	0.810	0.815	0.820	0.830	0.840	0.870
Performing High-Yield Bonds Rated Baa	0.76	0.79	0.80	0.81	0.83	0.84	0.85	0.87	0.88	0.90
Performing High-Yield Bonds Rated B	0.72	0.75	0.76	0.77	0.78	0.79	0.80	0.82	0.83	0.85
Distressed Bank Loans Valued Below $0.85	0.58	0.62	0.63	0.64	0.67	0.68	0.69	0.71	0.72	0.74
Performing High-Yield Valued Below Caa	0.45	0.49	0.50	0.51	0.56	0.58	0.60	0.62	0.64	0.67
Distressed Bonds	0.35	0.39	0.40	0.41	0.47	0.48	0.50	0.54	0.56	0.57
Reorganized Equities	0.31	0.37	0.38	0.39	0.44	0.46	0.47	0.51	0.52	0.54

Source: Moody's Investors Service, "Moody's Approach to Rating Market-Valued CDOs,"
April 13, 1998.

To get a handle on what this all means, Exhibit 2 shows Moody's advance rates in the simplest case of a one-tranche structure — one with subordination provided only by the advance rate.

In producing this table, Moody's assumed the following regarding portfolio diversification:

1. Maximum allowable investment in one issuer = 5%
2. Maximum allowable investment in any one industry = 20%
3. Maximum allowable investment in any one asset type = 100%

Thus, the least diversified portfolio consists of 20 issuers, 5 industries, and one asset type.

If an asset class consists of performing high-yield bonds rated B, and the deal is carved only into a bond rated A2 and equity, then (from Exhibit 2) Moody's advance rate would be 0.79. Thus, the market value of the deal times the advance rate (0.79 in this case) must be greater than the value of the bonds. If a deal has several tranches, then the par value of the debt within each rating is weighted to find the weighted average advance rate. Thus, if the liabilities consisted of equal parts bonds rated A2 (with an advance rate of 0.79) and those rated Baa2 (with an advance rate of 0.83), then the weighted average advance rate would be 0.81. Note that if there were greater diversification within this deal, then the advance rates would be somewhat higher.

We used this information to create a sample deal. We assumed that the deal originally consisted of $500 million in assets, with $375 million of bonds rated A2 and $125 million of equity (shown in Exhibit 3). Initially, the value of the assets times the advance rate is $395 million (in the Exhibit 3 column labeled "Adjusted" MV of Assets). This is obviously greater than the $375 million in bonds. The deal has 25% equity to begin ($125 million /$500 million).[2]

A Simple Example

In an effort to illustrate and test deal mechanics, Exhibit 3 shows the effect of an unrealistically rapid deterioration. We assume that the assets earn 1% per month, and that the value of the assets declines by 3% per month. Net, net—the value of the assets is declining by 2% per month. In addition, the rated debt holders are paid 0.66% per month. For simplicity, we assume all interest payments on the collateral are collected monthly, and the interest payments on the debt are disbursed monthly.[3] After month 3 of declining market prices, the value of the assets is $463.32 million. Applying the 0.79 advance rate, the "adjusted" value of the assets is $366.02 million, against $375 million of bonds. The structure fails the market value test: the adjusted market value of the securities is less than the par value of the bonds. The deal must begin to liquidate.

Let's walk through the process. The shortfall between the "Adjusted" MV (market value) of assets and debt is $8.98 million (shown in the Exhibit 3 column labeled "Difference"). Since the advance rate is 0.79, each dollar of liquidation is the equivalent of curing only $0.21 of the shortfall.[4] To bring the new adjusted MV of assets into line with the bonds, we must liquidate assets to cure the shortfall. We must liquidate $8.98 million/0.21 or $42.75 million of collateral [(shortfall)/(1 − advance rate)]. Thus, the new MV of the assets is $420.56 million, and the new "adjusted" MV (AMV) of the assets is $332.25 million. This is identical to the post liquidation par value of the liabilities.

Assume in the following month that the assets again earn 1%, their value again declines by 3%, and bondholders are again paid 0.66%. There will be another shortfall, this time of $8.38 million. Thus, $39.89 million must be liquidated to bring the new "adjusted" MV of the assets in line with the par value of the bonds.

---

[2] This deal starts life with a 4% capital cushion [($395 million adjusted MV of assets − $375 million rated bonds)/$500 million deal size]. In market value deals, the senior tranche is often a blank line, allowing the manager to lever and delever easily, eliminating the need for a capital cushion.

[3] In real deals interest is paid quarterly, not monthly. The accrued interest on the assets is included in the market value of the assets, and the accrued interest on the liabilities is added to the par value of the bond, for the purposes of applying the market value test.

[4] Intuitively, for each dollar of assets that is liquidated, the liabilities are paid down by $1.00, while the adjusted MV of the assets declines by $0.79.

Exhibit 3: Illustration of Market Value Deal Mechanics
(Assume 3% Drop in MV Per Month, Assets Yield 1% per Month, 0.66% Income Paid per Month on A2 Bonds)

Month	Market Value of Assets	"Adjusted" MV of Assets*	Par Value of Bonds Rated A2	Diff	Liq	New MV of Assets	New AMV of Assets	New Par on Bond	% Equity Before Liq	% Equity After Liq	New Par on Bond
0	500.00	395.00	375.00	20.00	0.00	500.00	395.00	375.00	0.25	0.25	375.00
1**	487.53	385.14	375.00	10.14	0.00	487.53	385.14	375.00	0.23	0.23	375.00
2	475.30	375.49	375.00	0.49	0.00	475.30	375.49	375.00	0.21	0.21	375.00
3	463.32	366.02	375.00	-8.98	42.75	420.56	332.25	332.25	0.19	0.21	332.25
4	409.96	323.87	332.25	-8.38	39.89	370.07	292.35	292.35	0.19	0.21	292.35
5	360.74	284.98	292.35	-7.37	35.10	325.64	257.25	257.25	0.19	0.21	257.25
6	317.43	250.77	257.25	-6.49	30.89	286.54	226.36	226.36	0.19	0.21	226.36
7	279.31	220.66	226.36	-5.71	27.18	252.13	199.19	199.19	0.19	0.21	199.19
8	245.78	194.16	199.19	-5.02	23.92	221.86	175.27	175.27	0.19	0.21	175.27
9	216.27	170.85	175.27	-4.42	21.04	195.22	154.23	154.23	0.19	0.21	154.23
10	190.30	150.34	154.23	-3.89	18.52	171.78	135.71	135.71	0.19	0.21	135.71

*Adjusted MV of assets = MV of assets × 0.79

**To illustrate calculations:

Market value of assets = +500 million × 0.97 = +485 million

+500 million × 0.01 = +5 million

−375 million × 0.66% = −2.475

= 487.53

There are a number of things to note from this example. First, the deal liquidates very quickly in an environment of unfavorable performance. In this simplified example, the par value of the bonds has amortized down to $154.23 million after 10 months. However, despite a very quick deterioration in market value, the rated debt holders have completely received 100% return of principal and timely payment of interest. Second, there is always a very hefty capital cushion. In this example, the equity before liquidation never drops lower than 19%. By definition, the equity after liquidation must be a minimum of (1 – the advance rate), or 21% in this case.

Market value deals are actually marked-to-market no less frequently than once a week, and the tests are applied at that time. Some are marked-to-market daily. When the test is failed, the excess indebtedness must be repaid within 10 to 15 business days.

Extra Protection

Investors should be aware that in addition to the protection provided by advance rates, Fitch IBCA also has a required quarterly minimum net worth test to protect the rated debt. This requires that 60% of the original equity remains to protect the senior tranche, and 30% to protect the subordinated tranche. If the equity falls below that, noteholders of the senior tranche may vote to accelerate payment of the debt, at which point the asset manager must liquidate assets and fully pay down the debt related to the test that has failed. In our simple 1 bond CBO (shown in Exhibit 3), assume that Fitch IBCA would require a 50% minimum net worth. This would mean that if the equity falls below $62.5 million ($125 million × 50%), the noteholders could vote to liquidate the deal. In our example, this would happen at the end of month 6, where, after the adjustments required to pass the market value test, the value of the equity would be $60.18 million ($286.54 million – $226.36 million).

HOW ADVANCE RATES ARE DERIVED

Advance rates are the crucial variable in market value deals. It is useful to look more closely at how these are derived. Advance rates are actually a combination of three factors — price volatility of the securities, correlation among securities, and liquidity. It's interesting to look at how the rating agencies view each of these variables.

Both Moody's and Fitch IBCA use historical volatility as the basis for deriving volatility estimates. This volatility is then stressed depending on the length of the historical record and the desired rating of the CBO/CLO tranche. Because there is a very complete record for the returns on high-yield bonds (that is, high quality information collected over a large number of years) only a relatively small stress factor is applied to the historical volatility for this instrument. At the other end of the spectrum, a relatively large stress factor is applied to distressed instruments, especially reorganized equities.[5] The higher the desired rating, the greater the stress factor, which reflects the fact that higher rated tranches are expected to hold up under greater standard deviations of stress. Fitch is very explicit on that final point. A security rated A must be able to sustain market value declines 3 times as large as needed for the security to obtain a single B rating. For an AAA rating, the security must be able to sustain market value declines 5 times as large as would be needed to obtain a B rating.

The choice of correlations is problematic. Historical correlations are useful, but correlations often rise sharply during periods of crisis. Thus, Moody's uses correlations that are higher than those prevailing during "normal" periods, but not as high as those observed during the most stressful periods. They assume correlation of 55% between firms within the same industry, and 40% among those in different industries.

For most securities, the bid-ask spread is small relative to ordinary price volatility. However, market value transactions lend themselves to using less liquid assets which also have irregular cash flows. For these securities, liquidity can become a key consideration, especially during periods of financial stress. Both Moody's and Fitch IBCA make assumptions as to what losses would be during periods of market stress. So, for performing high-yield bonds, Moody's assumes a 5% liquidity "haircut", while for distressed bonds, it's crewcut is 10%. For performing bank loans the haircut is 7%, while for distressed bank loans it is increased to 12.5%. Reorganized equities get scalped at 20%.

So these three factors — price volatility, correlation among securities and liquidity together — account for the advance rates shown in Exhibit 2.

ARE ADVANCE RATES CONSERVATIVE?

To test how conservative advance rates actually are, we looked at monthly performance for a readily available set of data — high-yield bonds. Through Ryan Labs we obtained the performance of the Lehman and Merrill Lynch indices, going back to 1985. These two plus Salomon are the three indices most commonly used by investors. The Salomon data did not go back as far, hence we did not include it in this analysis. We use monthly observations because the market values are evaluated at least weekly, and a portfolio normally has 10 to 15 business days to liquidate assets to correct the deficiency. Thus, if the portfolio passes the test one period, and then the market value of the portfolio deteriorates, it could take a maximum of just over four weeks to find and correct the deficiency (1 week maximum until the next test, 15 business days to correct the deficiency). This suggests that monthly intervals are the correct benchmark period for looking at how conservative advance rates are.

---

[5] Note that the prices or returns on less liquid assets are often not of the highest quality. That is, the series may reflect a number of observations in a row in which the price is the same, or the return is 0. Moody's drops those observations from the analysis, boosting volatility on these less liquid securities.

Exhibit 4: High-Yield Indices
(Merrill Lynch versus Lehman Brothers)

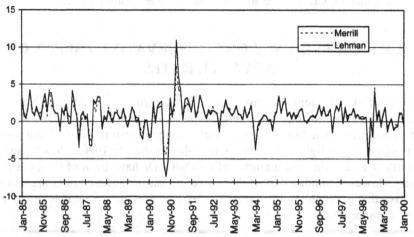

Exhibit 4 shows month-by-month returns on the Lehman and Merrill indices going back to the beginning of 1985. These two are similar in that they are both representative of the market, and their returns are usually close. Both indices include all publicly traded domestic debt with a fixed-rate coupon, a minimum maturity of one year, and a maximum credit quality of Ba1. Both indices exclude payment-in-kind (PIK) bonds, and Eurobonds. However, there are still a number of differences. Lehman requires a minimum of $100 million outstanding for inclusion, while Merrill only requires $10 million. Lehman does not have a minimum credit quality for inclusion, and includes securities in default, whereas Merrill does not include securities in default (rated DDD1 or less).

There are 181 observations (monthly 1985-1999 = 15 years × 12 observations/year = 180 observations + Jan of 2000 = 181 observations). Exhibit 5 restates these 1-month returns as a histogram, an exhibit which shows the distribution of 1-month returns. Note from this histogram that there was only 1 month in which the total return on the Lehman index was less than –7% (the worst single month was September of 1990 at –7.30%). The worst month on the Merrill index was –4.35%. Given that Lehman also includes defaulted securities and Merrill does not, we would expect that the Lehman index would display a higher variance of returns.

The worst three months on the indices were August, September, and October of 1990. The Lehman index was down 5.69% in August, 7.30% in September, and 5.25% in October of 1990. During the worst 3-month period in the history of the market, the total loss was 17.2%. The Merrill index also showed these to be the worst three consecutive months on record: down 3.83% in August, 4.35% in September, and 2.54% in October, for a cumulative decline of 10.35%. This period corresponded to the beginning of the recession. We showed earlier that the advance rates are meant to correspond to 1-month price changes. However, the advance rates are more severe than the worst 3-month period in the history of the market. Clearly, the advance rates are very conservative.

FURTHER EVIDENCE OF CONSERVATIVE ASPECT OF ADVANCE RATES

Want proof of the extent of conservatism in the rating methodology? Note that Moody's has never downgraded a single tranche of a market value CBO, whereas Fitch has downgraded only one such tranche. Many investors will find that particularly surprising in light of asset price volatility in the late 1990s. Clearly, part of the answer is that the vast majority of CBOs/CLOs have been of the cash flow variety. However, another part of the answer is that the advance rates are so conservative that price volatility in recent years is well within the range anticipated by the advance rates.

Exhibit 5: Return Distribution on High Yield Indices
(Number of Observations)

1-month Return Range	Merrill Lynch	Lehman Brothers
−8 to −7	0	1
−7 to −6	0	0
−6 to −5	0	3
−5 to −4	2	0
−4 to −3	2	4
−3 to −2	4	4
−2 to −1	9	8
−1 to 0	17	16
0 to 1	58	59
1 to 2	59	47
2 to 3	20	22
3 to 4	5	11
4 to 5	4	4
5 to 6	0	1
6 to 7	0	0
7 to 8	1	0
8 to 9	0	0
9 to 10	0	0
10 to 11	0	1
11 to 12	0	0
Total Obs:	181	181
Mean	0.902	0.891
Std	1.519	1.964

Number of Observations Range	Merrill	Lehman
−6 to −8	0	1
−4 to −6	2	3
−2 to −4	6	8
−2 to 0	26	24
0 to 2	117	106
2 to 4	25	33
4 to 6	4	5
6 to 8	1	0
8 to 10	0	0
10 to 12	0	1
Total:	181	181

Source: Ryan Labs Inc.

The one bond that was downgraded by Fitch was a mezzanine tranche originally rated single B, and downgraded to CCC+. The downgrade was triggered by a failure to meet the December 31, 1999 minimum net worth tests. Note that the other tranches of the deal (rated A, BBB, and BB) were not downgraded, nor even put on Rating Alert-Negative. Moreover, within 30 days of the December 31 test date, the minimum net worth requirement was met, and the deal was back into compliance with all covenants. The A rated bonds were paid off, and the rating on the BBB, BB, and CCC+ tranches were affirmed.

COMPARISON TO HEDGE FUND

Now that we all have such a good understanding of how market value deals work, it is useful to contrast them to hedge funds. From the bondholder's point of view, making an investment in a market value CBO is quite different from giving money to a hedge fund and betting that it will perform. First, note what happens to leverage in the two different investment situations. As the value of assets decline, hedge fund equity becomes smaller, and hence the asset package becomes more highly leveraged (to the extent allowed by bank lines of credit). In a market value CBO, the percent equity in the deal cannot fall below the threshold of 1 minus the advance rate. Thus, the minimum equity in the deal is a constant, pre-specified percent, and the market value tests are designed to insure this minimum equity threshold. (We saw in Exhibit 3 that the percent equity in the deal, after liquidation, is never lower than 21%, with a 79% advance rate.)

Second, the equity financing in a CBO is permanent, whereas in a hedge fund, equity can leave, thus forcing liquidations. In a CBO, the only forced liquidations are those designed to protect the bondholders.

CONCLUSION

Many CBO investors have steered away from the debt in market value deals, believing that purchasing the debt is like making an investment in a hedge fund. As a result, market value deals trade at similar or slightly wider spreads than cash flow deals launched at the same time. We believe that the protections built into market value deals are quite powerful from the bondholder's point of view, and that this paper will eventually trade tighter than cash flow paper with the same rating issued at the same time.

Residential Real Estate Backed ABS

Chapter 18

Mortgage Credit Analysis

Joel W. Brown, CFA
Mortgage Credit Analyst
Stein, Roe & Farnham, Inc.

William M. Wadden IV
Senior Vice President and Principal
Stein, Roe & Farnham, Inc.

INTRODUCTION

In 1983, the first CMO was introduced and it vastly increased the appeal of residential mortgages to the investment community. CMOs allowed for the tranching of principal and interest payments to fit specific investor profiles. As a result of CMO development, prepayment analysis gained momentum. The sophistication of prepayment analysis grew as fast as computer technology permitted, and Wall Street firms spent millions of dollars in this area of research. During the late-1980s, the securitization of non-agency jumbo whole loans not only utilized time tranching but credit tranching as well. Cash flow payment priority was split between senior and subordinate tranches whereby subordinate investors absorbed credit losses of the underlying mortgage loans. Whereas initial CMO innovation allowed the interest rate risk of agency mortgages to be tranched, subsequent innovation in senior/subordinate structures allowed non-agency whole-loan mortgages to be credit tranched according to a variety of credit ratings. This permitted investors to adjust the level of mortgage credit risk suitable for their investment mandate. By the mid-1990s, the mortgage and mortgage-related asset-backed market evolved to the point where non-prime collateral had also become a permanent part of the mortgage credit landscape. The non-prime market includes Alternative-A quality documentation (Alt-A), home equity loans, home improvement loans, manufactured housing, and 125% high LTV loans.

Mortgage credit analysis has not evolved to the same level of sophistication as prepayment analysis. In fact, highly leveraged credit-sensitive mortgage securities are created without modeling delinquency and loss rates in an equally sophisticated manner as is done for voluntary prepayments. The goal of this chapter is to demystify the jargon of mortgage credit analysis as well as to present a preferred approach for forecasting delinquency and loss rates.

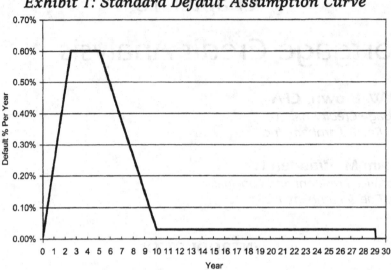

Exhibit 1: Standard Default Assumption Curve

THE SDA CURVE

The Public Securities Association introduced the Standard Default Assumption (SDA curve) in 1993.[1] Exhibit 1 illustrates the shape of this curve. The SDA curve standardized default projections for prime mortgages, and it is useful for forecasting default rates on non-agency whole loan REMICs. The SDA curve relates to defaults just as a PSA curve relates to prepayments; it is a forecasted speed for removing loans from a pool. With the SDA curve, default prompts the removal of a mortgage from a loan pool. In the real world of mortgage servicing, however, default is neither a delinquency nor liquidation. Instead, default signifies when foreclosure proceedings commence on a property. In the corporate bond market, default signifies the inability of a company to meet an interest or principal payment. In the mortgage market, a delinquency signifies the borrower's inability to make a timely payment. Thus, corporate bond credit terminology is not fungible to the mortgage credit market.

The mortgage credit analyst must forecast losses as well as defaults. By itself, the SDA curve is insufficient to forecast losses. Three other assumptions are necessary before obtaining a final loss curve:

1. the liquidation timeline
2. whether a servicer advances principal and interest on a defaulted loan
3. loss severity[2]

---

[1] Andrew K. Feigenberg and Adam S. Lechner, "A New Default Benchmark for Pricing Nonagency Securities," Salomon Brothers (July 22, 1993).

[2] Jerome S. Fons and James Schmidbauer, "Moody's Approach to Rating Residential Mortgage Pass-Through Securities," Moody's Investors Service (November 8, 1996).

The liquidation timeline is the number of days required to foreclose and dispose of a property. The disposition might require the lender to acquire the property and hold it in their inventory for some time before it can be sold (REO), or use an alternative foreclosure process such as a deed in lieu of foreclosure.[3] Servicers may advance principal and interest payments to a security holder that a non-defaulted loan would otherwise pay. When the proceeds of a liquidated property do not cover the unpaid principal balance of a mortgage loan, a loss occurs. Loss severity is largely due to an impairment of a home's value, recovery of principal and interest advances, costs to remarket the property (brokers fees and commissions), and legal fees incurred from the foreclosure process.

CONSTANT DEFAULT RATE APPROACH

Most non-agency mortgage credit analysis relies on the *constant default rate* (CDR) approach to forecast mortgage defaults. CDR is computed as follows:

$$CDR = 100 \times \left[1 - \left(1 - \frac{D_t}{P_{t-1}S_t} \right)^{12} \right]$$

where

D_t = defaulted loan balance in month t
P_t = pool balance in month t
S_t = scheduled principal payment in month t

As the above formula suggests, a CDR is merely a constant annualized rate at which defaulted loans are removed from their pool. A slight modification to the constant loan removal approach is to allow CDRs to gradually ramp upward during the first 12 to 24 months of a pool's life until reaching a plateau. Within the home equity sector, an analyst might fashion a base case assumption that ramps from 0% to 4% CDR over an 18-month period, then remain at 4% CDR for the rest of the transaction. To run a default stress on the transaction, the analyst will incrementally raise the CDR plateau until the first loss occurs.

A NEW APPROACH

We suggest that, by itself, the CDR approach (or its ramped version) is not a complete mortgage credit analysis tool. We will demonstrate a preferred method of mortgage credit analysis that has three principal improvements over the customary CDR framework:

• focus on variables that can be measured from actual pool performance

---

[3] Jack C. Harris and Jack P. Friedman, *Real Estate Handbook, Fourth Edition* (Barrons, 1993).

> • focus on estimating loss curves as opposed to default curves
> • model transactions in dollars

Defaults are Unobservable

Investors have a strong incentive to compare actual defaults versus their own estimated defaults. However, how does an analyst determine actual defaults? In order to properly compute a CDR it is necessary to have: (1) a list of newly foreclosed loans, (2) the amount of time it took to liquidate or dispose of the property, (3) the principal and interest advanced, and (4) the gross liquidation proceeds. The effort required to calculate a CDR is not trivial. Market participants must have access to loan level data obtained from mortgage servicing "tapes" in order to correctly compute an actual CDR. Oftentimes more than one set of tapes is required to track the above variables. Furthermore, it is difficult for investors to gain access to these tapes.

Neither are investors able to observe defaults from monthly remittance reports. The remittance report displays principal and interest payments received by each tranche, fundamental credit trends on the mortgage pool, month-to-month prepayments, and REMIC expenses. CDR, or the data necessary for its calculation, is rarely included in a remittance report. This is peculiar since CDR forecasting has ostensibly become a fundamental part of the forecasting process for non-prime and subordinate mortgages.

To illustrate, Exhibit 2 displays the remittance report for Advanta's 1997-1 home equity loan REMIC. The report identifies the stock of delinquencies (30-59, 60-89, and 90+ day), foreclosures, real estate owned (REO), and liquidations. Although this is one of the better remittance reports available, it does not itemize newly foreclosed or liquidated properties. Some remittance reports identify the number and quantity of newly foreclosed loans, but do not contain all of the data required for a CDR calculation such as liquidation timelines. Several mortgage companies, notably Citicorp Mortgage, PNC, and RFC, provide access to loan level information for CDR calculations. However, within the sub-prime mortgage universe, this level of information usually does not exist.

Liquidations and Losses are Observable

While default rates are unobservable, the monthly remittance report does provide figures for liquidated loan amounts and final losses. One of the main purposes of this chapter is to clarify and refine mortgage credit terminology, eliminating confusion among analysts regarding exactly what variables to use as the building blocks of loss forecasting. Instead of using the term CDR, we prefer to define two new terms, which we will refer to as the *charge-off-rate* (COR) and the *loss rate* (LR).

The COR is the annualized rate of loan liquidations. The LR is the product of COR times the loss severity, and represents the annualized rate of losses. Although CDR is usually the core default model in credit sensitive mortgage securities, in practice, COR actually becomes the monitoring tool. These newly coined terms are mathematically defined by the following formulas:

Exhibit 2: *ADVANTA Mortgage Loan Trust 1997-1 Mortgage Loan Asset-Backed Certificates Series 1997-1*

Statement To Certificateholders

Distribution Date: December 27, 1999

DELINQUENT LOAN INFORMATION	30-59 DAYS	60-89 DAYS	90+ DAYS (Excluding F/C, REO & BANKRUPTCY)	LOANS IN BANKRUPTCY	LOANS IN REO	LOANS IN FORECLOSURE
GROUP 1						
PRINCIPAL BALANCE	3,301,696.44	941,404.09	838,993.29	7,760,042.35	2,822,331.52	5,800,546.82
PERCENTAGE OF POOL BAL.	2.41%	0.69%	0.61%	5.66%	2.06%	4.23%
NUMBER OF LOANS	64	14	17	142	54	111
PERCENTAGE OF POOL LOANS	2.67%	0.58%	0.71%	5.92%	2.25%	4.63%
GROUP 2						
PRINCIPAL BALANCE	2,354,380.80	434,838.32	500,139.13	6,091,800.19	2,711,702.82	5,150,247.38
PERCENTAGE OF POOL BAL.	3.84%	0.71%	0.82%	9.95%	4.43%	8.41%
NUMBER OF LOANS	29	4	6	60	28	57
PERCENTAGE OF POOL LOANS	4.39%	0.61%	0.91%	9.09%	4.24%	8.64%
COMBINED						
REO BOOK VALUE					7,063,774.27	

GENERAL MORTGAGE LOAN INFORMATION:	GROUP I	GROUP II	TOTAL
BEGINNING AGGREGATE MORTGAGE LOAN BALANCE	140,886,676.31	63,121,656.45	204,008,332.76
PRINCIPAL REDUCTION	3,790,575.73	1,887,296.44	5,677,872.17
ENDING AGGREGATE MORTGAGE LOAN BALANCE	137,096,100.58	61,234,360.01	198,330,460.59
BEGINNING AGGREGATE MORTGAGE LOAN COUNT	2,462	676	3,138
ENDING AGGREGATE MORTGAGE LOAN COUNT	2,399	660	3,059
CURRENT WEIGHTED AVERAGE COUPON RATE	10.65%	11.17%	10.81%
NEXT WEIGHTED AVERAGE COUPON RATE	10.64%	11.20%	10.81%

Exhibit 2 (Continued)

MORTGAGE LOAN PRINCIPAL REDUCTION INFORMATION:	GROUP I	GROUP II	TOTAL
SCHEDULED PRINCIPAL	245,905.84	33,311.49	279,217.33
CURTAILMENTS	-	-	-
PREPAYMENTS	2,586,759.04	1,339,677.68	3,926,436.72
REPURCHASES/SUBSTITUTIONS	-	-	-
LIQUIDATION PROCEEDS	957,910.85	514,307.27	1,472,218.12
OTHER PRINCIPAL	-	-	-
LESS: REALIZED LOSSES	504,553.17	135,356.32	639,909.49
LESS: DELINQUENT PRINCIPAL NOT ADVANCED BY SERVICER	-	-	-
TOTAL PRINCIPAL REDUCTION	3,286,022.56	1,751,940.12	5,037,962.68

SERVICER INFORMATION:	GROUP I	GROUP II	TOTAL
ACCRUED SERVICING FEE FOR THE CURRENT PERIOD	39,788.53	14,254.34	54,042.87
LESS: AMOUNTS TO COVER INTEREST SHORTFALLS	598.43	605.69	1,204.12
LESS: DELINQUENT SERVICE FEES	18,914.25	12,046.35	30,960.60
COLLECTED SERVICING FEES FOR CURRENT PERIOD:	20,275.85	1,602.30	21,878.15
ADVANCED PRINCIPAL	33,735.40	8,333.23	42,068.63
ADVANCED INTEREST	403,698.79	267,499.22	671,198.01

$$\text{Charge Off Rate (COR)} = 100 \times \left[1 - \left(1 - \frac{L_t}{P_{t-1}S_t} \right)^{12} \right]$$

$$\text{Loss Severity} = \frac{L - LP}{L}$$

$$\text{Loss Rate (LR)} = \text{COR} \times \text{Loss Severity}$$

where

L_t = liquidated loan balance in month t
LP = liquidation proceeds
P_t = pool balance in month t
S_t = scheduled principal payment in month t

Loss severity is 100% when there are no liquidation proceeds, and zero severity occurs when liquidation proceeds equal the liquidated loan balance.

Losses Are Deducted From Credit Enhancement

In most non-prime mortgage securities, losses are deducted from excess spread. These structures typically use excess spread as the first layer of credit enhancement to cover losses, backed up by overcollateralization and/or subordination. Excess spread is the difference between the mortgage interest collected from borrowers, less the interest payments made to bondholders and any fees paid from the trust. Without explicitly incorporating all of the variables influencing ultimate losses, it is impossible for an analyst to determine that a given default rate can be adequately handled by excess spread. Due to the timing difference between a defaulted loan and its ultimate liquidation, it is difficult to determine that a given level of defaults can be absorbed by excess spread without causing deterioration in other forms of credit enhancement.

COR is Dependent on Voluntary Prepayments and Liquidation Timelines

During 1998 and 1999, some large monoline finance companies failed.[4] One of the prime reasons for failure was due to gain-on-sale accounting assumptions. More specifically, their CDR assumptions broke down. The CDR assumptions failed because voluntary prepayment rates rose and liquidation timelines lengthened. Unexpected changes in voluntary prepayments and liquidation timelines can have a significant impact on the economics of a mortgage securitization.

---

[4] Some of the specialty finance companies that filed for bankruptcy or faced significant reorganization included: AMRESCO (HEL), First Plus Financial (125 LTV), IMC Mortgage (HEL), Southern Pacific Funding (HEL), and UCFC (HEL & MH).

Exhibit 3: CDR versus COR Voluntary CPR Stress

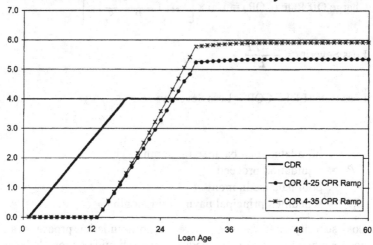

Exhibit 4: CDR versus COR Timeline Stress

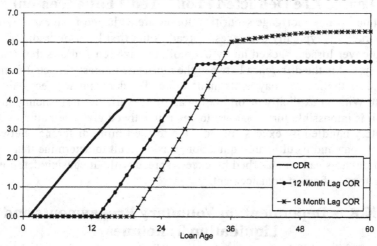

Exhibits 3 and 4 illustrate our point. In each of these illustrations, principal payments were calculated using a pool of home equity loans with an 11% gross WAC and 300 month WAM. We also assumed a CDR forecast that ramped from 0% to 4% over 18 months. In Exhibit 3, we examine the more minor impact of voluntary prepayment stress on COR calculations. In this example, COR is calculated as a function of two different voluntary CPR vectors. The base case vector ramps from 4% to 25% CPR over 18 months, while the faster vector ramps from 4% to 35% over the same time period. The 10% higher CPR plateau causes the COR calculation to peak at a higher level, 5.9%, versus the base case, which produces a COR of 5.4%. The liquidation timeline pushes a defaulted dollar into the future until it becomes liquidated. Prepayments cause the remaining balance to decline over time. Therefore, a defaulted dollar becomes a larger percentage of the remaining principal balance when it is liquidated. Furthermore, the difference between the CDR and COR increase as prepayments rise. This effect is seen in Exhibit 3, where the COR is higher than the CDR when the ramp-up period and liquidation timeline are complete.

The more significant influence occurs when the liquidation timeline lengthens. Exhibit 4 shows two COR functions, both created from the same 0-4% CDR ramp and 4%-25% base case voluntary CPR vector. The first COR function is determined using a 12-month liquidation timeline. The second COR function represents an 18-month liquidation timeline. Lengthening the liquidation time-line by only six months causes the COR to rise to 6.4% from 5.4%. Again, the COR increases as the timeline lengthens, because the remaining loan balance is given a chance to decline further with six months additional time. As an aside, loss severity will also rise as the timeline stretches because principal and interest advances become more expensive to the transaction. Longer liquidation time-lines are usually indicative of a less efficient mortgage servicing and loss mitiga-tion operation.

Assuming a 12-month lagged COR has a 35% loss severity, an 18-month lagged COR might produce a 45% loss severity. Correlating these two factors causes the loss rate (LR) to increase from 1.88% to 2.87%. Such an increase in the liquidation timeline can put serious pressure on a home equity deal, since these transactions have only 2.0%-2.5% of excess spread.

Transactions Should be Evaluated in Dollars

Observing actual dollars at work provides the mortgage credit analyst with much deeper insight into a transaction. This added dimension helps to eliminate the noise that ongoing principal balance reductions can have on percentage based credit statistics. For instance, when a pool's principal balance is high, even a rela-tively low delinquency percentage can lead to a large amount of delinquent loans that is burdensome to the servicer.

Forecasting losses in dollars, and then comparing those losses to credit enhancement levels is the ultimate goal of a mortgage credit analyst. Exhibits 5 and 6 take the COR vectors previously shown and converts charge-offs into future dollar amounts of losses. These losses are subtracted from excess spread to deter-mine net excess spread. Exhibit 5 shows the net dollars of excess spread remain-ing after losses have been charged off from our hypothetical transaction, assuming the transaction generates 2.5% of excess spread and loss severity is 35%. The dollar amount of net excess spread declines as higher voluntary prepay-ments produce lower amounts of remaining principal balance. A 10% increase in voluntary prepayment cuts the dollar amount of net excess spread virtually in half, causing a real squeeze in credit enhancement.

Exhibit 5: Net Excess Spread versus Voluntary CPR Stress

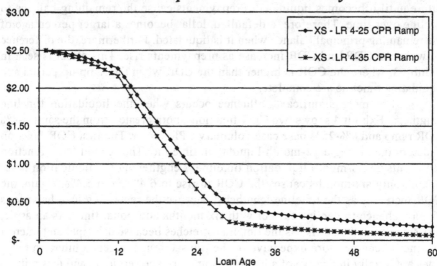

Exhibit 6: Net Excess Spread versus Timeline Stress

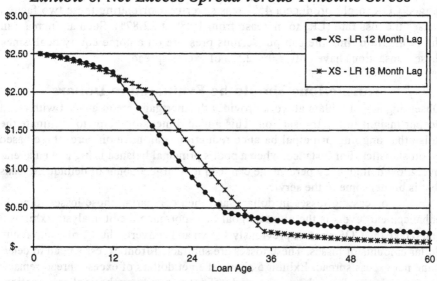

Exhibit 6 demonstrates how a longer liquidation timeline affects the timing of net excess spread. As liquidation timelines increase, losses are lower early on. This delay causes the losses to be applied versus a lower amount of excess spread, thus causing a real squeeze of excess spread later in the transaction. Both of these graphs show little net excess spread dollars by the third year.

Exhibit 7: Transition Probability Matrix

From	Current	30-59	60-89	90-119	120-149	150-179	Charge Off
To: Current	96.63%	31.37%	6.15%	6.43%	1.00%	0.00%	0.00%
30-59	1.72%	27.00%	7.12%	0.00%	0.00%	0.00%	0.00%
60-89	0.00%	37.00%	12.00%	10.13%	0.00%	0.00%	0.00%
90-119	0.00%	0.00%	74.73%	26.01%	4.00%	0.00%	0.00%
120-149	0.00%	0.00%	0.00%	57.43%	12.00%	0.00%	0.00%
150-179	0.00%	0.00%	0.00%	0.00%	83.00%	7.00%	0.00%
Charge Off	0.00%	0.00%	0.00%	0.00%	0.00%	93.00%	0.00%
Pay Off	1.65%	4.63%	0.00%	0.00%	0.00%	0.00%	0.00%

TRANSITION MATRIX APPROACH

Up to now, we have defined more precise terminology for evaluating and measuring mortgage credit risk. Establishing better terminology is just a beginning, because mortgage credit analysts still need better tools to forecast delinquency and loss rates. The use of transition probability matrices offers one promising approach. This procedure measures the probability of a mortgagor "rolling" (or transitioning) from one credit status to another. To imagine how this works, consider a borrower who is 30-59 days delinquent. A transition matrix contains the complete set of mathematical probabilities of this borrower rolling from his current status to any of the other possible states: (1) performing, (2) more severely delinquent (60-89 days), (3) refinanced, or (4) bankrupt. Also contained within the matrix, are probabilities of status changes from those states to the remaining others. Exhibit 7 is an example of a transition matrix table for a 125% High LTV securitization.

This transition matrix was developed using empirical mortgage payment history. It required loan level detail, which was obtained from the mortgage servicer's loan tapes. Due to the simplicity of loss mitigation options, 125% high LTV loans are an ideal collateral class to forecast delinquencies and losses with transition matrix technology. This mortgage sub-sector has no foreclosure or REO process, and the loss mitigation effort is more transparent because of the sequential order of realized delinquency experience. Either delinquent borrowers cure, or they progressively become more delinquent. Loans are then liquidated after missing seven consecutive payments.

It is not as cut-and-dry to develop a transition matrix for a pool of first-lien mortgages (such as home equity loans). Within the foreclosure bucket, a range of delinquency periods exists, each requiring a different loss mitigation approach. This produces a unique roll rate emanating from each sub-delinquency category. To complicate matters further, state laws dictate foreclosure timelines unique to each state.

The graph presented in Exhibit 8 uses transition probabilities from Exhibit 7. We connected actual delinquency figures to the matrix to develop a forward-looking delinquency forecast measured as a percent of remaining principal balance. CPR and COR forecasts can be developed with this framework too. Furthermore, it is very easy to observe the effect on delinquency and loss rates by changing any one of the variables in the matrix. The mortgage credit analyst can appreciate the transition matrix framework compared to more simplistic approaches. For instance, some CDR based models forecast delinquencies as a percentage of defaults. This type of forecast is both backward looking and unintuitive. Due to the complex delinquency and loss based trigger and step-up formulas embedded in securitizations, it is imperative that analysts make use of the best possible delinquency forecast.

Although the initial motivation for developing a transition matrix is for credit forecasting, there is a hidden benefit in that it can be used to quantitatively compare performance amongst different servicers. A transition matrix may help identify whether delinquency transition differences are due to unique loan and geographical concentrations, or unique servicing practices. However, if loan attributes are identical, a transition matrix will measure the effectiveness of loss mitigation strategies on roll rates and timeline management among servicers.

Thus far the most sophisticated transition matrix has been developed from Markov chain analysis. This work is very promising, but analysis is limited to only a few servicers and collateral programs. We have uncovered one shortcoming to the transition matrix approach: delinquency, COR, and CPR achieve a level state after several months into the forecast due to constant transition ratios.

Exhibit 8: Delinquency

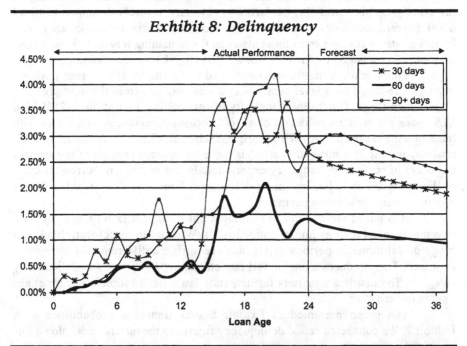

We do not think that transition matrix analysis is fully mature today. There is more room for development and sophistication in this area of research. Non-agency mortgage servicers have much more data available to analyze than agency programs, and many of the non-prime mortgage programs have been around long enough from which useful data are available. In the future, we will likely see transition matrices with time dependent features such as pool seasoning, and geographic factors will influence the foreclosure timelines. The greater number of variables within a transition matrix framework will provide mortgage credit analysts a robust tool for delinquency and loss forecasts.

CONCLUSION

The mortgage credit market will benefit from more sophisticated credit analysis techniques. This can occur through remittance reporting, standardizing terminology, and improving forecasting techniques. These issues are critical for loss dependent structures and collateral, and they will help improve mature sectors such as prime non-agency deals. By itself, the CDR approach does not do a complete job of evaluating mortgage credit risk. The mortgage credit analyst must go beyond default forecasting, and further evaluate the impact that other risks, such as prepayment and liquidation timelines, will ultimately have on losses. It is imperative that anyone participating in the loss dependent sector of the mortgage credit market understand the intricacies of CDR and COR measurement. Market participants will face extreme difficulty in this sector without understanding the mechanics of loss dependent variables.

Chapter 19

Securities Backed by Closed-End Home Equity Loans

R. Russell Hurst
Vice President
First Union Securities, Inc.

INTRODUCTION

This chapter provides investors with an understanding of the U.S. home equity loan (HEL) securitization market and the tools that an investor will need in order to identify and understand the investment opportunities in the HEL market. To gain a firm understanding of HEL asset-backed securities (ABS), an investor must know the fundamental characteristics of the loans, the structure and its characteristics that may affect the credit protection of the security purchased, the credit standing and economic motive of all parties to a transaction, and the legal concepts used to achieve bankruptcy remoteness and sale treatment by the seller/originator.

WHAT IS THE U.S. HOME EQUITY LOAN TODAY?

In the early 1990s, HEL referred to a traditional second lien mortgage with the proceeds primarily used for home improvement, college education, or debt consolidation. Although second mortgage HELs are still originated, more than 95% of the current nonprime HEL product described above is a first lien mortgage product. A simple but important distinction between HEL mortgage products and other similar securitized nonprime nonconforming mortgage products is that the proceeds from a HEL mortgage are not used to purchase a new home but to refinance an existing mortgage. The payment behavior of nonprime purchase money mortgages and home improvement loans (HILs) differ from HELs primarily due to the circumstances of the borrowers. The proceeds of an HEL loan may be used in part to finance home improvements but most likely will not be used in its entirety for that purpose. The prepayment behavior of HELs is closely related to the characteristics of the borrower. HELs are typically used to

- consolidate consumer debt in a lower-rate, tax-deductible form
- monetize equity in the home

337

- reduce a homeowner's monthly mortgage payment by extending the loan's term
- finance home improvements
- finance temporary liquidity needs such as for education or medical expenses

The traditional second mortgage is still included in the HEL category, but HELs now commonly refer to first lien mortgages to borrowers with some combination of impaired credit history and/or debt-to-income ratios that exceed agency guidelines. These borrowers are commonly referred to as *nonprime* or *B* and *C* *borrowers*. The originators of HELs use proprietary credit scoring techniques to grade each borrower on their ability to repay debt with letter gradations from A to D. The criteria vary by company, and each company has made some disclosure of the characteristics of each class of borrower. The nuances of underwriting standards among home equity lenders is useful when trying to differentiate the quality of one pool of collateral from another. The underwriting guidelines by credit class of borrower in Exhibit 1 are fairly representative of the collateral in the market.

As the credit profile of the borrower becomes increasingly risky or complex, a greater reliance is placed on the equity in the property mortgaged. This equity improves the chances of fully recovering the full principal value of the loan in foreclosure as well as the foreclosure costs including lost interest. An incrementally higher rate is also charged to financially weaker borrowers, which helps to ensure a higher return on a portfolio of nonprime HELs.

The U.S. economy has enjoyed six consecutive years of low inflation, low interest rates and sustained growth, all of which have had a favorable effect on property values in the United States. In addition to contributing to the growth in the HEL market, these factors have reduced the severity of losses in this market. Another, often overlooked, aspect of this market is that bankruptcy law in the United States does not allow a bankruptcy election more than once every seven years. This places the lender in a powerful position with regard to the borrower and may partly explain why bankruptcies are acceptable to this group of lenders. Thus, bankruptcy law is a great motivator for the borrower to make payments and serves to shorten the foreclosure period, thereby reducing the cost of foreclosure (time value of money).

The most prevalent forms of HELs include the following:

- *Closed-end HELs*, where the loan amount and term to maturity are set at origination and bear a fixed rate, constitute most of the market.

- *Adjustable-rate, closed-end HELs* (HEL ARMs) have a set term to maturity and usually have both periodic and lifetime caps. The loans generally allow for the accretion of interest to the principal while the interest rate is at the cap. The additional principal is repaid from future payments when the interest rate is reset or when the rate recedes from the capped level. If the interest rate remains at the cap for the life of the loan, there is usually a provision to extend the maturity. The loans are structured in a manner that renders this extension risk as highly improbable.

Exhibit 1: Representative Home Equity Underwriting Guidelines

Grade	Quality	Credit History and Ratios
A	Good	• No late payment on mortgages • Maximum of two or three late payments on revolving credit and no more than three 30-day late payments on installment debt; perhaps one 60-day late payment • Chapter 7 or 13 bankruptcy must be discharged for one to three years with credit reestablished for two years • Maximum debt-to-income ratio of 45% • Maximum loan-to-values ranging from 85% to 95%
B	Satisfactory	• Maximum of three or four 30-day late payments on mortgage payments in the past 12 months • For nonmortgage debt, pattern of 30 delinquencies and limited 60-day delinquencies with isolated 90-day delinquency • Bankruptcies acceptable with one to two years reestablished credit • Maximum debt-to-income ratio of 50% • Maximum loan-to-value of 85%
C	Fair	• Maximum 210 total days delinquent with limited 60-day and isolated 90-day delinquencies on mortgage debt • Discretionary with cross section of 30-, 60-, and 90-day delinquencies • Bankruptcies acceptable with one to two years reestablished credit • Maximum debt-to-income ratio of 55% • Maximum loan-to-value of 80%
D	Poor	• No more than 120-day mortgage or rent delinquency in the past 12 months and property not in foreclosure • Delinquent or charged-off receivables • Bankruptcies acceptable if discharged or dismissed • Maximum debt-to-income ratio of 60% • Maximum loan-to-value of 65%

Source: First Union Securities, Inc.

- *Home equity lines of credit* (HELOCs) are open-end, revolving loans, where the borrower receives an HEL line of credit that can be partially or completely drawn down and partially or completely paid back over time. HELOCs carry floating rates, usually with high lifetime caps and no interim caps. Because of the open-end, revolving structure of the HELOC collateral, which is similar to that of credit cards, these loans are not discussed in this chapter.

BASIC STRUCTURE

HELs are financial assets or receivables originated by a bank, a finance company, or other financial institution. HELs are then sold to a bankruptcy-remote special-purpose vehicle (SPV). Certain conditions must be met to achieve a "true sale," and reputable counsel provides legal opinions that confirm these conditions, such as the arm's length requirement and the transfer of the legal title to the asset, have in fact been met.

HEL issues usually take the form of a real estate mortgage investment conduit (REMIC), which allows cash flows to be redirected to create several tranches of certificates with expected average lives at many points on the yield curve. REMICs were created as a new issuance vehicle by the Tax Reform Act of 1986 to solve many of the problems experienced with collateralized mortgage obligations (CMOs) that used a multiclass trust structure. The first passthrough was issued in 1970, followed by the first CMO in 1983. As the moniker implies, CMOs were technically debt instruments rather than passthrough certificates and were successful in avoiding tax liability to the issuing trust. Issuers had to maintain a portion of residual interests, record CMOs as liabilities in their financial statements, and satisfy minimum capital requirements. The CMO structure also created a mismatch between the monthly receipts on the collateral and the quarterly payments on the bonds. In 1985, use of the owner trust structure solved some of these problems by allowing the sale of the residual interest to others and removal from the issuer's balance sheet. The new residual interest holder then became liable for interest rate shortfalls on any of the owner trust tranches. Buyers for the residuals were scarce and as a result the market for this type of CMO was not liquid.

REMICs changed all this. To qualify for REMIC status, a multiclass offering can have multiple classes of *regular interests* but only one class of *residual interest*. The legislation defines a "regular interest" as a fixed principal amount with periodic interest payments or accruals on the outstanding principal balance. Buyers of regular interests are taxed as holders of debt obligations and the buyers of the residual interest pay taxes on the earnings, if any, of the trust. Due to its flexibility in meeting investor demand, the CMO and HEL markets have used the REMIC structure almost exclusively since 1991.

Following these guidelines, the trust issues either debt or passthrough certificates (a ratable equity interest in the pool or some portion of the pool), the proceeds of which are used to buy the pool of assets to be securitized. To facilitate the selling of certificates or debt to the market, some combination or variation of the following provides credit enhancement:

- *Excess spread:* Revenue less expenses of the trust.

- *Reserve account:* Excess spread captured and held in the trust as some predetermined or calculated level to pay any cash flow shortfalls in the trust.

- *Subordinated protection:* The amount by which the collateral value exceeds any class of liability.

- *Senior/subordinated structures:* Certain classes of securities have a senior claim to others on the cash flow of the trust. The purest form of this structure is referred to as *sequential*, where any principal payments received by the trust are used to fully pay down the principal of the most senior class prior to any of the junior classes. All classes receive principal payments sequentially according to their rank of claim to the cash flow of the trust. The lowest-ranking class will be the last to receive a principal payment as well as the last to have its principal fully retired. This is commonly referred to as the *waterfall*. Any amount left over is referred to as the *residual* and flows to the equity holder. A minimal amount of true equity is provided at the formation of the SPV and is necessary to comply with certain legal and tax requirements of the trust. The residual can be, and often is, separated from the true equity in the trust and retained by the seller/servicer. Retention of this amount by the seller/servicer provides a primary motivation to maximize the cash flow in the trust (i.e., accelerate collections and minimize losses) so that the value of the residual is realized.

- *Third-party guarantee:* This can take the form of bond insurance, a letter of credit, or a corporate guarantee of all or any class of a securitization. The motivations vary but the result is a better economic execution for the issuer, which may have to provide less collateral to the trust or may achieve a better pricing on insured bonds than an uninsured funding execution. The issuer may not have access to the market by any other means. Firms active in the guaranty of HEL transactions include Capital Markets Assurance Corp. (CapMac), Financial Guaranty Insurance Co. (FGIC), Mortgage Bond Insurance Associates (MBIA), Financial Security Assurance (FSA), and Capital Guaranty Assurance (CGA).

The most important basic feature of an asset-backed security that should not be underemphasized or overlooked when viewing the home equity securitization market for investment purposes is the true sale of the assets into a bankruptcy-remote SPV (the issuer). This issue as it relates to the recent economic hard times and bankruptcy of sellers/servicers will be discussed in more detail later. From a pure credit perspective, these structures have survived bankruptcy, minimal degradation of servicing cash flow, and there is some evidence that retained residual interests are providing the proper motivation, even in bankruptcy, for the seller/servicer to continue servicing and collections in an efficient manner. In this regard, having tested the structure is a positive for the market and should provide an additional level of comfort to the investor.

Not surprisingly, because growth in the HEL market followed the growth in the mortgage-backed securities (MBS) market, many of the features are patterned after those used in the MBS market and are aimed at smoothing prepayment volatility such that payment windows for each class are shortened. This will reduce the risk that the investment will experience a shorter or longer average life than expected. The most common structures are discussed below.

- Senior/subordinated with up to 10 fixed-rate senior tranches with different average lives ranging out to 10 years. This is a lesser number of fixed-rate subordinated tranches with different average lives and backed by a fixed-rate pool of HELs. There is also a larger longer service average life floating-rate tranche backed by a floating-rate pool of HELs.

• Senior/subordinated with some combination of fixed, floating, HEL, and HIL collateral.

• Single class with 100% surety bond.

• Senior/subordinated with 100% surety bond on a subordinate piece.

Exhibit 2 illustrates the principal paydown of The Money Store 98-B home equity securitization and the total collateral cash flow and its allocation to principal payment and the expenses of the program.

Exhibit 3 illustrates the total collateral cash flow of The Money Store 98-B home equity securitization and its allocation to principal payment and the expenses of the program. This exhibit illustrates the excess spread concept.

An increasingly important structural feature for analyzing the cash flow expectations of HEL securitizations is the step-down provision. Due to the senior/subordinated structure, where all excess spread and principal payments are used to repay the senior tranche(s), subordinated tranche protection increases as a percentage of total certificate outstandings. This increased percentage protection is more than necessary to support the rating of the senior tranches. Step-downs were created as a method to redirect some of the excess spread cash flow to the subordinated tranches while protecting the rating on the senior ranking tranches throughout the life of the transaction.

Exhibit 2: HEL Principal Paydown — The Money Store 98-B

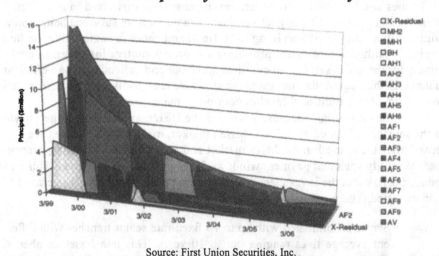

Source: First Union Securities, Inc.

Exhibit 3: The Money Store 98-B HEL Cash Flow

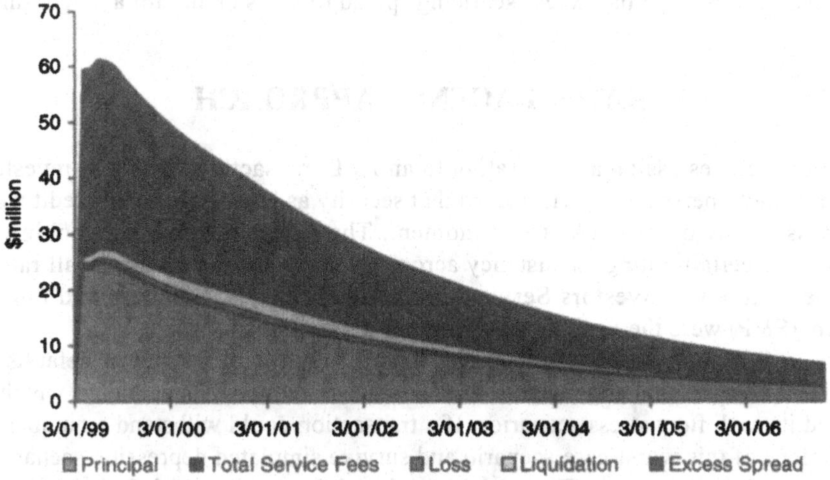

Source: First Union Securities, Inc.

Step-downs allow the redirection of a portion of the excess spread to subordinated tranches as long as the collateral is performing within the parameters described later. If the deal deteriorates due to higher-than-expected losses, the redirection of cash flows, or step-down, would not be allowed until the conditions were met. If step-down conditions are not met and the collateral exceeds the collateral quality triggers, cash flow would be redirected to the senior tranche until the collateral met the predetermined conditions. The step-down is set to occur usually 3–4 years from the date the deal was issued and requires the collateral pool outstandings to exceed a certain percentage of the original collateral balance, usually 50%, as well as meet certain asset quality tests as of a certain date. Failure to meet the step-down tests would alter the cash flow assumptions on which the senior, mezzanine, and subordinated tranches were priced, resulting in a shorter average life for the senior and mezzanine tranches and a longer average life for the subordinated tranches. The closer an issue comes to failing the tests should be an uncertainty properly priced into the spread of that issue compared with other issues that clearly will not fail the test.

In summary, structural protections include the excess spread at the first layer of protection, subordination, cash collateral accounts, step-down provisions, third-party credit enhancement, and the bankruptcy remoteness of the issuer. In general, ratings from two or three of the rating agencies for the typical HEL securitization will range from AAA for the senior tranches to as low as B- for the most subordinated tranche. In 1998, 42% of all HEL securitizations were floating rate. All of the HEL structures shift credit volatility to the subordinated tranches in varying degrees and ensure in all but the most extreme cases that the senior AAA tranches have sufficient credit protection to remain rated AAA while outstanding.

Slower prepayments generate additional credit support. When prepayments slow, the absolute value of the excess servicing spread remains higher for a longer time.

RATING AGENCY APPROACH

Rating agencies assign a AAA rating to an HEL transaction so that an investor, from a credit perspective, will regard that security as having the same credit worthiness as any other AAA at that moment. The rating agencies are looking to achieve a certain rating consistency across all fixed-income sectors at all rating grades. Moody's Investors Service, Inc. (Moody's), and Standard and Poor's Corp. (S&P) were the first to rate structured transactions.

S&P's approach to structured finance began with a study of defaults in the Great Depression and resulted in a worst-case economic scenario on which it based its cash flow stress scenarios. If a transaction could withstand a number of iterations of this worst-case scenario and survive simulated depression scenarios, it deserved a AAA rating. The model introduced the concept of default frequency and loss severity. This basic model has been applied in modified form to each class of ABS rated by S&P. The result for all ABS, including the HEL sector, is that a AAA will survive 3–5 times historical losses. S&P constructs a prime pool for residential mortgages. As the characteristics of the prime pool differ from the pool to be securitized, penalties are assessed to default frequency and loss severity assumptions used in the cash flow scenarios. Lesser-quality pools require a greater amount of credit loss protection for the senior tranche to achieve a AAA rating than that required for the prime pool. Factors considered in analyzing the mortgage pool include historical level of delinquencies, loss severity, lien type, loan type, number of loans, geographical concentration, quality of borrower and step-downs. The IBCA Fitch and the Duff and Phelps models followed an approach similar to that of S&P in developing their cash flow models.

Moody's started out on a somewhat different route toward the same end. By looking at historical defaults for each rating level, Moody's thought that Aaa structured financed issues should have the same probability of default as a Aaa corporate and so on for each rating grade. Taking this approach to its logical extreme, Moody's studied the Great Depression as well as other recessions in the twentieth century and observed how the collateral being securitized behaved in stressful economic situations. This resulted in the identification of a positive correlation between collateral performance and economic events, allowing Moody's to use a Monte Carlo model to generate a worst-case loss distribution for the collateral pool. Moody's then quantified the loss protection needed for that pool to achieve Aaa loss protection (approximately three standard deviations from the expected loss). Aa transactions provided enough protection to cover 2.5 standard deviations, and single A covered 2.0 standard deviations. Although Moody's approach is similar, the data available for this type of analysis have greatly improved for each asset class (and for the other forms of derivatives in the structure, such as swaps). This approach is also called the *expected value approach.* Currently, Moody's sets credit enhancement levels so that the annual change in yield on the rated security, due to defaults in the collateral pool and other credit events that would cause a loss of cash flow to the trust, is equivalent to the target levels in Exhibit 4.

HEL COLLATERAL PERFORMANCE

Exhibits 5 and 6, taken from First Union Securities home equity prepayment model, show that collateral performance has been excellent and is well within the worst-case parameters set by the rating agencies. Loss information on HEL product is presented by year of origination (vintage) to avoid any understatement of losses because of new issue volume. Exhibit 5 shows that net losses are low the first year after origination and increase rapidly for the next two years. From the peak in the 36th month, the losses recede for two years before percentage net losses increase again.

By examining the loss curve of each issue, an investor can decide, on a relative basis, whether the spread received is appropriate for the collateral's risk profile. Loss curves differ by issuer and vintage because of the targeted niche borrower, underwriting guidelines and, in some cases, servicing and collection.

It is particularly useful to look at cumulative HEL collateral losses by year of origination for the entire HEL universe as shown in Exhibit 6.

HELs originated in 1993 and 1994 have had significantly better loss experience than the product originated in 1995–1998. In all likelihood, this is the result of the increased competition and market growth during the latter period. Lower interest rates and aggressive origination by brokers also explain why a lower-quality product was originated. It is also useful to compare cumulative loss curves by year of origination for the same issuer to see if the loss experiences on collateral pools originated in the same year differ dramatically from each other.

Exhibit 4: Yield Change Limits for Moody's Rated HEL Transactions

Rating	Yield Change (bps)
Aaa	0.06
Aa2	1.30
A2	9.00
Baa2	27.00
Ba2	106.00
B2	231.00

Source: Moody's Investor Service, Inc.

Exhibit 5: Annualized HEL Net Loss Rate by Vintage

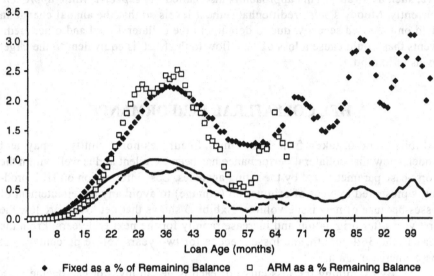

ARM: Adjustable-rate mortgage.

Source: First Union Securities, Inc.

Exhibit 6: Cumulative HEL Losses by Vintage

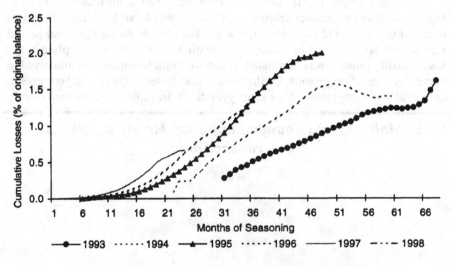

Source: First Union Securities, Inc.

Exhibit 7: Seasoned HEL Transaction Comparison

	ContiMortgage 1997-1 A4	Advanta 1993-1 A1	Saxon 1997-3 AF1
Weighted Average Coupon			
Original	11.556	10.340	10.094
Current	11.360	10.092	10.044
Certificate Coupon			
Original	6.680	5.950	5.816
Current	6.680	5.950	5.097
Servicing Fee			
Original	1.500	0.500	0.534
Current	0.500	0.500	0.533
Net Annualized Losses			
Original	0.000	0.000	0.000
Current	1.480	0.440	0.040
Net Excess Spread			
Original	3.376	3.890	3.744
Current	2.700	3.202	4.374
Level of Credit Enhancement Class A			
Original	11.500	100.000	9.230
Current	23.116	100.000	17.474
Original Rating	Aaa	Aaa	Aaa
Current Rating	Aaa	Aaa	Aaa

Note: All numbers are stated as percentages.

Source: First Union Securities, Inc.

An increase in 60-day delinquencies, sustained for more than a month or two, is a good predictor of increased losses and whether a certain collateral pool is beginning to deteriorate. If the pool is in fact deteriorating, the increase in 60-day delinquencies will be followed by an increase in 90-day delinquencies and finally an increase in losses.

Loss curve analysis of the collateral pool is fundamental to understanding whether the probability of default has increased or decreased since the origination of the transaction. In most cases, the subordinated protection increases as the senior bonds pay down (see Exhibit 7).

There has *not* been a performance downgrade of a public HEL issue since the inception of the asset-backed market. However, variations in collateral performance will cause issues of the same average life to trade at different spreads to the Treasury market. This is also true for insured transactions though to a lesser degree than for senior/subordinated transactions.

HEL PREPAYMENT EXPERIENCE

Prepayments are extremely important to determining the value of any mortgage-backed investment. Exhibit 8, from First Union Securities prepayment model, shows the prepayment of the rated universe of HEL product from 1994 to 1998.

Exhibit 8: Aggregate Historical CPR versus Model CPR

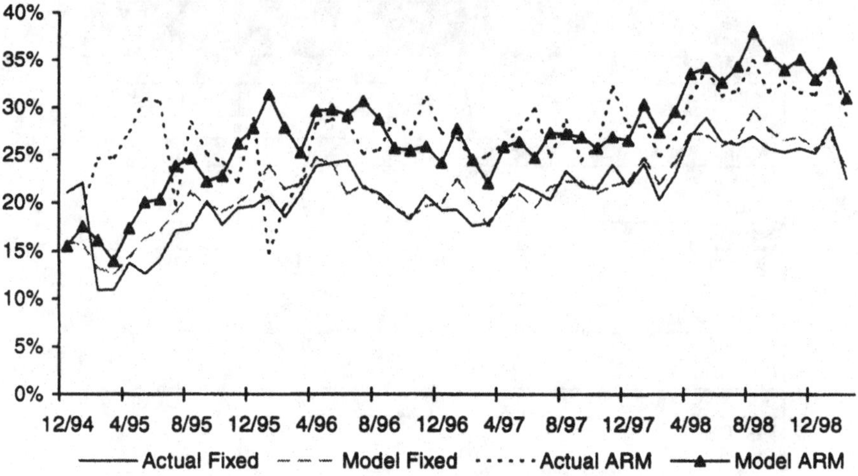

ARM: Adjustable-rate mortgage; CPR: Conditional prepayment rate.
Source: First Union Securities, Inc.

The prepayment of HEL product has proved to be much more stable than that of the MBS market and has resulted in securitization with less negative convexity. Investor acceptance of HEL prepayment characteristics contributed to market growth in 1997–1998. From a credit perspective, prepayments will accelerate the retirement of the senior-most tranches and increase the subordinated protection available to classes of the same rank when measured as a percentage of current outstandings. Due to B and C borrowers' limited refinancing opportunities, refinancing rates must fall 200 bps–300 bps to significantly increase prepayments due to refinancing in the HEL market versus the 25 bps–50 bps that move the private MBS market. Examination of this data shows that HEL product originated prior to 1997 has had the highest prepayment experience. HELs originated in 1996 and earlier had higher coupons than current HEL product. Coupons originated as of this writing are lower because of a lower absolute level of interest rates. Intense competition in the market for product and market share has also accelerated prepayments.[1]

SEPARATING HEL CREDIT RISK FROM THE MARKET PRICING OF THAT RISK

For HEL securitizations, credit risk includes collateral performance, cash flow allocations, asset-quality triggers, access to established reserves, sufficiency of any

[1] For greater detail on HEL prepayment behavior, see James S. Anderson and Webster Hughes, *Prepayment Models and Home Equity Analysis*, First Union Securities, Inc., Asset-Backed/Quantitative Research, October 1998.

subordinated tranche protection, credit worthiness of any third-party guarantor or substitute credit provider, legal integrity of the structure, and administrative risk.

The bankruptcy of a servicer does not, as a stand-alone event, increase the credit risk of any particular HEL investment. It does raise the concern that the servicing of the collateral may become less efficient while being transferred to a back-up servicer and that collections may be less efficient and result in slower collections due to a significantly pared down servicing operation or the lack of economic incentive if the servicing is allowed to remain with the bankrupt entity while it is reorganized or sold to a third party. This is appropriately referred to as *administrative risk.*

Insured transactions provide solid protection from administrative risk. Insurers become insiders, use covenant protection to a greater degree than for senior/subordinated structures and promise timely payment of principal and interest as scheduled. For an HEL passthrough, interest due on the outstanding principal will be paid to certificate holders when due, and payment of any principal amount after the collateral is fully depleted (the only time principal is "due" in a passthrough). Although there is no promise to pay if collections slow down, the insurers, to protect their own interests, have teams of auditors that continually review collateral performance and the servicing process. The insurers stand ready to take control of collateral if covenants are breached and the result is to significantly reduce administrative risk in the insured transaction. The insurers are in the business of insuring investment-grade or better transactions and are heavily regulated by the rating agencies as to capital sufficiency. Insured transactions, without the insurance, would result in a senior tranche rating of AA or A and investment grade or better for the subordinated tranches. Insured transactions provide multiple levels of protection to the investor.

Without a fundamental change in credit risk, HEL credit spreads are affected by the market pricing of that risk. Supply and demand drives the market pricing of credit risk between sectors and includes the market's reaction to world events, the health of the U.S. economy, capital flows around the world, or the market's reaction to headline risk within a sector.

HEADLINE RISK AND HARD TIMES

The public and private asset-backed market has been largely free of event risk. The distinction between event and headline risk is important. *Event risk* in the corporate market represents an event that when announced has immediate credit rating implications for a company's outstanding debt or the debt of an industry, which, in most cases, would result in a downgrade (or an upgrade) of the company or companies affected by the event. The most obvious example would be mergers and acquisitions. *Headline risk* may immediately affect the credit spread of a security but does not have immediate upgrade or downgrade implications.

None of the recent bankruptcy announcements by sellers/servicers in the HEL market have resulted in the downgrading of the related HEL securitizations.

Since its inception, the ABS market has had a remarkable track record of credit stability. Exhibit 9 shows that over the 5-year period 1994–1998 no asset-backed security rated by Moody's has defaulted in the public or private market at any rating level. In fact, that statement holds true for the asset-backed market since inception. Moody's first downgrade of a public asset-backed security occurred in February 1998, then again in April 1998 when it downgraded the lower-rated B-1 and B-2 tranches of BankAmerica Manufactured Housing Contract 1996-1. Prior to 1997, only three ABS had been downgraded by Moody's. In 1997, Moody's downgraded four tranches of three private nonprime automobile transactions (Aegis, Autoflow and AJ Acceptance). In 1998, Aegis was downgraded further, as well as a private LSI nonprime auto tranche, and three private securities backed by charged-off credit card accounts issued by Commercial Financial Services (CFS). The undetected fraud in the CFS SMART transactions will result in the first ABS default. Even in this situation, collections on the receivables continue and payments to certificate holders continue. Technically, in a senior/subordinated structure, a default will only occur when passthrough payments fail to make a payment while a certificate balance is still outstanding. This can only occur when current pay collateral is fully depleted.

At this juncture, investors have become conditioned to the headline risk present in the HEL market. Some investors regard headline risk spread widening as a buying opportunity. A pattern has emerged whereby announcements have been made by sellers/servicers in financial difficulty that they are either seeking a strategic partner, seeking to restructure or sell certain parts of their operations, plan to reduce growth, or plan to eliminate or decrease their most costly source of loan origination (in most cases, third-party broker originated product). A few months after this announcement, sellers/servicers that did not find a partner or alternate sources of financing have announced bankruptcy. Significant headline risk announcements by sellers/servicers are summarized in Exhibit 10.

Exhibit 9: Credit Stability of ABS versus Comparable Corporates (as of June 30, 1998)

Original Rating	Average 5-Year Default Rate		Percent Downgraded after 5 Years		Percent Upgraded after 5 Years	
	CORP	ABS	CORP	ABS	CORP	ABS
Aaa	0.10%	0.00%	28.40%	0.00%	0.00%	0.00%
Aa	0.40%	0.00%	28.90%	0.00%	5.50%	12.80%
A	0.50%	0.00%	20.80%	0.70%	10.20%	11.60%
Baa	1.70%	0.00%	17.80%	1.90%	20.90%	4.10%
Ba	11.40%	0.00%	23.50%	5.70%	17.90%	0.00%

ABS: All public and private asset-backed securities rated by Moody's; CORP: All public corporate bonds rated by Moody's.

Source: Moody's Investors Services, Inc. and First Union Securities, Inc.

Exhibit 10: 1998/1999 Headline Risk Announcements

Aames Financial	Third-quarter 1998 earnings down more than 95%, with much of the reduction attributed to losses on hedging positions. Servicing operation might be sold. Has exited the securitization market.
Amresco	Announced $50 million–$60 million loss for 1998 and major reorganization and closing of its wholesale and retail operations.
Cityscape	Filed for bankruptcy in October 1998.
ContiFinancial	Made first-quarter 1999 announcement that it is seeking a strategic partner following a large loss in the third quarter of 1998 and announcement of major restructuring.
FirstPlus	Announced $82 million third-quarter 1998 loss. Reduced staff more than 50%. Eliminated wholesale division. Terminated agreement to sell servicing operation to Superior Bank. Proposed merger with Life Financial canceled. Did no securitizations in the fourth quarter. Sold U.K. operations and its conforming loan business. Filed for bankruptcy the first week of March 1999.
IMC Mortgage	Third-quarter 1998 earnings down more than 80% from last year. Had severe liquidity problems. Completed previously announced agreement with Greenwich Street Capital Partners to purchase 95% interest in company and assume control in February 1999.
IndyMac	Announced fourth-quarter 1998 loss and laid off 280 employees. Reducing servicing portfolio. Exiting manufactured housing business.
Southern Pacific	Wrote down earnings during the summer. Sought to raise capital through whole loan sales. Sought strategic partner and then filed for bankruptcy in October 1998.
United Companies	Major reorganization announced in the fourth quarter and announced it was looking for a partner. Filed for bankruptcy the first week of March 1999.

Source: First Union Securities, Inc.

These events will affect the liquidity and pricing of all HEL product. Some issues, with strong sellers/servicers or those owned by investment-grade parents, and insured issues will recover to a normalized spread more quickly than those with servicers experiencing some form of financial stress. In reality, investors prefer not to own a HEL issue when the servicer files for bankruptcy, not because there is an immediate risk of downgrade or default (there is not), but because the investor prefers not to have to deal with the spread widening that accompanies the announcement (i.e., the headline risk).

For an issue sponsored by a seller/servicer that has just filed for bankruptcy, the spread widening is less severe for insured issues. At this point, the market goes through a discovery period with regard to the affected issues and trading in these issues may be light to nonexistent. For the insured issues, investors are uncertain whether the insurer will require that the servicing be transferred to the backup servicer and whether servicing continues smoothly with no discernible slowdown in collections or confusion surrounding the transfer. Liquidity should return to the market for these issues, albeit at a modestly wider spread.

For senior/subordinated structures, the discovery and return to liquidity in the market will take longer and, in the case of Southern Pacific's senior/subordinated issues, has taken 3–6 months. In this case, the bankruptcy court allowed Southern Pacific to retain a substantial of amount of its servicing in an effort to maximize the value of residuals held by the bankruptcy estate. Despite pared-down operations, the retention of the residual by the bankruptcy estate has apparently provided the necessary motivation for Southern Pacific to continue servicing the affected issues in an efficient manner. As a result, some investors have returned cautiously to the market for these securities and currently view the available spreads as cheap. The failure of a servicer/seller should worry the investor to the extent it causes a deterioration in the performance of the collateral. This could be the result of a lost economic incentive for diligent collection of payments or rapid resolution of problem loans. This collateral degradation, if sustained, fundamentally changes the credit protection afforded the issuer and the investor should be compensated for this uncertainty.

In some senior/subordinated issues, backup servicers were not required and the concept of a special servicer was not contemplated. For most commercial mortgage-backed securities, a special servicer is paid a fee and a success fee for collecting seriously delinquent loans or loans in foreclosure. The documents of an HEL issue do not allow a step-up in servicing fees as an incentive for another servicer to step in and take over servicing. As a result, provisions such as these are now being incorporated into some of the new senior/subordinated deals in the market. The insurers have long used the two-tier fee concept.

In a perverse way, all of this has been a positive for the HEL market. The experience of seller/servicer bankruptcy, together with the maintenance of existing ratings, has satisfactorily tested the structural safeguards put in place in HEL transactions and validated the principal tenet of asset securitizations — that the deals are isolated from the insolvency of the issuer. This should result in a higher confidence level in the transactions and in further modification, or fine-tuning, of the documentation used in future transactions.

Chapter 20

Home Equity Line of Credit (HELOC) Securitizations

W. Alexander Roever, CFA
Managing Director
Head of ABS Research
Banc One Capital Markets, Inc.

John N. McElravey
Director, ABS Research
Banc One Capital Markets, Inc.

Glenn M. Schultz, CFA
Director, ABS Research
Banc One Capital Markets, Inc.

INTRODUCTION

As housing values have appreciated over the past decade, homeowners have borrowed large amounts of money against the equity in their homes. Outstanding home equity debt totaled $420 billion as of year-end 1997 according to the Federal Reserve. This borrowing generally is used as a substitute for other types of consumer credit, either to finance new consumption or to pay down other outstanding consumer credit balances. The securitization of home equity debt has created one of the largest segments of the asset-backed securities (ABS) market. In 1998, residential loan backed ABS accounted for 37% of total new issuance in the public market.

Several factors make home equity borrowing attractive to consumers. One is tax deductibility. The Tax Reform Act of 1986 phased out federal tax deductions for nonmortgage consumer debt, such as credit cards and auto loans, and increased their after-tax cost. Home equity borrowing allows the funds to be used for just about any reason, but maintains its privileged tax status. Another attractive aspect is that home equity lending allows borrowers to access the equity accumulated in their homes. Homeowners' equity represents one of the largest components of household wealth in the United States.[1] Home equity borrowing

---

[1] Glenn B. Canner, *et. al.*, "Recent Developments in Home Equity Lending," *Federal Reserve Bulletin* (April 1998), pp. 241-251.

353

provides a means for homeowners to monetize the equity in their homes that would otherwise be relatively illiquid.

HOME EQUITY LINES OF CREDIT

When ABS investors, analysts, and traders mention the home equity market, they generally are referring to securities backed by closed-end loans, which are the primary type of collateral in this sector. However, another class of home equity credit exists that receives comparatively little attention. Home equity lines of credit (HELOCs) are revolving lines of credit available to homeowners that can be drawn and repaid based on the equity in their homes. While HELOCs represent only about 4% of total home equity securitizations outstanding, they do represent a potentially large source of collateral for future transactions. Over the last ten years, HELOCs represented between 20% and 25% of total home equity origina-tions (see Exhibit 1). The majority of HELOCs that have been originated are still held on the balance sheets of commercial banks, thrifts, and credit unions (see Exhibit 2). Depository institutions hold 80% to 85% of all outstanding lines, and this market share has been relatively stable over the past ten years. Finance com-panies hold about 8% of outstanding HELOCs. Meanwhile, only 7% of lines out-standing have been securitized.

Exhibit 1: HELOCs as a Percentage of All Home Equity Originations

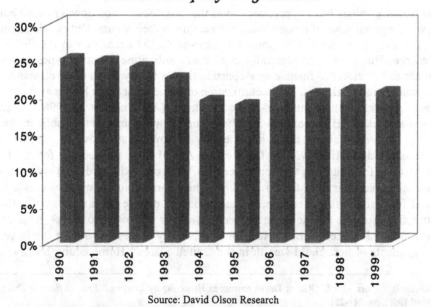

Source: David Olson Research

Exhibit 2: Estimated Share of HELOCs Outstanding by Institutional Holder

Institution	1990	1991	1992	1993	1994	1995	1996	1997	1998
Commercial Banks	59%	56%	57%	58%	62%	61%	62%	63%	61%
Thrift Institutions	14%	16%	17%	14%	14%	14%	13%	11%	13%
Credit Unions	10%	10%	9%	9%	9%	9%	9%	9%	9%
Finance Companies	12%	11%	11%	11%	6%	7%	8%	8%	8%
Securitized Pools	5%	6%	6%	7%	8%	9%	7%	7%	8%
Other	1%	1%	1%	1%	1%	1%	0%	1%	1%
Total	100%	100%	100%	100%	100%	100%	100%	100%	100%
Total Amount (billion$)	113.9	124.7	129.5	125.7	123.7	129.4	137.0	153.4	172.0

Source: David Olson Research, Banc One Capital Markets, Inc.

Depository institutions seem to predominate this area of lending for several reasons. First, lines of credit are generally more complex to administer, and more costly to originate and service, than traditional closed-end loans. As a result, larger banks are more likely than smaller banks or finance companies to offer this product. Second, because the loan is a revolving account, a relationship between borrower and lender can give a competitive advantage over specialty finance firms. A bank or thrift, for example, should have better information about the credit quality of a customer because of other loan or deposit accounts held at that institution. Third, home equity lines provide another cross-selling opportunity for the bank. Finally, HELOCs may be accessed several times per year, primarily through drafts or checking accounts, or by personal withdrawals. Depository institutions already have an infrastructure in place to facilitate customers to make withdrawals and deposits.

CHARACTERISTICS OF HELOCS AND BORROWERS

The characteristics of the collateral and the borrower profile would make HELOCs attractive for securitization. Typically, the revolving period for HELOCs extends for 10 to 15 years. At the end of the revolving period, the loans provide for an amortization period, extending for as much as 10 years, or a balloon payment at maturity. According to the 1998 Home Equity Loan Study from the Consumer Bankers Association (CBA), nearly all HELOCs carry variable rates.[2] Closed-end loans are predominantly fixed rate with only 9% of closed-end loans carrying variable rates. About three-quarters of all lines reset monthly using the Prime Rate reported in *The Wall Street Journal* (see Exhibit 3). The average spread over *The Wall Street Journal* Prime Rate declined over the last few years, falling to 127 basis points over prime in 1997.

[2] Richard F. DeMong and John H. Lindgren, *1998 Home Equity Loan Study*, Consumer Bankers Association, 1998.

Exhibit 3: HELOC Characteristics
Variable Rate Index

	1997	1996
The Wall Street Journal Prime Rate	78%	90%
Bank Prime Rate	6%	2%
90 Day Treasury Bill	2%	2%
180 Day Treasury Bill	4%	0%
Federal Reserve Treasury Bill Discount Rate	2%	2%
Other	10%	5%
Total	100%	100%

Average HELOC Spread Over The Wall Street Journal Prime Rate (Basis Points)

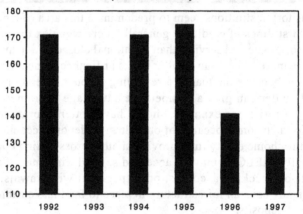

Variable Rate Adjustment Period

	1997	1996
Daily	20%	11%
Weekly	0%	3%
Monthly	78%	81%
Quarterly	2%	5%
Total	100%	100%

Source: CBA 1998 Home Equity Loan Study

Exhibit 4 provides a graphical description of the uses of home equity lines. The primary reason for home equity borrowing is debt consolidation, which represented 40% of HELOC borrowing in 1997. Many consumers replaced higher interest rate credit card debt with lower interest rate home equity borrowing that has the added benefit of being tax deductible. Prior to 1992, the primary reason for home equity borrowing was home improvement, which in 1997 accounted for 23% of the lines extended. Other uses of home equity lines include automobile purchases (7%), education (6%), and other major purchases (6%). The uses of closed-end loans are broadly similar to the responses given for lines of credit. Overall, the shift from home improvement, where the underlying real estate is being upgraded, to debt consolidation suggests that the risk profile associated with home equity lending has increased somewhat over time.

As they have on closed-end home equity loans, average loan-to-value ratios (LTVs) have been rising on HELOCs. LTVs reached an average of 77% in 1997, up from 72% in 1995. These levels are comparable to the LTVs on closed-end loans. At the same time, the number of lenders that offer at least some high LTV HELOCs has increased. According to the CBA survey, 25% of lenders offer at least some lines with LTVs greater than 100%. (See Exhibit 5.)

Given the shift to debt consolidation and higher LTVs, it appears that the level of risk may have increased somewhat in the home equity sector. However, the superior demographic characteristics and financial circumstances of HELOC borrowers relative to traditional closed-end loan borrowers provide some additional credit support. According to the results from the 1997 Surveys of Consumers conducted by the University of Michigan's Survey Research Center and the Federal Reserve Board, HELOC borrowers were older, had more expensive homes, more home equity, higher household incomes, and more education than closed-end loan borrowers.[3] These same characteristics are found in the CBA survey.[4] The relative affluence, and corresponding credit quality, of the HELOC borrowers may be one reason that many banks and thrifts prefer to keep these lines on balance sheet rather than securitize them.

Delinquency and charge-off rates are generally superior to other types of consumer credit. Average delinquencies on HELOCs from the CBA Survey were 1.11% in 1997. This compares to non-credit card consumer debt delinquencies of about 3% and credit card delinquencies of nearly 5% for the same period. The story for charge-offs is similar. Average charge-offs on HELOCs were 0.11% in 1997 compared to about 1% for non-credit card consumer debt and more than 5% for credit cards. Given the credit performance of collateral and borrower demographics, the ABS market would welcome more HELOC issuance.

Exhibit 4: Uses of Home Equity Loans

	Percent
Debt Consolidation	40
Home Improvement	23
Automobile	7
Major Purchase	6
Education	6
Business Expenses & Investment	5
Other or Don't Know	13
Total	100

Source: CBA 1998 Home Equity Loan Study

[3] Canner, et. al., "Recent Developments in Home Equity Lending," pp. 244-246.
[4] DeMong and Lindgren, *1998 Home Equity Loan Study*, p. 13.

Exhibit 5: HELOC LTVs and Percent of Institutions Offering High LTV HELOCs

Industry Average HELOC LTVs

1995	72%
1996	73%
1997	77%

Percent of Institutions Offering High LTV HELOCs

Maximum LTV	
< 100%	63%
101% - 124%	10%
125%	10%
> 125%	5%

Source: CBA 1998 Home Equity Loan Study

Exhibit 6: HELOC Pricing History

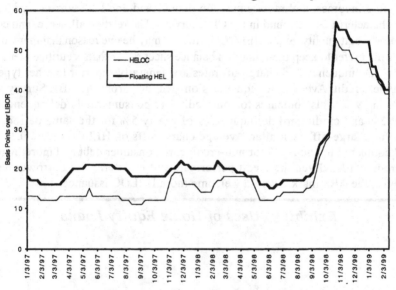

HELOC STRUCTURES

HELOC ABS are structured as floating-rate certificates, and are priced at a spread above 1-month LIBOR. For this reason they are often compared to floating-rate tranches of closed-end home equity transactions. Exhibit 6 illustrates recent pricing spread history for both products. These two assets have historically priced comparably to one another; however, HELOCs have generally commanded a slight premium versus a closed-end product because of better obligor quality and stronger servicer profiles.

But, because HELOC loans more closely resemble credit card accounts than mortgage loans, the structures used to securitize these loans differ dramatically from those employed in the closed-end home equity market. Due to the open-ended nature of the collateral, HELOC transactions usually rely on revolving trust structures. Unlike the static issuance vehicles used to securitize closed-end loan pools, a revolving trust allows for the securitization of outstanding principal amounts while providing obligors the ability to draw against their lines of credit.

To achieve this, a HELOC trust is generally divided into two interests: a certificate, or investor interest, and a seller interest. This multiple interest structure is common to most types of revolving ABS transactions. The certificate interest is the portion of the trust assets that collateralize the HELOC certificates sold in the term ABS market. The seller interest is the difference between the collateral pool balance and the certificate interest balance. The size of the seller interest will fluctuate over time since the investor interest will either remain constant or decline, depending on whether the certificates are in a revolving or amortization phase, while the pool balance will increase or decrease, depending on the relative amount of draws or paydowns during a given month. Typically, there is a required minimum level for the seller interest that is often sized to 2% of the initial pool balance, and then may decline as the investor interest amortizes.

Principal Repayment

Given the similarities between HELOC and revolving ABS structures, it should not be surprising that HELOC certificates repay principal in a manner that is more akin to a revolving ABS than to a typical MBS. As such, the life of HELOC can be divided into three phases: a revolving period, a managed amortization period, and a rapid amortization period. While not all HELOC transactions feature revolving periods, most feature some combination of managed and rapid amortization periods.

Revolving Period

During a revolving period, the certificates are typically locked out from receiving principal payments. Instead, principal collected on the underlying loans, in excess of new draws, can be captured in a trust funding account. This cash can then be used to fund future draws or purchase new loans. At the end of the revolving period, cash remaining in the funding account may be used to paydown outstanding certificate balances.

Managed Amortization Period

Most transactions provide for a managed amortization period of five years. During the managed amortization period, principal payments are equal to some fraction of principal paid on the loans, net of all new draws. Principal paid may include both scheduled and unscheduled payments. If new draws exceed principal collections during a given month, there may be no principal payment for that month.

When evaluating prepayment risk during the managed amortization period it is helpful to understand the cash flow conventions used in the HELOC sector. The rate at which additional balances are created is referred to as the *constant draw rate* (CDR) and the rate at which balances are paid down is the *constant prepayment rate* (CPR). The formulas for both the CDR and the CPR are given below:

$$CDR = 1 - (1 - \text{Single monthly draw rate})^{12}$$

$$CPR = 1 - (1 - \text{Single monthly mortality rate})^{12}$$

where

$$\text{Single monthly draw rate} = 1 - \frac{\text{Total \$ amount drawn during month}}{\text{Beginning monthly pool balance}}$$

$$\text{Single monthly mortality rate} = 1 - \frac{\text{Total \$ amount paid down}}{\text{Beginning monthly pool balance}}$$

The *single monthly draw rate* (SMD) is the increase in pool balance expressed as a percentage of the pool balance at the beginning of the month. Conversely, the *single monthly mortality rate* (SMM) is the decrease the pool balance expressed as a percentage of the pool balance at the beginning of the month. Finally, both the CDR and CPR are annualized expressions of the monthly draw and payment rates. The annualized prepayment rate realized by the investor during the managed amortization period is given by the following:

$$\text{Max } \{0, 1 - (1 - [(SMM - SMD)/\text{Beginning monthly pool balance}])^{12}\}$$

Rapid Amortization Period

A rapid amortization can occur either as a normal phase late in the life of a HELOC, or can be triggered by a decline in credit quality or other event. Normally, a rapid amortization period will follow a revolving or managed amortization period, and is characterized by the distribution of a high fixed percentage of gross principal collections (*not* net of draws) to certificate holders.

During rapid amortization, the rate of principal repayment can be affected by the trust's historical draw experience and the size of the seller's interest. If borrowers make more draws than principal payments during the life of a transaction, the seller interest will grow relative to the investor's interest. Because certificate holders are allocated a fixed percentage of all principal collections, HELOC ABS issued from trusts with larger seller interests will experience faster repayment during rapid amortization than those certificates issued by trusts with smaller seller interests. This implies that the utilization rate of the underlying loans affects the rate at which investors will receive principal payments, and that higher utilization rates at the time of securitization may be correlated with slower repayment rates.

Rapid amortization can also be used as a protective structural device for investors and third party credit enhancers. Rapid amortization can be triggered by a number of events, typically including:

- Failure on the part of the servicer to make timely payments or deposits under the pool and servicing agreement, or to observe or perform in a material respect the covenants or agreements set forth in the transaction documentation;
- Breach of representations or warranties made by the seller or servicer;
- The occurrence of certain events of bankruptcy, insolvency or receivership relating to the seller;
- Violation of certain collateral performance related either in the transaction documentation or surety agreement.

Credit Enhancement

The most common form of credit enhancement for HELOCs consists of a mono-line insurance policy. Other structural tools like overcollateralization, spread accounts, and excess spread are often used in conjunction with a wrapped structure. However, in wrapped transactions these devices are sized and exist primarily for the benefit of the insurer. Investors should look to the insurance provider as their primary source of enhancement.

Overcollateralization can be created by allocating principal payments to the certificates using a fixed allocation percentage method. Certificate holders are allocated a fixed percentage of collections, which reduces the size of the investor interest relative to the size of the overall collateral pool, thereby growing the amount of collateral relative to the certificates. Once the desired overcollateralization target is achieved, some principal collections may be redirected to the holder of the seller interest.

Spread accounts build to a predetermined level by capturing the excess spread in the transaction and depositing the funds into an trust account. To the extent that the investor interest and principal collection amounts are insufficient to pay the certificate holders, the spread account will be drawn upon. In the event that the spread account is drawn down below its target level, excess spread will again be captured to fund the spread account back to targeted levels.

Available Funds Caps

HELOCs, like floaters structured from closed-end adjustable rate HELs, are subject to basis risk in the form of both index risk and reset risk. Index risk arises when the coupon on the underlying collateral is tied to an index other than that of the certificate. While HELOC certificates almost always pay a coupon spread over 1-month LIBOR, the underlying loans are more likely tied to the prime rate or some other index.

Reset risk is the difference between the frequency of the investor coupon resets and the frequency of the resets of the underlying collateral. Reset risk is often mitigated in HELOC structures since approximately 80% of HELOC loans reset their coupons monthly.

Thus, index risk is responsible for most of the basis risk present in HELOC transactions. The combination of basis risk with available funds caps embedded in a structure can potentially cause problems for investors, and should be closely examined. An available funds cap can limit the coupon payment on a structured security, if the dollar amount of the coupon to be paid exceeds the dollar amount of funds available from collections. A mismatch between the index used to reprice the collateral and the index used to reprice the security potentially increases the risk of an available funds cap being triggered. To mitigate this risk, many — but not all — transactions have interest carryover provisions that allow for the carryover of the previous period's interest shortfall. These provisions generally specify that any carryover will earn interest at the then-current coupon rate.

To evaluate the likelihood of hitting an available funds cap, investors must compute both the available funds margin and the available funds cap.[5] Also, when considering the likelihood of hitting the available funds cap and the subsequent interest carryover provisions, it is important to bear in mind several facts, including:

- That the monoline wrap does not apply to interest carried over from one period to the next;
- The interest carryover is paid from the excess spread in the transactions and often subordinate in the waterfall, and therefore is likely to persist for more than one period; and
- The payment of the interest carryover may not be mandatory, and in the event of an interest carryover balance upon the maturity of the transaction, the investor will forego the carryover balance to the extent that funds are insufficient to pay the balance in full.

SUMMARY

The securitization of revolving home equity lines of credit has been relatively limited compared to the outstanding supply of HELOCs and the growth in securitization of closed-end home equity loans. This shortage is due more to financial

---

[5] The available funds margin (AFM) is the amount available to pay the bondholders coupon and the servicing and surety fees as well as other fees. The available funds margin is calculated as follows:

AFM = Gross coupon − Servicing fees − Surety fees − Other fees − (Coupon index − Margin)

The available funds cap (AFC) is the maximum amount available to pay the bondholders coupon. The available funds cap is calculated as follows:

AFC = Gross coupon − Servicing spread − Surety fees − Other fees

institutions deciding to carry them on the balance sheet than it is to any lack of investor demand for the product. In general, the credit quality of the collateral, the demographics of the borrowers, and a lack of supply have led to HELOCs commanding a slight pricing premium to floating rate closed-end product. Given the solid collateral performance and floating rate nature of the collateral, we believe that ABS investors would welcome additional issuance from this market niche.

Chapter 21

Securities Backed by Manufactured Housing Loans

James S. Anderson
Managing Director
Asset-Backed Research
First Union Securities, Inc.

Kristina L. Clark
Associate
Fixed-Income Research
First Union Securities, Inc.

INTRODUCTION

This chapter provides investors with an overview of the manufactured housing industry, as well as the collateral underlying manufactured housing asset-backed securities (ABS). For investors already familiar with manufactured housing ABS, we discuss current issues in the industry and their impact on ABS as well as introduce a source of higher-level analytics and surveillance.

The manufactured housing industry has undergone dramatic changes since the late 1970s and early 1980s. Government regulations and advances in home design have greatly improved product quality and safety. Competitive financing and changes in consumer demand have led to a shift in sales from smaller, less expensive single-section homes to larger, more expensive multisection homes (see Exhibit 1). New manufactured homes are being designed to resemble more closely traditional site-built homes, offering amenities such as vaulted ceilings, fireplaces, and walk-in closets. Manufacturers have been working with land developers and dealers to change the negative stereotype of "trailer parks" by promoting the construction of "manufactured housing communities," which include swimming pools, clubhouses, and recreational facilities.

As the manufactured housing industry evolved and demand for such accommodations increased, loans providing underlying financing became more common collateral for securitization. As with other ABS classes, manufactured housing ABS are subject to the growing pains of the underlying industry, and although the manufactured housing industry has come a long way, competition and credit standards pose a continuing challenge to analyzing pool performance.

365

Exhibit 1: Average Size and Sales Price of Manufactured and Site-Built Homes

($)	1992	1993	1994	1995	1996	1997
Manufactured Homes						
Total						
Average Sales Price	28,400	30,500	33,500	36,300	38,400	41,100
Average Square Footage	1,255	1,295	1,330	1,355	1,380	1,420
Cost per Square Foot	22.63	23.55	25.19	26.79	27.83	28.94
Single Section						
Average Sales Price	20,600	21,900	23,900	26,700	28,200	29,000
Average Square Footage	1,035	1,065	1,085	1,115	1,120	1,125
Cost per Square Foot	19.90	20.56	22.03	23.95	25.18	25.78
Multisection						
Average Sales Price	37,200	39,600	42,900	45,900	47,300	49,500
Average Square Footage	1,495	1,525	1,565	1,585	1,600	1,615
Cost per Square Foot	24.88	25.97	27.41	28.96	29.56	30.65
Site-Built Homes						
Average Sales Price	144,100	147,700	154,100	158,700	166,200	176,200
Land Price	36,025	36,925	38,525	39,675	41,550	44,050
Price of Structure	108,075	110,775	115,575	119,025	124,650	132,150
Average Square Footage	2,095	2,095	2,115	2,115	2,125	2,150
Cost per Square Foot	51.59	52.88	54.65	56.28	58.66	61.47

Source: Manufactured Housing Institute.

Fortunately for investors, the issuers in this industry are not novice securitizers. Companies such as Green Tree (now wholly owned by Conseco, Inc.), Oakwood Homes Corp., Vanderbilt Mortgage and Finance, Inc., and GreenPoint Credit Corp. (with the recent addition of Bank of America Corp.'s manufactured housing operation) have extensive experience securitizing this industry. By the end of 1998, much of the industry had reorganized and refocused. The credit crunch in the third quarter of 1998 and less-than-stellar performance from 1995–1996 collateral pools have forced the industry to change, and the result has been a clearer focus on borrower and collateral quality.

WHAT IS A MANUFACTURED HOUSE?

According to the Department of Housing and Urban Development (HUD), manufactured houses are single-family homes constructed on a chassis at a factory and shipped in one or more sections to a housing site, then installed on a semipermanent foundation. Single-section manufactured homes are typically 12–14 feet wide and 40–64 feet long. Multisection homes are created by joining two or more single sections along their length or by stacking them to create additional stories.

Manufactured housing is generally less expensive (15%–40%) and smaller than comparable site-built housing. In 1997, the average manufactured home had 1,420 square feet of living space and cost $41,100 compared with the average site-built home (2,150 square feet costing $132,150, excluding land). Although commonly referred to as mobile homes, most manufactured homes are permanent residences. Transporting a manufactured home can cost $2,000–$6,000, depending on the size of the home and the location.

There has been a shift in sales from smaller, less expensive single-section homes to larger, more expensive multisection homes (see Exhibit 2).

MANUFACTURED HOUSING LOAN PRODUCTS

Manufactured homes can be purchased separately or with land. In a land and home purchase, the unit is permanently affixed to the site, and the entire property is taxed as real estate. Loans for land and home purchases typically have more financing options and more closely resemble mortgages for traditional site-built homes. The number of land and home contracts has increased in recent years along with the growth in popularity of more expensive multisection homes. This trend has had a positive impact on loan pools as historical performance shows consumers who borrow to purchase the home and the land are more reliable than consumers who borrow to purchase only the home.

Homes purchased separately are typically financed through a retail installment sales contract or a personal property loan. Typically, a UCC filing on the home (similar to the documentation for an automobile loan) takes the place of a deed of trust. These loans are commonly referred to as chattel loans. Historically, terms for a chattel loan were 15–20 years with a 10% down payment. Recently, however, lenders have begun offering terms of 25–30 years with as low as a 5% down payment in an effort to increase market share.

WHO ARE THE BORROWERS?

Although the characteristics of a typical manufactured housing buyer have been changing since the late 1980s and early 1990s, two population segments show particular growth. The first segment consists of retirees and baby boomers. A total of 27% of the heads of manufactured housing households are retired, and occupants older than 70 years account for 21% of all manufactured housing residents (see Exhibit 3). Manufactured housing combined with home healthcare has become for some a favorable alternative to nursing home care.

Exhibit 2: Manufactured Housing Loan Characteristics

	Single Section	Multisection	U.S. Average Site Built
Loan Rate versus Conventional (bps)	338	288	
Average Loan Term (months)	200	240	360
Average Monthly Payment ($)	260	406	831

Source: Green Tree Financial Corp.

Exhibit 3: Manufactured Housing Borrower Demographics

(%)	Single Section	Multisection
Average Age		
18–34	71.0	23.5
35–54	24.2	67.9
55+	4.8	8.6
Average Years Same Job		
0–5	72.3	29.1
5–10	23.4	59.5
10+	3.4	11.4
Family Income		
$15,000–$25,000	64.7	12.8
$25,000–$50,000	34.5	84.6
$50,000+	0.8	2.6

Source: Manufactured Housing Institute.

The second growth segment is Generation X as they move into the first-time home-buying market. Because rents have been rising for the past decade, manufactured housing offers a strong alternative to apartments in addition to substantial cost savings in relation to site-built homes.

For both segments, the average annual income is $21,500 with 21% exceeding $40,000. The average household net worth is $58,000 with 27% exceeding $100,000.

In the late 1980s and the early 1990s, interest rates for manufactured housing loans for lower-income borrowers were as high as 14%. These exorbitant rates negated cost savings from choosing manufactured housing instead of site-built homes, further inhibiting the industry's growth. Finance companies claimed the high rates reflected the greater risk of delinquency and default associated with manufactured housing borrowers, a stereotype plaguing the industry. Reports at that time disproved the claim and illustrated that average delinquencies on manufactured home loans were significantly less than delinquencies on comparable mortgages. Finance companies have since realized their prejudice and, during the past few years, rates for manufactured housing loans have fallen closer in line with mortgage rates.

Increases in the popularity and acceptance of multisection homes have exposed the industry to higher-credit borrowers than those that sought a single-section home (see Exhibit 3). The typical multisection homeowner is older, has a longer employment history, and has a larger income. In contrast, the traditional single-section borrower is younger, has a shorter employment history, and has a smaller income.

OVERVIEW OF MANUFACTURED HOUSING ABS

Manufactured housing ABS volume has grown dramatically, culminating in a 17% increase in volume from 1997 to 1998. The rapid expansion reflects changing characteristics in the industry. Some of the most prevalent changes include the following:

- Increasing demand for low-cost housing alternatives
- Refinancings due to increased industry competition
- Larger loan balances due to increased desire for larger or multisectional homes
- Longer loan terms to help borrowers manage monthly payments
- Maturing of the industry and its key players
- Industry support provided by government agencies such as HUD

The majority of manufactured housing ABS issuance has been in the public market. As of June 22, 1999, issuance volume had reached a level comparable to total issuance in 1995. At this rate, the asset class will have more than doubled in size in only four years. The asset class has proven its ability to grow in the face of volatility and unsure market conditions as evidenced by record growth despite the tough third quarter of 1998 experienced by all ABS market participants.

Manufactured housing ABS has been a significant portion of total ABS issuance since 1995. Although the aggregate market has seen the emergence of many new asset classes from 1995 to 1998, manufactured housing ABS has remained a consistent 5%–6% of the total market. While auto-backed issues and home equities (HEQs) have remained similarly consistent, asset classes such as credit cards and student loans have decreased as a percentage of total issuance.

Although manufactured housing competition continues to increase and more issuers continue to come to market, an overwhelming majority of new issuance still comes from key market players such as Green Tree, Oakwood, Vanderbilt and GreenPoint. Green Tree, in particular, consistently appears at the top of the league table.

With $4 billion of total manufactured housing ABS volume in 1995, Green Tree accounted for 62% of the asset class's total new issuance that year. Although still the largest issuer of manufactured housing ABS, Green Tree's share of new issuance fell from 53% in 1997 to 47% in 1998 (Exhibit 4).

Exhibit 4: Change in Market Share by Key Players

	1996	1997	1998	1999
Green Tree Financial Corp.	63%	53%	47%	1%
Associates	16%	8%	0%	0%
Oakwood Homes Corp.	8%	9%	9%	8%
Vanderbilt Mortgage and Finance, Inc.	5%	10%	8%	11%
Others	5%	12%	11%	0%
BankAmerica Housing Services	3%	8%	13%	0%
Merit	0%	0%	0%	5%
Bombardier Capital Mortgage Securitization Corp.	0%	0%	6%	2%
GreenPoint Credit Corp.	0%	0%	6%	23%

Note: GreenPoint acquired BankAmerica Housing Services on Sept. 30, 1998.

Source: *Asset-Backed Alert* and First Union Securities, Inc.

POOL CHARACTERISTICS

Most loan pools today contain a mixture of single- and multisection manufactured home loans. Placement of the homes also varies with some of the collateral on private lots and others in communities. Loans collateralized by larger homes and those supported by land in addition to the home are generally preferred as collateral rather than a loan on a smaller, unattached unit. Historically in pools, there has been a prevalence of multisection homes as collateral, even when single-section home sales exceeded multisection home sales. Multisection homes accounted for 60.9% of total shipments in 1997, whereas single-section home shipments have slipped since 1995. Issuers tend to place higher-credit collateral in their securitization pools to obtain and sustain tranche ratings. By the end of the first quarter of 1999, multisection homes in securitization pools on average were 67.7% of the underlying collateral.

The majority of loans placed in pools are for new property as opposed to used or secondary market collateral. New homes have constituted 76% or more of total loan pools since 1995. Also evident is a steady increase in used homes as a percentage of the total, which is due to the growth of the secondary market. Also spurring used homes as acceptable collateral is the increasing quality of manufactured homes over the past five years. With better quality standards supported by manufactured housing manufacturers and government housing agencies, it is reasonable that the newer homes would last longer and depreciation rates would be less than those for homes manufactured and sold a few years ago. As manufactured housing increasingly becomes a more acceptable alternative to site-built homes, secondary market activity should increase and thus more used homes should be financed.

To date, collateral on private lots has been more prevalent than properties situated in communities. This aversion to manufactured housing communities is an offshoot of the old trailer park image. As more upscale communities are tailored for manufactured homes, we expect to see an increase of community-based collateral.

The average life of a typical manufactured housing loan currently ranges from seven to eight years, but this is lengthening. Due to increased demand for larger or multisection homes, loan balances have also been rising. Concurrent with rising financing amounts, borrowers have been demanding longer loan terms to accommodate budgets and to simulate site-built home mortgages. There has also been a heightening of industry competition to meet the requirements of increased business flow. A relaxation of credit underwriting has plagued the industry of late. This issue is discussed in greater detail later in this chapter.

DRAWING BORROWERS AND THE EFFECT ON SECURITIZATION POOLS

During the mid-1990s as the demand for manufactured housing increased, retailers and financiers began implementing aggressive lending terms to capture greater market share. Higher advance rates, extended loan terms and buy-down programs were used to attract customers and increase underwriting volume. Traditional 15–

20-year loan terms were extended to 25–30 years and industry standard down payments of 10%–15% were lowered to 5% in some cases. The increase in more expensive multisection home purchases and the availability of "5% down" financing have led to a greater percentage of loans with loan-to-value (LTV) ranges of 95% and higher. The proportion of high-LTV loans has risen on average from 0% to 5% of the total in 1994 to 30%-40% in 1998 and 1999, depending on the lender.

Not surprisingly, as a result of looser credit standards, defaults and the number of used and repossessed homes on the market have risen and affected pool performance. To assuage losses, many lenders have switched from wholesale to retail channels to clear repos. In retail disposition, homes are often placed on a consignment basis on a dealer's lots. The dealer receives a commission for the sale of the home and the lender provides financing for the new buyer. Pricing trends suggest many repossessed homes on consignment are sold at or above their true market price. The problem with using retail disposition as a form of loss mitigation is that lenders run the risk of replacing old bad loans with new bad loans. In fact, statistics show consumers with a weak credit history are more likely to purchase repossessed manufactured homes.

With new unit shipments leveling off, many lenders have turned to refinancing as a source of increased volume. Larger loan balances, combined with relatively low interest rates, have created an incentive for many borrowers to refinance. Naturally, this trend in loans appeared within securitization pools and resulted in increasing delinquencies, prepayments, and defaults. Although data shows that borrowers in the high advance rate category typically perform better than the average manufactured housing borrower, some have argued the lack of equity in the home raises the likelihood of default should the borrower run into financial trouble.

In 1997, the manufactured housing financing industry began reorganizing and consolidating. This was accelerated by market volatility in the third quarter of 1998, which hindered many specialty finance companies from securitizing. Reorganization and consolidation have continued as weaker players drop out because of their inability to successfully execute in the market.

What Happened to Green Tree?

Green Tree Financial Corp., the market's top securitizer for manufactured housing, experienced trouble and controversy related to its collateral and use of gain-on-sale accounting. In 1996, the company was forced to take a $150 million cash charge resulting from the miscalculation of assumptions on loans originated in 1995 and 1996. Although the charge was small in relation to the $26 billion in loans under management, the action highlighted the importance of conservatively measuring the gain on sale of securitized assets. Unfortunately for Green Tree, its trouble did not stop there. As a result of similar prepayment miscalculations, the company revised 1996 and 1997 earnings down $400 million. Lawsuits were brought by shareholders who believed management did not efficiently report troubles in the company. Controversy accelerated when it was revealed that former Chairman Larry Coss' salary was a percentage of reported earnings, an amount that reached $102 million in 1996.

Exhibit 5: An Example of Buy-Down Terms

Original Loan Amount ($)	Loan Term (years)	Interest Rate	Monthly Payment ($)	Points	Buy-Down Amount ($)
50,000	20	10.00%	482.51	0.0	0
50,000	20	9.75%	474.26	1.0	500
50,000	20	9.50%	466.07	2.0	1,000
50,000	20	9.25%	457.93	3.0	1,500
50,000	20	9.00%	449.86	4.0	2,000
50,000	20	8.75%	441.86	5.0	2,500
50,000	20	8.50%	433.91	6.0	3,000
50,000	20	8.25%	426.02	7.0	3,500
50,000	20	8.00%	418.22	8.0	4,000

Source: First Union Securities, Inc.

Green Tree has since rebounded from the negative press associated with its gain-on-sale treatment, but an example has been made of the potential problems that can arise from misjudging these calculations.

Buy-Down Programs

In a buy-down program, the lender offers the borrower a rate lower than the prevailing rate by charging the borrower points in exchange for the lower rate. The points are either added to the loan amount or financed by the lender under a separate agreement. Standard practices in the industry are a 1.0 point charge for every 25 bps reduction in rate. Exhibit 5 provides an example of buy-down terms for a 20-year, $50,000 loan with a base rate of 10%. By reducing monthly payments, buy-down programs enable lenders to offer financing to homebuyers who might otherwise not qualify for a manufactured housing loan. The low rate also makes it difficult for competitors to refinance the loan, which decreases the likelihood of prepayment.

Buy-down loans that are securitized result in tighter spreads due to the lower weighted average coupon (WAC). While the likelihood of prepayments is less, this is offset by an increase in potential loss severity. When buy-down loans are sold to a trust, the lender receives the face value of the loan plus any points financed. If a buy-down loan defaults, the sale of the asset must cover the loan amount plus points and liquidation costs. Depending on depreciation and the timing of default, it is likely the necessary recovery amount will exceed the value of the underlying asset.

ISSUER PROFILES

Throughout late 1998 and 1999, the manufactured housing industry has undergone restructuring and reorganization. Bank of America sold its housing operation to GreenPoint, Green Tree merged with Conseco, Inc., in July 1998 and small players such as United Companies Financial Corp. exited the market. Throughout this process, underwriting standards and dealer networks stood out as keys to industry success. This has brought intense focus on the key industry issuers and how they differentiate themselves.

Green Tree Financial Corp. (Conseco Finance)

Green Tree, founded in 1975, is a diversified finance company with nationwide operations serving the consumer and commercial markets. The company has more than 20,000 independent retail dealer relationships and seven business lines with more than 8,000 employees in more than 200 offices nationwide. The company is known for its well-developed dealer network. With finance receivables in excess of $33 billion, Green Tree is the nation's second largest issuer of asset-backed securities, totaling $13.4 billion in 1998. In July 1998, the company merged with Conseco, a specialist in supplemental health insurance, retirement annuities, and universal life insurance.

Green Tree has been and remains the dominant player in the manufactured housing securitization market. In 1998, the company's securitizations totaling $5.5 billion represented roughly 50% of the manufactured housing securitization market. As a result, Green Tree has played a major role in determining market standards for securitization structures and collateral characteristics. Green Tree also leads the market in structural sophistication and has begun to provide a guaranty on subordinated pieces rather than retaining them.

Green Tree's recovery rate on deals from 1995 through 1998 averaged 56.1%, which ranks in the middle of the industry. Green Tree's deals consist primarily of new units on private lots. Average loans size has trended upward, which parallels the industry overall. WACs have fallen as LTVs have increased, again reflecting overall industry trends.

Oakwood Homes Corp.

Oakwood Homes, headquartered in Greensboro, N.C., is one of only a few vertically integrated housing companies. Oakwood engages in the production, sale, financing and insuring of manufactured housing units. Founded in 1946, Oakwood (NYSE-OH) is the nation's third largest manufacturer of factory-built homes. With 32 nationwide manufacturing plants and 359 company-owned retail sales centers, Oakwood sells more homes each year than any other retail competitor. Furthermore, the company's financial services business unit completes the sale process by providing customer financing as well as insurance coverage. The company markets its retail businesses under the names Oakwood, Freedom, Victory, Golden West, Schult, Crest, Suburban, and Destiny homes.

Since the issuance of the company's first securitization in 1994, Oakwood has significantly increased its manufactured housing securitization program. With a total of $3.7 billion in securitizations, Oakwood is recognized as a quarterly securitizer and maintains a stable presence in the manufactured housing securitization market. According to the rating agencies, the loans in Oakwood's securitizations are typically of lower credit quality as Oakwood liberally uses the 95% LTV program. In addition, Oakwood's securitizations generally have higher credit support levels than others in this market. Although Oakwood has a relatively high default rate, its recovery rate remains well in excess of other market leaders such as Green Tree.

This is attributable to Oakwood's strong dealer network fostered through its vertical integration. This structure allows for increased success with repos, unit trading, secondary market creation, and the avoidance of liquidation through wholesaling, but it may not be enough to sustain collateral troubles over an extended time.

Oakwood announced in mid-June 1999 that earnings for the third quarter, ended June 30, would fall short of analysts' expectations by as much as 50% ($0.55/share). Management also announced a decision to explore strategic alternatives, including a management-led buyout. The earnings shortfall stemmed from "unanticipated softness" in both retail and wholesale sales that, as previously noted, has of late generally affected the industry. Another announcement was made on July 17, 1999 stating that third-quarter earnings will be 65%–75% below analysts' estimates. The company's Baa3/BBB- ratings have been placed on negative watch by both Moody's Investor Services, Inc., and Standard & Poor's Corp. Recent troubles, however, have not hindered Oakwood from continuing to access the securitization market.

Vanderbilt Mortgage and Finance, Inc.

Vanderbilt is the captive finance arm and wholly owned subsidiary of Clayton Homes, Inc. (NYSE-CMH), a vertically integrated manufactured housing company operating in 28 states. Vanderbilt engages in manufacturing, retailing, financing and insuring homes as well as operating manufactured housing communities. As a financial services group, Vanderbilt provides financing and insurance for consumers buying manufactured homes from Clayton-owned retail offices and select independent retail centers. The company's current servicing portfolio contains more than 140,000 loans, totaling more than $3 billion.

Since 1995, Vanderbilt has established itself as a quarterly issuer and has increased its market presence in the manufactured housing securitization market. Historically, the issues have been considered by rating agencies as being at the higher end of the credit spectrum. Average loan maturity is below the norm, reducing depreciation risk, and the company has not been as involved in the 95% LTV program, thus reducing the relative delinquency and loss risk of the pools. In addition, the company does not repurchase defaulted loans from its securitizations, but instead relies on the dealers to perform this task. As a result, losses are absorbed at the dealer level rather than in Vanderbilt's securitizations. In 1998, total issuance of manufactured housing securitizations exceeded $850 million.

Vanderbilt tends to use predominantly community-based loans as opposed to private-lot-based loans in its securitizations. Its weighted average LTVs are lower than Oakwood's, but higher than Green Tree's, reflecting Vanderbilt's middle-of-the-market strategy.

GreenPoint Credit Corp.

GreenPoint Credit, headquartered in San Diego, is a wholly owned subsidiary of GreenPoint Financial Corp. (NYSE-GPT) specializing in the manufactured housing lending industry. It is the second largest originator and servicer of manufactured housing loans, with annual originations of more than $2.6 billion and a servicing portfolio of more than $10 billion. GreenPoint Credit, with 1,500 employees across a national sales and service network of 45 offices, has relationships with 5,000 dealers.

On November 18, 1998, GreenPoint brought its first manufactured housing securitization to market. The $728 million offering consisted of fixed and floating loans purchased from Bank of America as part of the acquisition of BankAmerica Housing Services. Since the first securitization, GreenPoint has issued two others in 1999 for a total of more than $2.3 billion.

On December 7, 1998, the company announced it had acquired the dealer origination segment of NationsCredit Manufactured Housing Corp.'s manufactured housing business. NationsCredit's business was part of NationsBank prior to its merger with Bank of America. On an annual basis, NationsCredit has originated approximately $400 million through its dealer channel. The purchase provided GreenPoint with access to NationsCredit's dealer business throughout the United States. In addition, the agreement called for a future correspondent relationship in which manufactured housing loans originated through Bank of America's branches will be sold to GreenPoint.

The WAC of the GreenPoint deals is lower than that of its competition's deals. GreenPoint also has had more than 80% of new home collateral for all four deals. Like Vanderbilt, GreenPoint's pool collateral is predominantly located in housing parks or communities as opposed to in private lots. This parallels the trend in the manufactured housing industry toward planned communities built with the help of developers and with full recreational equipment for the community and residents.

Bombardier Capital

Bombardier Capital is the financial services arm of global transportation equipment manufacturer, Bombardier, Inc. An international provider of financial solutions, Bombardier Capital offers a full line of lending, leasing, and asset management services to the consumer, inventory, commercial, and industrial markets. The company employs more than 1,100 people at multiple locations in the United States, Canada, and Europe.

Bombardier Capital has been in the manufactured housing business for more 10 years. In 1997, the company launched a manufactured housing retail financing business to provide financing services. The business expanded to double its market share in early 1999 with the purchase of NationsCredit Manufactured Housing's manufactured housing inventory finance portfolio.

Bombardier Capital's portfolio prior to the acquisition encompassed $200 million in assets under management and 540 manufactured housing retailers. The purchased portfolio included floor plan financing loans outstanding of $195 million with approximately 290 retailers at the end of 1998.

The company began to securitize in 1998 and, to date, has issued four securitizations totaling $849.3 million. Almost all of Bombardier Capital's collateral consists of new homes, and weighted average LTVs are lower than much of the competition's.

MANUFACTURED HOUSING PREPAYMENT MODELS

The Asset-Backed and Quantitative Research groups at First Union Securities have developed prepayment models for a variety of mortgage and mortgage-related asset types.[1] There are two models reflecting differing origination and underwriting criteria for manufactured housing originators and servicers. We have tested each model against all publicly issued ABS and have determined the best fit for each particular collateral group. Below we highlight some of the findings regarding manufactured housing prepayments.

Exhibits 6 and 7 show the prepayment and delinquency/loss for the universe of manufactured housing ABS. Though the data goes back to 1990, the bulk of the information is from 1993 onward. Note the high original WACs from 1990 to 1992, as well as the repricing of manufactured housing loans since 1993. It is not surprising the life speed of 1994 production shows a higher rate than subsequent years, given the higher WAC of that year's production. Moreover, the 12-month speeds for 1994 and 1995 vintages are somewhat above the total life speed. This reflected the interest rate environment, turnover, and competition.

The 1995 vintage at 4.26% exhibits the highest cumulative net loss of any year. The loss curves in Exhibit 7 are interesting in that there is a peak in Year 3, followed by a decline until the loans are seasoned (6–7 years). By this time, the factors (current pool collateral balance) are in the 0.2–0.3 range, possibly indicating adverse borrower selection and burnout in seasoned pools.

In Exhibits 8 and 9, the historical data on Green Tree shows fairly consistent collateral performance, with prepayments over the past two years oscillating in a fairly narrow range around a 12% constant prepayment rate (CPR); this is consistent with Green Tree's FASB 125 assumption of 200 MHP. The effect of competition and the subsequent rise in prepayments is apparent in Exhibit 8. Delinquencies (60+ days) have been between 1.5% and 2.0% over the same time frame, with the peak occurring out about 2.5 years. Annualized net losses peak at Year 3 at just under 2.5%. There is some collateral performance tail risk as cumulative net losses rise after Year 5, though thus far exhibiting a much smaller cumulative net loss than the universe as a whole.

Other issuers show a higher base prepayment rate than Green Tree and the manufactured housing universe in general. It seems as if this asset class in general exhibits fairly stable prepayments and therefore better convexity characteristics than other competing mortgage-backed product.

---

[1] The basic framework of our approach may be found in our October 1998 report *Prepayment Models and Home Equity Analysis.*

Exhibit 6: Prepayments for the Universe of Manufactured Housing Asset-Backed Securities

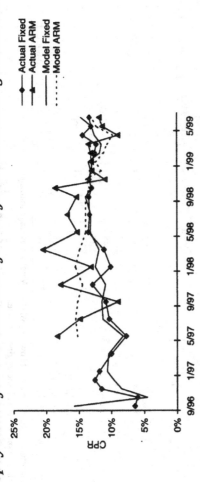

Legend: Actual Fixed, Actual ARM, Model Fixed, Model ARM

Historical CPR by Vintage

Vintage	1 Month	3 Month	12 Month	Life	Current WAC	Original WAC	Current Balance ($000)
1990	11.75	14.62	14.45	16.65	14.06	14.17	88,463
1991	19.06	18.71	19.83	15.92	12.24	12.36	144,786
1992	13.58	14.78	14.25	12.70	11.75	11.91	376,634
1993	13.11	14.14	13.65	11.69	10.25	10.28	865,743
1994	14.76	15.98	15.76	13.02	11.12	11.18	2,275,494
1995	13.67	15.41	14.97	11.81	10.88	11.01	4,233,066
1996	13.09	14.41	13.58	10.37	10.31	10.36	5,313,833
1997	13.24	14.01	12.93	10.56	10.25	10.23	7,488,201
1997	9.14	10.77	12.81	11.42	9.36	10.66	245,760
1998	10.04	9.14	8.91	7.69	9.59	9.59	10,083,876
1998 ARM	11.53	9.37	14.98	9.08	8.99	9.09	629,553

Projected CPR by Vintage

Vintage	Base Case				−100 bps	+100 bps
	1 Month	3 Month	6 Month	12 Month	12 Month	12 Month
1990	14.57	13.49	12.64	11.88	13.35	10.65
1991	15.01	13.82	12.93	12.15	13.93	10.92
1992	14.58	13.46	12.63	11.87	13.90	10.50
1993	13.23	12.13	11.40	10.76	12.73	9.67
1994	14.96	13.78	12.98	12.28	14.46	11.07
1995	16.10	14.86	14.07	13.47	15.76	12.15
1996	15.06	13.88	13.15	12.61	14.84	11.40
1997	13.93	13.04	12.58	12.33	14.56	11.11
1997	15.60	14.71	14.30	14.27	16.05	13.16
1998	8.87	8.55	8.56	9.07	10.69	8.15
1998 ARM	11.93	11.49	11.54	12.10	13.66	10.86

ARM: Adjustable-rate mortgage; CPR: Constant prepayment rate; WAC: Weighted average coupon.

Source: First Union Securities, Inc.

Exhibit 7: Delinquency/Loss for the Universe of Manufactured Housing Asset-Backed Securities

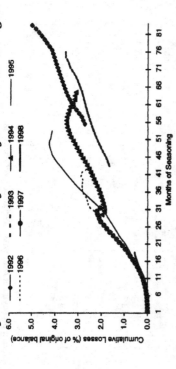

Delinquency/Loss by Vintage

| Vintage | As % of Remaining Balance | | | | | | | | As % of Original Balance | | | | Sample Size |
| | 30 Days | 60 Days | 90+ | REO | Annualized Net Loss Rate | | | | Annualized 1-Month Net Loss | Cumulative Net Loss | WALA | Factor* | |
					1 Month	3 Month	6 Month	12 Month					
1990	1.16	0.94	0.53		1.66	2.50	2.51	2.48	0.30	11.17	108	0.18	5
1991	1.16	0.62	0.17		0.96	1.22	1.55	1.62	0.21	5.48	95	0.22	4
1992	1.02	0.56			0.93	1.51	1.51	1.36	0.28	4.63	83	0.30	6
1993	1.13	0.88	0.75		1.28	1.24	1.11	1.04	0.53	3.09	70	0.41	4
1994	1.31	0.91	1.25		1.52	1.91	1.72	1.64	0.72	3.91	59	0.47	14
1995	1.95	1.44	0.67		2.23	2.56	2.48	2.37	1.32	4.38	47	0.59	20
1996	1.78	1.48	1.58	1.61	2.15	2.51	2.37	2.24	1.56	2.67	36	0.73	21
1997	2.07	1.51	1.16	0.94	1.96	2.24	1.96	1.50	1.60	1.65	23	0.82	28
1997	5.53	0.53								0.00	23	0.77	4
1998	2.82	1.16	1.50	0.40	1.00	0.77	0.58	0.37	0.91	0.48	13	0.91	24
1998 ARM	4.92	0.75	0.72		1.34	1.34	1.34	1.34		0.00	10	0.89	5

ARM: Adjustable-rate mortgage; REO: Real estate owned; WALA: Weighted average loan age.
*Factor: Remaining balance compared with the original balance.

Source: First Union Securities, Inc.

Exhibit 8: Green Tree Financial Corp. Aggregate Historical CPR versus Model CPR

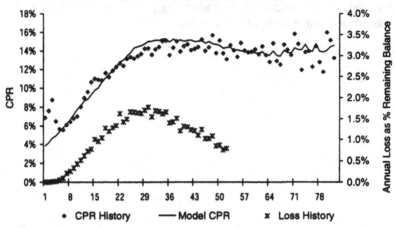

CPR: Constant prepayment rate.

Source: First Union Securities, Inc.

Exhibit 9: Green Tree Financial Corp. Cumulative Losses

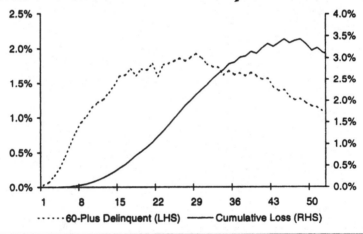

CONCLUSION

Manufactured housing ABS have been a consistent investment vehicle since 1995. The diverse nature of the underlying collateral allows issuers and underwriters to create securities with favorable convexity characteristics and solid credit support. As with many specialty finance sectors, investors must understand and account for the competitive landscape affecting the origination and ongoing performance of these ABS. The growth of the secondary market, alternative distribution methods, and mortgage-like financing terms continue to draw consumers into this product. As demand for the underlying product remains strong, the asset class should be a viable option for investors.

Chapter 22

Securities Backed by Tax Liens

Christopher Flanagan*

Ralph DiSerio*

Ryan Asato*

INTRODUCTION

Real estate property taxes are the primary source of local revenues for the nation's counties, cities, and local governments. Approximately 75% of all local revenues are raised through the assessment and collection of such taxes, which are estimated to total $180 billion annually. Nationwide, 5% to 6% of these taxes remain uncollected.

A tax lien typically attaches to real estate upon the delinquency of the taxes due on the parcel. Tax liens not only represent delinquent tax amounts, but accrued interest, penalties, and fees as well. Interest rate and penalty structures will vary according to individual state statutes, but most are normally set high in order to encourage fast redemption (repayment) of the tax lien. A tax lien generally has priority over all other existing liens on the property (including mortgages), except for prior liens of the federal government.

In this chapter we describe the tax lien ABS sector, providing an overview of the assets and structures that make up this growing segment of the market.

OVERVIEW OF TAX LIENS

Cash Flow and Risk/Return Profiles of Tax Liens

Tax liens possess characteristics that are unlike those of traditional loans and leases backing ABS transactions. In particular, tax lien cash flows are very different from a typical self-amortizing, monthly pay loan or lease. Upon purchase of a tax lien, there is only a one-time, lump-sum payment received by the investor. That payment does not take place until redemption in full of the tax lien is made. The cash flow is similar to a zero-coupon bond that has stated maturity.

* This chapter is based on an article appearing in *Real Estate ABS Monitor* (published by Merrill Lynch) and coauthored by Messrs. Flanagan, DiSerio, and Asato while employed as analysts at Merrill Lynch.

Exhibit 1: Hypothetical Tax Lien Rates of Return

Scenario	Lien Balance	Redemption Period	Accrued Interest	4% Penalty	Annual Return
Scenario 1	$5000	1	$42	$200	58%
Scenario 2	$5000	12	$500	$200	14%

When combined with the interest rate and penalty structure provided for by most state statutes, this cash flow profile can result in some very attractive rates of return for the investor. Exhibit 1 shows the hypothetical rates of return available to an investor that purchases a New Jersey tax lien with an interest rate of 10% and a flat penalty of 4% under two redemption scenarios. The first scenario assumes a 1-month redemption period, while the second scenario assumes 12 months until redemption occurs. As illustrated, the presence of the flat penalty boosts the annual return to 58% under the fast redemption scenario. Unlike most other mortgage-related collateral, fast repayment speeds are beneficial to this asset type.

Despite the potential for high rates of return, tax liens are generally low balance ($3,000 average) and extremely low lien-to-value (5% to 10% average). As a result, foreclosures of tax liens have been extremely limited historically due to ultimate repayment by either property owners or other interested parties, such as mortgage holders. In one recent rating agency study, it was found that property owners redeem over 95% of outstanding tax liens. In short, tax liens offer investors the opportunity to earn high yields with little risk of loss.

Tax Lien Sales to Investors

About 30 states permit local governments to convert their tax receivables into cash by selling tax liens to investors. Six additional states currently have pending legislation that will enable them to do so in the near future. The sale process is most frequently in the form of a public auction, but can also be structured as sealed bid offers or negotiated bulk purchases. Tax certificates representing these sales are generally awarded to the bidder that agrees to pay off all delinquent tax amounts, while accepting the lowest rate of interest, with a statutory maximum rate generally set at 18%. In some states, an interest rate floor in the form of a flat penalty will enhance yields if repayment of the tax liens is very fast. In Florida, for example, an investor would receive the greater of the bid rate or a 5% flat penalty.

Tax Certificate Mechanics

Individual state statutes typically govern how tax lien programs work and how long the taxpayer has to make payments before a foreclosure action can be commenced. Under these state statutes local governments may set up individualized processes to manage and control the programs. State statutes also dictate collection and notification procedures that can be utilized by the purchaser of tax certificates as well as the method to be used for initiating foreclosure proceedings if repayment is never made. Effective servicing of tax liens requires a thorough knowledge of these state specific procedures.

In the discussion that follows, we use Florida and New Jersey (two states whose tax liens are most frequently securitized) statutes to describe the process under which tax certificate holders manage and realize value from their investments.

During a 24-month statutory holding period in Florida and New Jersey, delinquent tax payers may extinguish the tax lien on their property by paying back all outstanding taxes plus interest, penalties, and fees to the municipality. If the property holder redeems in this manner, the municipality fully reimburses the tax certificate holder. It is important to note that it is the municipality that actually collects delinquent payments from the taxpayer.

If a redemption has not taken place by the end of the holding period, however, the tax certificate holder may file for a tax deed in Florida or pursue a foreclosure action in New Jersey. In either case, these legal remedies allow the tax certificate holders to recover their investment from the value of the underlying property. In Florida and New Jersey, tax deed and foreclosure actions can only be commenced if subsequent tax liens on the property have been satisfied. Tax certificate holders are also motivated to purchase subsequent liens because they typically earn 18% interest, further enhancing investment yield.

History indicates that the vast majority of tax liens do not get to the point where legal action is required. Even if property owners fail to make payment, mortgage holders or other investors in the property are likely to pay off delinquent taxes in order to take control of the legal process and protect their interests.

Competitive Environment

The market to purchase tax lien certificates remains highly fragmented. Historically, municipalities sold their liens to individual local investors seeking highly protected assets with superior returns. More recently, this risk/return profile has drawn interest from institutional players with deeper pockets. Capital Asset Research Corporation (CARC, 50% owned by MBIA) is the current industry leader. They have been purchasing tax liens for over five years and have several securitizations under their belt. CARC's share, however, remains at only 2% of the market. The growing list of institutional players interested in this segment include JE Roberts, TransAmerica, Breen Capital, Coast Asset, Bank United, Plymouth Financial, and Countrywide.

SECURITIZATION OF TAX LIENS

Tax Lien Sellers

Tax lien securitizations have been done at the county/municipal level and the individual investor level. In the former case, ABS investors purchase the county/

municipality's entire portfolio of tax liens at the end of the fiscal year. In the latter case, ABS investors purchase an institutional investor's portfolio of tax liens, which may be located in several different jurisdictions. In 1999, CARC and Breen Capital have brought fairly sizable institutional portfolio deals to the market. Increasing institutional interest in this asset class suggests that private sector transactions like these may be the fuel that drives the growth engine of this asset class.

Credit and Cash Flow Structure

As with other new ABS asset classes, tax lien ABS are most frequently offered in a 144A format. In addition, most early transactions employed a bond insured credit enhancement structure. More recently, however, senior subordinated transactions have become more commonplace. Exhibit 2 shows deal characteristics from a typical $300 million private sector senior subordinated tax lien ABS.

As illustrated, the typical senior subordinated tax lien ABS is credit tranched from AAA down to BBB. Credit support is derived from the levels of subordination indicated at each rating level, which in this case includes 6% initial overcollateralization (OC). OC is a particularly important concept in these transactions. In addition to providing credit support, OC also allows the notes to receive more than their pro-rata share of cash flow, which is applied according to the waterfall shown in Exhibit 3. A full turbo cash flow structure and a 25% auction call result in extremely short and stable WAL tranches, as illustrated later in this chapter. In this example, all the rated notes have the same 27 month principal window and the same 1.2 year WAL. (Note that level 4 in the waterfall applies all remaining cash flow as principal on a pro-rata basis.)

Exhibit 2: Characteristics of a Typical Senior Subordinate Tax Lien ABS

	Class A	Class M1	Class M2	Class B	OC
Class Size ($mm)	$214.5	$37.5	$18.0	$12.0	$18
Class Size (%)	71.5%	12.5%	6.0%	4.0%	6.0%
Credit Support (%)	28.5%	16.0%	10.0%	6.0%	NA
Principal Window (Exp)	1-27	1-27	1-27	1-27	NA
Interest Accrual	30/360	30/360	30/360	30/360	NA
Interest Payment	Fixed	Fixed	Fixed	Fixed	NA
WAL (yrs)	1.2	1.2	1.2	1.2	NA
Expected Final	11/01	11/01	11/01	11/01	NA
Ratings (S&P/Moodys)	AAA/Aaa	AA/Aa2	A/A2	BBB/Baa2	NA
Spread over EDSF	65	85	110	275	NA
Interest Reserve	6 months interest, replenishable				
Working Cap Reserve	$2.5 mm				
Subs Lien Purch Reserve	$75 mm				
Collateral Profile	$225 mm tax liens, 75% FLA, 25% NJ, 8% Avg LTV, 6.2% Avg Bid Rate, 5 mo Avg Age				
Pricing Assumptions	FLA Liens: 50% CLR, 200% purchase rate; NJ Liens: 35% CLR & 35% purchase rate, 25% Auction Call				

Exhibit 3: Tax Lien ABS Senior Subordinate Cash Flow Waterfall

All Cash Flow Applied in Following Order of Priority:	
Level 1:	Pay Trust Expenses Including Trustee and Servicing Fees
Level 2:	Pay Interest on Notes in Credit Priority Order
Level 3:	Replenish Interest and Working Capital Reserve Funds
Level 4:	Pay Principal on Notes on a Pro-Rata Basis
Level 5:	Reimburse Realized Losses on Notes in Credit Priority Order

Additional Structural Requirements

The unique features of tax lien collateral call for additional structural elements to be present in tax lien ABS transactions. Since tax liens have no scheduled cash flow until redemption and tax lien ABS generally pay interest quarterly, a *replenishable interest reserve fund* will usually be maintained by the trust. Rating agencies generally size this reserve fund to cover at least six months worth of interest. Interest reserve fund levels will reflect the historical redemption rates of the tax liens relative to the amount of interest payable over the accrual period.

A *replenishable working capital reserve fund* is also generally maintained by the trust. These funds are used by the servicer to pay lien administration expenses such as tax deed, foreclosure, and REO costs. Rating agencies size the working capital reserve fund based on the individual state statutes that are relevant to the transaction and the amount of tax lien collateral expected to remain delinquent at the end of the statutory holding period.

In our example transaction, a $75 million reserve fund has also been set aside to purchase subsequent tax liens. In many states like Florida and New Jersey, for example, tax deed and foreclosure actions can only be commenced if subsequent tax liens have been satisfied. These funds allow the trust to maintain its priority lien status in the underlying properties and enhance the transactions yield because subsequent liens generally earn 18% interest. Rating agencies size the subsequent lien reserve fund based on the individual state statutes that are applicable to the transaction and the expected redemption rates of the tax lien collateral.

The higher yields provided by subsequent tax lien purchases and the turbo pay structure provide additional credit support to the transaction through the creation of overcollateralization. As shown in Exhibit 4, OC builds slowly at first due to the limited amount of subsequent liens purchased by the trust in the first 12 months of the transaction (subsequent liens are not purchased in Florida until the original tax lien is 24 months old and roughly 25% to 30% of the Florida liens are 13 months seasoned). After 27 months (the expected call date), however, overcollateralization represents approximately 40% of the collateral pool (assuming the pricing speed and no losses). This level of OC is particularly meaningful since it virtually ensures that a successful auction call will take place. Collateral values would have to fall to 60 cents on the dollar before an auction would not be economically viable for a purchaser.

Exhibit 4: Tax Lien ABS OC Buildup

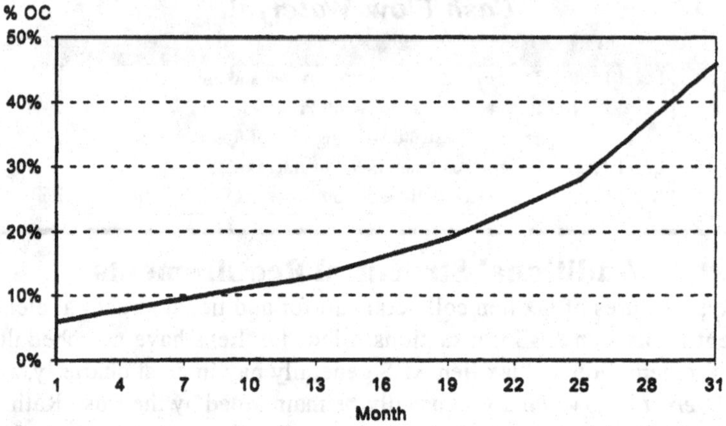

Exhibit 5: Tax Lien ABS Breakeven Cumulative Losses

Scenario	AAA	AA	A	BBB
1 - Pricing Speed Minus 10%	26%	16%	12%	8%
2 - Pricing Speed	30%	19%	14%	11%
3 - Pricing Speed Plus 10%	39%	26%	20%	16%

Assumptions: 0% recovery on defaulted tax lien collateral, losses start in month 12, and OC builds to 11% in scenario 1, 13% in scenario 2, and 16% in scenario 3.

Credit Strength of Tax Lien ABS

Subordination and rapid OC buildup provide tax lien ABS with a very durable credit enhancement structure. Even under stressed redemption, recovery, and loss timing assumptions, the credit enhancement structures of tax lien ABS are able to absorb a significant level of cumulative losses without investors being impacted. Exhibit 5 shows breakeven cumulative losses at various redemption speeds for the sample transaction described in Exhibit 2. Note that assumptions with respect to recovery rates and loss timing are intentionally conservative. Although the average lien to value of the sample collateral pool is 8%, it is assumed that each lien that fails to redeem receives no recovery value. In addition, losses are assumed to start in month 12 even though the statutory holding period in Florida and New Jersey is 24 months.

PERFORMANCE VARIABLES

Given the relative newness and private nature of this asset class, few lien level performance models have been made available to the public. It is difficult, therefore, to quantify the impact that some collateral characteristics will have on credit and redemption performance. From looking at aggregate performance data, however, we are comfortable that the main variables impacting the credit and redemption performance of tax liens include lien seller, lien to value, jurisdiction, and seasoning.

Tax Lien Seller

At this point it is worth noting the difference in collateral quality between private sector and municipal deals. In the former case, most institutional investors have developed specific criteria that preclude the inclusion of high risk collateral in transactions and that risk base price those liens that have less desirable characteristics. In the latter case, the municipality's entire portfolio is generally securitized, including liens with less desirable characteristics. Municipal tax lien transactions will typically have weaker property type and lien to value distributions, and by definition, are less geographically diverse.

The Importance of Lien to Value

Although there are large amounts of structural credit support available in most tax lien securitizations, the main protection afforded investors is the amount of unencumbered value in the underlying properties. Lien to value is by far the most important variable to impact the credit and redemption performance of tax liens. In most private sector transactions, the net equity positions in the properties are very strong. Weighted average lien to value ratios generally average between 5% and 10%. Very few properties in private sector transactions have lien to value ratios that are greater than 25%. Typically, high lien to value (greater than 25%) concentrations are less than 10%. As indicated in our tax lien ABS breakeven analysis, loss severities of 100% must be assumed at the collateral level before losses start to impair the credit enhancement provided by the tax lien ABS structure. More importantly, the threat of losing the property at a tax deed or foreclosure auction is significant motivation for either the property owner or other interested party (a mortgage holder, for example) to repay the delinquent taxes. Most private sector tax lien purchasers have very little loss history to report as a result of high back-ended redemption rates.

Since lien to value is a key variable governing both credit and redemption performance, institutional tax lien investors generally go to great lengths in their origination and servicing procedures to ensure that property values are accurate. Most institutional tax lien investors have procedures in place that require elevated levels of due diligence based upon property type, assessed value, lien amount, and municipality. For example, the lien to value on a $2,000 lien on a residential property with assessed value of $125,000 in Dade County Florida will most likely rely on the county's assessed value. This is because of the low lien amount and the fact that assessed values on Florida residential properties are generally very accurate (the assessed value typically underestimates market value in Florida by approximately 10% to 15%). In contrast, a $100,000 lien on an $500,000 industrial site in Newark, NJ would probably require a drive-by appraisal to estimate value and a commercial inspection report to validate property conditions. Servicers are also vigilant about monitoring equity levels over time. Most have procedures in place that require appraisal updates at regular intervals of time.

Investment banks also put a good deal of effort into validating the level of net equity in the properties through their own due diligence process. In one recent tax lien transaction, we selected random and adverse samples of liens backed by residential and commercial properties representing roughly 2.5% of the securitized portfolio. On the residential properties, broker price opinions were obtained, while on the commercial properties, assessed values were confirmed with the relevant county. Every property received a drive-by inspection to validate property conditions. The results of our review showed that on average, stated lien to value ratios on the sample were overstated (to high) by approximately 5% regardless of property type. This due diligence result is one of the strongest we have seen.

Reasons for Delinquency

Given the low lien to value ratios, why would property owners be delinquent on their taxes? We have talked to various originators and servicers of tax liens and have found the following to be common causes of delinquency:

- Ineffective servicing on the part of the municipality
- The property is not a primary residence. The property owner is not present to pay the bill. This is a particularly frequent occurrence in Florida.
- Taxpayers are experiencing short-term financial distress or face more pressing financial needs.
- Commercial property owners may use the delinquency as an alternative form of financing. As rates get bid down on properties, the tax lien may be cheaper than a no documentation loan.
- Property value is less than the total of all encumbrances on the property. This would not necessarily hurt the tax lien holder as the tax lien represents the most senior lien on the property. In fact, it is likely that the holder of a mortgage on the property would pay the tax lien in order to preserve the value of the mortgage.

Jurisdiction and Seasoning Impact Redemption Performance

While limiting the potential for future losses, low lien to value ratios are also the main driver of tax lien redemption (repayment) performance. Most historical data show extremely fast redemption rates, particularly in the early months of delinquency or as the liens move close to tax deed or foreclosure status. Exhibit 6 shows static pool redemption performance for Florida tax liens over a 3-year period. All three static pools share a remarkably consistent story. During the first year of delinquency, the data show a 60% constant liquidation rate. This fast early redemption rate is likely explained by the fact that many property owners may just be finding out about the delinquent tax and the penalties incurred. During the second year of delinquency, redemptions slow to a 50% constant liquidation rate. However, as the tax liens move closer to tax deed status in month 24, redemptions spike up into the 90% constant liquidation rate range. The redemption seasoning pattern of these tax liens is front and back loaded due to the statutory penalty structure and statutory holding period in place in the state of Florida. Tax liens located in other jurisdictions may show different redemption seasoning patterns due to statutes that are specific to those jurisdictions.

PRICING ASSUMPTIONS

The key pricing assumptions for a tax lien transaction are the *constant liquidation rate* and *subsequent purchase rate*. The constant liquidation rate, or CLR, represents the annualized percentage of outstanding lien redemptive value (delinquent tax amount plus interest and penalties) which pays off in any monthly period and is broadly analogous to a CPR in a mortgage deal. Subsequent purchase rates represent the annualized percentage of outstanding lien redemptive value that is purchased monthly in order to maintain the trust's senior interest in the underlying property. Subsequent purchase rates are similar to draw rates in HELOC transactions.

Exhibit 6: Florida Tax Lien Liquidation Rates

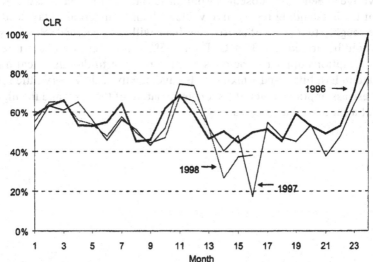

Exhibit 7: Tax Lien ABS WAL Sensitivity to Changing CLR Assumptions

Scenario	A	B	C	D	E
Florida Tax Liens	40%	45%	50%	55%	60%
Florida Tax Deeds	90%	90%	90%	90%	90%
New Jersey Tax Liens	25%	30%	35%	40%	45%
Tax Lien ABS WAL	1.3	1.3	1.2	1.1	1.0

Assumes subsequent purchases occur at pricing assumptions, issuer exercises the right to retire bonds on optional termination date.

Exhibit 8: Tax Lien ABS WAL Sensitivity to Changing Subsequent Purchase Rate Assumptions

Scenario	A	B	C	D	E
Florida Tax Liens	100%	150%	200%	250%	300%
New Jersey Tax Liens	25%	30%	35%	40%	45%
Tax Lien ABS WAL	1.3	1.2	1.2	1.1	1.1

Assumes CLRs occur at pricing assumptions, issuer exercises the right to retire bonds on optional termination date.

Given that state specific statutory procedures control the redemption process, pricing assumptions on tax lien transactions are made on a state specific basis. Assuming the collateral composition outlined in the example provided in Exhibit 2, we would price the Florida tax liens to a 50% CLR and Florida tax deeds to a 90% CLR. Given historical data, the 50% CLR for liens appears to be a conservative speed. The subsequent purchase rate for Florida is assumed to be 200% of the outstanding redemptive value of liens transferred to tax deed status because roughly two years of subsequent liens will have accrued. New Jersey tax liens would be priced to a 35% CLR and 35% subsequent purchase rate. Both these assumptions appear to be conservative relative to the historical data. As illustrated in Exhibits 7 and 8 tax lien ABS average lives show very little sensitivity to these assumptions given the short-term nature of the asset and the high likelihood of a successful auction call.

Commercial Mortgage-Backed Securities

Chapter 23

Commercial Mortgage-Backed Securities

Anthony B. Sanders, Ph.D.
Professor of Finance and Galbreath Distinguished Scholar
The Ohio State University

INTRODUCTION

Commercial mortgage-backed securities (CMBS) represent an interesting departure from residential MBS. With residential MBS, the underlying collateral is loans on residential properties (1-4 units). With CMBS, the underlying collateral is loans on retail properties, office properties, industrial properties, multifamily housing, and hotels. Unlike residential mortgage loans, commercial loans tend to be "locked out" from prepayment for 10 years. Counterbalancing the reduction of prepayment risk for CMBS is the increase in default risk.

Both CMBS and real estate investment trusts (REITs) have grown tremendously since 1995 as investors' tastes for new real estate-related products have increased. Investment banks were able to apply what they have learned from residential MBS and apply it (with some interesting twists) to the commercial real estate loan market. Not only is the U.S. market continuing to expand, but also CMBS is growing at an ever-increasing rate in Europe (albeit at a much smaller scale). This chapter focuses on the interesting twists that make CMBS such a fascinating product.

THE CMBS DEAL

A CMBS is formed when an issuer deposits commercial loans into a trust. The issuer then creates securities in the form of classes of bonds backed by the commercial loans. As payments on the commercial loans (and any lump-sum repayment of principal) arc received,. they are distributed (passed through) to the bondholders according to the rules governing the distribution of proceeds.

Bond Passthrough Rates

An example of a recent CMBS deal can be used to highlight the distribution of cash flows to the bondholders and the rules governing the distribution. The

GMAC 1999-C3 deal, underwritten jointly by Deutsche Bank and Goldman Sachs, is summarized in Exhibit 1. The balance of the bonds as of the cutoff date (9/10/99) is $1,152,022,048. The gross weighted-average coupon (WACg) is 7.90% and the net weighted-average coupon (WACn) is 7.79%. The weighted-average maturity (WAM) is 117 months

The bonds are sequential-pay. The passthrough rate for class A-1-a is 6.97% and fixed. The passthrough rates for classes A-1-b, A-2, B, C, G, H, J, K, L, M, and N are equal to the lesser of the fixed passthrough rate and net WAC of the mortgage pool. For example, the A-1-b bondholders will receive the lesser of the fixed passthrough rate (7.27%) and the net WAC (7.79%). Passthrough rates for classes D, E, and F are equal to the WAC of the mortgage pool.

Class X is an interest-only class. Class X receives the excess of the net WAC received from tile pool over the weighted-average passthrough rate paid to the sequential-pay bonds. Class X's notional balance equals the outstanding balance of the sequential-pay bonds.

CMBS Ratings and Subordination Levels

The rating agencies play a critical role in the CMBS market. The role of the rating agency is to provide a third-party opinion on the quality of each bond in the structure (as well as the necessary level of credit enhancement to achieve a desired rating level). The rating agency examines critical characteristics of the underlying pool of loans such as the *debt service coverage ratio* (DSCR) and the *loan-to-value ratio* (LTV). If the target ratios at the asset level are below a certain level, the credit rating of the bond is reduced. Subordination can be used at the structure level to improve the rating of the bond. For example, suppose that a certain class of property requires a DSCR of 1.50× to qualify for an A rating; if the actual DSCR is only 1.25×, additional subordination can be added at the deal level to bring the rating to an A rating.

The credit ratings for the bonds in the GMAC 1999-C3 deal are presented in Exhibit 1. Fitch rated the first three bonds (A-1-a, A-1-b, and A-2) AAA Moody's rated the same bond classes as Aaa. The B through F bonds have progressively lower ratings. The subordination level decline with the bond ratings: 27% subordination for the AAA bond down to 10.5% for the BBB– bond. The subordination levels continue to drop for the C bond (17.5%) through the N bond (0%).

Prioritization of Payments

The highest-rated bonds are paid-off first in the CMBS structure. Any return of principal caused by amortization, prepayment, or default is used to repay the highest-rated tranche first and then the lower-rated bonds. Any interest received on outstanding principal is paid to all tranches. However, it is important to note that many deals vary from this simplistic prioritization assumption.

For example, consider the GMAC 1999-C3 deal. The bonds that are rated AAA by Fitch (classes A-1-a, A-1-b, and A-2) are the Senior Certificates. Classes

B through M are organized in a simple sequential structure. Principal and interest are distributed first to the class B and last to the class N. Unfortunately, the Senior Certificates are not as simple in their prioritization.

The loans underlying the GMAC 1999-C3 are divided into two groups. Group 2 consists of the multifamily loans and Group 1 consists of the remaining loans (retail, office, warehouse, and so on). In terms of making distributions to the Senior Certificates, 61% of Group 1's distribution amount is transferred to Group 2's distribution amount. Group 1's distribution amount is used to pay:

1. Interest on bond classes A-1-a, A-1-b, and the portion of interest on the Class X on components A-1-a and A-1-b pro rata, and
2. Principal to the Class A-1-a and A-1-b in that order.

Loan Group 2's distribution amount is used to pay:

1. Interest on Class A-2 and the portion of interest on the Class X components from A-2 to N pro rata, and
2. Principal to the Class A-2;

In the event where the balances of all the subordinated classes (Class B through Class M) have been reduced to zero because of the allocation of losses, the principal and interest will be distributed on a pro rata basis to Classes A-1-a, A-1-b, and A-2.

Exhibit 1: Bonds for GMAC 1999-C3 deal

Bond	Moody Rating	Fitch Rating	Original Amount	Subordination Original	Coupon	Coupon Type
A-1-a	Aaa	AAA	$50,000,000	0.2700	0.0697	Fixed
A-1-b	Aaa	AAA	$190,976,000	0.2700	0.0727	Fixed
A-2	Aaa	AAA	$600,000,000	0.2700	0.0718	Fixed
B	Aa2	AA	$51,840,000	0.2250	0.0754	Fixed
C	A2	A	$57,601,000	0.1750	0.0779	Fixed
D	A3	A−	$20,160,000	0.1575	0.0779	WAC-0b
E	Baa2	BBB	$37,440,000	0.1250	0.0779	WAC-0b
F	Baa3	BBB−	$23,040,000	0.1050	0.0779	WAC-0b
G	NA	NA	$57,601,000	0.0550	0.0697	Fixed
H	NA	NA	$8,640,000	0.0475	0.0697	Fixed
J	NA	NA	$11,520,000	0.0375	0.0697	Fixed
K	NA	NA	$14,400,000	0.0250	0.0697	Fixed
L	NA	NA	$11,520,000	0.0150	0.0697	Fixed
M	NA	NA	$5,760,000	0.0100	0.0697	Fixed
N	NA	NA	$11,524,048	0.0000	0.0697	Fixed
X	NA	NA	$1,152,022,048n	NA	0.0053	WAC/IO
R	NA	NA	$0r	NA	0	

Source: Charter Research.

Loan default adds an additional twist to the structuring. Any losses that arise from loan defaults will be charged against the principal balance of the lowest rated CMBS bond tranche that is outstanding (also known as the *first loss piece*). For the GMAC 1999-C3 deal, losses are allocated in reverse sequential order from Class N through Class B. After Class B is retired, classes A-1-a, A-1-b, and A-2 bear losses on a pro-rata basis. As a consequence, a localized market decline (such as a rapid decline in the Boston real estate market) can lead to the sudden termination of a bond tranche. Hence, issuers seek strategies that will minimize the likelihood of a "microburst" of defaults.

As long as there is no delinquency, the CMBS are well behaved. Unfortunately, delinquency triggers intervention by the servicer (whose role will be discussed later in the chapter). In the event of a delinquency, there may be insufficient cash to make all scheduled payments. In this case, the servicer is supposed to advance both principal and interest. The principal and interest continue to be advanced by the servicer as long as these amounts are recoverable.

Call Protection

In the residential MBS market, the vast majority of mortgages have no prepayment penalties. In the CMBS market, the vast majority of mortgages have some form of prepayment penalty that can impact the longevity and yield of a bond. Call protection can be made at both the loan level and in the CMBS structure. At the loan level, there exist several forms of call protection: prepayment lockout, yield maintenance, defeasance, and prepayment penalties.

Prepayment lockout is where the borrower is contractually prohibited from prepaying the loan during the lockout period. The lockout is the most stringent form of call protection since it removes the option for the borrower to prepay before the end of the lockout period. The prepayment lockout is commonly used in newer CMBS deals.

Under *yield maintenance,* the borrower is required to pay a "make whole" penalty to the lender if the loan is prepaid. The penalty is calculated as the difference between the present value of the loan's remaining cash flows at the time of prepayment and principal prepayment. Yield maintenance was a common form of call protection in older CMBS deals but it is less common in newer deals.

Defeasance is calculated in the same manner as yield maintenance. However, instead of passing the loan repayment and any penalty through to the investor, the borrower invests that cash in U.S. Treasury securities (strips/bills) to fulfill the remaining cash flow structure of the loan. The Treasuries replace the building as collateral for the loan. The expected cash flows for that loan remain intact through to the final maturity date. Like yield maintenance, it was more popular with older CMBS deals and is less common in newer deals.

With *prepayment penalties,* the borrower must pay a fixed percentage of the unpaid balance of the loan as a prepayment penalty if the borrower wishes to refinance. The penalty usually declines as the loan ages (e.g., starting with 5% of the outstanding principal in the first year, 4% in the second year, etc., until the penalty evaporates).

Exhibits 2 and 3 examine the largest 20 loans underlying the GMAC 1999-C3 deal. In terms of call protection, each of the loans is locked-out. The average lockout has about 114 months remaining. Hence, the loans underling this CMBS deal have just less than 10 years of prepayment protection.

In addition to call protection at the loan level, call protection is available in structural form as well. Since CMBS bond structures are sequential-pay, lower-rated tranches cannot pay down until the higher-rated tranches are retired. This is the exact opposite of default where principal losses hit the lowest-rated tranches first.

Timing of Principal Repayment

Unlike residential mortgages that are fully amortized over a long time period (say, 30 years), commercial loans underlying CMBS deals are often *balloon loans*. Balloon loans require substantial principal payment on the final maturity date although the loan is fully amortized over a longer period of time. For example, a loan can be fully amortized over 30 years but require a full repayment of outstanding principal after the tenth year. The purpose of a balloon loan is to keep the periodic loan payment of interest and principal as low as possible.

Exhibit 2: The Twenty Largest Loans Underlying the GMAC 1999-C3 Deal

	Name	Location, MSA	Category	Loan Amount
1	Biltmore Fashion	Phoenix, Arizona	Retail	$80,000,000
2	Prime Outlets	Niagara Falls, New York	Retail	$62,835,426
3	Equity Inns	Various	Hotel	$46,511,317
4	One Colorado	Pasadena, California	Retail	$42,628,093
5	Comerica Bank	San Jose, California	Office	$33,640,510
6	120 Monument	Indianapolis, Indiana	Office	$28,955,362
7	125 Maiden	New York, New York	Office	$28,500,000
8	Texas Development	Houston, Texas	Apartment	$26,926,701
9	Sherman Plaza	Van Nuys, California	Office	$25,984,904
10	Alliance TP	Various	Apartment	$24,888,157
11	Bush Tower	New York, New York	Office	$23,000,000
12	County Line	Jackson, Mississippi	Retail	$20,990,264
13	Sherwood Lakes	Schererville, Indiana	Apartment	$20,162,442
14	Laurel Portfolio	Various	Apartment	$17,950,331
15	Sweet Paper	Various	Warehouse	$17,420,000
16	Sheraton Portsmouth	Portsmouth, New Hampshire	Hotel	$15,949,087
17	Trinity Commons	Fort Worth, Texas	Retail	$15,242,981
18	Village Square	Indianapolis, Indiana	Apartment	$14,993,950
19	Golden Books	Fayetteville, North Carolina	Warehouse	$14,493,350
20	Air Touch	Dublin, Ohio	Office	$13,992,523

Source: Charter Research.

Exhibit 3: Loan Characteristics for the Twenty Largest Loans Underlying the GMAC 1999-C3 Deal

	Name	Coupon	Maturity	Current Occupancy	DSCR	LTV	Prepay Lockout
1	Biltmore Fashion	7.68%	07/01/09	96.00%	1.43	60.40%	114
2	Prime Outlets	7.60%	05/01/09	96.00%	1.36	72.70%	109
3	Equity Inns	8.37%	07/01/09	NA	1.90	49.50%	114
4	One Colorado	8.29%	07/01/09	91.00%	1.25	72.30%	114
5	Comerica Bank	7.55%	05/01/08	99.00%	1.43	65.20%	32
6	120 Monument	8.09%	06/01/09	100.00%	1.23	74.40%	113
7	125 Maiden	8.12%	09/01/09	97.00%	1.31	73.80%	116
8	Texas Development	7.44%	05/01/09	NA	1.34	72.00%	114
9	Sherman Plaza	7.68%	08/01/09	95.00%	1.24	68.40%	115
10	Alliance TP	7.32%	08/01/09	NA	1.19	86.40%	112
11	Bush Tower	7.99%	08/01/09	97.00%	1.27	46.00%	115
12	County Line	7.91%	08/01/09	98.00%	1.39	84.00%	115
13	Sherwood Lakes	6.99%	02/01/08	94.00%	1.32	76.70%	94
14	Laurel Portfolio	7.37%	05/01/09	NA	1.22	73.60%	112
15	Sweet Paper	8.26%	06/01/09	NA	1.25	71.40%	113
16	Sheraton Portsmouth	8.53%	05/01/09	71.00%	1.28	72.50%	116
17	Trinity Commons	7.93%	08/01/09	97.00%	1.44	68.80%	115
18	Village Square	7.80%	10/01/07	97.00%	1.28	79.30%	93
19	Golden Books	8.50%	08/01/09	100.00%	1.69	67.40%	119
20	Air Touch	7.98%	08/01/09	100.00%	1.20	77.70%	117

Notes: A * in the Prepay Lockout column denotes that yield maintenance is used in conjunction with Prepay Lockout.

Source: Charter Research.

Balloon loans pose potential problems for investors due to the large, lump-sum payment that must be refinanced. If there is a change in the quality of the underlying asset (e.g., a decline in the real estate market, increased competition leading to a decline in lease rates, etc.), there is a danger that the loan will not be refinanced; this can result in default. In order to prevent this type of loan failure at the balloon date from occurring, there are two types of loan provisions: the internal tail and the external tail.

The *internal tail* requires the borrower to provide evidence that an effort is underway to refinance the loan prior to the balloon date (say, 1 year prior to the balloon date). The lender would require that the borrower obtain a refinancing commitment before the balloon date (say, 6 months prior to the balloon date). With an *external tail,* the maturity date of the CMBS deal is set to be longer than that of the underlying loans. This allows the borrower more time to arrange refinancing while avoiding default on the bond obligations. The servicer advances any missing interest and scheduled principal in this buffer period.

Exhibit 4: Aggregate Loan Amounts by State for GMAC 1999-C3 Deal

State	Loan Amount	No. of Loans	% of Pool
California	$257,522,410	33	22.35%
Texas	$162,355,125	26	14.09%
New York	$130,070,471	7	11.29%
Arizona	$99,942,794	5	8.68%
Indiana	$68,623,516	5	5.96%
Ohio	$44,982,528	5	3.90%
Mississippi	$23,067,864	2	2.00%
New Jersey	$22,983,973	5	2.00%
Other	$342,473,371	50	29.73%
Total	$1,152,022,052	138	100.00%

Source: Charter Research.

THE UNDERLYING LOAN PORTFOLIO

There are two sources of risk relating to the underlying loan portfolio. The first risk is prepayment risk and the second risk is default/delinquency risk.

Diversification

A factor that is often considered when analyzing the risk of a CMBS deal is the diversification of the underlying loans across space. The reasoning for what is termed "spatial diversification" is that the default risk of the underlying pool of loans is lessened if the loans are made on properties in different regions of the country. Rather than have the entire portfolio of loans being subject to an idiosyncratic risk factor (e.g., the decline in oil prices and the collapse of the Houston real estate market), the portfolio can spread its risks across numerous economies. Thus, a collapse of the Houston real estate market (which may lead to higher defaults on commercial loans) will be less of a concern if the commercial property markets in Chicago, Kansas City, New York, and Seattle remain strong.

The strategy of spatial diversification can be seen in Exhibit 4. Approximately 22% of the loans underlying the GMAC 1999-C3 are on properties in California, 14% on properties in Texas, and 11% on properties in New York. The remaining loans are spread out among other states such as New Hampshire, Missouri, Illinois, and Mississippi. Thus, the GMAC 1999-C3 deal has achieved a significant degree of spatial diversification. Although a 22% concentration factor for California is still quite large, it is considerably less than a 100% concentration-factor (which is often referred to as a "pure play" strategy). Furthermore, California, Texas, and New York represent the states where most of the commercial loans are being originated.

Exhibit 5: Aggregate Loan Amounts by Property Type for GMAC 1999-C3 Deal

Property Type	Loan Amount	No. of Loans	% of Pool
Apartment	$259,779,802	39	22.55%
Office	$322,053,844	36	27.96%
Retail	$350,683,062	34	30.44%
Warehouse	$99,126,075	15	8.60%
Hotel	$105,832,139	8	9.19%
Other	$14,547,130	6	1.26%
Total	$1,152,022,052	138	100.00%

Source: Charter Research.

Exhibit 6: Characteristics for Loans Underlying the GMAC 1999-C3 Deal by Property Type

Property Type	Coupon	Due	Current Occupancy	DSCR	LTV	Prepay Lockout
Apartment	7.62%	06/29/09	92.92%	1.29	76.51%	113
Office	7.79%	04/03/09	96.17%	1.33	67.84%	107
Retail	7.95%	09/19/09	95.21%	1.36	69.77%	116
Warehouse	8.13%	06/27/09	99.56%	1.42	68.28%	115
Hotel	8.50%	12/31/08	75.18%	1.65	58.93%	109
Other	7.83%	05/13/09	95.11%	1.54	67.00%	113

Source: Charter Research.

In addition to spatial diversification, CMBS pools can be diversified across property types. Rating agencies tend to give lower levels of credit-enhancement to deals that contain diversification across property types since a pool that is diversified across residential, office, industrial, and retail will likely avoid the potential of a national glut in one of the sectors (such as the retail market).

The degree of property type diversification can be seen in Exhibit 5. Approximately 90% of the loans are on retail, apartments, and office properties with retail having the largest percentage (30.44%). As a consequence, the GMAC 1999-C3 deals have reduced the risk of default by not being heavily concentrated in only one of the property groups.

The loan characteristics of the pool underlying the GMAC 1999-C3 pools are presented in Exhibit 6. The hotel properties are viewed as being the most risky given that they have the highest coupon (8.50%), the highest DSCR (1.65×), and the lowest LTV (58.93%). The apartment properties are viewed as the safest risk with the lowest coupon (7.62%), the lowest DSCR (1.29×), and the highest LTV (76.51%). As can be seen in Exhibits 5 and 6, 90% of the underlying loans are in the three least-risky property types: apartment, office, and retail.

Cross-Collateralization

Diversification of the underlying collateral is one way of reducing default risk. Another way to reduce default risk is to use cross-collateralization. *Cross-collateralization* means that the properties that serve as collateral for the individual loans are pledged against each loan. Thus, the cash flows on several properties can be used to make loan payments on a property which has insufficient funds to make a loan payment. This "pooling" mechanism reduces the risk of default. To add some additional enforcement penalties to the cross-collateralization mechanism, the lender can use cross-default which allows the lender to call each loan within the pool, when any one defaults.

Loan Analysis

There are several products available that provide analysis of the underlying collateral for CMBS deals. An example of a package that allows for the analysis of the CMBS deal and the underlying collateral is Conquest, an on-line service provided by Charter Research in Boston. Conquest provides for a detailed examination of each loan in the underlying portfolio. In addition to simply describing the loan data (DSCR, LTV, loan maturity, prepayment lock type, etc.), Conquest provides default risk (delinquency) analysis as well. Using vendors such as Torto Wheaton, Conquest forecasts the growth in net operating income and value for each property in the underlying portfolio.

Torto Wheaton, for example, provides 10-year forecasts of net operating income and value by geographic area (MSA) property type (office, industrial, retail, and apartments). These forecasts are updated quarterly. Torto Wheaton provides five scenarios ranging from best to worst cases. Given these five scenarios, the user is able to examine the future path of debt service coverage and loan to value for each loan in the pool. Thus, the user is able to examine default and extension risk tendencies on a loan-by-loan basis. This information is aggregated to the deal level so that changes in the riskiness for each of the underlying loans is reflected in the cash flows for each tranche at the deal level.

Stress Testing at the Loan Level

Stress testing the collateral in a CMBS deal is important from both the underwriter and investor perspective. By allowing the forecasts on net operating income and value to be varied over time, underwriters and investors can better understand the default risk and extension risk likelihoods and how these in turn impact CMBS cash flows.

For CMBS markets, stress tests must be performed in a manner that is consistent with modern portfolio theory. While diversification across property type and economic region reduces the default risk of the underlying loan pool, the effects of diversification are negated if the stress test ignores the covariance between the properties. For example, there should be some degree of common variance across all properties (reflecting general economic conditions). Furthermore, there should be some degree of common variance across property type and economic regions.

The Torto Wheaton approach of generating five forecast paths by property type and geographic location permits the construction of a distribution of future outcomes for property value and net operating income growth for the loan pool. Based on Torto Wheaton forecasts, the user can determine the degree to which the portfolio is diversified (by reducing the variance of the distribution of future outcomes). An index of diversification can be created that allows users to compare the degree of diversification across different CMBS deals. Thus, stress testing the underlying properties can be measured in the aggregate by how much the diversification index is changed.

In addition to being able to create a diversification index, the user can construct a default risk/extension risk index as well. As the underlying loans are stressed, a distribution of outcomes in terms of default and extension risk can be obtained. This would allow users to compare CMBS deals not only for the diversification of the underlying loan portfolio, but compare CMBS deals for sensitivity to the stress test.

Historical Aspect on Loan Performance

While a detailed analysis of loan performance models is beyond the scope of this chapter, it is important to recognize that CMBS deals are not free of prepayment, default, and delinquencies. In Exhibit 7, the historical default and prepayment information for deals with a cutoff date in 1994 (from the Conquest database) are presented. As one can see, there is a wide range in terms of the ratio of performing loans to original loans in the pool. The KPAC 1994-M1 deal has the lowest performing loan ratio of 11.48%. On the other hand, the DLJ 1994-MF 11 has a performing loan ratio of 98.72%. The average performing loan ratio is 46.34% for the 13 deals from 1994.

Exhibit 7: Historical Default and Prepayment for CMBS Deals with Cutoff Dates in 1994

Deal	Loans	Performing	Matured	Prepaid	Bankrupt	Fore.	REO*
ASC 1994-C3	40	21	3	13	0	3	0
ASC 1994-MD1	9	7	1	1	0	0	0
ASFS 1993-2	30	19	4	5	1	1	0
ASFS 1994-C2	39	6	26	7	0	0	0
CLAC 1994-1	89	37	33	19	0	0	0
CSFB 1994-CFB1	63	21	8	34	0	0	0
DLJ 1993-MF 17	42	38	0	4	0	0	0
DLJ 1994-MF 11	78	77	0	1	0	0	0
KPAC 1994-M1	61	7	13	41	0	0	0
MCFI 1994-MC1	44	9	9	26	0	0	0
MLMI 1994-M1	80	32	28	20	0	0	0
SASC 1994-C1	185	67	51	53	0	0	14
SASC 1995-C1	142	30	21	71	0	5	15

Source: Charter Research.

Exhibit 8: Percentage Disposition of Loans Underlying 1994 CMBS Deals

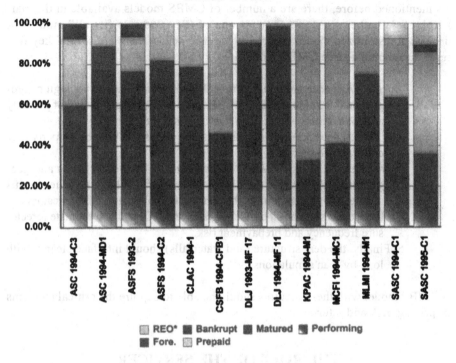

Source: Charter Research

It should be noted that the average performing loan ratio of 46.34% could be explained, in part, by underlying loan maturity. On average, 20.58% on the loans underlying deals from 1994 matured. Mortgage prepayments account for approximately 30.33% of the original loans terminating. Foreclosures, defaults, and real estate owned (REO) comprise only 2.50% of the 13 deals from 1994. Interestingly, the DLJ CMBS deals have a very high performance loan ratio (90% and 98%) with few loan maturities and prepayments (and no defaults or foreclosures).

Despite the historical performance of these deals, analysts must be careful about projecting these results for current deals. Prepayment lockouts, which are more popular now than they were in 1994, will be more effective in determining prepayments than simple yield maintenance provisions. Also, longer-term mortgage loans will extend the duration of the underlying loan pool (keeping the performance loan ratio higher for a longer period of time). Finally, improvements in underwriting and the investor's ability to understand the underlying collateral should improve default and foreclosure risk over time.

CREATING A CMBS MODEL

As mentioned before, there are a number of CMBS models available in the marketplace. Whether someone chooses one of the "one size fits all" models or designs a customized model tailored to specific needs, there are several key features that should be in a CMBS model.

1. An econometric model of historical loan performance using logit or proportional hazards model. This permits a better understanding of property and loan attributes that predict default and prepayment.
2. If default does occur, empirical estimates of loss severity by property type and state are needed.
3. Database of actual *NOI and Value volatility* by property type and geographic location (see the discussion of Torto Wheaton earlier in this chapter). This step permits the construction of default risk indicators.
4. Monte carlo simulation of interest rates and NOI paths to estimate foreclosure frequency and prepayment risk.
5. Finally, the deal structure (and waterfalls) should interface cleanly with loan-by-loan simulations.

A CMBS model with these features should be able to capture the critical elements of pricing, risk and return.

THE ROLE OF THE SERVICER

The servicer on a CMBS deal plays an important role. The servicer collects monthly loan payments, keeps records relating to payments, maintains escrow accounts, monitors the condition of underlying properties, prepares reports for trustee and transfers collected funds to trustee for payment.

There are three types of servicers: the subservicer, the master servicer and the special servicer. The *subservicer* is typically loan originator in a conduit deal who has decided to sell the loan but retain the servicing. The subservicer will then send all payments and property information to the *master servicer*. The master servicer oversees the deal and makes sure the servicing agreements are maintained. In addition, the master servicer must facilitate the timely payment of interest and principal. When a loan goes into default, the master servicer has the responsibility to provide for servicing advances.

Unlike the subservicer and the master servicer, the *special servicer* enters the picture when a loan becomes more than 60 days past due. Often, the special servicer is empowered to extend the loan, restructure the loan and foreclose on the loan (and sell the property). This critical role is of great importance to the subordinated tranche owners because the timing of the loss can significantly impact the loss severity, which in turn can greatly impact subordinated returns. Thus, first-loss investors usually want to either control the appointment of the special servicer or perform the role themselves. This creates a potential moral hazard problem since the special servicer may act in their own self-interest and potentially at the expense of the other tranche holders.

INNOVATIONS IN THE CMBS MARKET: "BUY-UP" LOANS

A recent innovation in the CMBS market is the "buy-*up*" loan. Most participants in the mortgage market are familiar with the "buy-*down*" loan in the residential market. With a buydown loan, a borrower pays "points" upfront to reduce the mortgage interest rate. The resulting loan, having a lower interest rate, is less sensitive to prepayment and has a greater duration than a higher interest rate loan. The buy-up loan in the commercial mortgage market is the exact opposite, but with a twist.

Consider a borrower who approaches a commercial mortgage lender for a $1 million loan. They agree on an 8.00% interest rate with the loan being fully amortized over 30 years (using monthly amortization). The resulting monthly mortgage payment would $7,337.65. The DSCR for the loan (based on annual NOI of $100,000) is 1.14× while the LTV is 71.40%. (See Exhibit 9.)

Suppose that the rating agency requires additional loan subordination (or gives a lower rating) if the loan in question has an LTV in excess of 65%. However, the subordination level would be reduced (and/or the rating increased) if the loan has an LTV of 65% or less. With a buy-up loan, the monthly payments of $7,337.65 are discounted at an interest rate of 9.00% (instead of 8.00%) resulting in a present value of the loan being $911,936.30. Although the DSCR remains the same, the LTV declines to 64.9%, thus qualifying the loan for lower subordination levels (and/or a higher rating).

Exhibit 9: A Comparison of a Standard Loan and a Buy-up Loan

	Standard	Buy-up
NOI (annual)	$100,000.00	$100,000.00
Loan size	$1,000,000.00	$911,936.30
Amount to borrower	$1,000,000.00	$1,000,000.00
Loan term	360	360
Mtg rate	8.00%	9.00%
Monthly payment	$7,337.65	$7,337.65
DSCR	1.14	1.14
LTV - PV of loan	71.4	64.9
LTV - amt to borrower	71.4	71.4

The problem facing the rating agency is selecting the correct LTV. Clearly, for the purpose of correctly identifying default risk; the LTV should be used that is based on the actual amount disbursed to the borrower, not the present value of the mortgage payments. The definition of LTV caused some problems when buy-up loans were first used since it was unclear which definition of LTV the lender was using. Once the rating agencies recognized there were multiple definitions of LTV, the lenders began to report both LTVs.

Technically, the difference between the amount disbursed to the borrower ($1,000,000) and the present value of the buy-up loan ($911,936.30) is the buy-up premium. The documents on a CMBS deal containing buy-up loans will most likely say that the buy-up loan is locked out; furthermore, in case of prepayment, the borrower would owe both the buy-up loan amount and the buy-up premium. The higher interest rate on the buy-up loan (with its lockout provision) means that there is more interest for an IO class.

SUMMARY

The purpose of this chapter is to provide a broad overview of the CMBS market from the point of view of a sample CMBS deal. Although CMBS deals tend to be prepayment insensitive, bonds (or tranches) will still be somewhat sensitive to interest rate changes since lockouts usually dissolve after 10 years. Default risk is a concern with CMBS and the underlying collateral needs to be examined on a loan-by-loan basis. Products currently available make this task much more tractable.

Chapter 24

Structure, Valuation, and Performance of CMBS

Rich Gordon
Director
First Union Securities, Inc.

Lang Gibson
Vice President
First Union Securities, Inc.

INTRODUCTION

In this chapter we discuss the structural features, relative value, risk/return characteristics, hedging strategies, and regulatory environment for CMBS.

RISK, RETURN, AND PRICING IN THE CMBS MARKET

Because of their contractual and structural prepayment protection and sensitivity to credit risk, CMBS spreads are more correlated with corporate bond and swap spreads than residential mortgage securities. From October 1997 to August 1998, the spread between AAA CMBS and AAA corporates held constant at 40 bps. During the bond market discord from August to November 1998, spreads widened to as high as 140 bps in October and have moved in a range of 40 bps–80 bps since November 1998.

The wider spreads found in CMBS versus same-rated corporates can be explained by the following factors:

- *Analytical challenge of studying multiple loans versus corporate cash flow (dependence on ratings).* CMBS require more analysis, so they have wider spreads to compensate investors for analytical complexity. However, the advantage to the investor is that the large number of loans provides ample time to react to credit degradation, whereas corporates have significant event risk.

407

- *Liquidity premium.* Although liquidity risk took its toll on all spread markets in October 1998, the problem was exacerbated for CMBS, which were hit by a combination of factors: greater financing costs, higher hedge costs as swap spreads widened, dealers aggregating collateral for much larger deals over a longer period than with current smaller joint-issuer deals, and a higher composition of leveraged investors in the CMBS market than is the case now.
- *The unwillingness of natural mortgage security buyers to learn a new collateral class.* Although the rating agencies are conservative in their criteria, many traditional residential mortgage-backed securities (RMBS) buyers have not yet become active in the market. CMBS still tend to trade wider than corporates due in part to a narrower market sponsorship. Therefore, there is an opportunity for those investors willing to learn the characteristics of this younger market.
- *Extension risk.* Most commercial mortgages are underwritten with a stated final maturity of 15–30 years and a balloon payment due after 10 years. The lockout protection in the underlying commercial real estate loans provides excellent protection from prepayment risk, whereas extension will only occur to the extent that borrowers cannot make their balloon payment and make arrangements with the servicer to extend their repayment schedules.
- *Price compression due to prepayments from credit losses.* Although CMBS structures have multiple layers of prepayment protection, unscheduled prepayments can occur. Because of the possibility of unscheduled prepayments, CMBS price appreciation slightly lags that of its bulleted counterparts. Unlike RMBS, this price compression as the bond rises above par is meager. For instance, the AAA tranches might widen about 2 bps per point rise above a price of $103.

As of September 1, 1999, spreads on rated CMBS tranches varied between 125 bps and 375 bps. For example, in the CMFUN 1999-1 deal (Exhibit 1), the 10-year AAA tranche has a 133 bps spread to Treasurys (38 bps swapped back to LIBOR), whereas the BBB- tranche has a 313 bps spread to Treasurys (203 bps swapped back to LIBOR).

Institutional investors that would normally purchase mortgage securities or corporate bonds should consider CMBS as a yield-enhancing investment. Compared with RMBS, CMBS provide significantly higher risk-adjusted returns due to the substantially greater prepayment/extension protection and average life stability. Compared with noncallable corporate bonds, CMBS provide more than adequate spreads to compensate for marginally lower average life stability. Furthermore, with the entry of the Lehman CMBS index into its aggregate fixed-income index, more investors will have to buy CMBS to track and meet their benchmarks.

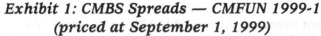

Exhibit 1: CMBS Spreads — CMFUN 1999-1
(priced at September 1, 1999)

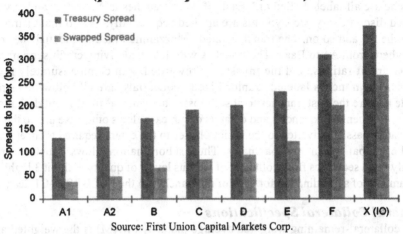

Source: First Union Capital Markets Corp.

VALUATION METHODOLOGY

In this section, we outline an analytic framework for the evaluation of CMBS. We believe this methodology provides a sound and consistent framework for the analysis of these structured products. Using FUCMC's proprietary *Bond Analyzer*, we will show how the various risk/return attributes of CMBS tranches can be evaluated.

The process essentially breaks down into three major steps:

- Understand the deal's general structure and the major characteristics of the underlying collateral
- Assess the structural prepayment protection of the deal and tranche being evaluated
- Run loss scenarios to determine the level of credit risk in the tranche

We look at each of these points in detail, using two deals as examples, FULB 1997-C1 and CMFUN 1999-1.

Understanding a Deal's General Structure and the Major Characteristics of the Underlying Collateral

Assess Structural Elements and Levels of Subordination in the Deal

CMBS deal structures are far simpler than most RMBS collateralized mortgage obligation (CMO) structures. The major structural component of a CMBS deal is credit tranching. To have AAA rated tranches, there must be enough credit support from tranches that absorb any losses on the underlying collateral first. In the top right corner of Exhibit 2, we break down FULB 1997-C1 into three major components of credit tranching. Tranches A1, A2, and A3 and the interest-only (IO) tranche are all labeled "Senior." Each of these tranches is Aaa rated, and any permitted discretionary prepayments are applied sequentially, first to the A1 tranche, then the A2 and so on. The tranches rated "Mezzanine Fixed Sequential" are rated anywhere from Aa to Baa3. The tranches with less underlying credit support have lower credit ratings, and the investor is rewarded with commensurately higher yields. The tranches labeled "Junior Fixed Sequentials" are all below investment grade and are the first tranches to absorb losses to principal from credit defaults.

When delinquencies and defaults occur, cash flows otherwise due to the subordinated class are diverted to the senior classes to the extent required to meet scheduled principal and interest payments. Thus, subordination allows issuers to create highly rated securities from collateral of various levels of quality. Exhibit 3 highlights the amount of subordination for each of the tranches in the FULB 1997-C1 deal.

General Collateral Specifications
The collateral-remaining weighted average maturity (WAM) is the weighted average time remaining to the balloon date (see the top left corner of Exhibit 2). This section of Exhibit 2 also provides the gross weighted average coupon (WAC) of the underlying collateral and the weighted average final maturity. The number of loans in the underlying pool shows diversification risk. Conduit deals usually have a larger number of smaller deals, whereas fusion deals have a few large loans. The deal we are analyzing has 279 loans, for an average loan size of approximately $4.5 million. Deals with fewer loans are usually considered less liquid and trade at wider spreads. However, buyers who look at the more credit-sensitive tranches sometimes prefer fusion deals because it is easier to analyze the fewer underlying loan credits.

Collateral Concentration by Property Type
The "Top 5 Property Types" (Exhibit 2) shows the respective concentrations of each type of commercial credit exposure to the overall pool of collateral. Heavier concentrations in multifamily loans are usually considered desirable because the loans are relatively short term and the landlord can raise rents to keep up with rising costs. Although multifamily properties are usually more leveraged than other types, historical losses have been lower. The credit strength of retail properties is determined by looking at the strength of retail tenants. Retail properties pose turnover risk. Turnover on retail properties occurs less often than on multifamily properties, but the costs to re-lease are higher. Hotels are analyzed on a going-concern basis because the value of the property lies in the cash flow stability and occupancy rates on the underlying rooms. Office and industrial properties enjoy cash flow stability from long-term leases but carry the highest risk and greatest cost of re-leasing to a different tenant after the lease expires. Indeed, the property is typically adapted to the requirements of a particular lessee, and refitting and re-leasing to a different concern can be costly. It is important for the CMBS investor to be comfortable with the underlying collateral mix as a large concentration to risky sectors is undesirable.

Exhibit 2: Bond Analyzer Commercial Mortgage Collateral Summary

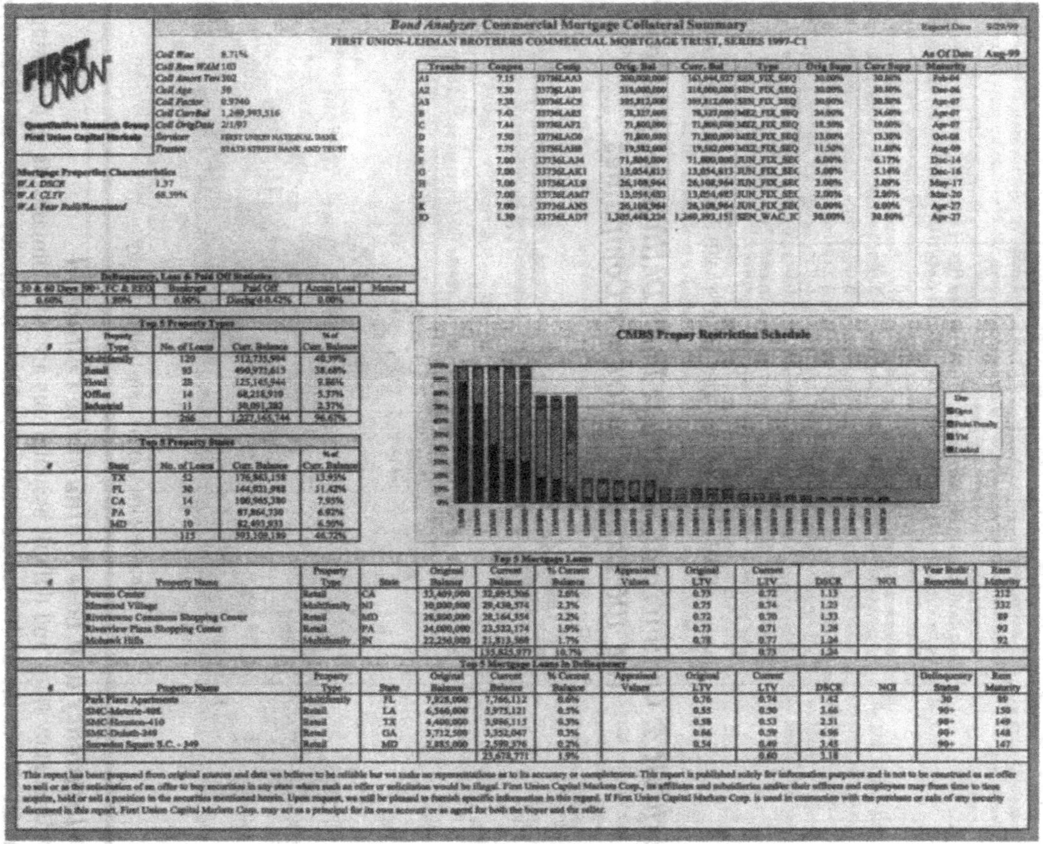

Exhibit 3: FULB 1997-C1 Subordination Levels

Tranche	S&P Rating	Original Balance	Original Support
A1	Aaa	200,000	30.0%
A2	Aaa	318,000	30.0%
A3	Aaa	395,812	30.0%
B	Aa2	78,327	24.0%
C	A2	71,800	18.5%
D	Baa2	71,800	13.0%
E	Baa3	19,582	11.5%
F	BB	71,800	6.0%
G	BB-	13,055	5.0%
H	B	26,109	3.0%
J	B-	13,054	2.0%
K	144A	26,109	0.0%
IO	Aaa	1,305,448	30.0%

Source: First Union Capital Markets Corp.

Exhibit 4: Commercial Mortgage Loan Delinquency Rates for the 100 Largest Insurance Companies

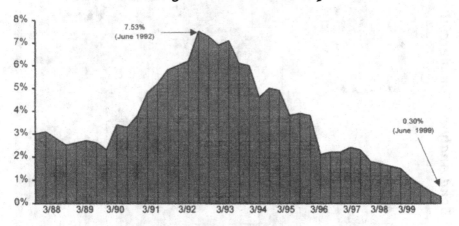

Source: First Union Capital Markets Corp.

Delinquency and Loss Status of the Collateral

Delinquency rates and default assumptions are key components in assessing the credit risk in the underlying collateral pool. Delinquency rates can be analyzed empirically to determine how future real estate cycles might affect CMBS valuations. Exhibit 4 demonstrates how commercial loan delinquencies have fallen steadily since 1992 to 0.30% as of June 1999.

In the FULB 1997-C1 deal, only 0.6% of the underlying collateral is 30–60 days past due, 0.42% has been discharged, and no losses have been taken to date.

Geographic Concentration of the Underlying Collateral

It is preferable that the collateral location be reasonably diversified. Collateral concentrations in states or regions where land prices hyperappreciated prior to the origination of the commercial loans may expose the security holder to greater credit and prepayment risks. In the case of FULB 1997-C1, no more than 14% of the collateral is concentrated in one state, and the top five property states represent four distinct geographic regions.

Look at the Major Credit Characteristics of the Collateral Pool and of the Largest Loans in the Pool

Two primary ratios are used to assess the credit of commercial loans: the *debt service coverage ratio* (DSCR) and the *loan-to-value ratio* (LTV). The DSCR reflects the free cash flow generated by the commercial property divided by the debt service requirement. Because of the going-concern nature of commercial properties, this cash flow coverage ratio is really the key to the mortgagee getting paid on the loan. In the pool of collateral in FULB 1997-C1, the weighted average DSCR is 1.37. Obviously, DSCRs of less than 1.0 are cause for concern; it means the property is not providing enough cash flow to cover the debt service payments. Look at the DSCR on the top five mortgage loans in the pool (Exhibit 2). If the largest loans in the pool show signs of credit weakness, such that individual defaults could have a deleterious effect on performance, investors need to factor potential distress on those loans into their analysis and pricing.

LTV is another indicator of risk. When property is liquidated after default, higher LTVs usually result in greater losses on a percentage basis. Again, we look at the characteristics of the largest loans in the pool for signs of potential problems in the future.

The rating agencies set minimum DSCRs and maximum LTVs for different rating classifications based on their analysis of historical loan performance data, qualitative and quantitative reviews of the collateral, and consideration of the security structure. Investors should consider not only the weighted average DSCR and LTV for a deal but also the dispersion.

In the credit tranching process, the goal is to minimize the total cost of funds for the issuer. Consequently, the issuer tries to maximize the size of the higher-rated tranches, which carry lower yields, and minimize the size of the lower-rated tranches, which carry higher yields. However, the size of each tranche is dictated by the leverage ratios required for a targeted rating.

Assessing Structural Prepayment Protection

One of the greatest attractions of CMBS product is the high degree of prepayment protection inherent in the underlying loans. These protections make CMBS a more positively convex product than the majority of RMBS cash flows and structures.

Basic Forms of Call Protection

The basic forms of call protection in a commercial loan are as follows:

Lockouts Most loans prohibit discretionary prepayments for 2–5 years.

Defeasance After the lockout period ends, many loans currently being originated require that, if the loan is prepaid, the cash flows to the mortgagee (and ultimately the security holder) must be maintained. To do this, the mortgagor buys
Treasury strips that exactly replicate the cash flows of principal and interest from
the prepaid loan. This defeasance serves not only to maintain the cash flow
stream but also to improve the underlying credit quality because risk-free government debt is substituted for the credit risk of the underlying borrower. The period
that defeasance covers can vary but typically lasts 2–5 years after the lockout
period ends. Defeasance improves the "swapability" of the bond to floating rate
because the cash flow stream is maintained, and investors have come to prefer
defeasance to yield maintenance.

Yield Maintenance Yield maintenance compensates the mortgagee by forcing
the mortgagor that is prepaying the loan to "make whole" the mortgagee on an
economic basis for the loss of income from the prepayment. The prepayment penalty under a yield maintenance clause can be calculated in several stipulated
methods. The most common is for the prepaying mortgagor to pay the mortgagee
a penalty equal to the net present value of the future cash flows from the mortgage loan discounted at a rate equal to the yield of the Treasury bond with the
same average life as the loan. The lower the yield, the greater the prepayment
penalty. This means that as the market rallies and rates fall, the prepayment penalties under most yield maintenance provisions become progressively more onerous. The downside to yield maintenance is that the mortgagee "loses the asset"
when it gets prepaid.

Points Prepayment penalties in the form of points are sometimes included in
CMBS structures. Point prepayment penalties are typically in place for several
years after yield maintenance or defeasance expires. Point penalties usually
decline over time.

Factors that Could Trigger an Unscheduled Prepayment

Unlike RMBS, CMBS prepayments are quite insensitive to the level of interest
rates. For CMBS, the majority of prepayments are related to credit losses. Other
than these credit-induced prepayments, discretionary prepayments are interest-
rate-sensitive only to the extent that rates have dropped enough to make the prepayment, with its associated penalties, economically viable. For the most part,
such interest-rate-driven prepayments will occur only in booming real estate markets and/or after prepayment penalties have wound down. The following factors
could trigger an unscheduled prepayment:

Exhibit 5: Unscheduled Prepayment Scenario

Property Book Value	$10 million
Borrowed Amount	$7 million (70% LTV ratio)
Marginal Tax Rate	40%
Five Years Later	
Property Market Value	$15 million
Prepayment Penalty	$1 million
Refinance Amount	$10.5 million (70% LTV)
Rationale for Prepayment Quantified	
Gain after Penalty	$4 million (133% ROE)
Tax Deduction	$400,000
Total Gain (with tax benefit)	$4.4 million (147% ROE)

LTV: Loan-to-value; ROE: Return on equity.
Source: First Union Capital Markets Corp.

Credit Losses When a default occurs in a pool of CMBS collateral, any loss is absorbed first by the most junior subordinated tranche in the deal. Although the junior tranche absorbs any principal shortfall from the loss, two other tranches also see an impact to cash flow. The credit loss essentially becomes an unscheduled prepayment, and this prepayment is applied as a par redemption to the first sequential tranche in the deal. The other tranche that is directly affected is the WAC IO because the coupon on the IO is reduced as the defaulted loan leaves the pool, diminishing the value of the IO strip.

Real Estate Market Induced Prepayment Prepayments may arise if the economy boosts real estate values and the borrower has an opportunity to refinance the loan with penalties and then leverage the investment economically. The major factors driving such a prepayment include the following:

1. Higher real estate values, which provide a gain to pay for any penalties
2. Lower interest rates, which have an effect similar to that of RMBS
3. Higher marginal tax bracket, which increases the value of a tax deduction for paying prepayment penalties

Exhibit 5 shows the rationale for making an unscheduled prepayment. Lower interest rates five years out provide further incentive to refinance for the same reason a residential mortgage borrower would refinance.

Prepayment Protection Features Winding Down Commercial real estate loans have a wide variety of prepayment penalty structures. In most instances, CMBS are locked out for the first 2–5 years. After the lockout, the yield maintenance period kicks in until several months before maturity, which is usually the 10-

year balloon payment. In place of or in addition to yield maintenance, there may be defeasance and prepayment penalties after the lockout. In either case, as these penalties become less onerous, falling rates may induce the borrower to prepay the loan to the extent the interest savings outweigh the after-tax penalty expense.

To show the structural prepayment protection in CMBS, we looked at the cash flows of the A2 tranche from FULB 1997-C1. When the deal was issued in 1997, the A2 was a 7.75-year bond. The prepayment protection remaining on the whole deal is shown in the CMBS Prepay Restriction Schedule of Exhibit 2. The schedule shows when hard lockout, yield maintenance, and point penalties provide protection from discretionary prepayments.

Next, we ran the A2 tranche on the *Bond Analyzer* under three different prepayment methodologies (Exhibit 6). First, we looked at a scenario where prepayments occur only after all of the forms of prepayment protection expire. Then, we looked at the prepayments and average life variability of the tranche if prepayments occurred after the yield maintenance protection expired. Finally, we looked at the worst case, which assumes prepayments occur after the expiry of the hard lockout period.

We can see in Exhibit 6 the value of yield maintenance. The average life of the cash flows drifts little when the yield maintenance is applied. Sometimes discretionary prepayments are made during the yield maintenance period. However, the structural protection and onerous prepayment penalties imposed in CMBS transactions give comfort to investors that the actual cash flow variability risk is much closer to the first and second potential outcomes.

Exhibit 6: Weighted Average Life Drift — FULB 1997-C1 A2

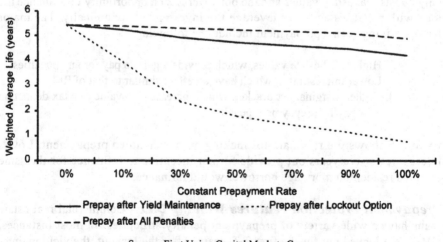

Source: First Union Capital Markets Corp.

Exhibit 7: CMBS Yield Compression under Stressed CDR Scenarios — CMFUN 1999-1 (as of Sept. 1, 1999)

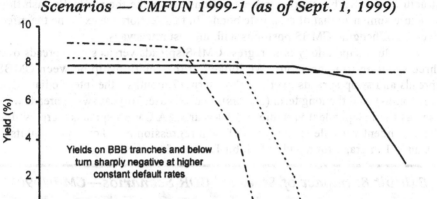

Source: First Union Capital Markets Corp.

Stressing the Credit Protection of Individual Tranches

Exhibit 7 depicts how various tranches in the CMFUN 1999-1 deal absorb losses under onerous credit loss scenarios. We used the *Bond Analyzer* to shock tranches under scenarios of rising *constant default rates* (CDRs). Similar to constant prepayment rates (CPRs) in RMBS, the CDR is an annual measure of loss. For instance, a 4% CDR implies that the collateral suffers 4% in defaults annually, an average level not seen since the early 1990s. We also assume a *loss severity rate* (LSR) of 45%, which is higher than indicated in the empirical analysis provided by one rating agency, Fitch IBCA. An LSR of 45% implies that if a $1 million loan defaults, $450,000 is lost.

Using the *Bond Analyzer*, it was found that due to the 26.5% AAA credit support structured into the deal, the AAA 10-year tranche has a constant 7.54% yield over all default scenarios. The A tranche's yield only deteriorates slightly at a 5% CDR assumption, whereas the BBB tranche is hit after 3% CDR and the BBB- tranche starts suffering at 2% CDR. Exhibit 8 enumerates the yields, spreads, and principal outstanding under the different CDR scenarios.

HEDGING CMBS WITH INTEREST RATE SWAPS

Interest rate swaps have become the preferred risk management tool in the marketplace. This is due in part to the relative delinking of Treasury-based products and spread products in the market since the beginning of 1997. Most risk managers use interest rate swaps to hedge part of the interest rate risk in bulleted credit structures. CMBS have structural protections that make the product's cash flow structure similar to that of corporate bonds. In this section, we examine the effectiveness of hedging CMBS positions with interest rate swaps.

Our methodology is to regress CMBS spreads versus swap spreads over three separate time horizons. We looked at the relationship between CMBS spreads and swap spreads over the short term (7 months), the intermediate term (13 months), and the long term (3 years). In each case, 10-year swap spreads were used as the independent variable and 10-year AAA CMBS spreads were used as the dependent variable. The results of each regression are shown in Exhibits 9, 10, and 11 in graph form and in Exhibit 12.

Exhibit 8: Impact of Stressed CDR Scenarios—CMFU9901

	Yield (%)				Spreads (bps)				Principal Outstanding (%)			
Tranche:	A2	C	E	F	A2	C	E	F	A2	C	E	F
Rating:	AAA	A	BBB	BBB-	AAA	A	BBB	BBB-	AAA	A	BBB	BBB-
0% CDR	7.54	7.91	8.31	9.12	157	193	233	313	100%	100%	100%	100%
1% CDR	7.54	7.91	8.26	9.04	157	193	227	305	100%	100%	100%	100%
2% CDR	7.54	7.90	8.21	8.85	157	192	221	285	100%	100%	100%	100%
3% CDR	7.54	7.88	8.09	4.27	158	190	207	-174	100%	100%	100%	27%
4% CDR	7.54	7.85	2.03	-8.77	158	186	-396	-1,471	100%	100%	21%	0%
5% CDR	7.54	7.25	-9.70	-15.82	158	124	-1,564	-2,172	100%	87%	0%	0%
6% CDR	7.54	2.71	-15.50	-22.72	159	-329	-2,141	-2,860	100%	31%	0%	0%

CDR: Constant default rate.

Source: First Union Capital Markets Corp.

Exhibit 9: 10-Year AAA CMBS versus Swap Spreads (January 1999-August 1999)

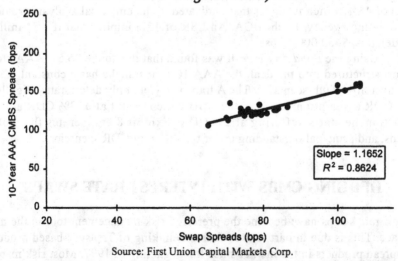

Slope = 1.1652
$R^2 = 0.8624$

Source: First Union Capital Markets Corp.

Exhibit 10: 10-Year AAA CMBS versus Swap Spreads (August 1998-August 1999)

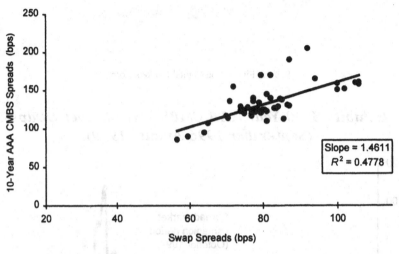

Source: First Union Capital Markets Corp.

Exhibit 11: 10-Year AAA CMBS versus Swap Spreads (September 1996-August 1999)

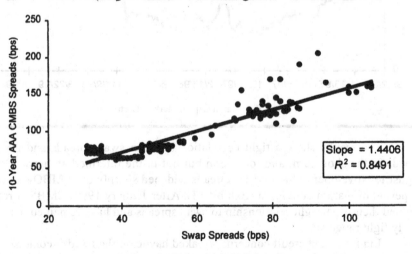

Source: First Union Capital Markets Corp.

Exhibit 12: Summary of Relationship between 10-Year CMBS Spreads and 10-Year Swap Spreads

Period length	R-Squared
Short Term (7 months)	86%
Intermediate Term (13 months)	48%
Long Term (3 Years)	85%

Source: First Union Capital Markets Corp.

Exhibit 13: 10-Year AAA CMBS Spreads over Swaps (September 1996-August 1999)

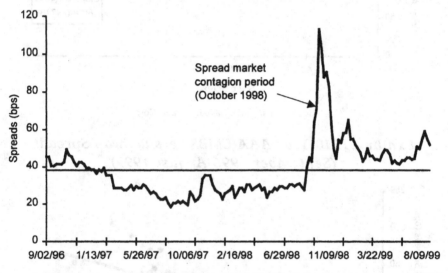

Source: First Union Capital Markets Corp.

The results show a tight correlation between swap spreads and CMBS spreads in the short term and long term but not in the intermediate term. From August to November 1998, CMBS spreads widened sharply over LIBOR during the period of market contagion (Exhibit 13). After January 1999, CMBS spreads resumed their usual tight relationship to swap spreads and have remained in a relatively tight range since then.

Liquidity and credit concerns wreaked havoc on the fixed-income spread sector markets from August to November 1998, and CMBS was one of the hardest-hit sectors. However, fundamental structural changes in the CMBS market and the general market climate since then lead us to conclude a similarly sharp disconnect between CMBS spreads and swap spreads is unlikely to occur in the future. These reasons include the following:

Exhibit 14: Adjusted Carry on CMBS Position with Different Haircuts*

Percentage of Haircut	Effective Financing Cost	Asset Yield after Swap	Financing Adjusted Carry
5%	5.25/0.95 = L + 27 bps	L + 42 bps	+15 bps
10%	5.25/0.90 = L + 58 bps	L + 42 bps	−16 bps
15%	5.25/0.85 = L + 92 bps	L + 42 bps	−50 bps

*Assuming 5.25% LIBOR and 10-year AAA CMBS swaps out at LIBOR + 42 bps.
Source: First Union Capital Markets Corp.

Stable financing costs. Higher perceived levels of general credit risk manifest themselves in both wider swap spreads and greater percentage haircuts on financing rates, particularly on more analytically complex products such as CMBS. A haircut of 15% rather than 5% triples the amount of equity the investor must provide for the position and means the effective financing cost of the position increases by approximately 65 bps (Exhibit 14). This happens because the leveraged investor foregoes the earning power of the money invested as equity. The economic opportunity cost of the equity money is approximately LIBOR, which is assumed to be the level of foregone return on the money.

Changes in the haircut increase the cost of financing, similar to the effect of wider swap spreads increasing the hedge cost on the asset side of the transaction. Both erode the income that the position generates. Taken together, the combination can create negative carry, which was the case in 1998. Mark-to-market losses and margin calls in 1998 were the final dagger, and many leveraged investors were forced to sell at distressed levels into an already illiquid market. This fire-sale environment caused CMBS to underperform both Treasurys and LIBOR more than most other spread sectors did in 1998. The CMBS market is generally less leveraged than it was last year, which should curtail any downside spread volatility.

Reduced aggregation risk. Another factor that increased CMBS spread volatility in 1998 was aggregation risk. In 1998, dealers were aggregating collateral for $3–$4 billion deals. In 1999, most deals were smaller, and dealers were partnering up, thereby reducing their downside risk and decreasing the potential spread volatility.

Improved credit climate. Most important, the credit climate is fundamentally different now than it was in 1998 when Russia's default, the Asian flu, and the collapse of Long Term Capital Management sent shock waves through the credit markets, highlighting a high level of inherent credit and liquidity risk. No such credit distress exists now, and this is reflected by the fact that haircuts on CMBS have not been changed.

Exhibit 15: CMFUN 1999-1

Tranche	Rating	Size	Avg. Life	ERISA	SMMEA
A1	AAA	210,400	5.4	Yes	Yes
A2	AAA	816,866	9.5	Yes	Yes
B	AA	76,870	9.7	No	Yes
C	A	62,894	9.7	No	No
D	A–	20,965	9.8	No	No
E	Baa3	48,917	10.1	No	No
F	BBB–	17,471	10.9	No	No
G	144A	59,400	11.8	No	No
H	144A	10,482	13.6	No	No
I	144A	10,482	13.8	No	No
J	144A	20,965	14.7	No	No
K	144A	6,988	16.3	No	No
L	144A	8,735	16.8	No	No
M	144A	26,206	19.7	No	No
X (IO)	AAA	1,398,640	9.4	Yes	Yes

ERISA: Employment Retirement Income Security Act; SMMEA: Secondary Mortgage Market Enhancement Act.

Source: First Union Capital Markets Corp.

We conclude CMBS have shown the type of relationship to swap spreads that renders hedging with swaps an extremely useful method of reducing potential spread volatility. Going forward, we do not expect CMBS spreads can or will dislocate from the swaps market to nearly the degree that occurred in 1998.

REGULATORY ISSUES

The more senior tranches of CMBS deals receive favorable regulatory treatment. The Employee Retirement Income Security Act of 1974 (ERISA) sets forth six general conditions that must be satisfied by employee benefit or retirement plans and insurance company separate accounts. In general, the senior tranches rated AAA are ERISA-eligible; however, investors should verify exemption with their legal advisers. In the example CMBS deal (Exhibit 15), the A1, A2, and all of the IO tranche, which represent 73% of the deal, are ERISA-eligible.

The Secondary Mortgage Market Enhancement Act (SMMEA) was amended in December 1996 to add qualifying CMBS paper. To qualify, the paper must be rated in the top two classes by at least one rating agency and meet certain criteria. In the CMFUN 1999-1 deal, the A1, A2, B, and all of the IO tranche are SMMEA-eligible. Again, investors should verify the interpretation of SMMEA eligibility with the appropriate governing authority or regulatory body.

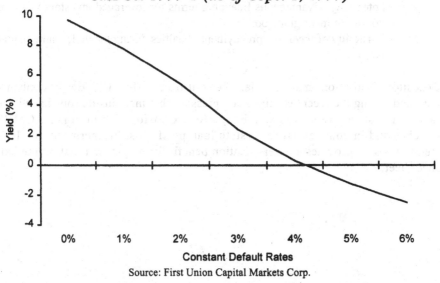

Exhibit 16: CMBS IO Sensitivity to Defaults —
CMFUN 1999-1 (as of Sept. 1, 1999)

Source: First Union Capital Markets Corp.

CMBS INTEREST-ONLY (IO) TRANCHES

Unlike RMBS IOs, which are extremely sensitive to interest-rate-driven, discretionary prepayment rates and have been labeled "derivatives," CMBS IOs are far less sensitive to interest rate volatility. Similar to RMBS IOs, CMBS IOs represent payment of a portion, say 100 bps, of the collateral coupon rate. The payment of this cash flow only disappears to the extent that the collateral disappears. In the case of CMBS IOs, the collateral is much more likely to disappear under default scenarios than interest-rate-driven prepayment scenarios.

CMBS IOs are typically rated AAA based on priority of cash flow rather than credit, although it is default risk that drives the valuation. For instance, looking at the CMFUN 1999-1 deal under CDR scenarios between 0% and 6%, we see that yield compression is mostly a result of default rates (Exhibit 16). However, varying CPR assumptions between 0% and 100% can vary yields between 50 bps and 200 bps depending on the deal structure. At 0% CDR, the tranche yields 375 bps over Treasurys for a 9.72% yield. On average, the yield declines 200 bps for every 1% jump in the CDR assumption.

Besides offering a substantial yield advantage versus other fixed-income investments, other advantages include the following:

- ERISA and SMMEA eligibility due to CMBS IOs nonsubordinated position in the structure

- Unlikely future downgrading as the priority of the IO never changes even if the credit quality of the collateral declines
- Potentially advantageous financing terms for leveraged investors vis-à-vis non-investment-grade bonds
- Possibility of receiving prepayment penalties during the yield maintenance period

Depository institutions may especially benefit from CMBS IOs. Besides enhancing yield during the recent earnings compression that most institutions have been facing, the structure serves as a hedge for extension risk in non-IO CMBS tranches and in commercial real estate loan portfolios. Furthermore, the IO's credit exposure provides a diversification benefit for prepayment risk in the balance sheet.

Chapter 25

Floating-Rate Commercial Mortgage-Backed Securities

Patrick Corcoran, Ph.D.
Vice President
J.P. Morgan Securities Inc.

Joshua Phillips*
Vice President
Nomura Securities International

INTRODUCTION

This chapter examines the growing market for floating-rate CMBS. It compares their features to the better known fixed-rate market, surveys some recent deals, summarizes rating agency approaches, and offers opinions about future direction and relative value.

BORROWER PREFERENCES FOR FLOATING-RATE FINANCE

A borrower preference for floating-rate financing rather than traditional fixed-rate debt can arise for several reasons. First, a borrower may be in the process of renovating or repositioning a property. Since improvements are expected in both cash flow and the certainty of the cash flow stream, the borrower does not desire to lock in long-term financing terms that fail to fully reflect the property's anticipated improvement. Hence, the borrower opts for a short-term financing.

A second broad motive for short-term financing comes from acquisitions. Acquisition activity as of this writing is being fueled by consolidation in the REIT sector, where the securities valuation of many entities continue at discounts to the value of properties owned. Short-run borrowing needs of property acquirers are not well met by traditional 10-year fixed-rate commercial mortgages, featuring strong prohibitions against prepayment.

---

* Mr. Phillips was an associate at J.P. Morgan Securities when this chapter was written.

A final motive for short-term financing arises from the judgment that long-term financing is at the time of this writing too expensive. A sharp increase in borrowing rates in 1999-2000 has led to an increase in floating-rate loans secured by both transitional and completely stabilized properties.

A Credit Perspective: Transitional Property versus Stabilized Property Financing

Thus, depending on borrower motive, floating-rate CMBS deals can include loans on either fully stabilized properties or transitional properties. However, floating-rate deals often differ from traditional fixed-rate deals because of their typical emphasis on transitional property loan collateral.

Transitional properties involving renovation or repositioning can be thought of as containing two elements. First, there is a stabilized property component represented by value corresponding to in-place cash flows. Second, there is an improvement component, which may arise in several different ways. First, changing market conditions within the broad property type or alternatively at the local market level may warrant a repositioning of the property. In a strong rental market, a typical indicator is leases that are well below market rents. Depending on the details, such repositioning will involve improved marketing or management, new "concepts," alternative ideas about site plans or tenancy, local market studies, and so on, in addition to actual physical renovations. Second, rising demand for space in the local market may highlight the benefit of a renovation or expansion of the facility. Here, the most obvious costs relate to physical expansion or improvement in the property.

In either case, the improvement component's value added is the difference between the total costs of the investment and the higher value realized in the repositioned or expanded property. In some ways, this value-added paradigm resembles that for new construction activity. However, repositioning or expanding existing properties with in-place cash flows should generally be considered as a lower risk than stand-alone construction projects.

Property improvements or renovations are subject to a different risk/return dynamic over the property market cycle. This can be seen in Exhibit 1. The solid line shows our proprietary "Credit Drift" for office property exposure. It is designed to measure the attractiveness of office property exposure taken in fixed-rate commercial mortgages. Notice that the Credit Drift measure turned positive in 1993, indicating that commercial mortgage exposure had turned attractive, following the real estate debacle of the early 1990s. Essentially, this turning point was supported by two distinct developments. First, in the property rental market, rents stopped falling and vacancies peaked at elevated levels and began to decline. Second, property prices had fallen to about 50% of replacement cost levels. The latter development was particularly striking. Since the difference between property prices and new development costs represents the gross profit margin to the developer, the large negative margin pointed to an absence of development activity for some time to come.

Exhibit 1: Credit Drift Scores for Stabilized Property and Repositioning/Improvement Activity (Downtown Office)

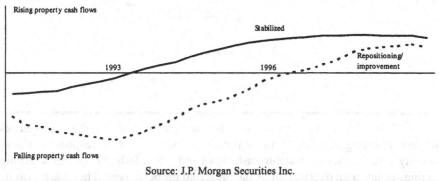

Source: J.P. Morgan Securities Inc.

Both of these factors were very positive for intermediate-term commercial mortgage exposure to stabilized properties. However, deeply discounted property prices were not positive for repositioning or additions to existing properties. After all, one could buy a property with "embedded" improvements at 50% of new development costs. So it made no sense to buy an older property and undertake new improvements at 100% of cost. A positive backdrop for renovation /repositioning activity had to await a substantial recovery of property prices several years later.

Exhibit 1 also shows an experimental measure designed to signal the attractiveness of shorter-term exposure to repositioning/improvement activity. This measure only turned positive several years later. Any particular transitional property will represent a mix of the stabilized property and pure improvement components, depending on their relative importance in the project. Since the mix can vary widely, so do the risk characteristics.

The environment as of this writing provides a contrast with 1993. Property prices have returned to a positive margin above new development costs. In addition, while rents and property cash flows are growing somewhat more slowly than in earlier years as a result of ample new construction, cash flows remain steady. Thus, the Credit Drift reading (Exhibit 1) corresponding to loan exposure in stabilized office properties remains healthy. Moreover, the transitional index, measuring the attractiveness of repositioning/improvement activity, is currently looking almost as strong as the index for stabilized properties (Exhibit 1).

In summary, transitional properties represent a combination of stabilized property exposure and exposure to repositioning and improvement activity. Since stabilized properties and any renovation component represent different risk exposures, our rating methodology offers the potential for evaluating a wide range of different risk profiles. Second, the wider range in signals for repositioning activity (Exhibit 1) highlights greater risk in transitional properties than in stabilized properties. However, in our view, the negative performance in the early 1990s downturn in real estate (Exhibit 1) overstates this additional risk in the more stable modern CMBS market.

Exhibit 2: National Credit Drift for Transitional versus Stabilized Properties

	Stabilized	Repositioning
Office	1.9	2.2
Suburban Office	2.0	1.5
Retail	4.0	5.0
Apartment	5.8	1.9
Industrial	3.8	2.8

Source: J.P. Morgan Securities Inc.

Exhibit 2 shows the Credit Drift readings for both stabilized properties and repositioning activity. In these indices, scores of 1-3 correspond to rising property cash flows, 4-6 to stable cash flows and 7-9 to falling cash flows. Strong readings point to an overweight of the indicated property type. They must also be balanced against the higher risk of repositioning activity. In apartment, industrial and suburban office loans, repositioning activity posts stronger scores than stabilized properties. In the downtown office sector, where scores are very strong, repositioning activity is only slightly less bullish than stabilized properties. In the case of retail properties, the repositioning index is somewhat behind a roughly neutral reading for stabilized properties.

Overall, the improving pattern in the repositioning index (Exhibit 1) evident in downtown office properties is also mirrored in the other property types. The property market in early 2000 is generally much more favorable to such activity than was the case as recently as 1994-1995.

FIXED AND FLOATING-RATE CMBS: RATING AGENCY APPROACHES

In looking at the early RTC CMBS deals, the rating agencies observed that floating-rate deals had higher default probabilities, other things equal, than comparable fixed-rate deals. They worried that interest rate spikes could increase the likelihood of term defaults. As a result, they encouraged borrowers to buy caps protecting them from rate spikes.

As a result of their default analysis, the rating agencies underwrite floating-rate deals more stringently than fixed-rate deals through the use of so-called "loan constants." The loan constants, which are different for the various property types, are designed to mimic the impact of a stress scenario in which floating rates spike or property income drops sharply. The constant is the sum of an assumed interest rate and amortization rate. Calculations of debt service coverage ratios (DSCR) look at the ability of net property cash flow (as underwritten by the agencies) to cover the assumed debt service, as measured by the loan constant. Typically, the rating agency DSCR is the most important input into the credit enhancement models that determine bond tranching.

Exhibit 3: Fixed versus Floating-Rate Rating Agency Underwriting Analysis

Appraised property value	= $140
Loan face amount	= $100
Issuer underwritten cash flow	$11.50
Rating agency underwritten cash flow	$11.00

Fixed-rate underwriting
Rating agency loan constant = 9.75%

$$\text{Agency DSCR} = \frac{\$11}{(0.0975)(\$100)} = 1.1282\times$$

Floating-rate underwriting
Rating agency loan constant = 11.50%

$$\text{Agency DSCR} = \frac{\$11}{(0.1150)(\$100)} = 0.9565\times$$

Source: J.P. Morgan Securities Inc.

Suppose for a particular fixed-rate loan, the loan constant is 9.75% (see Exhibit 3). For the same face loan amount, the loan constant in a floating-rate loan might be 11.50%. If rating agency underwritten cash flow were equal to 11.0% of the loan's face amount, the calculated DSCR for the floater would be 0.9565× (see Exhibit 3). However, for the fixed-rate loan, the DSCR would be 1.1282×. This simple calculation illustrates the most important reason why subordination levels for floating-rate CMBS are substantially above fixed-rate conduit paper.

If the borrower chooses to buy an interest rate cap (covering both the loan's term and any extension options), the borrower's situation improves somewhat. In this case, the rating agency takes the debt service to be equal to the capped interest rate plus assumed amortization. However, the agencies will not allow caps to reduce the loan constant below that used in fixed-rate deals.

COMPARING LOAN COLLATERAL IN FIXED AND FLOATING RATE DEALS

Loan Count and Average Loan Balance

Exhibit 4 shows some basic features of four floating-rate deals issued in the second half of 1999. The most obvious aspect, relative to fixed-rate conduit CMBS, is the relatively small number of loans and the relatively large loan size. There is an immediate implication for investors. Similar to fixed-rate large loan deals, the analysis must focus squarely on specific credit and loan collateral characteristics. This is true in analyzing both prepayment and credit loss scenarios. Unlike a conduit deal of 150-200 loans with average loan balance of $5 million, little comfort can be derived from statistical analysis and the law of large numbers. From the rating agency perspective, this means that significantly less credit is given for diversification benefits compared to those typically present in a fixed-rate conduit deal.

Within the four floating-rate deals, there is also substantial variation in average loan size. The DLJ 1999 FL-1 is most similar to conduit specifications with an average loan balance of $12.5 million. Although the GMAC 1999 FL-1 has a similar average loan size to the DLJ deal, it actually consists of a $130 million investment-grade large loan and 29 conduit loans averaging about $8-9 million per loan. By contrast, the COMM 2000 FL-1 and CDC 1999 FL-1 deals are large loan deals. Both of these deals have average loan balances around $50 million (Exhibit 4). Moreover, the COMM 2000 FL-1 deal has about three-quarters of its loan collateral in the form of loan participations. In each of these instances, notes junior to those included in the Trust are held outside the Trust. Finally, lumpiness in the floating-rate deals also shows up in the relatively high percentage of the deals accounted for by the top five and top ten loans (Exhibit 4), as well as in the uneven distribution of loan balances by property type.

Exhibit 4: Recent Floating Rate Deals

Overview	GMAC 1999 FL-1	DLJ 1999 STF-1	COMM 2000 FL-1	CDC 1999 FL-1	1999 Conduit Average
Deal Size	$374.16	$428.53	$1,002.88	$549.14	$912.40
	11/16/99	11/30/99	1/26/00	12/16/99	
No. of loans	30	35	19	11	201
No. of prop	58	35	37	39	221
Avg Loan size (MM)	$12.5	$12.2	$52.8	$49.9	$4.5
Hard Lockboxes	2%	38%	68%	95%	N/A
Top 5 loan %	70%	53%	60%	70%	
Top 10 loan %	86%	79%	90%	96%	33.4%
Property Types	Conduit Only				
Office	48	22	33	33	18.9
Retail	5	10	19	22	25.9
Multifamily	30	41	4	6	31.0
Industrial	5	0	0	4	8.8
Hotel	0	27	11	34	8.9
Other	12	0	32	0	6.5
Rating Agencies					
Moody's	X	X	X	X	
S&P	X		X		
Fitch	X			X	
Duff					
Issuer					
DSCR	1.35	1.16	2.13	1.47	1.42
LTV	68.3%	69.2%	52.0%	57.7%	69.6%

Source: J.P. Morgan Securities Inc.

Exhibit 5: Rating Agency Analysis of Recent Floating Rate Deals

Moody's	GMAC 1999 FL-1	DLJ 1999 STF-1	COMM 2000 FL-1	CDC 1999 FL-1
DSCR Whole Loans	1.09(conduit only)	1.22	1.19	1.18
LTV (%) Whole Loans	93.8%(conduit only)	89.9%	84.9%	87.0%
DSCR Inv Grade loans	1.64			
LTV (%) Inv Grade Loans	64.2%			
DSCR Participation			1.52	
LTV (%) Participation			66.4%	
WA Gross Margin (bps)	260	311	220	332
WAM (wo extensions)	22	20	28	29
WAM (w/ max extension)	26	37	38	36
Adjustment to Cash Flow	(Conduit Only)			
In Place Cash flow	−3.5%	17.1%	−7.4%	−7.1%
Stabilized Cash flow		−18.4%	N/A	−22.2%
Herfindel Score	26	15	10	8
AAA subordination Levels	44.5%	50.0%	30.25/45.3%*	47.0%
Stabilized/transitional	Largely stabilized	Largely not stabilized	Largely stabilized	Largely not stabilized

* The 45% level is the subordination level had the junior interests in the participation's been included in the trust.

Source: J.P. Morgan Securities Inc., Moody's Investors Services

Stabilized and Repositioned Properties

The fall 1998 crisis caused several investment banks to finance substantial inventories of loans, many involving turnaround properties, as floating-rate deals. Examples included several large balance sheet floaters by Lehman Brothers and CSFB. Despite the volatile capital markets environment, however, these early floater deals issued in late 1998 and early 1999, were supported by strong real estate credit fundamentals — as highlighted in Exhibits 1 and 2. As credit spreads tightened between the end of 1998 and late 1999, the deals paid down fairly quickly and performed strongly.

These earlier floating-rate deals are not examined in this chapter because they are not indicative of more recent floater deals that began to emerge in the second half of 1999. On average, the latter floaters have less of an improvement/turnaround component than earlier floaters. Nonetheless, the variation in underlying property collateral can be substantial.

At one end of the spectrum is largely stabilized property collateral. According to Moody's presale report, the properties underlying COMM 2000 FL-1 were "virtually . . . all stabilized." Consistent with the largely stabilized loans/properties are low rating agency subordination levels and a relatively light rating agency haircut to stabilized cash flow (see Exhibit 5).

The relatively low subordination levels for AAAs in COMM 2000 FL-1 benefit substantially from the use of the Note A/Note B loan structure. The participation structure effectively takes what would otherwise have been junior loan principal outside the Trust and leaves the amount of AAA bonds approximately unchanged, thereby reducing subordination. If the junior Note B interests are counted as additional credit support to the AAA bond classes, total subordination (both within and outside the Trust) is 45.3%. This compares with a 30.0% within-the-trust credit support level. However, the higher 45.3% credit support number highlights the fact that rating agency credit support levels have been within a very tight band, even though loan collateral has varied rather widely.

An example of a deal with largely stabilized properties but some transitional properties is GMAC 1999 FL-1. According to the Fitch presale report, about 71.5% of the properties were considered "stable," meaning that the properties have relevant historical operating history that the rating agency used as the basis of its underwriting, parallel to the approach taken in fixed-rate conduit deals. The rating agency considered the remaining 28.5% of the properties as having "low cash flow volatility." This category includes properties that are nearing the end of a successful repositioning strategy. Such properties are often fairly far along in a "lease-up" period and showing material improvement between trailing 12-month and current annualized revenue numbers. The preponderance of stabilized and "low volatility" properties in the GMAC 1999 FL-1 deal also shows up in a relatively modest cash flow haircut (Exhibit 5).

Somewhat further along the spectrum is the DLJ 1999 STF-1 deal. This deal appears to correspond largely to properties in the lease-up phase. This means that various improvements to properties have already been made and that what remains is for the properties to work their way through lease-up (i.e., getting from occupancies near pre-improvement levels to new "stabilized" occupancy and rent levels in the improved property). One way this shows up is in a substantial difference between underwritten net cash flow and DSCR and underwriter projections of "stabilized" cash flow and DSCR. In the case of DLJ 1999 STF-1, projected stabilized net cash flow is about 45% higher than current underwritten cash flow. This clearly represents a substantial improvement component.

Notice that the rating agency treatment of DLJ 1999 STF-1 haircuts stabilized net property cash flow by 18.4% (Exhibit 5) while actually giving a positive adjustment to in-place cash flow. By contrast, the COMM 2000 FL-1 deal, where the properties are largely stabilized, receives a modest 7.4% haircut (Exhibit 5).

The CDC 1999 FL-1deal, like the DLJ deal, contains properties that have been recently renovated or re-tenanted. In addition, some properties are currently undergoing renovation or other repositioning of the property. In this deal, Moody's identified a larger number of properties in non-stabilized condition than Fitch IBCA. In addition, Fitch IBCA put most of the transition properties in its "low volatility" bucket. According to Moodys, as a result of those properties still undergoing repositioning, four loans representing 24% of the pool balance include future funding obligations subject to various criteria. The aggregate amount of this subordinate financing totals to about $31 million, compared to collateral pool balances of about $600 million. For one large retail loan, advances of up to $10.5 million may be made, and principal repayment of these balances (if extended) will be made *pari passu* with the loan included in the Trust.

According to Moody's presale report, the CDC deal features underwritten net cash flows, once the properties become completely stabilized, that are about 24% larger than in-place cash flows. This is a smaller increase than the DLJ deal, but it also features future renovation and property repositioning (with additional lending and structural complexities) rather than pure lease-up risk.

Low Leverage versus High or Low Leverage

In early floating-rate deals in late 1998 and early 1999, leverage was unquestionably higher than that of typical fixed-rate conduit deals. For example, in SASCO 1999-C3, Moody's stressed LTV was 122% while the Fitch IBCA stressed debt service coverage ratio was 0.65×. These levels compare with typical 1999 fixed-rate conduit marks of 88% (LTV) and 1.15× (DSCR).

In the floating-rate deals examined in this chapter, however, it is not so clear that leverage is indeed higher. Of course, since fixed-rate deals involve purely stabilized properties, we can only compare floating-rate deals with largely stabilized properties to fixed-rate conduit deals. Let's use the GMAC 1999 FL-1 as an example, since it involves largely stabilized properties.

Exhibit 6 shows that this deal's leverage is only slightly above the average for 1999 fixed-rate conduit deals. Following our earlier discussion of rating agency underwriting approaches, we approximate loan constants to roughly calculate the Fitch stressed DSCR on a fixed-pool basis. In addition, we show the Moody's stressed LTV measure. Both rating agency measures show only slightly higher leverage than average fixed-rate conduit deals in 1999.

Call Protection

In fixed-rate conduit CMBS deals, call protection consists of lock-out, defeasance, and yield maintenance charges which either forbid or strongly discourage prepayment. By contrast, floating-rate loan collateral generally has much weaker call protection.

Exhibit 6: Leverage in GMAC 1999-FL1

	Floating-rate	Fixed-rate equivalent	1999 fixed-rate conduit average
Fitch Stressed DSCR			
Large loan	1.19×	1.40×	
Conduit loans	0.92×	1.08×	1.15×
Total	1.01×	1.17×	
Moody's Stressed LTV	93.8%		88.0%

Source: J.P. Morgan Securities Inc., Fitch-IBCA, Moody's Investor Services

Exhibit 7: Call Protection in Recent Floating-Rate Deals

	GMAC 1999 FL-1	DLJ 1999 STF-1	COMM 2000 FL-1	CDC 1999 FL-1
Yield Protection on Loans	• 35% of the loans have no call protection • 65% of the loans lockout • 1 to 15 months.	• All loans with lockout • Average lockout term 1.29 years • Lockout terms range from 1 to 1.67 years	• Lockout in year one • Afterwards fixed penalties	• Yield maintenance based on "LIBOR flat"
Stabilized/ transitional	Largely stabilized	Largely not stabilized	Largely stabilized	Largely not stabilized

Source: J.P. Morgan Securities Inc.

Floating-rate loans are typically in the 2- to 5-year maturity range. Call protection is a less important issue than in traditional 10-year fixed-rate mortgages. If a borrower prepays to take advantage of lower borrowing costs, investors in the fixed-rate loan are missing a component of the interest income stream for a much longer period and the present value of the missing cash flow is commensurately higher. In the floating-rate loan, resets in the floating interest rate remove one of several possible reasons that borrower financing costs could fall, thereby creating incentives to prepay the loan. The relative absence of call protection in floating-rate CMBS is similar to other floating-rate product, such as credit card or auto loan paper. In floating-rate CMBS, moreover, weak call protection meets the need for flexibility in seeking long-term takeout financing, repositioning a renovated property, or financing a portfolio acquisition short-term.

Since lock-out is necessary in selling a deal's IO on favorable terms, some lock-out may be negotiated with the borrower, but extension options are also common. Following the pattern in the fixed-rate market, loan terms are more likely to be customized with larger loans and borrowers.

In addition, there may naturally tend to be a trade-off in floating-rate deals between call protection and credit characteristics. For example, a borrower who uses a floating-rate loan to temporarily fund the acquisition of fully stabilized properties is much more likely to want complete flexibility and, depending on his short term plans, may be reluctant to accept lock-out. For example, in the case of the GMAC 1999 FL-1 deal with its generally stabilized or near-stabilized properties, call protection varied widely (Exhibit 7). 35% of the loans were without call protection while the remaining loans used lock-out (rather than prepayment premiums) ranging from 1 month to 15 months.

The GMAC deal is also unusual in combining a very large investment-grade loan with conduit collateral. The large loan is about one-third of the entire pool. In this situation, the rating agencies would be reluctant to assign bond sizing levels that gave "full credit" to the investment-grade loan without having confidence that it would be around for a while. This means that it would be difficult to do such a deal without having significant call protection on the large loan. In the large loan, lock-out is 15 months on a 24-month term. In essence, the heterogeneous character of the loan collateral in the GMAC deal forces the strong call protection on the large loan.

Another deal with mostly stabilized properties is the COMM 2000 FL-1 transaction. Here again, there was substantial variation among the loans (Exhibit 7). Call protected loans generally had a year of lock-out combined with decreasing fixed penalties over the next two years.

On the other hand, if properties are just beginning "lease up" after improvements have been finished, the borrower will want to wait until the end of this phase before considering permanent financing. In the DLJ 1999 STF-1 deal, where the properties appeared to be generally in the early "lease-up" phase, a year or so of lock-out was uniformly afforded on 2-year loans. Since the loans are very unlikely to be prepaid in the middle of the lease-up period, both the ease of obtaining the lock-out and the value of the protection are very different from the case where the property collateral is entirely stabilized.

The CDC1999 FL-1 deal affords an example of more flexible call protection in a deal with many non-stabilized properties. The approach used here was a modified form of yield maintenance using "Libor flat" (Exhibit 7) to discount the loan's floating-rate cash flow stream. The theory here is similar to using "Treasury flat" in fixed-rate yield maintenance. Clearly, no loan ever improves in quality to the point that the Treasury rate is the correct discount rate for the remaining cash flows. However, since improvements in property and loan quality are correlated with higher likelihood to prepay, Treasury flat helps to deal with the adverse selection problem. (See discussion below on this issue.) The same can be said for Libor flat. Libor-based rates are roughly equivalent to the credit of an AA-rated bank. Thus, the Libor flat discount rate is not as tough a hurdle as Treasury flat for fixed-rate loans.

Clearly, loan collateral in floating rate deals can vary greatly. As emphasized in our discussion of credit earlier, the mix of risk characteristics between stabilized properties and improvements are very different as well. The rating agencies underwrite the in-place cash flow for stabilized properties in floaters in the same way as for fixed-rate deals. However, they are much tougher on cash flows that are attributed to property improvements during lease-up. In a lease-up phase that is well along and appears to be moving ahead successfully, the agency may give credit for in-place cash flows but no credit for vacant space.

Extension Options

Like call protection, extension options can also be related to whether the collateral is stabilized or transitional loans/properties. In general, the demand for extension options by borrowers is likely to be greater with transition properties than fully stabilized properties. As shown in Exhibit 8, it is the deals with largely stabilized property collateral (GMAC 1999FL-1 and COMM2000FL-1) that exhibit the lower shares of loans with extension options. The other two deals with more transitional property loans have the larger shares of loans with extension options.

Exhibit 8: Extension Provisions in Recent Floating-Rate Deals

	GMAC 1999 FL-1	DLJ 1999 STF-1	COMM 2000 FL-1	CDC 1999 FL-1
Percent of loans with extension options	28.8%	100.0%	43.5%	60.7%
Extension terms	Average 11.3 months	All loans with options Range 6-12 months Four loans with second extension option	Average 24.1 month option	All loans 12 month option

Source: J.P. Morgan Securities Inc.

BONDS AND STRUCTURING ISSUES IN FLOATING-RATE CMBS

In looking at structural questions in floating-rate CMBS, the issues can be broadly divided into two categories. First, floating-rate deals are lumpy deals with much larger average loan size than fixed-rate conduits and far fewer loans. Since 1998, the market has been wary of lumpiness in fixed-rate deals. In response to this development, there have been a variety of structural innovations such as Note A/ Note B structures to reduce the lumpiness of larger loans in fixed-rate conduit and fusion deals. Since floating-rate deals are lumpy, lumpiness has been an issue just as it has in fixed-rate deals.

Second, the weaker call protection in floating-rate deals brings out the so-called "adverse selection" problem. This describes the tendency for improving loan credits and properties to have a higher probability of prepayment while deteriorating loans are more likely to extend at the balloon date. As compared with fixed-rate deals, this issue assumes larger importance in the floating-rate market both because of weaker call protection and widespread extension options. In an extreme scenario, when rapid early prepays combine with a high percentage of extensions, the loan coupon payments could be inadequate to pay the interest on the lower rated bonds, thereby hurting B-piece returns in such scenarios.

To provide a greater comfort level for subordinate bond buyers, recent deals have varied the bond structure from strict senior/subordinated sequential pay. As a practical matter, in the current market environment, this involves negotiations with B-piece investors and a balancing act with the rating agencies, who allow more favorable allocations of higher-rated bonds in the presence of a strict sequential pay structure. However, if a better reception by B-piece investors can be secured through a partial tilt to a pro-rata allocation of non-default related prepayments, proceeds from the deal may possibly be increased despite fewer highly rated bonds being allocated in the structure.

For example, the 1999 CDC deal allowed lower-rated bonds to share on a pro-rata basis in unscheduled principal payments not related to default (Exhibit

9). In the case of defaults, recoveries of principal are returned on the normal sequential senior/sub basis. Similarly, the DLJ 1999 STF-1 deal pays on a pro-rata scheme (Exhibit 9). Interestingly, both these deals are ones with a greater share of transition properties rather than largely stabilized collateral.

In our view, demand by B-piece buyers for pro-rata structuring of non-default prepays is likely to be larger the larger the "window" in which adverse selection can operate. This window includes both periods that are freely open to call and also extension period options. Moreover, adverse selection seems likely to play out most forcefully in extension options when the collateral corresponds largely to non-stabilized properties. In these deals, the greater uncertainty surrounding the success of the turnaround activity, compared to risks on stabilized properties, suggests greater scope for adverse selection to operate.

Exhibit 9: Structural Provisions in Recent Floating-Rate Deals

	GMAC 1999 FL-1	DLJ 1999 STF-1	COMM 2000 FL-1	CDC 1999 FL-1
Overall Structure	Sequential	Pro-Rata	Sequential; several loans are participations	Pro-Rata Contingent on a rule-set that once violated permanently reverts to sequential-pay
Scheduled Principal	sequential	Pro-rata if current balance is greater than .325 of original After the factor reaches .325 the deal is sequential	Sequential	Modified sequential
Unscheduled Principal			Paid pro-rata between senior interests and junior interests (outside the trust) before an event of default	
Prepayment premiums	No prepay premiums Lockout only Exit fees ranging from 1-4%	No prepay premiums lockout only	All to the IO	Allocated between the IO and a "remainder" class
Other Unique Features			72% of the loans are participation loans Junior interest held outside the trust.	

Source: J.P. Morgan Securities Inc.

In cases where borrowers owning stabilized properties are reluctant to agree to lock-out, this by itself may raise the demand by B-piece buyers for pro-rata sharing of prepay principal returns. In addition, specific deal features can also play a role. As discussed above in the GMAC deal, for example, rating agency issues essentially forced strong call protection on the large loan in the deal. When the latter feature is combined with the largely stabilized collateral, the likely result is to reduce pressure from B-piece buyers for pro-rata sharing arrangements. And, in fact, we find the deal is sequential (Exhibit 9).

The COMM 2000 FL-1 deal allows junior Note B loan interests outside the Trust to share in non-default unscheduled principal paydowns (Exhibit 9). Once these arrangements had been negotiated at the loan level, they were not subject to change as a result of discussions with potential B-piece buyers. In addition, if the junior interests had been included within the Trust in a conventional CMBS structure, the importance of B-pieces in the CMBS structure would have been far larger.

In terms of mechanics, pro rata allocation rules can be based upon loan pool statistics or, alternatively, they can operate at the individual loan level, reflecting rating agency concerns about particular loans. An example of a pool-based rule can be seen in the DLJ 1999 STF-1 deal (Exhibit 8). If the aggregate loan balance in the deal falls below 32.5%, principal allocations revert to straight sequential pay.

In summary, pro rata principal allocation rules help B-piece buyers deal with the adverse selection problem. From the perspective of the AAA investors, compensation for the departure from strict sequential pay comes in the form of both higher subordination levels and reduced prepayment risk.

CONCLUSION AND RELATIVE VALUE IN FLOATING-RATE CMBS

AAA subordination in the floating-rate deals examined in this chapter falls within a tight 44% to 50% range, even though the collateral ranges from largely stabilized to largely transitional. This compares with AAA subordination levels in the mid-twenties in typical fixed-rate conduit deals. As discussed above, this higher subordination represents a rating agency response to (1) lower loan count, (2) weaker diversification, as well as (3) more stringent underwriting by the Agencies for floaters.

Loan collateral in late 1999 floaters has moved much closer to fixed-rate conduit collateral than was the case in earlier 1998-1999 floaters. We expect this process to continue to evolve. In particular, we expect to see some floating-rate deals with larger loan counts, better diversification, and closer conformity in general to fully stabilized fixed-rate conduit collateral.

Historically, defaults came "early and often" in 1970s and 1980s vintage loans as well as the RTC CMBS deals (including floaters) in the early 1990s. By contrast, the non-RTC CMBS market, which began in 1993-1994, has been marked by an absence of early term defaults and stellar loan performance in general. In our view, rating agency underwriting of floating-rate loans is conservative. Thus, even in deals that move closer to fixed-rate collateral in loan count and diversifcation, subordination levels should remain significantly higher than those on fixed-rate deals. From a credit standpoint, in our opinion, this points to good relative value in AAA paper backed by stabilized properties.

Since collateral varies widely within floating-rate deals, there is a need for careful analysis of transitional property collateral. While loans backed by transitional properties are somewhat higher risk than stabilized property collateral, the additional risk is mitigated by the strong performance of property rental markets in the modern real estate markets since 1993. Credit Drift scores for repositioning activity can be used with scores for stabilized property markets to assess opportunities in transitional properties. Attention must also be paid to the fine points of repositioning plans and improvements.

As shown in Exhibit 10, pricing of AAA floating-rate securities examined have been quite close to fixed-rate 5-year AAA CMBS, on a swap-adjusted basis. (Note this is a plain vanilla swap and not a "balanced guaranteed" or true asset swap.) Pricing of the fixed-rate AAAs is as of Friday the week the floating rate deals priced. The GMAC 1999 FL-1 and COMM 2000 FL-1, the two deals with largely stabilized property collateral, both priced slightly tighter in spread than the fixed-rate AAAs, on a swap-adjusted basis. On the other hand, the two deals with transitional property collateral, DLJ 1999 STF-1 and CDC 1999 FL-1, priced wider in swap-adjusted spread than the fixed-rate paper. While these differentials in swap-adjusted spread are in the "right direction," the differentials look small, in our opinion, compared to differences in collateral.

Another indication that floating-rate deals with transitional collateral are not always "efficiently" priced can be seen in the SASCO 1999-C3 deal, also shown in Exhibit 10. Even though this deal priced in October 1999, it is similar to earlier higher-leverage floaters with highly transitional collateral. Despite this, it priced at a swap-adjusted spread tight to generic 5-year fixed-rate AAA paper.

Exhibit 10: Pricing of Floating-Rate AAA bonds

	GMAC 1999 FL-1	DLJ 1999 STF-1	COMM 2000 FL-1	CDC 1999 FL-1	SASCO 1999-C3
AAA Libor spread (bps)	+36	+40	+30	+45	+40
AAA Average life (years)	1.52	1.50	2.10	1.98	1.58
Pricing date	11/16/99	11/30/99	1/26/00	12/16/99	10/20/99
2yr AAA credit card Libor spread (bps)	+14	+14	+10	+12	+17
5yr AAA CMBS fixed-rate spread minus swap spread (not balanced guaranteed, bps)	+39	+34.5	+32	+27.5	+43

Source: J.P. Morgan Securities Inc., Commercial Mortgage Alert

Exhibit 11: 3-Year Credit Cards: Floating-Rate versus Fixed-Rate-Swap Spread

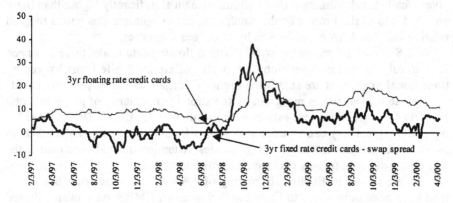

(5 day moving averages in bps)

The long position in 5-year fixed-rate AAA CMBS and short a plain vanilla swap is not of course a true floating-rate exposure. A true floating-rate exposure would require an asset swap linked to the 5-year fixed-rate CMBS. While such "balanced guaranteed" swaps have been written on 10-year fixed-rate AAA CMBS, they have not been written on 5-year paper. The obvious reason is that the five-year fixed-rate bond occupies a more vulnerable position to default-related prepays in the deal structure.

Thus, with rough parity in swap-adjusted spread between fixed- and floating-rate AAAs (Exhibit 10), floating-rate investors would generally opt for the AAA floater. At rough spread parity, the fixed-rate AAA CMBS looks expensive relative to AAA floating-rate bonds, in our opinion. In part, this pricing may reflect the less lumpy, more diversified collateral in fixed-rate conduit pools, pointing to reduced volatility in bond cash flows.

The pricing configuration for fixed and floating-rate AAA CMBS bears some resemblance to pricing in AAA credit card paper. Exhibit 11 compares spreads on 3-year floaters to swap-adjusted fixed-rate spreads. Over the 1997-2000 interval, floating-rate credit card paper has persistently looked a few basis points cheap to fixed-rate paper. Since the floating-rate side of the credit card market is better developed than in CMBS, the result seems to reflect demand-supply dynamics of investors and issuers in fixed and floating-rate debt and less than complete integration in pricing.

Analysis of ABS

Chapter 26

Performance, Risk, Structure, and Valuation of Credit-Sensitive ABS

Lang Gibson
Vice President
First Union Securities, Inc.

INTRODUCTION

As investors search for higher returning fixed-income investments, they are increasingly considering the more credit-sensitive (e.g., subordinated and mezzanine) tranches of asset-backed securities (ABS), which offer attractive risk-adjusted returns. The relative attractiveness of lower-rated ABS versus similarly rated corporates is that ABS performance measurement and credit stress testing can be quantified, leaving less to subjective judgment. Furthermore, although ABS and corporates face event risk, the collateral supporting ABS deals is far more diversified than that of corporates, which has a performance based on the expected cash flows and earnings volatility of one company. Indeed, historical defaults and credit downgrades demonstrate the superior protection afforded to all rated ABS tranches. As investors remain weary of rising interest rates and general market uncertainty, credit-sensitive ABS diversify the risk and return in a portfolio. In addition, for financial institutions, credit-sensitive ABS act as a surrogate for loans and may substantially increase the yield in the securities portfolio. Lastly, in times of higher prepayments, credit-sensitive ABS, which are issued at a discount, act as a convexity hedge as the discount is returned earlier than expected at issuance.

This chapter focuses on how these instruments can be analyzed to ensure a manager has performed proper due diligence for investing in a higher-return/higher-risk sector. The chapter is divided into the following topics:

- spread performance
- risk overview
- summary of the senior/subordinated structure and credit triggers in ABS
- stress-test results for the credit-sensitive tranches of bellwether issuers of credit card, auto, equipment, manufactured housing, and home equity ABS

Exhibit 1: Credit-Sensitive ABS Historical Spread Performance

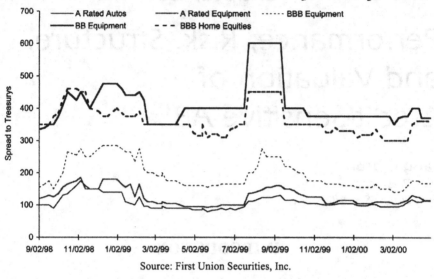

Source: First Union Securities, Inc.

SPREAD PERFORMANCE AND OUTLOOK

Exhibit 1 depicts how spreads for the credit-sensitive tranches of auto, equipment, and home equity ABS deals have performed between September 2, 1998 and April 28, 2000. The data show substantial spread widening during the 1998 market contagion period when Russia defaulted on its loans and Long-Term Capital Management (LTCM) was bailed out. Until the second half of 1998, hedge funds had always been big buyers of credit-sensitive ABS, helping to keep spreads tight. Once the LTCM crisis reduced hedge funds' ability to highly leverage their investments in ABS and they took huge losses on their short Treasury hedge positions, the bid for credit-sensitive ABS dissipated and spreads widened. BBB rated home equity and equipment paper spreads widened to maximum levels of 460 bps and 285 bps, respectively, from pre-crisis levels of 335 bps and 150 bps. In 1998, home equity spreads were particularly exacerbated by issuers filing for bankruptcy as their aggressive underwriting standards came back to haunt them. Meanwhile, A rated auto and equipment ABS widened to 175 bps and 185 bps, respectively, from precrisis levels of 90 bps and 120 bps.

The second credit-sensitive ABS spread blowout was in the third quarter of 1999 in response to Y2K concerns. BBB rated home equity and equipment paper widened to the same levels seen at the end of 1998 versus early 1999 lows of 310 bps and 155 bps, respectively. Meanwhile, A rated auto and equipment paper did not widen nearly as wide as the levels seen in the 1998 market contagion period. They widened to only 130 bps and 160 bps, respectively, versus early

1999 levels of 79 bps and 93 bps. As Y2K fears subsided in the fourth quarter of 1999, spreads came back to earth and credit-sensitive ABS have been increasingly supported by collateralized bond obligation (CBO) arbitrage funds as opposed to hedge funds, for which capital and leverage have remained at significantly reduced levels since 1998. In fact, hedge fund assets are approximately one-fifth of what they were precrisis. Credit-sensitive ABS spreads have risen slightly during the first few months of 2000 in sympathy with the rest of the market. However, as of April 28, 2000, BBB rated home equity and equipment paper was trading at 360 bps and 167 bps, whereas A rated auto and equipment paper was trading at 115 bps and 113 bps, respectively.

A predominant theme emanating from ABS conferences in 1999 and 2000 is the attractive relative value opportunities available in credit-sensitive ABS paper. Spread tightening in this market, especially real estate ABS, was correctly predicted by the ABS research community in 1999. However, in early 2000 real estate ABS spreads started to widen again due to credit risk and extension risk concerns.

Positive elements for ABS include the following:

1. Ongoing trends
   - significant tightening of underwriting standards
   - industry turmoil of 1998 and 1999 continuing to dissipate
   - improved credit performance
   - general flattening of the credit curve across ABS sectors as they become more transparent
   - better models providing enhanced clarification on the impact of potential defaults and delinquencies

2. Trends from end-1999 announcements
   - proposed Bank for International Settlements (BIS) rules to lower required regulatory capital for paper rated A to AAA
   - proposed Department of Labor (DOL) rules allowing pension funds to invest in non-real-estate subordinated paper

From a regulatory standpoint, the BIS proposal of late 1999 to allow ABS ratings to determine capital charges promises to bring a new breed of bank and insurance company investors to the ABS market, especially tranches rated A through AAA. Whereas most ABS now require 8% capital, under the proposal, AAAs and AAs will require only 1.6% capital while As will require only 4% capital. Furthermore, the DOL is proposing, as of late 1999, that corporate pension funds be able to invest in subordinated credit cards, autos, and commercial mortgage-backed securities (CMBS) for the first time. Meanwhile, the Bond Market Association is pushing the DOL to include subordinated home equity and high loan-to-value (LTV) paper as permitted investments for pension funds.

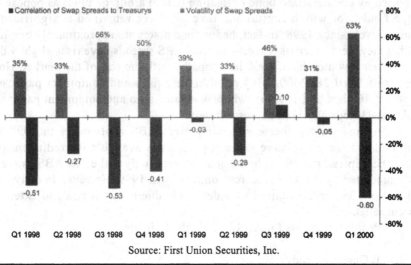

*Exhibit 2: Swap Spread Volatility and Correlation —
Q1 1998 to Q1 2000*

Source: First Union Securities, Inc.

RISK OVERVIEW

General credit spread volatility should be considered for market timing in any fixed income spread sector. For example, credit spread volatility was at exceptionally high levels during the first half of the year 2000. In Exhibit 2, we use daily swap spreads as a proxy for ABS credit spreads in general; there has been substantial academic and Street research showing how highly correlated these are. Over the first half of 2000, daily swap spread action was off the charts. Over this period, daily 5-year swap spread volatility was 63% versus 56% and 50% in the third and fourth quarters of 1998 (the market contagion period) and up from 31% in the fourth quarter of 1999.

In normal times, we would expect swap spread changes to be negatively correlated with Treasury yield changes, which keeps swap yields relatively stable despite volatility in the Treasury market. When Treasury rates fall, swap spreads usually widen and vice versa. However, we had never seen such a negative correlation as this, primarily due to a whipsawing Treasury curve. Over the first half of 2000, the correlation was negative 0.60 versus close to zero correlation in each of the two previous quarters. Even at the height of the 1998 market contagion period, the correlation never fell below negative 0.53 (third quarter of 1998). As volatility and correlations revert back to the mean from such lofty levels as seen in the first half of 2000, we would expect swap and ABS spreads to trade at lower levels.

Although credit-sensitive ABS spread volatility rose slightly in the first half of 2000 (Exhibit 3), return/risk measures were attractive during this period (Exhibit 4). Many investors are increasingly looking at the spread-to-spread volatility ratio, an offshoot of the Sharpe ratio, to determine value between sectors and securities. The ratio is calculated by dividing the period's average spread by the same period's annualized spread volatility. For instance, as of May 2000, the average annualized spread volatility of the five sectors tracked in Exhibit 1 was 68% versus 59% in the second half of 1999. Meanwhile, the average spread-to-spread volatility ratio had only fallen from 4.16 to 3.96.

Exhibit 3: Credit-Sensitive ABS Spread Volatility — Second Half of 1998 to First Half of 2000

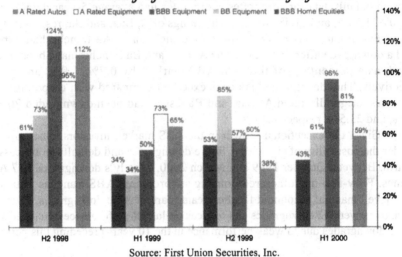

Source: First Union Securities, Inc.

Exhibit 4: Risk-Adjusted Performance — Second Half of 1998 to First Half of 2000

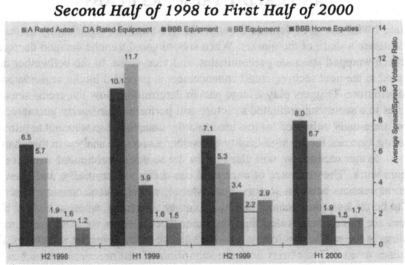

Source: First Union Securities, Inc.

From a credit standpoint, credit-sensitive ABS had performed well as of end-1999. Using Moody's Investors Service, Inc.'s ABS ratings, our analysis focused on default and downgrade history. As of the third quarter of 1999 and since the inception of Moody's ABS ratings in 1986, there had been no defaults, public or private, on Moody's rated ABS tranches. The first default of an ABS rated by Moody's after this period was the lower-rated tranches of three credit card ABS issued by Commercial Financial Service (CFS). However, the average 5-year default rate of 0% for ABS rated from Ba to Aaa over this period compared favorably with default data for corporates. Corporates had average 5-year default rates of 0.50%, 1.70%, and 11.4% for original ratings of A, Baa, and Ba, respectively.

Furthermore, as of the same period, no Aaa or Aa tranche had experienced a downgrade after five years. The A, Baa, and Ba tranches have been downgraded, as a percentage of the total ABS market, by 0.7%, 1.9%, and 5.7%, respectively. This downgrade history is excellent compared with corporates. For corporates, originally rated A, Baa, and Ba issues had been downgraded 20.8%, 17.8%, and 23.5%, respectively.

Given the exceptional growth in the ABS market, investors must seriously consider the possibility of significant future downgrades and defaults in a recession scenario. Between October 1999 and March 2000, Moody's downgraded 137 ABS tranches. Fifty-two manufactured housing subordinated ABS tranches issued by Green Tree Financial accounted for the greater part of these downgrades. Over this period, there were 62 downgrades due to weak collateral performance compared with only 18 downgrades due to weak performance in the 10 years preceding this period.

SUMMARY OF THE SENIOR/SUBORDINATED STRUCTURE AND CREDIT TRIGGERS IN ABS

The late 1990s saw good demand for subordinated tranches, significantly increasing this structure's share of the market. When subordinated tranche demand decreases, insurance wrapped issuance predominates, and vice-versa. In the bellwether deals analyzed in the next section, credit enhancement is provided by the senior/subordinated structure. Triggers play a large part in determining how the credit-sensitive tranches in a senior/subordinated structure will perform. Third-party guarantees, or wraps, are usually only used for less creditworthy issuers and so were not required by the rating agencies for the high-quality bellwether issuers we analyze in this chapter.

In this section, we will clarify how the senior/subordinated structure and triggers work. The structure of each deal can differ substantially, and there are different nuances between sectors. For instance, manufactured housing structures tend to be far less complicated than home equity structures, whereas both of these sectors are more complicated than the other three sectors we evaluate. A major problem is the public disclosure provided on the more complex structures. Prospectuses often fail to clarify how the subordinated and mezzanine tranches will perform in different credit scenarios. However, for most deals, our data source

(Intex) does clarify the structure, although the data may be difficult to access. From a valuation standpoint, it is important to have a model that incorporates all the structural features embedded in the bond.

In a senior/subordinated structure, the higher-rated tranches have a senior claim to the lower-rated mezzanine and subordinated tranches, which have a senior claim to the unrated, residual and equity tranches on the cash flow underlying the deal. This cash flow prioritization is referred to as the *sequential payment*, or *waterfall*. The lowest ranking class is the last to receive a principal payment and the last to have its principal fully retired. Any amount left over flows to the equity, or residual, holder. The rating agencies decide how much principal can be allocated to each tranche and thus determine the amount of support in each tranche. Deals with more creditworthy collateral require less support than less creditworthy collateral. For instance, the bellwether bonds we analyze in the next section have comparatively sound collateral and so require less support. Therefore, for the same credit stress-test scenario, the lower-rated tranches will experience principal loss or delay before the credit-sensitive tranches of a deal with poorer collateral. As the residual is often retained by the issuer, there is an incentive for the issuer to maximize the cash flow in the deal. Furthermore, issuers who rely substantially on securitization to fund their originations will do everything possible to protect the credit-sensitive tranches in their deals. Otherwise, these issuers risk losing access to the market and greatly deteriorating their franchise value.

In the first 2-3 years of most senior/subordinated deals, excess spread and principal payments are directed to the most senior tranches so that support levels as a percentage of the remaining balance increase and thus ensure adequate protection of the senior tranches. *Step-downs* were created as a method to redirect some of the excess spread cash flow to the subordinated tranches while protecting the ratings on the most senior tranches. Step-downs, which allow the credit-sensitive tranches to be paid off in a reasonable timeframe pro rata with the senior tranches, occur at the crossover date, which is normally after 2-3 years of aging.

After the crossover date, the credit-sensitive tranches are then exposed to credit triggers canceling the step-down feature. Once a trigger is hit, cash flows are again redirected to the most senior tranches until the credit conditions are satisfied. When the trigger is activated, the cash flows are again paid off sequentially to the tranches according to seniority as happens before the crossover date. Often, credit events can be satisfied in future periods and the step-down process continues allowing the lower-rated tranches to be paid down. However, serious credit events may be irreversible. Every deal has different credit events that initiate the trigger. For instance, home equity deals usually have some combination of delinquency and loss triggers. 1997 and earlier vintage equipment deals often had residual value tests. However, due to the relative smoothness of equipment loss curves, recent deals have replaced triggers with credit enhancement floors. Lastly, credit card deals typically have to meet certain excess spread levels. Triggers follow three steps in credit-sensitive tranche performance:

- Headline news announcements warn investors of the potential for triggers to be hit thus putting pressure on spreads.
- When the trigger is first hit, the average life may extend substantially.
- If the trigger continues to be hit, the tranche could lose principal.

Any reversal of credit events can reverse this process and allow the subordinated tranche to trade at normal levels again. In other words, the triggers are "correctable." A strategy that many investors use to trade credit-sensitive tranches with the potential of hitting a trigger is to buy the bond well before the crossover date, then sell the bond as credit starts deteriorating but substantially before the trigger is hit, thus avoiding headline risk. Then the investor would go onto the next credit-sensitive ABS tranche and execute the same strategy. The objective is to stay invested in high-yielding credit-sensitive paper while avoiding credit events. However, it is critical that the investor has full disclosure of the deal's performance with access to Intex and/or dealer surveillance reports. Furthermore, the investor needs a bond model that can accurately stress test the bond to time entry and exit prudently.

STRESS-TEST RESULTS FOR THE CREDIT-SENSITIVE TRANCHES OF BELLWETHER ISSUERS

In this last section, we will stress test the annual constant default rates (CDRs) for five subordinated tranches and four mezzanine tranches of bellwether issuers in five ABS sectors.

CDR assumes a percentage default rate over the life of the bond. The annualized realized loss is the product of the CDR and a severity rate. In each sector, we use constant conservative severity assumptions across all scenarios to focus the analysis on the impact to bond valuation of the assumed CDR. Whereas we assume a 100% severity rate for credit cards, we assume only a 50% severity rate for autos, equipment, and home equities. Manufactured housing falls between the two at a 70% severity rate. In our home equity deal, we will also stress test delinquencies, which are a key driver of performance.

All five deals analyzed have 2–3 years of aging, because this is a critical time to stress test deals as crossover dates approach. We perform this credit analysis with First Union Securities' proprietary *Bond Analyzer*, which uses all structural features provided by Intex, including triggers, as well as our proprietary prepayment and loss models.

Using the *Bond Analyzer*, our objective is to determine first where the deal's triggers cause the credit-sensitive tranches to extend in average life, if applicable, and second where the yield starts deteriorating due to principal losses. Depending on how much the bond is at a discount, the yield will first decline due to average life extension (as the investor would have to wait longer to receive back all cash flows) and then decline due to principal loss. Although we do not evaluate premium bonds here (as subordinated tranches are issued at a discount and so premiums in the secondary market are rare), these would experience rising yields as the average life extends and then yields would decline only once principal losses occur. The first scenario shows the yield at 0% CDR over the life of the deal. The second and/or third scenarios show the lowest CDR before the average life or yield is significantly affected due to the trigger. The subsequent four or five scenarios have CDR assumptions rising in 0.5% increments from the average life and yield breakpoint levels hit in the preceding scenarios. Pricing is as of May 3, 2000.

Exhibit 5 presents stress-test results for the A rated subordinated tranche (Class B) of a Citibank credit card deal, CBCT 97-02. The trigger in this deal occurs when the average 3-month excess spread is less than or equal to zero. Before the trigger is hit, the yield falls from 7.26% at 0% CDR to 7.05% at 3.8% CDR. For CBCT 97-02, Class B, after 3.8% CDR, the trigger is hit and the yield falls to 5.02% at a 4.0% CDR. Although 4.0% annual defaults could occur in a recession scenario, it is highly unlikely to occur over an extended period of time. Credit card triggers are hit at comparatively lower CDR levels than other ABS classes as the loans have substantially shorter maturities and we assume a 100% severity rate. Unlike some triggers, this trigger does not cause the average life to extend as the CDR rises.

Exhibit 6 presents stress-test results for the A rated mezzanine tranche (Class C) and BBB rated subordinated tranche (Class D) of a Ford Motor Co. auto deal, FAOT 98-A. The trigger in this deal is the reserve account falling to zero. Both tranches extend in average life marginally as the CDR increases. Whereas Class C's yield is not affected by the trigger until after 26.2% CDR, Class D's yield is affected after 6.6% CDR. Class C's yield falls from the base-case yield of 7.66% to 6.67% at 26.5% CDR (after the trigger is hit) and then to 1.99% at the point 28.5% CDR is reached. These CDRs are extremely unlikely, therefore it is likely the yield will remain close to the base case of 7.66%, except for the impact of large interest rate movements (the duration is only 1.5). Class D's yield falls from 8.08% in the base case to 8.04% at 6.6% CDR just before the trigger is hit. At 7.0% CDR, an increase of 0.4% CDR, the yield declines to −3.32%. If the CDR is stressed at 9.0%, the yield falls to −8.52%. So the reserve account trigger causes tremendous sensitivity between 6.6% and 7.0% CDR, at which point the yield decline starts leveling off for this tranche.

Exhibit 5: Citibank Credit Card CDR Stress Test

CBCT 97-02 Class B (A rated)	Subordinated Tranche						
	Scenario 1	Scenario 2	Scenario 3	Scenario 4	Scenario 5	Scenario 6	Scenario 7
CDR	0.0%	3.8%	4.0%	4.5%	5.0%	5.5%	6.0%
Severity	100.0%	100.0%	100.0%	100.0%	100.0%	100.0%	100.0%
Yield	7.26%	7.05%	5.02%	−4.83%	−17.18%	−33.65%	−59.62%
Principal Recovered	100.0%	100.0%	96.5%	81.8%	67.2%	52.6%	38.1%
Average Life (years)	1.78	1.71	1.69	1.62	1.53	1.44	1.34
Duration	1.63	1.57	1.56	1.56	1.57	1.59	1.59

CDR: Constant default rate.

Source: First Union Securities, Inc.

Exhibit 6: Ford Motor Co. Auto CDR Stress Test

FAOT 98-A Class C (A rated)	Mezzanine Tranche						
	Scenario 1	Scenario 2	Scenario 3	Scenario 4	Scenario 5	Scenario 6	Scenario 7
CDR	0.0%	26.2%	26.5%	27.0%	27.5%	28.0%	28.5%
Severity	50.0%	50.0%	50.0%	50.0%	50.0%	50.0%	50.0%
Yield	7.66%	7.35%	6.67%	5.52%	4.36%	3.18%	1.99%
Principal Recovered	100.0%	100.0%	98.5%	95.8%	93.2%	90.6%	87.9%
Average Life (years)	1.66	2.19	2.21	2.23	2.26	2.29	2.33
Duration	1.51	1.97	1.98	2.00	2.02	2.04	2.06

FAOT 98-A Class D (BBB rated)	Subordinated Tranche						
	Scenario 1	Scenario 2	Scenario 3	Scenario 4	Scenario 5	Scenario 6	Scenario 7
CDR	0.0%	6.6%	7.0%	7.5%	8.0%	8.5%	9.0%
Severity	50.0%	50.0%	50.0%	50.0%	50.0%	50.0%	50.0%
Yield	8.08%	8.04%	−3.32%	−4.62%	−5.92%	−7.22%	−8.52%
Principal Recovered	100.0%	100.0%	74.9%	72.4%	69.8%	67.2%	64.6%
Average Life (years)	2.12	2.36	2.37	2.41	2.44	2.44	2.51
Duration	1.88	2.07	2.07	2.11	2.13	2.13	2.17

CDR: Constant default rate.

Source: First Union Securities, Inc.

Exhibit 7: Newcourt Credit Group Inc. Equipment CDR Stress Test

NRAT 97-01 Class B (A rated)	Mezzanine Tranche						
	Scenario 1	Scenario 2	Scenario 3	Scenario 4	Scenario 5	Scenario 6	Scenario 7
CDR	0.0%	24.7%	25.0%	25.5%	26.0%	26.5%	27.0%
Severity	50.0%	50.0%	50.0%	50.0%	50.0%	50.0%	50.0%
Yield	7.63%	7.32%	6.10%	3.60%	1.62%	−1.09%	−3.95%
Principal Recovered	100.0%	100.0%	98.2%	94.7%	92.0%	88.5%	85.0%
Average Life (years)	0.90	1.22	1.26	1.34	1.40	1.48	1.56
Duration	0.82	1.09	1.10	1.11	1.12	1.13	1.14

NRAT 97-01 Class C (BBB rated)	Subordinated Tranche						
	Scenario 1	Scenario 2	Scenario 3	Scenario 4	Scenario 5	Scenario 6	Scenario 7
CDR	0.0%	21.4%	21.5%	22.0%	22.5%	23.0%	23.5%
Severity	50.0%	50.0%	50.0%	50.0%	50.0%	50.0%	50.0%
Yield	8.08%	7.70%	7.55%	3.38%	−1.17%	−6.19%	−11.81%
Principal Recovered	100.0%	100.0%	99.8%	94.1%	88.3%	82.6%	76.8%
Average Life (years)	0.84	1.17	1.18	1.31	1.43	1.55	1.67
Duration	0.77	1.04	1.05	1.07	1.08	1.10	1.13

CDR: Constant default rate.

Source: First Union Securities, Inc.

Exhibit 7 presents stress-test results for the A rated mezzanine tranche (Class B) and BBB rated subordinated tranche (Class C) of a Newcourt Credit Group equipment deal, NRAT 97-01. The trigger in this deal is the reserve account having zero value as was the case in the auto deal. Later vintage Newcourt deals have been structured with credit enhancement floors instead of triggers. Both tranches extend in average life slightly as the trigger approaches. For NRAT 97-01, the Class B yield is affected by the trigger after 24.7% CDR, and the Class C yield is affected after 21.4% CDR. Class B's average life extends from 0.90 year to 1.22 years once the trigger is hit, then extends to 1.56 years at 27.0% CDR. Stressing the CDR an additional 0.3% past the trigger point, the yield falls from 7.63% in the base case to 6.10% at 25.0% CDR. Class C takes only a slightly lower CDR threshold to activate yield degradation and average life extension. Average life extends from 0.84 year in the base case to 1.67 years at 23.5% CDR. At 22.0% CDR, an additional 0.6% CDR after the trigger is hit, the yield falls to 3.38% from 8.08% in the base case.

Exhibit 8 presents the stress-test results for the A rated mezzanine tranche (Class M1) and the BBB rated subordinated tranche (Class B1) of a Green Tree Financial manufactured housing deal, GTMH 97-01. The trigger in this deal is a combination of delinquency, current loss, and cumulative loss. Although the crossover date is not until February 2002, the current loss trigger, which is at the point that current loss falls below 2.25%, is already hit. In this deal, average life extension is significant as the triggers approach. Class M1's average life extends from 8.40 years in the base case to 14.85 years at 6.8% CDR. Even at 3.0% CDR, the average life extends to 11.94%. The yield is affected due to loss of principal after 6.8% CDR. Between 6.8% CDR and 7.5% CDR, the yield falls from 8.35% to 7.49%. At 8.5% CDR, the yield falls to 5.44%. Class B1 experiences significant average life extension from 3.35 years to 15.17 years between 2.8% and 3.0% CDR. This extension causes the yield on the discount-priced bond to fall from 11.75% to 8.77%. Yield degradation from principal loss occurs between 5.5% and 6.0% CDR when the yield declines from 8.68% to 6.63%.

Exhibit 8: Green Tree Financial Corp. Manufactured Housing CDR Stress Test

GTMH 97-01 Class M1 (A rated)	Mezzanine Tranche						
	Scenario 1	Scenario 2	Scenario 3	Scenario 4	Scenario 5	Scenario 6	Scenario 7
CDR	0.0%	3.0%	6.8%	7.0%	7.5%	8.0%	8.5%
Severity	70.0%	70.0%	70.0%	70.0%	70.0%	70.0%	70.0%
Yield	8.94%	8.47%	8.35%	8.20%	7.49%	6.54%	5.44%
Principal Recovered	100.0%	100.0%	100.0%	91.8%	60.2%	32.3%	8.6%
Average Life (years)	8.40	11.94	14.85	15.26	15.09	14.47	13.78
Duration	5.14	7.34	8.21	8.26	8.25	8.28	8.41

GTMH 97-01 Class B1 (BBB rated)	Subordinated Tranche						
	Scenario 1	Scenario 2	Scenario 3	Scenario 4	Scenario 5	Scenario 6	Scenario 7
CDR	0.0%	2.8%	3.0%	5.5%	6.0%	6.5%	7.0%
Severity	70.0%	70.0%	70.0%	70.0%	70.0%	70.0%	70.0%
Yield	11.18%	11.75%	8.77%	8.68%	6.63%	2.91%	-6.93%
Principal Recovered	100.0%	100.0%	100.0%	100.0%	4.1%	3.7%	3.3%
Average Life (years)	3.95	3.35	15.17	17.07	16.79	12.84	8.19
Duration	3.01	2.63	8.08	8.65	8.80	8.71	5.56

CDR: Constant default rate.

Source: First Union Securities, Inc.

Exhibit 9: Saxon Mortgage Funding Corp. Home Equity CDR and Delinquency Stress Test

SAST 97-01 Class MF2 (A rated)	Mezzanine Tranche						
	Scenario 1	Scenario 2	Scenario 3	Scenario 4	Scenario 5	Scenario 6	Scenario 7
CDR	0.0%	8.2%	8.5%	9.0%	9.5%	10.0%	10.5%
Severity	50.0%	50.0%	50.0%	50.0%	50.0%	50.0%	50.0%
Delinquencies	0.0%	20.0%	30.0%	40.0%	50.0%	60.0%	70.0%
Yield	8.48%	8.45%	7.43%	6.05%	5.07%	4.38%	3.63%
Principal Recovered	100.0%	99.7%	92.9%	81.7%	72.7%	67.4%	62.3%
Average Life (years)	4.84	4.71	5.73	6.35	7.01	7.28	7.41
Duration	3.33	3.26	4.05	4.41	4.76	5.05	5.26

SAST 97-01 Class BF (BBB rated)	Subordinated Tranche						
	Scenario 1	Scenario 2	Scenario 3	Scenario 4	Scenario 5	Scenario 6	Scenario 7
CDR	0.0%	7.1%	7.5%	8.0%	8.5%	9.0%	9.5%
Severity	50.0%	50.0%	50.0%	50.0%	50.0%	50.0%	50.0%
Delinquencies	0.0%	20.0%	30.0%	40.0%	50.0%	60.0%	70.0%
Yield	9.53%	9.61%	4.75%	−1.51%	−20.12%	−38.14%	−44.30%
Principal Recovered	100.0%	100.0%	72.9%	36.8%	1.9%	0.0%	0.0%
Average Life (years)	5.30	4.97	5.84	6.16	4.64	3.84	3.51
Duration	3.71	3.51	4.42	6.74	7.04	3.95	3.75

CDR: Constant default rate.

Source: First Union Securities, Inc.

Exhibit 9 presents the stress-test results for the A rated mezzanine tranche (Class MF2) and the BBB rated subordinated tranche (Class BF) of a Saxon Mortgage home equity deal, SAST 97-01. The trigger in this deal is delinquencies and losses, so we stress test both CDRs and delinquencies. For consistency, we stress test both tranches between 20% and 70% delinquencies. Neither tranche has the large average life variability seen in the manufactured housing deal. For SAST 97-01, Class MF2's yield and average life are affected negatively after 8.2% CDR, whereas Class BF is affected by the trigger after 7.1% CDR. Class MF2 sees its yield compress from 8.45% to 7.43% and its average life extend from 4.71 years to 5.73 years between 8.2% and 8.5% CDR. As the CDR is stressed further, the yield deteriorates slowly as the average life extends slowly until they are at 3.63% and 3.51 years, respectively, at 10.5% CDR. Class BF's yield contracts from 9.61% to 4.75%, whereas its average life extends from 4.97 years to 5.84 years between 7.1% CDR and 7.5% CDR. From 7.5% CDR, as CDR increases, the yield deteriorates at an increasing rate, whereas the average life caps out at 7.04 years when 8.5% CDR is breached.

CONCLUSION

The credit-sensitive tranches of ABS offer attractive yields largely uncorrelated with factors driving volatility in the traditional fixed-income market. Furthermore, credit-sensitive ABS offer more diversification, lower defaults and better rating downgrade performance than similarly rated corporates. However, investors should perform proper due diligence on these investments by understanding how they may perform in a turning credit cycle.

We have presented in this chapter many of the factors that should be considered when investing in credit-sensitive ABS. These factors include macro sector performance and risk (including historical spread performance, volatility, defaults, and credit downgrades), the impact on the lower-rated tranches of the sequential pay-down structure in a senior/subordinated structure, and state-of-the-art credit stress testing with a model that embeds the impact of a deal's structural features.

Chapter 27

Identifying Relative Value in the ABS Market

Lisa N. Wilhelm
Managing Director
Asset Backed Finance
Banc One Capital Markets, Inc.

W. Alexander Roever, CFA
Managing Director
Head of ABS Research
Banc One Capital Markets, Inc.

INTRODUCTION

For bond investors, relative value is a beautiful thing. Indeed, finding a bond that offers an above-average rate of return in exchange for a given level of risk is the holy grail of most portfolio managers. But, because investors have individual preferences and risk tolerances, value — like beauty — can be in the eye of the beholder. Just as philosophers may disagree over what constitutes beauty, investors often differ over what constitutes relative value. After all, every bond trade requires both a buyer and a seller, each of whom has simultaneously evaluated the same security and concluded, respectively, that the bond is cheap or rich.

This apparent paradox demonstrates that relative value is not a market-wide phenomenon but, instead, a concept unique to each investor. Relative-value analysis should be viewed as an investor-specific process for identifying those securities that are most likely to provide a superior return over a given horizon for a given level of risk. But, with respect to measuring both return and risk, ABS can provide some unique challenges relative to other fixed-income securities. Most of these challenges are by-products of securitization, the process that transforms cash flows received from relatively risky forms of collateral into less risky securities. Securitization shapes and transfers risk through the use of financial and legal structuring techniques. In doing so it can create opportunities and pose problems that investors inexperienced with ABS may have trouble spotting. The purpose of this chapter is to provide investors with a usable set of tools for identifying relative value in the asset-backed securities market.

457

The ABS market contains a rich array of security types supported by many diverse kinds of collateral. There are numerous ways to stratify this market. The most meaningful cut, from a relative-value perspective, is by coupon type. Although there are often opportunities between the fixed- and floating-rate market that can be exploited through the use of derivatives, the vast majority of comparisons are made between assets of similar coupon type. As a reflection of this concentration on coupon type, the chapter is organized into two parts focused on identifying relative value in fixed- and floating-rate ABS.

RELATIVE VALUE IN FIXED-RATE ABS

Embedded in the price of every bond are views about the timing and certainty of its expected cash flows, as well as an expectation of its future performance versus similar instruments. All else being equal, bonds that are more creditworthy, bonds with known payment timing, and bonds with better total-return characteristics will command higher prices than otherwise similar bonds lacking these attributes.

These same principles hold in the ABS market. But, the diversity of collateral types securitized, the wide range of collateral maturities, the delinquency and loss profiles of the collateral, the variety of structures employed, the sensitivity of the structures to changes in collateral payment rates, and a host of other factors can complicate relative-value analysis. This analysis can be simplified for fixed-rate ABS by evaluating three attributes of each security: cash-flow profile, volatility of collateral cash flows, and underlying credit profile.

Cash-Flow Profiles

In the bond market, the trading price of a security is determined by adding a spread to the yield of a benchmark security, then discounting the future cash flows at the combined yield. By convention, the benchmark security is usually the U.S. Treasury note or bond with a maturity that most closely matches the average life of the bond being priced. This pricing convention can cause problems in the ABS market, where, for almost any given average life, there are many bonds and many different cash-flow profiles.

Cash-flow profiles common in ABS include bullets, passthrough securities, and sequential-pay bonds. These profiles are largely reflective of the term of the underlying assets and the structures employed in securitization. Most short-lived collateral types such as credit card or trade receivables usually rely on revolving structures and produce ABS with bullet profiles. Longer-dated collateral, such as auto or mortgage loans, are securitized using structures that pass through cash flows as they are collected. Depending on the structure employed, either pure passthrough or time-tranched ABS can be based on these types of collateral.

Because bonds with different profiles behave differently and are exposed to different levels of market risk over time, investors will usually express their preference for a given profile in the price of the bond. All else being equal, and given a positively sloped yield curve, investors will usually pay more for bonds with bullet profiles and less for bonds with amortizing profiles. Since bullets and amortizing bonds with identical average lives price off the same benchmark, the investor's preference is reflected as wider spreads for bonds with more widely dispersed payments.

Exhibit 1 illustrates how different cash-flow profiles behave over time, and how this affects the relative value of the securities. The exhibit presents three bonds which initially have identical average lives. Bond A is a bullet. Bond B is a sequential-pay bond that receives no principal until the end of the second year. Bond C is a passthrough structure that begins receiving principal the first year. All three bonds pay a 5% coupon annually and sell for par.

Exhibit 1: Behavior of Cash-Flow Profiles over Time

Period	Term Structure (%)	Expected Cash Flows Bond A	Bond B	Bond C
1	4.00	$5.00	$5.00	$25.00
2	4.50	5.00	38.33	24.00
3	5.00	105.00	36.66	23.00
4	5.25		35.01	22.00
5	5.50			21.00

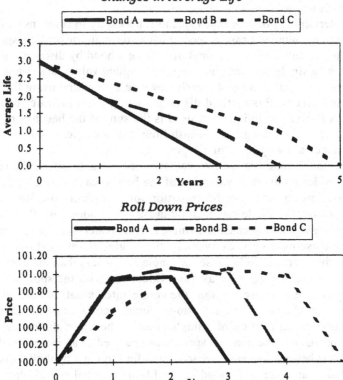

Changes in Average Life

Bond A —— Bond B —— Bond C

Roll Down Prices

Bond A —— Bond B —— Bond C

As time passes, each structure will age differently, and these differences have implications for the returns investors can earn on the bonds. After one year has passed, bonds A and B have a remaining average life of two years, but bond C has a remaining average life of 2.5 years. If the curve is upward sloping, bonds A and B will reprice off a lower-yielding benchmark than bond C, which should result in bonds A and B having a higher price than bond C. This upward change in price due to aging is known as "rolling down the yield curve." Bonds that age faster have better "roll" characteristics and, all else being equal, will earn greater total returns. Since amortizing bonds roll slower than bullet bonds, they tend to have lower returns than otherwise identical bullet bonds. Sequential-pay bonds that are locked out from principal payments for a period of time will roll like bullets during the lockout period and like amortizing bonds during their payout phase. Over a horizon that is longer than its lockout period, a sequential-pay bond will roll less than an otherwise identical bullet and, therefore, have a lower return.

To offset the disadvantage posed by wider principal payment windows, investors will usually require a higher yield. Since convention requires bonds, regardless of profile, to be spread off the yield of a benchmark with the same average life, wider yields translate into wider nominal spreads. As a rule, the wider the principal payment window, the wider the nominal spread must be to offset this disadvantage.

Determining just how much spread is necessary to compensate for differences in payment windows can be accomplished through use of static spread analysis. Unlike the conventional method of valuing a bond by discounting all of its cash flows by a single rate and summing the resultant values, static spread analysis requires that each of a bond's cash flows be discounted using the spot rate method. Essentially, this method discounts using a unique rate for each of a bond's cash flows. The unique rate used is the sum of the benchmark spot rate corresponding to the timing of each cash flow, plus a single, uniform — or static — spread added to every benchmark spot rate.

Exhibit 2 contrasts the two valuation methods. In effect, the single-rate method provides an average valuation of the bonds' cash flows, while the spot method calculates a time-specific valuation for each cash flow. Relative to the spot-rate method, the single-rate method undervalues bond cash flows occurring prior to the average life, because the single rate is greater than the spot rates associated with these payments. Conversely, the single-rate method overvalues the flows after the average life because the single rate is less than the corresponding spot rates. By comparing these average valuations with the spot valuations, it becomes possible to judge whether the single-rate valuation has, on balance, overvalued or undervalued the cash flows. Since static spread is measured over the yield curve rather than off of a single point on the curve, differences between the static spreads and the nominal spreads can be used as an indicator of whether the investor is being adequately compensated for buying a nonbullet bond. If the static spread of an amortizing bond is equal to its nominal spread, then the overvalued and undervalued cash flows have offset one another and the bond is priced fairly. If the static spread is greater than the nominal spread, then the undervalued cash flows are on balance greater than the overvalued cash flows and, therefore, the bond's price understates its value. Conversely, if a static spread is less than the nominal spread, the bond is overvalued.

Static-spread analysis is a useful, albeit imperfect, tool for relative-value analysis. Since it assumes a fixed term structure, it essentially ignores the effects that changing interest rates will have on bond values. For this reason, it is useful to use static-spread analysis in conjunction with traditional risk measures such as duration and convexity. One way to make static-spread analysis more robust is to repeat the calculations using several different term structures. This approach can help investors to quantify the effects that yield-curve reshaping (such as flattening, steepening, or inversion) will have on bonds with differing cash-flow profiles.

Cash-Flow Volatility

Another drawback to static-spread analysis is that it assumes cash flows are fixed. This assumption can be problematic for passthrough ABS with collateral that is subject to early repayment. For these bonds, changes in the rate of repayment can significantly alter a security's cash flow profile and, therefore, its relative attractiveness. All else being equal, bonds with relatively stable and predictable cash flows offer greater value than those with less predictable payments.

Exhibit 2: Single-Rate Versus Spot-Rate Valuation

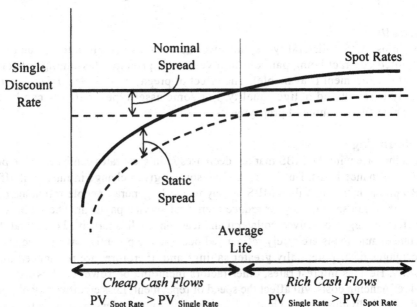

Prepayments are an important fact of life in the ABS market. They may indeed be the single most important determinant of a fixed-rate bond's relative value. Assumptions about collateral repayment determine the average lives and benchmarks used to price most ABS. Variations in collateral prepayment rates from their expected levels can negatively impact investors. If actual prepayment rates prove slower than expected prepayment rates, too short an average life will have been used in pricing the bond and returns earned will be less than expected. If the actual speed of prepayments exceeds expectations, it is possible that investors may have to reinvest bond proceeds at interest rates lower than on the bonds they purchased. This is particularly a risk for ABS supported by interest rate-sensitive collateral such as various kinds of mortgage products. Many factors can affect ABS prepayment rates as explained in the following sections.

Normal Turnover
Normal economic activity causes some level of prepayment for nearly every type of financial asset securitized. Examples of this include equipment lease contracts that are terminated because the lessee upgrades equipment or auto loans that are repaid by insurance proceeds following an accident or theft.

Curtailments
These partial prepayments occur when borrowers pay more than their scheduled monthly payment. They are common in some consumer asset types like mortgages and auto loans, but usually contribute only a small amount to overall prepayments.

Defaults
With most ABS collateral types, borrower defaults will result in the value of the defaulted contract being paid out to investors as principal (assuming sufficient credit enhancement is available). The effect of prepayment-driven defaults varies widely by asset and obligor quality. For some asset types, defaults can be the most significant source of prepayments.

Refinancing
As is the case with the MBS market, decreases in interest rates can incentivize people to refinance loans. But for several reasons, a given change in rates will affect ABS prepayments less than MBS prepayments. In general, people refinance only when they can save money, or reduce their debt-service payment. The savings are greatest on large, long-lived collateral and least on small, short-lived collateral. For instance, auto loans are rarely refinanced because the potential savings are small. Mortgages offer potentially greater savings and, therefore, are refinanced more readily. Besides interest rates, other factors including borrower creditworthiness and refinancing costs will affect the speed of repayment. Less creditworthy obligors and other individuals facing high refinancing costs will be less prone to refinance.

Exhibit 3: Projected Loss Multiples

Rating	Minimum Loss Multiple
AAA	4 – 5 × Base-Case Losses
AA	3 – 4 ×
A	2 – 3 ×
BBB	1.75 – 2 ×
BB	1.5 – 1.75 ×

Source: Standard & Poor's, by permission.

Credit Profile

The third piece of the ABS relative-value puzzle is the credit profile. The credit profile serves as an indicator of the certainty of ultimate principal repayment and goes beyond the concept of credit ratings. At least four dimensions of credit have implications for the relative risk of any ABS: structural enhancement, collateral seasoning, servicer quality, and liquidity considerations.

Structural Enhancement

The credit rating of every ABS is a function of the structure of the securitization from which it was issued. When assembling transactions, investment bankers — on behalf of the sponsor — work with the rating agencies to design the most efficient and cost-effective securitization structure. Such a structure is usually achieved by maximizing the number of bonds issued and minimizing the overall interest cost and levels of credit enhancement. One of the primary tasks of the rating agency is to determine the appropriate level of credit enhancement necessary for the ABS sold to achieve the desired credit rating. The enhancement can come from either external or internal sources. External enhancement typically takes the form of a specialized insurance policy or letter of credit. Common types of internal enhancement include reserve accounts, overcollateralization, and subordination.

For ABS that rely on internal enhancement, the rating agencies calculate or "size" the amount of credit enhancement needed for each class of bonds to achieve the rating by scaling the enhancement to a multiple of projected losses, as shown in Exhibit 3. The goal of the sizing process is to provide every rated ABS with a cushion of credit enhancement and liquidity capable of absorbing losses and promoting timely coupon payments. Higher ratings require higher enhancement multiples.

When evaluating two or more bonds with otherwise identical features, those bonds which feature greater credit enhancement will have less credit risk and, therefore, offer greater value. If the rating agencies are consistent in the way they rate new securities, bonds with similar loss profiles should initially have similar levels of credit enhancement. However, investors should be cognizant that the level of actual losses sustained by the collateral may differ from the loss assumptions embedded in the credit enhancement. If the actual collateral performance proves substantially better or worse than projected performance for a sustained period, then the ABS might, respectively, become a candidate for a rating upgrade or downgrade.

Exhibit 4: Stress-Testing Alternative

Issue	Issue Date	Weighted Average Seasoning at Issue	Current Weighted Average Seasoning*	Cumulative Losses*	Credit Enhancement for Seniors*	Enhancement as a Multiple of Losses
Chase Manhattan Grantor Trust Series 1995-B	11/15/95	11 months	34 months	0.32%	6.25%	19.5×
Ford Credit Grantor Trust Series 1995-B	11/15/95	4 months	27 months	1.80%	8.53%	4.7×

* As of 10/31/97

Rather than waiting for a rating agency to initiate a ratings review, investors may want to take a more proactive approach to structural analysis. After all, they ultimately bear the risks and stand to reap the rewards created by disparities between expected and actual collateral performance. Among the structural analysis tools available to investors are *stress testing* and *loss-multiple analysis*.

Stress testing requires modeling every aspect of a securitization from its collateral to its capital structure and cash-flow allocation mechanisms, then stressing the collateral's performance until the ABS suffers a loss. Structures that can suffer higher levels of stress are superior. While stress testing can provide a very accurate indication of how well protected ABS are from collateral losses, they can be difficult and time-consuming to construct properly; meanwhile, the bonds in question may be sold away before a conclusion can be reached.

A simpler and quicker alternative to stress testing evaluates credit enhancement levels as a multiple of actual or expected losses. Exhibit 4 illustrates two very similar bonds, Chase Manhattan Grantor Trust 1995-B, Class A and Ford Credit Grantor Trust 1995-B, Class A. Based on their loss-coverage multiples, the Chase bonds appear to offer a greater margin of safety.

Even though the use of loss multiples can be an extremely helpful tool, investors should exercise caution to ensure they are making a fair comparison. Differences in the structure of credit enhancement need to be taken into account when comparing coverage multiples from different bonds. For example, while some ABS have credit enhancement levels that remain relatively constant over the life of the bonds, other structures feature enhancement levels that may change during the life of the bond. For instance, many bonds are protected by mechanisms that cause changes in the level of enhancement relative to the remaining bonds. Structural devices like spread accounts (reserve accounts that are funded with excess spread), minimum reserve-account requirements, and subordinate bonds with principal-lockout features will all change the levels of enhancement over the life of an ABS. Other mechanisms such as loss and delinquency triggers can, if invoked, also increase enhancement levels. Investors should take care to incorporate the effects of these structural devices into their analysis.

Exhibit 5: Behavior of Pool Loss Rates over Time

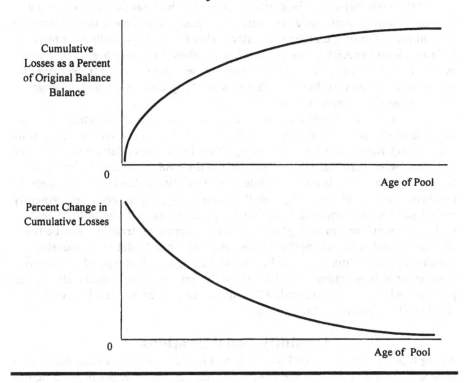

Collateral Seasoning

It is exceptionally rare for loan defaults and losses to be spread evenly over the life of a collateral pool. Instead, many collateral types when pooled tend to exhibit a loss life cycle in which the rate of loss is greatest in the early months, then slows as the bonds age. This relationship can be seen in static-loss curves, which depict the relationship between the age of a collateral pool and the cumulative losses it has sustained. The two graphs in Exhibit 5 illustrate a typical static loss curve and the behavior of a pool's loss rates over time.

Analysis of a pool's static losses can aid in relative-value decisions. For instance, by helping to identify where a collateral pool stands in its loss cycle, pool analysis can provide an indication of future collateral performance, which investors can then use in determining the adequacy of credit enhancement. Also, static-pool analysis can be useful over time for monitoring the performance of firms that originate and service ABS collateral. Increases in static losses from series to series can signal important changes in credit and collection procedures and other business practices at an originator/servicer. Unless credit enhancement levels change in step, newer series will be less creditworthy than vintage series, even though ABS from the different series continue to carry the same rating.

Servicer Quality

One of the main benefits of securitization is that the financial assets serving as collateral are, by virtue of a true sale to a bankruptcy-remote third party, put beyond the reach of the seller's creditors. This true-sale procedure protects the collateral securing ABS in the event the seller should fall into bankruptcy. However, if the seller also functions as the servicer on a transaction it is important for investors to realize that their investment is not fully insulated against changes in the seller/servicer's credit quality.

Despite its bankruptcy-remote status, securitized collateral remains exposed to its servicer's ability to perform. Failure of a servicer to perform its duties adequately can often result in significantly worse collateral performance and, thereby, compromise the credit quality of the ABS. Should a servicer become financially strained, it is quite possible that its operating standards could become compromised. To mitigate against this possibility, rating agencies typically embed servicer performance tests into ABS transactions. If one of these tests is violated, a servicer can be replaced. However, servicing transfers can be time-consuming and collateral performance could continue to deteriorate during the transition period. Ultimately, the best protection against this type of servicer risk is to invest in transactions for which the seller/servicer is in a financially secure position. All things considered, ABS subject to greater levels of servicer risk should reflect that risk in their pricing.

Liquidity Considerations

A long time truism of the bond market is that liquidity is always available until it is needed. This quip hints at the fickle and credit-sensitive nature of bond liquidity. In the bond market, liquidity is reflected in pricing and, therefore, has implications for relative value. Bonds with greater liquidity command tighter spreads to their benchmark than relatively illiquid securities.

Among the many factors affecting liquidity in the ABS market are collateral type, issue size, and issuer reputation. Bonds supported by mature and widely understood collateral types will almost always price better than similar bonds backed by less closely followed assets. Similarly, ABS issued from large securitizations will tend to have greater liquidity because the large issues are more widely held and therefore more investors are generally aware of the bonds and their performance. Along the same lines, securities originated by frequent or well known issuers tend to have a wider following and command better pricing.

On the negative side, ABS liquidity is very occasionally subject to "headline" risk, in which negative news regarding an originator, a collateral type, or some other aspect of a securitization causes a dramatic and sudden drop in demand. An excellent example of this occurred in early 1997 when several bankruptcies rocked the subprime auto finance industry. Reacting to the news, spreads on all subprime auto ABS, not just those of the firms affected, widened significantly.

In spite of its potentially negative effects, illiquidity is not always a bad thing. Investors who are by nature buy-and-hold or who have the ability to allocate some portion of their portfolios in illiquid instruments, may be able to enhance their long-term returns by systematically purchasing illiquid ABS at relatively cheap prices.

RELATIVE VALUE IN FLOATING-RATE ABS

In the previous section, we discussed variables important to measuring relative value in fixed-rate ABS. Credit quality assessment, cash-flow profiles, and cash-flow volatility are also key inputs to accessing relative value in floating-rate ABS. Factors unique to floaters include some characteristics of basis risk, the need to recalibrate deals to a common benchmark, and the calculation of spread duration.

Floating-rate ABS structures are common in those sectors where the finance charges or interest payments earned on the underlying receivables are also floating. These finance charges and interest payments float at a fixed spread over a predetermined market index. Examples of ABS sectors with floating-rate collateral include credit cards, adjustable-rate home equity loans, home equity lines of credit, trade receivables, and student loans. Floating-rate tranches have also been carved out of the short-term cash flows off fixed-rate collateral. In 1996, for example, Chrysler's four auto loan deals included a floating-rate sequential tranche collateralized with fixed-rate auto loans. Floating-rate tranches off fixed-rate home equity loans are another example. For the purposes of this chapter, references to home equity floaters will apply to structures collateralized with adjustable-rate home equity loans and not floaters structured off of fixed-rate loans.

Yield spreads for floating-rate ABS are quoted in terms of a discount margin to the underlying reset index. A floating-rate bond's discount margin is the difference between the yield on the reset index and the yield on the security. The term of the reset index typically matches the coupon reset and payment frequency. For example, most credit card floaters are quoted at a discount margin to one-month LIBOR, corresponding to a monthly coupon reset and a monthly coupon payment to bondholders. The coupon rate and amount adjusts monthly based upon the value of the underlying reset index. The coupon formula is stated as a fixed spread to the underlying reset index.

Basis Risk

Basis risk refers to a possible mismatch between adjustments to the ABS coupon rate paid to the investor and the yield on the underlying portfolio of collateral. Before paying a coupon to the investor, the yield on a portfolio of collateral must pay fees for servicing, surety, and other functions, and cover principal losses. The amount of yield remaining after fees, principal losses, and the bond coupon are paid is referred to as excess spread for most asset types, and the available funds margin[1] for home equity floaters. Losses, delinquencies, and non-interest rate related fees on underlying collateral cause much of the variation in excess spreads and the available funds margin. Basis risk refers to that portion of the mismatch unrelated to collateral performance.

Basis risk is driven by factors that are uncertain at the time of purchase, such as the frequency and magnitude of changes in the level of rates and the shape of the Treasury and Eurodollar yield curves. A few sources of basis risk are common over most collateral asset types, such as index risk and reset risk. Collateral containing "teaser" rates or interest rate caps can also introduce basis risk.

Index Risk

Index risk represents the yield curve risk between the coupon rate paid to bondholders and the portfolio yield generated by the underlying receivables. Many fixed-rate and most floating-rate ABS structures have exposure to index risk. In credit card ABS structures, finance charges on outstanding credit card balances reset at a fixed spread over the prime rate while the coupon on the ABS securities collateralized with those balances resets at a spread to 1-month LIBOR. The mortgages collateralizing home equity floaters may be indexed off 6-month LIBOR or a constant-maturity Treasury index and support a coupon on the ABS indexed to 1-month LIBOR.

In both examples, a mismatch exists between the coupon rate paid to investors and the index which sets the portfolio yield. Coupons paid reset off the front of the Eurodollar curve. Yet the interest income supporting those coupons is driven by a constant-maturity Treasury (CMT) index or the prime rate, which both move with the Treasury yield curve. The positive yield curve slope usually protects investors from index risk. Investor coupons typically float over an index with a shorter term than the index associated with the collateral. Conversely, an inverted yield curve could increase the effects of index risk.

Reset Risk

Most floating-rate ABS structures are also exposed to reset risk, defined as the mismatch between the frequency of investor coupon resets and the frequency of the resets on the underlying collateral. Finance charges on seasoned credit card balances reset daily over the prime rate versus monthly coupon resets on ABS collateralized with credit card receivables. Interest rates on adjustable-rate home equity loans reset annually or twice per year, versus monthly coupon resets on home equity floaters. Since home equity floaters are collateralized with new production loans, reset dates on the underlying mortgages can be lumped together rather than equally distributed across the calendar.

Reset risk is mitigated for most asset classes by the wide margins between the coupons paid to investors and interest earned on the underlying col-

---

[1] The available funds margin (AFM) is the amount available to pay the bondholder's coupon, the servicing fees, and other fees:

AFM = Gross Coupon − Servicing − Other Fees − Surety Spread − (Coupon Index − Margin)

lateral. The wide margins reflect the difference in credit quality between the security, which is often rated triple-A, and the underlying consumer or commercial borrower. For instance, home equity floaters collateralized with B and C loans run little reset risk due to very wide margins. Mortgage rates on collateral typically reset at 500-700 basis points above either 6-month LIBOR or 1-year CMT versus a coupon rate indexed to 1-month LIBOR plus 50 to 100 basis points.

An illustration of the sizable available funds margin on home equity floaters can be found in the Exhibit 6 description of the Aames 97-1 Class A bond. The Aames 97-1 bond is indexed to 1-month LIBOR + 20 basis points, whereas the underlying mortgage collateral is indexed to both 6-month LIBOR (79%) and 1-year CMT (21%). If 1-month LIBOR increases while both 6-month LIBOR and 1-year CMT remain constant, the amount available to pay the coupon, the available funds cap,[2] has decreased. All other things equal, an investor would require a wider discount margin on a bond for which the underlying collateral exhibits an unevenly distributed reset schedule.

Teaser Risk
Teaser risk refers to the impairment on the portfolio yield from below-market rates earned on underlying receivables. Some credit card issuers offer "teaser" rates to attract new cardholders. The issuer guarantees a below-market rate of interest on credit card balances for six months or one year. When credit card receivables with teaser rates are added to a revolving master trust by the issuer, ABS bondholders are at risk of falling portfolio yields. As the proportion of receivables with teaser rates increases in a revolving master trust, portfolio yields and excess spreads fall and investors usually require wider spreads to hold the securities.

Exhibit 6: ABS Floater Characteristics

Issue FUSAM 1997-4	AAMES 1997-1
Class A	A
Coupon 1-month LIBOR + 21 basis points	1-month LIBOR + 20 basis points
Average Life 10-year soft bullet	3.12 years at 25 CPR
Collateral Description Revolving structure of credit card receivables	Type: Adjustable Rate
Portfolio Yield: 17.42% (3-month average)	Gross Weighted Average Coupon 10.38%
Base Rate: 7.93% (3-month average)	Weighted Average Gross Margin 6.71%
Excess spread: 2.93% (3-month average)	Net Weighted Average Coupon: 9.88% Weighted Average Life Cap: 17% Servicing Fee: 0.5%
Index 1 month LIBOR: 5.65% Prime Rate: 8.50%	6 month LIBOR: 5.90% (79%) 1 Year CMT: 0.49% (21%) Blended Rate: 5.81%

[2] The available funds cap (AFC) is the maximum amount available to pay the coupon:
AFC = Gross Coupon − Servicing − Other Fees − Surety Spread

Teaser risk is defined differently for adjustable-rate mortgage collateral. ARM issuers also entice borrowers with a below-market — teaser — interest rate for an initial period ranging from six months to three years. When the teaser period expires, interest on the underlying mortgage resets to market levels. Teaser risk represents the reduction in the available funds margin from which coupons and fees for surety, servicing, and other functions get paid. Yield enhancements in the form of overcollateralization and acceleration features mitigate the risk that the available funds margin will not cover expenses associated with the transactions. The excess interest generated by overcollateralization is used to pay down principal on the structures.

Cap Risk

Cap risk measures the impact of periodic and lifetime caps on floating-rate collateral. Most floating-rate collateral is subject to some form of cap on interest rates charged the borrower. For example, state usury laws usually place a cap on rates that finance companies can charge consumer borrowers. Home equity floaters have periodic and lifetime caps that limit the amount that mortgage rates can increase at each reset and over the life of the mortgage. Some ABS structures have caps on coupons paid to investors. For example, some credit card issues have embedded coupon caps ranging from 11% to 14%. Many cap options embedded in ABS deals are out of the money and have little impact on relative value and bond pricing. That said, investors need to be aware of how cap options are valued in the market.

Home equity floater structures usually include multiple periodic cap options and a lifetime cap option. Most 6-month LIBOR ARMs have 100 basis point periodic caps, which equate to a 200 bp annual cap. Caps on 1-year CMT ARMs average 200 bp annually. Lifetime caps limit rate adjustments over the life of the mortgage and typically range from 15% to 18%. Home equity floaters collateralized with B and C loans run little risk of hitting the available fund cap due to the high yields on the underlying mortgages relative to the coupon on the ABS. For example, the weighted average life cap of the Aames 97-1 (Exhibit 7) collateral is 17%, which translates into a life cap for the Class A bond of 16.5%. By subtracting the indexed coupon on Class A from the life cap, we calculated a life cap margin[3] of 1,061 basis points. This means that 1-month LIBOR would have to increase 1,061 basis points or reach 16.3% before the class-A bond would hit the life cap. The Aames example is not uncommon for most home equity floaters in the ABS sector. Life caps are so far out of the money that cap option values are only one to two basis points.

The average life of a security also affects the valuation of the embedded short-cap options. The longer the length of the cap, the higher the probability that

---

[3] The life cap margin is the difference between the life cap and the indexed investor coupon, where the life cap is defined as the difference between the weighted average life cap (WALC) and all the fees:

Life Cap = Weighted Average Life Cap (WALC) – Servicing – Other Fees – Surety Spread

Life Cap Margin (LCM) = Life Cap – (Index – Margin)

the cap will be hit at some point and the higher the time value of the cap option. Therefore the term structure of spreads on home equity floaters should be steeper than the term structure of floaters with no embedded options.

Evaluating ABS Floaters Relative to Common Benchmarks

Bond investors are accustomed to comparing two or more securities on the basis of a spread to the underlying Treasury yield curve. Because spreads on floating-rate securities are referencing dissimilar indices, yields should be restated as an effective money-market yield. The three most common references for floating-rate ABS are 1-month LIBOR, 3-month LIBOR, and 91-day Treasury bills. The most common reference index for floating-rate instruments is 1-month LIBOR because it corresponds to monthly coupon payments to investors and on the underlying collateral. The effective money-market yield allows the investor to compare the relative value of floating-rate ABS products indexed with more than one benchmark.

Exhibit 7 illustrates the steps to convert nominal yield spreads off different indices into an effective money-market yield. The first step is to restate the discount margin as an effective nominal yield by adding the discount margin to the index yield. Next, convert the effective nominal yield to an effective money market yield by restating the yield on an actual/360 discounting basis. Yields on floating-rate structures priced and reset off the Eurodollar curve are typically stated using actual/360 discounting. Therefore, when comparing yields on securities indexed off more than one LIBOR rate, this final calculation is unnecessary.

The floating-rate investor can also look at the different reset indexes as a means of making a directional interest rate or curve play. Investors with a bullish outlook should, all else being equal, prefer longer reset periods. As interest rates fall, the investor's coupon resets down less frequently and the return on the instrument should exceed that of a security with a shorter reset period.

Exhibit 7: Restating Yields on Floating-Rate ABS
Prices as of September 30, 1997

		Reset Margin	Index Yield	DM	Effective Nominal Yield	Effective Money Market Yield
SLMA 97-3 A2 7.2 year average life	Weekly reset quarterly pay Interest paid actual/actual	+64 > 3-month T-bill Available funds cap	5.03%	+64	5.68%	5.60% Conversion formula: 5.68% × 360/365 = 5.60%
MBNAM 97-JA 7.0 year average life	Monthly reset, monthly pay Interest paid actual/360	+12 > 1 month LIBOR no cap	5.66%	+12	5.78%	5.78% LIBOR floaters are usually actual/360; therefore, no restatement required

Bearish investors would pursue the opposite strategy, preferring securities, again all things being equal, with more frequent reset periods. As interest rates increase, the more frequent reset provides the investor with a higher yield and a higher return. Investors expecting the yield curve to flatten might use floating-rate instruments with frequent reset periods as the short end of a barbell strategy.

The preceding discussion is simplistic in that it does not account for the term structure of nominal yields corresponding to the frequency of the reset. The Eurodollar curve off which LIBOR is based is usually positively sloped. Therefore, the investor accepts a smaller nominal yield in exchange for more frequent resets. In order to assess accurately the possible outcomes associated with the strategies discussed earlier, the investor should perform horizon analysis to determine whether the nominal yield differences are offset by expected rate moves.

The availability of floating-rate ABS product indexed off both the Treasury curve and the Eurodollar curve provides investors with tools to take a position on the TED spread. The TED spread is the price spread between the 3-month Treasury bill futures contract and the 3-month Eurodollar futures contract. An increase in market volatility accompanied by a widening in the TED spread will cause a floater indexed off Treasury bills to underperform the LIBOR floater. The discount margin on the Treasury bill floater will widen to keep effective nominal yields in line with LIBOR floaters.

The opposite also holds true. A decrease in market volatility accompanied by a falling TED spread allows the spreads on Treasury bill floaters to decline as nominal yields decline on LIBOR floaters. Clearly, spread volatility on Treasury bill floaters exceeds that of LIBOR floaters. Unfortunately, opportunities for investors to trade volatility in the floaters market through the TED spread are limited. At this time, Sallie Mae is the only sizable ABS issuer with Treasury-indexed floating-rate coupons.

Term Structure of Discount Margins

Similar to yield spreads on fixed-rate ABS, there is a term structure to spreads for floating-rate ABS. Investors are compensated for a longer period of credit exposure and structure risk with a wider spread over the benchmark index. Exhibit 8 illustrates the term structure of spreads on floating-rate credit cards and home equity floaters as of September 30, 1997.

Spread Duration

One reason why the term structure of discount margins is typically upward sloping is that floating-rate investors — like their fixed-rate counterparts — want to be compensated for bearing the greater price risk inherent in longer-lived bonds. Although floaters are, by virtue of their periodic coupon resets, largely insulated from interest rate risk, discount margins can be affected by changes in credit quality and average life. The impact of changes in discount margin on the price of a bond can be estimated through the use of spread duration. Because spread is a component of a fixed-rate bond's aggregate yield, a fixed-rate bond's spread duration is no different than its modified or effective duration. Therefore, the expected change in price from a given change in the yield is a product of the duration times the change in yield.

Exhibit 8: Term Structure of Spreads on Floating-Rate Credit Card ABS and Home Equity Floater ABS: September 30, 1997

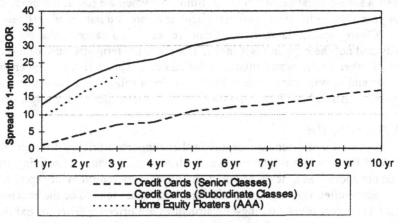

Exhibit 9: Spread Durations on Floating-Rate ABS

Issue:	MBNMA 97-J		MBNAM 97-E	
Class:	Class A		Class A	
Reference Index:	1-mo LIBOR		3-mo LIBOR	
Average Life:	6.8 yr		4.4 yr	
Index Duration:	0.08 years		0.25 years	
Pricing Spread less 10 basis points:	2 DM	100-18	−2 BM	100-12+
Pricing Spread:	*12 DM*	*100-00*	*8 DM*	*100-00*
Pricing Spread plus 10 basis points:	22 DM	99-14	18 DM	99-19+
Price change from 10 bp move (32nd)	18/32nds		12.5/32nds	
Price change from 10 bp move (%):	0.563%		0.391%	
Implied Spread Duration	5.63 years		3.91 years	

Analysis as of 10/16/97

For fixed-rate securities:

$$\text{Price Change} = \text{Effective Duration} \times \text{Change in Yield Spread} \qquad (1)$$

Therefore,

$$\text{Price Change/Change in Yield Spread} = \text{Spread Duration} \qquad (2)$$

Equation (1) does not hold true for floating-rate securities when the maturity of the security exceeds the term of the reset index. If we applied the same concept to floating-rate ABS, the price change from a change in the yield spread would be negligible since the duration of the floating-rate ABS reflects the duration of the reset index on the coupon. Exhibit 9 illustrates that the impact on price from a change in spread results in a spread duration very close to that of a fixed-rate bond with the same maturity. When we adjust the spread on the MBNAM 97-J Class A by 10 basis points, and plug the price change into equation (2) above, we calculate a spread duration of 5.6 years. Similarly, when we repeat the process for the 4.4 year average life 97-E deal, we calculate a spread duration of 3.91 years.

Clearly, spread duration on a floater reflects the duration to the underlying maturity and not the coupon reset index. Therefore the term structure of discount margins further compensates investors for additional price risk on longer-dated structures and provides for price appreciation from rolldown. Said another way, floating-rate ABS do benefit from rolldown as the average life of a security shortens.

Cash-Flow Profiles

The term structure of discount margins further supports a pricing differential for bullet ABS floaters relative to amortizing structures. Because amortizing structures do not shorten as quickly as bullet structures, they require wider spreads.

Soft-bullet, floating-rate credit card ABS issues tend to be the benchmark against which most other floating-rate structures are priced. Earlier, in Exhibit 8, we illustrated spread curves for home equity floaters and credit card floaters. The spread differential associated with bullet versus amortizing structures is not directly comparable for these two sectors due to the embedded prepayment options and cap options in securities collateralized with residential home mortgages. Better comparisons include the Class A2 floating-rate tranches in the Chrysler (PRAT) 96-1, 96-2, 96-3, and 96-4 auto loan ABS, and the AT&T Capital Equipment (CAPRT) 97-1 Class A-5.

The Class A2 notes in each of the PRAT 96 issues had an original average life of one year with a 12-month payment window. PRAT 96-1 Class A2 and its three sisters priced two to three basis points wider than comparable spreads on floating-rate credit card soft bullets. The CAPRT 97-1 equipment lease ABS included a 1.6-year average life floating-rate note (Class A5) with a 4-year window that priced five basis points wider than cards.

To ascertain the breakeven spread between soft bullet and amortizing floaters, investors can compare horizon returns. If the return on the bullet exceeds the return on the amortizer, then the investor is not adequately compensated for the loss of rolldown and should prefer the soft bullet. Conversely, when the horizon return on the amortizing note exceeds the return on the bullet, the investor is adequately compensated for the lack of rolldown. The investor is indifferent between the two structures when horizon returns are equal.

CONCLUSION

Characteristics such as cash-flow profile, the volatility of collateral cash flows, and servicer creditworthiness can all significantly impact the relative attractiveness of both floating- and fixed-rate ABS. As with any fixed income investment, investors should demand higher yields as compensation for any factor that negatively affects the timing or certainty of future cash flows. In this chapter we have described relative value tools intended to help investors quantify whether the prospective returns offered by an ABS are adequate compensation for the risks embedded in the security. Although such tools are helpful, they can, at their best, only provide a consistent framework with which to evaluate ABS. Only once an insurer considers such an evaluation in the context of their own risk biases and constraints can a determination of value be made.

Chapter 28

Analysis of ABS

Frank J. Fabozzi, Ph.D., CFA
Adjunct Professor of Finance
School of Management
Yale University

Shrikant Ramamurthy
Senior Vice President
Fixed Income Research
Prudential Securities Inc.

Laurent Gauthier
Vice President
Fixed Income Research
Prudential Securities Inc.

INTRODUCTION

In this chapter we will explain and illustrate the methodology for valuing asset-backed securities and measures of relative value. We begin by reviewing static cash flow yield analysis and the limitations of the spread measure that is a result of that analysis — the nominal spread. We then look at a better spread measure called the zero-volatility spread, but point out its limitation as a measure of relative value for ABS products where the embedded option has value. Finally, we look at the methodology for valuing ABS products where the embedded option has value — the Monte Carlo simulation model. A byproduct of this model is a spread measure called the option-adjusted spread. This measure is superior to the nominal spread and the zero-volatility spread for ABS products where the embedded option has a value because it takes into account how cash flows may change when interest rates change. That is, it recognizes the borrower's prepayment option and how that affects prepayments when interest rates may change in the future. While the option-adjusted spread is far superior to the two other spread measures, it is based on assumptions that must be understood by a portfolio manager and the sensitivity of the ABS's value and option-adjusted spread to changes in those assumptions must be investigated.

STATIC CASH FLOW YIELD ANALYSIS

The yield on any financial instrument is the interest rate that makes the present value of the expected cash flow equal to its market price plus accrued interest. For ABS, the yield calculated is called a *cash flow yield*, although some firms refer to it as the *yield to maturity*. The problem in calculating the cash flow yield of an ABS is that because of prepayments (voluntary and involuntary) the cash flow is unknown. Consequently, to determine a cash flow yield some assumption about the prepayment rate and recovery rate in the case of defaults must be made.

The cash flow for an ABS is typically monthly. The convention is to compare the yield on an ABS to that of a Treasury coupon security by calculating the ABS's bond-equivalent yield. The bond-equivalent yield for a Treasury coupon security is found by doubling the semiannual yield. However, it is incorrect to do this for an ABS because the investor has the opportunity to generate greater interest by reinvesting the more frequent cash flows. The market practice is to calculate a yield so as to make it comparable to the yield to maturity on a bond-equivalent yield basis. The formula for annualizing the monthly cash flow yield for an ABS is as follows:

$$\text{Bond-equivalent yield} = 2[(1 + i_M)^6 - 1]$$

where i_M is the monthly interest rate that will equate the present value of the projected monthly cash flow to the market price (plus accrued interest) of the ABS.

All yield measures suffer from problems that limit their use in assessing a security's potential return. The yield to maturity for a Treasury, agency, or corporate bond has two major shortcomings as a measure of a bond's potential return. To realize the stated yield to maturity, the investor must: (1) reinvest the coupon payments at a rate equal to the yield to maturity and (2) hold the bond to the maturity date. The reinvestment of the coupon payments is critical and for long-term bonds can be as much as 80% of the bond's return. The risk of having to reinvest the interest payments at less than the computed yield is called *reinvestment risk*. The risk associated with a decline in the value of a security due to a rise in interest rates is called *interest rate risk* and later in this chapter we will discuss how to quantify that risk.

These shortcomings are equally applicable to the cash flow yield measure for an ABS: (1) the projected cash flows are assumed to be reinvested at the computed cash flow yield and (2) the ABS is assumed to be held until the final payout based on some prepayment assumption. The importance of reinvestment risk, the risk that the cash flow will be reinvested at a rate less than the cash flow yield, is particularly important for amortizing ABS products, because payments are monthly and both interest and principal must be reinvested. Moreover, an additional assumption is that the projected cash flow is actually realized. If the prepayment experience and the recovery rate realized are different from that assumed, the cash flow yield will not be realized.

Given the computed cash flow yield and the average life for an ABS based on some prepayment assumption and default/recovery assumption, the next step is to compare the yield to the yield for a comparable Treasury security. "Comparable" is typically defined as a Treasury security with the same maturity as the (weighted) average life of the ABS. The difference between the cash flow yield and the yield on a comparable Treasury security is called the *nominal spread*.

Unfortunately, it is the nominal spread that some managers will use as a measure of relative value for all ABS. However, this spread masks the fact that a portion of the nominal spread may be compensation for accepting prepayment risk. Instead of nominal spread, managers need a measure that indicates the potential compensation after adjusting for prepayment risk for ABS products where the prepayment option has value. This measure is called the *option-adjusted spread*. Before discussing this measure, we describe another spread measure commonly quoted for ABS products called the *zero-volatility spread*. This measure takes into account another problem with the nominal spread. Specifically, the nominal spread is computed assuming that all the cash flows for an ABS should be discounted at only one interest rate. That is, it fails to recognize the term structure of interest rates.

ZERO-VOLATILITY SPREAD

The proper procedure to compare an ABS to a Treasury is to compare it to a portfolio of Treasury securities that have the same cash flow. The value of the ABS is then equal to the present value of all of the cash flows. The ABS's value, assuming the cash flows are default-free, will equal the present value of the replicating portfolio of Treasury securities. In turn, these cash flows are valued at the Treasury spot rates.

The *zero-volatility spread* is a measure of the spread that the investor would realize over the entire Treasury spot rate curve if the ABS being analyzed is held to maturity. It is not a spread off one point on the Treasury yield curve, as is the nominal spread. The zero-volatility spread (also called the *Z-spread* and the *static spread*) is the spread that will make the present value of the cash flows from the ABS when discounted at the Treasury spot rate plus the spread equal to the price of the ABS. A trial-and-error procedure (or search algorithm) is required to determine the zero-volatility spread.

In general, the shorter the average life of the ABS, the less the zero-volatility spread will deviate from the nominal spread. The magnitude of the difference between the nominal spread and the zero-volatility spread also depends on the shape of the yield curve. The steeper the yield curve, the greater the difference.

If borrowers in the underlying loan pool have the right to prepay but do *not* typically take advantage of a decline in interest rates below the loan's rate to refinance, then the zero-volatility spread is the appropriate measure of relative value and the zero-volatility spread should be using in valuing cash flows to determine the value of an ABS. This is the case, for example, for automobile loan ABS. While borrowers have the right to refinance when rates decline below the loan rate, they typically do not. In contrast, for home equity loan ABS, borrowers do tend to refinance when interest rates decline below the loan rate. The next methodology and spread measure are used for ABS products with this characteristic.

VALUATION USING MONTE CARLO SIMULATION AND OAS ANALYSIS

In fixed income valuation modeling, there are two methodologies commonly used to value securities with embedded options — the lattice model (such as the binomial and trinomial models) and the Monte Carlo model. The latter model involves simulating a sufficiently large number of potential interest rate paths in order to assess the value of a security on these different paths. This model is the most flexible of the two valuation methodologies for valuing interest rate sensitive instruments where the history of interest rates is important. ABS products where the embedded option has value are commonly valued using this model. As explained below, a byproduct of this valuation model is the option-adjusted spread (OAS).

A lattice model is used to value callable agency debentures and corporate bonds. This valuation model accommodates securities in which the decision to exercise a call option is not dependent on how interest rates evolved over time. That is, the decision of an issuer to call a bond will depend on the level of the rate at which the issue can be refunded relative to the issue's coupon rate, and not the path interest rates took to get to that rate. ABS products which allow prepayments have periodic cash flows that are interest rate path-dependent. This means that the cash flow received in one period is determined not only by the current interest rate level, but also by the path that interest rates took to get to the current level. Prepayments for such ABS products are interest rate path-dependent because this month's prepayment rate depends on whether there have been prior opportunities to refinance since the underlying loans were originated. Moreover, the cash flows to be received in the current month by investors in an ABS tranche depend on the outstanding balances of the other tranches in the deal. Thus, we need the history of prepayments to calculate these balances.

Conceptually, the valuation of ABS using the Monte Carlo model is simple. In practice, however, it is very complex. The simulation involves generating a set of cash flows based on simulated future refinancing rates, which in turn imply simulated prepayment and default/recovery rates. The objective is to figure out how the value of the collateral gets transmitted to the tranches. More specifically, the objective is to find out where the value goes and where the risk (prepayment risk and credit risk) goes so that one can identify the tranches with low risk and high value.

Simulating Interest Rate Paths and Cash Flows

The typical model that Wall Street firms and commercial vendors use to generate these random interest rate paths takes as input today's term structure of interest rates and a volatility assumption. The term structure of interest rates is the theoretical spot rate (or zero coupon) curve implied by today's Treasury securities. The simulations should be calibrated so that the average simulated price of a zero-coupon Treasury bond equals today's actual price.

Some models use the on-the-run Treasury issues in the calibration process. Other dealers use off-the-run Treasury issues.[1] Some dealers and vendors of analytical systems use the LIBOR curve instead of the Treasury curve — or give the user a choice to use the LIBOR curve. The reason is that some investors are interested in spreads that they can earn relative to their funding costs and LIBOR for many investors is a better proxy for that cost than Treasury rates.

Each model has its own model of the evolution of future interest rates and its own volatility assumptions. Typically, there are no significant differences in the interest rate models of dealer firms and vendors, although their volatility assumptions can be significantly different.

The volatility assumption determines the dispersion of future interest rates in the simulation. Today, many vendors do not use one volatility number for the yield of all maturities of the yield curve. Instead, they use either a short/long yield volatility or a term structure of yield volatility. A short/long yield volatility means that volatility is specified for maturities up to a certain number of years (short yield volatility) and a different yield volatility for greater maturities (long yield volatility). The short yield volatility is assumed to be greater than the long yield volatility. A term structure of yield volatilities means that a yield volatility is assumed for each maturity.

The random paths of interest rates should be generated from an arbitrage-free model of the future term structure of interest rates. By arbitrage-free it is meant that the model replicates today's term structure of interest rates, an input of the model, and that for all future dates there is no possible arbitrage within the model.

The simulation works by generating many scenarios of future interest rate paths. In each month of the scenario (i.e., path), a monthly interest rate and a refinancing rate are generated. The monthly interest rates are used to discount the projected cash flows in the scenario. The refinancing rate is needed to determine the cash flows because it represents the opportunity cost the borrower is facing at that time.

If the refinancing rates are high relative to the borrower's loan rate, the borrower will have no incentive to refinance. In the case of real-estate ABS, there is a disincentive to prepay (i.e., the homeowner may avoid moving in order to avoid refinancing). If the refinancing rate is low relative to the borrower's loan rate, the borrower has an incentive to refinance.

---

[1] The argument for using off-the-run Treasury issues is that the price/yield of on-the-run Treasury issues will not reflect their true economic value because the market price reflects their value for financing purposes (i.e., an issue may be on special in the repo market).

Exhibit 1: Simulated Paths of 1-Month Future Interest Rates

Month	Interest Rate Path Number						
	1	2	3	...	n	...	N
1	$f_1(1)$	$f_1(2)$	$f_1(3)$	...	$f_1(n)$	...	$f_1(N)$
2	$f_2(1)$	$f_2(2)$	$f_2(3)$	...	$f_2(n)$	...	$f_2(N)$
3	$f_3(1)$	$f_3(2)$	$f_3(3)$	...	$f_3(n)$	...	$f_3(N)$
...	...	...	...	...	...	...	...
t	$f_t(1)$	$f_t(2)$	$f_t(3)$	...	$f_t(n)$	...	$f_t(N)$
...	...	...	...	...	...	...	...
$M-2$	$f_{M-2}(1)$	$f_{M-2}(2)$	$f_{M-2}(3)$	...	$f_{M-2}(n)$	...	$f_{M-2}(N)$
$M-1$	$f_{M-1}(1)$	$f_{M-1}(2)$	$f_{M-1}(3)$	...	$f_{M-1}(n)$	...	$f_{M-1}(N)$
M	$f_M(1)$	$f_M(2)$	$f_M(3)$	...	$f_M(n)$	...	$f_M(N)$

Notation: $f_t(n)$ = 1-month future interest rate for month t on path n; N = total number of interest rate paths; M = number of months for the loan pool

Exhibit 2: Simulated Paths of Refinancing Rates

Month	Interest Rate Path Number						
	1	2	3	...	n	...	N
1	$r_1(1)$	$r_1(2)$	$r_1(3)$	...	$r_1(n)$	...	$r_1(N)$
2	$r_2(1)$	$r_2(2)$	$r_2(3)$	...	$r_2(n)$	...	$r_2(N)$
3	$r_3(1)$	$r_3(2)$	$r_3(3)$	...	$r_3(n)$	...	$r_3(N)$
...	...	...	...	...	...	...	...
t	$r_t(1)$	$r_t(2)$	$r_t(3)$	...	$r_t(n)$	...	$r_t(N)$
...	...	...	...	...	...	...	...
$M-2$	$C_{M-2}(1)$	$C_{M-2}(2)$	$C_{M-2}(3)$	...	$C_{M-2}(n)$	...	$C_{M-2}(N)$
$M-1$	$C_{M-1}(1)$	$C_{M-1}(2)$	$C_{M-1}(3)$	...	$C_{M-1}(n)$	...	$C_{M-1}(N)$
M	$C_M(1)$	$C_M(2)$	$C_M(3)$	...	$C_M(n)$	...	$C_M(N)$

Notation: $r_t(n)$ = refinancing rate for month t on path n; N = total number of interest rate paths; M = number of months for the loan pool

Prepayments (voluntary and involuntary) and recoveries are projected by feeding the refinancing rate and loan characteristics into a prepayment model and default model. Given the projected prepayments, the cash flows along an interest rate path can be determined.

To make this more concrete, consider a newly issued loan pool with a maturity of M months. Exhibit 1 shows N simulated interest rate path scenarios. Each scenario consists of a path of M simulated 1-month future interest rates.[2] So, our first assumption that we make to get Exhibit 1 is the volatility of interest rates.

Exhibit 2 shows the paths of simulated refinancing rates corresponding to the scenarios shown in Exhibit 1. In going from Exhibit 1 to Exhibit 2, an assumption must be made about the relationship between the Treasury rate and the refinancing rate. The assumption is that there is a constant spread relationship between the refinancing rate and the Treasury issue with a maturity that is the best proxy for the borrowing rate.

---

[2] The number of paths generated is based on a well known principle in simulation which will not be discussed here.

Exhibit 3: Simulated Cash Flows for the Collateral

Month	Interest Rate Path Number						
	1	2	3	...	n	...	N
1	$C_1(1)$	$C_1(2)$	$C_1(3)$	...	$C_1(n)$	...	$C_1(N)$
2	$C_2(1)$	$C_2(2)$	$C_2(3)$	...	$C_2(n)$	...	$C_2(N)$
3	$C_3(1)$	$C_3(2)$	$C_3(3)$	...	$C_3(n)$	...	$C_3(N)$
...	...	...	...	...	...	...	...
t	$C_t(1)$	$C_t(2)$	$C_t(3)$	...	$C_t(n)$	...	$C_t(N)$
...	...	...	...	...	...	...	...
M-2	$C_{M-2}(1)$	$C_{M-2}(2)$	$C_{M-2}(3)$	...	$C_{M-2}(n)$	...	$C_{M-2}(N)$
M-1	$C_{M-1}(1)$	$C_{M-1}(2)$	$C_{M-1}(3)$	...	$C_{M-1}(n)$	...	$C_{M-1}(N)$
M	$C_M(1)$	$C_M(2)$	$C_M(3)$	...	$C_M(n)$	...	$C_M(N)$

Notation: $C_t(n)$ = collateral's cash flow for month t on path n; N = total number of interest rate paths; M = number of months for the loan pool

Exhibit 4: Simulated Cash Flows for a Tranche

Month	Interest Rate Path Number						
	1	2	3	...	n	...	N
1	$TRC_1(1)$	$TRC_1(2)$	$TRC_1(3)$	...	$TRC_1(n)$	...	$TRC_1(N)$
2	$TRC_2(1)$	$TRC_2(2)$	$TRC_2(3)$	...	$TRC_2(n)$	...	$TRC_2(N)$
3	$TRC_3(1)$	$TRC_3(2)$	$TRC_3(3)$	...	$TRC_3(n)$	...	$TRC_3(N)$
...	...	...	...	...	...	...	...
t	$TRC_t(1)$	$TRC_t(2)$	$TRC_t(3)$	...	$TRC_t(n)$	...	$TRC_t(N)$
...	...	...	...	...	...	...	...
M-2	$TRC_{M-2}(1)$	$TRC_{M-2}(2)$	$TRC_{M-2}(3)$	...	$TRC_{M-2}(n)$	...	$TRC_{M-2}(N)$
M-1	$TRC_{M-1}(1)$	$TRC_{M-1}(2)$	$TRC_{M-1}(3)$	...	$TRC_{M-1}(n)$	...	$TRC_{M-1}(N)$
M	$TRC_M(1)$	$TRC_M(2)$	$TRC_M(3)$	...	$TRC_M(n)$	...	$TRC_M(N)$

Notation: $TRC_t(n)$ = tranche's cash flow for month t on path n; N = total number of interest rate paths; M = number of months for the loan pool

Given the refinancing rates, the collateral's cash flows on each interest rate path can be generated. This requires a prepayment and default/recovery model. So our next assumption is that the prepayment and default/recovery models used to generate the collateral's cash flows are correct. The resulting cash flows are depicted in Exhibit 3.

Given the collateral's cash flow for each month on each interest rate path, the next step is to use the rules for the structure to determine how the cash flow is distributed to the tranche of interest. Let us use TRC to denote the cash flow for the tranche. Exhibit 4 shows the simulated tranche's cash flows on each of the interest rate paths.

Calculating the Present Value of a Tranche for a Scenario Interest Rate Path

Given the tranche's cash flows on an interest rate path, the path's present value can be calculated. The discount rate for determining the present value is the simulated spot rate for each month on the interest rate path plus an appropriate spread.

The spot rate on a path can be determined from the simulated future monthly rates. The relationship that holds between the simulated spot rate for month t on path n and the simulated future 1-month rates is:

$$z_t(n) = \{[1 + f_1(n)][1 + f_2(n)]...[1 + f_t(n)]\}^{1/t} - 1$$

where

$z_t(n)$ = simulated spot rate for month t on path n

$f_j(n)$ = simulated future 1-month rate for month j on path n

Consequently, the interest rate path for the simulated future 1-month rates can be converted to the interest rate path for the simulated monthly spot rates as shown in Exhibit 5. Therefore, the present value of the cash flows for month t on interest rate path n discounted at the simulated spot rate for month t plus some spread is:

$$PV[TRC_t(n)] = \frac{TRC_t(n)}{[1 + z_t(n) + K]^t}$$

where

$PV[TRC_t(n)]$ = present value of tranche's cash flows for month t on path n

$TRC_t(n)$ = tranche's cash flow for month t on path n

$z_t(n)$ = spot rate for month t on path n

K = spread

The present value for path n is the sum of the present value of the cash flows for each month on path n. That is,

$$PV[Path(n)] = PV[TRC_1(n)] + PV[TRC_2(n)] + ... + PV[TRC_M(n)]$$

where $PV[Path(n)]$ is the present value of interest rate path n.

Exhibit 5: Simulated Paths of Monthly Spot Rates

Month	Interest Rate Path Number						
	1	2	3	...	n	...	N
1	$z_1(1)$	$z_1(2)$	$z_1(3)$	...	$z_1(n)$	...	$z_1(N)$
2	$z_2(1)$	$z_2(2)$	$z_2(3)$	...	$z_2(n)$	...	$z_2(N)$
3	$z_3(1)$	$z_3(2)$	$z_3(3)$	...	$z_3(n)$	...	$z_3(N)$
...	...	...	...	...	...	...	...
t	$z_t(1)$	$z_t(2)$	$z_t(3)$	...	$z_t(n)$	...	$z_t(N)$
...	...	...	...	...	...	...	...
M-2	$z_{M-2}(1)$	$z_{M-2}(2)$	$z_{M-2}(3)$	...	$z_{M-2}(n)$	...	$z_{M-2}(N)$
M-1	$z_{M-1}(1)$	$z_{M-1}(2)$	$z_{M-1}(3)$	...	$z_{M-1}(n)$	...	$z_{M-1}(N)$
M	$z_M(1)$	$z_M(2)$	$z_M(3)$	...	$z_M(n)$	...	$z_M(N)$

Notation: $z_t(n)$ = spot rate for month t on path n; N = total number of interest rate paths; M = number of months for the loan pool

Determining the Theoretical Value

The present value of a given interest rate path can be thought of as the theoretical value of a tranche if that path was actually realized. The theoretical value of the tranche can be determined by calculating the average of the theoretical values of all the interest rate paths. That is, the theoretical value is equal to

$$\text{Theoretical value} = \frac{\text{PV}[\text{Path}(1)] + \text{PV}[\text{Path}(2)] + \ldots + \text{PV}[\text{Path}(N)]}{N}$$

where N is the number of interest rate paths.

Option-Adjusted Spread

In the Monte Carlo model OAS is the spread that when added to all the spot rates on all interest rate paths that will make the average present value of the paths equal to the observed market price (plus accrued interest). Mathematically, OAS is the spread that will satisfy the following condition:

$$\frac{\text{PV}[\text{Path}(1)] + \text{PV}[\text{Path}(2)] + \ldots + \text{PV}[\text{Path}(N)]}{N} = \text{Market price}$$

where N is the number of interest rate paths.

The procedure for determining the OAS is straightforward, although time consuming. The next question, then, is how to interpret the OAS. Basically, the OAS is used to reconcile value with market price. On the right-hand side of the previous equation is the market's statement: the market price of the tranche. The average present value over all the paths on the left-hand side of the equation is the model's output, which we refer to as "value."

The OAS was developed as a measure of the spread that can be used to convert dollar differences between value and market price. But what is it a "spread" over? In describing the model above, we can see that the OAS is measuring the average spread over the Treasury spot rate curve, not the Treasury yield curve. It is an average spread since the OAS is found by averaging over the interest rate paths for the possible Treasury spot rate curves. Of course, if the LIBOR curve is used, the OAS is the average spread over that curve.

This spread measure is superior to the nominal spread which gives no recognition to the prepayment risk. The OAS is "option adjusted" because the cash flows on the interest rate paths are adjusted for the option of the borrowers to prepay.

Option Cost

The implied cost of the option embedded in an ABS can be obtained by calculating the difference between the OAS at the assumed yield volatility and the zero-volatility spread. That is,

Option cost = Zero-volatility spread – OAS

The option cost measures the prepayment (or option) risk embedded in the ABS. Note that the cost of the option is a byproduct of the option-adjusted spread analysis, not valued explicitly with some option pricing model.

When the option cost is zero because the borrower tends not to exercise the prepayment option when interest rates decline below the loan rate, then substituting zero for the OAS in the previous equation and solving for the zero-volatility spread, we get:

Zero-volatility spread = OAS

Consequently, when the value of the option is zero (i.e., the option cost is zero) for a particular ABS product, simply computing the zero-volatility spread for relative value purposes or for valuing that ABS product is sufficient. Even if there is a small value for the option, the zero-volatility spread should be adequate rather than going through the Monte Carlo/OAS analysis.

Simulated Average Life

The average life of an ABS is the weighted average time to receipt of principal payments (scheduled payments and projected prepayments). The average life reported in a Monte Carlo model is the average of the average lives along the interest rate paths. That is, for each interest rate path, there is an average life. The average of these average lives is the average life reported by the model.

Additional information is conveyed by the distribution of the average life. The greater the range and standard deviation of the average life, the more uncertainty there is about the security's average life.

Illustrations

We will illustrate many of the concepts described so far in this chapter with an analysis of four structured products: a home equity loan ABS, a manufactured housing ABS, agency passthrough securities, and an agency collateralized mortgage obligation (CMO). Exhibits 6, 7, 8, and 9 provide information about the four structured products and the analytical concepts discussed above (as well as several concepts to be discussed later in this chapter). The analysis was performed on April 4, 2000. Market implied volatility is assumed.[3]

Exhibit 6 shows the information for the home equity loan ABS — the Residential Asset Securities Corp. (RASC) issued in February 2000. The deal has six tranches. The weighted average life of the tranches is 3.2 years and the average option cost per tranche is 24 basis points.

Exhibit 7 shows the information for the Vanderbilt Mortgage and Finance manufactured housing loan deal issued in February 2000. The deal has six tranches with a weighted average life of 6.7 years. The average option cost per tranche is 18 basis points. Notice that the average option cost is lower than in the home equity loan deal. Also note that comparable tranches have lower option costs and a lower standard deviation for the average life in the manufactured housing deal versus the home equity loan deal as shown below:

---

[3] Market volatility is extracted from 1, 2, 3, 4, 5, 7, and 10-year interest-rate cap market prices. From these prices, a term structure of yield volatility is obtained.

Exhibit 6: Analysis of Home-Equity Loan

Issuer	Residential Asset Securities Corp. (RASC)	Prepay. Assumption* 25 HEP
Deal Date	February 2000	Credit Support Wrapped by AMBAC
Type	HEL REMIC	Volatility Assumption Market implied

Class	Size ($ mm)	Type	Coupon (%)	Maturity	Avg. Life	Price	Yield (%)	Spread to WAL (bps)	Zero-vol Spd. (bps)	OAS** (bps)	Option Cost*** (bps)	Eff. Dur.	Eff. Conv.	St. Dev. of Avg. Life
A1	220	AAA Seq	7.615	1/15	0.9	100-11	6.585	40****	50	45	5	0.9	-0.3	0.10
A2	100	AAA Seq	7.700	6/21	2.0	100-00	7.525	110	113	93	20	2.1	-0.5	0.45
A3	105	AAA Seq	7.735	11/25	3.1	100-04	7.612	122	130	92	38	3.2	-0.7	0.98
A4	105	AAA Seq	8.040	11/28	5.1	100-16	7.915	163	175	127	48	4.7	-0.6	2.35
A5	55	AAA Seq	8.195	1/31	7.9	100-20	8.126	200	212	176	36	6.3	0.6	2.63
A6	65	AAA NAS	7.905	1/31	6.2	100-24	7.763	155	162	144	18	4.9	0.3	0.74
Weighted avg.			7.794		3.2	100.34	7.358				24	3.0		

Analysis as of 4/4/00

* Yields and spreads are computed relative to a constant prepayment assumption.

** OASs and durations are calculated by a Monte Carlo simulation of rates which utilizes Prudential Securities Inc.'s home equity loan prepayment model.

*** Option cost is defined as the difference between the OAS at market volatility and at zero volatility.

**** The spread to WAL for this class is lower than the OAS because the spread and OAS are computed at different prepayment speeds. The spread is computed at a constant prepayment speed assumption, while the OAS is computed assuming that prepayment speeds vary by time and interest-rate scenario.

Exhibit 7: Analysis of Manufactured Housing

Issuer	Vanderbilt Mortgage and Finance	Prepay. Assumption*	250 MHP	
Deal Date	February 2000	Credit Support	Senior/sub structure	
Type	MH REMIC	Volatility Assumption	Market implied	

Class	Size ($ mm)	Type	Coupon (%)	Maturity	Avg. Life	Price	Yield (%)	Spread to WAL (bps)	Zero-vol Spd. (bps)	OAS** (bps)	Option Cost*** (bps)	Eff. Dur.	Eff. Conv.	St. Dev. of Avg. Life
A2	33.0	AAA Seq	7.580	8/12	3.0	100-16	7.434	103	105	78	27	2.4	-0.3	0.73
A3	32.0	AAA Seq	7.820	11/17	5.1	101-00	7.639	133	145	127	18	3.8	-0.2	2.18
A4	27.2	AAA Seq	7.955	12/24	9.2	101-20	7.877	169	190	175	15	5.8	-0.2	3.76
A5	9.1	AA Seq	8.195	11/32	12.0	102-12	7.989	200	220	212	8	7.9	0.2	3.18
M1	7.3	A Seq	8.635	11/32	8.7	101-16	8.502	240	254	239	15	6.3	0.3	1.53
B1	7.3	BBB Seq	9.250	9/15	6.1	100-09	9.330	310	314	292	22	4.7	0.0	0.54
B2	12.8	BBB Seq	9.250	11/32	10.2	99-02+	9.536	355	363	353	10	6.9	0.4	2.12
Weighted avg.			8.083		6.7	100.90	7.995				18	4.6		

Analysis as of 4/4/00

* Yields and spreads are computed relative to a constant prepayment assumption.

** OASs and durations are calculated by a Monte Carlo simulation of rates which utilizes Prudential Securities Inc.'s manufactured housing prepayment model.

*** Option cost is defined as the difference between the OAS at market volatility and at zero volatility.

Exhibit 8: Analysis of Agency Fixed-Rate MBS

Issuer   Fannie Mae

Volatility Assumption   Market implied

Class	Coupon (%)	Maturity	Avg. Life	Price	Yield (%)	Spread to WAL (bps)	Zero-vol Spd (bps)	OAS* (bps)	Option Cost** (bps)	Eff. Dur	Eff. Conv.
FNMA	6%	30-year	9.4	91-30	7.40	151	155	125	30	6.0	0.1
FNMA	6.5%	30-year	9.2	94-18	7.46	156	162	122	40	5.6	-0.1
FNMA	7%	30-year	8.7	96-27	7.59	166	174	122	52	5.1	-0.4
FNMA	7.5%	30-year	7.8	98-29	7.74	177	185	122	63	4.6	-0.8
FNMA	8%	30-year	6.7	100-23	7.86	183	194	124	70	3.9	-1.5

Analysis as of 4/4/00

* OASs and durations are calculated by a Monte Carlo simulation of rates which utilizes Prudential Securities Inc.'s Agency prepayment model.

** Option cost is defined as the difference between the OAS at market volatility and at zero volatility.

Exhibit 9: Analysis of Agency CMO

Issuer   FNMA   Type   Agency REMIC   Volatility Assumption   Market implied

Deal Date   January 2000   Prepay. Assumption*   153 PSA

Class	Size ($ mm)	Type	Coupon (%)	Maturity	Avg. Life	Price	Yield (%)	Spread to WAL (bps)	Zero-vol Spd (bps)	OAS** (bps)	Option Cost*** (bps)	Eff. Dur	Eff. Conv.	St. Dev. of Avg. Life
A	82.5	Seq	7%	4/28	5.6	98-02	7.50	135	148	98	50	3.8	-0.6	1.70
B	65.5	Seq	7%	1/26	3.9	98-20	7.43	120	130	84	46	3.0	-0.6	1.14
C	10.1	Seq	7%	5/27	10.5	96-01	7.64	175	178	122	56	6.2	-0.4	3.57
D	6.8	Seq	7%	4/28	13.1	95-04	7.67	180	193	137	56	7.3	0.1	4.31
VA	12.5	AD Seq	7%	8/10	5.8	99-04	7.23	110	118	107	11	4.0	0.1	0.48
VB	10.9	AD Seq	7%	12/15	13.0	96-22	7.47	160	173	139	34	7.1	0.8	2.40
Z	11.6	Z-Seq	7%	2/30	19.7	89-24	7.69	185	216	168	48	17.7	7.3	4.01
Weighted avg life:					6.8						Weighted avg OC	43		

Analysis as of 4/4/00

* Yields and spreads are computed relative to a constant prepayment assumption.

** OASs and durations are calculated by a Monte Carlo simulation of rates which utilizes Prudential Securities Inc.'s Agency prepayment model.

*** Option cost is defined as the difference between the OAS at market volatility and at zero volatility.

	Option cost		Average life std. dev.	
Average life	HEL	MH	HEL	MH
3-years	38	27	0.98	0.73
5-years	48	18	2.35	2.18

Information for several agency passthrough securities — Fannie Mae passthroughs with coupon rates from 6% to 8% — is shown in Exhibit 8. Notice from Exhibits 6, 7, and 8 that agency passthrough securities have higher option costs than the weighted average option costs of both the home equity loan deal and manufactured housing deal. Alternatively stated, there is more prepayment volatility in agency passthrough securities. The most relevant passthrough for comparison purposes would be the 8% coupon given that the price on this coupon security is comparable to both the home equity loan and manufactured housing loan structures that are presented — they are all slightly above par. The Fannie Mae 8% coupon passthrough has an option cost of 70 basis points versus 24 basis points on the home equity loan deal and 18 basis points on the manufactured housing loan deal.

The CMO deal analyzed is a Fannie Mae deal issued in January 2000 and backed by 7% collateral. Information about the deal is presented in Exhibit 9. The weighted average option cost on the collateral as well as option cost for individual tranches are higher in the CMO deal than for the home equity loan deal and the manufactured housing loan deal.

The value of the options embedded in the bonds shown in Exhibits 6, 7, 8, and 9 is mainly driven by two factors: the sensitivity of prepayments to interest rates and the maturity of these options. On one extreme, manufactured housing prepayments are typically insensitive to interest rates, while agency mortgage borrowers are much more able to benefit from refinancing opportunities. Home equity loan borrowers — first-lien mortgages for sub-prime borrowers — generally suffer from their lower credit scores, and are less able to profit from decreasing interest rates to refinance their loans.

The maturity of the loans is important since the longer the time that borrowers possess the option to prepay a loan, the more chance the option has to be exercised. In addition, depending on the seasoning of the underlying loans, prepayments may be more or less interest rate sensitive; after some time, borrowers are more able to refinance due to, for example, improved credit circumstances ("credit curing"). Finally, very seasoned loans exhibit prepayment burnout: the most savvy borrowers have already refinanced if the opportunity presented itself, and the remaining ones are less inclined to do so.

In a structured transaction, depending on the sequencing of cash flows, the value of the option can vary. The very short tranches have low optionality given no seasoning. The highest optionality is on the 3- and 5-year structures where borrowers are at the top of the prepayment ramp and the collateral is slightly seasoned. The longest tranches have low optionality because of prepayment burnout.

MEASURING INTEREST RISK

The two measures of interest rate risk used by managers are duration and convexity. Duration is a first approximation as to how the value of an individual security or the value of a portfolio will change when interest rates change. Convexity measures the change in the value of a security or portfolio that is not explained by duration.

Duration

The most obvious way to measure a bond's price sensitivity as a percentage of its current price to changes in interest rates is to change rates by a small number of basis points and calculate how its price will change. To do this, we introduce the following notation. Let

V_0 = initial value or price of the security
Δy = change in the yield of the security (in decimal)
V_- = the estimated value of the security if the yield is decreased by Δy
V_+ = the estimated value of the security if the yield is increased by Δy

There are two key points to keep in mind in the foregoing discussion. First, the change in yield referred to above is the same change in yield for all maturities. This assumption is commonly referred to as a "parallel yield curve shift assumption." Thus, the foregoing discussion about the price sensitivity of a security to interest rate changes is limited to parallel shifts in the yield curve. Second, the notation refers to the estimated value of the security. This value is obtained from a valuation model. Consequently, the resulting measure of the price sensitivity of a security to interest rate changes is only as good as the valuation model employed to obtain the estimated value of the security.

Now let's focus on the measure of interest. We are interested in the percentage change in the price of a security when interest rates change. This measure is referred to as *duration*. It can be demonstrated that duration can be estimated using the following formula:

$$\text{Duration} = \frac{V_- - V_+}{2 V_0 (\Delta y)}$$

To illustrate this formula, consider the FNMA 8% mortgage-backed security described in Exhibit 8. It is priced at 100-23, or 100.72 in decimal form. A 10 basis point rise in interest rates results in a new price of 100.31. A 10 basis point decline in rates results in a new price of 101.10. Therefore we have

V_0 = 100.72
V_+ = 100.31
V_- = 101.10
Δy = 0.1% or 0.001

$$\text{Duration} = \frac{101.10 - 100.31}{2(100.72)(0.001)} = 3.9$$

The duration of a security can be interpreted as the approximate percentage change in price for a 100 basis point parallel shift in the yield curve. Thus a bond with a duration of 3.9 will change by approximately 3.9% for a 100 basis point parallel shift in the yield curve. For a 50 basis point parallel shift in the yield curve, the bond's price will change by approximately 1.95%; for a 25 basis point parallel shift in the yield curve, 0.975%, and so on.

Modified Duration versus Effective Duration

One form of duration that appears in the fixed income literature is *modified duration*. Modified duration is the approximate percentage change in a bond's price for a 100 basis point parallel shift in the yield curve *assuming that the bond's cash flows do not change when the yield curve shifts*. What this means is that in calculating the values of V_- and V_+ in the duration formula, the same cash flows used to calculate V_0 are used. Therefore, the change in the bond's price when the yield curve is shifted by a small number of basis points is due solely to discounting at the new yields.

The assumption that the cash flows do not change when the yield curve shifts in a parallel fashion makes sense for option-free bonds such as noncallable Treasury securities. However, the same cannot be said for ABS products whose cash flows are sensitive to changes in interest rates. For these ABS products, a change in yield will alter the expected cash flows because it will change expected prepayments.

The Monte Carlo model that we described earlier in this chapter takes into account how parallel shifts in the yield curve will affect the cash flows. Thus, when V_- and V_+ are the values produced from the valuation model, the resulting duration takes into account both the discounting at different interest rates and how the cash flows can change. When duration is calculated in this manner, it is referred to as *effective duration* or *option-adjusted duration*.

Calculation of Effective Duration

To calculate effective duration, the value of an ABS must be estimated when rates are shocked up and down a given number of basis points. In terms of the Monte Carlo model, the yield curve used is shocked up and down and the new curve is used to generate the values to be used in the duration formula to obtain effective duration.

There are two important aspects of this process of generating the values when the rates are shocked that are critical to understand. First, the assumption is that the relationships assumed do not change when rates are shocked up and down. Specifically, the yield volatility is assumed to be unchanged to derive the new interest rate paths for a given shock (i.e., the new Exhibit 1), the spread between the loan rate and the appropriate Treasury rate is assumed to be unchanged in constructing the new Exhibit 2 from the newly constructed Exhibit 1, and the OAS is assumed to be constant. The constancy of the OAS comes into play because when discounting the new cash flows (i.e., the cash flows in the new Exhibit 4), the current OAS that was computed is assumed to be the same and is added to the new rates in the new Exhibit 1. In the duration example shown earlier, we implicitly assumed that OAS was constant. This effectively allowed us to calculate the price of the mortgage-backed security in both up and down scenarios.

Exhibits 6, 7, 8, and 9 show the effective duration for the bonds in each structure. Notice how the prepayment tranching for the home equity loan deal, the manufactured housing loan deal, and the CMO deal creates bonds with different effective durations within a deal.

Convexity

The duration measure indicates that regardless of whether interest rates increase or decrease, the approximate percentage price change is the same. However, this does not agree with the price volatility property of a bond. Specifically, while for small changes in yield the percentage price change will be the same for an increase or decrease in yield, for large changes in yield this is not true. This suggests that duration is only a good approximation of the percentage price change for a small change in yield.

The reason for this result is that duration is in fact a first approximation for a small change in yield. The approximation can be improved by using a second approximation. This approximation is referred to as "convexity." The use of this term in the industry is unfortunate since the term convexity is also used to describe the shape or curvature of the price/yield relationship. The convexity measure of a security can be used to approximate the change in price that is not explained by duration.

Convexity Measure

The convexity measure of a bond can be approximated using the following formula:

$$\text{Convexity measure} = \frac{V_+ + V_- - 2V_0}{2V_0(\Delta y)^2}$$

where the notation is the same as used earlier for duration.

For our FNMA MBS, we have

$$\text{Convexity measure} = \frac{101.10 + 100.31 - 2 \times 100.72}{2(100.72)(0.001)^2}$$

$$= -149$$

Note that dealers often quote convexity by dividing the convexity measure by 100. In the above example, convexity would be quoted as −1.49. Exhibits 6, 7, 8, and 9 use this convention to quote convexity.

The above example is one where a bond is said to have negative convexity. Let us examine another bond that has a different convexity characteristic, the A-5 tranche of the home equity loan deal in Exhibit 6. For that tranche, the following was determined for a 10 basis point rate change:

$$V_0 = 100.625$$
$$V_+ = 100.006$$
$$V_- = 101.257$$
$$\Delta y = 0.001$$

Then

$$\text{Convexity measure} = \frac{101.257 + 100.006 - 2 \times 100.625}{2(100.625)(0.001)^2}$$

$$= 65$$

Notice that when the convexity measure is positive, we have the situation where the gain is greater than the loss for a given large change in rates. That is, the bond exhibits *positive convexity*. We can see this in the example above. However, if the convexity measure is negative, we have the situation where the loss will be greater than the gain. A security with this characteristic is said to have *negative convexity* and it occurs with ABS products where the embedded option has value.

Exhibits 6, 7, 8, and 9 show the convexity measure for the bonds analyzed. Notice that some of the bonds have a positive convexity and others have a negative convexity.

Convexity Adjustment to Percentage Price Change

Given the convexity measure, the approximate percentage price change adjustment due to the bond's convexity (i.e., the percentage price change not explained by duration) is:

Convexity adjustment to percentage price change
$$= \text{Convexity measure} \times (\Delta y)^2 \times 100$$

The price of a bond for a given movement in interest rates can be proxied using both duration and the convexity measure by the following equation[4]

$$V_{new} = V_0[1 - D\Delta y + C(\Delta y)^2]$$

where

$$V_0 \quad = \text{ initial value or price before rate movement}$$
$$V_{new} = \text{ estimated value after rate movement}$$
$$D \quad = \text{ effective duration}$$

---

[4] This equation is a consequence of Taylor's formula for estimating a non-linear function.

C = effective convexity measure

Δy = change in the yield of the security (in decimal)

For example, a 20 basis point rise in interest rates can result in the following new price for our FNMA 8% MBS with an effective duration of 3.9 and an effective convexity of -149:

$$V_{new} = 100.72[1 - 3.9 \times (0.002) + (-149)(0.002)^2]$$
$$= 99.90$$

Chapter 29

A Framework for Evaluating Cleanup Calls in Amortizing ABS

Arthur Chu
Vice President
ABS/MBS Research
Lehman Brothers

INTRODUCTION

It is typical for amortizing ABS securitizations to contain a cleanup call that allows the issuer to purchase all outstanding bonds at par once the collateral factor reaches a certain level (usually 10%-20%). This cleanup call typically affects the senior last cash flow and subordinate securities, and, in certain markets such as the HEL ARM market, all securities in the transaction. For subordinates in particular, the call/maturity question can be worth several points in valuation. Despite the importance of the issue, the market tends to trade securities based on simple rules — discounts trade to maturity, while premiums trade to call.

The purpose of this chapter is to examine the issue of cleanup calls more closely, and to show that the rules that the market uses to decide the call/maturity issue do not adequately capture the economic decision of the issuer. In the following, we present a framework for understanding the cleanup call decision which is applicable to a wide variety of structures. We discuss the methodology in detail using the home equity loan market as an example, and also illustrate the methodology in the manufactured housing market. This framework gives a simple methodology for understanding some of the new call structures used by Household and by Conseco Finance, which have a large cleanup call percentage (15%-20%).

ESTABLISHING THE FRAMEWORK USING THE HOME EQUITY LOAN MARKET

Understanding the Role of Overcollateralization

The key parameter that is not considered in the current market pricing of cleanup calls is overcollateralization. A securitization provides an issuer with a leveraged position in the collateral, where the issuer is long the entire collateral and short the

ABS. In a typical HEL transaction, there will be an excess of collateral over bonds, which is called the overcollateralization (O/C). The O/C is analogous to the haircut in a repo transaction, and it is clear that, all else equal, a lower amount of overcollateralization is desirable, as it allows for greater leverage and higher returns on equity.

In general, the overcollateralization as a percentage of the outstanding balance will increase as a home equity loan deal seasons. At the cleanup call date, overcollateralization levels will be 5%-7% for typical fixed-rate transactions and 10%-12% for adjustable-rate transactions. As a percentage of the collateral balance, the O/C at the call date is at least double the O/C percentage at the time of deal issuance, and possibly greater than double the initial amount. This implies that the degree of leverage provided to the issuer by the securitization *decreases* as the deal seasons.

By calling the deal, the issuer can resecuritize the collateral and lower the amount of O/C trapped in the transaction. As discussed above, the O/C in a new deal may be half or even lower of the O/C in a deal at the call date. The O/C which is taken out can then be sold or pledged to other securitizations. As a stylized example, suppose that at the call date, the current O/C in the deal is 6%, but that the deal could be resecuritized, at the same funding cost, with 3% O/C. By calling the deal, the issuer removes 3% of the collateral and realizes a gain of approximately 3 points. (The gain is not quite 3 points, and we will be more precise about this in the next section.) Even if it costs the issuer more to fund the new securitization than the existing one, the gain obtained by releasing the overcollateralization may still make it economical to call the deal. This example illustrates the main point of our analysis — that the O/C can make the call far in-the-money even if funding costs go up. Thus, even in situations where bonds are discounts, deals may still be called.

Formulating the Call Decision

With this qualitative understanding in mind, we now provide a more quantitative exercise decision for the call. The decision process is as follows.

If the issuer does not call and leaves the securitization outstanding, the value of the issuers' position is just the present value of the future residual cash flows in the deal (the residual value). Typically, residual cash flows are risky — they are the first loss piece in the deal — and would trade at very high discount rates. We use a discount rate of 20% in the analysis below.

If the issuer does call she pays par for the face amount of the bonds, and owns the entire amount of the collateral. We emphasize again that the face amount of collateral exceeds the face amount of bonds — for example, if there is 3% overcollateralization, and the collateral is worth par, the net value of the position after calling is 3%. If the net value of the position after calling is greater than the residual value, then the issuer should call the deal.

The value of the collateral at the time of the call depends on the (1) credit performance of the deal, (2) the general prices of current coupon whole loans, and the (3) relative coupon of the collateral. Turning first to the credit performance of the deal, delinquent loans will trade at lower dollar prices than otherwise equivalent current loans. Exhibit 1 approximates the prices of delinquent collateral by delinquency buckets, and gives a reasonably representative total delinquency percentage at the time of call date. For these delinquency percentages and prices, the total package would trade at about 97% of the price of an otherwise equivalent pool of current loans. Next, current coupon fixed-rate whole loans at the time of this writing trade at about 103. We assume this price in calculating call strategies. Finally, the price of the collateral will change if rates rise or fall, according to the duration of the collateral at the call date.

Holding collateral performance constant (i.e., holding future losses and prepayments constant), the principal factor governing the value of the residual is the structure and the timing of the cash flows. Here is a recap of call structures:

The 10% Call Structure This is the structure in the majority of HEL securitizations. When the bond factor reaches 10%, the issuer has the right to purchase all of the collateral by paying par for the face amount of bonds. If the deal is not called, the issuer continues to receive excess cash flow. However, typically there are very few or no overcollateralization releases until all of the bonds are paid off.

The 15%-20% Call Structure[1] This is the structure used by Conseco Finance and Household. These issuers use a larger cleanup call so that it is not necessary to book a gain on sale at the time of securitization. The key point about this structure is that if the call is not exercised, all of the residual cash flow goes to pay down bonds. That is, if the deal is not called, the issuer receives no cash flow until all of the bonds are paid off. Additionally, these structures usually have high levels of O/C — the O/C at the call date for Conseco is 7.5%, while that for Household is 19%. The combination of high O/C and the turbo feature push the strike of the call further in the money than the standard 10% call.

Exhibit 1: Representative Prices and Percentages of Delinquent Loans

Delinquency Status	Price as % of price Of current loans	% of deal at cleanup call date
Current	100	84
30 days	97	3
60 days	94	2
90 days	85	5
90+ days	75	6
All	97.5%	100

[1] These structures actually incorporate an auction call where parties other than the issuer may bid for the collateral, which further increases the likelihood of the cleanup call being exercised.

In the typical 10% structure, at the call date, the overcollateralization will have reached a floor, so that the principal cash flows from the O/C will not be released to the issuer until all of the bonds are paid off. In the Conseco/Household structure, no residual cash flows will be released to the issuer until the bonds are paid off. This severely impairs the residual value if the deal is not called, effectively pushing the call option in-the-money.

Putting it All Together — How Much Do Rates Need to Rise for the Call to be Out-of-the-Money?

We calculate breakeven rate changes using the following methodology. First, we assume that, at the time of the call date, the collateral prepays at 30% CPR and has an annual loss rate of 3%. This performance reasonably mirrors that of a generic HEL pool, and, at any rate, the results of our analysis are not highly sensitive to these assumptions. Second, we project the future residual cash flows for a generic securitization structure using these collateral assumptions and discount the cash flows at 20%. This step gives us the residual value, or the value of not calling the transaction. Finally, we assume that current coupon whole loans trade at 103, and fix a certain delinquency and overcollateralization level. This allows us to calculate the price of the entire collateral pool (using Exhibit 1), and thus the takeout from calling the deal. We increase rates until the price of the collateral decreases enough that the residual value just equals the takeout from calling the deal.

As an example, suppose that a deal has a 10% cleanup call and 5% overcollateralization at the call date. Suppose further that the delinquency percentages are as shown in Exhibit 1. Then, assuming a price of non-delinquent collateral of 103, the value of the collateral would be $103 \times 97.5\% = 100.46$. The value of calling the deal would be

$$\text{value of the collateral} - \text{value of paying par for the bonds}$$
$$= (100.46 - 100 \times 95\%) = 5.46\%$$

On the other hand, under our assumptions, the residual value would be approximately 2.75% at the call date. Thus, calling the deal results in a gain of 2.71%. Assuming that the collateral has a duration of 2.2 years, rates could rise 2.71%/2.2 or 123 bp before the gain from calling the deal would be neutralized.

Exhibit 2 summarizes the main results of our analysis. In the exhibit we show the breakeven rate increases for the call not to be exercised, where we vary the percentage of delinquencies in the pool. The lower, dashed line assumes a 10% cleanup call and a 5% overcollateralization at the call date. This simulates a typical fixed-rate deal. The upper, solid line assumes a 20% cleanup call and a 7.5% overcollateralization at the cleanup date; in this case, we also assume that if the call is not exercised, then all of the residual cash flow goes to pay down the ABS. This situation simulates the Conseco/Household structure (i.e., the 15%-20% call structure).

Exhibit 2: Breakeven Rate Increases for Cleanup Call

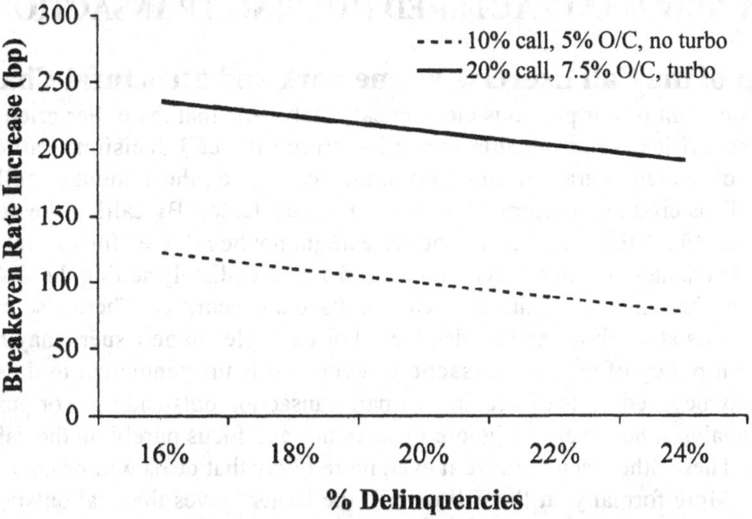

Three points are worth emphasizing. First, even for the 10% call structure, rates can rise fairly substantially before it becomes uneconomical to exercise the call. For example, at a total delinquency rate of 20%, rates can still rise 100 bp before the issuer is indifferent to exercising the 10% call. Second, while the rate increases do drop with increasing delinquencies, they are not extremely sensitive. For instance, for the 10% call structure, even at 24% total delinquencies, the breakeven rate change is still about 75 bp. Third, due to the high degree of O/C in the 20% call structure, this call is much further out of the money than the 10% call. At all delinquency levels, rates need to rise approximately 200 bp before it becomes uneconomical to call. As such, even though the call is larger, the higher strike actually makes it less valuable.

The breakeven rate changes imply that last cash flow securities can have very low dollar prices, and yet the deal may still be called by the issuer. For example, if a newly issued last cash flow HEL were trading at par in an unchanged rate environment, it would trade at approximately 93 if the market were to back up 100 bp. However, as Exhibit 2 shows, for typical O/C amounts, it could still be economical for the issuer to call the bonds in this type of backup. In the case of HEL floaters in particular, it is highly likely that deals will be called, even though delinquencies tend to be higher than on fixed-rate deals. In addition to the step-up coupons in the event that the deal is not called, ARM deals require a large amount of overcollateralization. Additionally, fast prepayments imply a short spread duration at the call date, so that spreads can widen substantially before offsetting the gain associated with O/C. For instance, in the event of 20% total delinquencies and a 10% O/C, spreads could widen about 250 bp before it would become uneconomical to call the deal.

ILLUSTRATING THE METHODOLOGY ON CLEANUP CALLS ON NEW MANUFACTURED HOUSING TRANSACTIONS

Recap of the Call Exercise Framework and Structural Changes

The basic point of our previous cleanup call analysis is that the dollar price of the called securities is not the sole factor governing the call decision. Rather, the amount of overcollateralization (O/C) in the deal — i.e., the amount of collateral "trapped" as credit enhancement — is the primary factor. By calling the deal, an issuer will "free" the O/C, which otherwise might not be released for several years. If there is enough O/C in the deal, the gain from immediately selling the O/C may be greater than the loss incurred by calling discount securities. There also may be other factors at work in the call decision. For example, some issuers may have a consistent policy of calling transactions, even if it is uneconomical to do so; or, there may be fixed costs of keeping a small transaction outstanding. For purposes of this analysis, however, we ignore these issues and focus purely on the call economics. These other factors make it even more likely that deals will be called.

More formally, at the call date, if the issuer leaves the deal outstanding, the value of its position is the present value of the projected residual cash flows. If the issuer calls the deal, he now owns all of the collateral (= the bonds + the residual), but has paid par for the bonds — i.e., the value of the issuer's position is the value of the collateral less the par amount of bonds. If the collateral value minus the par value of bonds exceeds the residual value, the deal should be called. We emphasize that if there is overcollateralization trapped in residual form, it would typically be discounted at a higher rate than if it were freed as collateral outside a deal; the reason for this is that the O/C is subordinated and is highly levered to losses. The ability to immediately free the O/C by calling the deal is the main factor which gives the call value.

In the Conseco Finance/Green Tree MH market, the key point is that nearly all Green Tree MH transactions from 1992-1999 had no overcollateralization, whereas the new deals have significant overcollateralization. In this structure, the call decision is governed purely by changes in funding costs — i.e., by the dollar prices of the called securities. Beginning with CNF 1999-6, the structure changed in three ways (see also Exhibit 3):

Exhibit 3: Comparison of Call Structures on Green Tree/Conseco Finance MH Transactions

	Old Deals (e.g. GT 1999-1)	New Deals (e.g. CNF 2000-1)
Cleanup call percentage	10%	20%
O/C target (% original balance)	0%	2%
O/C at call date (% current balance)	0%	10%
If deal not called...	(nothing special happens)	All residual cash flow pays down bond principal; issuer receives no residual until bonds are paid off

1. The cleanup call size was enlarged from 10% to 20% (in order to obtain financing status for the securitization).
2. The structure uses overcollateralization as a credit enhancement mechanism. O/C begins at 1.5% of the original balance, builds to 2% of the original balance, and does not step down over time. At the cleanup call date, the O/C is 10% (2%/20%) of the current balance.
3. If the cleanup call is not exercised, all residual cash flow — which is normally released to the issuer — goes to pay bond principal, until all bonds are paid off. This "turbo feature" defers all residual cash flows until a later point. As discussed above, residuals typically trade at very high yields, so this delay substantially impacts the present value of the residual cash flows.[2]

Implications of the Structure Change

Based on the framework discussed above, the presence of a large amount of O/C at the call date, as well as the diversion of residual cash flows, will both increase the issuer's incentive to call. The former increases the value of exercising the call (more collateral is freed), while the latter decreases the value of not exercising the call (the residual value is lowered). We now quantify the impact of these structural changes by estimating the breakeven rate changes needed to make the issuer indifferent between calling and not calling the transaction.

In order to calculate these breakeven rate changes, it is necessary to value the collateral and the residual at the call date. A key parameter in this valuation is the percentage of delinquent loans at the call date, since delinquent loans will trade at lower dollar prices than otherwise equivalent current loans.[3] Historical data suggest that Conseco Finance/Green Tree MH delinquencies will be very low at the time of the call. Exhibit 4 shows the percentage of 30-day, 60+ day (excluding repossessions), and repossession loans versus the pool factor for Green Tree MH securitizations. At the 20% pool factor point, these delinquency percentages are 100 bp, 75 bp, and 50 bp, respectively. In calculating the collateral value, we assume that 30-day delinquent loans trade at 75% of the value of current loans, 60-day delinquent loans trade at 50% of the value of current loans, and that repossessed seasoned loans trade at 25% of the value of current loans. Our results are highly insensitive to these assumptions, since the absolute level of delinquencies is low at the call date.

A final important point in the collateral valuation is that seasoned, current MH loans should command price payups over otherwise equivalent, new MH loans. At the time of the call date, seasoned loans will be 10-12 years old, and will have established a long mortgage payment history, as well as equity in the home. As such, the expected losses for these highly seasoned loans could be lower than for otherwise equivalent new loans, which would imply higher prices. Although the exact payups

---

[2] In addition, the new calls are "auction calls," so that third parties may bid on the collateral (and pay off the bonds in the process). This further enhances the probability of the call exercise.

[3] This is discussed in Lehman Brothers' *Relative Value* publication, February 7, 2000.

are difficult to ascertain (there is no liquid market for seasoned MH whole loans), in Exhibit 5 we calculate breakeven rate changes for different seasoned loan payups. In each of these calculations, we increase rates until the loss from paying par for discount bonds exactly offsets the gain by taking back the overcollateralization today. Even under the extremely conservative assumption of zero payup for seasoning, rates can rise more than 175 bp before the issuer is indifferent to calling the deal. Under modest payup assumptions (1-1.5 points), this breakeven increases to 210-225 bp.

Exhibit 4: Historical Delinquencies for Green Tree MH versus Pool Factor

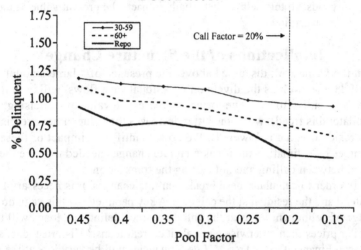

Exhibit 5: Breakeven Rate Changes versus Payups for Seasoned MH Collateral

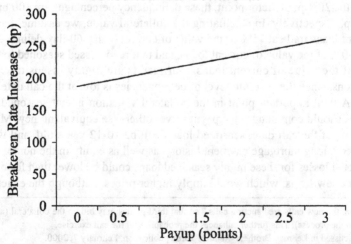

Exhibit 6: Market Pricing Differences for Last Cash Flow 10% and 20% Structures

10% call structure	Pricing Assumption	Call/Maturity	Avg. Life	Price	Convexity
–100 bp	170/C @ 225 MHP	Call	9.1 yr	105-16	
0 bp	162/C @ 175 MHP	Call	11.4	100-00	–2.5
+100 bp	177/C @ 160 MHP	Maturity	13.0	91-31	

20% call structure	Pricing Assumption	Call/Maturity	Avg. Life	Price	Convexity
–100 bp	165/C @ 225 MHP	Call	8.5 yr	105-00	
0 bp	158/C @ 175 MHP	Call	10.7	100-00	–2.3
+100 bp	164/C @ 160 MHP	Call	11.6	92-21	

The basic result of this analysis is that the cleanup call is an in-the-money option, and that the market should trade newer structures to call under a wide range of rate increases. This result is based purely on the economics of the call, and does not consider other factors, such as an issuer's potential desire to programatically call all deals regardless of the economics. Based on economics alone, though, a discount dollar price for a new, last cash flow MH sequential does not automatically imply that the deal will not be called. From a practical perspective, the implication is that the empirical convexity of last cash flow sequentials is actually slightly better in the new structure compared to the old structure.

To illustrate this point, in Exhibit 6 we calculate the expected prices for two types of last cash flow sequential MH securities, under +100 bp, unchanged, and –100 bp rate scenarios. The first type of security has a 10% cleanup call, but no overcollateralization, representing the older Green Tree MH structure. The second has a 20% cleanup call, but overcollateralization, representing the new structure. (Note that our pricing is not "constant OAS" pricing, simply because the market is not likely to trade the securities to constant OAS.) In the +100 scenario for the 20% call structure, we assume that the deal is priced to call, as the analysis above indicates that rates can rise significantly more than 100 bp before it becomes uneconomical to call. In contrast, we assume that in the +100 scenario, the 10% structure security is priced to maturity. As Exhibit 6 highlights, the empirical convexity that results for the 20% structure is –2.3, slightly better than the –2.5 for the 10% structure. In other words, even though the call option is larger, the local convexity characteristics are more favorable.

CONCLUSIONS AND RELATIVE VALUE IMPLICATIONS

In practice, the market will not begin trading discount securities to call until issuers actually call deals containing discount bonds. As a result, we do not expect the market to reprice the call/extension features of deals over the short term. From a fundamental perspective, though, the economics of the call are significantly different from what current market conventions imply, and we expect prices to ultimately reflect these economics. At similar nominal spreads, investors should prefer discount last cash flow securities to par priced last cash flows. In the subordinate market in particular, investors should look for discount securities which have significant amounts of overcollateralization trapped; these securities can likely be purchased to maturity but should, under a wide range of delinquency and rate scenarios, trade to call.

As a final note, we emphasize that the framework we have presented here is generic and applicable to not only home equity loans and manufactured housing, but also to other types of assets. For any type of cleanup call, the basic economic decision facing the issuer is to compare the present value of the residual to the gain produced by purchasing the bonds at par and selling the collateral. (Alternatively, the issuer may resecuritize the collateral, but the price of the collateral should closely reflect the gain implied by the securitization.) For asset classes with unique residual cash flow features (e.g., full turbo after the call date), or with large reserve funds/ overcollateralization at the call date, the deal may still be called even if the underlying securities are deeply discounted.

Accounting

Chapter 30

Accounting for Investments in MBS and ABS

Sunil Gangwani
Director
Securitization Transactions Team
Deloitte & Touche LLP

Allen S. Thomas
Partner
Securitization Transactions Team
Deloitte & Touche LLP

James Mountain
Partner
Capital Markets Group
Deloitte & Touche LLP

INTRODUCTION

This chapter provides a brief overview of certain U.S. generally accepted accounting principles (GAAP) applicable to investments in mortgage loans, mortgage servicing assets, and securitized debt instruments which are also known as mortgage-backed securities (MBS) and asset-backed securities (ABS). It does not address income tax issues. It is not meant to provide professional advice but instead it is intended to merely state certain facts and, in some cases, the concepts behind the pronouncements of the Financial Accounting Standards Boards (FASB).

The primary focus here will be on statements issued by the FASB. Specifically, this chapter addresses certain information set forth in the Statement of Financial Accounting Standards (SFAS) No. 65, "Accounting for Certain Mortgage Banking Activities;" SFAS No. 91, "Accounting for Nonrefundable Fees and Costs Associated

The information set forth herein has been gathered from various publications from the Financial Accounting Standards Board. The rules and regulations are subject to change from time to time. The authors strongly encourage readers to refer to the original information published by the FASB or to contact their accountants for appropriate advice. The authors would also like to thank Marty Rosenblatt of Deloitte & Touche LLP.

with Originating or Acquiring Loans and Initial Direct Costs of Leases;" SFAS No. 115, "Accounting for Certain Investments in Debt and Equity Securities;" SFAS No. 125, "Accounting for Transfers and Servicing of Financial Assets and Extinguishment of Liabilities;" and SFAS No. 134, "Accounting for Mortgage-Backed Securities Retained after the Securitization of Mortgage Loans Held for Sale by a Mortgage Banking Enterprise." Certain unique issues related to investments such as "residuals" and "interest-only" securities are addressed by Emerging Issues Task Force (EITF) Issue No. 89-4, "Accounting for Purchased Investment in a Collateralized Mortgage Obligation Instrument or in a Mortgage-Backed Interest Only Certificate" and EITF Issue No. 93-18, "Recognition of Impairment for an Investment in a Collateralized Mortgage Obligation Instrument or in a Mortgage-Backed Interest Only Certificate."

MBS and ABS are generally considered "debt instruments" for accounting purposes irrespective of the form of such securities. For example, an MBS from one transaction may be issued as an undivided interest (often characterized as "certificates") in a pool of mortgage loans while an MBS from another transaction may be issued as debt (often characterized as "notes" or "bonds") of a special purpose entity. For accounting purposes, both such investments are usually treated as "debt securities." Therefore, interest-only securities, floaters, inverse floaters, principal-only securities, senior classes, subordinate classes, certificated residual classes, etc. are considered debt securities despite the fact that some of these types of securities may be issued in "equity" form. (Note that certain residual interests may in fact be treated as equity.)

CLASSIFICATIONS

SFAS No. 115 requires investors to classify each security they hold into one of three categories: (a) held-to-maturity, (b) trading, or (c) available-for-sale. Each classification is based on the intent and ability of the investor at the date of acquisition.

> *Held-to-maturity (HTM):* Debt securities that are acquired with the "positive intent and ability" to hold until maturity are classified as held-to-maturity. Equity securities are not eligible for the HTM category. HTM securities are reported at amortized historical-cost basis. Fluctuations in market value due to changing economic conditions have no impact on the carrying value of such debt securities. Any unrealized gain is not reported. Any unrealized losses are not recognized unless the asset is permanently impaired. The sale of HTM securities prior to maturity, might call into question the classification of current and future securities purchased on a HTM basis.

> *Trading:* Debt securities that are acquired for the sole purpose of profiting from short term fluctuations in price are classified as trading securities. Most brokers/dealers, pension plans and investment companies have their

assets classified into this category. It is expected that this account will be the most active account for purchases and sales of securities. While the holding period of securities would typically be short, investors may also elect at the acquisition date to classify a security as trading, even if the holding period is expected to be long-term. Such assets are always reported at fair value. Any unrealized gain or loss is reported in earnings. Transfers to and out of the trading classifications should be rare.

Available-for-sale (AFS): Debt securities that are not classified in either of the above two categories are placed in the available-for-sale category. Many regulated organizations may have assets in this category as a result of regulatory changes that may require disposing of certain securities within a certain time frame. Also, certain debt securities must be classified into either the trading or AFS category if they can be contractually prepaid or otherwise settled in such a way that the holder would not recover substantially all of its investment. The assets are reported at fair value. Any unrealized gain or loss is reported in a separate component of shareholders' equity. If the investment is permanently impaired, the excess of amortized cost over fair value is recognized currently as a loss in the income statement.

Exhibit 1 summarizes such classifications. Since these classifications are made on an individual security basis and largely reflect ability and intent, the same type of debt security may be reported on a different basis in the same organization. This classification is determined at acquisition and should be reassessed on each reporting date. However, debt securities are generally not allowed to be freely moved from one category to another. The FASB has provided certain guidelines under which reclassification of a security is permitted.

Exhibit 1: Classification of Debt Securities

Impact	HTM	Trading	AFS
Balance Sheet	Historical cost – adjusted for amortization of discount or premium in accordance with effective interest method.	Fair value.	Fair value.
Income Statement	Interest income reported in earnings based on the effective interest method; Losses arising from permanent impairment of assets reported in earnings.	Interest income reported in earnings based on the effective interest method; Unrealized gain or loss arising from changes in market value reported directly in earnings.	Interest income reported in earnings based on the effective interest method; Unrealized gain or loss arising from changes in market value reported as other comprehensive income and a separate component of shareholder's equity. Permanent impairment losses reported in earnings.

The debt securities reported under the held-to-maturity category cause the least amount of fluctuation in earnings of an organization. Earnings are reported on an historical cost basis which is based on pricing factors at the time of acquisition. Factors such as current market value and current interest rates generally have no impact on earnings. However, prepayments and credit losses do impact earnings as described below. If an organization does not have the ability to hold the debt securities until maturity due to interest rate risk, prepayment risk, currency risk, liquidity risk or gap management, they should not be classified as HTM. For example, if a bank is expecting to sell certain securities to meet liquidity demands in the future, these debt securities should be classified as AFS or trading from the acquisition date. Similarly, if an organization does not have the positive intent to hold the debt securities until maturity, they should not be classified as HTM. Another example would be an organization's desire to sell securities in order to offset taxable losses or gains. For instance, if there are taxable losses, an organization cannot sell any appreciated debt securities from HTM to offset the taxable losses. If the intent is to offset taxable gains or losses by selling certain debt securities, those debt securities should be classified in the AFS or trading category from the acquisition date. Also, it was concluded by the FASB that hedging price and interest rate risk will be considered to be inconsistent with the intent to hold a debt security to maturity. When an organization adopts SFAS No. 133, "Accounting for Derivative Instruments and Hedging Activities," it will no longer be able to completely hedge price or interest rate risk of HTM securities. However, at the time of adopting SFAS No. 133, an organization has a one-time opportunity to reclassify any securities out of HTM into AFS or Trading.

Any movements via reclassification or direct sales from the HTM category are expected to be rare. If a debt security is reclassified, the FASB expects the existence of very compelling and unusual reasons for doing so. Reclassifications are permitted if: (a) there is permanent credit impairment of such securities, (b) regulatory requirements change the risk weighting significantly or otherwise cause business organizations to sell such securities, (c) tax law changes the tax exempt status of such securities, (d) a major business combination or disposition (such as a merger or an acquisition) causes the organization to dispose of certain securities to maintain existing interest rate or credit risk profiles and (e) other events that are isolated, non-recurring and unusual that could not have been reasonably anticipated. Transfer or sale of an HTM security for other than the specified reasons would call into question the original classification and "taint" all other HTM securities. Those other tainted HTM securities would need to be reclassified and no new securities could be classified as HTM for a certain period. Fortunately for securitization transactions, the sale of the "tail" portion of the debt securities is allowed without raising doubts about the initial classification of the entire portfolio. The "tail" portion is identified as the earlier to occur of (a) when 85% of the outstanding principal balance at the date of acquisition is paid down and (b) 90 days or less to the final maturity date of the debt security.

Exhibit 2: Historical Cost Method

Period	Scheduled Balance	Principal	Expected Interest	Payment	Carrying Value	12.893% Income	Unamortized Discount
0	$100,000	(98,000)	98,000	2,000			
1	98,776	1,224	1,000	2,224	96,828	1,053	1,947
2	97,539	1,237	988	2,224	95,644	1,040	1,894
3	96,290	1,249	975	2,224	94,448	1,028	1,842
4	95,028	1,262	963	2,224	93,238	1,015	1,790
5	93,754	1,274	950	2,224	92,015	1,002	1,739
6	92,467	1,287	938	2,224	90,779	989	1,688
...	...	...	...	...	...	...	...
48	25,036	1,955	270	2,224	24,919	289	117
49	23,062	1,974	250	2,224	22,962	268	100
50	21,068	1,994	231	2,224	20,985	247	84
51	19,055	2,014	211	2,224	18,986	225	69
52	17,021	2,034	191	2,224	16,965	204	56
53	14,966	2,054	170	2,224	14,923	182	44
54	12,892	2,075	150	2,224	12,859	160	33
55	10,796	2,096	129	2,224	10,773	138	24
56	8,680	2,116	108	2,224	8,664	116	16
57	6,542	2,138	87	2,224	6,532	93	10
58	4,383	2,159	65	2,224	4,378	70	5
59	2,202	2,181	44	2,224	2,201	47	2
60	0	2,202	22	2,224	(0)	24	0

Regardless of the specific classification, interest income including amortization of purchased discount or premium is reported in earnings. Exhibit 2 shows the "effective interest" or "level yield" method of amortization for a hypothetical amortizing mortgage-like debt security with an outstanding principal balance of $100,000, a coupon of 12.0% per annum, a term of 5 years and a gross purchase price of 98.0% ($98,000). Based on these characteristics, the investor receives a contractual payment of $2,224 per month for 60 months. The internal rate of return or yield to maturity of the debt security is 12.893% per annum. The reportable income is calculated as the product of the beginning carrying value of the debt security in a period and 12.893% per annum. The ending carrying value in that period is determined by adding the interest income to the previous carrying value and reducing the resulting amount by the total cash payment received. If this debt security were classified as held-to-maturity, the carrying value of the security will be reported as shown in Exhibit 2 in every reporting period. Exhibit 3 shows the impact of a decline in the fair value to 95.0% (representing an unrealized loss of $2,972 and a fair value of $91,475) at the end of the first quarter for the same security carried under the three different categories. Note that the change in the fair value does not change the carrying value of the assets held in the HTM category. Exhibit 4 shows the recording of transfers in the event of a reclassification.

Exhibit 3: Impact on Reported Earnings — Journal Entries

Original Entry		
Investments in MBS	$98,000	
Cash		$98,000
Held-to-Maturity[1]		
Cash	$6,673	
Interest income[2]		$3,121
Investments in MBS[3]		$3,552

[1] Requires disclosure of the fair value of this portfolio.
[2] Earnings (includes $158 amortization of discount).
[3] Principal amount received less amortization of discount.

Trading		
Cash	$6,673	
Interest income[4]		$3,121
Investments in MBS		$3,552
Loss from MBS[4]	$2,972	
Investments in MBS		$2,972

[4] Earnings will increase by a net of only $149.

Available-for-Sale		
Cash	$6,673	
Interest income		$3,121
Investments in MBS		$3,552
Other comprehensive income[5]	$2,972	
Investments in MBS		$2,972

[5] Separate component of equity (amount should be net of tax).

Exhibit 4: Reclassification of Debt Securities

From/To	HTM	Trading	AFS
HTM	—	Recorded at fair value. Unrealized gain or loss recognized in earnings at the time of reclassification.	Recorded at fair value. Unrealized gain or loss reported in a separate component of shareholder's equity.
Trading	Recorded at fair value. Unrealized gain or loss already reported in earnings; no reversals.	—	Recorded at fair value. Unrealized gain or loss already reported in earnings; no reversals.
AFS	Recorded at fair value. Unrealized gain or loss recognized to be continued in a separate component of shareholder's equity. This amount is amortized in accordance with the effective interest method.	Recorded at fair value. Unrealized gain or loss recognized in earnings at the time of reclassification.	—

Somewhat similar to the rules for debt securities SFAS No. 65, accounting for certain mortgage banking activities, requires mortgage bankers to classify whole mortgage loans into one of two categories: held for sale or held for long-term investment. Mortgage loans classified as held for sale are carried at the lower of cost or market value (LOCOM). If market value is less than cost, a valuation allowance is recorded for the difference, resulting in a charge to income. Changes in the required valuation allowance due to changes in market value are reflected in income as they occur. This means that recovery of a previous LOCOM mark down can be recognized as a gain. However, the loans should not be carried at an amount above cost.

Mortgage loans held for long-term investment are those where there is an ability and intent to hold the loans for the foreseeable future, or until maturity. Loans held for long-term investment are carried at amortized cost and evaluated for other than temporary impairment. If ultimate recovery of the carrying amount of the loan is doubtful, the loans should be written down to the expected collectible amount, which becomes the new cost basis. The write down is recorded as a loss and any subsequent recovery is not recognized until the loans are sold or mature. Unlike SFAS No. 115, there is no specific list of circumstances under which loans may be transferred between classifications, although such transfers should be infrequent. Selling or transferring a loan out of the held for long-term investment category would not "taint" the similar classification of any other loan.

ACCOUNTING FOR INCOME

The generally accepted method of accounting for amortization of discount and premium for mortgage loans and debt securities, as described earlier, is called the "effective interest" or "level yield" method. The initial carrying value of the mortgage loans used to calculate the effective yield (level yield" or "purchase yield") is the purchase price adjusted for (increased by) any direct costs and (decreased by) any nonrefundable origination fees associated with the mortgage loans. The initial carrying value of the debt securities is the purchase price plus accrued interest, if any, paid for such securities. The effective interest method determines the periodic income as either (a) the sum of coupon income and accretion of purchase discount, if any, or (b) the difference between coupon income and amortization of purchase premium, if any, in each case using the internal rate of return to determine the accretion of discount or amortization of purchase premium.

In Exhibit 2 it was assumed that the investor will receive only contractual payments and that the debt security is neither callable nor putable. However, in the case of mortgage loans and MBS, investors have implicitly written a call option to the mortgagors which makes them likely to prepay their loans at no additional cost (generally) to them in a declining interest rate environment. Prepayments are generally expected to rise in a declining interest rate environment because mortgagors can obtain other mortgage loans with lower prevailing interest rates. Prepaying the existing mortgage loans can therefore reduce their cost of borrowing. Since the borrowers in the underlying assets are long a call option, they have the right but not the obligation, to exercise the call. This arrangement makes it extremely difficult to predict the future cash flows to investors in mortgage loans and MBS and thus makes the yield to maturity only an estimate at any point in time. The FASB recognized the importance of the callable nature of mortgage-backed and asset-backed securities.

Effect of Prepayments

If a securitized instrument is purchased at par, changing prepayments does not impact the interest income based on the effective interest method. The interest income received over time is the same as the cash received based on the coupon and the then-outstanding face amount. However, if such an instrument is purchased at a discount from par, an increase in interest rates can adversely affect income because mortgagors are less likely to prepay their mortgages and the accretion of discount will occur over a longer period of time. Of course, the reverse is true as well (i.e. purchases at a premium can be adversely affected by a decrease in interest rates).

Methods of Accounting for Prepayable Securities

SFAS No. 91 allows two basic methods of accounting for interest income for mortgage loans and debt securities that are prepayable. The first method is based on the contractual cash flows determined at the time of purchase without regard to any prepayments that may arise in the future. As prepayments are experienced, the discount or premium related to such prepayments is adjusted in the interest income for that period.

The second method is based on the cash flows with estimated prepayments embedded in those cash flows. The FASB does not require estimation of prepayments under SFAS No. 91. The method may be used if a pool of underlying mortgage loans consists of a large number of mortgage loans or similar assets with substantially similar characteristics such that prepayments can be reasonably estimated. In every reporting period, investors are required to make adjustments to the effective yield to maturity and hence the future interest income based on the actual prepayment experience to date and the expected future prepayment experience of the underlying mortgage loans. Using the actual prepayments from the date of acquisition to the reporting date and the expected future prepayments from the reporting date onward, a new effective yield is calculated from the date of acquisition. The carrying value is adjusted to the amount that would have existed had the new effective yield been applied since acquisition. The difference between the new carrying value and the actual carrying value is charged or credited to interest income. This results in a "catch up" of effective yield in every reporting period.

If a debt security were purchased at a discount and if the prepayments were to accelerate, the new effective yield would be higher than the one calculated at acquisition. Consequently, the interest income in the future reporting periods would be higher than initially projected. If prepayments were to decelerate, the new effective yield would be lower than the one calculated at acquisition resulting in lower interest income for the subsequent reporting periods. This method is also known as the "retrospective method." All fixed rate MBSs and adjustable rate MBSs are required to follow the retrospective method (other than high-risk IO and certain other classes for which the return of substantially all of the initial investment is not guaranteed). Exhibit 5 depicts the impact of "catch up" for a hypothetical mortgage-like debt security. In the first and second quarter, the income on the security is $3,119 (interest income of $3,146 (at 13.266%) and a write-down of $27) and $2,955 (interest income of $2,841 (at 13.154%) and a write-up of $94), respectively. This method will have the most impact on period-to-period earnings in the middle of the life of the investment. Because the effective yield to maturity is adjusted, a portion of the total change in cash flows is amortized over the remaining life at a higher or lower yield. Shortly after acquisition, very little income has been recognized so the yield adjustment recognized most of the cash flow change over future periods. Near the end of the investment's life, a change in prepayments will have less impact on cash flows.

Accounting for Adjustable-Rate MBS

Adjustable-rate MBS (ARM) are complicated not just by prepayments but also by the fact that their coupons are tied to specific indices. If the index moves the coupon income of the ARM becomes subject to increase or decrease. Also, most ARMs are created with "teaser" rates which rates may be significantly below the current interest rates at the time of issuance (resulting from a desire to attract new borrowers in the underlying mortgage loans who cannot afford a higher initial payment that would have resulted from a fixed rate mortgage). The teaser rates are fixed for a short period of time (the teaser period) after origination of mortgages. However, after the lapse of the teaser period, the coupon rate is pegged to an index implying that the coupon equals the applicable index plus the specified margin (subject to certain caps and floors).

How does one compute the effective yield for an ARM with changing interest rates? For the purposes of amortizing the discount or premium, the FASB allows both (a) using an index rate at acquisition for the life of the ARM to project cash flows and (b) adjusting the coupon to the correctly indexed rate at the end of the teaser period and projecting the cash flows accordingly. The second strategy results in most of the original discount from discounted ARMs to be recognized in the teaser period. Floaters and inverse floaters coupons are tied to an index. In the case of floaters, the coupon moves in the same direction as the related index, whereas in the case of inverse floaters, the coupon moves in the opposite direction. Note that both can be leveraged in relation to the underlying index making a significant impact on the coupon income. Both are accounted for using the retrospective method.

Exhibit 5: Retrospective Method

Period	Prepayments	Effective Yield	Carrying Value	Cash	Income	Discount Amortization	Unamortized Discount
0			98,000				2,000
1	22%	13.266%	94,835	4,249	1,083	83	1,917
2	22%	13.266%	91,746	4,137	1,048	81	1,836
3	22%	13.266%	88,733	4,027	1,014	78	1,757
0			98,000				2,000
1	22%	13.154%	94,826	4,249	1,074	74	1,926
2	22%	13.154%	91,728	4,137	1,039	72	1,854
3	22%	13.154%	88,707	4,027	1,006	70	1,784
4	15%	13.154%	86,387	3,292	972	67	1,717
5	15%	13.154%	84,103	3,232	947	66	1,651
6	15%	13.154%	81,852	3,172	922	64	1,586
0			98,000				2,000
1	22%	13.356%	94,842	4,249	1,091	91	1,909
2	22%	13.356%	91,761	4,137	1,056	88	1,821
3	22%	13.356%	88,755	4,027	1,021	85	1,736
4	15%	13.356%	86,451	3,292	988	83	1,653
5	15%	13.356%	84,182	3,232	962	81	1,572
6	15%	13.356%	81,946	3,172	937	79	1,492
7	30%	13.356%	78,442	4,416	912	78	1,415
8	30%	13.356%	75,061	4,253	873	74	1,340
9	30%	13.356%	71,801	4,096	835	71	1,269

High-Risk Securities

The FASB has defined "high risk" securities as those securities where there is a potential for loss of substantially all of the original investment due to changes in (a) market interest rates, (b) prepayment rates or (c) temporary reinvestment earnings. For a debt security to not be considered a high risk security, the generally accepted threshold is recovery of 90% or more of the initial investment.

Under this definition, both interest-only (IO) and most residual securities are considered high risk securities and the accounting for such securities is therefore based on the "prospective method" as described under EITF Issue No. 89-4, "Accounting for Purchased Investment in a Collateralized Mortgage Obligation Instrument or in a Mortgage-Backed Interest Only Certificate." In the initial accrual period, interest income is accrued based on the initial carrying value and effective yield. Any cash received is first used to apply towards accrued interest and then to reduce the carrying value to zero. At each reporting date, the effective yield is adjusted prospectively from the reporting period based on the new estimate of prepayments. If the new effective yield is less than the then-current risk-free interest rate, the investment is considered impaired and written down to fair value, which becomes the new cost basis. The new effective yield is calculated based on the carrying value at the end of the previous reporting period, the new prepayment estimates and the contractual terms of the debt security. This procedure continues until all cash has been received. Note that this does not result in a write-up or a write-down of the carrying value in the reporting period. Only the future interest income is affected.

Exhibit 6 depicts the impact of the prospective method for a hypothetical mortgage-like debt security. In the second first and second quarters, the income from the debt security is $3,146 and $2,838, respectively. Also, as amended by SFAS No. 125, these types of debt securities may not be classified in the HTM category. Because of the high-risk and volatile nature of these debt securities, they are marked to market and classified in either the trading or AFS category.

Despite the fact that principal-only (PO) securities are very sensitive to changes in market interest rates and prepayments, they are not considered high-risk securities under the definition described above. Aside from the permanent credit impairment that may potentially result in a loss of some portion of the original investment, investors in these securities generally receive back their entire investment. The adverse changes in market interest rates or the prepayment rates may only affect the effective yield or the total return of such debt securities. Of course, the market value of the security will be affected by changing interest rates and prepayments. Any changes in the fair value may be carried over to earnings or to a separate component of the equity based on the classification of the security as trading, AFS or HTM.

In certain situations, increasing prepayments that result in reduced cash flows to the security holder can cause the effective yield to equal or fall below 0%. Prior to the release of EITF Issue No. 93-18 such debt securities were written down to the undiscounted cash flows (equivalent to 0% effective yield) of the debt securities, however, now such debt securities are tested against the comparable duration risk-free yield and consequently written down to fair value in such a way as to yield the market rate in the future.

Exhibit 6: Prospective Method

Period	Prepayments	Effective Yield	Carrying Value	Cash	Income	Discount Amortization	Unamortized Discount
0			98,000				2,000
1	22%	13.266%	94,835	4,249	1,083	83	1,917
2	22%	13.266%	91,746	4,137	1,048	81	1,836
3	22%	13.266%	88,733	4,027	1,014	78	1,757
4	15%	13.137%	86,413	3,292	971	66	1,691
5	15%	13.137%	84,127	3,232	946	65	1,626
6	15%	13.137%	81,876	3,172	921	63	1,562
7	30%	13.421%	78,375	4,416	916	81	1,481
8	30%	13.421%	74,998	4,253	877	78	1,403
9	30%	13.421%	71,741	4,096	839	75	1,328

Exhibit 7: Recognition of Interest Income

Debt security	Accounting Income
Planned Amortization Classes, Targeted Amortization Classes, Support Classes and other Fixed Rate Certificates	Retrospective method
Principal-Only Certificates	Retrospective method
Interest-Only Certificates	Prospective method
Residual Certificates	Prospective method
Adjustable Rate, Floater and Inverse Floater Certificates	Retrospective method
Originated Fixed Rate Loans	Retrospective method

Nuances

(1) Most MBS investors accrue income during a specified accrual period, however, the accrued income is paid out to the investors only after certain number of days (often called delay days in the MBS community). SFAS No. 91 does not provide guidance on the computational techniques to account for such delay days. Economically, it reduces the effective yield on the debt security;(2) SFAS No. 91 also does not provide guidance on computational techniques to take into account purchased accrued interest. A typical fixed rate MBS accrues interest for the entire calendar month prior to the month of actual payment. If such MBS settles on the 28th of the month, an investor will purchase twenty-seven days of accrued interest from the seller; and (3) Due to variations in prepayment speeds and index rates, it is possible for discount and premium ARMs to accrete their cost basis to more than the outstanding principal balance or the initial basis at acquisition, respectively. In such cases, the cost basis is capped at the outstanding principal balance (for discount ARMs) or the market value (%) at acquisition (for premium ARMs). For simplicity, all examples shown in this chapter are based on (a) no delay days and (b) no accrued interest.

INVESTMENTS BY SECURITIZERS IN RETAINED INTERESTS — RESIDUALS

Many organizations securitize their assets periodically. There are many reasons to access the capital markets via securitization. The most important reason being the availability of funds at lower costs.

However, there has been a lot of press talk about certain accounting procedures followed by lending institutions which primarily depend on securitization to access the capital markets. Many lenders have had to change their accounting resulting in a write down of their assets, in particular, the residual interests in securitizations held by them. When high yielding mortgage loans such as B&C/subprime quality loans are securitized, a residual security is created by virtue of the fact that the underlying assets generate higher coupon income than that needed for any on-going expenses and the interest on newly formed debt securities. The difference between the income on the assets and the expense on the liabilities represents "excess interest" needed for credit enhancement and is given the form of "residual security" or "residual interest." These residual interests are akin to interest-only strips and generally have no principal balance. If prepayment rates were to increase, the residual interests would be left with declining cash flow possibly causing a significant loss of the original investment. Per SFAS No. 125, these securities must be classified into trading or AFS category and marked to market in every reporting period.

Ideally, the "market" or fair value of the residual security used for accounting purposes should be the price at which it can be traded. Quoted market prices in active markets are the best indicators of fair value. However, residual securities trading is scarce and very specialized making the market for such debt securities very inactive and illiquid. If quoted market prices are unavailable, the FASB allows estimation of fair value based on reasonable assumptions about future cash flows. The process of projecting the future cash flows for residual securities is driven mainly by the following assumptions: the (a) prepayment rate and (b) expected credit loss rate in a pool of mortgage loans. Future cash flows using the above assumptions are then discounted back to the date of securitization at the prevailing discount rates. These discounted cash flows provide an estimate of the fair value of the residual security.

If a securitization is to be treated as a sale for accounting purposes, the recognition of "gain" or "loss" is not an election of the seller. A seller must recognize gain or loss immediately based on the allocation of the carrying value of the mortgage loans to the debt securities sold. A hypothetical securitization shown in Exhibit 8 depicts how pre-tax gain (loss) is calculated for a securitization assuming that the net carrying value of the mortgage loans is at par. The key factor here is to estimate the fair value of the residual class which often tends to drive a transaction. If the fair value is not available and if it cannot be estimated for a retained security, it should be recorded at zero.

The expected rate of return on the residual depends primarily on the expected credit loss experience and the expected prepayment experience of the underlying mortgage loans. Significant fluctuations in the earnings stream can result if the valuations are done incorrectly at the beginning of the process.

Upon acquisition, an effective yield is calculated for the residual security based on the reasonable assumptions about prepayment and credit loss rates. This effective yield is equal to the discount rate used at acquisition. In the above example, the prepayment rate was 25% per annum, the loss rate was 0.75% per annum taken as a haircut from interest income, and the discount rate for the residual security was 19.5% per annum. The effect of changing one of the assumptions (while keeping the others constant) from the base case is shown in Exhibit 9.

These securities are carried at fair value in either the trading or AFS category. Any unrealized gains or losses because of changes in the fair value of a trading security is recognized in earnings. For AFS securities, these changes are recognized in a separate component of equity called "comprehensive income." These debt securities are tested for other-than-temporary impairment by comparing the discounted present value of the expected cash flows at a comparable risk-free rate to the current carrying value of such debt security. The debt security is considered impaired if such difference is negative in which case the debt security should be written down to fair value. The write-down is a charge against earnings. The debt securities which are classified into the trading category need not be assessed for such impairment because any difference in fair value is already included in earnings.

Exhibit 8: Pre-tax Gain for Securitization

Class	Balance	Coupon	Price	FMV	Allocation	Basis	Sold
Loans	$100,000	9.0%	—	—		$100,000	Y
Class AAA	96,000	7.5	100%	$96,000	94.27%	94,266	Y
Class BB	4,000	7.5	96	3,840	3.77	3,771	Y
Residual		—		1,500	1.47	1,473	N
Servicing		0.5		500	0.49	490	N
	$100,000			$101,840	100.00%	$100,000	

Proceeds	$99,840
Allocated Carrying Value	(98,037)
Pre-tax Gain	$1,803

Journal Entries after a Securitization

Journal Entries	Debit	Credit
Cash	$99,840	
Class R certificates	1,473	
Servicing asset	490	
Mortgage loans		$100,000
Gain-on-sale		1,803
Class R certificates*	27	
Other comprehensive income		27

*Adjusting entries to mark the retained interest to fair value. Servicing asset (is not a security and) remains at carrying value.

Exhibit 9: Impact of Varying Assumptions on the Hypothetical Retained Interest

Loss Rate	0.00%	0.25%	0.50%	1.00%
Fair Value	$3,078	$2,548	$2,021	$981
% Change from Base Case	105%	70%	35%	−35%
Prepayment Rate	20.00%	22.50%	27.50%	30.00%
Fair Value	$1,717	$1,602	$1,405	$1,320
% Change from Base Case	14%	7%	−6%	−12%
Discount Rate	10.00%	12.50%	15.00%	17.50%
Fair Value	$1,853	$1,745	$1,648	$1,562
% Change from Base Case	24%	16%	10%	4%

At the time of this writing, the EITF has added to its agenda, EITF Issue No. 99-20, (Recognition of Interest Income and Impairment on Certain Investments). Initially, the scope of the project will be limited to retained interests classified as either held-to-maturity or available-for-sale. Existing GAAP does not provide robust guidance for the ongoing measurement of interest income and other adjustments for securitized debt instruments whose cash flows may change as a result of prepayments, credit losses, changes in an interest rate index and other reasons. Multiple interest income accounting models have been developed and applied for particular types of securities to deal with changes in their estimated future cash flows.

Servicing by Securitizers

Servicing is inherent in all financial assets. The servicing function includes, but is not limited to, collections of principal, interest and taxes from borrowers, disbursement of such funds to investors and related taxing authorities, monitoring delinquencies and performing foreclosures on behalf of investors. Servicing becomes a distinct asset only when it is contractually separated from the underlying financial assets or if it is purchased separately.

Per SFAS No. 125, if the seller retains the servicing function of the securitized mortgage loans and the contractual servicing fee is more than "adequate," a servicing asset must be recorded on the balance sheet. Conversely, if the servicing compensation is not adequate, a servicing liability must be recorded. How does one determine the "adequate compensation" for any portfolio? In general, it includes the cost of servicing plus some profit demanded by the marketplace. Note that the adequate compensation is not determined by the individual servicing operations. It is set by the marketplace. As a rule of thumb, larger balance mortgage loans demand smaller servicing fee and vice versa. For example, the servicing fee for non-conforming jumbo mortgage loans is generally 20 basis points whereas for conforming mortgage loans serviced by agency-approved servicers is expected to be higher than 20 basis points. In our example the contractual servicing fee is assumed to be 50 basis points. In most securitizations the servicers are entitled to late fees and any reinvestment earnings of the funds held. On the other hand, these servicers are also contractually obligated to advance certain payments for delinquent borrowers and, in some cases, for interest shortfalls caused by unexpected prepayments of principal in a securitization. For simplicity, it is assumed in our example that the extra income from late fees and reinvestment earnings will offset these expenses (and that the time value of the difference is zero). Let us further assume that there is an average bid (solicited or unsolicited) of 40 basis points to service the portfolio. If the seller retains the servicing function of the portfolio, the 10 basis points over and above the average bid indicates that a servicing asset must be booked after securitization. If the contractual servicing fee were only 25 basis points, the 15 basis points below the representative bid would indicate a servicing liability.

Exhibit 10: Servicing Assets and Liabilities

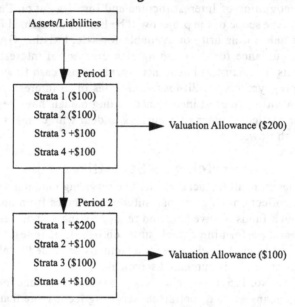

A servicing asset or liability is not amortized using any of the contractual, retrospective or prospective methods discussed earlier. In fact, both servicing assets and liabilities are amortized in proportion to and over the period of net estimated servicing income (excess of servicing revenues over the servicing costs) or net servicing loss (excess of servicing costs over the servicing revenues). In addition, the servicing asset or liability should be reassessed each period for impairment by comparing the carrying value against the fair value of the asset or liability. If the fair value is lower than the carrying value, the servicing assets are adjusted downward to the lower-of-cost-or-market and the difference is carried via valuation allowance into earnings. Subsequent writeups through earnings are allowed only to the extent of previous writedowns.

The determination of impairment in servicing assets requires stratification of underlying assets being serviced. The underlying assets must be broken down into categories representing significant risk in the portfolio such as fixed rate vs. adjustable rate mortgage loans, coupon, remaining term, geographic location, etc. The fair value in each individual category is compared to the carrying value of the corresponding category. The writedown is taken through a valuation allowance in each individual category. As shown in Exhibit 10, a writedown in one category must not be offset by an increase in the fair value (over the carrying value) in another category. For servicing liabilities, an increase in fair value implies an increase in the liability via a basis adjustment (no valuation allowance) with the loss carried through earnings. Servicing assets and liabilities must be accounted for separately.

Exhibit 11: Accounting for Servicing Asset by Sellers
(Portfolio $100 Million, 9.0% Coupon, 30 Years, 25% CPR)

Period	Servicing Fee (.5%)	Servicing Fee less Servicing Costs	% of Total Income	Carrying Value at 12%	Amortization of Servicing Asset	Income (Fee less Amortization)
0	$1,211,810					
1	$41,667	$16,667	2.45%	1,182,140	$29,670	$11,997
2	40,657	16,263	2.39%	1,153,188	28,951	11,706
3	39,672	15,869	2.33%	1,124,938	28,250	11,422
4	38,711	15,484	2.27%	1,097,373	27,566	11,146
5	37,773	15,109	2.22%	1,070,475	26,898	10,875
6	36,857	14,743	2.17%	1,044,230	26,246	10,612
7	35,964	14,386	2.11%	1,018,620	25,609	10,355
8	35,092	14,037	2.06%	993,632	24,988	10,104
9	34,241	13,696	2.01%	969,250	24,382	9,859
10	33,410	13,364	1.96%	945,459	23,791	9,619
11	32,600	13,040	1.92%	922,245	23,214	9,386
12	31,809	12,723	1.87%	899,595	22,650	9,158

Exhibit 12: Accounting for an IO Security

Period	Carrying Value	Interest-Only Amortization	Income
0	$1,211,810		
1	1,182,261	$29,549	$12,118
2	1,153,427	28,835	11,823
3	1,125,288	28,138	11,534
4	1,097,830	27,458	11,253
5	1,071,035	26,795	10,978
6	1,044,888	26,147	10,710
7	1,019,373	25,515	10,449
8	994,475	24,898	10,194
9	970,179	24,296	9,945
10	946,471	23,708	9,702
11	923,336	23,135	9,465
12	900,761	22,575	9,233

The income on IO securities is recognized either based on changes in fair value and the effective yield method (if classified as trading) or simply based on the effective yield method (if classified as available-for-sale). Because there are differences in the subsequent accounting for servicing and IO securities, sellers may structure contracts for the retained interests to provide smaller servicing assets and larger IO securities or vice versa. Exhibits 11 and 12 depict the differences in accounting for income from servicing assets and IO securities for the same expected cash flows. The different methods of accounting for servicing and IO securities in this above example result in the same aggregate amount of accounting income to be recognized over the life of the investment, however the timing of such income varies.

The servicing assets are adjusted for the difference between fair value and the carrying value as described above under the LOCOM method, but only if the fair value were less than the carrying value of the assets. Thus, in subsequent periods, gains are recognized only to the extent of previously recorded losses. On the other hand, in each reporting period, the IO securities are adjusted to fair value, for both gains and losses, in earnings (if classified as trading) or equity (if classified as available-for-sale). This is illustrated in Exhibit 11.

Index